Lecture Notes in Computer Science 1540

Edited by G. Goos, J. Hartmanis and J. van Leeuwen

T0223205

Springer

Berlin
Heidelberg
New York
Barcelona
Hong Kong
London
Milan
Paris
Singapore
Tokyo

Catriel Beeri   Peter Buneman   (Eds.)

Database Theory –
ICDT'99

7th International Conference
Jerusalem, Israel, January 10-12, 1999
Proceedings

 Springer

Series Editors

Gerhard Goos, Karlsruhe University, Germany
Juris Hartmanis, Cornell University, NY, USA
Jan van Leeuwen, Utrecht University, The Netherlands

Volume Editors

Catriel Beeri
The Hebrew University, Institute of Computer Science
Givat-Ram, Jerusalem 91940, Israel
E-mail: beeri@cs.huji.ac.il

Peter Buneman
University of Pennsylvania
Department of Computer and Information Science
Philadelphia, PA 19104-6389, USA
E-mail: peter@cis.upenn.edu

Cataloging-in-Publication data applied for

Die Deutsche Bibliothek - CIP-Einheitsaufnahme

Database theory : 7th international conference ; proceedings / ICDT
'99, Jerusalem, Israel, January 10 - 12, 1999. Catriel Beeri ; Peter
Buneman (ed.). - Berlin ; Heidelberg ; New York ; Barcelona ; Hong
Kong ; London ; Milan ; Paris ; Singapore ; Tokyo : Springer, 1998
   (Lecture notes in computer science ; Vol. 1540)
   ISBN 3-540-65452-6

CR Subject Classification (1998): H.2., F.1.3, F.4.1, I.2.1, H.4

ISSN 0302-9743
ISBN 3-540-65452-6 Springer-Verlag Berlin Heidelberg New York

© Springer-Verlag Berlin Heidelberg 1999
Printed in Germany

Typesetting: Camera-ready by author
SPIN 10693017   06/3142 – 5 4 3 2 1 0   Printed on acid-free paper

Foreword

Database research is a field of computer science where theory meets applications. Many concepts and methods, that were regarded as issues of theoretical interest when initially proposed, are now included in implemented database systems and related products. Examples abound in the fields of database design, query languages, query optimization, concurrency control, statistical databases, and many others.

The papers contained in this volume were presented at ICDT'99, the 7th International Conference on Database Theory, in Jerusalem, Israel, January 10–12, 1999. ICDT is an international forum for research on the principles of database systems. It is a biennial conference, and has a tradition of being held in beautiful European sites: Rome in 1986, Bruges in 1988, Paris in 1990, Berlin in 1992, Prague in 1995, and Delphi in 1997. From 1992, ICDT has been merged with another series of conferences on theoretical aspects of database systems, The Symposium on Mathematical Fundamentals of Database Systems (MFDBS), that was initiated in Dresden (1987), and continued in Visegrad (1989) and Rostock (1991). ICDT aims to enhance the exchange of ideas and cooperation in database research both within unified Europe, and between Europe and the other continents.

ICDT'99 was organized in cooperation with:
   ACM Special Interest Group on Management of Data (Sigmod)
   IEEE Israel Chapter
   ILA — The Israel Association for Information Processing
   EDBT Foundation

ICDT'99 was sponsored by:
   The Hebrew University of Jerusalem
   Tel Aviv University
   Tandem Labs Israel, a Compaq Company

This volume contains 26 technical papers selected from 89 submissions. In addition to the technical papers, the conference featured two invited presentations: *Issues Raised by Three Years of Developing PJama: An Orthogonally Persistent Platform for Java^{TM}* by Malcolm Atkinson and Mick Jordan, and *Novel Computational Approaches to Information Retrieval and Data Mining* by Christos H. Papadimitriou. The conference also featured a state-of-the-art tutorial on *Description Logics and Their Relationships with Databases* by Maurizio Lenzerini.

The conference organization committee consisted of Catriel Beeri and Tova Milo. Administrative support was provided by Dan Knassim, Ltd, of Ramat-Gan, Israel.

We wish to thank all the authors who submitted papers for consideration, the program committee members, and the external reviewers for their efforts and for their care in evaluating the submitted papers. We also wish to thank the organizing committee and the staff of Dan Knassim for their efforts with the local organization of the conference and Hartmut Liefke for his help in organizing the submissions and reviews. Last, but not least, we wish to express our appreciation and gratitude to the sponsoring organizations for their assistance and support.

Jerusalem, January 1999   Catriel Beeri and Peter Buneman
                                         Program Co-Chairs

The members of the program committee were:

Gustavo Alonso (Switzerland) Catriel Beeri (Israel) co-chair
Anthony Bonner (Canada)   Peter Buneman (USA) co-chair
Marco Cadoli (Italy)   Sophie Cluet (France)
Guozhu Dong (Australia)   Ronald Fagin (USA)
Erich Grädel (Germany)   Gosta Grahne (Canada)
Marc Gyssens (Belgium)   Yannis Ioannidis (Greece & USA)
Alon Levy (USA)   Alberto Mendelzon (Canada)
Guido Mörkotte (Germany)   Shelly Qian (USA)
Kenneth Ross (USA)   Timos Sellis (Greece)
Eric Simon (France)   Dan Suciu (USA)
S. Sudarshan (India)   Michael Taitslin (Russia)

External reviews were provided by:

Roberto Baldoni   Michael Benedikt   Alex Borgida
Diego Calvanese   Giuseppe De Giacomo Stijn Dekeyser
Alin Deutsch   Francoise Fabret   Wenfei Fan
Daniela Florescu   Minos N. Garofalakis Floris Geerts
Marc Gemis   Bart Goethals   Israel Gold
Sergio Greco   Vassos Hadzilacos   Colin Hirsch
Gerti Kappel   Bettina Kemme   David Kemp
Phokion Kolaitis   Bart Kuijpers   Laks V.S. Lakshmanan
Maurizio Lenzerini   Paolo Liberatore   Leonid Libkin
Paolo Merialdo   Tova Milo   Frank Neven
Otto Nurmi   Kenneth Oksanen   Luigi Palopoli
Guy Pardon   Jan Paredaens   Francesco Quaglia
Krithi Ramamritham   Sridhar Ramaswamy   Francesco Scarcello
Luc Segoufin   Kenneth C. Sevcik   Seppo Sippu
Eljas Soisalon-Soininen Val Tannen   Yannis Theodoridis
David Toman   Alejandro Vaisman   Jan Van den Bussche
Luc Vandeurzen   Panos Vassiliadis   Helmut Veith
Roger Weber   Limsoon Wong

Table of Contents

Invited Talks

Tutorial

Query Languages

Logic

Performance I

Concurrency and Distribution

Constraint Databases

Index Structures

Semi-structured Data

Mediation

Computational Issues

Views

Author Index

Issues Raised by Three Years of Developing PJama:

An Orthogonally Persistent Platform for Java™

Malcolm Atkinson and Mick Jordan*

University of Glasgow, Glasgow G12 8QQ, Scotland and Sun Microsystems
Laboratories, 901 San Antonio Road MS MTV29-110, Palo Alto, CA 94303

Abstract. Orthogonal persistence is based on three principles that have
been understood for nearly 20 years. PJama is a publically available
prototype of a Java platform that supports orthogonal persistence. It is
already capable of supporting substantial applications.

The experience of applying the principles of orthogonal persistence to
the Java programming language is described in the context of PJama.
For example, issues arise over achieving orthogonality when there are
classes that have a special relationship with the Java Virtual Machine.
The treatment of static variables and the definition of reachability for
classes and the handling of the keyword **transient** also pose design problems. The model for checkpointing the state of a computation, including
live threads, is analyzed and related to a transactional approach. The
problem of dealing with state that is external to the PJama environment is explained and the solutions outlined. The difficult problem of
system evolution is identified as a major barrier to deploying orthogonal
persistence for the Java language.

The predominant focus is on semantic issues, but with concern for reasonably efficient implementation. We take the opportunity throughout
the paper and in the conclusions to identify directions for further work.

1 Introduction

In three short years the Java programming language and associated class libraries, collectively referred to as the Java platform, has achieved an unprecedented degree of acceptance and adoption by academia and industry. The Java
language provides the programmer with a simple but powerful object model,
a strong type system, automatic storage management and concurrency through
lightweight threads. Within the closed world of an executing Java program, these
properties are extremely helpful, vital even, in the timely development of reliable
and robust applications. However, there is no satisfactory way of maintaining
these properties beyond the single execution of a Java virtual machine. Instead
the programmer must deal explicitly with saving the state of an application,

---

* Java and all Java-based trademarks and logos are trademarks or registered trademarks of Sun Microsystems, Inc. in the United States and other countries.

Catriel Beeri, Peter Buneman (Eds.): ICDT'99, LNCS 1540, pp. 1–30, 1998.
© Springer-Verlag Berlin Heidelberg 1998

using some combination of a variety of persistence mechanisms, for example, file input/output, object serialization, relational database connectivity, none of which provide complete support for the full computational model. This lack of completeness, while only a minor nuisance for simple applications, becomes a serious problem as application complexity increases.

Mindful of the limitations of the traditional approaches to persistence, the Forest project at Sun Microsystems Laboratories initiated a collaborative research project with the Persistence and Distribution Group at Glasgow University to apply the principles of orthogonal persistence [3] to the Java language. This project, PJama[1], begun shortly after the first public release of the Java platform in May 1995. It has been running in parallel with the mainstream development of the Java language, and a series of prototypes have been developed[2]. While these prototypes have validated the principles of orthogonal persistence, there remain a number of holes in the completeness property, and a number of issues that are still under debate. In this paper we use the term OPJ to denote the abstract notion of orthogonal persistence for the Java language, and PJama for our specific prototype implementations.

Over the past three years there have been some significant additions to the Java language, and substantial additions to the set of standard class libraries. In addition, many other class libraries have been added as standard extensions, and many third-party libraries have become available. Inevitably some of these changes have implications for orthogonal persistence. Most significantly, certain idioms that have become widespread in the class libraries are either at odds with orthogonal persistence or at least would not be required were orthogonal persistence a standard part of the platform.

Meanwhile, the phenomenal success of the Java platform has caused many object database vendors to develop systems for it. Some of these systems conform quite closely to the principles of orthogonal persistence, but are shaped by the object database viewpoint, primarily the model proposed by the Object Database Management Group (ODMG) [31]. Specifically, these systems all require that access to persistent objects is through a transaction interface. There are a number of unresolved issues in the relationship between the transaction approach and the Java language semantics, which we discuss in section 4.

This paper is a sequel to one that described our very early experiences with the first PJama prototype [18] and is based on [19]. We begin with a brief discussion of the standard support for persistence in the Java platform, and then review the principles of orthogonal persistence, and their application to the Java language. We then discuss the model of checkpointing the computational state and its relationship to the transactional approach. This is followed by a detailed discussion of the problem of handling state that is external to the Java environment, which is a small but significant issue for the OPJ programmer. We

---

[1] We originally used the name PJava but this was taken as the trade mark for Personal Java.

[2] The initial design and motivation is described in [1,2]. Some implementation issues are described in [29,11,30].

then briefly discuss the difficult problem of class and platform evolution in OPJ. Finally, we review performance issues before drawing conclusions. The reader is assumed to have a working knowledge of the Java language and the core class libraries. A number of issues requiring further research have been highlighted in the main text.

2 Persistence in the Java Platform

The fact that the Java language contains the keyword `transient` suggests the designers gave some thought to persistence. However the first version of the Java language specification, JLS 1.0 [15], only provides a hint as to how `transient` might be interpreted in a future version of the specification:

> "Variables may be marked `transient` to indicate that they are not part of the persistent state of an object. If an instance of the class `Point`:
>
> ```
> class Point {
>     transient float rho, theta;
> }
> ```
>
> were saved to storage by a system service, then only the fields x and y would be saved. This specification does not yet specify details of such services; we intend to provide them in a future version of this specification."

As we shall discuss later 5.4 the specification has now been defined, unfortunately in a way that is incompatible with orthogonal persistence.

In the initial release of the Java language, the basic form of persistence was a traditional programming-language mechanism, namely encoding and decoding basic types to and from output and input streams that can be connected to some external device, such as a file system or a network socket. Built on this was an *ad hoc* scheme for encoding and decoding a property table (`java.util.Properties`) to and from a stream.

Shortly afterwards the Java Database Connectivity (JDBC^{TM}) API was added to provide a standard way to communicate with a relational database. While providing access to existing relational data, JDBC can be used to save Java object state, and several object-relational mapping systems [33,36,28] are being developed that automate this process, which is very tedious to program manually.

With the JDK 1.1 release of the Java platform came the support for Java Object Serialization (JOS), a mechanism that supports the encoding and subsequent decoding of *nearly* any object to and from a stream. Unlike the property table encoding, which is text-based, JOS uses a binary encoding format. JOS is effectively the default persistence mechanism for the Java platform and is used extensively in the JavaBeans^{TM} framework [32]. It is also used as the argument marshalling protocol for the Java Remote Method Invocation framework [35].

2.1   Persistence and Application Development

The problems of dealing with persistent state have a profound impact on the overall approach that programmers bring to application development. In the absence of orthogonal persistence, every application must deal with converting the internal state into an appropriate external state and vice versa. It is believed that as much as 30% of the code of an application is occupied with this task.

We observe several costs with this approach:

- The application programmers encounter an additional conceptual load, which may include the need to understand two different models of the application domain, an additional technology and the interface mechanisms.
- The "business" logic of the application may be obscured or distored by the mechanisms for managing persistence, this often increases maintenance costs.
- The computation may be inefficient (with a long start up and shut down latency) because application programmers, in an attempt to minimise the previous two effects adopt a traditional structure (described below).

The model of "input, process, output", that is encouraged by the lack of orthogonal persistence, is very deeply ingrained in the programming language community, so deeply in fact that experienced programmers often have trouble understanding the concept of orthogonal persistence and want to see the "API". In [23] Liedke observes that novice programmers easily absorbed the concepts of orthogonal persistence but that seasoned programmers continued initially to design mappings between "internal" and "external" data structures.

It must be admitted that orthogonal persistence is an inherently language-based approach to data definition, in contrast to the file-format approach that so typifies the current computing landscape. Indeed the Java platform has itself contributed a multitude of new file formats.

It is not clear whether this tension will ever be resolved. What is clear however, is that orthogonal persistence fully supports the long-term preservation of the type safety and consistency of the Java language, whereas ad hoc persistence does not. Ultimately, if these values are deemed important, they must surely be propagated to the domain of persistent storage.

Another popular structure for applications is:

1. Run queries to extract data from various databases;
2. Perform processing;
3. Update one or more databases with the results;
4. Repeat from 1 until no more to do.

This form of application can utilise orthogonal persistence in one of two ways. It can be written using orthogonal persistence instead of the databases. The loop avoids much of the explicit extraction and all of the explicit update. Data translation and interworking between different persistent regimes is avoided. Alternatively, orthogonal persistence can be used to store intermediate results and parts of the data, while the basic loop also uses legacy systems in traditional databases.

Problem 2.1. It is an open question how best to advise application designers and programmers, so that they exploit the potential of orthogonal persistence in the context of legacy systems.

2.2 The Principles of Orthogonal Persistence

The concept of orthogonal persistence has been developed and refined over many years of research and development in the academic community [3]. While the general principles are language independent, they must be tailored appropriately when applied to a specific language.

Orthogonal persistence is defined by three principles:

- Type Orthogonality: persistence is available for all data irrespective of type.
- Transitive Persistence: the lifetime of all objects is determined by reachability from a designated set of root objects.
- Persistence Independence: it is indistinguishable whether code is operating on short-lived or long-lived data.

The notion of orthogonality is often referred to loosely as transparent persistence. Many systems claim transparency yet, on deeper investigation, the transparency does not fully embrace the spirit of orthogonal persistence. In particular, since there is some latitude in the application to a particular programming language, there is inevitably the opportunity for disagreement on exactly how the principles should be applied.

3 Applying the Principles to the Java Language

In this section, we discuss how the principles are applied to the Java language, using the PJama system as a base-line, since it specifically aims to provide orthogonal persistence for the Java platform.

3.1 Type Orthogonality

The Java language provides two kinds of type: primitive types, for example `int`, and reference types, namely: `array` types, `class` types and `interface` types. The values of a reference type are references to objects. All objects, including arrays, support the methods of class `Object`. Other than the issue of references to external state, discussed in section 5, there are few difficulties in making user-defined classes persistent.

The principal problem with user-defined classes is the specification of the `Object.hashCode` method, which does not require that the returned value be consistent across different applications or between different executions of the same application. The default implementation is based on the memory address of the object, which guarantees inconsistency if the hashcode is recomputed each time the object is brought into memory at a different address. We believe that the correct model for OPJ is to consider a persistent store as embodying a suspended virtual machine, which means that each execution is the same application in the sense of the JLS. Therefore, the value returned by Object.hashCode must be consistent across such executions. This issue is covered in detail in [4]. We have only recently modified PJama to maintain this invariant, which turns out to be important for some core classes.

Problem 3.1. Is the requirement for equivalence with a suspended virtual machine execution adequate to guarantee persistence independence?

Classes Requiring Special Support Some of the core classes, however, are a much more challenging proposition for OPJ. The classes Class, Thread and Throwable are intimately connected with the language definition and require special support from the virtual machine. Every object has an associated class, denoted by a unique instance of the class Class and this binding cannot be changed by program action. Every program consists of a number of independent threads of control, denoted by instances of the class Thread. The normal control flow may be short circuited by the **throw** statement, which takes a Throwable value as its argument, to the body of a matching **catch** clause of a **try** statement. The programmer may treat instances of Class, Thread and Throwable in a first-class way, store their values in other variables, pass them as arguments and so on. Therefore, by extension, the principle of type orthogonality must apply to instances of these types.

The Class Class Although not fully enforced by the Java language, the model of object-oriented programming is that a client access an object through an interface that defines its abstract state and behavior. In practice this is realized by a combination of instance variables in the object and methods that perform some computation. In general, the methods that access the state of the object may perform an arbitrary computation. In short, the methods defined in the class of an object play a crucial role in defining the object. There is no way that a user of the interface can separate the physical manifestation of the state in the instance variables from the code that uses it to provide the abstract state. Furthermore, once created, an object cannot change the binding of its methods. From this we can conclude that orthogonal persistence must maintain that binding in order to preserve the type consistency of the language. By extension this requires that the code of a class be made persistent along with its instances. We discuss the issues of class reachability in more detail in section 3.2.

The Class Thread The availability of user-defined threads as first-class objects only serves to emphasize the issue of the persistence of execution state. Even a language without such facility has an implicit thread that carries the execution state. The fundamental issue is where computation resumes after a checkpoint[3].

---

[3] A checkpoint occurs when called explicitly by an application (using PJStore.stabilizeAll() in PJama), on successful transaction commit and on normal program termination.

This is a complex issue that is discussed in more detail in section 5.4. Here we merely observe that, since the language permits the programmer to treat instances of class Thread like any other object from the perspective of assignment compatibility, the programmer can construct object structures that effectively capture execution state[4]. Therefore, OPJ must support this correctly. This is not a trivial matter, since thread state includes held locks in addition to the activation stack.

Owing to the complexity of the thread implementation in the JDK 1.1 virtual machine, PJama does not currently support persistent threads. Removing this limitation is high on our priority list.

The Class Exception Exception objects are usually thrown, caught and then discarded. However, it is possible to retain them and subsequently access their state, such as any message string, or the stack trace. JLS 1.0 does not define the format of the stack trace, but it does suggest there are limits to the duration of its validity. Experimentally, the information survives the stack being overwritten with subsequent activations. Currently, when an exception is made persistent in PJama, the stack trace information is lost on restart, although this could be fixed with some effort.

Problem 3.2. We refer to the set of classes whose run-time state and behaviour is intimately connected with the implementation of a Java Virtual Machine (JVM) as the *intrinsic classes*. Is this a set determined only by the Java languages definition? Is it possible (and acceptably efficient) to define abstract reflection interfaces over these classes (and their instances) so that if JVMs support these interfaces, orthogonal persistence can be implemented without the implementers of persistence having to modify a JVM? That is, can completely orthogonal persistence be implemented in a JVM-neutral way if suitable reflection interfaces are added to the intrinsic classes?

Static Variables Unlike C++ or C, the Java language has no isolated global variables, only variables declared **static** in a top-level class definition. There is one instance of such a static variable for every instance of the Class object[5]. Although the specification does not mandate such an implementation, it is intuitive to imagine static variables as if they were ordinary instance variables of the associated class's Class object. One common use for static variables is for data that pertains to all instances of the class. If the data reachable from the static variables contributes to the invariants of the class, it is important that it become persistent if instances of the class become persistent, otherwise the invariants assumed by the class will not hold on restart. In short, type orthogonality requires that static variables be made persistent along with a class's Class instance[6].

---

[4] For example, certain of the AWT classes do this.

[5] An instance of a Class object is constructed each time a class is loaded. Any given ClassLoader may only load a class once. However, an application may use multiple ClassLoaders to obtain independent instances of a class within one execution.

[6] Other aspects of static variables are discussed later in the paper.

PJama supports the persistence of static variables unless they are marked **transient**. This sets PJama apart from all other known persistence solutions for the Java platform, which treat static variables as implicitly transient.

Problem 3.3. The correct combination of persistence with static variables needs to be established.

3.2   Persistence by Reachability

Transitive persistence is defined as persistence by reachability from a designated set of roots. Reachability is already used in the Java language to determine the life-time of objects, and persistence by reachability is an obvious extension of this construct. However, the issue is quite complex owing to the interaction between dynamic class loading and the reachability of classes.

Reachability in the Java Language All Java objects are allocated on a heap and the lifetime of an object is determined automatically by reachability from the set of live threads and the static variables of the set of loaded classes. There is a subtlety relating to the set of loaded classes that was only clarified recently, namely exactly how the reachability of a Class instance is defined. If only the thread stacks act as roots, then many Class instances might become unreachable during execution, causing them to be garbage collected. However, later in the program execution a new instance of a garbage-collected class might be created, requiring the creation of a new Class instance. If class garbage collection is implemented as class unloading, which is desirable in certain environments, for example, browsers, then this may result in a class being loaded several times during program execution, with the attendant loss of state held in static variables due to static initialization occurring on each load. Since static variables are the only truly global state in a Java program, this behavior is sometimes undesirable and arguably a violation of the language semantics. The issue is further complicated by the provision for user-defined class loaders in the Java language.

The resolution of this problem states that a Class instance is unreachable if and only if its class loader is unreachable, and that the system class loader is always reachable. This effectively defines the (hidden) table of system-loaded classes, and their associated static variables, as an additional set of roots.

This issue is significant for orthogonal persistence as it strengthens the argument for maintaining the binding between an object and its Class instance, and for static variables to be persistent by default.

Class Reachability The requirement for persistence of instances of class Class, including the associated behavior as specified by the method bodies, is unassailable. However, because of the semantics of dynamic class loading in the Java language, it is still unclear how to treat the reachability that is implicit in the class definition, in particular in the field declarations, method signatures and method bodies. This implicit reachability is characterized by symbolic references to classes that may not yet have been loaded, because no active use[7] has yet been made of them. For example, the class of a local variable of a method that has not been invoked at the time of a checkpoint may not have been loaded.

An important issue is whether the transitive persistence principle should apply in this case. The case for answering "yes" is based on the belief that the complete behavior of the class must be captured with the object, and that the behavior of the named class contributes to this. The case for answering "no" is partly based on pragmatic issues such as the cost of loading such classes at the checkpoint, partly on consistency with the normal behavior of the Java platform and partly on the fact that it is impossible in general to determine the complete set of reachable classes. This is because of the dynamic class naming provided by the `Class.forName` method, which takes a `String` value, and by the reflection subsystem, which also allows references to classes named through `String` values. We argue that reference to a class name via a language identifier is strongly suggestive that reachability should be enforced, because the classfile was generated by compiling the referencing class against a specific instance of the referenced class, whereas there is no direct connection in the case of dynamic class naming.

The term "loading a class" is often used loosely to describe a sequence of disjoint actions that may, in practice, be separated in time. The JLS separates the specification of class loading into several stages, namely loading, linking, and initialization. Loading is the portion that generates a `Class` instance from a binary form of a class, typically a classfile. Linking is further divided into verification, preparation, and resolution. Resolution is the process that corresponds to the notion of class reachability as it is required to resolve all symbolic references to other classes. A symbolic reference corresponds directly to name used as an identifier in the source code. The JLS explicitly permits an implementation to resolve classes eagerly, although it requires that any errors detected during loading that might be thrown as exceptions, are actually thrown at a point in the program where some action is taken that might cause the loading to occur. Initialization is the process of executing static (class) variable initializers and static initialization blocks. Initialization is permitted to result only from an active use of the class, which is precisely defined in the JLS, but informally corresponds to instance creation, method invocation or assignment to a class variable.

The PJama prototype was designed and implemented prior to the release of the JLS and treats initialization as an integral part of the loading process. That is, if a class is deemed reachable by the resolution phase it will be loaded, linked and initialized. Therefore, the PJama prototype violates the JLS specification. This is rarely observable but occasionally causes messages related to initialization failures to appear during a checkpoint[8].

Note that OPJ must preserve the basic invariant of the class loading mechanism, which is that a class is loaded at most once in a given classloader. In the

---

[7] "Active use" is defined in the JLS.
[8] We will remedy this fault.

following sections, therefore, the term "load and resolve" should be understood to ignore already loaded classes. The term "promote" is used to denote the process of making any object or class persistent in the store. Similarly, promotion should be understood to ignore already promoted classes.

In PJama we have considered the following approaches to handling class reachability:

1. Use the reference virtual-machine class-loading algorithm. At a checkpoint promote those classes that are reachable from the persistent roots. As a result classes promoted to the persistent store might contain symbolic references to classes that had not been loaded at the time of the checkpoint. These references would remain until an active use of the referenced class occurred, during a later execution. Then the problem arises that the resolution might lead to an different (perhaps incompatible) version of the class than it would have at the time of the initial promotion, or it might fail to find the class at all. Either case is a loss of referential integrity.

2. As case 1 but eagerly load and resolve the transitive closure of referenced classes every time a class is loaded. This is the most extreme case permitted by the JLS, and would prevent unresolved references occurring in promoted classes, at the cost of increased execution time and an increased demand for heap space.

3. Similar to case 2, but defer the determination of the transitive closure until a checkpoint operation occurs, and limit the resolution process to those classes reachable from the persistent roots. This delays the cost of loading the additional classes until the last possible moment before they are needed to ensure referential integrity in the store, but may add considerable latency to the checkpoint operation. In addition, to comply with the JLS, the checkpoint operation would have to be defined as causing arbitrary loading in order for the programmer to be expected to catch any exceptions that occurred during the process.

4. Similar to case 3, but simply capture the class-files, as byte arrays in the persistent store, of those classes in the transitive closure that are not already loaded. That is, defer the actual loading, linking and initialization, until a subsequent active use of the class. Modify the class-loading algorithm to search this set before the normal class-searching algorithm. In effect this scheme captures part of the external file system in the persistent store.

Cases three and four can be altered slightly by defining reachability to be based on all classes that are currently loaded. This variant is called "conservative" by analogy with conservative garbage collection, because it may load more classes than strictly necessary. PJama currently uses the conservative variant of case three, but we now believe that case four would be a better choice, as it provides essentially the same consistency properties but at reduced cost at checkpoint time.

Note that none of the above cases deal with references to classes through dynamic class naming, for example `Class.forName(someString)`. If the programmer wishes to capture the set of classes that `someString` might name, then the programmer must arrange for such classes to be statically reachable (named explicitly as identifiers in the source code). Note that with OPJ, this can be done separately from the code that uses dynamic naming, for example, in an application-initialization class that is executed simply for the effect of forcing the classes to load and be made persistent.

Problem 3.4. A precise definition of persistence by reachability is required which takes into account the need to make behaviour completely persistent by preserving an appropriate set of classes.[9]

Problem 3.5. Given the previous definition, static initialization must occur exactly once at an appropriate time. That is, on the first active use of the class, in any execution against the persistent store.

3.3 Explicit Persistent Roots

When applying the principle of transitive persistence, it is possible to allow the programmer to define the roots explicitly, rather than simply use the roots defined by the Java language semantics. If threads cannot be made persistent, as is the case in many current systems, this is a pragmatic choice, as the only other option is to use the static variables in the set of loaded classes. Given the historical uncertainty over the semantics of class reachability, coupled with the fact that in the initial version of the Java language a static variable could not be marked transient, an explicit, user-programmed root table was the obvious way to proceed, and this is the current mechanism that is used by PJama.

Unfortunately, the existence of this table and the associated interface inevitably violates the third principle of persistence independence. Arguably, the explicit root table should be dropped in favor of the standard reachability rules of the Java language. However, because this would make all core classes implicitly persistent, it would require a complete solution to the issue of external state, described in detail in section 5. It would also make conservative class loading the default, as all loaded classes would be reachable, by definition. This issue seems to hinge primarily on the level of orthogonality of the system as a whole and on the quality of the evolution tools (see section 6).

Problem 3.6. The precise definition of persistence independence and persistence by reachability must encompass a mutually consistent definition of the persistent roots.

3.4 Persistence Independence

The purpose of this principle is to support the re-use of software irrespective of object lifetime. The fundamental requirement of persistence independence

---

[9] There are subtleties due to the possibility of multiple `ClassLoaders`. For example, if a second attempt is made to load a class of the same name using a different loader, and there is a preserved copy in the persistent store and a revised copy in the file space identified by the `CLASSPATH` which variant should be used?

is that source code should not have to be modified in order for a class to become persistent. Typically required modifications include inheriting from special classes, requiring specific constructors, requiring explicit method calls to transfer an object from persistent storage and so on.

The Java platform defines a public format for compiled classes [24]. This permits the source form of a class to undergo arbitrary transformations before execution, provided that the resulting classfile defines a class of the same name and also that it passes the verification tests of the Java virtual machine.

This has led to several systems that achieve a form of persistence independence by effectively rewriting the source code to insert the read and write barriers and other changes that are needed to support transparent persistence [27,36].

It is debatable whether such systems meet the principle of persistence independence. Certainly the source code does not need to be modified, which is the first priority of this principle. However, the goal of re-use, which is the larger purpose of this principle, is compromised by classfile transformation. Typically, the transformed bytecodes cannot be used outside of the particular persistence framework, which seriously damages the "write once, run anywhere" goal of the Java platform. For example, the popular JGL collection classes are available in two versions, standard and transformed, for use with Object Design's PSE system [27]. This bifurcation would become intolerable if variants were needed for a wide variety of different implementations of persistence.

In the general case, supporting a system of dynamically loaded classes that need post-processing requires bundling the pre-processor with the application and loading such classes with a customized class loader. Since this requires foresight on the part of the programmer it therefore violates the principle of persistence independence. It also rules out the core classes, which cannot be loaded by this mechanism. They may indeed be preloaded and therefore excluded from persistence via this implementation strategy. But they earn their presence in the core classes because they are frequently re-used.

Finally, complete transparency would require that the transformation step be completely hidden from debuggers, performance monitoring tools, the reflection system and so on. Achieving this degree of transparency is quite unprecedented at the current state of the art.

Problem 3.7. The principle of persistence independence requires careful definition so that it covers all relevant aspects of application programming without being over restrictive. A good definition is essential for ensuring the re-use of classes across persistent and non-persistent systems.

4   Controlling Checkpoints

The principles of orthogonal persistence are not explicit about whether the programmer has any control over when the state of the computation becomes durable, so that it will survive a shutdown of the system, intended or involuntary. In a perfect implementation of orthogonal persistence in a closed world, this would not be an issue. Provided that the system checkpoints its state with a sufficiently fine grain, the only slight discontinuity would be after a crash, and even then the system would recover transparently and continue from the last successful checkpoint [23].

In practice this idealized model is unrealistic, and must be modified to deal with external state that is defined outside the Java environment, but accessed within it. Handling external state is covered in detail in section 5.

However, even in a closed world, it is necessary to address how the programmer can control the checkpoint mechanism and to specify the special cases of shutdown and restart.

The precise details of the Java virtual machine start-up are defined by the JLS to be implementation dependent. The general scheme is to load a specific named class and then invoke its main method, which has a special signature, in a thread. It is implementation and application dependent whether other threads may be created prior to the invocation of main. A virtual machine terminates its activity and exits when one of the following two things happens:

- All the non-daemon threads terminate.
- A thread invokes the System.exit method and the exit operation is not forbidden by the security manager.

A daemon thread is defined by the fact that its existence does not influence the decision to exit the virtual machine.

Let us consider the start-up of a fresh orthogonally persistent Java virtual machine and a completely empty store, that is, the store contains no threads and no loaded classes and no other object instances. Assume that a class Main is indicated as the entry class and assume also that no additional threads are created. There are three cases to consider:

- The thread terminates normally without invoking a checkpoint.
- The thread terminates abnormally without invoking a checkpoint.
- The thread invokes a checkpoint, and then terminates abnormally.

Abnormal termination is defined as an uncaught exception in the thread, or a call to System.exit with a non-zero argument.

In the first case the thread will have caused the loading of some classes, often a very large number, and possibly created some persistent roots. We choose to interpret normal termination as requiring an implicit checkpoint. By definition, the terminated thread is not reachable, therefore the store will contain only passive objects and no persistent execution state.

In case two, we choose to interpret the abnormal termination as indicating that no implicit checkpoint should occur. Therefore the store remains unchanged.

In case three, the explicit checkpoint will find that the thread is active and reachable. Therefore the state of the thread should be made persistent in the store. The subsequent abnormal termination will, as in case two, avoid the implicit checkpoint.

Now consider the start-up of the virtual machine with the store in the state left by each of the above cases. In cases one and two the store contained no persistent threads and it is therefore necessary to create a new thread and also for the start-up process to be provided with the name of the entry class. This class may or may not already exist in the persistent store; if not it will be loaded.

Case three is more interesting. Since the persistent store contains a live thread, there is no need to create a new thread and also no need to specify an entry class. The virtual machine can simply resume the suspended thread. But what if an entry class is specified? This situation is interpreted as indicating that an additional thread should be created to invoke the given method, causing a total of two live threads. This case generalizes to a store that contains an arbitrary number of live threads.

The astute reader will have noted that in case three, the live thread in the store may resume and then terminate abnormally, as it did during the first activation. This is an example of a persistent bug, a known phenomenon of persistent systems [23]. However, if a new entry class is specified and executes in a fresh thread, this will not matter, as the new thread has the opportunity to alter the behavior of the system. Another mechanism for handling this case is outlined in section 5.4.

Problem 4.1. The semantics and utility of persistent active threads requires further exploration. Their interaction with JVM start up and shut down require a careful definition.

4.1 Transactional Interpretation

The decision to interpret successful termination as an implicit checkpoint and abnormal termination as abort is similar to the commit and abort operation of a transaction [16]. Indeed one can consider one execution of the JVM as a single flat transaction. In transactional terms the explicit checkpoint is like a chain transaction, which is a transaction that commits periodically, relinquishing the ability to abort those changes, but does not release control of the resources it is using. In the OPJ model, the virtual machine is the sole owner of all the resources and so a checkpoint is equivalent to a chain transaction. In particular an explicitly invoked check-point cannot be undone.

Although it is possible to construct an application system as a set of method invocations on an OPJ virtual machine, each acting as an ACID transaction, this approach has some drawbacks. First it assumes an external environment that is capable of activating the virtual machines, and so is not an appropriate model for some applications. Second, there is inevitably some latency and overhead in launching and closing down a virtual machine.

In languages that do not support concurrent threads, concurrency has to be simulated with multiple processes (virtual machines). This model is common, for example, in many object-oriented database systems, and has been carried over into their Java variants. However, since the Java language provides concurrency through lightweight threads, the multiple-process model is strictly unnecessary. A single JVM can support a range of independent activities, running as separate (groups of) threads, and, if the orthogonality of the system is complete, it will not matter when and by which threads checkpoints are initiated. However, all these threads are running in a shared object space and it is important that they do not accidently interfere with one another. The Java language supports this with explicit object locking through the use of **synchronized** methods and blocks. This puts the onus on the programmer to get the locking correct, a task that is known to be difficult and error prone [22]. In particular **synchronized** methods do not provide effective support for coordinating sequences of operations on a group of objects, owing to the inability to recover from deadlock caused by acquiring individual locks in an incorrect order.

Transactions, which originated in the database field, are explicitly designed to support an isolated, recoverable unit of work that consists of multiple operations. To ensure consistency, the transaction approach uses implicit object locking, holding locks until the transaction commits or aborts, thus ensuring an equivalent serial ordering exists. A key feature of the transaction approach is that the locking is dynamic and orthogonal to other properties of an object, whereas synchronized methods are a static, compile-time property.

This difference in the locking model is enough to suggest that adding transactions to the Java language is a significant change, and effectively defines a variant of the language. Another aspect of the transactional approach that significantly changes the programming model is the ability to abort (undo) part of a computation. This is a very powerful mechanism that comes at negligible additional cost, since it is already required to support the basic properties of atomicity and durability. However, we should note that extending this capability orthogonally to short-lived (transient) objects is not trivial for an implementation. Indeed, at the time of writing, none of the commercially available transaction systems for the Java platform undo transient state on a rollback or abort, and this limitation leads to many subtle bugs in applications involving transient state.

In parallel with the basic provision of orthogonal persistence for Java, the PJama project has from the outset also included research on a sophisticated extensible transaction model [2,12], although this has not yet been implemented in any of publicly available prototypes. However, whereas all commercial vendors of persistence solutions for the Java platform only provide persistence in a transactional framework, we believe that the provision of complete orthogonal persistence for the Java language is independent and more fundamental than a transaction mechanism.

Despite the potential pit-falls it is a fact that the Java language already supports a highly customizable concurrency control model, which is widely used in existing code, particularly in sophisticated applications which could not be constructed with flat ACID transactions. Adding orthogonal persistence to the Java platform opens up new territory by allowing the concurrency model to be fully exploited in long-lived applications. It seems to us that this territory should be explored in parallel with the development of transaction models.

It may turn out that the power and orthogonal properties of an extensible transaction model would be a significant addition to the Java language, but its adoption may require abandoning, or severely curtailing, its current approach to concurrency control. In this context, it is important to understand a fundamental difference in approach between the PJama extensible transaction model and that of the current crop of commercial systems. The latter is essentially aimed at controlled access to an external object space by multiple instances of a JVM, whereas the former is concerned with controlled access by multiple threads to the object space defined by a single virtual machine. In this sense the PJama extensible transaction model is more compatible with the Java language specification as it is designed to operate in a similar closed-world environment.

There are many open issues concerned with the relationship between the checkpoint model of orthogonal persistence and the transaction model, some of which are discussed in [5]. Regardless of how these issues are resolved, it seems likely that the basic principles of orthogonal persistence will play an important role in any transaction system. In particular, the much sought after feature of a "long-running transaction" can obviously benefit from complete orthogonal persistence.

Problem 4.2. There is a rich space of possible combinations of orthogonal persistence and transactions. Their combination with the Java languages concurrency model is not straightforward. There are both semantic and practical problems deserving further investigation here.

5   Handling External State

Almost all of the problems that application developers experience with orthogonal persistence are caused by the need to deal, explicitly or implicitly, with external state that is not under the control of the system. Even when an orthogonally persistent application supports a rich and long-lived set of objects, there will be times when it is necessary to communicate with external systems, some of which will not be written in the Java language. In fact, because of the safety properties of the Java language, part of the implementation of the runtime system must be written in another language.

5.1   Incompatible Models of External State

A general model for dealing with external state is to treat the application's accumulated information about external state as a cache that is discarded when a system shuts down, either purposely or due to a crash, and needs to be reconstructed when the system restarts. This will sometimes require saving the values representing the external state in a different form and using this to re-establish the active state during restart. For example, the operating system descriptor FD of an open file with pathname PN will not be valid across restarts, but PN can usually be used to re-open the file returning an equivalent descriptor FDnew[10]. Persistence at the operating-system level [13,21,23,25] attempts to reduce the

---

[10] The file may have changed or have been moved or deleted in the interim, of course.

external state to an absolute minimum. Network communications still present a problem, however.

Note that managing external state of this sort requires the programmer to do extra work. That is, the code cannot be persistence independent. In fact, this is an example where supporting orthogonal persistence requires the application programmer to do more work than in a transient program[11]. Using the open file as an example, it is likely that the name of the file to open is passed in as an argument to a method of the class that holds the file descriptor. In a transient application this execution path will always be followed, which will cause the file descriptor to be initialized each time, before it is used. However, an orthogonally persistent application logically continues from the point that it reached before the last checkpoint, and so will not usually retrace this execution path. Therefore, unless the programmer takes extra steps to ensure the validity of the file descriptor value, by re-opening the file during restart, the application will fail when it tries to use the FD value.

This is an example of a fundamental incompatibility between the programming model of orthogonal persistence and the traditional transient programming model. The incompatibility arises from the (natural) position taken in OPJ that variables are persistent by default, which clashes with the reality that in a transient program all variables are re-initialized on each run. Unless the programmer is aware of the possibility that the code might run in an orthogonally persistent environment, it is easy to forget to handle the subset of variables that are truly transient because they deal with external state. External state may change between activations of the OPJ system since it is managed independently. Indeed the reason that it is desirable for it to remain external is to take advantage of these other, pre-existing, systems.

This conflict between the transient and persistent programming models is visible in many places in the core-class libraries. A classic example is the standard technique for loading native-code libraries, which assumes that it is safe to do this in a **static** class initializer. However, in an OPJ system, a class is initialized exactly once, so on a second invocation of the program, the library is not loaded. There are many other instances of variables that hold values that are intrinsically transient, but they are not distinguished in the source code.

This is particularly unfortunate because the Java language provides a keyword to denote that a value should not be persistent, namely the **transient** modifier. In many cases, all that the programmer needs to do is to mark the variable as **transient** and then handle the restart case by checking for a distinguished value, typically null. Fortunately, this issue also applies to Java Object Serialization (JOS), which means that quite a lot of existing code that deals with external state already works correctly when used in a the normal transient Java platform or in the OPJ platform. However, the solution is not complete because serialization is itself not complete. Some classes cannot be serialized, and static variables are assumed by serialization to be transient. Often it is precisely these

---

[11] This extra work is undertaken as a matter of course in distributed and continuously running applications, in order to resume after partial failures.

classes and variables that deal with external state. Sadly, as explained in detail in 5.4, the transient modifier has now been specified in the latest version of the JLS in a way that is incompatible with its natural application for orthogonal persistence.

One other variant of external state that can cause incompatibilities with OPJ, is that which holds the context in which the application (virtual machine) is assumed to be executing. A classic example of this is the notion of a `locale`, which defines the human language with which the application should communicate with a user.

This differs from the previous kind of external state in an important way, namely that it is usually not the case that the internal form of the state is invalidated by a shutdown and subsequent restart. Rather the external context determines the particular set of objects that will be used (instantiated). Currently, in the Java platform, this kind of contextual choice is often achieved using the mechanism of dynamic class loading. For example, the `locale` (internationalization) support defines an elaborate algorithm for choosing which classes to load based on external values in the environment.

In general, this programming model is incompatible with OPJ, again for the reason that classes are not reloaded when a suspended execution resumes. This can be handled in the same manner as other external state, namely through use of the **transient** modifier and action handlers (see below). However it is not entirely clear that this information should always be transient. For example, if a user initiates an application in one physical locale, but resumes its execution in another, he/she probably does not want the application to change its behavior with respect to the language it uses to communicate. On the other hand if the user delegates the task to a co-worker whose native language is different, it would be appropriate to change the `locale`, even while running on the same machine.

The current mechanisms in the Java platform cannot capture this kind of contextual change. A better solution would be to preserve the `locale` by default in the persistent store, and provide an explicit mechanism that is application-driven to change the `locale` explicitly. This would result in incrementally capturing the information pertaining to different locales. Note that the problem is not per se the use of the algorithm to identify the classes for a `locale`, it is the assumption in the Java programming model that classes are always loaded whenever an application resumes. This assumption itself is driven by the traditional separation of code and data, a notion that is fundamentally at odds with object-oriented programming.

Finally, the exact behavior of many of the class libraries is dependent on external property files as defined by the class `java.util.Properties`. In OPJ one would expect that much of this configuration data would be stored and manipulated directly in class instances.

5.2 Native Code

The Java language semantics are mainly defined in a closed world that consists solely of Java entities. A major exception is the provision for a method to be annotated with the **native** modifier, which indicates that this method is implemented in some other language.

The language definition makes no attempt to embrace external notions such as graphics devices, network adaptors, or generalized input and output. Instead this is left to standard class libraries, some of which make use of the native modifier to escape the constraints of the Java language, and to exploit legacy code written in other languages, typically C.

The principles of orthogonal persistence apply straight-forwardly to the closed-world part of the Java platform, but it is much less obvious how to deal with the **native** modifier and the state that exists outside the Java environment. It is evident that a complete solution would require the principles of orthogonal persistence to be applied to the language used to implement the native code. In general this is impossible because the principle of transitive persistence cannot be applied to a weakly-typed language like C. However, we must mention the alternative approach taken by the persistent operating system community [13,21,23], which is essentially to define a machine-level semantic model in terms of tables of memory pages. This provides persistence by reachability of memory pages, but leaves it up to each language implementation how to map its semantic model to the memory-page abstraction. This can be challenging, for example, when considering the efficient implementation of garbage collection. There are other problems arising from the "page" versus "object" mis-match, in particular the handling of concurrency control. In addition, devices that do not map easily to the memory model, for example a network adaptor, still require special treatment.

In summary, there really is no escape from the problem of external state, and every implementation of orthogonal persistence must choose how much effort should be expended to achieve the ideal properties of the closed world. It must also provide interposition mechanisms, where they are appropriate, for application programs to define policy.

5.3   Completeness

A fundamental decision is where to drawn the line in providing complete support for orthogonal persistence. Our experiences with PJama and its associated user community are that the standard platform, namely the virtual machine and the core classes, must support orthogonal persistence completely. Most of the problems that users have complained about are directly or indirectly a consequence of lack of orthogonality in the standard platform. The chief problem area is the Abstract Window Toolkit (AWT), which is heavily used in most Java applications. Unfortunately, AWT relies extensively on native code, including third-party libraries, in particular native window-system implementations. The recent release of the "Swing" user-interface components [34], which maintain their state as Java objects, has alleviated the problems, but Swing still relies on several fundamental AWT mechanisms that, in turn, depend on native code.

The move to adopt a standard and more abstract interface to native code, embodied in the Java Native Interface (JNI), bodes well for handling arbitrary native code in an OPJ environment, because the required modifications can be achieved by modifying just the implementation of JNI itself.

5.4 Mechanisms for Handling External State

In principle the **transient** modifier could provide a basic mechanism for handling external state, if it is defined appropriately. The specification in JLS 1.0 is only suggestive of the behavior on output, or checkpoint in the case of OPJ, but it suggests that the persistent state of the object does not contain variables marked transient at all. The specification is silent on input or restart, but in keeping with the normal behavior of a transient program, we can surmise that a new object should be created and populated with the values of the persistent fields. From the OPJ perspective, however, a new object cannot be created because doing so would break the guarantees on object identity. Instead, we can simply arrange that any transient fields are set to a specific value. In any case, when readying the object for active use, it is not entirely obvious what the specific value for a field marked **transient** should be. There are several choices:

1. the default value for the type of the variable.
2. the value given by an initializing expression, if any.
3. the value after executing the default constructor.
4. the value of the field at the point when the last checkpoint occurred.

The simplest is undoubtedly choice 1, and this is the choice made by JOS, which has become the persistence service alluded to in JLS 1.0. Choices 2 and 3 would more closely approximate the state when a fresh object is created with the new operator, but suffer from having to execute arbitrary user-code to effect the initialization. Choice 4 is equivalent to ignoring the **transient** modifier.

When the object is active, the value of a transient field is part of the state of the object and presumably is a factor in any of its invariants. From this we can conclude that it will be necessary to re-establish the state (invariants) before methods of the object can execute correctly. In particular, the OPJ programming model requires that the state be re-established to a value *equivalent to* case 4.

There are two techniques for re-establishing the state. The first is to direct all access to the field through a check for an uninitialized state, e.g:

```
if (transientField == null) {
    transientField = reEstablishState();
}
```

Since a checkpoint might be initiated by a separate thread after the check for uninitialized state, care must be taken not to assign an intermediate value to `transientField`, which might lead to an initialized but incorrect value on subsequent restart.

This adds an overhead to all code that will access the field and is one reason why initializing expressions and constructors are useful, since they establish the state initially and so avoid the check. However, such checks offer a significant defence mechanism for objects that may be used with arbitrary and complex populations of other objects. Such sanity checks on critical state that may have been corrupted by independent action at least discover erroneous conditions and may lead to more robust applications.

The second technique is to factor out the code that re-establishes the state into a designated restart method, and arrange for this to be invoked before there is a possibility for a client to invoke one of the object's methods. Since this code might fail, and so raise an exception, or have arbitrary side-effects, there is an issue as to when this code is executed. In an OPJ system with a very large number of objects, it might be expensive and introduce unacceptable latency to process every object with a transient field on start-up, which suggests a lazy invocation scheme might be more appropriate. On the other hand it is not clear how the programmer is expected to deal with the apparently asynchronous invocation of the restart method.

JOS handles this situation as part of its general mechanism for interposition on the serialization and deserialization of an object. Since serialization processes an entire object graph from one explicit call by the user, and carefully defines the order of calls to user-defined restart handlers, the asynchronous invocation problem does not arise.

Since the OPJ model of persistence is implicit, a different approach is taken. This allows the programmer to adjust the state of the application on restart of the virtual machine, with the aim of re-establishing the state as closely as possible to that which pertained at the last successful checkpoint. In PJama this is achieved by action handlers, which are a generalization of the restart method, and also handle the checkpoint, shutdown, abort and recover situations.

Action handlers are defined by an interface, `PJActionHandler`, that declares the methods: `onStabilization`, `onStartup`, `onShutdown`, `onAbort` and `onRecoveryStartup` which are called by the PJama system when one of the corresponding events occur. Any class may implement this interface to manage its state. Handlers are executed synchronously and there is no system support for lazy, per-object invocation. Instead this must be programmed explicitly using transient fields and the guard check outlined earlier in this section.

Action handlers have been used in the PJama system to deal with several of the core classes that manage external state. For example the problem of ensuring that native code libraries are loaded on every run is handled generically by modifying the `Runtime` class to become an action handler, making the list of loaded library names persistent and reloading them on restart.

A typical idiom for using action handlers is to arrange that constructors of classes needing external state re-establishing on resumption register each new instance on a list. The code in the action handler then scans these lists re-establishing whatever external values are needed.

In an early version of PJama transient fields were reset to their default value after every checkpoint, but restart handlers were not run. This had the disastrous effect of breaking the invariants on the values of transient fields, causing applications to fail. In the current version, the values of transient fields are left unchanged across a checkpoint.

Problem 5.1. The model for writing resumable and resiliant code that copes with external autonomous state needs to be defined, explained and adopted.

The Misuse of the Transient Modifier   Much of the above discussion is centered around using the **transient** modifier as an integral part of the mechanisms for handling external state. Unfortunately, since JDK 1.1, the **transient** modifier has been given a semantics that supports a particular programming idiom that is specific to JOS, and is incompatible with orthogonal persistence.

In JDK 1.1, **transient** has been defined operationally as follows:

Variables marked **transient** in a class are not written to the output stream by a call of `defaultWriteObject()`. If a class does not define its own `writeObject` method (the usual case), then its fields are written to an object stream during serialization by a call of `defaultWriteObject`. Therefore, by the above definition, fields marked **transient** will not be written to the stream. This is consistent with the spirit of **transient** as suggested by the JLS 1.0, and compatible with orthogonal persistence.

However, even if a class does define its own `writeObject`, it is still possible to call the method `defaultWriteObject` explicitly. Given the above definition, this will write out all the fields that are not marked **transient**. So, imagine a class with ten fields, one of which the programmer wants to map explicitly to a representation in the persistent state. An economical way to achieve this is to mark the field **transient**, call `defaultWriteObject` to write out the other nine, and then write the **transient** field explicitly. Unfortunately, the **transient** field is not really transient in the sense of the JLS 1.0 specification, since the field is saved, albeit with a specialized representation. In particular, it is not transient in the sense of orthogonal persistence.

As an example, consider this extract of the `LinkedList` class from the JDK 1.2 `collections` package:

```
private transient Entry header = new Entry(null, null, null);
private transient int size = 0;
```

These fields represent the entire state of the object. Although one might expect this class to be a perfect example for the convenient automation offered by JOS, the programmer has chosen to serialize them explicitly, and is using the idiom to do so, even though there are no non-transient fields to write out. Note also that the transformation of the list representation is not related to handling external state. It is simply an optimization to reduce the storage costs in the persistent form, and avoid some of the overheads of default serialization. It is ironic that the overheads are caused in part by the elabo-rate interposition mechanisms such as `writeObject`.

A consequence of this idiom is that the natural interpretation of **transient** by OPJ must be avoided, otherwise all classes which use the above idiom will be invalid on restart after a checkpoint.

Since the concept of **transient** is so useful for dealing with external state, a replacement is required. In PJama, we have added a **markTransient** method that marks a field transient in the OPJ sense. The irony is that the **transient** modifier directly supports the OPJ principle of persistence independence, which is violated by **markTransient**. Yet in order to use the serialization idiom the programmer is already required to violate this principle comprehensively.

In fact, in JDK 1.2, an alternate mechanism [35] has been provided for specifying which fields to make persistent that might eventually free **transient** for use by OPJ. However, it requires more work by the programmer than the above idiom and, evidently, is not being adopted even in the core classes.

Problem 5.2. The difference between transient and requiring-special-translation needs to be recognised. Proper mechanisms for each of these are required.

6   Class Evolution

A consequence of the OPJ programming model is that an object, once created, cannot change its class. Since the class includes behavior, a persistent application system is intrinsically resistant to change, except by addition of new classes. This consistency, of course, is one of the strengths of the approach, but not all change can be achieved by class addition. Sometimes, it is necessary to alter the definition of a class and, in order to maintain the type consistency of the system, to alter all the existing instances to conform to the change.

There are two basic approaches to achieving class evolution in OPJ. The first is to treat it as an external action, one that is described and takes place outside the OPJ programming model. The second is to provide it as an internal action as part of the OPJ programming model, for example, by extending the Java reflection API to permit **Class** instances to be modified at run-time, as in Smalltalk. It is unclear what the overall impact of such a change would have on the Java platform, but, at a minimum, the implementation challenges alone would be significant for an OPJ environment that supported very large numbers of classes and instances. A more serious concern is maintaining global consistency in the face of a sequence of small changes. It is possible that the transaction approach can be used to manage a complex evolution.

Problem 6.1. Evolution based on reflection appears to be necessary if a continuous service and maintenance are both to be offered. Both the semantics of the reflection operations and their implementation require exploration and definition in the context of persistent programming languages.

The PJama experience with class evolution is very limited to date. We have recently implemented a comprehensive evolution tool using the external action approach [14]. It operates as an off-line activity on a quiescent store. The efficiency of the process is fundamentally limited by the implementation of the virtual machine and store layer in the current version of PJama. We expect to make substantial progress in this area as we begin to use a new store layer [30].

Evolution is, of course, not restricted to the classes of the application, but also affects the virtual machine itself. Indeed, during the development of the PJama prototype, there have been many occasions when a new version of the prototype required that the application completely rebuild its persistent store. This could be solved either by a specific store migration tool with each release, as is common in commercial database products, or by a general archive and restore utility that would save the application data in a form independent from a particular OPJ implementation. Because the intrinsic classes and other classes that use C data structures may be intimately inter-related with JVM details, this is not straightforward. There are for example complex bootstrap problems. It is desirable to discover either abstract reflection methods that can be implemented by such classes or some other well-defined interface to facilitate system evolution and platform migration.

Problem 6.2. Research is needed to discover mechanism that permit a populated persistent store to be detached from one implementation of a persistent language and recoupled to a different implementation of that language.

Evolution is also complicated by the increasing use of Java as an implementation language in the persistence layer itself, because this opens the possibility that an application might evolve a class in such a way that it either breaks or seriously degrades the performance of the system itself. The absence of clear layers in the current Java platform exacerbates this problem.

7   Automatic Storage Management

One of the potential benefits of orthogonal persistence for Java is the extension of automatic storage management to the domain of persistent objects. While there are no conceptual difficulties in this task the engineering involved in developing a robust and efficient solution is considerable. The current level of main-memory storage management for the Java platform is generally considered to be inadequate, and there continues to be much debate as to the best approach to the problem of garbage collection. Experience with garbage collection for large persistent stores is quite limited and still the subject of research.

The current PJama prototype retains the main-memory allocation system of Sun's reference JDK implementation, including its garbage collector for the transient heap. Allocation in the persistent space is implicitly part of the stabilization process, but is currently subject to size limitations per stabilization that can cause transactions with large numbers of new or modified objects to fail. Garbage collection of the persistent store is only available as an off-line process at present [29], which prevents continuous operation. We expect to remove both of these limitations when the new persistent store layer is deployed. Currently Gemstone/J provides the only commercially available persistence solution for Java with a concurrent persistent store garbage collector.

8 Performance of Orthogonal Persistence

Orthogonal persistence for the Java language is undoubtedly challenging to implement such that application performance is acceptable. Indeed, it is unlikely to ever compete on a purely CPU-bound application executing in a highly optimized virtual machine. Fortunately such applications exist only in the simplified world of naïve benchmarks.

The only realistic performance measure is total application cost. This includes application load time, initialization, and the cost of any layered subsystems, such as object-relational mapping layers, and a relational database or file system. There are inherent and significant costs in the multiple-process architectures that are implied in such solutions. We are in the process of performing a comparative study of the total application costs for a range of applications and persistence solutions and hope to report on this in the near future.

Two events have changed the performance overhead of PJama since we last reported our experiences [18]. The first is that since JDK 1.1 the standard interpreter loop has been rewritten in assembler code. This achieves roughly a factor of two speedup. The second is the emergence of Just-In-Time (JIT) compilers for Java bytecodes. The public release of PJama has not been modified to use an assembler interpreter loop. Nor have we felt it worthwhile to support a JIT, which would require modification to insert read and write barriers in the generated code. Internally, we have measured an assembler-loop version of PJama as incurring an over-head of 14one benchmark, which is consistent with the overhead reported in [18], but carries the caveat of a singleton experiment.

It is clear that the overhead of OPJ inevitably increases as the performance of the basic engine improves. Work is underway to exploit optimization techniques [26,17,7,10,9] to further reduce the overhead of OPJ and ultimately we expect to benefit from the more comprehensive dynamic optimization frameworks such as Java Hotspot^{TM} . However, we still believe that total application cost is the critical measure and that, as with automatic storage management, it is acceptable to use a percentage of the annual increase in computing power to simplify the development of robust and reliable software.

Problem 8.1. There are opportunities to exploit orthogonal persistence in optimizers. For example, analysis structures can easily be retained and re-used. There are also opportunities to increase persistent language performance by further research into optimizations that reduce barrier insertions, etc. Optimization in this context should be validated using total system measurements on appropriately realistic applications.

9 Distribution

It should be clear from the earlier discussion that, just as the Java language specification does not directly address the issue of distribution, neither does orthogonal persistence for Java. Although the specification permits an implementation that maintains sets of objects at different nodes in a network, nothing in the Java language specification allows these sets to be distinguished. Furthermore, stabilization would be required to be transparent across all the nodes, although, of course, it might fail more often than with a single node. This is the so-called one-world model of distribution, which is known to be unrealistic beyond relatively small and tightly-bound systems of nodes.

The standard mechanism for distribution in the Java platform is Java RMI, which is more akin to the federated model of distribution, where nodes are autonomous, and programmers must explicitly deal with communication failure and issues of object identity. Java RMI is actually a hybrid system, as it offers aspects of one-world model for objects that implement the java.rmi.Remote interface, including distributed garbage collection. However, programmers must explicitly handle method invocation failure due to communication problems, and some standard methods, for example, Object.hashCode, operate on the local proxy object and not on the object to which the proxy refers.

Since Java RMI, which is almost completely written in Java, uses the socket and input and output mechanisms of the Java core classes, it falls into the category of code that depends on external state discussed in section 5. Perhaps not surprisingly therefore, when standard Java RMI is used with the PJama virtual machine, it does not work correctly once the Java RMI classes are made persistent. To remedy this, the PJama system now includes a modified version of Java RMI that exploits the PJama action handler framework to work correctly when a persistent store is resumed. In addition, it supports the transparent persistence of both exported server objects and client stubs. This scheme is very easy to use in comparison with the programming-intensive mechanisms that are required by the Java RMI Activation framework, which is a new feature of Java RMI that provides similar capabilities in the JDK 1.2 release.

While the support for persistence of Java RMI objects is valuable, it would be preferable if a more orthogonal distribution mechanism were available for Java programmers. The arguments that support the principles of orthogonal persistence apply equally to the field of distribution despite the fact that the realities of latency and partial failure cannot be ignored completely. An example of the benefits that orthogonal persistence could provide to distribution is the provision of stable, globally unique, identity-based hashcodes [4]. Longer term, the extensible transaction model might be a useful mechanism for handling communication failure in addition to handling transaction conflicts and media failure.

10 Conclusions and Further Work

While the general principles of orthogonal persistence are well understood, there is only limited experience in applying them to specific languages. In applying the principles to the Java language, a number of subtle issues arise, which have only been resolved through the experience of application development. These experiences have confirmed the principles to be fundamentally sound and a significant contribution to simplifying the otherwise complex task of managing persistent state.

The work on PJama developing orthogonal persistence in the Java platform has been an interesting as, unlike earlier experiences with academic research languages, we were not only presented with a langauge specification that was a fait accompli, but that languages platform has been evolving rapidly. It is significant that we have been able to show that the existing langauge and its evolutions can be supported. There are certainly several cases where forethought about persistence would have yielded improvement, but for most of the language its integration with orthogonal persistence has been straightforward. This could be said to vindicate the claim in [3] that orthogonal persistence was now ready for industrial use.

Our experiences have demonstrated that the principles of orthogonal persistence must be applied uniformly to the entire Java platform, as application developers inevitably stumble into any omissions, ironically often as a direct consequence of transitive persistence.

It is perhaps surprising to find that support for concurrent transactions within a multithreaded Java application has not become a central issue. We remain committed to research into flexible transaction models that can operate well in this context, but we have also found that there is a demand for durability and recovery where applications have been built using Java's isolation and consistency mechanisms. It is not yet clear how the two approaches can be reconciled.

The open nature of the Java language, which contributed greatly to its speedy adoption, requires that a simple solution be found to the problem of handling state that is external to the Java environment. A combination of the **transient** modifier and action handlers that are invoked at critical points in the execution of an OPJ system solves these problems in an economic and efficient manner.

Several challenges remain before the promise of the OPJ model can be deployed routinely in a wide variety of application environments. First, the implementation of OPJ must be complete and include support for threads. Second, and largely a matter of engineering, the implementation must be scalable and deliver performance that is competitive with standard Java environments. Finally, and the most critical barrier to adoption, there must be an effective solution to the problem of system evolution.

The main text has highlighted a number of specific topics which deserve further attention. In addition there are three more general areas worthy of investigation.

1. Appropriate handling of bulk types. Earlier work [8,20] has suggested that standard data structures (collection classes and indexes) can represent bulk values and that queries can be evaluated by converting them using reflection into code appropriate to both the query and the underlying data structure. The development of this approach into "industrial-strength" bulk data handling, say for SQLJ and OQL, has yet to be demonstrated. This will probably depend on a suitable polymorphism extension [6].
2. Appropriate software engineering approaches. The software engineering methodologies that are currently in use are tuned to the two traditional

data processing models described above (input-compute-output and query-compute-update-repeat). More incremental and event driven models of processing become available with orthogonal persistence and it is necessary to develop corresponding software engineering methodologies. Until such approaches, or at least the underlying design patterns, are made explicit, it will be difficult to get application programmers to convert from the traditional processing models and to benefit from orthogonal persistence.

3. Program development and administration systems are needed for persistent programming. For example, new build models that include evolution must be supported, tools are needed to visualize the content and operation of the persistent store, and installation technology is needed to ship and install replacement sets of classes and objects in populated production stores.

Acknowledgments

The authors are indebted to the entire PJama team, Laurent Daynès, Misha Dmitriev, Neal Gafter, Craig Hamilton, Gordon Haywood, Brian Lewis, Bernd Mathiske, Tony Printezis and Susan Spence. Part of this work is supported by a grant from the British Science and Engineering Research Council.

Trademarks

Sun, Sun Microsystems, Java, JavaBeans, Java Blend, JDK, Java Foundation Classes, Java Hotspot, and Solaris are trademarks or registered trademarks of Sun Microsystems Inc. in the United States and other countries.

References

1. M. P. Atkinson, L. Daynès, M. J. Jordan, T. Printezis, and S. Spence. An Orthogonally Persistent Java. *SIGMOD Record*, December 1996.
2. M. P. Atkinson, M. J. Jordan, L. Daynès, and S. Spence. Design Issues for Persistent Java: a Type-Safe Object-Oriented Orthogonally Persistent System. In *Proceedings of the Seventh International Workshop on Persistent Object Systems (POS7), Cape May, New Jersey, USA*. Morgan Kaufmann, 1996.
3. M. P. Atkinson and R. Morrison. Orthogonal Persistent Object Systems. *VLDB Journal*, 4(3), 1995.
4. M.P. Atkinson and M.J. Jordan. Stable Identity Methods for PJama. Technical Report in preparation, Sun Microsystems Laboratories, 1998.
5. S. Blackburn and J. Zigman. Concurrency — The fly in the ointment? In M.P. Atkinson, M.J. Jordan, and R. Morrison, editors, *Proceedings of the Third International Workshop on Persistence and Java (PJW3)*, Morgan Kaufmann, 1998.
6. G. Bracha, M. Odersky, D. Stoutamire, and P. Wadler. Making the future safe for the past: Adding Genericity to the Java Programming Language. In *Proceedings of OOPSLA '98, Vanvouver, Canada*, October 1988.

7. K. Brahnmath, N. Nystrom, A. Hosking, and Q.I. Cutts. Swizzle-barrier optimization for Orthogonal Persistence for Java. In M.P. Atkinson, M.J. Jordan, and R. Morrison, editors, *Proceedings of the Third International Workshop on Persistence and Java*, pages xx–yy. Morgan Kaufmann Publishers, Inc., September 1998.

8. R.L. Cooper, M.P. Atkinson, A. Dearle, and D. Abderrahmane. Constructing Database Systems in a Persistent Environment. In *Proceedings of the Thirteenth International Conference on Very Large Databases, Brighton, UK*, pages 117–125, September 1987.

9. Q. Cutts and A.L. Hosking. Analysing, profiling and optimising orthogonal persistence for java. In *Proceedings of the Second International Workshop on Persistence and Java (Half Moon Bay, California)*, number SMLI TR-97-63 in Sunlabs Technical Reports, 901 San Antonio Road MS MTV29-01, Palo Alto, CA 94303, USA, August 1997. Sun Microsystems Inc. To appear.

10. Q.I. Cutts, S. Lennon, and A. Hosking. Reconciling Buffer Management with Persistence Optimisations. In M.P. Atkinson, M.J. Jordan, and R. Morrison, editors, *Proceedings of the Eighth International Workshop on Persistent Object Systems*, pages xx–yy. Morgan Kaufmann Publishers, Inc., August 1998.

11. L. Daynès and M. P. Atkinson. Main-Memory Management to support Orthogonal Persistence for Java^{TM}. In *Proceedings of the Second International Workshop on Persistence and Java (PJW2)*, Half Moon Bay, CA, USA, August 1997.

12. L. Daynès, M.P. Atkinson, and P. Valduriez. Efficient Support for Customizing Concurrency Control in Persistent Java. In *International Workshop on Advanced Transaction Models and Architectures (ATMA), Goa, India*, 1996.

13. A. Dearle, R. di Bona, J. Farrow, F. Henskens, A. Lindstrom, J. Rosenberg, and F. Vaughan. Grasshopper: An Orthogonally Persistent Operating System. *Computing Systems*, 7(3):289–312, 1994.

14. M. Dmitriev. The First Experience of Class Evolution Support in PJama. In M.P. Atkinson, M.J. Jordan, and R. Morrison, editors, *Proceedings of the Third International Workshop on Persistence and Java (PJW3)*, pages xx–yy. Morgan Kaufmann, 1998.

15. J. Gosling, B. Joy, and G. Steele. *The Java Language Specification*. Addison-Wesley, 1996.

16. J. Gray and A. Reuter. *Transaction Processing: Concepts and Techniques*. Morgan Kaufmann Publishers, Inc., 1993.

17. A. Hosking, N. Nystrom, Q. Cutts, and K. Brahnmath. Optimizing the read and write barrier for orthogonal persistence. In *Proceedings of the Eighth International Workshop on Persistent Object Systems*, Tiburon, California, August 1998. To appear.

18. M. J. Jordan. Early Experiences with Persistent Java. In *Proceedings of the First International Workshop on Persistence and Java (Drymen, Scotland) (PJW1)*, MS MTV29-01, 901 San Antonio Road, Palo Alto, CA 94303, USA, 1996. Sun Microsystems Laboratories.

19. M.J. Jordan and M.P. Atkinson. Orthogonal Persistence for Java — A Mid-term Report. In M.P. Atkinson, M.J. Jordan, and R. Morrison, editors, *Proceedings of the Third International Workshop on Persistence and Java (PJW3)*, pages xx–yy. Morgan Kaufmann, 1998.

20. G. Kutlu and J.E.B. Moss. Exploiting Reflection to add Persistence and Query Optimization to a Statically Typed Object-Oriented Language. In M.P. Atkinson, M.J. Jordan, and R. Morrison, editors, *Proceedings of the Eighth International*

   Workshop on Persistent Object Systems (Tiburon, California), pages xx–yy. Morgan Kaufmann Publishers, Inc., August 1998.
21. C. Landau. The Checkpoint Mechanism in KeyKOS. In *Proceedings of the IEEE Second International Workshop on Object Orientation in Operating Systems*, September 1992.
22. D. Lea. *Concurrent Programming in Java — Design Principles and Patterns*. Addison-Wesley, 1997.
23. J. Liedtke. A persistent System in Real Use — Experiences of the First 13 years. In *Proceedings of the Third International Workshop on Object-Orientation in Operating Systems*, 1993.
24. T. Lindholm and F. Yellin. *The Java Virtual Machine Specification*. Addison-Wesley, 1996.
25. D. B. Lomet and G. Weikum. Efficient and TRansparent Application Recovery in Client-Server Information Systems. In *Proceedings of ACM SIGMOD Conference 1998*, May 1998.
26. N. Nystrom, A.L. Hosking, Q.I. Cutts, and A. Diwan. Partial Redundancy Elimination for Access Path Expressions. In *Proceedings of OOPSLA'98*, pages xx–yy. ACM, October 1998.
27. Object Design Inc. Object PSE Pro for Java, 1997.
28. Oracle Corporation. SQLJ User Guide and Reference, Oracle 8. Technical report, Oracle Corporation, 1987.
29. T. Printezis. Analysing a Simple Disk Garbage Collector. In *Proceedings of the First International Workshop on Persistence and Java (Drymen, Scotland) (PJW1)*, MS MTV29-01, 901 San Antonio Road, Palo Alto, CA 94303, USA, 1996. Sun Microsystems Laboratories.
30. T. Printezis, M. P. Atkinson, L. Daynès, S. Spence, and P. Bailey. The Design of a new Persistent Object Store for PJama. In *Proceedings of the Second International Workshop on Persistence and Java (PJW2)*, Half Moon Bay, CA, USA, August 1997.
31. R.G.G. Cattell (Ed.). *The Object Database Standard: ODMG 2.0*. Morgan Kaufmann, 1997.
32. Sun Microsystems Inc. JavaBeans™, Revision 1.01, July 1997.
33. Sun Microsystems Inc. Java Blend™, 1998.
34. Sun Microsystems Inc. Java Foundation Classes, 1998.
35. Sun Microsystems Inc. Java Object Serialization Specification Beta Draft, Revision 1.4.1, February 1998.
36. F. Xhumari, C. Souza Dos Santos, and M. Skubiszewski. Java Universal Binding. In *Proceedings of the Second International Workshop on Persistence and Java, Sun Microsystems Technical Report TR-97-63*, number SMLI TR-97-63 in Sunlabs Technical Reports, MS MTV29-01, 901 San Antonio Road, Palo Alto, CA 94303-4900, USA, 1997. Sun Microsystems Laboratories.

Novel Computational Approaches to Information Retrieval and Data Mining

Christos H. Papadimitriou*

University of California, Berkeley, USA
christos@cs.berkeley.edu

Abstract. The realities and opportunities of the global information environment enable and necessitate new techniques and approaches, they expand the scope and the methodology of database theory. This talk surveys recent results of this nature, by the author and/or several collaborators, in two areas. In information retrieval, spectral methods have been introduced which extract the hidden semantics of a corpus by analysing the eigenvalues of related matrices. In fact, the performance of such methods can be theoretically predicted to be favorable in a certain statistical sense. A different spectral method has also been introduced successfully in the analysis of hypertext so as to identify authoritative sources of information. In data mining —the search for interesting patterns in data— we argue that a meaningful definition of "interesting" requires consideration of the optimization problem the enterprise is facing. This "microeconomic" view leads quickly to certain novel and interesting computational problems.

* Research partially supported by the National Science Foundation.

Description Logics and Their Relationships with Databases

Maurizio Lenzerini

Dipartimento di Informatica e Sistemistica
Università di Roma "La Sapienza"
Via Salaria 113, I-00198 Roma, Italy
lenzerini@dis.uniroma1.it

Abstract. Description Logics are logics for representing and reasoning about classes of objects and their relationships. They can be seen as successors of semantic networks and frame systems, and have been investigated for more than a decade under different points of view, in particular, expressive power and computational complexity of reasoning. In this short paper, we introduce Description Logics, we compare Description Logics with Database models, and then discuss how Description Logics can be used for several tasks related to data management, in particular information integration, and semi-structured data modeling.

1 Introduction

The idea of developing knowledge representation systems based on a structured representation of knowledge was first pursued with *Semantic Networks* and *Frames*. Semantic Networks [28] represent knowledge under the form of a labeled directed graph. Specifically, each node is associated with a concept, and the arcs represent the various relations between concepts. *Frames* [31] represent concepts (or classes) and are characterized by a number of elements called slots, each of which corresponds to an attribute that the members of the class can have.

The attempt to provide a formal ground to Semantic Networks and Frames led to the development of the system KL-ONE [11]. More recently, *Description Logics*[1] (DLs) have been proposed as successors of KL-ONE, with an explicit model-theoretic semantics. The family of DL systems includes systems like KRYPTON [10], NIKL [26], BACK [32], LOOM [30], CLASSIC [8], KRIS [4], and others (see [33,35]).

In DLs the domain of interest is modeled by means of *concepts* and *relationships*, which denote classes of objects and relations, respectively. Generally speaking, a DL is formed by three basic components:

- A *description language*, which specifies how to construct complex concept and relationship expressions (also called simply concepts and relationships),

---

[1] See http://dl.kr.org for the home page of Description Logics.

Catriel Beeri, Peter Buneman (Eds.): ICDT'99, LNCS 1540, pp. 32–38, 1998.

by starting from a set of atomic symbols and by applying suitable constructors.
- A *knowledge specification mechanism*, which specifies how to construct a DL knowledge base, in which properties of concepts and relationships are asserted.
- A set of *reasoning procedures* provided by the DL.

The set of allowed constructors characterizes the expressive power of the description language. Various languages have been considered by the DL community, and recent papers aim at formally studying their expressive power under different points of view [7,3,13].

We provide here an example of description language, in particular the one of the DL $\mathcal{DLR}_{reg}$, used in [15]. We assume to deal with a finite set of atomic relationships and concepts[2], denoted by $\mathbf{P}$ and A respectively. We use $\mathbf{R}$ to denote arbitrary relations[3] (of given arity between 2 and n_{max}), E to denote regular expressions, and C to denote arbitrary concepts, respectively built according to the following syntax

$$\mathbf{R} ::= \top_n \mid \mathbf{P} \mid (\$i/n{:}C) \mid \neg\mathbf{R} \mid \mathbf{R}_1 \sqcap \mathbf{R}_2$$
$$E ::= \varepsilon \mid \mathbf{R}|_{\$i,\$j} \mid E_1 \circ E_2 \mid E_1 \sqcup E_2 \mid E^*$$
$$C ::= \top_1 \mid A \mid \neg C \mid C_1 \sqcap C_2 \mid \exists E.C \mid \exists[\$i]\mathbf{R} \mid (\leq k\,[\$i]\mathbf{R})$$

where i and j denote components of relations, i.e. integers between 1 and n_{max}, n denotes the arity of a relation, i.e. an integer between 2 and n_{max}, and k denotes a nonnegative integer.

We consider only concepts and relationships that are *well-typed*, which means that

- only relations of the same arity n are combined to form expressions of type $\mathbf{R}_1 \sqcap \mathbf{R}_2$ (which inherit the arity n), and
- $i \leq n$ whenever i denotes a component of a relation of arity n.

The semantics of expressions is specified through the notion of interpretation. An *interpretation* $\mathcal{I} = (\Delta^{\mathcal{I}}, \cdot^{\mathcal{I}})$ is constituted by an *interpretation domain* $\Delta^{\mathcal{I}}$ and an *interpretation function* $\cdot^{\mathcal{I}}$ that assigns to each concept C a subset $C^{\mathcal{I}}$ of $\Delta^{\mathcal{I}}$, to each regular expression E a subset $E^{\mathcal{I}}$ of $\Delta^{\mathcal{I}} \times \Delta^{\mathcal{I}}$, and to each relation $\mathbf{R}$ of arity n a subset $\mathbf{R}^{\mathcal{I}}$ of $(\Delta^{\mathcal{I}})^n$, such that the conditions in Figure 1 are satisfied. We observe that $\top_1$ denotes the interpretation domain, while $\top_n$, for $n > 1$, does *not* denote the n-Cartesian product of the domain, but only a subset of it, that covers all relations of arity n. It follows, from this property, that the "$\neg$" constructor on relations is used to express difference of relations, rather than complement.

---

[2] In general, DLs consider also individuals besides concepts and relationships, although we do not deal with them in this paper.
[3] Although most DLs deal only with binary relationships (called *roles*), $\mathcal{DLR}_{reg}$ does not impose this limitation.

$$T_n^{\mathcal{I}} \subseteq (\Delta^{\mathcal{I}})^n$$
$$\mathbf{P}^{\mathcal{I}} \subseteq T_n^{\mathcal{I}}$$
$$(\$i/n:C)^{\mathcal{I}} = \{(d_1, \ldots, d_n) \in T_n^{\mathcal{I}} \mid d_i \in C^{\mathcal{I}}\}$$
$$(\neg \mathbf{R})^{\mathcal{I}} = T_n^{\mathcal{I}} \setminus \mathbf{R}^{\mathcal{I}}$$
$$(\mathbf{R}_1 \sqcap \mathbf{R}_2)^{\mathcal{I}} = \mathbf{R}_1^{\mathcal{I}} \cap \mathbf{R}_2^{\mathcal{I}}$$

$$\varepsilon^{\mathcal{I}} = \{(x, x) \mid x \in \Delta^{\mathcal{I}}\}$$
$$(\mathbf{R}|_{\$i,\$j})^{\mathcal{I}} = \{(x_i, x_j) \mid$$
$$(x_1, \ldots, x_n) \in \mathbf{R}^{\mathcal{I}}\}$$
$$(E_1 \circ E_2)^{\mathcal{I}} = E_1^{\mathcal{I}} \circ E_2^{\mathcal{I}}$$
$$(E_1 \sqcup E_2)^{\mathcal{I}} = E_1^{\mathcal{I}} \cup E_2^{\mathcal{I}}$$
$$(E^*)^{\mathcal{I}} = (E^{\mathcal{I}})^*$$

$$\top_1^{\mathcal{I}} = \Delta^{\mathcal{I}} \qquad\qquad (\neg C)^{\mathcal{I}} = \Delta^{\mathcal{I}} \setminus C^{\mathcal{I}}$$
$$A^{\mathcal{I}} \subseteq \Delta^{\mathcal{I}} \qquad\qquad (C_1 \sqcap C_2)^{\mathcal{I}} = C_1^{\mathcal{I}} \cap C_2^{\mathcal{I}}$$
$$(\exists E.C)^{\mathcal{I}} = \{d \in \Delta^{\mathcal{I}} \mid \exists d' \in C^{\mathcal{I}}.(d, d') \in E^{\mathcal{I}}\}$$
$$(\exists [\$i] \mathbf{R})^{\mathcal{I}} = \{d \in \Delta^{\mathcal{I}} \mid \exists (d_1, \ldots, d_n) \in \mathbf{R}^{\mathcal{I}}.d_i = d\}$$
$$(\leq k\,[\$i]\mathbf{R})^{\mathcal{I}} = \{d \in \Delta^{\mathcal{I}} \mid \#\{(d_1, \ldots, d_n) \in \mathbf{R}_1^{\mathcal{I}} \mid d_i = d\} \leq k\}$$

Fig. 1. Semantic rules for $\mathcal{DLR}_{reg}$ ($\mathbf{P}$, $\mathbf{R}$, $\mathbf{R}_1$, and $\mathbf{R}_2$ have arity n)

Using (concept and relationship) expressions, knowledge about concepts and relationships can be expressed through the notion of knowledge base. In $\mathcal{DLR}_{reg}$, a knowledge base is constituted by a finite set of *inclusion assertions* of the form

$$\mathbf{R}_1 \sqsubseteq \mathbf{R}_2$$
$$C_1 \sqsubseteq C_2$$

where $\mathbf{R}_1$ and $\mathbf{R}_2$ are of the same arity.

An interpretation $\mathcal{I}$ *satisfies* an assertion $\mathbf{R}_1 \sqsubseteq \mathbf{R}_2$ (resp. $C_1 \sqsubseteq C_2$) if $\mathbf{R}_1^{\mathcal{I}} \subseteq \mathbf{R}_2^{\mathcal{I}}$ (resp. $C_1^{\mathcal{I}} \subseteq C_2^{\mathcal{I}}$). An interpretation that satisfies all assertions in a knowledge base S is called a *model* of S.

The fundamental reasoning tasks considered in the context of Description Logics are *knowledge base satisfiability, concept and relationship satisfiability*, and *logical implication*. A knowledge base S is satisfiable if it admits a model. A concept C is satisfiable in S if S admits a model in which C has a nonempty interpretation (similarly for relationships). S logically implies an inclusion assertion $C_1 \sqsubseteq C_2$ if in all models of S the interpretation of C_1 is a subset of the interpretation of C_2.

Much of the research efforts in DLs in the last decade have been devoted to characterizing the trade-off between the expressive power of DLs and the decidability/complexity of reasoning. We refer to [24,23] for a survey on this subject.

2   Description Logics and Database Models

A knowledge base S in $\mathcal{DLR}_{reg}$ can be seen as a database schema, in such a way that a model of S corresponds to a database conforming to the schema, i.e. a database satisfying all the constraints represented by S. Under this view, a DL can be considered as a data model. An inclusion assertion $A \sqsubseteq C$ (where A is atomic) specifies *necessary* conditions for an object to be an instance of the concept A, and thus corresponds naturally to the constraints imposed on classes by a schema expressed in a traditional database model. The pair of inclusions $A \sqsubseteq C$ and $C \sqsubseteq A$ specifies both *necessary and sufficient* conditions for the instances of A, and thus corresponds to the concept of *view* used in databases.

Several papers discuss more precisely the relationship between DLs and data models and languages (see, for example, [6,29,20]). All of them emphasize that DLs provides modeling features, such as the possibility of expressing incomplete information, that are generally not supported by traditional data models. Notably, the reasoning capabilities of DLs can be very useful for supporting inferencing on a database schema. In this respect, it is important to notice that reasoning in Databases is usually done by referring to finite models only. The assumption of dealing with finite structures is, however, by no means common in Description Logics, and needs to be taken explicitly into account when devising reasoning procedures to be used in data modeling. We refer to [19,14] for methods for finite model reasoning in DLs.

3   Information Integration

Several advanced applications of databases require to integrate information coming from different sources [34], so as to provide a uniform access to data residing at the sources. DLs have been used for information integration in various ways. For example, [22,21] use DLs for specifying and reasoning about the interrelationships between classes of objects in different sources. [27,18] use a specific DL for describing the conceptual schema of an integration application, and for specifying the content of the sources, as views of the conceptual schema.

In all the approaches, the reasoning capabilities of DLs are used to support the task of query answering. In particular, the notions of query containment and query rewriting have been shown to be crucial for devising effective algorithms that reason about the content of the sources and their relationships with the query. Recent results on these aspects for the case of DL-based integration are reported in [5,15].

4   Semi-structured Data Modeling

The ability to represent data whose structure is less rigid and strict than in conventional databases is considered a crucial aspect in many application areas, such as digital libraries, internet information systems, etc.. Following [1], we define semi-structured data as data that is neither raw, nor strictly typed as in conventional database systems. Recent proposals of models for semi-structured data represent data as graphs with labeled edges, where information on both the values and the schema of data are kept [2,12,25]. For several tasks related to data management, it is important to be able to check subsumption between two schemas, i.e. to check whether every graph conforming to one schema always conforms to another schema.

A model of a DL knowledge base can be naturally seen as a labeled graph. Moreover, the possibility of expressing both incomplete information and sophisticated constraints at the schema level makes the family of DLs a good candidate for modeling semi-structured data schemas. Again, the reasoning capabilities of DLs can be profitably exploited for reasoning about semi-structured data schemas and queries, as discussed in [17,16].

References

1. Serge Abiteboul. Querying semi-structured data. In *Proceedings of the Sixth International Conference on Database Theory (ICDT-97)*, pages 1–18, 1997.
2. Serge Abiteboul, Dallan Quass, Jason McHugh, Jennifer Widom, and Janet L. Wiener. The Lorel query language for semistructured data. *International Journal on Digital Libraries*, 1(1):68–88, 1997.
3. Franz Baader. A formal definition for the expressive power of terminological knowledge representation languages. *Journal of Logic and Computation*, 6:33–54, 1996.
4. Franz Baader and Bernhard Hollunder. A terminological knowledge representation system with complete inference algorithm. In *Proc. of the Workshop on Processing Declarative Knowledge (PDK-91)*, number 567 in Lecture Notes In Artificial Intelligence, pages 67–86. Springer-Verlag, 1991.
5. Catriel Beeri, Alon Y. Levy, and Marie-Christine Rousset. Rewriting queries using views in description logics. In *Proceedings of the Sixteenth ACM SIGACT SIGMOD SIGART Symposium on Principles of Database Systems (PODS-97)*, pages 99–108, 1997.
6. Alexander Borgida. Description logics in data management. *IEEE Transactions on Knowledge and Data Engineering*, 7(5):671–682, 1995.
7. Alexander Borgida. On the relative expressiveness of description logics and predicate logics. *Artificial Intelligence*, 82:353–367, 1996.
8. Alexander Borgida, Ronald J. Brachman, Deborah L. McGuinness, and Lori Alperin Resnick. CLASSIC: A structural data model for objects. In *Proceedings of the ACM SIGMOD International Conference on Management of Data*, pages 59–67, 1989.
9. Ronald J. Brachman and Hector J. Levesque. *Readings in Knowledge Representation*. Morgan Kaufmann, Los Altos, 1985.
10. Ronald J. Brachman, Victoria Pigman Gilbert, and Hector J. Levesque. An essential hybrid reasoning system: Knowledge and symbol level accounts in KRYPTON. In *Proceedings of the Ninth International Joint Conference on Artificial Intelligence (IJCAI-85)*, pages 532–539, Los Angeles, 1985.
11. Ronald J. Brachman and James G. Schmolze. An overview of the KL-ONE knowledge representation system. *Cognitive Science*, 9(2):171–216, 1985.
12. Peter Buneman, Susan Davidson, Mary Fernandez, and Dan Suciu. Adding structure to unstructured data. In *Proceedings of the Sixth International Conference on Database Theory (ICDT-97)*, pages 336–350, 1997.

13. Marco Cadoli, Luigi Palopoli, and Maurizio Lenzerini. Datalog and description logics: Expressive power. In *Proceedings of the Sixth International Workshop on Database Programming Languages (DBPL-97)*, 1997.
14. Diego Calvanese. Finite model reasoning in description logics. In Luigia C. Aiello, John Doyle, and Stuart C. Shapiro, editors, *Proceedings of the Fifth International Conference on the Principles of Knowledge Representation and Reasoning (KR-96)*, pages 292–303. Morgan Kaufmann, Los Altos, 1996.
15. Diego Calvanese, Giuseppe De Giacomo, and Maurizio Lenzerini. On the decidability of query containment under constraints. In *Proceedings of the Seventeenth ACM SIGACT SIGMOD SIGART Symposium on Principles of Database Systems (PODS-98)*, pages 149–158, 1998.
16. Diego Calvanese, Giuseppe De Giacomo, and Maurizio Lenzerini. Representing and reasoning on the structure of documents: A description logics approach. Submitted for publication, 1998.
17. Diego Calvanese, Giuseppe De Giacomo, and Maurizio Lenzerini. What can knowledge representation do for semi-structured data? In *Proceedings of the Fifteenth National Conference on Artificial Intelligence (AAAI-98)*, pages 205–210, 1998.
18. Diego Calvanese, Giuseppe De Giacomo, Maurizio Lenzerini, Daniele Nardi, and Riccardo Rosati. Description logic framework for information integration. In *Proceedings of the Sixth International Conference on Principles of Knowledge Representation and Reasoning (KR-98)*, pages 2–13, 1998.
19. Diego Calvanese, Maurizio Lenzerini, and Daniele Nardi. A unified framework for class based representation formalisms. In J. Doyle, E. Sandewall, and P. Torasso, editors, *Proceedings of the Fourth International Conference on the Principles of Knowledge Representation and Reasoning (KR-94)*, pages 109–120, Bonn, 1994. Morgan Kaufmann, Los Altos.
20. Diego Calvanese, Maurizio Lenzerini, and Daniele Nardi. Description logics for conceptual data modeling. In Jan Chomicki and Günter Saake, editors, *Logics for Databases and Information Systems*, pages 229–264. Kluwer Academic Publisher, 1998.
21. Tiziana Catarci and Maurizio Lenzerini. Representing and using interschema knowledge in cooperative information systems. *Journal of Intelligent and Cooperative Information Systems*, 2(4):375–398, 1993.
22. Christine Collet, Michael N. Huhns, and Wei-Min Shen. Resource integration using a large knowledge base in Carnot. *IEEE Computer*, 24(12):55–62, 1991.
23. Francesco M. Donini, Maurizio Lenzerini, Daniele Nardi, and Werner Nutt. The complexity of concept languages. *Information and Computation*, 134:1–58, 1997.
24. Francesco M. Donini, Maurizio Lenzerini, Daniele Nardi, and Andrea Schaerf. Reasoning in description logics. In Gerhard Brewka, editor, *Principles of Knowledge Representation*, Studies in Logic, Language and Information, pages 193–238. CSLI Publications, 1996.
25. Mary F. Fernandez, Daniela Florescu, Jaewoo Kang, Alon Y. Levy, and Dan Suciu. Catching the boat with strudel: Experiences with a web-site management system. In *Proceedings of the ACM SIGMOD International Conference on Management of Data*, pages 414–425, 1998.
26. Thomas S. Kaczmarek, Raymond Bates, and Gabriel Robins. Recent developments in NIKL. In *Proceedings of the Fifth National Conference on Artificial Intelligence (AAAI-86)*, pages 978–985, 1986.
27. Thomas Kirk, Alon Y. Levy, Yehoshua Sagiv, and Divesh Srivastava. The Information Manifold. In *Proceedings of the AAAI 1995 Spring Symp. on Information Gathering from Heterogeneous, Distributed Enviroments*, pages 85–91, 1995.

28. Fritz Lehmann. Semantic networks. In Fritz Lehmann, editor, *Semantic Networks in Artificial Intelligence*, pages 1–50. Pergamon Press, 1992.
29. Alon Y. Levy and Marie-Christine Rousset. CARIN: A representation language combining Horn rules and description logics. In *Proceedings of the Twelfth European Conference on Artificial Intelligence (ECAI-96)*, pages 323–327, 1996.
30. Robert MacGregor and R. Bates. The Loom knowledge representation language. Technical Report ISI/RS-87-188, University of Southern California, Information Science Institute, Marina del Rey, Cal., 1987.
31. Marvin Minsky. A framework for representing knowledge. In J. Haugeland, editor, *Mind Design*. The MIT Press, 1981. A longer version appeared in *The Psychology of Computer Vision* (1975). Republished in [9].
32. Joachim Quantz and Carsten Kindermann. Implementation of the BACK system version 4. Technical Report KIT-Report 78, FB Informatik, Technische Universität Berlin, Berlin, Germany, 1990.
33. Charles (ed) Rich. Special issue on implemented knowledge representation and reasoning systems. *SIGART Bulletin*, 2(3), 1991.
34. Jeffrey D. Ullman. Information integration using logical views. In *Proceedings of the Sixth International Conference on Database Theory (ICDT-97)*, number 1186 in Lecture Notes in Computer Science, pages 19–40. Springer-Verlag, 1997.
35. William A. Woods and James G. Schmolze. The KL-ONE family. In F. W. Lehmann, editor, *Semantic Networks in Artificial Intelligence*, pages 133–178. Pergamon Press, 1992. Published as a special issue of *Computers & Mathematics with Applications*, Volume 23, Number 2–9.

An Equational Chase for Path-Conjunctive Queries, Constraints, and Views

Lucian Popa and Val Tannen

University of Pennsylvania,
Department of Computer and Information Science,
200 South 33rd Street, Philadelphia, PA 19104, USA
{lpopa, val}@saul.cis.upenn.edu

Abstract. We consider the class of *path-conjunctive* queries and constraints (dependencies) defined over complex values with dictionaries. This class includes the relational conjunctive queries and embedded dependencies, as well as many interesting examples of complex value and oodb queries and integrity constraints. We show that some important classical results on containment, dependency implication, and chasing extend and generalize to this class.

1 Motivation

We are interested in distributed, mediator-based systems [Wie92] with multiple layers of nodes implementing mediated views (unmaterialized or only partially materialized) that integrate heterogenous data sources. Most of the queries that flow between the nodes of such a system are not formulated by a user but are instead generated automatically by composition with views and decomposition among multiple sources. Unoptimized, this process causes queries to quickly snowball into forms with superfluous computations. Even more importantly, without additional optimizations this process ignores intra- and inter-data source integrity constraints [1].

It has been recognized for some time that exploiting integrity constraints (so-called semantic optimization) plays a crucial role in oodbs [CD92] and in integrating heterogenous data sources [QR95,LSK95]. Relational database theory has studied extensively such issues [Mai83,Ull89,AHV95] but in the recent literature the use of constraints in optimization has been limited to special cases (see the related work in section 7). In contrast, we propose here a foundation for a systematic and quite general approach encompassing the old relational theory and a significant class of non-relational queries, constraints and views. A novel property of our approach, one that we hope to exploit in relation to rule-based optimization as in [CZ96], is that optimizing under constraints or deriving other constraints can be done *within* the equational theory of our internal framework by rewriting with the constraints themselves.

---

[1] In this paper, we use the terms *constraints* and *dependencies* interchangeably.

Catriel Beeri, Peter Buneman (Eds.): ICDT'99, LNCS 1540, pp. 39–57, 1998.

In this opening section we plan to show two motivating examples: one illustrating the important effect of constraints on query optimization, the other—coming from the announced paradigm of distributed mediator-base systems—concerned with deriving constraints that hold in views. The novel ideas to look for in these examples are (1) the use of the constraints themselves as "rewrite" rules (what we call the *equational chase*) (2) the ability to "compose" views with constraints yielding other constraints that can be checked directly (3) the ease with which we handle the heterogenous nature of the examples' schema (figure 1) which features a relation interacting with a class.

Both examples are resolved with the general techniques that we develop in this paper. For simplicity these examples are shown in the syntax of the ODMG [Cat96] proposal although the actual method is developed and justified primarily for our more general internal framework (see section 3). Consider the schema in figure 1. It is written following mostly the syntax of ODL, the data definition language of ODMG, extended with referential integrity (foreign key) constraints in the style of data definition in SQL. It consists of a class Dept whose objects represent departments, with name, manager name, and DProjs, the set of names of all the projects done in the department. It also consists of a relation Proj whose tuples represent projects, with name, customer name, and PDept, the name of the department in which the project is done.

```
Proj : set<struct{              class Dept
    string PName;                 (extent depts  key DName){
    string CustName;                attribute string DName;
    string PDept;}>                 relationship set<string> DProjs
  primary key PName;                  inverse Proj(PDept);
  foreign key PDept                 attribute string MgrName;}
    references Dept::DName;        foreign key DProjs
  relationship PDept                 references Proj(PName);
    inverse Dept::DProjs;
```

Fig. 1. The Proj-Dept schema, expressed in extended ODMG

The meaning of the referential integrity (RICs), inverse relationship, and key constraints specified in the schema is expressed by the following logical statements.

(RIC1) $\forall(d \in \text{depts})\ \forall(s \in d.\text{DProjs})\ \exists(p \in \text{Proj})\ s = p.\text{PName}$

(RIC2) $\forall(p \in \text{Proj})\ \exists(d \in \text{depts})\ p.\text{PDept} = d.\text{DName}$

(INV1) $\forall(d \in \text{depts})\ \forall(s \in d.\text{DProjs})\ \forall(p \in \text{Proj})$
$$s = p.\text{PName} \ \Rightarrow\ p.\text{PDept} = d.\text{DName}$$

(INV2) $\forall(p \in \text{Proj})\ \forall(d \in \text{depts})$
$$p.\text{PDept} = d.\text{DName} \ \Rightarrow\ \exists(s \in d.\text{DProjs})\ p.\text{PName} = s$$

(KEY1) $\forall(d \in \text{depts})\ \forall(d' \in \text{depts})\ d.\text{DName} = d'.\text{DName}\ \Rightarrow\ d = d'$

(KEY2) $\forall(p \in \text{Proj})\ \forall(p' \in \text{Proj})\ p.\text{PName} = p'.\text{PName}\ \Rightarrow\ p = p'$

A query equivalence. In the presence of the constraints above, the following OQL[2] query:

```
define ABC_DP as select distinct  struct(PN: s, DN: d.DName)
                      from  depts d, d.DProjs s, Proj p
                      where  s = p.PName  and  p.CustName = "ABC"
```

is equivalent to the (likely better) query:

```
define ABC_P as select distinct struct(PN: p.PName, DN: p.PDept)
                     from  Proj p
                     where  p.CustName = "ABC"
```

Because it involves both a class and a relation, and because it doesn't hold if the constraints are absent, the equivalence between ABC_DP and ABC_P does not appear to fit within previously proposed optimization frameworks. We will see that the equational chase method that we develop in this paper can be used to obtain this equivalence. Each of the constraints determines a semantics-preserving transformation rule. Specifically, one step of chasing with a constraint of the form

$$\forall(r_1 \in R_1) \cdots \forall(r_m \in R_m)\, [\, B_1\ \Rightarrow\ \exists(s_1 \in S_1) \cdots \exists(s_n \in S_n)\ B_2\,]$$

produces the transformation

```
select distinct  E              select distinct  E
from   R₁ r₁,..., Rm rm    ⤇     from   R₁ r₁,..., Rm rm, S₁ s₁,..., Sn sn
where  B₁  and  C               where  B₁  and  B₂  and  C
```

This transformation may seem somewhat mysterious, but we shall see that it can be justified by *equational* rewriting with the constraint itself put in an equational form and with the (idemloop) law (see section 3). We shall also see that when restricted to the relational model, the method amounts exactly to the *chase* [BV84]. Anyway, chasing ABC_DP with (INV1) gives

```
select distinct  struct(PN: s, DN: d.DName)
from   depts d, d.DProjs s, Proj p
where  s = p.PName and p.PDept = d.DName and p.CustName = "ABC"
```

while chasing ABC_P with (RIC2) and then with (INV2) gives

```
select distinct  struct(PN: p.PName, DN: p.PDept)
from  Proj p, depts d, d.DProjs s
where  p.PDept = d.DName and p.PName = s and p.CustName = "ABC"
```

These two queries are clearly equivalent.

---

[2] OQL is ODMG's query language.

A constraint derivation for views. Consider again the `Proj`-`Dept` schema in figure 1 and the following view, which combines *un*nesting, *j*oining, and *p*rojecting:

```
define UJP_View as
  select distinct
    struct(PN: p.PName, CN: p.CustName, MN: d.MgrName)
  from  Proj p, depts d, d.DProjs s,
  where  s = p.PName
```

We will establish that the functional dependency `PN` → `MN` holds in this view, namely

(FD) $\forall(v \in \text{UJP\_View}) \ \forall(v' \in \text{UJP\_View}) \ v.\text{PN} = v'.\text{PN} \ \Rightarrow \ v.\text{MN} = v'.\text{MN}$

Note that standard reasoning about functional dependencies is not applicable because of the nature of the view. Indeed we shall see that in addition to the key dependencies we will also use (INV1) to establish (FD).

We perform the derivation in two phases. First we *compose* (FD) with the view, obtaining a constraint on the original `Proj`-`Dept` schema. This is done by substituting the definition of `UJP_View` for the name `UJP_View` in (FD) and then rewriting the resulting constraint to the following form:

(FD-RETRO) $\forall(p \in \text{Proj}) \ \forall(d \in \text{depts}) \ \forall(s \in d.\text{DProjs})$
$\forall(p' \in \text{Proj}) \ \forall(d' \in \text{depts}) \ \forall(s' \in d.\text{DProjs})$
$s = p.\text{PName} \ \wedge \ s' = p'.\text{PName} \ \wedge \ p.\text{PName} = p'.\text{PName} \ \Rightarrow$
$d.\text{MgrName} = d'.\text{MgrName}$

Thus, (FD) holds in the view iff (FD-RETRO) holds in `Proj`-`Dept`. In the second phase we show that (FD-RETRO) follows from the constraints in the `Proj`-`Dept` schema. The equational chase method applies to constraints as well as to queries. Specifically, one step of chasing with a constraint of the form

$$\forall(r_1 \in R_1) \cdots \forall(r_m \in R_m) \ [\ B_1 \ \Rightarrow \ \exists(s_1 \in S_1) \cdots \exists(s_n \in S_n) \ B_2 \ ]$$

produces the transformation

$$\forall(r_1 \in R_1) \cdots \forall(r_m \in R_m) \ [\ B_1 \ \Rightarrow \ \exists(t_1 \in T_1) \cdots \exists(t_p \in T_p) \ B_3 \ ]$$
$$\overset{\Leftrightarrow}{\longmapsto}$$
$$\forall(r_1 \in R_1) \cdots \forall(r_m \in R_m) \ \forall(s_1 \in S_1) \cdots \forall(s_n \in S_n)$$
$$[\ B_1 \wedge B_2 \ \Rightarrow \ \exists(t_1 \in T_1) \cdots \exists(t_p \in T_p) \ B_3 \ ]$$

Again, the rewriting that produces (FD-RETRO) and the transformation of constraints we just saw may seem somewhat mysterious, but they too have a simple and clear justification in terms of equational rewriting (see section 3).

Now, chasing (twice) with (INV1), then with (KEY2) and finally with (KEY1), transforms (FD-RETRO) into

(TRIV) $\forall(p \in \text{Proj})$ $\forall(d \in \text{depts})$ $\forall(s \in d.\text{DProjs})$
           $\forall(p' \in \text{Proj})$ $\forall(d' \in \text{depts})$ $\forall(s' \in d.\text{DProjs})$
           $s = p.\text{PName} \wedge p.\text{PDept} = d.\text{DName} \wedge$
           $s' = p'.\text{PName} \wedge p'.\text{PDept} = d'.\text{DName} \wedge$
           $p.\text{PName} = p'.\text{PName} \wedge p = p' \wedge$
           $d = d' \Rightarrow d.\text{MgrName} = d'.\text{MgrName}$

(Along the way, some simple facts about conjunction and equality came into play.) But (TRIV) is a constraint that holds in *all* instances, regardless of other constraints (such a constraint or dependency is traditionally called *trivial*). Therefore, (FD-RETRO) follows from (INV1, KEY2, KEY1).

How general is this method? The rest of the paper is concerned with proposing an answer to this question. We give first an overview, then we use our internal framework to justify the soundness of the method illustrated in the previous examples, and finally using *path-conjunctions* we identify a class of queries, constraints and views for which this method leads to decision procedures and complete equational reasoning.

2   Overview (of the Rest of the Paper)

In section 3 we present some aspects of our internal framework, called CoDi [3]. This is a language and equational theory that combines a treatment of dictionaries with our previous work [BBW92,BNTW95,LT97] on collections and aggregates using the theory of *monads*. In addition we use dictionaries (finite functions), which allow us to represent oodb schemas and queries. While here we focus on set-related queries, we show elsewhere[4] that the (full) CoDi collection, aggregation and dictionary primitives suffice for implementing the quasi-totality of ODMG/ODL/OQL [Cat96]. Using boolean aggregates, CoDi can represent constraints like the ones we used in the examples in section 1 as equalities between boolean-valued queries. We also give the basic equational laws of CoDi while the rest of the axiomatization can be found in [PT98]. In section 3 we also show how that the transformations shown in section 1 correspond to precise rewrites in CoDi. This suggests the definition of a general notion of chase by rewriting, which connects dependencies to query equivalence (and therefore containment via intersection). This generalizes the relational chase of [ABU79,MMS79,BV84] for conjunctive queries (with equality) [CM77,ASU79] and embedded dependencies [Fag82]. In the same section we discuss composing dependencies with views. Our main results are in sections 4 and 5. In section 4 we exhibit a class of queries

---

[3] From "Collections and Dictionaries"
[4] "An OQL interface to the K2 system", by J. Crabtree, S. Harker, and V. Tannen, forthcoming.

and dependencies on complex values with dictionaries called *path-conjunctive* (PC queries and embedded PC dependencies (EPCDs)) for which the methods illustrated in earlier sections are complete, and in certain cases decidable. Theorem 1 in section 4 extends and generalizes the containment decidability/NP result of [CM77]. Theorem 3 and corollary 1 in section 5 extend and generalize the corresponding results on the chase in [BV84]. Theorem 1 and theorem 3 also state that CoDi's equational axiomatization is complete for deriving dependencies and containments, which extends and generalizes the corresponding completeness results on algebraic dependencies from [YP82,Abi83], although in a different equational theory. Proposition 1 which in our framework is almost "for free" immediately implies an extension and generalization of the corresponding SPC algebra [AHV95] result of [KP82] (but not the SPCU algebra result).

Due to the space restrictions, the proofs of the theorems stated here and some technical definitions are in the companion technical report [PT98]. This report also contains more results (that we summarize in section 6) and more examples. Related work and further investigations are in section 7.

3 Chase and View Composition in CoDi

We want to "rewrite" queries using constraints and we want to "compose" views with constraints. But constraints are logical assertions and queries and views are functional expressions (at least when we use OQL, SQL, or various algebras). The reconciliation could be attempted within first-order logic using appropriate translations of queries and views. Since we deal with complex values (nested sets and records) and with oo classes, some kind of "flattening" encoding (eg. [LS97]) would be necessary. Here we take the opposite approach, by translating constraints into a functional algebra, CoDi where queries and views are comfortably represented. We shall see that the fragment of logic that we need for constraints also has a natural representation.

The three major constructs in our functional algebra are the following (given here with their semantics, for $S \stackrel{\text{def}}{=} \{a_1, \dots, a_n\}$):

$$\underline{\mathsf{BigU}}\,(x \in S)\,R(x) \stackrel{\text{def}}{=} \bigcup_{i=1}^{n} R(a_i) \qquad \underline{\mathsf{All}}\,(x \in S)\,B(x) \stackrel{\text{def}}{=} \bigwedge_{i=1}^{n} B(a_i)$$

$$\underline{\mathsf{Some}}\,(x \in S)\,B(x) \stackrel{\text{def}}{=} \bigvee_{i=1}^{n} B(a_i)$$

$R(x)$ and S are set expressions, i.e. with types of the form $\{\sigma\}$ and $B(x)$ is a boolean expression. The variable x is *bound* in these constructs (as in lambda abstraction) and we represent by $R(x)$ and $B(x)$ the fact that it may occur in R and B. $B(a), R(a)$ are the results of substituting a for x. We shall use the generic notation $\underline{\mathsf{Loop}}$ to stand for $\underline{\mathsf{BigU}}$, $\underline{\mathsf{All}}$, or $\underline{\mathsf{Some}}$ and we shall consider mostly expressions of the form

$$\underline{\mathsf{Loop}}\,(x \in S)\,\underline{\mathsf{if}}\,B(x)\,\underline{\mathsf{then}}\,E(x)$$

which is an abbreviation for

$$\underline{\mathsf{Loop}}(x_1 \in S_1) \cdots \underline{\mathsf{Loop}}(x_n \in S_n(x_1, \ldots, x_{n-1}))$$
$$\underline{\mathsf{if}}\ B(x_1, \ldots, x_n)\ \underline{\mathsf{then}}\ E(x_1, \ldots, x_n)\ \underline{\mathsf{else}}\ \underline{\mathsf{null}}$$

where $\underline{\mathsf{null}}$ is another generic notation [5] standing for $\underline{\mathsf{empty}}$ in a $\underline{\mathsf{BigU}}$, for $\underline{\mathsf{true}}$ in an $\underline{\mathsf{All}}$ and for $\underline{\mathsf{false}}$ in a $\underline{\mathsf{Some}}$. We shall also use $\mathsf{sng}\,E$, denoting a singleton set. The syntax for tuples (records) is standard. We also use an equality test: $\mathsf{eq}(E_1, E_2)$ and boolean conjunction. As for expressive power (so far), note that $\underline{\mathsf{BigU}}$ is the operation ext/Φ of [BNTW95], shown there to have (with singleton and primitives for tuples and booleans) the expressive power of the relational algebra over flat relations and the expressive power of the nested relational algebra over complex objects.

Dictionaries We denote by $\sigma \mathbin{\Diamond\!\!\!>} \tau$ the type of dictionaries (finite functions) with keys of type σ and entries of type τ. $\mathsf{dom}\,M$ denotes the set of keys (the *domain*) of the dictionary M. $K\,!\,M$ denotes the entry of M corresponding to the key K (lookup!). This operation *fails* unless K is in $\mathsf{dom}\,M$ and we will take care to use it in contexts in which it is guaranteed not to fail. We model oo classes with extents using dictionaries whose keys are the oids. The extents become the domains of the dictionaries and the implicit oid dereferencing in OQL is translated by a lookup in the dictionary. For example, depts d and d.DProjs s in ABC_DP, section 1, become $d \in \mathsf{dom}\,\mathsf{Dept}$ and $s \in d\,!\,\mathsf{Dept.DProjs}$, see below.

Example. Refering to the schema in figure 1, the type specs translate in CoDi as

Proj : $\{\langle \mathsf{PName} : \mathsf{string}, \mathsf{CustName} : \mathsf{string}, \mathsf{PDept} : \mathsf{string}\rangle\}$

Dept : $Doid \mathbin{\Diamond\!\!\!>} \langle \mathsf{DName} : \mathsf{string}, \mathsf{DProjs} : \{\mathsf{string}\}, \mathsf{MgrName} : \mathsf{string}\rangle$

the query ABC_DP translates in CoDi as the expression

$\underline{\mathsf{BigU}}\,(d \in \underline{\mathsf{dom}}\,\mathsf{Dept})\,\underline{\mathsf{BigU}}\,(s \in d\,!\,\mathsf{Dept.DProjs})\,\underline{\mathsf{BigU}}\,(p \in \mathsf{Proj})$
$\underline{\mathsf{if}}\ \mathsf{eq}(s,\,p.\mathsf{PName})\ \underline{\mathsf{and}}\ \mathsf{eq}(p.\mathsf{CustName},\ \texttt{"ABC"})\ \underline{\mathsf{then}}\ \mathsf{sng}\langle \mathsf{PN} : s, \mathsf{DN} : d\,!\,\mathsf{Dept.DName}\rangle$

and the constraint (INV2) translates in CoDi as the *equation*

$\underline{\mathsf{All}}\,(p \in \mathsf{Proj})\,\underline{\mathsf{All}}\,(d \in \underline{\mathsf{dom}}\,\mathsf{Dept})$
$\quad \underline{\mathsf{if}}\ \mathsf{eq}(p.\mathsf{PDept},\,d\,!\,\mathsf{Dept.DName})\ \underline{\mathsf{then}}\ \underline{\mathsf{Some}}\,(s \in d\,!\,\mathsf{Dept.DProjs})\,\mathsf{eq}(p.\mathsf{PName},\,s)$
$\qquad\qquad\qquad = \underline{\mathsf{true}}$

---

[5] These generic notations are not *ad-hoc*. We show in [LT97] that they correspond to *monad algebras* which here are structures associated with the set monad and are "enriched" with a nullary operation.

Expressing constraints this way will allow us to achieve both our objectives: rewriting queries (and constraints!) with constraints and composing views with constraints. All our manipulations are justified by CoDi's *equivalence laws* and we show the basic ones in figure 2. Some of these laws are derived from the theory of monads and monad algebras and the extensions we worked out in [BNTW95,LT97]. The important new axiom is (idemloop). Its validity is based on the fact that x does not occur in E and that union, conjunction, and disjunction are all idempotent operations. The rest of the equational axiomatization is in [PT98]. Some laws, such as (commute) and (from [PT98]) the laws governing eq, the conditional, and , and the congruence laws are used rather routinely to rearrange expressions in preparation for a more substantial rewrite step. When describing rewritings we will often omit mentioning these ubiquituous rearrangements.

(sng)	$\underline{\mathsf{BigU}}\,(x \in S)\,\underline{\mathsf{sng}}(x) = S$
(monad-β)	$\underline{\mathsf{Loop}}\,(x \in \underline{\mathsf{sng}}(E))\,E'(x) = E'(E)$
(assoc)	$\underline{\mathsf{Loop}}\,(x \in (\underline{\mathsf{BigU}}\,(y \in R)\,S(y)))\,E(x) = \underline{\mathsf{Loop}}\,(y \in R)\,(\underline{\mathsf{Loop}}\,(x \in S(y))$ $E(x))$
(null)	$\underline{\mathsf{Loop}}\,(x \in \underline{\mathsf{empty}})\,E(x) = \underline{\mathsf{null}}$
(cond-loop)	$\underline{\mathsf{Loop}}\,(x \in S)\,\underline{\mathsf{if}}\,B\,\underline{\mathsf{then}}\,E(x) = \underline{\mathsf{if}}\,B\,\underline{\mathsf{then}}\,\underline{\mathsf{Loop}}\,(x \in S)\,E(x)$
(commute)	$\underline{\mathsf{Loop}}\,(x \in R)\,\underline{\mathsf{Loop}}\,(y \in S)\,E(x,y) = \underline{\mathsf{Loop}}\,(y \in S)\,\underline{\mathsf{Loop}}\,(x \in R)$ $E(x,y)$
(idemloop)	$\underline{\mathsf{Loop}}\,(x \in S)\,\underline{\mathsf{if}}\,B(x)\,\underline{\mathsf{then}}\,E = \underline{\mathsf{if}}\,\underline{\mathsf{Some}}\,(x \in S)\,B(x)\,\underline{\mathsf{then}}\,E$

Fig. 2. Equivalence laws

Example. We show how we obtained (FD-RETRO) from (FD) (see section 1). First, we express UJP_View in CoDi:

$\underline{\mathsf{BigU}}\,(p \in \mathtt{Proj})\,\underline{\mathsf{BigU}}\,(d \in \underline{\mathsf{dom}}\,\mathtt{Dept})\,\underline{\mathsf{BigU}}\,(s \in d\,!\,\mathtt{Dept.DProjs})$
    $\underline{\mathsf{if}}\,\mathsf{eq}(s,\,p.\mathtt{PName})\,\underline{\mathsf{then}}\,\underline{\mathsf{sng}}\langle\mathtt{PN}:p.\mathtt{PName},\mathtt{CN}:p.\mathtt{CustName},\mathtt{MN}:d\,!\,\mathtt{Dept.MgrName}\rangle$

Translating (FD) into CoDi (as we did for (INV2)), then substituting the first occurrence of UJP_View with its definition and using (assoc) we obtain:

$\underline{\mathsf{All}}\,(p \in \mathtt{Proj})\,\underline{\mathsf{All}}\,(d \in \underline{\mathsf{dom}}\,\mathtt{Dept})\,\underline{\mathsf{All}}\,(s \in d\,!\,\mathtt{Dept.DProjs})$
$\underline{\mathsf{All}}\,(v \in \underline{\mathsf{if}}\,\mathsf{eq}(s,\,p.\mathtt{PName})\,\underline{\mathsf{then}}\,\underline{\mathsf{sng}}\langle\mathtt{PN}:p.\mathtt{PName},\mathtt{CN}:p.\mathtt{CustName},\mathtt{MN}:d\,!\,\mathtt{Dept.MgrName}\rangle)$
$\underline{\mathsf{All}}\,(v' \in \mathtt{UJP\_View})\,\underline{\mathsf{if}}\,\underline{\mathsf{eq}}(v.\mathtt{PN},\,v'.\mathtt{PN})\,\underline{\mathsf{then}}\,\mathsf{eq}(v.\mathtt{MN},\,v'.\mathtt{MN})$

$= \underline{\mathsf{true}}$

After some manipulations of conditionals we apply, in sequence, (monad-β), (null) and (cond-loop), and obtain:

$\underline{\text{All}}\,(p \in \text{Proj})\,\underline{\text{All}}\,(d \in \underline{\text{dom}}\,\text{Dept})\,\underline{\text{All}}\,(s \in d\,!\,\text{Dept.DProjs})\,\underline{\text{All}}\,(v' \in \text{UJP\_View})$
$\quad\quad \underline{\text{if}}\ \text{eq}(s, p.\text{PName})\ \underline{\text{and}}\ \text{eq}(p.\text{PName}, v'.\text{PN})\ \underline{\text{then}}\ \text{eq}(d\,!\,\text{Dept.MgrName}, v'.\text{MN})$
$=\ \underline{\text{true}}$

A similar rewriting in which the other occurrence of UJP_View is substituted with its definition yields the direct translation in CoDi of (FD-RETRO). Note that these transformations explain tableau view "replication" [KP82].

The form in which we have written the constraints turns out to be convenient if we want them rewritten but not if we want to rewrite *with* them. In order to replace equals by equals within the scope of $\underline{\text{Loop}}(x \in S)$ bindings, we will use a form of equations "guarded" by set membership conditions for the variables:

$$x_1 \in S_1, \ldots, x_n \in S_n(x_1, \ldots, x_{n-1}) \vdash E_1(x_1, \ldots, x_n) = E_2(x_1, \ldots, x_n)$$

The congruence rules for the $\underline{\text{Loop}}$ construct together with some additional rules that can be found in [PT98] allow us to rewrite the set membership conditions within the scope of $\underline{\text{All}}$ and vice-versa. Thus we have the following:

Lemma 1 (Two Forms for Constraints). *The following two equations are derivable from each other in CoDi's equational theory:*

$$\underline{\text{All}}\,(x \in S)\,\underline{\text{if}}\ B(x)\ \underline{\text{then}}\ C(x)\ =\ \underline{\text{true}}$$

$$x \in S \vdash B(x)\ =\ B(x)\ \underline{\text{and}}\ C(x)$$

The Equational Chase Step. Consider the constraint (d) and the expression G:

$(d)\quad x \in R_1 \vdash B_1(x)\ =\ B_1(x)\ \underline{\text{and}}\ \underline{\text{Some}}\,(y \in R_2(x))\,B_2(x, y)$

$G\ \overset{\text{def}}{=}\ \underline{\text{Loop}}\,(x \in R_1)\,\underline{\text{if}}\ B_1(x)\ \underline{\text{then}}\ E(x)$

Rewriting G with (d) we obtain

$\underline{\text{Loop}}\,(x \in R_1)\,\underline{\text{if}}\ B_1(x)\ \underline{\text{and}}\ \underline{\text{Some}}\,(y \in R_2(x))\,B_2(x, y)\ \underline{\text{then}}\ E(x)$

Commutativity of conjunction and nesting of conditionals yields

$\underline{\text{Loop}}\,(x \in R_1)\,\underline{\text{if}}\ \underline{\text{Some}}\,(y \in R_2(x))\,B_2(x, y)\ \underline{\text{then}}\ \underline{\text{if}}\ B_1(x)\ \underline{\text{then}}\ E(x)$

Finally, applying (idemloop) from right to left gives

$G'\ \overset{\text{def}}{=}\ \underline{\text{Loop}}\,(x \in R_1)\,\underline{\text{Loop}}\,(y \in R_2(x))\,\underline{\text{if}}\ B_1(x)\ \underline{\text{and}}\ B_2(x, y)\ \underline{\text{then}}\ E(x)$

Therefore, the equation $G = G'$ is derivable in CoDi's equational theory (and hence follows semantically) from (d). We say that G' is the result of (one-step) chasing G with (d). G could be a query but it could also be the boolean-valued expression A when we translate constraints as equations $A = \underline{\text{true}}$. Chasing a constraint means chasing the expression A.

Query Containment. The chase step illuminates the connection between query containment and constraints (in the relational case a similar connection was put in evidence in [YP82,Abi83]). Consider

$$Q_i \stackrel{\text{def}}{=} \underline{\text{BigU}}\,(x \in R_i)\,\underline{\text{if}}\,B_i(x)\,\underline{\text{then}}\,\text{sng}(E_i(x)) \qquad (i = 1, 2)$$

and observe that we can express intersection by

$$Q_1 \cap Q_2 \;=\; \underline{\text{BigU}}\,(x \in R_1)\,\underline{\text{BigU}}\,(y \in R_2)$$
$$\underline{\text{if}}\,B_1(x)\,\underline{\text{and}}\,B_2(y)\,\underline{\text{and}}\,\underline{\text{eq}}(E_1(x),\,E_2(y))\,\underline{\text{then}}\,\text{sng}(E_1(x))$$

Now consider the constraint $cont(Q_1, Q_2)$ defined as

$$x \in R_1 \;\vdash\; B_1(x) \;=\; B_1(x)\,\underline{\text{and}}\,\underline{\text{Some}}\,(y \in R_2)\,B_2(y)\,\underline{\text{and}}\,\underline{\text{eq}}(E_1(x),\,E_2(y))$$

It is easy to see that one step of chasing Q_1 with $cont(Q_1, Q_2)$ yields $Q_1 \cap Q_2$. Since $Q_1 \subseteq Q_2$ is equivalent to $Q_1 = Q_1 \cap Q_2$, it follows that containments can be established by deriving certain constraints. In fact, we show in sections 4 and 5 that for path-conjunctive queries containment is *reducible* to path-conjunctive dependencies.

The Relational Case. Conjunctive (tableau) queries [AHV95] are easily expressible in CoDi (using variables that range over tuples rather than over individuals, much as in SQL and OQL). Embedded dependencies (tuple- and equality-generating) are expressible just as we have expressed the constraints of the schema in figure 1 [6]. It turns out that mirroring in CoDi one step of the relational chase of a tableau query Q (or another embedded dependency) with an embedded dependency (d) corresponds exactly to the equational chase step that we have described above! Moreover, the special case of chasing with trivial dependencies explains equationally tableaux query containment and tableaux minimization. When $cont(Q_1, Q_2)$ is trivial, it corresponds precisely with a containment mapping ([CM77]). We show in section 4 (and in full details in [PT98]) that this is the case for the more general class of path-conjunctive queries and dependencies. Moreover, we show that CoDi is complete for proving triviality and containment/equivalence for this class.

---

[6] Since we are using tuple variables, full relational dependencies still require existential quantification in CoDi. With extra care, a generalization of full dependencies is still possible (section 5).

4   Path-Conjunctive Queries, Dependencies, and Views

A *schema* consists simply of some names (roots) R and their types. An *instance* consists of complex values (with dictionaries) of the right type for each root name. We will distinguish between *finite* and *unrestricted* instances, where $\{\sigma\}$ means *all* sets. We now define:

Paths: $\qquad\qquad\qquad P ::= x \mid R \mid P.A \mid \underline{\text{dom}}\, P \mid x\,!\,P \mid \underline{\text{true}} \mid \underline{\text{false}}$

Path-Conjunctions: $\quad C ::= \underline{\text{eq}}(P_1, P_1') \underline{\text{ and }} \cdots \underline{\text{ and }} \underline{\text{eq}}(P_n, P_n')$

Path-Conjunctive (PC) Queries: $\quad Q ::= \underline{\text{BigU}}\,(x \in P)\,\underline{\text{if}}\, C(x)\,\underline{\text{then}}\,\underline{\text{sng}}(E(x))$
where [7]: $\quad E ::= P \mid \langle A_1 : P_1, \ldots, A_n : P_n \rangle$

Path-Conjunctive View: $\quad$ a view expressed using a PC query.

Embedded Path-Conjunctive Dependency (EPCD):

$\quad d ::= \quad \underline{\text{All}}\,(x \in P_1)\,\underline{\text{if}}\,C_1(x)\,\underline{\text{then}}\,\underline{\text{Some}}\,(y \in P_2(x))\,C_2(x, y) \;=\; \underline{\text{true}}$

or equivalently (see lemma 1):

$\quad d ::= \quad x \in P_1 \vdash C_1(x) \;=\; C_1(x) \underline{\text{ and }} \underline{\text{Some}}\,(y \in P_2(x))\,C_2(x, y)$

Equality-Generating Dependency (EGD): $\quad$ an EPCD of the form

$$\underline{\text{All}}\,(x \in P_1)\,\underline{\text{if}}\,C_1(x)\,\underline{\text{then}}\,C_2(x) \;=\; \underline{\text{true}}$$

Restrictions. All PC queries and EPCDs are subject to the following restrictions.

1. A *simple* type is defined (inductively) as either a base type or a record type in which the types of the components are simple types (in other words, it doesn't involve set or dictionary types). Dictionary types $\sigma \Join \tau$ are restricted such that σ is a simple type. The paths P_i, P_i' appearing in path conjunctions must be of simple type. The expression E appearing in PC queries must be of simple type.

2. A *finite set type* is a type of the form $\{\tau\}$ where the only base type occurring in τ is bool or $\langle\rangle$ (the empty record type). We do not allow in PC queries or EPCDs bindings of the form $x \in P$ such that P is of finite set type [8].

3. $x\,!\,P$ can occur only in the scope of a binding of the form $x \in \underline{\text{dom}}\,P$ [9].

---

[7] Although we don't allow record constructors in paths, their equality is still representable, componentwise.

[8] Finite set types cause some difficulties in our current proof method. However there are more serious reasons to worry about them: it is shown in [BNTW95] that they can be used to encode set difference, although the given encoding uses a language slightly richer than that of PC queries.

[9] This restriction could be removed at the price of tedious reasoning about partiality, but we have seen no need to do it for the results and examples discussed here.

Views. The following shows that composing EPCDs with PC views yields EPCDs. Thus all subsequent results regarding implication/triviality of EPCDs can be used to infer implication/triviality of EPCDs over views as well.

Proposition 1. *Composing an EPCD over a schema* S *with a PC view from* R *to* S *yields an expression that is provably equivalent to an EPCD over* R. *Moreover composing EGDs with PC views gives expressions provably equivalent to EGDs.*

The **main result** of this section is about containment of queries and triviality (validity, holds in all instances) of dependencies.

Theorem 1 (Containment and Triviality). *Containment of PC queries and triviality of EPCDs are reducible to each other. Both hold in all (unrestricted) instances iff they hold in all finite instances. Both are decidable and in NP. CoDi's equational axiomatization is complete for deriving them.*

As for relational tableau queries, the proof of the theorem relies on a reduction to the existence of certain kinds of *homomorphisms* between *tableaux*. Except that here we must invent a more complex notion of tableau that takes set and dictionary nesting into consideration. In CoDi, the (PC) tableau corresponding to the PC query $\underline{\mathsf{BigU}}\,(x \in P)\,\underline{\mathsf{if}}\ C(x)\ \underline{\mathsf{then}}\ \mathsf{sng}(E(x))$ is just a piece of syntax consisting of several expressions $T ::= \{x \in P\ ;\ C(x)\}$. Note that relational tableaux can also be represented this way, with the variables in x corresponding to the rows. We define a homomorphism between two tableaux to be a mapping between variables satisfying certain PTIME-checkable conditions. The precise definition is given in [PT98]. A basic insight about relational tableaux is that they can be considered themselves as instances. In the presence of nested sets and dictionaries, we must work some to construct from any tableau T a canonical instance, $Inst(T)$ such that a valuation from T_2 into $Inst(T_1)$ induces a homomorphism from T_2 to T_1. [10] Deciding containment then comes down to testing for the existence of a homomorphism, which is in NP. Since the problem is already NP-hard in the relational case [CM77], containment of PC queries is in fact NP-complete. The full details are given in [PT98]. As for the reductions between containment and triviality, we show that for PC queries $Q_1 \subseteq Q_2$ iff $cont(Q_1, Q_2)$ is trivial, hence triviality of EPCDs is also NP-hard. Conversely, we associate to an EPCD (d) two queries [11], where A are fresh labels:

$$front(d) \stackrel{\text{def}}{=} \underline{\mathsf{BigU}}\,(x \in P_1)\,\underline{\mathsf{if}}\ C_1(x)\ \underline{\mathsf{then}}\ \mathsf{sng}\langle A : x\rangle$$

$$back(d) \stackrel{\text{def}}{=} \underline{\mathsf{BigU}}(x \in P_1)\underline{\mathsf{BigU}}(y \in P_2(x))\ \underline{\mathsf{if}}\ C_1(x)\ \underline{\mathsf{and}}\ C_2(x,y)$$
$$\underline{\mathsf{then}}\ \mathsf{sng}\langle A : x\rangle$$

and we show that (d) is trivial iff $front(d) \subseteq back(d)$, hence triviality of EPCDs is NP-complete.

---

[10] Intuitively, $Inst(T)$ is the minimal instance that contains the "structure" of T, and we can express syntactical conditions on T as equivalent conditions on $Inst(T)$.

[11] Since x may have non-simple type variables, these queries do not obey the restriction we imposed for PC queries. Nonetheless, their containment is decidable. This encourages the hope that the simple type restriction can be removed for this theorem.

In the case of **EGDs**, we can improve on complexity and we can even remove the restriction to simple types.

Theorem 2 (Trivial EGDs). *A non-simple EGD (with equality at non-simple types) holds in all (unrestricted) instances iff it holds in all finite instances. Triviality of non-simple EGDs is decidable in PTIME. CoDi's equational axiomatization is complete for deriving all trivial non-simple EGDs.*

5 Path-Conjunctive Chase

The chase as defined in section 3 is only a particular case. In general we need to be able to map the bound variables to other variables. Moreover, we need a precise definition of when the chase step should *not* be applicable because it would yield a query or dependency that is trivially equivalent to the one we already had. As with relational tableau queries, it suffices to define the chase on tableaux: chasing a PC query means chasing the corresponding PC tableau, while chasing an EPCD (d) means chasing the PC tableau that corresponds to *front(d)*. For example, just for the particular case justified in section 3 chasing the tableau $\{x \in P_1 ; C_1(x)\}$ with the dependency

(d) $\underline{\text{All}}\,(x \in P_1)\,\underline{\text{if}}\,C_1(x)\,\underline{\text{then}}\,\underline{\text{Some}}\,(y \in P_2(x))\,C_2(x,y)\ =\ \underline{\text{true}}$

yields the tableau $\{x \in P_1, y \in P_2(x) ; C_1(x)\,\underline{\text{and}}\,C_2(x,y)\}$. The complete definition of the chase step involves homomorphisms and due to lack of space we give it in [PT98]. Like the particular case we've shown, the complete definition is such that a chase step transforms a PC query (an EPCD) into one provably equal (equivalent) in the CoDi equational axiomatization. Most importantly, the complete definition is such that if $Inst(T) \not\models d$ then the chase step with d is applicable to T.

A *chase sequence* with a set of EPCDs D is a sequence of tableaux obtained by successive chase steps each with some dependency $d \in D$ (same d can be used repeatedly). We say that a sequence starting with T *terminates* if it reaches a tableau T' that cannot be chased with any $d \in D$ (and therefore $Inst(T') \models D$). Although in general T' depends on the choice of terminating chase sequence, we shall denote it by $chase_D(T)$ and extend the same notation to queries and dependencies.

Theorem 3 (Containment/Implication by Chasing). *Let D be a set of EPCDs.*

1. *Let Q_1, Q_2 be PC queries such that some chasing sequence of Q_1 with D terminates (with $chase_D(Q_1)$). The following are equivalent and the unrestricted and finite version of each of (a)–(d) are equivalent as well:*

   (a) $Q_1 \subseteq_D Q_2$ (b) $chase_D(Q_1) \subseteq Q_2$

   (c) $chase_D(cont(Q_1, Q_2))$ *is trivial*   (d) $D \models cont(Q_1, Q_2)$

   (e) $cont(Q_1, Q_2)$ *(hence $Q_1 \subseteq Q_2$) is provable from D in CoDi*

2. *Let d be an EPCD such that some chasing sequence of d with D terminates. The following are equivalent and the unrestricted and finite version of each of (a)–(d) are equivalent as well:*

(a) $D \models d$ (b) $chase_D(d)$ *is trivial*

(c) $chase_D(front(d)) \subseteq back(d)$ (d2) $front(d) \subseteq_D back(d)$

                (e)   *d is provable from D in CoDi*

Full EPCDs. This is a class of dependencies that generalizes the relational full dependencies [AHV95] (originally called total tgd's and egd's in [BV84]). Since we work with "tuple" variables, the definition needs a lot more care than in the first-order case.

Definition 1 (Full Dependencies). *An EPCD*

$$\underline{\text{All}}\,(r \in R)\,\underline{\text{if}}\,B_1(r)\,\underline{\text{then}}\,\underline{\text{Some}}\,(s \in S(r))\,B_2(r,s)\; =\; \underline{\text{true}}$$

is full if for any variable s_i in s there exists a path $P_i(r)$ such that the following EGD is trivial

$$\underline{\text{All}}\,(r \in R)\,\underline{\text{All}}\,(s \in S(r))\,\underline{\text{if}}\,B_1(r)\,\underline{\text{and}}\,B_2(r,s)\,\underline{\text{then}}\,\underline{\text{eq}}(s_i,\,P_i(r))\; =\; \underline{\text{true}}$$

Theorem 4 (Full Termination). *If D is a set of full EPCDs and T is a PC tableau then any chase sequence of T with D terminates.*

Corollary 1. *PC query containment under full EPCDs and logical implication of EPCDs from full EPCDs are reducible to each other, their unrestricted and finite versions coincide, and both are decidable.*

Proposition 2. *Let D be a set of full EPCDs and (d) be another EPCD. Let T be the tableau part of (d) that gets chased. Then deciding whether $D \models d$ can be done in time*

$$c_1\,|D|\,(nh)^{c_2 ws}$$

where c_1 and c_2 are two constants, $|D|$ is the number of EPCDs in D, n is the number of variables in T, s is the maximum number of variables of an EPCD in D, while w and h are two schema parameters: w is the maximum number of attributes that a record type has in the schema (including nested attributes at any depth) and h is the maximum height of a type in the schema.

Therefore, the complexity of the chase decision procedure for full EPCDs is not worse than in the relational subcase [BV84] (recall also the lower bound of [CLM81]). For EGDs, which are always full, it is easy to see that the problem is actually in PTIME, as in the relational case.

The chase with full EPCDs also enjoys the following nice properties:

Theorem 5 (Confluence). *Consider two terminal chase sequences of a PC tableau T with a set D of full EPCDs, ending in T_1 and T_2 respectively. Then $Inst(T_1)$ and $Inst(T_2)$ must be isomorphic.*

Note that we cannot hope that T_1 and T_2 are "equal" (even modulo variable renaming) because the path-conjunctions may be different, although logically equivalent.

Proposition 3 (Semantic Invariance). *Let D_1 and D_2 be two semantically equivalent (hold in the same instances) sets of full EPCDs and let T_1 and T_2 be the resulting tableaux of two arbitrary terminal chase sequences of a given tableau T with D_1 and, respectively, D_2. Then $Inst(T_1)$ and $Inst(T_2)$ must be isomorphic.*

6   Other Results

The companion technical report [PT98] contains several other results that space restrictions prevent us from outlining here. In particular, we show in [PT98] how to extend and generalize the complete proof procedure result of Beeri and Vardi [BV84] for the case when the chase may not terminate. The result also applies to query containment. Note that since we are not in the first-order case, even the r.e.-ness is non-obvious. The equational axiomatization of CoDi is complete in this case too. Moreover, we show in [PT98] that the containment parts of theorems 1 and 3 (as well as the result for the non-terminating chase) also hold, with similar proofs, for boolean-valued-Some queries in PC form, where containment means boolean implication.

We have shown how to use dictionaries to model oo classes but in fact they are much more versatile. In [PT98] we give examples of queries, views, and constraints that use dictionaries to model indexes. We also use the chase to characterize nesting of relations into nested sets or dictionaries, as well as unnesting of the corresponding structures.

7   Related Work and Further Investigations

Related work. The monad algebra approach to aggregates [LT95] is related to the monoid comprehensions of [FM95b] but it is somewhat more general since there exist monads (trees for example) whose monad algebras are not monoids. The maps of [ALPR91], the treatment of object types in [BK93] and in [DHP97], that of views in [dSDA94], and that of arrays in [LMW96] are related to our use of dictionaries. An important difference is made by the operations on dictionaries used here.

The idea of representing constraints as equivalences between boolean-valued (OQL actually) queries already appears in [FRV96]. The equational theory of CoDi proves almost the entire variety of proposed algebraic query equivalences beginning with the standard relational algebraic ones, and including [SZ89a], [SZ89b,CD92,Clu91,FM95b,FM95a] and the very comprehensive work by Beeri and Kornatzky [BK93]. Moreover, using especially (commute), CoDi validates and generalizes standard join reordering techniques, thus the problem of join associativity in object algebras raised in [CD92] does not arise. Our PC queries are less general than COQL queries [LS97], by not allowing alternations of conditionals and BigU. However we are more general in other ways, by incorporating dictionaries and considering constraints. Containment of PC queries is in NP while a double exponential upper bound is provided for containment of COQL queries. In [Bid87] it is shown that containment of conjunctive queries for the Verso complex value model and algebra is reducible to the relational case. Other studies include semantic query optimization for unions of conjunctive queries [CGM88], containment under Datalog-expressible constraints and views [DS96], and containment of non-recursive Datalog queries with regular expression atoms under a rich class of constraints [CGL98]. We are not aware of any extension of the chase to complex values and oodb models. Hara and Davidson [HD98] provide a complete intrinsic axiomatization of generalized functional dependencies for complex value schemas without empty sets. Fan and Weinstein [FW98] examine the un/decidability of logical implication for path constraints in various classes of oo-typed semistructured models.

Further investigations. We conjecture that the simple type restriction can be removed without affecting the containment/triviality result (Theorem 1). When equality at non-simple types is allowed, the chase is incomplete. However, the chase seems to be able to prove the two containments that make a set or dictionary equality. This suggests that a complete proof procedure might exist that combines the chase with an extensionality rule. Another important direction of work is allowing alternations of conditionals and BigU and trying to extend the result of [LS97] from weak equivalence to equivalence. The axiomatization of inclusions in [Abi83] can be soundly translated into CoDi's equational theory. We conjecture that CoDi is a conservative extension of this axiomatization. An interesting observation is that the equational chase does not require the PC restrictions, but just a certain form of query and dependency. It is natural to ask how far we can extend the completeness of this method. Most EPCDs in our examples are full. Some of those who are not may be amenable to the ideas developed for special cases with inclusion dependencies [JK84,CKV90]. Another question regards the decidable properties of classes of first-order queries and sentences that might correspond (by encoding, eg. [LS97]) to PC queries and EPCDs. Other encodings might allow us to draw comparisons with the interesting results of [CGL98].

It is an intriguing question why the powerful relational optimization techniques using tableaux and dependencies have not made their way into commercial optimizers. There seem to be two reasons for this. One is that queries crafted by users tend not to introduce spurious joins and tend to take advantage of certain constraints (even implicit ones!). The other reason is that the techniques have generally exponential algorithms. But do these reasons carry through to the paradigm of distributed mediator-based systems that interests us? We have already argued that in such systems there are a lot of (secondary) queries that are generated by not-so-smart software components. The complexity issue remains a serious one and only an experimental approach might put it to rest. Recall that the algorithms are exponential in the size of queries and dependencies, not of data. Note also that standard relational optimization using dynamic programming is also exponential in theory, yet practical. Finally, some work on PTIME subcases exists [CR97,Sar91] and might be extended. On a more practical note, rewriting with individual CoDi axioms generates too large a search space to be directly useful in practical optimization. An important future direction is the modular development of coarser derived CoDi transformations corresponding to various optimization techniques in a rule-based approach.

Anecdote We were happily proving equalities in CoDi by rewriting with dependencies and (idemloop) for quite some time before we realized the connection with the chase!

Many thanks to Serge Abiteboul, Peter Buneman, Sophie Cluet, Susan Davidson, Alin Deutsch, Wenfei Fan, Carmem Hara, Rona Machlin, Dan Suciu, Scott Weinstein, and the paper's reviewers.

References

[Abi83]   S. Abiteboul. Algebraic analogues to fundamental notions of query and dependency theory. Technical report, INRIA, 1983.

[ABU79]   A. V. Aho, C. Beeri, and J. D. Ullman. The theory of joins in relational databases. *ACM Transactions on Database Systems*, 4(3):297–314, 1979.

[AHV95]   Serge Abiteboul, Richard Hull, and Victor Vianu. *Foundations of Databases*. Addison-Wesley, 1995.

[ALPR91] M. Atkinson, C. Lecluse, P. Philbrow, and P. Richard. Design issues in a map language. In *Proc. of the 3rd Int'l Workshop on Database Programming Languages (DBPL91)*, Nafplion, Greece, August 1991.

[ASU79]   A. V. Aho, Y. Sagiv, and J. D. Ullman. Equivalences among relational expressions. *SIAM Journal of Computing*, 8(2):218–246, 1979.

[BBW92]   Val Breazu-Tannen, Peter Buneman, and Limsoon Wong. Naturally embedded query languages. In J. Biskup and R. Hull, editors, *LNCS 646: Proceedings of 4th International Conference on Database Theory, Berlin, Germany, October, 1992*, pages 140–154. Springer-Verlag, October 1992. Available as UPenn Technical Report MS-CIS-92-47.

[Bid87]   N. Bidoit. The verso algebra or how to answer queries with fewer joins. *Journal of Computer and System Sciences*, 35:321–364, 1987.

[BK93]   Catriel Beeri and Yoram Kornatzky. Algebraic optimisation of object oriented query languages. *Theoretical Computer Science*, 116(1):59–94, August 1993.

[BNTW95] Peter Buneman, Shamim Naqvi, Val Tannen, and Limsoon Wong. Principles of programming with collection types. *Theoretical Computer Science*, 149:3–48, 1995.

[BV84]   Catriel Beeri and Moshe Y. Vardi. A proof procedure for data dependencies. *Journal of the ACM*, 31(4):718–741, 1984.

[Cat96]   R. G. G. Cattell, editor. *The Object Database Standard: ODMG-93*. Morgan Kaufmann, San Mateo, California, 1996.

[CD92]   Sophie Cluet and Claude Delobel. A general framework for the optimization of object oriented queries. In M. Stonebraker, editor, *Proceedings ACM-SIGMOD International Conference on Management of Data*, pages 383–392, San Diego, California, June 1992.

[CGL98]   Diego Calvanese, Giuseppe De Giacomo, and Maurizio Lenzerini. On the decidability of query containment under constraints. In *Proc. 17th ACM Symposium on Principles of Database Systems*, pages 149–158, 1998.

[CGM88]   U.S. Chakravarthi, J. Grant, and J. Minker. Foundations of semantic query optimization for deductive databases. In J. Minker, editor, *Foundations of Deductive Databases and Logic Programming*, pages 243–273, San Mateo, California, 1988. Morgan-Kaufmann.

[CKV90]   Stavros S. Cosmadakis, Paris C. Kanellakis, and Moshe Y. Vardi. Polynomial-time implication problems for unary inclusion dependencies. *Journal of the ACM*, 37(1):15–46, 1990.

[CLM81]   A. K. Chandra, H. R. Lewis, and J. A. Makowsky. Embedded implicational dependencies and their inference problem. In *Proceedings of ACM SIGACT Symposium on the Theory of Computing*, pages 342–354, 1981.

[Clu91]   S. Cluet. *Langages et Optimisation de requetes pour Systemes de Gestion de Base de donnees oriente-objet*. PhD thesis, Universite de Paris-Sud, 1991.

[CM77]   Ashok Chandra and Philip Merlin. Optimal implementation of conjunctive queries in relational data bases. In *Proceedings of 9th ACM Symposium on Theory of Computing*, pages 77–90, Boulder, Colorado, May 1977.

[CR97]   C. Chekuri and A. Rajaraman. Conjunctive query containment revisited. In *LNCS 1186: Database Theory - ICDT'97, Proceedings of the 6th Int'l Conference*, pages 56–70, Delphi, 1997. Springer-Verlag.

[CZ96]   M. Cherniack and S. B. Zdonik. Rule languages and internal algebras for rule-based optimizers. In *Proceedings of the SIGMOD International Conference on Management of Data*, pages 401–412, Montreal, Quebec, Canada, 1996.

[DHP97]   S. B. Davidson, C. Hara, and L. Popa. Querying an object-oriented database using CPL. In *Proceedings of the 12th Brazilian Symposium on Databases*, pages 137–153, 1997. Also available as technical report MS-CIS-97-07, University of Pennsylvania.

[DS96]   Guozhu Dong and Jianwen Su. Conjunctive query containment with respect to views and constraints. *Information Processing Letters*, 57(2):95–102, 1996.

[dSDA94] C. Souza dos Santos, C. Delobel, and S. Abiteboul. Virtual schemas and bases. In *Proceedings ICEDT*, March 1994.

[Fag82]   Ronald Fagin. Horn clauses and database dependencies. *Journal of the ACM*, 29(4):952–985, 1982.

[FM95a]   L. Fegaras and D. Maier. An algebraic framework for physical oodb design. In *Proc. of the 5th Int'l Workshop on Database Programming Languages (DBPL95)*, Umbria, Italy, August 1995.

[FM95b]   Leonidas Fegaras and David Maier. Towards an effective calculus for object query languages. In *Proceedings of ACM SIGMOD International Conference on Management of Data*, pages 47–58, San Jose, California, May 1995.

[FRV96]   D. Florescu, L. Rashid, and P. Valduriez. A methodology for query reformulation in cis using semantic knowledge. *International Journal of Cooperative Information Systems*, 5(4), 1996.

[FW98]   W. Fan and S. Wenstein. Interaction between path and type constraints. Technical Report MS-CIS-98-16, University of Pennsylvania, 1998.

[HD98]   Carmem Hara and Susan Davidson. Inference rules for nested functional dependencies. Technical Report MS-CIS-98-19, University of Pennsylvania, 1998.

[JK84]   D. S. Johnson and A. Klug. Testing containment of conjunctive queries
           under functional and inclusion dependencies. *Journal of Computer and
           System Sciences*, 28:167–189, 1984.
[KP82]   A. Klug and R. Price. In determining view dependencies using tableaux.
           ACM Transactions on Database Systems, 7:361–381, 1982.
[LMW96]   L. Libkin, R. Machlin, and L. Wong. A query language for multidimensional
           arrays: Design, implementation and optimization techniques. In *SIGMOD
           Proceedings, Int'l Conf. on Management of Data*, 1996.
[LS97]   Alon Levy and Dan Suciu. Deciding containment for queries with complex
           objects. In *Proc. of the 16th ACM SIGMOD Symposium on Principles of
           Database Systems*, Tucson, Arizona, May 1997.
[LSK95]   A. Levy, D. Srivastava, and T. Kirk. Data model and query evaluation
           in global information systems. *Journal of Intelligent Information Systems*,
           1995.
[LT95]   S. K. Lellahi and V. Tannen. Enriched monads. Technical Report ??, LRI,
           Univ. Paris-Sud, February 1995.
[LT97]   Kazem Lellahi and Val Tannen. A calculus for collections and aggregates.
           In E. Moggi and G. Rosolini, editors, *LNCS 1290: Category Theory and
           Computer Science Proceedings of the 7th Int'l Conference, CTCS'97*, pages
           261–280, Santa Margherita Ligure, September 1997. Springer-Verlag.
[Mai83]   David Maier. *The Theory of Relational Databases*. Computer Science Press,
           Rockville, Maryland, 1983.
[MMS79]   D. Maier, A. O. Mendelzon, and Y. Sagiv. Testing implications of data
           dependencies. *ACM Transactions on Database Systems*, 4(4):455–469, 1979.
[PT98]   Lucian Popa and Val Tannen. Chase and axioms for PC queries and de-
           pendencies. Technical Report MS-CIS-98-34, University of Pennsylvania,
           1998. Available online at http://www.cis.upenn.edu/~techreports/.
[QR95]   X. Qian and L. Raschid. Query interoperation among object-oriented and
           relational databases. In *Proc. ICDE*, 1995.
[Sar91]   Y. Saraiya. *Subtree elimination algorithms in deductive databases*. PhD
           thesis, Stanford University, 1991.
[SZ89a]   G. Shaw and S. Zdonik. Object-oriented queries: equivalence and opti-
           mization. In *Proceedings of International Conference on Deductive and
           Object-Oriented Databases*, 1989.
[SZ89b]   G. Shaw and S. Zdonik. An object-oriented query algebra. In *Proc. DBPL*,
           Salishan Lodge, Oregon, June 1989.
[Ull89]   Jeffrey D. Ullman. *Principles of Database and Knowledge-Base Systems*,
           volume 2. Computer Science Press, 1989.
[Wie92]   Gio Wiederhold. Mediators in the architecture of future information sys-
           tems. *IEEE Computer*, pages 38–49, March 1992.
[YP82]   Mihalis Yannakakis and Christos Papadimitriou. Algebraic dependencies.
           Journal of Computer and System Sciences, 25:2–41, 1982.

Adding For-Loops to First-Order Logic
Extended Abstract

Frank Neven[1]*, Martin Otto[2], Jurek Tyszkiewicz[3]**, and
Jan Van den Bussche[1]

[1] Limburgs Universitair Centrum, {fneven,vdbuss}@luc.ac.be
[2] RWTH Aachen, otto@informatik.rwth-aachen.de
[3] Warsaw University, jty@mimuw.edu.pl

Abstract. We study the query language BQL: the extension of the relational algebra with for-loops. We also study FO(FOR): the extension
of first-order logic with a for-loop variant of the partial fixpoint operator.
In contrast to the known situation with query languages which include
while-loops instead of for-loops, BQL and FO(FOR) are not equivalent.
Among the topics we investigate are: the precise relationship between
BQL and FO(FOR); inflationary versus non-inflationary iteration; the
relationship with logics that have the ability to count; and nested versus
unnested loops.

1 Introduction

Much attention in database theory (or finite model theory) has been devoted to
extensions of first-order logic as a query language [AHV95,EF95]. A seminal paper in this context was that by Chandra in 1981 [Cha81], where he added various
programming constructs to the relational algebra and compared the expressive
power of the various extensions thus obtained. One such extension is the language that we denote here by BQL: a programming-language-like query language
obtained from the relational algebra by adding *assignment statements*, *composition*, and *for-loops*. Assignment statements assign the result of a relational
algebra expression to a relation variable; composition is obvious; and for-loops
allow a subprogram to be iterated exactly as many times as the cardinality of
the relation stored in some variable.

For-loops of this kind have since received practically no attention in the
literature. In contrast, two other iteration constructs, namely least or inflationary
fixpoints, and while-loops, have been studied extensively. In the present paper
we will make some steps toward the goal of understanding for-loops in query
languages as well as fixpoints and while-loops.

---

* Research Assistant of the Fund for Scientific Research, Flanders.
** Research begun at RWTH Aachen, supported by a German Research Council DFG
grant, continued at the University of Warsaw, supported by the Polish Research
Council KBN grant 8 T11C 002 11, and on leave at the University of New South
Wales, supported by the Australian Research Council ARC grant A 49800112 (1998–
2000).

Catriel Beeri, Peter Buneman (Eds.): ICDT'99, LNCS 1540, pp. 58–69, 1998.
© Springer-Verlag Berlin Heidelberg 1998

The variant of BQL with while-loops instead of for-loops, called RQL, was introduced by Chandra and Harel [CH82]. In the same paper these authors also introduced, in the context of query languages, the extension of first-order logic with the least fixpoint operator; we will denote this logic here by FO(LFP). By using a *partial* fixpoint operator we obtain a logic, called FO(PFP), with the same expressive power as RQL.

Here, we will introduce the FOR operator, which iterates a formula (called the "body formula") precisely as many times as the cardinality of the relation defined by another formula (called the "head formula"). In contrast to the equivalence of RQL and FO(PFP), FO(FOR) is not equivalent to, but strictly stronger than, BQL. The reason for this turns out to be the presence of free variables acting as parameters; the restriction of FO(FOR) that disallows such parameters is equivalent to BQL.

The question whether FO(LFP) is strictly weaker than FO(PFP) is a famous open problem, since Abiteboul and Vianu showed that it is equivalent to whether PTIME is strictly contained in PSPACE [AV95]. In FO(LFP) we can equivalently replace the least fixpoint operator by the *inflationary* fixpoint operator IFP. So the PTIME versus PSPACE question is one of inflationary versus non-inflationary iteration. Since the FOR operator is non-inflationary in nature, one may wonder about the expressive power of the inflationary version of FOR, which we call IFOR. We will show that FO(IFOR) lies strictly between FO(IFP) and FO(FOR). Since in FO(FOR) we can define parity, FO(FOR) is not subsumed by FO(PFP), and conversely FO(PFP) can only be subsumed by FO(FOR) if PSPACE equals PTIME, since FO(PFP) equals PSPACE on ordered structures and FO(FOR) is contained in PTIME.

A natural question is how FO(FOR) relates to FO(IFP, #), the extension of FO(IFP) with counting. Actually, FO(FOR) is readily seen to be subsumed by FO(IFP, #). We will show that this subsumption is strict, by showing that one cannot express in FO(FOR) that two sets have the same cardinality.[1] We also will show that the restriction of FO(IFP, #) that allows modular counting only, is strictly subsumed by FO(FOR).

The main technical question we will focus on in this paper is that of nesting of for-loops. It is known that nested applications of while-loops in RQL, or of the PFP operator in FO(PFP), do not give extra expressive power; a single while-loop or PFP operator suffices [EF95]. In the case of BQL, however, we will show that nesting does matter, albeit only in a limited way: one level of nesting already suffices. In the case of FO(FOR), there are two kinds of nesting of the FOR operator: in body formulas, and in head formulas. Regarding bodies, we will show that nested applications of the FOR operator in body formulas again do matter, although here we do not know whether nesting up to a certain level is sufficient. Regarding heads, we will show that the restriction of FO(FOR) that allows only head formulas that are "pure" first-order, is weaker than full FO(FOR). By "pure" we mean that the formula cannot mention relation variables from

---

[1] The analogous result for BQL (which is weaker than FO(FOR)) was stated by Chandra in the early eighties [Cha81,Cha88], but no proof has been published.

surrounding FOR operators; from the moment this is allowed, we are back to full FO(FOR).

In this extended abstract, the proofs of our results are only sketched.

2   Preliminaries

Throughout the paper we will use the terminology and notation of mathematical logic [EFT94]. A *relational vocabulary* τ is what in the field of databases is known as a relational schema; a *structure* over τ is what is known as an instance of that schema with an explicit domain. (Structures are always assumed to be finite in this paper.) The query language of first-order logic (the relational calculus) is denoted by FO.

Let us briefly recall the syntax and semantics of FO(PFP) and FO(IFP). Let $\varphi(\bar{x}, \bar{y}, X, \overline{Y})$ be an FO formula over $\tau \cup \{X, \overline{Y}\}$, where X is an n-ary relation variable, $\bar{x}$ is of length n, and $\overline{Y}$ is a tuple of relation variables. On any τ-structure $\mathcal{A}$ expanded with interpretations for the first- and second-order parameters $\bar{y}$ and $\overline{Y}$, φ defines the stages $\varphi^0(\mathcal{A}) := \emptyset$ and $\varphi^i(\mathcal{A}) := \{\bar{a} \mid \mathcal{A} \models \varphi[\bar{a}, \varphi^{i-1}(\mathcal{A})]\}$ for each $i > 0$. If there exists an i_0 such that $\varphi^{i_0}(\mathcal{A}) = \varphi^{i_0+1}(\mathcal{A})$, then we say that *the partial fixpoint of φ on $\mathcal{A}$ exists*, and define it to be $\varphi^{i_0}(\mathcal{A})$, otherwise we define it as the empty set. We obtain FO(PFP) by augmenting FO with the rule $[\mathrm{PFP}_{\bar{x}, X}\varphi](\bar{t})$, which expresses that $\bar{t}$ belongs to the partial fixpoint of φ. For FO(IFP) we consider the stages $\tilde{\varphi}^0(\mathcal{A}) := \emptyset$ and $\tilde{\varphi}^i(\mathcal{A}) := \tilde{\varphi}^i(\mathcal{A}) \cup \{\bar{a} \mid \mathcal{A} \models \varphi[\bar{a}, \tilde{\varphi}^{i-1}(\mathcal{A})]\}$, for each $i > 0$. Here, there always exists an i_0 such that $\tilde{\varphi}^{i_0}(\mathcal{A}) = \tilde{\varphi}^{i_0+1}(\mathcal{A})$. We call $\tilde{\varphi}^{i_0}(\mathcal{A})$ *the inflationary fixpoint of φ on $\mathcal{A}$.* We obtain FO(IFP) by augmenting FO with the rule $[\mathrm{IFP}_{\bar{x}, X}\varphi](\bar{t})$, which expresses that $\bar{t}$ belongs to the inflationary fixpoint of φ.

3   Query Languages with For-Loops

Let τ be a vocabulary. The set of BQL *programs over τ* is inductively defined as follows:

(i) if X is a relation variable of arity n and e is a relational algebra expression of arity n over the vocabulary τ and the relation variables, then $X := e$ is a BQL program;

(ii) if P_1 and P_2 are BQL programs then $P_1; P_2$ is a BQL program; and

(iii) if P is a BQL program then **for** $|X|$ **do** P **od** is a BQL program.

The semantics of BQL programs of the form (i) or (ii) is defined in the obvious way; for BQL programs of the form (iii) the subprogram P is iterated as many times as the cardinality of the relation stored in variable X prior to entering the loop.

Example 1. Let $\tau_G = \{E\}$ be the vocabulary of graphs; so E is the binary edge relation. Consider the following BQL programs:

$$X := \{x \mid x = x\}; \ Y := \emptyset; \ \textbf{for } |X| \textbf{ do } Y := \neg Y \textbf{ od},$$

$$X := E; \text{ for } |X| \text{ do } X := \{(x,y) \mid X(x,y) \lor (\exists z)(X(x,z) \land E(z,y))\} \text{ od}.$$

The first program computes, in variable Y, the parity of the number of vertices of the graph, and the second program computes the transitive closure of E. Formally we should have used relational algebra expressions in the assignment statements, but we use relational calculus formulas instead.   □

By a standard simulation technique [CH82], one can simulate every FO(IFP) formula by a BQL program. It is well known that it is not expressible in FO(PFP) whether the cardinality of a set is even. Hence, FO(PFP) does not subsume BQL and BQL strictly subsumes FO(IFP).

We next introduce the logic FO(FOR). The crucial construct in the formation of FO(FOR) formulas is the following: suppose $\varphi(\bar{x}, \bar{y}, X, \overline{Y})$ and $\psi(\bar{z}, \bar{u}, \bar{y}, \overline{Y})$ are formulas and $\bar{x}$, $\bar{u}$ and X are of the same arity. Then the following FO(FOR) formula ξ is obtained from ψ and φ through the FOR-constructor:

$$\xi(\bar{u}, \bar{y}, \overline{Y}) = \left[\mathrm{FOR}_{\bar{x}, X}^{\# \bar{z}: \psi} \varphi\right](\bar{u}).$$

The formula ψ is called the *head formula*, and φ is called the *body formula* of ξ. For each τ-structure $\mathcal{A}$ expanded with interpretations for the parameters $\bar{y}$ and $\overline{Y}$, and for any tuple of elements $\bar{a}$: $\mathcal{A} \models \xi[\bar{a}]$ iff $\bar{a} \in \varphi^m(\mathcal{A})$ where m equals the cardinality of the set $\{\bar{c} \mid \mathcal{A} \models \psi[\bar{c}, \bar{a}]\}$. Here φ^m is as defined in Section 2.

Example 2. Consider the following FO(FOR) formulas over τ_G:

$$\xi_1(u, v) \quad \equiv \quad [\mathrm{FOR}_{x,y,X}^{\# s,t:E(s,t)} E(x,y) \lor (\exists z)(X(x,z) \land E(z,y))](u,v)$$

and

$$\xi_2(x) \quad \equiv \quad \neg(\exists z)[\mathrm{FOR}_{z,Z}^{\# y: E(x,y)} \neg Z(z)](z).$$

The formula ξ_1 defines the transitive closure of E, and ξ_2 expresses that vertex x has even outdegree.   □

Note that all queries definable in FO(FOR) are in PTIME. We will show that there are PTIME queries that are not definable in FO(FOR). However, for every PTIME query $\mathcal{Q}$ on graphs there is a formula $\varphi \in$ FO(FOR) such that $\mathcal{Q}(G) \neq \varphi(G)$ for a vanishingly small fraction of n element graphs G. Indeed, Hella, Kolaitis and Luosto showed that a canonical ordering is definable on almost all graphs in FO(IFP) plus the even quantifier [HKL96]. For future reference we call the query that expresses this ordering the *HKL query*. Clearly, it is definable in FO(FOR), too. Since FO(FOR) can also easily simulate FO(IFP), which is known to capture PTIME in the presence of ordering, FO(FOR) thus captures PTIME on almost all graphs.

3.1   BQL versus FO(FOR)

Every BQL query is also definable in FO(FOR). The converse, however, does not hold. For non-Boolean queries this is readily seen. The relation variables in a BQL program always hold relations that are closed under indistinguishability in first-order logic with a fixed number of variables. To see this, let P be a BQL program and let k be the maximum number of variables needed to express the assignment expressions of P in FO. Then, for any structure $\mathcal{A}$, the value of any relation variable of P is definable by an FO^{2k}-formula. (FO^{2k} denotes the $2k$-variable fragment of FO.) The query defined by ξ_2 in Example 2, however, is not closed under FO^{2k}-indistinguishability for any k. Indeed, let $\mathcal{G}_k$ be the graph depicted in Figure 1. No FO^{2k} formula can distinguish the node p from node p', but they are clearly distinguished by ξ_2 .

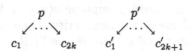

Fig. 1. The graph $\mathcal{G}_k$

To separate BQL from FO(FOR) with a Boolean query, we need to do more work. Let $\mathcal{Q}_1$ be the query *Is there a node with even outdegree?* This query is definable in FO(FOR) by the sentence $(\exists x)\xi_2(x)$. However, this query is not expressible in BQL. Indeed, let $\mathcal{S}$ be the class of graphs that are disjoint unions of stars with the same number of children. Hence, each graph $\mathcal{G}_{p,c} \in \mathcal{S}$ is characterized by the number of stars p and the number of children c. On $\mathcal{S}$, there are, up to equivalence, only a finite number of FO^{2k} formulas. Hence, there are only a finite number of possible values for the relation variables of BQL programs. On large enough graphs the values of the relation variables in the bodies of for-loops will thus start to cycle. Moreover, this behavior can be described by modular equations:

Lemma 3. *For any natural numbers k and v, there exist polynomials $q_1, \ldots, q_N$ in p and c and natural numbers d_1, d_2 such that for all $p, p', c, c' \geq d_1$: if*

$$q_j(p,c) \equiv q_j(p',c') \pmod{d_2} \qquad for\ j = 1 \ldots N,$$

then for every BQL program P with at most k individual and v relational variables, P accepts $\mathcal{G}_{p,c}$ iff P accepts $\mathcal{G}_{p',c'}$. Moreover, every polynomial is of the form $p \cdot q(p,c)$.

Now, suppose P is a BQL program with k individual and v relational variables that computes $\mathcal{Q}_1$. Take p as a multiple of d_2 and take c arbitrary but large enough. Then all above described polynomials are equivalent to 0 modulo d_2. Hence, P accepts $\mathcal{G}_{p,2c}$ iff P accepts $\mathcal{G}_{p,2c+1}$. This leads to the desired contradiction. We thus obtain:

Theorem 4. BQL *is strictly weaker than* FO(FOR).

It is natural to ask whether there is a fragment of FO(FOR) which is equivalent to BQL. The FO(FOR) formula ξ_2 of Example 2 uses an individual parameter x in its head formula. Hence, to find a fragment of FO(FOR) equivalent to BQL, one could try to exclude individual parameters from head formulas. This, however, is not enough, since they can be simulated by relational parameters in the head and individual parameters in the body (details omitted).

Proposition 5. *The fragment of* FO(FOR) *that does neither allow individual parameters in heads nor in bodies of for-loops is equivalent to BQL.*

3.2   Inflationary versus Non-inflationary Iteration

If we replace in the definition of the semantics of the FOR operator, the stages φ^m by $\tilde{\varphi}^m$ (cf. Section 2), we obtain the inflationary version of FOR which we denote by IFOR. It is routine to verify that FO(IFOR) collapses to FO on sets. Hence, one cannot express in FO(IFOR) that the cardinality of a set is even. This implies that FO(IFOR) is strictly weaker than FO(FOR). On the other hand, FO(IFOR) is strictly more expressive than FO(IFP). Indeed, consider the vocabulary $\tau = \{U, R\}$ with U unary and R binary, and let Q_2 be the following query: $Q_2(\mathcal{A})$ is true iff $R^{\mathcal{A}}$ is a chain and $|U^{\mathcal{A}}| \geq |R^{\mathcal{A}}|$, and is false otherwise (here $|U^{\mathcal{A}}|$ denotes the cardinality of the set $U^{\mathcal{A}}$). Using pebble games [EF95], one can show that Q_2 is not definable in FO(IFP). However, it can be defined in FO(IFOR) by the formula

$$\texttt{chain} \wedge (\forall z) \left((\exists y) R(y, z) \rightarrow [\texttt{IFOR}_{x, X}^{\#x : U(x)} \texttt{first}(x) \vee (\exists y)(X(y) \wedge R(y, x))](z) \right),$$

where $\texttt{chain}$ is an FO(FOR) sentence saying that R is a chain and $\texttt{first}(x)$ defines the first element of the chain. The above implies:

Proposition 6. FO(IFOR) *lies strictly between* FO(IFP) *and* FO(FOR).

3.3   A Comparison with Logics That Count

Inflationary fixpoint logic with counting [GO93,Ott96], denoted by FO(IFP, #), is a two sorted logic. With any structure $\mathcal{A}$ with universe A, we associate the two-sorted structure $\mathcal{A}^* := \mathcal{A} \cup \langle \{0, \ldots, n\}; \leq \rangle$ with $n = |A|$ and where $\leq$ is the canonical ordering on $\{0, \ldots, n\}$. The two sorts are related by *counting terms*: let $\varphi(x, \bar{y})$ be a formula, then $\#_x[\varphi]$ is a term of the second sort. For any interpretation $\bar{b}$ for $\bar{y}$, its value equals the number of elements a that satisfy $\varphi(a, \bar{b})$. The IFP operator can be applied to relations of mixed sort.

Every FO(FOR) formula can be readily simulated in FO(IFP, #), and this subsumption is strict.

Theorem 7. FO(FOR) *is strictly weaker than* FO(IFP, #).

Proof. (sketch) Consider the vocabulary $\tau = \{U, V\}$ with U and V unary. The *equicardinality query* evaluates to true on $\mathcal{A}$ if $|U^{\mathcal{A}}| = |V^{\mathcal{A}}|$. It is easily definable in FO(IFP, #) as $\#_x[U(x)] = \#_x[V(x)]$. This query, however, is not definable in FO(FOR). The proof proceeds along the lines of the proof of Theorem 4. Structures over τ have only a constant number of automorphism types. This implies that there are only a constant number of FO(FOR)-definable relations (every FO(FOR)-definable relation is closed under all automorphisms of the structure at hand). Hence, for large enough structures, the values of the relations defined by body formulas of for-loops start to cycle. This behavior can be described by modular equations similar to those of Lemma 3. More precisely, for any FO(FOR) sentence ξ there exist polynomials $q_1, \ldots, q_N$ in n and m and natural numbers d_1 and d_2 such that for all $n, n', m, m' \geq d_1$: if

$$q_j(n, m) \equiv q_j(n', m') \pmod{d_2} \qquad \text{for } j = 1 \ldots N,$$

then $\xi \models \mathcal{A}_{n,m}$ iff $\xi \models \mathcal{A}_{n',m'}$. Here, $\mathcal{A}_{n,m}$ is the τ-structure where $|U|^{\mathcal{A}} = n$, $|V|^{\mathcal{A}} = m$, $U^{\mathcal{A}} \cap V^{\mathcal{A}} = \emptyset$, and where the domain of $\mathcal{A}$ equals $U^{\mathcal{A}} \cup V^{\mathcal{A}}$. Then $\xi \models \mathcal{A}_{n,n}$ iff $\xi \models \mathcal{A}_{n,m}$ for $m = n + d_2$ and $n \geq d_1$. Hence, no FO(FOR) sentence can define the equicardinality query.   □

We conclude this section with three remarks,

(i) It can be shown that on monadic structures FO(FOR) collapses to FO plus modulo counting.

(ii) Though FO(IFP, #) is strictly more expressive than FO(FOR), the logic FO(IFP) extended with modulo counting is strictly weaker than FO(FOR). Indeed, the query $\mathcal{Q}_2$ from Section 3.2 is not expressible in FO(IFP) plus modulo counting. We omit the details.

(iii) Note that FO(IFP, #) formulas are not evaluated on the τ-structures themselves but on the extension of these τ-structures with a fragment of the natural numbers. Hence, to be able to compare FO(FOR) with FO(IFP, #) in an honest way, we should make this second sort also available to FO(FOR) formulas. It now turns out that when FO(FOR) formulas are evaluated on these number-extended structures, FO(FOR) becomes in fact equal to FO(IFP, #).

4   Nesting of For-Loops

4.1   Nesting in BQL

The *nesting depth* of a BQL program P, denoted by *depth*(P), is inductively defined as follows:

(i) the depth of an assignment statement is 0;
(ii) *depth*$(P_1; P_2) := \max\{depth(P_1), depth(P_2)\}$; and
(iii) *depth*(**for** $|X|$ **do** P **od**) := *depth*$(P) + 1$.

For $i \geq 0$, let BQL$_i$ be the fragment of BQL consisting of BQL programs of nesting depth smaller or equal to i. We also refer to BQL$_1$ as *unnested* BQL. We show:

Theorem 8. *Unnested BQL is strictly weaker than BQL.*

Proof. (sketch) Take the vocabulary $\tau = \{E, C\}$, with E binary and C unary. We now consider graphs of the form of a chain, where to each node of the chain a separate set is attached. The chain is distinguished in the structure by the unary relation C. The sets are of various sizes bounded above by the length of the chain. Let n be the length of the chain, and let α_i be the size of the i-th set. Then this structure is denoted by $\alpha = (\alpha_1, \ldots, \alpha_n)$; this is an element of $[1, n]^n$. In Figure 2, an example of such a structure is depicted. Now, let Q_3 be the binary query defined as follows: $Q_3(\alpha) := \{(i, \alpha_i) \mid i \in \{1, \ldots, n\}\}$. By the numbers i and α_i we mean respectively the i-th and α_i-th element of the chain. Observe that this query is injective. This query is expressible in BQL. We omit the details.

Towards a contradiction, let P be an unnested BQL program that computes Q_3. Let k be the maximum number of variables that are needed to express the assignments of P in FO.

For any $k > 2$ and any n large enough there always exist two nonisomorphic graphs $\alpha, \beta \in [2k, n]^n$ in which the cardinalities of the relations occurring in the heads of all the for-loops in P are equal. Indeed, the number of possible sequences of cardinalities of heads in P grows polynomially with n, while there are exponentially many elements in $[2k, n]^n$.

These α and β are indistinguishable in FO^{2k}. Moreover, $P(\alpha)$, the result of P on input α, is indistinguishable in FO^{2k} from $P(\beta)$, the result of P on input β, since in both structures P is evaluated as *the same* sequence of FO^k-definable substitutions. $P(\alpha)$ and $P(\beta)$ are indistinguishable subsets of chains of equal length, so they must in fact be *equal*. Hence, the query expressed by P is not injective. This leads to the desired contradiction. $\square$

Fig. 2. $\alpha = (\alpha_1, \ldots, \alpha_n)$

Note that the query Q_3 used in the above proof is not a Boolean query. It remains open whether there exists a Boolean query that separates BQL from unnested BQL.

We next show that the nesting hierarchy is not strict.

Theorem 9. BQL *is equivalent to* BQL_2.

Proof. (sketch) By structural induction we show that every BQL program P is equivalent to one of the form

$$P_1; \textbf{ while } Y \neq \emptyset \textbf{ do } P_2 \textbf{ od}, \qquad\qquad (\star)$$

where P_1 is a relational algebra program; P_2 is an unnested BQL program; and the variable Y becomes empty on any structure after at most a polynomial number of iterations, so that the while-loop can be implemented by a for-loop. The important property is that if Q_1 and Q_2 are two programs of the form $(\star)$, then $Q_1; Q_2$ and **while** $X \neq \emptyset$ **do** Q_1 **od** are also equivalent to a program of the form $(\star)$, provided X becomes empty in polynomially many iterations. We call an RQL program that only contains while-loops that iterate on any structure only a polynomial number of times a *PTIME* RQL program.

The key case is when P is **for** $|X|$ **do** P' **od**, with P' already of the form $(\star)$ by induction. Let k be the maximum number of variables that are needed to express the assignments of P in FO, and let v be the number of relation variables occurring in P.

To simulate P, we first compute the $2k$-variable Abiteboul-Vianu invariant $\pi_{2k}(\mathcal{A})$ [AV95] of the input structure $\mathcal{A}$ by a PTIME RQL program. This provides us with an ordering of the FO^{2k}-equivalence classes. Using this ordering, an ℓ-ary relation over the invariant can now encode any number between 0 and $2^{\ell \cdot |\pi_{2k}(\mathcal{A})|} - 1$. In case $|X| < 2^{v \cdot |\pi_{2k}(\mathcal{A})|}$, using relations as counters, we can simulate the for-loop of P by a while-loop of the desired form. If, on the other hand, $|X| \geq 2^{v \cdot |\pi_{2k}(\mathcal{A})|}$, then we know that the execution of the loop gets into a cycle, because there are only $2^{v \cdot |\pi_{2k}(\mathcal{A})|}$ assignments of values to v relation variables. Let t be the number of iterations needed before the values of the relations of P' get into the cycle and let p be the cycle size. Then we can simulate P by iterating the body first t times and then $(|X| - t) \bmod p$ times. The former can be done as in the previous case (the value of t is less than $2^{v \cdot |\pi_{2k}(\mathcal{A})|}$). For the latter we make use of the equality $|X| = \sum_{[\bar{a}] \subseteq X} |[\bar{a}]|$, where $[\bar{a}]$ is the FO^{2k}-equivalence class of $\bar{a}$.

The program iterating P' exactly $(|X| - t) \bmod p$ times is shown in Figure 3. Note that this is the only place where a real for-loop appears in the simulation.

$X' := X$; counter $:= 0$;
while $X' \neq \emptyset$ **do**
    $[\bar{a}] :=$ least class in X' according to the ordering of $\pi_{2k}(\mathcal{A})$;
    $X' := X' - [\bar{a}]$;
    for $|[\bar{a}]|$ **do** counter $:= (\text{counter} + 1) \bmod p$ **od**;
od;
while counter $\neq 0$ **do**
    P'; counter $:=$ counter $- 1$;
od;
P_{rest};

Fig. 3. The program iterating P' exactly $(|X| - t) \bmod p$ times.

Here, P_{rest} is the PTIME RQL program that iterates P' precisely $p - (t \bmod p)$ times. We omit the description of the programs that compute the threshold t

and the cycle size p. It can be shown that they are equivalent to a program of the form $(\star)$.

It remains to be noticed that the test whether $|X| < 2^{v \cdot |\pi_{2k}(\mathcal{A})|}$ can be simulated by a program of the form $(\star)$ in the standard way. Now, using the transformations of while-loops specified above one can reduce all while-loops to one. This ends the induction step. $\square$

4.2 Nesting in FO(FOR)

Nesting in the head. Let FH-FO(FOR), FO(FOR) *with first-order heads*, be the fragment of FO(FOR) that does not allow for-loops in its head formulas. Consider the sentence

$$\xi := \neg(\exists v)\left[\mathrm{FOR}_{v,V}^{\#x:\psi(x)}\neg V(v)\right](v)$$
$$\text{where } \psi(x) = \neg(\exists w)\left[\mathrm{FOR}_{w,W}^{\#y:E(x,y)}\neg W(w)\right](w).$$

It expresses the query *Are there an even number of nodes with even outdegree?* We can simulate the for-loop in the head by introducing an extra for-loop that computes in its first iteration the relation defined by the head of ξ and computes in its second iteration the body of ξ using the relation it computed in its first iteration. This construction can be generalized to arbitrary FO(FOR) formulas. Hence, nesting in the head is dispensable:

Proposition 10. FO(FOR) *is equivalent to* FH-FO(FOR).

The above described construction, however, introduces relational parameters in head formulas. We next show that in general one cannot get rid of these parameters. Let PFH-FO(FOR), FO(FOR) *with pure first-order heads*, be the fragment of FH-FO(FOR) that forbids relational variables in head formulas of for-loops.

To prove inexpressibility results for PFH-FO(FOR), we introduce an extended version of the k-pebble game [EF95]. First, the Duplicator has to preserve partial isomorphisms between the pebbles as in the ordinary k-pebble game. But on top of that, he must also make sure that for any FO^k formula $\varphi(\bar{x}, \bar{y})$, if we fill in some pebbled elements $\bar{a}$ from the first structure $\mathcal{A}$ and take the corresponding pebbled elements $\bar{b}$ in the second structure $\mathcal{B}$ (or vice versa) then $|\{\bar{a}' \mid \mathcal{A} \models \varphi[\bar{a}, \bar{a}']\}| = |\{\bar{b}' \mid \mathcal{B} \models \varphi[\bar{b}, \bar{b}']\}|$. This game provides us with the following tool:

Lemma 11. *Let $\mathcal{Q}$ be a Boolean query. If for every k, there exist structures $\mathcal{A}_k$ and $\mathcal{B}_k$ such that $\mathcal{Q}(\mathcal{A}_k) \neq \mathcal{Q}(\mathcal{B}_k)$, and the Duplicator has a winning strategy in the extended k-pebble game on $\mathcal{A}_k$ and $\mathcal{B}_k$, then $\mathcal{Q}$ is not definable in PFH-FO(FOR).*

Proof. (sketch) The key observation is that any PFH-FO(FOR) formula ξ is equivalent to a formula of infinitary logic with counting, where the counting quantifiers $\exists^k \bar{x}$ (meaning there exactly k tuples $\bar{x}$ such that ...) are applied to FO formulas only. It is routine to verify that the lemma holds for this logic. $\square$

Consider the following Boolean query over the vocabulary of graphs: $Q_4(\mathcal{G})$ is true iff

(i) every connected component of $\mathcal{G}$ is ordered by the HKL query (cf. the paragraph before Section 3.1);
(ii) the number of elements in each connected component is larger than the number of connected components; and
(iii) there are exactly two isomorphism types of connected components and they appear in equal numbers of copies.

This query can be shown to be definable in FO(FOR). Using Lemma 11, however, we can show that Q_4 is not definable in PFH-FO(FOR), as follows.

By a counting argument one can show that for any k, there are two non-isomorphic connected graphs G_k and H_k over which every FO^k formula is equivalent to a quantifier free one, and moreover for every such FO^k formula φ it holds that $|\{\bar{g} \mid G_k \models \varphi[\bar{g}]\}| = |\{\bar{g} \mid H_k \models \varphi[\bar{g}]\}|$. Additionally, G_k and H_k can be ordered by the HKL query and $|H_k|, |G_k| > 2k + 2$.

Let $\mathcal{A}_k$ be the disjoint union of $k+1$ copies of G_k and $k+1$ copies of H_k, and let $\mathcal{B}_k$ be the disjoint union of k copies of G_k and $k+2$ copies of H_k. The Duplicator has a winning strategy for the extended k-pebble game on these structures: it suffices to ensure that the partial isomorphism required for the game can always be extended to a partial isomorphism defined for all the members of the connected components in which the pebbles are located. Because initially there are no pebbles on the board and there are enough copies of the graphs H_k and G_k in both structures, the Duplicator can maintain this strategy. It can be shown that under this strategy the conditions of the extended k-pebble game are always satisfied. The key observation is that the cardinalities of definable relations are functions of the cardinalities of certain quantifier free definable relations over the components. In the absence of pebbles these cardinalities are equal in components isomorphic to G_k and H_k, and the components which contain parameters are isomorphic.

We obtain:

Theorem 12. PFH-FO(FOR) *is strictly weaker than* FO(FOR).

Nesting in the body. Let FB-FO(FOR), FO(FOR) with first-order bodies, be the fragment of FO(FOR) that does not allow for-loops in body formulas.

We next show that FO(FOR) is strictly more expressive than FB-FO(FOR). Let $n * \mathcal{G}$ denote the disjoint union of n copies of graph $\mathcal{G}$.

Let Q_5 be the following query over the vocabulary of graphs: $Q_5(\mathcal{G})$ is true iff

(i) $\mathcal{G} \cong n * \mathcal{H}$;
(ii) $\mathcal{H}$ can be ordered by the HKL query;
(iii) $n < |\mathcal{H}|$.

This query can be shown to be definable in FO(FOR). Q_5 is not definable in FB-FO(FOR).

The key observation is that if $\mathcal{H}$ satisfies extension axioms for sufficiently many variables (at least as many as there are in the sentence), then the unnested bodies of **for** loops start to cycle within a bounded number of iterations already, while Q_5 requires counting up to $|\mathcal{H}|$.

Consequently, no FB-FO(FOR) sentence can define Q_5. We obtain:

Theorem 13. FB-FO(FOR) *is strictly weaker than* FO(FOR).

References

[AHV95] S. Abiteboul, R. Hull, and V. Vianu. *Foundations of Databases*. Addison-Wesley, 1995.

[AV95] S. Abiteboul and V. Vianu. Computing with first-order logic. *Journal of Computer and System Sciences*, 50(2):309–335, 1995.

[CH82] A. Chandra and D. Harel. Structure and complexity of relational queries. *Journal of Computer and System Sciences*, 25(1):99–128, 1982.

[Cha81] A. Chandra. Programming primitives for database languages. In *Conference Record, 8th ACM Symposium on Principles of Programming Languages*, pages 50–62, 1981.

[Cha88] A. Chandra. Theory of database queries. In *Proceedings of the Seventh ACM Symposium on Principles of Database Systems*, pages 1–9. ACM Press, 1988.

[EF95] H.-D. Ebbinghaus and J. Flum. *Finite Model Theory*. Springer, 1995.

[EFT94] H.-D. Ebbinghaus, J. Flum, and W. Thomas. *Mathematical Logic*. Undergraduate Texts in Mathematics. Springer-Verlag, second edition, 1994.

[GO93] E. Grädel and M. Otto. Inductive definability with counting on finite structures. In E. Börger, editor, *Computer Science Logic*, volume 702 of *Lecture Notes in Computer Science*, pages 231–247. Springer-Verlag, 1993.

[HKL96] L. Hella, Ph. G. Kolaitis, and K. Luosto. Almost everywhere equivalence of logics in finite model theory. *Bulletin of Symbolic Logic*, 2(4):422–443, 1996.

[KV95] Ph. G. Kolaitis and Jouko A. Väänänen. Generalized quantifiers and pebble games on finite structures. *Annals of Pure and Applied Logic*, 74(1):23–75, 1995.

[Ott96] M. Otto. The expressive power of fixed-point logic with counting. *Journal of Symbolic Logic*, 61(1):147–176, 1996.

Definability and Descriptive Complexity on Databases of Bounded Tree-Width

Martin Grohe and Julian Mariño

Institut für mathematische Logik Eckerstr. 1, 79104 Freiburg, Germany
{grohe,marino}@sun2.mathematik.uni-freiburg.de

Abstract. We study the expressive power of various query languages on relational databases of bounded tree-width.

Our first theorem says that fixed-point logic with counting captures polynomial time on classes of databases of bounded tree-width. This result should be seen on the background of an important open question of Chandra and Harel [7] asking whether there is a query language capturing polynomial time on unordered databases. Our theorem is a further step in a larger project of extending the scope of databases on which polynomial time can be captured by reasonable query languages.

We then prove a general definability theorem stating that each query on a class of databases of bounded tree-width which is definable in monadic second-order logic is also definable in fixed-point logic (or datalog). Furthermore, for each $k \geq$ 1 the class of databases of tree-width at most k is definable in fixed-point logic. These results have some remarkable consequences concerning the definability of certain classes of graphs.

Finally, we show that each database of tree-width at most k can be characterized up to isomorphism in the language C^{k+3}, the $(k + 3)$-variable fragment of first-order logic with counting.

1 Introduction

The tree-width of a graph, which measures the similarity of the graph to a tree, has turned out to be an indispensable tool when trying to find feasible instances of hard algorithmic problems. As a matter of fact, many NP-complete problems can be solved in linear time on classes of graphs of bounded tree-width (see [5] for a survey). Numerous examples can easily be obtained by a result of Courcelle [8] saying that any query definable in monadic second-order logic (MSO) can be evaluated in linear time on graphs of bounded tree-width. Courcelle's MSO allows to quantify over sets of edges and sets of vertices; this makes it quite powerful. For instance, hamiltonicity of a graph is defined by an MSO-sentence saying that "there exists a set X of edges such that each vertex is incident to exactly two edges in X, and the subgraph spanned by the edge-set X is connected". The importance of these results relies on the fact that many classes of graphs occurring in practice are of small tree-width.

The notion of tree-width of a graph has been introduced (under a different name) by Halin [15] and later re-invented by Robertson and Seymour [20]. It has a straightforward generalization to relational databases (due to Feder and Vardi [10], also see [11]). It

Catriel Beeri, Peter Buneman (Eds.): ICDT'99, LNCS 1540, pp. 70–82, 1998.
© Springer-Verlag Berlin Heidelberg 1998

is easy to see that most of the results on graphs of bounded tree-width generalize to relational databases. Among them is Courcelle's theorem. It immediately implies that on a class of databases of bounded tree-width each first-order query can be evaluated in linear time.[1]

Our main task is to study the expressive power of fixed-point logic with and without counting on databases of bounded tree-width. Of course, our results transfer to the query languages datalog and datalog with counting, both under the inflationary semantics, which are known to have the same expressive power as the corresponding fixed-point logics ([1,12]).

Theorem 1. *Let $k \geq 1$. Fixed-point logic with counting captures polynomial time on the class of all databases of tree-width at most k.*

In other words, a "generic" query on a class of databases of bounded tree-width is computable in polynomial time if, and only if, it is definable in fixed-point logic with counting. It is important to note here that we are considering classes of unordered databases; on ordered databases the result is a just a special case of the well-known result of Immerman and Vardi [16,24] saying that fixed-point logic captures polynomial time on ordered databases. The problem of capturing polynomial time on unordered databases goes back to Chandra and Harel [7]. Our result should be seen as part of a larger project of gradually extending the scope of classes of databases on which we can capture polynomial time by "nice" logics. The main motivation for this is to get a better understanding of "generic polynomial time", which may contribute to the design of better query languages. Though it is known that fixed-point logic with counting does not capture polynomial time on all databases [6], it has turned out to be the right logic in several special cases. The best previously known result is that it captures polynomial time on the class of planar graphs [14]. Our Theorem 1 is somewhat complementary by a result of Robertson and Seymour [22] saying that a class C of graphs is of bounded tree-width if, and only if, there is a planar graph that is not a minor (see below) of any graph in C.

We next turn to fixed-point logic without counting. Although this weaker logic does certainly not capture polynomial time on databases of bounded tree-width, it remains surprisingly expressive.

Theorem 2. *Let $k \geq 1$ and τ a database schema.*

(1) The class of all databases over τ of tree-width at most k is definable in fixed-point logic.

(2) Each MSO-definable query on the class of databases of tree-width at most k is definable in fixed-point logic. More precisely, for each MSO-definable class D of databases the class

$$\{D \in \mathcal{D} \mid D \text{ is of treewidth at most } k\}$$

is definable in fixed-point logic.[2]

---

[1] More precisely, for each first-order formula $\varphi(\bar{x})$ there is a linear-time algorithm that, given a database D and a tuple $\bar{a}$, checks whether $D \models \varphi(\bar{a})$.

[2] For convenience we have only formulated the result for Boolean queries, but the generalization to arbitrary queries is straightforward.

This theorem has some nice applications to graphs. To obtain the full strength of Courcelle's MSO with quantification over edge-sets, we consider graphs as databases over the schema $\{V, E, I\}$ with unary V, E and a binary I. A graph is then a triple $G = (V^G, E^G, I^G)$, where V^G is the vertex-set, E^G is the edge-set, and $I^G \subseteq V^G \times E^G$ the binary incidence relation between them.[3] Thus Theorem 2 implies, for example, that hamiltonicity is fixed-point definable on graphs of bounded tree-width.

Recall that a graph H is a *minor* of a graph G if it is obtained from a subgraph of G by contracting edges. It can easily be seen that for each fixed graph H there is an MSO-sentence saying that a graph G contains H as a minor. In their Graph Minor Theorem, Robertson and Seymour [23] proved that for each class C of graphs closed under taking minors there are finitely many graphs $H_1, \ldots, H_n$ such that a graph G is in C if, and only if, it contains none of $H_1, \ldots, H_n$ as a minor. (Actually, a restricted version of this theorem, proved in [21], suffices for our purposes.) Together with the fact that the class of all planar graphs is fixed-point definable [14] and the abovementioned result of Robertson and Seymour that a class C of graphs is of bounded tree-width if, and only if, there is a planar graph that is not a minor of any graph in C, we obtain a quite surprising corollary:

Corollary 1. *Let C be a class of planar graphs that is closed under taking minors. Then C is definable in fixed-point logic.*

As another by-product of our main results, we obtain a theorem that continues a study initiated by Immerman and Lander [17,18]. C^k denotes the k-variable (first-order) logic with counting quantifiers.

Theorem 3. *Let $k \geq 1$. For each database D of tree-width at most k there is a C^{k+3}-sentence that characterizes D up to isomorphism.*

On the other hand, Cai, Fürer, and Immerman [6] proved that for each $k \geq 1$ there are non-isomorphic graphs G, H of size $O(k)$ that cannot be distinguished by a C^k-sentence.

2   Preliminaries

A *database schema* is a finite set τ of relation symbols with associated arities. We fix a countable domain *dom*. A *database instance*, or just *database*, over the schema $\tau = \{R_1, \ldots, R_n\}$ is a tuple $D = (R_1^D, \ldots, R_n^D)$, where R_i^D is a finite relation on *dom* of the arity associated with R_i. The *active domain* of D, denoted by A^D, is the set of all elements of *dom* occurring in a tuple contained in any of the R_i^D. For convenience, we usually write $a \in D$ instead of $a \in A^D$; we even write $\bar{a} \in D$ instead of $\bar{a} \in (A^D)^k$ for k-tuples $\bar{a}$. By $\bar{a}$ we always denote a tuple $a_1 \ldots a_k$, for some $k \geq 1$. The *size* of a

---

[3] It is more common in database theory to encode graphs as databases over $\{V, R\}$, where V is unary and R binary. But it is easy to see that there is a first-order definable transformation between graphs (V, R) and the corresponding (V, E, I) and vice-versa, and it changes the tree-width by at most 1.

database D, denoted by $|D|$, is the size of its active domain. In general, $|S|$ denotes the size of a set S.

If D is a database over τ, X a k-ary relation symbol not contained in τ, and X^* a k-ary relation over *dom*, then (D, X^*) denotes the database over $\tau \cup \{X\}$ defined in the obvious way. Occasionally we also need to expand a database D by distinguished elements, for a tuple $\bar{a} \in dom$ we write $(D, \bar{a})$ for the expansion of D by $\bar{a}$. An isomorphism between $(D, a_1 \dots a_l)$ and $(E, b_1 \dots b_l)$ is a bijective $f : A^D \cup \{a_1, \dots, a_l\} \rightarrow A^E \cup \{b_1, \dots, b_l\}$ such that $f(a_i) = b_i$ for $i \leq l$ and f is an isomorphism between D and E.

A *subinstance* of a database D over τ is a database E over τ such that for all $R \in \tau$ we have $R^E \subseteq R^D$. For $B \subseteq dom$ we let $\langle B \rangle^D$ denote the subinstance E of D where for all $R \in \tau$, say, of arity r, we have $R^E = R^D \cap B^r$. We often omit the superscript D and just write $\langle B \rangle$ if D is clear from the context.

The union, intersection, difference of a family of databases over the same schema is defined relation-wise. For example, the union of two databases D and E over τ is the database $D \cup E$ over τ with $R^{D \cup E} = R^D \cup R^E$ for all $R \in \tau$. If D is a database and $B \subseteq dom$ we let $D \setminus B = \langle A^D \setminus B \rangle^D$. Furthermore, for an l-tuple $\bar{a} \in dom$ we let $D \setminus \bar{a} = D \setminus \{a_1, \dots, a_l\}$.

An *ordered database* is a database D over a schema that contains the binary relation symbol $\leq$ such that $\leq^D$ is a linear order of the active domain of D.

We assume that the reader is familiar with the notions of a *query* and *query language*. Most of the time, we restrict our attention to *Boolean queries*,[4] which we just consider as isomorphism closed classes of databases over the the same schema. A Boolean query *on* a class $\mathcal{D}$ of databases is a Boolean query $\mathcal{Q}$ which is a subclass of $\mathcal{D}$.

We say that a query language L *captures* a complexity class K if for each query $\mathcal{Q}$ we have: $\mathcal{Q}$ is definable in L if, and only if, it is computable in K. We say that L *captures* K *on* a class $\mathcal{D}$ of databases if for each query $\mathcal{Q}$ on $\mathcal{D}$ we have: $\mathcal{Q}$ is definable in L if, and only if, it is computable in K.

For example, a well-known result of Immerman and Vardi [16,24] says that *least fixed-point logic* captures polynomial time on the class of all ordered databases.

2.1 Fixed-Point Logics

We assume a certain familiarity with first-order logic FO. The query languages we are mainly interested in are *inflationary fixed-point logic* IFP and *inflationary fixed-point logic with counting* IFP+C.

The set of IFP-*formulas* is obtained adding the following formula-formation rule to the usual rules to form first-order formulas:

Given a formula φ over the schema $\tau \cup \{X\}$, where X is a k-ary relation symbol for some $k \geq 1$, and two k-tuples $\bar{x}, \bar{z}$ of variables, we may form the new formula $[\mathsf{IFP}_{\bar{x}, X} \varphi] \bar{z}$ over τ.

---

[4] This restriction is inessential and can easily be removed. But it simplifies things a little bit.

The semantics of IFP is, as usually, given by a satisfaction relation $\models$. In particular, consider an IFP-formula $\varphi(\bar{x}, \bar{y})$ over a schema $\tau \cup \{X\}$, such that the free variables of φ occur in the tuples $\bar{x}, \bar{y}$, and a database D over τ. For each tuple $\bar{b} \in D$ we let $X_0^{\bar{b}} = \emptyset$ and $X_{i+1}^{\bar{b}} = X_i^{\bar{b}} \cup \{\bar{a} \in D \mid (D, X_i^{\bar{b}}) \models \varphi(\bar{a}, \bar{b})\}$ (for $i \geq 0$). Furthermore, we let $X_\infty^{\bar{b}} = \bigcup_{i \geq 1} X_i^{\bar{b}}$. Then $D \models [\text{IFP}_{\bar{x}, X} \varphi(\bar{x}, \bar{b})]\bar{c}$ if, and only, $\bar{c} \in X_\infty^{\bar{b}}$ (for all $\bar{c} \in D$).

To define IFP+C we need to introduce a second countable domain *num* disjoint from *dom*. We think of *num* as a copy of the non-negative integers, and we usually do not distinguish between an element of *num* and the corresponding integer. We also need variables of sort *num* which we denote by μ, ν. The symbols x, y, z always refer to variables of sort *dom*. If we do not want to specify the sort of a variable, we use symbols u, v, w. Furthermore, we let $\leqslant$ denote a binary relation symbol which is supposed to range over *num*.

For each database D over τ we let N^D be the initial segment $\{0, \ldots, |D|\}$ of *num* of length $|D| + 1$, and we let $\leqslant^D$ be the natural order on N^D. We let $D^\# = (D, \leqslant^D)$ considered as a database of schema $\tau^\# = \tau \cup \{\leqslant\}$ on the domain $dom \cup num$. Note that the active domain of $D^\#$ is $A^D \cup N^D$. We can now consider IFP on databases with this extended domain.

The set of IFP+C-formulas is defined by the same rules as the set of IFP-formulas and the following additional rule:

> If φ is a formula and x, μ are variables then $\exists^{=\mu} x \varphi$ is a new formula. (Recall that by our convention x ranges over *dom* and μ over *num*.)

To define the semantics, let $\varphi(x, \bar{w})$ be a formula over $\tau^\#$ whose free variables all occur in $x, \bar{w}$, let D be a database over τ, and $\bar{d} \in A^D \cup N^D$, $i \in N^D$. Then $D^\# \models \exists^{=i} x \varphi(x, \bar{d})$ if, and only if, the number of $a \in A^D$ such that $D^\# \models \varphi(a, \bar{d})$ is i.

So far, our IFP+C-formulas only speak about databases $D^\#$. However, for formulas φ without free *num*-variables, we can let $D \models \varphi \iff D^\# \models \varphi$. This way, IFP+C-formulas also define queries in our usual framework of databases on the domain *dom*.

IFP+C has turned out to capture polynomial time on several classes of databases. It follows easily from the Immerman-Vardi-Theorem mentioned earlier that IFP+C captures polynomial time on the class of all ordered databases. The following Lemma, which is based on the notion of *definable canonization* introduced in [13,14], can be used to extend this result to further classes of databases. The straightforward proof can be found in [13].

For an IFP+C-formula $\varphi(\bar{w})$ and a database D we let $\varphi(\bar{w})^{D^\#} = \{\bar{d} \in D^\# \mid D^\# \models \varphi(\bar{d})\}$. Note, in particular, that if $\bar{w}$ is an l-tuple of *num*-variables, then $\varphi(\bar{w})^{D^\#}$ is an l-ary relation on *num*.

Lemma 1. *Let $\tau = \{R_1, \ldots, R_n\}$ be a database schema, where R_i is r_i-ary, and let $\mathcal{D}$ be a class of databases over τ. Suppose that there are IFP+C-formulas $\varphi_1(\bar{\mu}_1)$, ..., $\varphi_n(\bar{\mu}_n)$, where μ_i is an r_i-tuple of num-variables, such that for all $D \in \mathcal{D}$ the database*

$$(\varphi_1(\bar{\mu}_1)^{D^\#}, \ldots, \varphi_n(\bar{\mu}_n)^{D^\#})$$

(which is a database over τ on the domain num) is isomorphic to D.
Then IFP+C captures polynomial time on $\mathcal{D}$.

The reason that this holds is that we can speak of the order $\leqslant^D$ on N^D in IFP+C. Thus essentially the hypothesis of the lemma says that we can define ordered copies of all databases $D \in \mathcal{D}$ in IFP+C.

3 Tree Decompositions

Deviating from the introduction, from now on we find it convenient to consider *graphs* as databases over $\{V, E\}$, where V is unary and E is binary. Without further explanation, we use usual graph theoretic notions such as paths, cycles, etc. A *tree* is a connected, cycle-free graph.

Definition 1. *A* tree-decomposition *of a database D is a pair $(T, (B_t)_{t \in T})$, where T is a tree and $(B_t)_{t \in T}$ a family of subsets of A^D such that $\bigcup_{t \in T} \langle B_t \rangle^D = D$ and for each $a \in D$ the subgraph $\langle \{t \mid a \in B_t\} \rangle^T$ of T is connected.*

The B_t are called the blocks *of the decomposition.*

The width *of $(T, (B_t)_{t \in T})$ is $\max\{|B_t| \mid t \in T\} - 1$. The* tree-width *of D, denoted by $\mathrm{tw}(D)$, is the minimal width of a tree-decomposition of D.*

On graphs, this notion of tree-decomposition coincides with the usual notion introduced by Robertson and Seymour [20].

The first thing we will do now is present two basic and well-known lemmas that give rise to a fixed-point definition of the class of databases of tree-width at most k. This requires some additional notation. We recommend the reader to really get familiar with this notation and the lemmas, since they will be used again and again throughout the whole paper. For other basic facts about tree-decompositions and tree-width we refer the reader to [9]. Similar techniques as we use them here have been employed by Bodländer in [3,4].

Definition 2. *Let $k \geq 1$ and D a database. A* k-preclique *of D is a $(k+1)$-tuple $\bar{a} \in D$ of distinct elements such that D has a tree-decomposition $(T, (B_t)_{t \in T})$ of width at most k with $B_t = \{a_1, \ldots, a_{k+1}\}$ for some $t \in T$.*

Lemma 2. *Let $k \geq 1$ and D a database of tree-width at most k and size at least $(k+1)$.*

(1) D has a tree-decomposition $(T, (B_t))$ with $|B_t| = k+1$ for all $t \in T$ and $B_t \neq B_u$ for all distinct $t, u \in T$.

In other words, D has a tree-decomposition whose blocks are pairwise distinct k-precliques. We call such a tree-decomposition a regular *tree-decomposition.*

(2) For each k-preclique $\bar{a}$ of D there is a regular tree-decomposition $(T, (B_t)_{t \in T})$ of D such that there is a $t \in T$ with $B_t = \{a_1, \ldots, a_{k+1}\}$.

Proof. To prove (1), let $(T, (B_t)_{t \in T})$ be a tree-decomposition of D of width k such that among all tree-decompositions of D of width k:

(i) $|T|$ is minimal.

(ii) Subject to (i), $\sum_{t \in T} |B_t|$ is maximal.

(i) clearly implies that there are no adjacent $t, u \in T$ such that $B_t \subseteq B_u$, because otherwise we could simply contract the edge tu in T and obtain a smaller tree. Now suppose $|B_t| < k + 1$ for some $t \in T$. Let u be a neighbor of t and $a \in B_u \setminus B_t$. We can simply add a to B_t and obtain a new tree-decomposition with a larger sum in (ii). This contradicts our choice of $(T, (B_t))$.

(2) can be proved similarly.   □

With each database D over τ we associate its *Gaifman graph* $G(D)$ with vertex set $V^{G(D)} = A^D$ and an edge between two vertices a, b if there is a tuple $\bar{c}$ in one of the relations of D such that both a and b occur in $\bar{c}$. Now we can transfer graph theoretic notions such as connected components or distances to arbitrary databases; we just refer to the respective notions in the Gaifman graph.

By comp(D) we denote the set of active domains of the connected components of a database D. Hence the connected components of D are the subinstances $\langle C \rangle$ for $C \in$ comp(D).

Let $l \geq 1$, D a database, and $\bar{a} \in D$ an l-tuple of vertices. For $b \in D$ we let $C_b^{-\bar{a}}$ denote the (unique) $C \in$ comp($D \setminus \bar{a}$) with $b \in C$; if $b \in \{a_1, \ldots, a_l\}$ then $C_b^{-\bar{a}}$ is the empty set. Note that comp($D \setminus \bar{a}$) = $\{C_b^{-\bar{a}} \mid b \in D\}$. Furthermore, we let $C_b^{+\bar{a}} = C_b^{-\bar{a}} \cup \{a_1, \ldots, a_l\}$.

For an l-tuple $\bar{a}$, an $i \leq l$, and any c we let $\bar{a}/i$ denote the $(l-1)$-tuple obtained from $\bar{a}$ by deleting the ith component and $\bar{a}(c/i)$ the l-tuple obtained from $\bar{a}$ by replacing the ith component by c.

Observe that a k-preclique of a database D either separates D or is the block of a leaf in every regular tree-decomposition of D where it occurs as a block. Also note that a database has tree-width at most k if, and only if, it has size at most k or contains a k-preclique.

The following lemma (for graphs) is essentially due to Arnborg, Corneil, and Proskurowski [2].

Lemma 3. *Let $k \geq 1$, D a database, and $\bar{a} \in D$ a $(k + 1)$-tuple of distinct elements.*

(1) The tuple $\bar{a}$ is a k-preclique of D if, and only if, $\bar{a}$ is a k-preclique of $\langle C_b^{+\bar{a}} \rangle$ for all $b \in D$.

(2) For all $b \in D \setminus \bar{a}$, the tuple $\bar{a}$ is a k-preclique of $\langle C_b^{+\bar{a}} \rangle$ if, and only if, there are $i \leq k + 1$ and $c \in C_b^{-\bar{a}}$ such that $\bar{a}/i$ isolates a_i in $\langle C_b^{+\bar{a}} \rangle$ (that is, a_i is not adjacent to any $d \in C_b^{-\bar{a}}$ in the Gaifman graph of D) and $\bar{a}(c/i)$ is a k-preclique of $\langle C_b^{+\bar{a}/i} \rangle (= \langle C_b^{+\bar{a}} \rangle \setminus a_i)$.

(3) For all $b \in \{a_1, \ldots, a_{k+1}\}$, the tuple $\bar{a}$ is a k-preclique of $\langle C_b^{+\bar{a}} \rangle$.

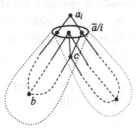

Figure 1.

Proof. Note first that if $(T, (B_t)_{t \in T})$ is a tree-decomposition of a database D and E is a subinstance of D then $(T, (A^E \cap B_t)_{t \in T})$ is a tree-decomposition of E of at most the same width.

Then the forward direction of (1) is obvious. For the backward direction we can simply paste together decompositions of the $C_b^{+\bar{a}}$ in which $\{a_1, \ldots, a_{k+1}\}$ forms a block along these blocks.

For the forward direction of (2), let $(T, (B_t)_{t \in T})$ be a regular tree-decomposition of $\langle C_b^{+\bar{a}} \rangle$ that contains a $t \in T$ with $B_t = \{a_1, \ldots, a_{k+1}\}$. Since $\bar{a}$ does not separate $\langle C_b^{+\bar{a}} \rangle$, t must be a leaf of T. Let u be the neighbor of t in T. Let $i \in \{1, \ldots, k+1\}$ such that $a_i \in B_t \setminus B_u$ and $c \in B_u \setminus B_t$. The claim follows.

For the backward direction, let $(T, (B_t)_{t \in T})$ be a tree-decomposition of $\langle C_b^{+\bar{a}/i} \rangle$ that contains a $t \in T$ with $B_t = \{a_1, \ldots, a_{i-1}, c, a_{i+1}, \ldots, a_{k+1}\}$. We add a new vertex u to T and make it adjacent to t. Furthermore, we let $B_u = \{a_1, \ldots, a_{k+1}\}$. We obtain a tree-decomposition of $C_b^{+\bar{a}}$ of the desired form.

(3) is trivial, since $C_b^{+\bar{a}} = \{a_1, \ldots, a_{k+1}\}$ in this case. $\qquad\square$

Combining (1) and (2) we obtain the following:

Corollary 2. *Let $k \geq 1$, D a database, $\bar{a} \in D$ a $(k+1)$-tuple of distinct elements, and $b \in D \setminus \bar{a}$.*

Then $\bar{a}$ is a k-preclique in $\langle C_b^{+\bar{a}} \rangle$ if, and only if, there is an $i \leq (k+1)$ and a $c \in C_b^{-\bar{a}}$ such that $\bar{a}/i$ isolates a_i in $\langle C_b^{+\bar{a}} \rangle$ and $a(c/i)$ is a k-preclique in all subinstances $\langle C_d^{+\bar{a}(c/i)} \rangle$, where $d \in C_b^{-\bar{a}/i}$.

Note that the subinstances $\langle C_d^{+\bar{a}(c/i)} \rangle$ are smaller then $\langle C_b^{+\bar{a}} \rangle$.

This gives rise to an inductive definition of the relation P consisting of all $(\bar{a}, b)$, where $\bar{a}$ is a $(k+1)$-tuple and b a single element, with the property that $\bar{a}$ is a preclique in $\langle C_b^{+\bar{a}} \rangle$: We start by letting P consist of all $(\bar{a}, a_i)$, where $\bar{a}$ is a $(k+1)$-tuple and $1 \leq i \leq k+1$. Then we repeatedly add all pairs $(\bar{a}, b)$ for which there exists an $i \leq k+1$ and a $c \in C_b^{-\bar{a}}$ such that $\bar{a}/i$ isolates a_i in $\langle C_b^{+\bar{a}} \rangle$ and we already have $(a(c/i), d) \in P$ for all $d \in C_b^{-\bar{a}/i}$. This inductive definition can easily be formalized in IFP. Thus we have:

Lemma 4. *There are IFP-formulas $\varphi(\bar{x}, y)$ and $\psi(\bar{x})$ such that for all databases D, $(k+1)$-tuples $\bar{a} \in D$ and $b \in D$ we have*

$$D \models \varphi(\bar{a}, b) \iff \bar{a} \text{ is a } k\text{-preclique in } \langle C_b^{+\bar{a}} \rangle,$$
$$D \models \psi(\bar{a}) \iff \bar{a} \text{ is a } k\text{-preclique.}$$

As a corollary we obtain the first part of Theorem 2.

Corollary 3. *Let τ be a database schema and $k \geq 1$. Then the class of all databases over τ of tree-width at most k is definable in IFP.*

4   Canonizing Databases of Bounded Tree-Width

In this section we sketch a proof of Theorem 1. The basic idea of the proof is the same as used in the proof that IFP+C captures polynomial time on the class of trees given in [13].

Let us fix a $k \geq 1$. Without loss of generality we restrict our attention to databases over the schema $\{R\}$, where R is a binary relation symbol.

We want to apply Lemma 1 to the class $\mathcal{D}$ of databases over $\{R\}$ of tree-width at most k. We shall define a formula $\varphi(\mu, \nu)$ such that for all databases $D \in \mathcal{D}$ we have $D \cong \varphi(\mu, \nu)^{D^{\#}}$.

For the course of our presentation, let us fix a database $D \in \mathcal{D}$; of course the formula φ we are going to obtain does not depend on D but works uniformly over $\mathcal{D}$.

Inductively we are going to define a $(k + 4)$-ary relation $X \subseteq (A^D)^{k+2} \times (N^D)^2$ with the following property:

For all $\bar{a}, b \in D$ such $\bar{a}$ is a k-preclique in $\langle C_b^{+\bar{a}} \rangle$ we have:

(i) There is an isomorphism f between $(\langle C_b^{+\bar{a}} \rangle, \bar{a})$ and $(X\bar{a}b\_\_, 1 \ldots k + 1)$, where $X\bar{a}b\_\_ = \{ij \in (N^D)^2 \mid \bar{a}bij \in X\}$.
(Recall that $(\langle C_b^{+\bar{a}} \rangle, \bar{a})$ denotes the expansion of the database $\langle C_b^{+\bar{a}} \rangle$ by the distinguished elements $\bar{a}$.)
(ii) For all $b' \in C_b^{+\bar{a}}$ we have $X\bar{a}b\_\_ = X\bar{a}b'\_\_$.

We start our induction by letting X be the set of all tuples $\bar{a}bij$ where $\bar{a} \in D$ is a $(k + 1)$-tuple of distinct elements, $b \in \{a_1, \ldots, a_{k+1}\}$, and $i, j \in \{1, \ldots, k + 1\}$ are chosen such that $a_i a_j \in R^D$.

For the induction step, recall Corollary 2. We consider $\bar{a}, c \in D, i \in \{1, \ldots, k+1\}$ such that

- $\bar{a}/i$ isolates a_i in $C_c^{+\bar{a}}$,
- for all $d \in C_c^{-\bar{a}/i}$, $\bar{a}(c/i)$ is a k-preclique of $\langle C_d^{+\bar{a}(c/i)} \rangle$ and the relation $X\bar{a}(c/i)d\_\_$ has already been defined,
- $X\bar{a}c\_\_$ has not been defined yet.

Note that these conditions imply, by Corollary 2, that $\bar{a}$ is a k-preclique in $\langle C_c^{+\bar{a}} \rangle$.

Let $\bar{a}' = \bar{a}(c/i)$. For the $d \in C_c^{-\bar{a}/i}$ we remember that $X\bar{a}'d\_\_$ is a database over $\{R\}$ whose active domain is contained in N^D. On N^D we have the order $\leqslant^D$ available. Hence we can view these two relations together as an ordered database over the schema $\{R, \leqslant\}$. Ordered databases, in turn, can be ordered lexicographically.

Let $C_1, \ldots, C_l$ be a list of the components $\langle C_d^{+\bar{a}'} \rangle$, for $d \in C_c^{-\bar{a}/i}$. For $1 \leq i \leq l$ and $d \in C_i$, let $X_i = X\bar{a}d\_\_$. By (ii), X_i does not depend on the choice of d. Some of the X_i may appear more than once, because different components may be isomorphic. We produce another list $Y_1, \ldots, Y_m$ (where $m \leq l$) that is ordered lexicographically (with respect to the order explained in the previous paragraph) and that only contains each entry once, and we let n_i be the number of times Y_i occurs in the list $X_1, \ldots, X_l$. (The list $Y_1, \ldots, Y_m$ can actually be defined in IFP+C; counting is crucially needed to obtain the multiplicities n_i.)

Let C denote the subinstance of D obtained by pasting the components $C_1, \ldots, C_l$ together along the tuple $\bar{a}'$. Using the Y_i and n_i we define a binary relation Y on N^D such that $(C, \bar{a}')$ is isomorphic to $(Y, 1 \ldots k + 1)$. It is clearly possible to do the arithmetic necessary here within the formal framework of our logic IFP+C.

In a second step we add an element representing a_i in an appropriate position and rearrange Y to obtain an $X' \bar{a} c_{--}$ that satisfies (i). However, (ii) is not guaranteed so far because our definition may depend on the choices of c and i. So finally we let $X \bar{a} c_{--}$ be the lexicographically first among all the $X' \bar{a} c'_{--}$, for all suitable choices of c' and i. For all $b \in C_c^{-\bar{a}}$ we let $X \bar{a} b_{--} = X \bar{a} c_{--}$.

This completes the induction step.

We eventually reach a situation where we have defined $X \bar{a} b_{--}$ for all k-precliques $\bar{a}$ and for all b. Similarly as in the definition of Y above, for each k-preclique $\bar{a}$ we can now define a binary $Z_{\bar{a}}$ on N^D such that $(D, \bar{a})$ is isomorphic to $(Z_{\bar{a}}, 1 \ldots k + 1)$. In other words, for all $\bar{a}$ we obtain an ordered copy of D whose first $(k + 1)$-elements represent $\bar{a}$. We pick the lexicographically smallest among all the $Z_{\bar{a}}$ to be our canonical copy.

This definition can be formalized in IFP+C and gives us the desired formula φ. $\square$

Theorem 3 can be proved by a similar induction, though its proof is simpler because we do not have to define a canonical copy of our database, but just determine its isomorphism type. Due to space limitations, we omit the proof.

5 Monadic Second Order Logic

The set of MSO-*formulas* is obtained adding the following formula-formation rule to the usual rules to form first-order formulas:

Given a formula φ over $\tau \cup \{X\}$, where X is a unary relation symbol, we may form a new formula $\exists X \varphi$ over τ.

Furthermore, we use the abbreviation $\forall X \varphi$ for $\neg \exists X \neg \varphi$.

The semantics of MSO is obtained by inductively defining a relation $\models$, the only interesting step being

$$D \models \exists X \varphi \iff \text{There is a subset } X^* \subseteq A^D \text{ such that } (D, X^*) \models \varphi.$$

In this section we want to prove the second part of Theorem 2: *On a class of databases of bounded tree-width, each MSO-definable query is IFP-definable.*

To prove Courcelle's [8] result that each MSO-definable query on graphs of bounded tree-width is computable in linear time one may proceed as follows: The first step is to compute a tree-decomposition of the input graph in which each vertex has valence at most 3. Then the crucial observation is that if we have such a tree-decomposition, we can describe each MSO-formula by a finite tree-automaton. It is not hard to simulate such an automaton in linear time.

We proceed in a similar spirit, having to deal with two problems. The first is that we do not know how to define a tree-decomposition of a database in IFP. But inductively climbing along the precliques is almost as good. The second problem is that we cannot guarantee a bounded valence, that is, we cannot give a bound on the number of compo-nents $C_b^{+\bar{a}}$ that may occur in Lemma 3(1). However, in the proof sketched above this is needed to make the automaton finite. To overcome this problem we first need to prove the following "padding lemma".

The *quantifier-rank* of an MSO-formula is the maximal number of nested (first and second-order quantifiers) occurring in the formula. For a database D and an l-tuple $\bar{a} \in D$ we let $\mathrm{tp}_r(D, \bar{a})$ be the set of all MSO-formulas $\Phi(\bar{x})$ of quantifier-rank r such that $D \models \Phi(\bar{a})$. The tuple $\bar{a}$ may be empty, in this case we just write $\mathrm{tp}_r(D)$. We let

$$\mathrm{types}(\tau, l, r) = \{\mathrm{tp}_r(D, \bar{a}) \mid D \text{ database over } \tau, \bar{a} \in D \ l\text{-tuple}\}.$$

Note that this set is finite for all τ, l, r.

Lemma 5. *Let τ be a database schema and $l, r \geq 1$. Then there is an integer $K = K(\tau, l, r)$ such that for all databases D, E over τ and l-tuples $\bar{a} \in D$, $\bar{b} \in E$ the following holds: If for all $\theta \in \mathrm{types}(\tau, l, r)$ we have*

$$\min\left(K, |\{C \in \mathrm{comp}(D \setminus \bar{a}) \mid \mathrm{tp}_r(\langle C^{+\bar{a}} \rangle^D, \bar{a}) = \theta\}|\right)$$
$$= \min\left(K, |\{C \in \mathrm{comp}(E \setminus \bar{b}) \mid \mathrm{tp}_r(\langle C^{+\bar{b}} \rangle^E, \bar{b}) = \theta\}|\right)$$

then $\mathrm{tp}_r(D, \bar{a}) = \mathrm{tp}_r(E, \bar{b})$.

The proof of this lemma is an induction on r. It uses the Ehrenfeucht-Fraïssé game characterizing MSO-equivalence.

The essence of the lemma is that to compute $\mathrm{tp}_r(D, \bar{a})$ we only need a finite amount of information on the types of the components $\langle C^{+\bar{a}} \rangle^D$.

We can arrange this information in a large disjunction of formulas saying:

If there are k_1 components C such that $\langle C^{+\bar{x}} \rangle = \theta_1$ and k_2 components C such that $\langle C^{+\bar{x}} \rangle = \theta_2$ and ... and k_m components C such that $\langle C^{+\bar{x}} \rangle = \theta_m$ then the type of the whole database is θ.

Here $\theta_1, \ldots, \theta_m$ range over the set $\mathrm{types}(\tau, l, r)$. The k_i are integers between 0 and $K(\tau, l, r)$, and in case $k_i = K(\tau, l, r)$ then the ith conjunct is to be read "if there are at least k_i components" (that is, we only count up to $K(\tau, l, r)$).

Recall Lemma 3. Using it we define, by a simultaneous induction, $(k + 2)$-ary re-lations X_θ, for $\theta \in \mathrm{types}(\tau, k + 1, r)$. The intended meaning of $\bar{x}y \in X_\theta$ is "$\bar{x}$ is a k-preclique in $\langle C_y^{+\bar{x}} \rangle$ and $\mathrm{tp}_r(\langle C_y^{+\bar{x}} \rangle, \bar{x}) = \theta$". It is not hard to formalize such an induc-tive definition in IFP. Since for all $r, D, \bar{a}$ the type $\mathrm{tp}_r(D)$ is determined by $\mathrm{tp}_r(D, \bar{a})$, we have proved the following lemma.

Lemma 6. *Let τ be a database schema, $r, k \geq 1$, and $\theta \in \mathrm{types}(\tau, 0, r)$. Then there is an IFP-sentence φ_θ such that for all databases D over τ of tree-width at most k we have*

$$\mathrm{tp}_r(D) = \theta \iff D \models \varphi_\theta.$$

Theorem 2(2) follows, since each MSO-sentence Φ over τ of quantifier-rank r is equivalent to the (finite) disjunction

$$\bigvee_{\substack{\theta \in \mathrm{types}(\tau, 0, r), \\ \Phi \in \theta}} \varphi_\theta.$$

6   Conclusions

We have studied the concept of tree-width of a relational database and seen that from a descriptive complexity theoretic perspective classes of databases of bounded tree-width have very nice properties.

Of course our results are of a rather theoretical nature. The more practically minded will ask whether databases occurring in practice can be expected to have small tree-width. Probably, this will not be the case for the average database. However, if in a specific situation it is known that the databases in question will have a small tree width, then it may be worthwhile to explore this. It seems plausible to us that in particular data carrying not too much structure can be arranged in a database of small tree-width.

This point of view may be supported by a different perspective on tree-width, which roughly says that tree-width is a measure for the "global connectivity" of a graph (or database). Essentially, the tree-width of a graph is the same as its *linkedness*, which is the minimal number of vertices required to split the graph and subsets of its vertex-set into more or less even parts (see [19])

References

1. S. Abiteboul and V. Vianu. Fixpoint extensions of first order logic and datalog-like languages. In *Proceedings of the 4th IEEE Symposium on Logic in Computer Science*, pages 71–79, 1989.
2. S. Arnborg, D. Corneil, and A. Proskurowski. Complexity of finding embeddings in a k-tree. *SIAM Journal on Algebraic Discrete Methods*, 8:277–284, 1987.
3. H.L. Bodländer. NC-algorithms for graphs with small treewidth. In J. van Leeuwen, editor, *Proceedings of the 14th International Workshop on Graph theoretic Concepts in Computer Science WG'88*, volume 344 of *Lecture Notes in Computer Science*, pages 1–10. Springer-Verlag, 1988.
4. H.L. Bodländer. Polynomial algorithms for graph isomorphism and chromatic index on partial k-trees. *Journal of Algorithms*, 11:631–643, 1990.
5. H.L. Bodländer. Treewidth: Algorithmic techniques and results. In *Proceedings 22nd International Symposium on Mathematical Foundations of Computer Science, MFCS'97*, volume 1295 of *Lecture Notes in Computer Science*, pages 29–36. Springer-Verlag, 1997.
6. J. Cai, M. Fürer, and N. Immerman. An optimal lower bound on the number of variables for graph identification. *Combinatorica*, 12:389–410, 1992.
7. A. Chandra and D. Harel. Structure and complexity of relational queries. *Journal of Computer and System Sciences*, 25:99–128, 1982.
8. B. Courcelle. Graph rewriting: An algebraic and logic approach. In J. van Leeuwen, editor, *Handbook of Theoretical Computer Science*, volume 2, pages 194–242. Elsevier Science Publishers, 1990.
9. R. Diestel. *Graph Theory*. Springer-Verlag, 1997.
10. T. Feder and M.Y. Vardi. Monotone monadic SNP and constraint satisfaction. In *Proceedings of the 25th ACM Symposium on Theory of Computing*, pages 612–622, 1993.
11. E. Grädel. On the restraining power of guards, 1998.
12. E. Grädel and M. Otto. Inductive definability with counting on finite structures. In E. Börger, G. Jäger, H. Kleine Büning, S. Martini, and M.M. Richter, editors, *Computer Science Logic, 6th Workshop, CSL '92, San Miniato 1992, Selected Papers*, volume 702 of *Lecture Notes in Computer Science*, pages 231–247. Springer-Verlag, 1993.

13. M. Grohe. Finite-variable logics in descriptive complexity theory, 1998.
14. M. Grohe. Fixed-point logics on planar graphs. In *Proceedings of the 13th IEEE Symposium on Logic in Computer Science*, pages 6–15, 1998.
15. R. Halin. S-Functions for graphs. *Journal of Geometry*, 8:171–186, 1976.
16. N. Immerman. Relational queries computable in polynomial time. *Information and Control*, 68:86–104, 1986.
17. N. Immerman. Expressibility as a complexity measure: results and directions. In *Proceedings of the 2nd IEEE Symposium on Structure in Complexity Theory*, pages 194–202, 1987.
18. N. Immerman and E. Lander. Describing graphs: A first-order approach to graph canonization. In A. Selman, editor, *Complexity theory retrospective*, pages 59–81. Springer-Verlag, 1990.
19. B. Reed. Tree width and tangles: A new connectivity measure and some applications. In R.A. Bailey, editor, *Surveys in Combinatorics*, volume 241 of *LMS Lecture Note Series*, pages 87–162. Cambridge University Press, 1997.
20. N. Robertson and P.D. Seymour. Graph minors II. Algorithmic aspects of tree-width. *Journal of Algorithms*, 7:309–322, 1986.
21. N. Robertson and P.D. Seymour. Graph minors IV. Tree-width and well-quasi-ordering. *Journal of Combinatorial Theory, Series B*, 48:227–254, 1990.
22. N. Robertson and P.D. Seymour. Graph minors V. Excluding a planar graph. *Journal of Combinatorial Theory, Series B*, 41:92–114, 1986.
23. N. Robertson and P.D. Seymour. Graph minors XX. Wagner's conjecture, 1988. unpublished manuscript.
24. M. Y. Vardi. The complexity of relational query languages. In *Proceedings of the 14th ACM Symposium on Theory of Computing*, pages 137–146, 1982.

Decidability of First-Order Logic Queries over Views

James Bailey[1] and Guozhu Dong[2]

[1] Department of Computer Science, King's College London
Strand, London WC2R 2LS, United Kingdom, `james@dcs.kcl.ac.uk`
[2] Department of Computer Science, The University of Melbourne
Parkville 3052, Australia, `dong@cs.mu.oz.au`

Abstract. We study the problem of deciding satisfiability of first order logic queries over views, our aim being to delimit the boundary between the decidable and the undecidable fragments of this language. Views currently occupy a central place in database research, due to their role in applications such as information integration and data warehousing. Our principal result is the identification of an important decidable class of queries over unary conjunctive views. This extends the decidability of the classical class of first order sentences over unary relations (the Löwenheim class). We then demonstrate how extending this class leads to undecidability. In addition to new areas, our work also has relevance to extensions of results for related problems such as query containment, trigger termination, implication of dependencies and reasoning in description logics.

Key words: satisfiability, decidability, first order logic, database queries, database views, conjunctive queries, unary views, inequality, the Löwenheim class.

1 Introduction

The study of views in relational databases has recently attracted considerable attention, with the advent of applications such as data integration and data warehousing. In such domains, views can be used as "mediators" for source information that is not directly accessible to users. This is especially helpful in modelling the integration of data from diverse sources, such as legacy systems and/or the world wide web.

Much of this recent research has been on fundamental problems such as containment and rewriting/optimisation of queries using views [12]. In this paper, we examine the use of views in a somewhat different context, such as for mediating and monitoring constraints on data sources where only views are available. An important requirement is that the resulting query/constraint language be *decidable*. We give results on the decision problem in this paper. As a by-product, our results also help us to analyse the specific problems mentioned above.

Catriel Beeri, Peter Buneman (Eds.): ICDT'99, LNCS 1540, pp. 83–99, 1998.
© Springer-Verlag Berlin Heidelberg 1998

1.1   Statement of the Problem

Consider a database with a schema over a set of base relations $R_1, \ldots, R_p$ and a set of views $V_1, \ldots, V_n$ defined over them. A *first order view query* is a first order query *solely* in terms of the given views. For example, given the views

$$V_1(X,Y) \leftarrow R(X,Y), S(Y,Y,Z), T(Z,A,X), \neg Q(A,X)$$
$$V_2(Z) \leftarrow R(Z,Z)$$

then $\exists X, Y((V_1(X,Y) \vee V_1(Y,X)) \wedge \neg V_2(X)) \wedge \forall Z(V_2(Z) \Rightarrow V_1(Z,Z))$ is an example first order view query, but $\exists X, Y(V_1(X,Y) \vee R(Y,X))$ is not.

First order view queries are realistic for applications where the source data is unavailable, but summary data (in the form of views) is. Since most database languages are based on first order logic (or extensions thereof), we choose this as the language for manipulating the views.

Our purpose in this paper is to determine, for what types of view definitions, satisfiability (over finite models) is decidable for the language. If views can be binary, then this language is as powerful as first order logic over binary base relations, and hence undecidable (even with only identity views). The situation becomes much more interesting, when we restrict the form views may take - in particular, when their arity must be unary. Such a restriction has the effect of constraining which parts of the database can be "seen" by a query and the way different parts of the database may interact.

1.2   Contributions

Our main contribution is the definition of a language called the *first order unary conjunctive view language* and a proof of its decidability. As the name suggests, it uses unary arity views defined by conjunctive queries. It is a maximal decidable class in the sense that increasing the expressiveness of the view definition results in undecidability. Some interesting aspects of this result are:

- It is well known that first order logic over solely monadic relations is decidable, but the extension to dyadic relations is undecidable [3]. The unary conjunctive view language can be seen as an interesting intermediate case between the two, since although only monadic predicates (views) appear in the query, they are intimately tied to database relations of higher arity.
- The language is able to express interesting properties such as generalisations of unary inclusion dependencies [6] and containment of monadic datalog queries under constraints. This is discussed in Section 4.

1.3   Paper Outline

The paper is structured as follows: Section 2 defines the unary conjunctive view language and shows its decidability. Section 3 shows that extensions to the language, such as negation, inequality or recursion in views, result in undecidability. Section 4 looks at applications of the results. Section 5 gives some comparisons to other work and section 6 summarises and then looks at future work.

2   Unary Conjunctive Views

The first language we consider is first order queries (without inequality) over unary conjunctive views. Each view has arity one and it is defined by a union of some arbitrary conjunctive queries. Some example views are

$$V_1(X) \leftarrow R(X,Y), R(Y,Z), R(Z,X)$$
$$V_2(X) \leftarrow S(X,X,Y), T(Z,X), R(Y,Y)$$
$$V_2(X) \leftarrow S(X,X,X)$$
$$V_3(X) \leftarrow T(X,Y), R(Y,X), S(X,Y,Z)$$

and an example first order query over them is

$$\exists X (V_1(X) \wedge \neg V_3(X) \wedge \forall Y (V_2(X) \Rightarrow (\neg V_1(Y) \vee V_3(Y))))$$

Note that this sentence can of course be rewritten to eliminate the views, since each view is just a positive existential query (e.g. $V_1(X)$ can be rewritten as $\exists Y, Z (R(X,Y) \wedge R(Y,Z) \wedge R(Z,X))$). Observe that there is no restriction on the number of variables that can be used by a view. Since this language can express the property that a graph has a clique of size $k+1$, it is not subsumed by any finite variable logic L_k (for finite k) [7]. Of course, having unary arity does have a price. In particular, some restrictions inherent in this language are

- *Limited negation:* Since negation can only be applied to the unary views, properties such as transitivity $(\forall X, Y (edge(X,Y) \wedge edge(Y,Z) \Rightarrow edge(X,Z)))$ cannot be expressed.
- *No Inequality:* It isn't possible to test inequality of variables and in particular it is impossible to write a sentence specifying that a single attribute X of a relation functionally determines the others (namely $\neg \exists X, Y, Z (edge(X,Y) \wedge edge(X,Z) \wedge Y \neq Z)$.

Our results in this paper verify that this language indeed has these two limitations, since the language itself is decidable, whereas adding $\neq$ or $\neg$ results in undecidability. Given these limitations, a proof of decidability might seem to be straightforward. However, this turns out not to be the case. Our plan is to show that the first order view queries have a bounded model property, for arbitrary fixed view definitions. To accomplish this, we need to construct a small model using a bounded number of constants from a large model. Difficulties arise, however, from the fact that sentences such as $\neg \exists X (V_1(X) \wedge V_2(X) \wedge \neg V_3(X) \wedge \neg V_4(X))$ can be expressed. Such sentences act like constraints on the space of possible models. When constructing the small model, we need to map different constants in the large model to identical ones, and we must do so without violating such constraints. We achieve this by using a procedure similar to chasing, plus an interesting duplicating and wrap-around technique. The rest of this section is devoted to describing this procedure and technique.

Theorem 1. *Satisfiability for the first order unary conjunctive view query language is decidable. In fact it is in $SPACE(2^{(m \times p)^m})$, but $NTIME(2^{p/\log p})$ hard, for queries using views of maximum length m over p relations.*

Proof. Let ψ be an arbitrary first order view query in the language. The first step consists of transforming ψ to ψ' in order to eliminate the union of views, that is, ψ' is equivalent to ψ and ψ' only uses views without union. ψ' is easily constructed by replacing each $V(X)$ in ψ using the disjunct $V_1(X) \vee V_2(X) \ldots \vee V_w(X)$, where (i) V's definition uses union, (ii) $V_1, \cdots, V_w$ is an enumeration of the conjunctive views in the definition of V, and (iii) no union is used in defining each V_i. Let there be n views in ψ' over the p relations. Let m be the maximum number of variables (including duplicates) used in defining any view body. For example, $m = 7$ for the views listed at the beginning of section 2. In addition to these views, we define all possible other views using at most m variables (including duplicates). Let N denote the total number of non isomorphic views obtained. Then it can be easily verified that $N \leq (m \times p)^m \times m$. We then "and" the formula $(V_x \vee \neg V_x)$ with ψ', for each view V_x that didn't originally appear in $V_1, \ldots V_n$. The purpose of defining these "redundant" views is to ensure maximum coverage of equivalence classes (whose definition will be given shortly).

It is possible to interpret ψ' in two possible ways. The standard way is by treating it as a first order formula over base-relation schema $\{R_1, ..., R_p\}$ (and indeed this corresponds to our intended meaning). It is also possible to interpret it in a non standard way, as a first order formula over the view schema $\{V_1, ..., V_N\}$, where each V_i is treated as a *materialised view*. Let us define a function $f : I_{base} \rightarrow I_{view}$, which relates base-relation models to view models. f is clearly a total function, since any base-relation model clearly has a view-model counterpart. f is not an onto function though, since some view-model interpretations could not be realised by the underlying base relations.

We now define equivalence classes and equivalence class states for the query ψ'. An *equivalence class* is simply a formula over the N views

$$C(X) = \{< X > \mid {}^{(\neg)}V_1(X) \wedge^{(\neg)} V_2(X) \wedge \cdots \wedge^{(\neg)} V_N(X)\},$$

where each $V_j(X)$ can appear either positively or negatively. Examples of such a class include $\{< X > \mid V_1(X) \wedge V_2(X) \wedge \cdots \wedge V_N(X)\}$ and $\{< X > \mid {}^{(\neg)}V_1(X) \wedge V_2(X) \wedge \cdots \wedge V_N(X)\}$. These equivalence classes can be enumerated as $C_1, C_2, \ldots, C_{2^N}$.

Using standard techniques, which we explain below, any instance which satisfies ψ' can be completely described by the behaviour of these equivalence classes. An equivalence class C_i appears positively in a model for ψ' if the formula $\exists X C_i(X)$ is true and it appears negatively if the formula $\neg \exists C_i(X)$ is true. An *equivalence class state* is a partition of all the equivalence classes into two groups - those appearing positively and those appearing negatively. We number the positive classes in such a state by $C_1, \ldots, C_{n_1}$ and the negative classes $C'_1, \ldots, C'_{n_2}$. Clearly $n_1 + n_2 = 2^N$. Thus an equivalence class state is described by the formula

$$\exists X C_1(X) \wedge \exists X C_2(X) \wedge \ldots \wedge \exists X C_{n_1}(X)$$
$$\wedge \neg \exists X C'_1(X) \wedge \neg \exists X C'_2(X) \wedge \ldots \wedge \neg \exists X C'_{n_2}(X).$$

Let $\phi_1, \cdots, \phi_{2^{2^N}}$ be an enumeration of the equivalence class states. Since the equivalence class states are mutually exclusive, it follows that ψ' is satisfiable iff one of $(\psi' \wedge \phi_i)$ is satisfiable. Hence to test satisfiability of ψ', it suffices to be able to test satisfiability of a single $\psi' \wedge \phi_i$ expression.

For the situation where we consider views in $\psi' \wedge \phi_i$ as arbitrary relations, we observe that $\phi_i \Rightarrow \psi'$ is valid if $\phi_i \wedge \psi'$ is satisfiable (see lemma 2 in appendix).

Therefore, given that ϕ_i is satisfiable by some realisable view instance I_v, if $\phi_i \wedge \psi'$ is satisfiable by some arbitrary view instance I_v' (not necessarily realisable), then $\phi_i \wedge \psi'$ is satisfiable by I_v. The converse is obviously true. Thus the satisfiability of $\phi_i \wedge \psi'$ can be tested by considering its truth over all possible small models of ϕ_i. Lemma 1 shows that we can test satisfiability of a ϕ_i by considering all small instances using at most $k = 2^{2 \times (m \times p)^m \times m} \times ((m \times p)^m \times m \times m)^{2m+3}$ constants, which is $\mathcal{O}(2^{(m \times p)^m})$.

Overall, to test satisfiability of ψ', we need to search for satisfiable ϕ_i's by testing all possible models of bounded size. This size bound then provides us with the upper bound of $SPACE(2^{(m \times p)^m})$ for the decision procedure.

Hardness: In [3], it is shown that satisfiability is $NTIME(2^{c \times l / \log l})$ hard for first order queries over unary relations, a special case of our language. Here c is some constant and l is the length of the formula. Since the number of relations is $\leq l$, our problem is $NTIME(2^{c \times p / \log p})$ hard. ∎

We next sketch a proof for the lemma we have just needed. The key insight is that for a query ψ, there is a bound m on the number of variables a view may have. This allows a complex chasing over "justifications" of constants that only "wraps around" at "distances" $\geq m$. (Given a set of tuples, we view a tuple as one generalised edge, and define distance as the length of shortest paths.)

Lemma 1. *Let ϕ be an equivalence class state formula over N views of maximum definition length m using p relations. If ϕ is satisfiable, then it has a model using at most $k = 2^{2 \times (m \times p)^m \times m} \times ((m \times p)^m \times m \times m)^{2m+3}$ constants.*

Proof. (sketch) The proof is quite complex and so we begin with an overview. We first show how any model for ϕ can be described by a structure H called a *justification hierarchy*, which links tuples in the model together according to their distribution in equivalence classes. We then show how to build a new justification hierarchy H', which is a maximal (enlarged) version of H, has some "nicer" properties and is also a model for ϕ. After this, we build another hierarchy H'' which consists of a number of distinct copies of H', each of which is pruned to a certain depth. The constants at the lowest level are justified by the constants at the roots of the copies. H'' can be associated with a new model I'' such that it uses no more than k constants, and I'' is also a model of ϕ. Some of the steps are further explained in the appendix.

Observe that, if the only positive class in ϕ is $\exists X (\neg V_1(X) \wedge ... \wedge \neg V_N(X))$, then ϕ is unsatisfiable since it says (i) that there are no constants in the database and (ii) there must exist a constant. So we can assume that ϕ contains some other positive class.

Justification Hierarchies: Recall that the positive equivalence classes are numbered $C_1, ..., C_{n_1}$ and observe that any constant in a model for ϕ appears in exactly one equivalence class. Given an arbitrary constant a_1 in class C_i, there must exist at least one associated *justification set* for the truth of $C_i(a_1)$. A justification set is simply a set of tuples, in the given model, which make $C_i(a_1)$ true. A minimal justification set is a justification set containing no redundant tuples (such a set is not in general unique). We will henceforth regard all justifications as being minimal.

A justification hierarchy for an equivalence class C_i is a hierarchy of justification sets. At the top is a justification set for some constant a in equivalence class C_i. The second level consists of justification sets for the equivalence class of each constant appearing in the justification set for $C_i(a)$. The third level consists of justification sets for the equivalence class of each new constant appearing at level two etc. The hierarchy extends until every constant in the hierarchy has been justified. Figure 1 shows a justification hierarchy for an equivalence class state ψ in the instance $I = \{(1,2),(2,3),(3,4),(4,5),(5,1)\}$. ψ is defined by

$$\exists X(V_1(X) \wedge V_2(X)) \wedge \neg\exists X(V_1(X) \wedge \neg V_2(X))$$
$$\wedge\neg\exists X(\neg V_1(X) \wedge V_2(X)) \wedge \neg\exists X(\neg V_1(X) \wedge \neg V_2(X))$$

where $V_1(X) \leftarrow R(X,Y)$ and $V_2(X) \leftarrow R(Y,X)$. (ψ contains one positive class and three negative ones.)

In general, to describe a model for ϕ, we will need a set of justification hierarchies, one for each positive equivalence class.

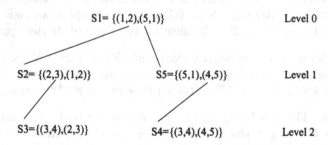

Figure 1: Example justification hierarchy for query ψ

Maximal Justification Hierarchies: Suppose we have a model I, and we have constructed exactly one justification hierarchy for each positive class. Let H consist of these justification hierarchies. By copying justification sets if necessary, we can assume that the justification hierarchies have a balanced structure. Here "balanced" refers to the notion that a hierarchy can be viewed as tree, whose edges link justification sets.

The next step consists of renaming the constants in the hierarchy to remove 'unnecessary' equalities among the constants in justifications. We build a new justification hierarchy set of the same height. We do this by iterating over all justifications: for each constant a, we replace all constants used in the justification of a using new constants. Call this new hierarchy the *maximised justification hierarchy set* (abbreviated MJHS).

Copying and Pruning Justification Hierarchies: Let I_{max} be a maximised hierarchy set for a model of ϕ. Let n_l be the number of constants at height m. Then

$n_l \leq$ (no. of hierarchies in MJHS) $\times$ ((no. of views) $\times$ (max. length of a view))^m
$\leq 2^N \times (N \times m)^m$.

In this step, we make n_l copies, denoted by $I_1, I_2, \ldots I_{n_l}$, of I_{max}, using a different set of constants for each copy. Let I_{union} be the union of $I_1 \cup I_2 \cup \ldots \cup I_{n_l}$. Then it can be verified that ϕ will still be true for this new instance. Next, all levels below m in the hierarchy are removed and constants at level m are "wrapped-around" by re-justifying them with the root of one of the copies for the same class. Again it can be verified that ϕ will still be true for this new instance.

The number of constants in I_{union} is bounded by $\leq$ num_copies $\times$ (max num. of constants in a justification hierarchy of height $m + 3$). Thus this number is

$\leq n_l \times (2^N \times (N \times m)^{m+3})$
$\leq (2^N \times (N \times m)^m) \times (2^N \times (N \times m)^{m+3})$
$\leq 2^{2N} \times (N \times m)^{2m+3}$
$\leq 2^{2 \times (m \times p)^m \times m} \times ((m \times p)^m \times m \times m)^{2m+3}$, which is $\mathcal{O}(2^{(m \times p)^m})$.

∎

Theorem 1 also holds for infinite models, since even if the initial justification hierarchies are infinite, the method used in lemma 1 can still be used to exhibit a finite model. We thus obtain finite controllability (every satisfiable formula is finitely satisfiable).

Proposition 1. *The first order unary conjunctive view language is finitely controllable.* ∎

3   Extending the View Definitions

The previous section showed that the first order language using unary conjunctive view definitions is decidable. A natural way to increase the power of the language is to make view bodies more expressive (but retain unary arity for the views). Unfortunately, as we will show, this results in satisfiability becoming undecidable.

The first extension we consider is allowing inequality in the views, e.g.,

$$V(X) \leftarrow R(X, Y), S(X, X), X \neq Y$$

Call the first order language over such views the *first order unary conjunctive$^{\neq}$ view language*. This language allows us to check whether a two counter machine computation is valid and terminates. This leads to the following result:

Theorem 2. *Satisfiability is undecidable for the first order unary conjunctive$^{\neq}$ view query language.*

Proof. The proof is by a reduction from the halting problem of two counter machines (2CM's) starting with zero in the counters. Given any description of a 2CM and its computation, we can show how to a) encode this description in database relations and b) define queries to check this description. We construct a query which is satisfiable iff the 2CM halts. The basic idea of the simulation is similar to one in [8], but with the major difference that *cycles are allowed* in the successor relation, though there must be at least one good chain. See appendix for further details. ■

The second extension we consider is to allow "safe" negation in the conjunctive views, e.g.

$$V(X) \leftarrow R(X,Y), \neg S(X,X)$$

Call the first order language over such views the *first order unary conjunctive⁻ view language*. It is also undecidable, by a result in [2].

Theorem 3. *[2] Satisfiability is undecidable for the first order unary conjunctive⁻ view query language.* ■

A third possibility for increasing the expressiveness of views would be to keep the body as a pure conjunctive query, but allow views to have *binary* arity, *e.g.*

$$V(X,Y) \leftarrow R(X,Y)$$

This doesn't yield a decidable language either, since this language has the same expressiveness as first order logic over binary relations, which is known to be undecidable.

Proposition 2. *Satisfiability is undecidable for the first order binary conjunctive view language.* ■

A fourth possibility is to use unary conjunctive views, but allow recursion in the view bodies, e.g.

$$V(X) \leftarrow edge(X,Y)$$
$$V(X) \leftarrow V(X) \wedge edge(Y,X)$$

Call this the first order unary conjunctive^{rec} language. This causes undecidability also.

Theorem 4. *Satisfiability is undecidable for the first order unary conjunctive^{rec} view language.*

Proof. (sketch): The proof of theorem 2 can be adapted by removing inequality and instead using recursion to ensure there is a connected chain in *succ*. It then becomes more complicated, but the main property needed is that *zero* is connected to *last* via the constants in *succ*. This can be done by

$$conn\_zero(X) \leftarrow zero(X)$$
$$conn\_zero(X) \leftarrow conn\_zero(Y), succ(Y,X)$$
$$\exists X(last(X) \wedge conn\_zero(X))$$

■

4 Applications

4.1 Containment

We now briefly examine the application of our results to conjunctive query containment. Theorem 1 implies we can test whether $Q_1(X) \subseteq Q_2(X)$ under the constraints $C_1 \wedge C_2 \ldots \wedge C_n$ where $Q_1, Q_2, C_1, \ldots, C_n$ are all first order unary conjunctive view queries. This just amounts to testing whether the sentence $\exists X(Q_1(X) \wedge \neg Q_2(X)) \wedge C_1 \wedge \ldots \wedge C_n$ is unsatisfiable.

We can similarly test containment and equivalence of monadic datalog programs under first order unary conjunctive view constraints. Monadic datalog is datalog with intensional relations having unary arity. To illustrate the idea, the *conn_zero* view defined above could be written

$$\forall X(conn\_zero(X) \Leftrightarrow (zero(X) \vee tmp(X))$$

where *tmp* is the view

$$tmp(X) \leftarrow conn\_zero(X) \wedge succ(Y, X)$$

Containment of monadic datalog programs was studied in [5], where it was shown to be EXPTIME hard and solvable in 2-EXPTIME using automata theoretic techniques. These complexity results are in line with theorem 1, since the decision problem we are addressing is more general.

Of course, we can also show that testing the containment $Q_1 \subseteq Q_2$ is undecidable if Q_1 and Q_2 are first order unary conjunctive view$^{\neq}$ queries, first order unary conjunctive view$^{\neg}$ queries and first order unary conjunctive^{rec} view queries. containment problem $Q \subseteq \emptyset$.

Containment of queries with negation was first considered in [10]. There it was essentially shown that the problem is decidable for queries which do not apply projection to subexpressions with difference. Such a language is disjoint from ours, since it cannot express a sentence such as $\exists Y V_4(Y) \wedge \neg \exists X(V_1(X) \wedge \neg V_2(X))$ where V_1 and V_2 are views which may contain projections.

4.2 Dependencies

Unary inclusion dependencies were identified as useful in [6]. They take the form $R[X] \subseteq S[Y]$. If we allow R and S above to be unary conjunctive views, we get *unary conjunctive view containment dependencies*. Observe that the unary views are actually unary projections of the join of one or more relations.

We can also define a special type of dependency called a *proper* unary conjunctive inclusion dependency, having the form $Q_1(X) \subset Q_2(X)$. The need for such a dependency could arise in security applications where it is necessary to restrict redundancy. If $\{d_1, \ldots, d_k\}$ is a set of such dependencies, then it is straightforward to test whether they imply another dependency d_x by testing the satisfiability of an appropriate first order unary conjunctive view query.

Theorem 5. *Implication is decidable for unary conjunctive view containment dependencies with subset and proper subset operators.* ∎

Similarly, we can consider unary conjunctive$^{\neq}$ containment dependencies. The tests in the proof of theorem 2 for the 2CM can be written in the form $Q_1(X) \subseteq Q_2(X)$, with the exception of the non-emptiness constraints, which must use the proper subset operator.

Theorem 6. *Implication is undecidable for unary conjunctive$^{\neq}$ (or conjunctive$^{\neg}$) view containment dependencies with the subset and the proper subset operators.* ∎

4.3 Termination

The languages in this paper have their origins in [2], where active database rule languages based on views were studied. The decidability result for first order unary conjunctive views can be used to positively answer an open question raised in [2], which essentially asked whether termination is decidable for active database rules using unary conjunctive views.

5 Related Work

Satisfiability of first order logic has been thoroughly investigated in the context of the classical decision problem [3]. The main thrust there has been determining for which quantifier prefixes first order languages are decidable. We are not aware of any result of this type which could be used to demonstrate decidability of the unary conjunctive view language. Instead, our result is best classified as a new decidable class generalising the traditional decidable unary first-order language (the Löwenheim class). Use of the Löwenheim class itself for reasoning about schemas is described in [11], where applications towards checking intersection and disjointness of object oriented classes are given.

As observed earlier, a main direction of work concerning views has been in areas such as containment. An area of emerging importance is description logics and coupling them with with horn rules [9,4]. In [4], the query containment problem is studied in the context of the description logic $\mathcal{DLR}_{reg}$. There are certain similarities between this and the first order (unary) view languages we have studied in this paper. The key difference appears to be that although $\mathcal{DLR}_{reg}$ can be used to define view constraints, these constraints cannot express unary conjunctive views (since assertions do not allow arbitrary projection). Furthermore, $\mathcal{DLR}_{reg}$ can express functional dependencies on a single attribute, a feature which would make our language undecidable (see proof of theorem 2). There is a result in [4], however, showing undecidability for a fragment of $\mathcal{DLR}_{reg}$ with inequality, which could be adapted to give an alternative proof of theorem 2 (though there inequality is used in a slightly more powerful way).

A recent work that deals with complexity of views is [1]. There, results are given for the *view consistency* problem. This involves determining whether there exists an underlying database instance that realises a *specific* (bounded) view instance . The problem we have looked at in this paper is slightly more complicated; testing satisfiability of a first order view query asks the question whether there exists an (*unbounded*) view instance that makes the query true. This explains how satisfiability can be undecidable for first order unary conjunctive$^{\neq}$ queries, but view consistency for non recursive datalog$^{\neq}$ views is in NP.

6   Summary and Further Work

Table 1 provides a summary of our decidability results. We can see that they are tight in the sense that the unary conjunctive view language cannot be obviously extended without undecidability resulting. In one sense the picture is negative - we cannot expect to use view bodies with negation, inequality or recursion or allow views to have binary arity if we are aiming for decidability. On the other hand, we feel that the decidable case we have identified, is sufficiently natural and interesting to be of practical use.

Table 1:
Summary of Decidability Results for First Order View Languages

Unary Conjunctive View	Decidable
Unary Conjunctive$^{\neq}$ View	Undecidable
Unary Conjunctive^{rec} View	Undecidable
Unary Conjunctive$^{\neg}$ View	Undecidable [2]
Binary Conjunctive View	Undecidable

As part of future work we intend to investigate relationships to description logics and also look at further ways of introducing negation into the language. One possibility is to allow views of arity zero to specify description logic like constraints, such as $R_1(X,Y) \subseteq R_2(X,Y)$. We would also like to narrow the complexity gap which appears in theorem 1 and gain a deeper understanding of the expressiveness of the view languages we have studied.

Acknowledgements: We wish to thank several people for discussions about the novelty of the problem at the initial stage of this work, including Michael Benedikt, Erich Grädel, and Phokion Kolaitis. Guozhu Dong benefited from discussions with Jianwen Su, and part of his work was done while visiting Simon Fraser University and George Mason University during his study leave.

References

1. S. Abiteboul and O. Duschka. Complexity of answering queries using materialized views. In *Proceedings of the 17th ACM SIGMOD-SIGACT-SIGART Symposium on Principles of Database Systems*, pages 254–263, Seattle, Washington, 1998.
2. J. Bailey, G. Dong, and K. Ramamohanarao. Decidability and undecidability results for the termination problem of active database rules. In *Proceedings of the 17th ACM SIGMOD-SIGACT-SIGART Symposium on Principles of Database Systems*, pages 264–273, Seattle, Washington, 1998.

3. E. Boerger, E. Graedel, and Y. Gurevich. *The Classical Decision Problem.* Springer-Verlag, 1996.
4. D. Calvanese, G. De Giacomo, and M. Lenzerini. On the decidability of query containment under constraints. In *Proceedings of the 17th ACM SIGMOD-SIGACT-SIGART Symposium on Principles of Database Systems*, pages 149–158, Seattle, Washington, 1998.
5. S. Cosmadakis, H. Gaifman, P. Kanellakis, and M. Vardi. Decidable optimization problems for database logic programs. *Proceedings of the ACM Symposium on the Theory of Computing*, pages 477–490, 1988.
6. S. Cosmadakis, P. Kanellakis, and M. Vardi. Polynomial time implication problems for unary inclusion dependencies. *Journal of the ACM*, 37(1):15–46, 1990.
7. N. Immerman. Upper and lower bounds for first-order expressibility. *Journal of Computer and System Sciences*, 25:76–98, 1982.
8. A. Levy, I. S. Mumick, Y. Sagiv, and O. Shmueli. Equivalence, query reachability, and satisfiability in datalog extensions. In *Proceedings of the twelfth ACM SIGACT-SIGMOD-SIGART Symposium on Principles of Database Systems*, pages 109–122, Washington D.C., 1993.
9. A. Levy and M. Rousset. The limits on combining recursive horn rules with description logics. In *Proceedings of the 13th National Conference on Artificial Intelligence (AAAI-96)*, Portland, Oregon, 1996.
10. Y. Sagiv and M. Yannakakis. Equivalences among relational expressions with the union and difference operators. *Journal of the ACM*, 27(4):633–655, 1980.
11. D. Theodoratos. Deductive object oriented schemas. In *Proceedings of ER'96, 15th International Conference on Conceptual Modeling*, pages 58–72, 1996.
12. J. D. Ullman. Information integration using logical views. In *Proceedings of the Sixth International Conference on Database Theory, LNCS 1186*, pages 19–40, Delphi, Greece, 1997.

Appendix

Lemma 2. *Suppose we treat the unary view symbols as arbitrary base relations. If $\psi' \wedge \phi_i$ is satisfiable, then $\phi_i \Rightarrow \psi'$ is valid.*

Proof. (Sketch) Suppose there exists an instance I for which $\psi' \wedge \phi_i$ is true. By deleting "extra" constants, we can transform I into a *minimal* model I_{min} such that each positive class contains exactly one constant. Then $\psi' \wedge \phi_i$ is also true in I_{min}. (One can verify this by translating $\psi' \wedge \phi_i$ into relational algebra. Then constants in the same equivalence class always travel together when we evaluate the subexpressions.) Let I' be any instance for which ϕ_i is true. Then I_{min} is isomorphic to a submodel of I', and we can view I' as the result of adding constants to the positive classes of I_{min}. Similar to deleting constants, adding constants doesn't alter the truth value of ψ'. Hence the formula $\phi_i \wedge \neg\psi'$ is unsatisfiable, or equivalently, the formula $\phi_i \Rightarrow \psi'$ is valid. ∎

Some Further Descriptions of Procedures Used in Lemma 1

Building a Justification Hierarchy Each level of the hierarchy contains justification sets for constants in the model for ψ (call this model I). Lower levels justify constants which appear in higher levels.

The base case: Choose a constant (say a_1) in $C_i(I)$. Choose a justification set for a_1 in I (say S_{a_1}). Insert S_{a_1} at level zero.

The recursive case: For each tuple t in the hierarchy at level i containing a constant a_k such that S_{a_k} doesn't appear at any level $\leq i$, create a justification set S_{a_k} at level $i + 1$.

Maximisation Procedure It is possible to define conjunctive query paths through a justification hierarchy between the root node and the leaf nodes. The distance between two constants in the hierarchy is a measure of the number of joins required to link these constants together. To ensure correctness, we would like the distance between a constant at the root node and a constant at level m to be m. Since constants within a justification hierarchy may appear in several justification sets, this property may not be true. The following procedure replaces duplicate constants in the hierarchy with new ones, without compromising the truth of ψ. The distance requirement is then satisfied.

Suppose that each of the hierarchies has height of at least $m + 3$.

```
/* Rename */
For i = 1 to (m + 2) do
    Let x be a constant in a justification set S_q at level i such that x ≠ q.
    If x appears at a level < i then
        choose an entirely new constant k
        For each S_t at level i containing x and t ≠ x do
            S_t = S_t[x\k];
            S_x at level i + 1 = S_x[x\k];
        end For
end For
```

Rename is a function which isomorphically substitutes new constants for all those currently in the hierarchy. Note that if x gets renamed to k, then S_x gets renamed to S_k.

Copying and Pruning Algorithm

Make a number of distinct copies of the hierarchies, as explained in the proof Call the result of the above step H'
Suppose the constants at height $m + 1$ in H' by $a_0, a_1, \ldots, a_k$
For $j = 1$ to k
    suppose (i) C_s is the equivalence class of a_j and (ii) b is the constant being justified at root of hierarchy for C_s in $I_{(j+1) \bmod k}$
    delete S_{a_j} at level $m + 1$
    S_{a_j} at level $m + 1 = S_b[b\backslash a_j]$
End For
remove all levels of hierarchy at height $> m + 1$

One can now envisage the model for ψ as a collection of interlinked justification hierarchies. Constants at level m of each hierarchy are justified by the root node of another hierarchy.

Correctness proof for this construction is quite lengthy, and so will be deferred to the full version of the paper.

Proof Details of Theorem 2 A two-counter machine is a deterministic finite state machine with two non-negative counters. The machine can test whether a particular counter is empty or non-empty. The transition function has the form

$$\delta : S \times \{=, >\} \times \{=, >\} \to S \times \{pop, push\} \times \{pop, push\}$$

For example, the statement $\delta(4, =, >) = (2, push, pop)$ means that if we are in state 4 with counter 1 equal to 0 and counter 2 greater than 0, then go to state 2 and add one to counter 1 and subtract one from counter 2.

The computation of the machine is stored in the relation $config(T, S, C_1, C_2)$, where T is the time, S is the state and C_1 and C_2 are values of the counters. The states of the machine can be described by integers $0, 1 \ldots, h$ where 0 is the initial state and h the halting (accepting) state. The first configuration of the machine is $config(0, 0, 0, 0)$ and thereafter, for each move, the time is increased by one and the state and counter values changed in correspondence with the transition function.

We will use some relations to encode the computation of 2CMs starting with zero in the counters. These are:

- $S_0, \ldots, S_h$: each contains a constant which represents that particular state.
- $succ$: the successor relation. We will make sure it contains one chain starting from $zero$ and ending at $last$ (but it may in addition contain unrelated cycles).
- $config$: contains computation of the 2CM.
- $zero$: contains the first constant in the chain in $succ$. This constant is also used as the number zero.
- $last$: contains the last constant in the chain in $succ$.

Note that we sometimes blur the distinction between unary relations and unary views, since a view V can simulate a unary relation U if it is defined by $V(X) \leftarrow U(X)$.

The unary and nullary views (the latter can be eliminated using quantified unary views) are:

- $halt$: true if the machine halts.
- bad: true if the database doesn't correctly describe the computation of the 2CM.
- $dsucc$: contains all constants in $succ$.
- dT: contains all time stamps in $config$.
- dP: contains all constants in $succ$ with predecessors.
- $dCol_1, dCol_2$: are projections of the first and second columns of $succ$.

When defining the views, we also state some formulas (such as *hasPred*) over the views which will be used to form our first order sentence over the views.

- The "domain" views (those starting with the letter *d*) are easy to define, e.g.

$$dP(X) \leftarrow succ(Z, X)$$
$$dCol_1(X) \leftarrow succ(X, Y)$$
$$dCol_2(X) \leftarrow succ(Y, X)$$

- *hasPred* says "each nonzero constant in *succ* has a predecessor:"

$$hasPred : \forall X (dsucc(X) \Rightarrow (zero(X) \lor dP(X)))$$

- *sameDom* says "the constants used in *succ* and the timestamps in *config* are the same set":

$$sameDom : \forall X (dsucc(X) \Rightarrow dT(X)) \land \forall Y (dT(Y) \Rightarrow dsucc(Y)))$$

- *goodzero* says "the zero occurs in *succ*":

$$goodzero : \forall x (zero(x) \Rightarrow dsucc(x))$$

- *nempty* : each of the domains and unary base relations is not empty

$$nempty : \exists X (dsucc(X))$$

- Check that each constant in *succ* has at most one successor and at most one predecessor and that it has no cycles of length 1.

$$bad \leftarrow succ(X, Y), succ(X, Z), Y \neq Z$$
$$bad \leftarrow succ(Y, X), succ(Z, X), Y \neq Z$$
$$bad \leftarrow succ(X, X)$$

Note that the first two of these rules could be enforced by the functional dependencies $X \rightarrow Y$ and $Y \rightarrow X$ on *succ*.
- Check that every constant in the chain in succ which isn't the last one must have a successor

$$hassuccnext : \forall Y (dCol_2(Y) \Rightarrow (last(Y) \lor dCol_1(Y)))$$

- Check that the last constant has no successor and zero (the first constant) has no predecessor.

$$bad \leftarrow last(X), succ(X, A)$$
$$bad \leftarrow zero(X), succ(A, X)$$

- Check that every constant eligible to be in last and zero must be so.

$$eligiblezero : \forall Y (dCol_1(Y) \Rightarrow (dCol_2(Y) \lor zero(Y)))$$
$$eligiblelast : \forall Y (dCol_2(Y) \Rightarrow (dCol_1(Y) \lor last(Y)))$$

- Each S_i and $zero$ and $last$ contain ≤ 1 element.

$$bad \leftarrow S_i(X), S_i(Y), X \neq Y$$
$$bad \leftarrow zero(X), zero(Y), X \neq Y$$
$$bad \leftarrow last(X), last(Y), X \neq Y$$

- Check that $S_i, S_j, last, zero$ are disjoint ($0 \leq i < j \leq h$):

$$bad \leftarrow zero(X), last(X)$$
$$bad \leftarrow S_i(X), S_j(X)$$
$$bad \leftarrow zero(X), S_i(X)$$
$$bad \leftarrow last(X), S_i(X)$$

- Check that the timestamp is the key for $config$. There are three rules, one for the state and two for the two counters; the one for the state is:

$$bad \leftarrow config(T, S, C_1, C_2), config(T, S', C_1', C_2'), S \neq S'$$

- Check the configuration of the 2CM at time zero. $config$ must have a tuple at $(0, 0, 0, 0)$ and there must not be any tuples in config with a zero state and non zero times or counters.

$$V_{z_s}(S) \leftarrow zero(T), config(T, S, \_, \_)$$
$$V_{z_{c_1}}(C) \leftarrow zero(T), config(T, \_, C, \_)$$
$$V_{z_{c_2}}(C) \leftarrow zero(T), config(T, \_, \_, C)$$
$$V_{y_s}(T) \leftarrow zero(S), config(T, S, \_, \_)$$
$$V_{y_{c_1}}(C_1) \leftarrow zero(S), config(T, S, C_1, \_)$$
$$V_{y_{c_2}}(C_2) \leftarrow zero(S), config(T, S, \_, C_2)$$
$$goodconfigzero : \forall X (V_{z_s}(X) \Rightarrow S_0(X) \wedge$$
$$(V_{z_{c_1}}(X) \vee V_{z_{c_2}}(X) \vee V_{y_s}(X) \vee V_{y_{c_1}}(X) \vee V_{y_{c_2}}(X)) \Rightarrow zero(X))$$

- For each tuple in $config$ at time T which isn't the halt state, there must also be a tuple at time $T + 1$ in $config$.

$$V_1(T) \leftarrow config(T, S, C_1, C_2), S_h(S)$$
$$V_2(T) \leftarrow succ(T, T2), config(T2, S', C_1', C_2')$$
$$hasconfignext : \forall T ((dt(T) \wedge \neg V_1(T)) \Rightarrow V_2(T))$$

- Check that the transitions of the 2CM are followed. For each transition $\delta(j, >, =) = (k, pop, push)$, we include three rules, one for checking the state, one for checking the first counter and one for checking the second counter. For the transition in question we have for the state

$$V_\delta(T') \leftarrow config(T, S, C_1, C_2), succ(T, T'), S_j(S), succ(X, C_1), zero(C_2)$$
$$V_{\delta_s}(S) \leftarrow V_\delta(T), config(T, S, C_1, C_2)$$
$$goodstate_\delta : \forall S (V_{\delta_s}(S) \Leftrightarrow S_k(S))$$

and for the first counter, we (i) find all the times where the transition is definitely correct for the first counter

$$Q_{1_\delta}(T') \leftarrow config(T, S, C_1, C_2),$$
$$succ(T, T'), S_j(S), succ(X, C_1),$$
$$zero(C_2), succ(C_1'', C_1), config(T', S', C_1'', C_2')$$

(ii) find all the times where the transition may or may not be correct for the first counter

$$Q_{2_\delta}(T') \leftarrow config(T, S, C_1, C_2), succ(T, T'), S_j(S), succ(X, C_1), zero(C_2)$$

and make sure Q_{1_δ} and Q_{2_δ} are the same

$$goodtrans_{\delta_{c_1}} : \forall T(Q_{1_\delta}(T) \Leftrightarrow Q_{2_\delta}(T))$$

Rules for second counter are similar.
For transitions $\delta_1, \delta_2, \ldots, \delta_k$, the combination can be expressed thus:

$$goodstate : goodstate_{\delta_1} \wedge goodstate_{\delta_2} \wedge \ldots \wedge goodstate_{\delta_k}$$
$$goodtrans_{c_1} : goodtrans_{\delta_{1_{c_1}}} \wedge goodtrans_{\delta_{2_{c_1}}} \wedge \ldots \wedge goodtrans_{\delta_{k_{c_1}}}$$
$$goodtrans_{c_2} : goodtrans_{\delta_{1_{c_2}}} \wedge goodtrans_{\delta_{2_{c_2}}} \wedge \ldots \wedge goodtrans_{\delta_{k_{c_2}}}$$

– Check that halting state is in $config$.

$$hlt(T) \leftarrow config(T, S, C_1, C_2), S_h(S)$$
$$halt : \exists X hlt(X)$$

Given these views, we claim that satisfiability is undecidable for the query $\psi = \neg bad \wedge hasPred \wedge sameDom \wedge halt \wedge goodzero \wedge goodconfigzero \wedge \wedge nempty \wedge hassuccnext \wedge eligiblezero \wedge eligiblelast \wedge goodstate \wedge goodtrans_{c_1} \wedge goodtrans_{c_2} \wedge hasconfignext$ ∎

Urn Models and Yao's Formula

Danièle Gardy and Laurent Némirovski

Laboratoire PRiSM, Université de Versailles Saint-Quentin,
45 avenue des Etats-Unis, 78035 Versailles, France

Abstract. Yao's formula is one of the basic tools in any situation where one wants to estimate the number of blocks to be read in answer to some query. We show that such situations can be modelized by probabilistic urn models. This allows us to fully characterize the distribution probability of the number of selected blocks under uniformity assumptions, and to consider extensions to non-uniform block probabilities. We also obtain a computationnally efficient approximation of Yao's formula.

1 Introduction

Evaluating the performances of any database is an intricate task, with many intermediate computations. One frequent step consists in evaluating the number of memory blocks that must be read in order to obtain a specified subset of some set, for example by a selection. A first answer was given by Yao in [Ya], at least for the expectation of the number of selected blocks, and under uniformity and independance assumptions.

The mathematical treatment of Yao was based on a very simple expression for the number of ways of choosing i objects among j; this allowed him to obtain the average number of desired blocks, but he did not characterize further the probability distribution. Getting enough information on the probability distribution is important, because the mean value is not enough to characterize a random variable : If substituting the mean value for the random variable itself, when computing some query costs, certainly allows fast evaluation of some costs in a situation where the accent is not on the detailed study of the number of retrieved blocks, but rather on quick computations for choosing an execution plan, at the same time one must have some confidence that using this average value will not induce too much error and lead us to choose a wrong plan!

Extending Yao's approach to try and get more information on the distribution, such as its higher order moments, would quickly lead to intricate computations, which may finally succeed in giving a mathematical expression in the uniform case, but which would probably not express the underlying mathematical phenomenon in an intuitive, easy to understand form, and which would fail when considering non-uniform distributions on blocks. We shall see that, when using the right framework (random allocations and probabilistic urn models), it is easy to obtain all the desired information on the random variable *number of retrieved*

Catriel Beeri, Peter Buneman (Eds.): ICDT'99, LNCS 1540, pp. 100–112, 1998.

blocks; as a consequence, we can check that in many situations the random variable is quite close to its expectation, which justifies the use of this expectation instead of the random variable itself. More precisely, we give the variance of the number of selected blocks, and we can obtain higher order moments, if desired. However, this seems less useful that getting the approximate distribution, for large numbers of blocks m and of selected objects n : This distribution is Gaussian, and its mean and variance are very easy to compute.[1]

Our first mathematical tool is a random allocation model that is an extension of a well-known occupancy urn model : When allocating a given number of balls into a sequence of urns, what can we say about the random variable *number of empty urns?* Our second tool is a systematic use of the methods of the analysis of algorithms, i.e. generating functions, and asymptotic approximations by complex analysis.

Numerical computations show that our approximation of the expectation is both very close to the exact value and much quicker to compute than Yao's formula : In many situations *it is not worthwhile to use the exact formule* , which differs from our approximation by a negligible amount, and which requires a significant computation time. We compute our approximation of Yao's formula with a constant number of operations, while the exact formule requires $O(n)$ operations. Another interesting consequence is that our mathematical model easily lends itself to extensions such as non-uniform distributions. We consider in this paper piecewise distributions, and show that we can extend our results to obtain again an asymptotic Gaussian limiting distribution, whose mean and variance can be efficiently computed.

The plan of the paper is as follows : We present in Section 2 our urn model for the classical problem (uniform placement of objects in blocks), then study the distribution of the number of selected blocks. We discuss in Section 3 the adequacy of an extension of Yao's formula (presented in [GGT]) to the case where the probabilities of blocks are no longer uniform. This leads us to an extension to piecewise distributions in Section 4. We also give in this section a sketch of our proofs; we refer the interested reader to [GN2] for detailed proofs. We conclude by a discussion of our results and of possible extensions in Section 5. A preliminary version of these results is presented in [GN1].

2   Yao's Formula Revisited

2.1   Notations and Former Result.

Consider a set $\mathcal{E}$ of objects, whose representation in memory requires a specified number of pages. A query on the set $\mathcal{E}$ selects a subset $\mathcal{F}$ of $\mathcal{E}$; now assume that the cardinality of the answer set $\mathcal{F}$ is known; how many pages must be read to

---

[1] We recall that a Gaussian distribution is fully determined by its first two moments, i.e. by its expectation and its variance.

access all the objects of $\mathcal{F}$? It is usual to assume that placement of the objects of $\mathcal{F}$ is done randomly and uniformly : each object of $\mathcal{F}$ has the same probability to be on any page. We shall use the following notations :

- the total number of objects is p, these p objects are on m memory pages; each block contains $b = p/m$ objects (in this section we assume that all the blocks have the same capacity);
- the query selects n objects;
- the number of blocs containing the n objects selected by the query is a random variable with integer values X.

Yao gave in [Ya] the expectation of X, by computing the probability that a given page is *not* selected : This probability is equal to the number of allocations of the n selected objects among $m - 1$ pages, divided by the total number of configurations, i.e. by the number of allocations of n objects among m pages; hence

$$E[X] = m \left(1 - \frac{\binom{p-b}{n}}{\binom{p}{n}} \right). \tag{1}$$

2.2   Occupancy Urn Models.

This familiar problem lends itself to a detailed probabilistic analysis, based on a random allocation model that is a variation of one of the basic urn occupancy models. We refer the reader to the survey book of Johnson and Kotz [JK] for a general presentation of urn models and give directly the urn model that we shall use :

Take a sequence of m urns and a set of n balls, then allocate an urn to each ball. The trials are independent of each other; at each trial all urns have the same probability $1/m$ to receive the ball. When the n balls are allocated, define the random variable X as the number of empty urns.

The translation to our database problem now should be obvious : The m urns are the pages; the n balls are the selected objects; the empty urns are the pages that contain no selected object, i.e. that won't be accessed. A few years before Yao, Cardenas [Ca] gave a formula for the expectation of X that is a direct application of the classical urn model :

$$E[X] = m \left(1 - \left(1 - \frac{1}{m} \right)^n \right). \tag{2}$$

Much is known for this model : exact formulae for the moments of X and for the probability distribution, asymptotic normality and convergence towards a Gaussian process in what Kolchin et al. [KSC] call the *central domain*, where the ratio n/m is constant, or at least belongs to an interval $[a_1, a_2]$, $0 < a_1 \leq a_2 < +\infty$. However, there is a difference between the database situation we want to model and the urn model : We have imposed no limitation on urn capacities, while pages have a finite capacity b. Assuming that pages have unbounded capacity is not realistic from a database point of view, and we turn now to an extension of the model where *each urn can receive no more than b balls*.

What happens to the assumptions of independence and uniformity when considering bounded urns? It seems obvious that, if urns have a finite number b of cells, each of which can receive exactly one ball, and if at some point an urn U_1 is still empty while an urn U_2 has received one or more balls, the probability that the next ball will be allocated to U_1 is no longer equal to the probability that it will be allocated to U_2. However, we may still consider that, at any time, the *empty cells* have the same probability to receive the next ball; hence the probability of any urn at that point is proportional to the number of its empty cells. Now the independence assumption becomes : The allocation of any ball into a *cell* is independent of former allocations. In other words, independence and uniformity still hold, but for cells instead of urns. Returning to our database formulation, a cell is one of the objects of the set $\mathcal{E}$, and the objects that are selected for the query are chosen independently of each other, and independently of their placement on pages, which is exactly the usual assumption.

2.3   Analysis of the Bounded-Capacity Urn Model.

Let X be the random variable *number of selected blocks, or of non empty urns*. We introduce now the generating function enumerating the set of possible allocations of balls into urns, which will give us a tool for studying the probability distribution of X. Define $N_{l,n}$ as the number of allocations of n balls into l of the m urns, in such a way that none of the l urns is empty, and define $F(x,y) = \sum_{l,n} N_{l,n}\, x^l\, y^n/n!$: We use the variables x to "mark" the non empty urns, and y to mark the balls. The probability that an allocation gives l urns with at least one ball, conditioned by the number n of balls, the average number of non empty urns, and its variance all can be obtained by extracting suitable coefficients of the function $F(x,y)$ or of some of its derivatives. We compute $F(x,y)$ by symbolic methods, and obtain, when desired, approximate expressions of coefficients by asymptotic analysis; see for example [FS] for an introduction to these tools. We have that

$$F(x,y) = \big(1 + x((1+y)^b - 1)\big)^m. \tag{3}$$

The probability that l blocks are selected, the average number of selected blocks and its variance are obtained from the coefficients of $F(x,y)$ and of its derivatives :

$$\mathrm{Pr}\,(l/n) = \frac{[x^l y^n]F(x,y)}{[y^n]F(1,y)} = \frac{\binom{m}{l}}{\binom{p}{n}}\sum_{i=0}^{l}(-1)^{l-i}\binom{l}{i}\binom{ib}{n}; \tag{4}$$

$$E[X] = m\left(1 - \frac{\binom{p-b}{n}}{\binom{p}{n}}\right); \tag{5}$$

$$\sigma^2[X] = m(m-1)\frac{\binom{p-2b}{n}}{\binom{p}{n}} - m^2 \left(\frac{\binom{p-b}{n}}{\binom{p}{n}}\right)^2 + m\frac{\binom{p-b}{n}}{\binom{p}{n}}. \qquad (6)$$

For large m and n, the formulae (5) have an approximate expression in terms of the ratio n/m. Although it is possible to consider an arbitrary relationship between the orders of growth of n and m, we shall limit ourselves to the case where n/m is constant; in other words we are in the central domain of Kolchin et al. We give below approximate values for the moments $E[X]$ and $\sigma^2[X]$; we shall see later on (see Section 2.4) that these approximations are very close to the actual values.

$$E[X] \sim m\left(1 - \left(1 - \frac{n}{bm}\right)^b\right); \qquad (7)$$

$$\sigma^2[X] \sim m\left(1 - \frac{n}{bm}\right)^b \left(1 - \frac{bn}{bm-n}\left(1 - \frac{n}{bm}\right)^b\right). \qquad (8)$$

What about the limiting distribution in the central domain? Applying former results [Ga], we see that the limiting distribution of the random variable X exists, and is a Gaussian distribution whose mean and variance satisfy the formulae (7) and (8).

2.4 Numerical Applications.

We first evaluate the possibility of using the approximate formula (7) instead of Yao's exact formula, whose computation is much more complicated and requires a time that cannot be neglected. We have fixed the total number of blocks at $m = 500$, and varied the size b of the blocks. For comparison purposes, we have also indicated the values corresponding to the infinite case, which give a lower bound for the expected number of blocks. Table 1 gives the numerical results, which are also the basis for the plots of Figure 1. The exact and approximate values are very close to each other; as a consequence, in the sequel we shall no longer bother with the exact values, but rather use the approximate expressions. However, as was already noticed by Yao, the infinite urn case is *not* a good approximation, at least for low sizes b of blocks.

Our next objective was to check the quality of the Gaussian approximation. We give in Figure 2 the exact distribution of the number of selected blocks, as well as the Gaussian distribution with the same mean and variance. As the former values of m and n would have given us some extremely low probabilities, we have chosen here $m = 100$ and $b = 5$, with a total of $n = 200$ balls. For these rather small values of m and n, we can check that the approximation by a Gaussian distribution is already quite good; of course it is still better for larger values of the parameters m and n.

n	Yao (exact)			Yao (approximate)			Unbounded urns
	b=2	b=5	b=10	b=2	b=5	b=10	(Cardenas)
200	180.0	170.5	167.7	180	170.4	167.5	164.9
400	320.1	291.0	282.9	320	290.8	282.8	275.5
600	420.1	373.3	360.9	420	373.2	360.7	349.5
800	480.0	427.4	412.7	480	427.3	412.5	399.2
1000	500	461.2	446.4	500	461.1	446.3	432.4

Table 1. Number of selected blocs, for a uniform distribution and several sizes of blocks

We can now be reasonably sure that the random variable *number of expected blocks* behaves as a Gaussian distribution, which has some important consequences: For a Gaussian distribution, we can quantify precisely the probability that we are at a given distance from the average value E, using the variance σ^2.

It is worth noting that our asymptotic formulae make for very quick computations, in contrast to Yao's formula. For $n = 1000$ the computation of Yao's formula requires 2.5s, the bound obtained by assuming that the urns are infinite is 0.15s, and the asymptotic formula is obtained in at most 0.017s. Our formula need a constant number of operations when n and m increase. Yao's formula requires n divisions and $n - 1$ multiplications for the same computation.

3   How Well-Fitted to Object Databases Is Yao's Formula?

It may happen that the database has different block sizes, or that the objects in the database are clustered according to the values of some attribute; then the probability that a block is selected is no longer uniform, and Yao's formula no longer gives a valid estimation of the average number of selected blocks. An extension of Yao's formula to deal with such a situation was proposed by Gardarin et al. in [GGT], where they consider blocks of different sizes in an object-oriented database, and suggest that Yao's formula be applied on each group of equal-sized blocks:

Let C be a collection of j partitions, where each partition has p_i objects and requires m_i blocks. Assume that n objects are chosen at random in the collection C; then the average number of selected blocks is

$$\sum_{i=1}^{j} m_i \left(1 - \frac{\binom{p_i - p_i/m_i}{n_i}}{\binom{p_i}{n_i}} \right), \text{with } n_i = n * p_i/p. \tag{9}$$

The proof of this formula relies on the assumption that the placement of objects into blocks is uniform, and that each object has the same probability of beeing selected, independently of the others; as a consequence the number n_i of selected

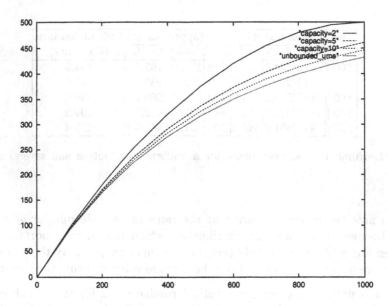

Fig. 1. Number of selected blocks, plotted against the number of selected objects, for several sizes of blocks

objects in the i-th partition is $n * p_i/p$. We argue that this does not always hold, for example in the simple example we give below.

Consider a database containing information relative to persons, and the query Q *"Find all people having a salary at least equal to 1000 $"*. If we know the number n of persons satisfying this query, and if the placement of persons on pages (blocks) is random, then the average number of blocks to retrieve is given by Yao's formula. Now assume that the database also contains data relative to cars, that each car has an owner, and that the persons are partitioned according to their owning, or not, a car : some blocks will contain data relative to the persons who own a car, and to their cars, and others blocks will contain data relative to the persons who do not own a car. Then we have introduced a correlation between the salary and ownership of a car : We expect the proportion of people satisfying our query Q to be larger among car owners than among the other people. This means that the blocks containing data on car owners have a greater probability of being selected than the other blocks.

The formula (9) does not take into account this phenomenon, and may lead to biased results, all the more when clustering is done according to an attribute that appears in the query. In the following section, we consider the case where the probability that a block is selected can take a finite number of values, i.e. where we can partition the blocks according to their probability.

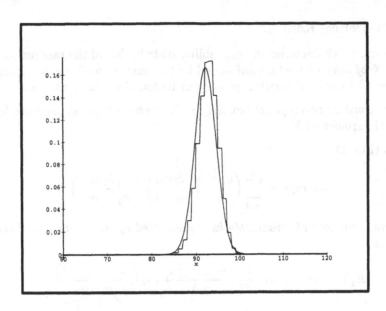

Fig. 2. Probability distribution of the number of selected blocks and of the Gaussian distribution with same mean and variance

4   Piecewise Uniform Distributions

We now define a model to deal with non-uniformity of database objects or of blocks. We shall assume that *the probability distribution on the blocks is piecewise uniform,* and that *the objects are stocked in blocks that may have different capacities.* This leads us to extend our urn model to allow different probabilities for urns. On each trial, the ball falls into the urn U with a probability $\Pr (U)$. We should mention at once that this assumption does not contradict our former assumption that urns have a finite capacity : The *conditional* probability that an urn U receives the next ball, knowing that it already holds j balls, is of course related to j!

We assume that there are i distinct kinds of blocks $(1 \leq i \leq j)$; there are m_i blocks of the kind i, each of which holds b_i objects. We translate this into an urn model, where the urns of type i each have b_i cells, and where each cell can hold at most one ball.

The total number of blocks (urns) is $m = \sum_{1 \leq i \leq j} m_i$; the cumulated number of objects (balls) in blocks of type i is $m_i b_i$, and the total number of objects in the database is $p = \sum_{1 \leq i \leq j} m_i b_i$. We shall denote by π_i the probability that a selected object is stocked in a block of type i; of course $\sum_{1 \leq i \leq j} \pi_i = 1$. This can be illustrated using the example of Section 3, where we separate the persons owning a car from those who don't: π_1 would be the probability of having a car, knowing that the person earns more than 1000 \$: $\pi_1 = \Pr (Car/Sal > 1000\ \$)$ and $\pi_2 = \Pr (\rceil Car/Sal > 1000\ \$) = 1 - \pi_1$.

4.1   Theoretical Results.

In this part, we characterize the probability distribution of the random variable *number X of selected blocks*, conditioned by the number n of selected objects; a brief sketch of the mathematical proofs can be found in the section 4.3.

When we consider two types of blocks ($j = 2$), we have exact expressions for the mean and variance of X :

Proposition 41 *Let*

$$f(m_1, m_2) := \sum_{i=0}^{n} \binom{b_1 m_1}{i} \binom{b_2 m_2}{n-i} \left(\frac{\pi_1 b_2 m_2}{\pi_2 b_1 m_1} \right)^i . \tag{10}$$

The average number of selected blocks, conditioned by the number n of selected objects, is

$$E[X] = m - \left(m_1 \frac{f(m_1 - 1, m_2)}{f(m_1, m_2))} + m_2 \frac{f(m_1, m_2 - 1)}{f(m_1, m_2)} \right). \tag{11}$$

This formula can be extended to give the variance, and to include general j [GN2], but the usefulness of such an extension may be discussed : We have seen that exact computation of Yao's formula, which involves a binomial coefficient, is already costly, and we have here sums of products of such terms! We shall rather concentrate our efforts on obtaining asymptotic expressions, which can be computed with a reasonable amount of effort, and which give good accuracy in many cases, as we shall see in Section 4.2.

We now turn to the asymptotic study, and notice at once that, in difference to the uniform case where we had to deal with two variables n and m, we now have to deal with $j + 1$ variables : the number n of selected objects and the numbers m_i of blocks of type i, for the j types. These variables may grow at different rates; moreover we have $2j$ parameters π_i and b_i. We shall limit ourselves to the easiest generalization of the uniform case : *The number m_i of blocks of each type is proportional to n.* Under this assumption, we have the following result :

Theorem 41 *When the number of blocks of each type is proportional to the total number n of selected objects, the random variable X asymptotically follows a Gaussian limiting distribution, with mean and variance*

$$E[X] \sim \sum_{i=1}^{j} \frac{m_i}{(1 + \pi_i \rho / b_i m_i)^{b_i}}; \tag{12}$$

$$\sigma^2[X] \sim \sum_{i=1}^{j} \frac{m_i}{(1 + \pi_i \rho / b_i m_i)^{b_i}} \left(1 - \frac{1}{(1 + \pi_i \rho / b_i m_i)^{b_i}} \right) \tag{13}$$

$$- \rho \frac{\left(\sum_{i=1}^{j} \frac{\pi_i}{(1 + \pi_i \rho / b_i m_i)^{b_i + 1}} \right)^2}{\left(\sum_{i=1}^{j} \frac{\pi_i}{(1 + \pi_i \rho / b_i m_i)^2} \right)^2}.$$

In these formulae, ρ is a function of n, and is the unique positive solution of the equation in y: $\sum_{i=1}^{j} \pi_i y / n(1 + \pi_i y / b_i m_i) = 1$.

4.2 Numerical Applications.

We have first considered two types of urns ($j = 2$), with $m_1 = 100$ and $b_1 = 10$ for the first type, $m_2 = 200$ and $b_2 = 15$ for the second type. We have also considered different values for the probabilities π_1 and π_2 that an object belongs to a block of the first or second type. Table 2 gives the average value of X in several cases : The first three columns give the exact values for different π_i, the next three columns the approximate values under the same assumptions, and the last column is obtained by the formula (9) of Gardarin et al (which does not allow us to consider different probabilities π_i). When the number n of selected objects is relatively low, the last formula gives results that may be considered as valid in the first case, but that differ sensibly from the actual ones in the other cases, where the probability distribution is more biased. (For n greater than 1500, almost all blocks are selected anyway, and the different formulae give comparable results.) Another noteworthy remark is that, here again, the asymptotic approximation is of quite good quality, and that the time for computing this approximation is far lower than the corresponding time for the exact case. The time necessary to compute $f(m_1, m_2)$, and then $E[X]$, is $O(n)$ for the exact formula, and $O(1)$ for the asymptotic formula approximation. For the numerical examples we have considered (see Table 2), the computation time of the asymptotic formulae is at most 0.017s, the formula of Gardarin at al. (which leads to somewhat imprecise results) requires a few seconds, and the time for the exact formula can be as much as a few minutes! As a consequence, we have used the approximate formulae for the curves of Figure 3.a, which presents the average number of selected blocks for probabilities $\pi_1 = 9/10$ and $\pi_2 = 1/10$; we have also plotted the estimation from Gardarin et al., which is always larger than the exact result.

n	Exact values			Approximate values			Uniformity
	$\pi_1 = 1/4$ $\pi_2 = 3/4$	$\pi_1 = 4/5$ $\pi_2 = 1/5$	$\pi_1 = 9/10$ $\pi_2 = 1/10$	$\pi_1 = 1/4$ $\pi_2 = 3/4$	$\pi_1 = 4/5$ $\pi_2 = 1/5$	$\pi_1 = 9/10$ $\pi_2 = 1/10$	
200	147.6	122.2	108.1	147.4	122.1	108.0	147.8
400	224.1	178.3	148.5	224.0	178.4	148.5	224.3
600	263.0	218.2	182.7	262.8	218.2	182.7	263.1
800	282.3	249.7	218.7	282.2	249.6	218.7	282.4
1000	291.7	272.5	251.8	291.7	272.4	251.8	291.8
1200	296.2	286.8	276.1	296.2	286.7	276.1	296.3
1500	298.9	296.6	294.0	298.9	296.6	293.9	298.9
2000	299.9	299.8	299.7	299.9	299.8	299.7	299.9

Table 2. Average number of selected blocks for two types of blocks with different probabilities

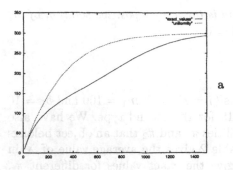
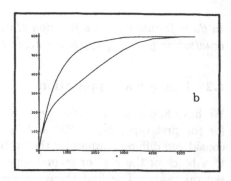

a

b

Fig. 3. a: Average number of selected blocks, for two types of blocks with probabilities $\pi_1 = 9/10$ and $\pi_2 = 1/10$, plotted against the same number under a uniform distribution. b: Three types of blocks

The average value of X is a simple function of the parameter ρ, which is obtained by solving a polynomial equation of degree j whose coefficients are expressed with the parameters n, m_i, b_i and π_i. If a comparatively simple expression of ρ exists when $j = 2$, such a formula either becomes quite complicated, or does not exists, for larger j, and we then use a numerical approximation of ρ. We present in Figure 3.b results for three types of blocks, which require a numerical approximation of the solution ρ. Here again, we have plotted the results against the result from Gardarin et al. in [GGT], and have checked that our formulae give a lower average number. We can check that the simplification that allowed them to compute their formula, by making strong assumptions of uniformity, gives a result that is always greater than the exact one; such a systematic overestimation, as noted long ago by Christodoulakis [Ch2], can lead to errors in the further process of optimization.

4.3   Sketch of Proofs.

We give here the main ideas and the sketch of the proofs of our theorems; the interested reader can find the complete proofs and detailed computations in [GN2]. We start from the generating function $F(x,y)$, with x marking the number of non empty urns, i.e. of selected blocks, and y marking the total number of balls in the m urns :

$$F(x,y) = \prod_{i=1}^{j} \left(x + (1 + \pi_i\, y)^{b_i} - 1\right)^{m_i}. \tag{14}$$

The right coefficients of the generating function and of its derivatives give us the desired information on the probability distribution, for example its value at some point, its average value and its variance. To obtain the limiting distribution, we use Levy's theorem on the convergence of characteristic functions. The characteristic function of the distribution of X, conditioned by the number n of selected objects, is obtained from the quotient of the two coefficients $[y^n]F(x, y)$ and $[y^n]F(1, y)$. We approximate these coefficients by a saddle point method, treating x as a parameter; in a second step we choose $x = e^{-t/\sigma[X]}$ to obtain the characteristic function, and check that it converges for large n towards the function of a Gaussian distribution of suitable expectation and variance.

An alternative proof is obtained by applying recent results of Bender and Richmond [BR] to our generating function $F(x, y)$.

5   Discussion and Extensions

We have shown that an adequate modelization allows us to compute much more than the average number of blocks to be retrieved, in a situation where all the blocks have the same probability to be selected. We have computed the variance of this number and its limiting distribution. In our opinion, the points that are relevant to practical applications are the following : The limiting distribution is Gaussian with mean and variance of the same order, the exact distribution is close to the limiting one for reasonable values of the parameters, and the approximate values of the expectation and variance are given by very simple formulae. This means that, when in a situation where one wants to use Yao's formula, one can use the average value with confidence that the actual number is not too far from it, and that we do not even need to use the exact average value (whose computation, involving binomial coefficients, i.e. factorials, can be costly), but can use a very efficient approximation.

We have also shown that extensions of Yao's formula to non-uniform probabilities are best done by the urn model. For piecewise distributions, we have given the exact and approximate mean and variance, and proved that the limiting distribution is again Gaussian : Once more, we are in a situation where using the expectation instead of the random variable is not likely to induce much error.

Former results on non-uniform distributions are few, and are much less precise than ours. To the best of our knowledge, they have been limited to the expectation of the number of retrieved blocks: For example, Christodoulakis gave in [Ch1] upper and lower bounds for this expectation. Our approch differs from the usual one in that we do not assume independency of the variables under study, although allowing dependencies may lead to greater generality, we still have to define and obtain conditional probabilities (the π_i of Section 4), which may limit the use of our results.

The fact that most of our results are asymptotic, i.e valid for large numbers of blocks and of selected objects, may at first glance seem a restriction. However, numerical computations have shown that the exact and approximate values are very close to each other for parameters as low as a few hundred, which is certainly relevant to most databases. If this is not the case, then one should use the exact formulae, which still give feasible computations for low values of the parameters. If one wishes for a mathematical justification of our approximations, then one might try and quantify the speed of convergence towards the limiting distribution (reasonably fast in urn models).

From a mathematical point of view, there is still work to be done : If urn models with uniform probabilities (and unbounded urns) are quite well-known, to our knowledge the extensions relative to bounded urns and non-uniform probabilities are not so well characterized. An interesting problem is to define a class of probability distributions on the urns that still give rise to a Gaussian behaviour, and with a variance low enough that the bound on the error when using the average value instead of the random variable remains within acceptable bounds.

References

[BR]   A.BENDER and L.B. RICHMOND. Multivariate asymptotique for product of large powers with applications to Lagrange inversion. Technical report, University of Waterloo, April 1998.

[Ca]   A.F. CARDENAS. Analysis and performance of inverted data base structures. *Comm. ACM*, 19(5), 1975.

[Ch1]   S. CHRISTODOULAKIS. Issues in query evaluation. *Database Engineering*, 5(3):220–223, September 1982.

[Ch2]   S. CHRISTODOULAKIS. Estimating block selectivities. *Information Systems*, 9(1):69–79, 1983.

[FS]   P. FLAJOLET and R. SEDGEWICK. *An introduction to the analysis of algorithms*. Addison-Wesley, 1996.

[GGT]   G. GARDARIN, J.-R. GRUSER, and Z.H. TANG. A cost model for clustered object oriented databases. In *21st VLDB Conference, Zürich, Switzerland*, pages 323–334, 1995.

[Ga]   D. GARDY. Normal limiting distributions for projection and semijoin sizes. *SIAM Journal on Discrete Mathematics*, 5(2):219–248, May 1992.

[GN1]   D. GARDY and L. NEMIROVSKI. Formule de Yao et modèles d'urnes. In *14st BDA Conference, Hammamet, Tunisia*, (to appear) 1998.

[GN2]   D. GARDY and L. NEMIROVSKI. Une application des modèles d'urnes aux bases de données : la formule de Yao et ses extensions. Technical report, Laboratoire PRISM, Université de Versailles, October 1998.

[JK]   N.L. JOHNSON and S. KOTZ. *Urn models and their application*. Wiley & Sons, 1977.

[KSC]   V. KOLCHIN, B. SEVAST'YANOV, and V. CHISTYAKOV. *Random Allocations*. Wiley & Sons, 1978.

[Ya]   S.B. YAO. Approximating block accesses in data base organizations. *Comm. ACM*, 20(4), 1977.

On the Generation of 2-Dimensional Index Workloads

Joseph M. Hellerstein[1]*, Lisa Hellerstein[2]**, and George Kollios[2]***

[1] University of California, Berkeley
EECS Computer Science Division
Berkeley CA 94720-1776, USA
jmh@cs.berkeley.edu
[2] Polytechnic University
Dept. of Computer and Information Science
Six MetroTech Center
Brooklyn, NY 11201-3840, USA
hstein@duke.poly.edu, gkollios@db.poly.edu

Abstract. A large number of database index structures have been proposed over the last two decades, and little consensus has emerged regarding their relative effectiveness. In order to empirically evaluate these indexes, it is helpful to have methodologies for generating random queries for performance testing. In this paper we propose a domain-independent approach to the generation of random queries: choose randomly among all logically distinct queries. We investigate this idea in the context of range queries over 2-dimensional points. We present an algorithm that chooses randomly among logically distinct 2-d range queries. It has constant-time expected performance over uniformly distributed data, and exhibited good performance in experiments over a variety of real and synthetic data sets. We observe nonuniformities in the way randomly chosen logical 2-d range queries are distributed over a variety of spatial properties. This raises questions about the quality of the workloads generated from such queries. We contrast our approach with previous work that generates workloads of random spatial ranges, and we sketch directions for future work on the robust generation of workloads for studying index performance.

1 Introduction

Multidimensional indexing has been studied extensively over the last 25 years; a recent survey article [5] describes over 50 alternative index structures for the two-dimensional case alone. Two-dimensional indexing problems arise frequently, especially in popular applications such as Geographic Information Systems (GIS)

* Supported by NASA grant 1996-MTPE-00099, NSF grant IRI-9703972, and a Sloan Foundation Fellowship.
** Supported by NSF grant CCR-9501660.
*** Supported by NSF grant IRI-9509527.

Catriel Beeri, Peter Buneman (Eds.): ICDT'99, LNCS 1540, pp. 113–130, 1998.
© Springer-Verlag Berlin Heidelberg 1998

and Computer Aided Design (CAD). A frustrating aspect of the multidimensional indexing literature is that among the many proposed techniques, there is still no "clear winner" even for two-dimensional indexing. Performance studies that accompany new index proposals typically offer little help, presenting confusing and sometimes conflicting results. Significantly absent from many of these studies is a crisp description of the distribution of queries that were used for testing the index. The need for rigorous empirical performance methodologies in this domain has been noted with increasing urgency in recent years [20,6].

Recent work on generalized indexing schemes presents software and analytic frameworks for indexing that are *domain-independent*, *i.e.*, applicable to arbitrary sets of data and queries [11,10]. As noted in [10], there is a simple logical characterization of the space of queries supported by an index over a data set D: they form a set $S \subseteq P(D)$, *i.e.*, a set of subsets of the data being indexed. Note that this logical view of the query space abstracts away the semantics of the data domain and considers only the membership of data items in queries – a query is defined by the set of items it retrieves. This abstraction leads to simplified systems [11], frameworks for discussing the hardness of indexing problems [10,19,15], and domain-independent methodologies for measuring the performance of queries over indexes [14].

A natural extension of this idea is to test indexes in a similarly domain-independent manner, by choosing randomly from the space of logical queries. In particular, a random logical query is simply a randomly chosen element of the set $S \subseteq P(D)$ of queries supported by the index. In this paper we consider randomly generating logical queries in this fashion for indexes that support range queries over two-dimensional points.

We begin by presenting a simple algorithm for generating random logical 2-d range queries, and we study its performance both analytically and empirically. While in the worst case the algorithm takes expected time $\theta(n^2)$ for databases of n points, in the case of uniformly distributed point sets it runs in constant expected time. We conducted experiments over standard geographic databases, and over synthetic data sets of various fractal dimensions: in all these cases, the running time of the algorithm was within a factor of two over its expected time on uniformly distributed points, suggesting that the algorithm performance is efficient and robust in practice.

We continue by considering the spatial properties of randomly generated logical queries. We note that the queries in a randomly generated set of logical 2-d range queries, although likely to be diverse with respect to the set of points they contain, may not be diverse with respect to natural properties such as area, cardinality, and aspect ratio. For example, given a data set consisting of uniformly distributed 2-d points, the expected area of a random logical range query over those points is 36% of the total data space (the unit square), and the variance is only 3%. Thus simply testing a data structure using random logical range queries will shed little light on how the data structure performs on queries of differing area. Moreover, doing so is unlikely to expose the performance of the data structure on "typical" queries, which are likely to be more selective.

To illuminate this issue further, we contrast these observations with properties of previously-proposed query workloads. These workloads provide explicit control over domain-specific properties like cardinality and area, but are not necessarily diverse with respect to logical properties like the set of points they contain, or the cardinality of queries. Thus these workloads may not provide good "coverage" of an index's behavior in different scenarios, and may also not be representative of "typical" real queries either. These observations raise a number of research issues, which broadly amount to the following challenge: in order to allow experimentalists to do good work analyzing the performance of indexes, we need better understanding and control of the techniques for generating synthetic workloads.

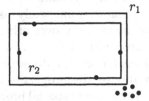

Fig. 1. Random Rectangle vs. Random Query Rectangle: the outer and inner rectangles represent the same query, though they are distinct rectangles.

1.1   Related Work

Previous work on spatial index benchmarking used queries generated from domain-specific distributions, based on geometric properties (area, position, aspect ratio, etc.) For example, many studies generated random rectangles in the plane, and used these to query the index. Note that the spaces of random rectangles in the plane and random queries are quite different: this is illustrated in Figure 1. From a spatial perspective, r_1 and r_2 are distinct two-dimensional *rectangles*. From a strictly logical perspective, however, r_1 and r_2 are identical *queries*, since they describe the same subset of data. We are careful in this paper to distinguish *random rectangles* in the plane from *random query rectangles*, which are chosen from the space of logically distinct rectangular range queries. It is inaccurate to consider random rectangles to be good representatives of randomly chosen logical queries; we discuss this issue in more detail in Section 5.

The original papers on many of the well-known spatial database indexes use domain-specific query benchmarks. This includes the papers on R-trees [9], R*-trees [2], Segment Indexes [13], and hBΠ-trees [3]. For some of those papers, the construction of the random rectangles is not even clear; for example, the R-tree paper describes generating "search rectangles made up using random numbers...each retrieving about 5% of the data", and goes into no further detail as to how those rectangles are chosen. The hBΠ-tree authors gave some consideration to the relationship of queries and data set by forming each rectangle "by taking a randomly chosen existing point as its center" [3]; a similar technique was used in [1]. Domain-specific techniques were also used in spatial index analysis papers, including Greene's R-tree performance study [8], and the various papers on fractal dimensions [4,1] (which only used square and radius query ranges). The domain-specific approach has been studied in greater detail by Pagel and colleagues. Their work provides an interesting contrast to the work presented here, and we discuss this in depth in Section 5.

1.2   Structure of the Paper

In Section 2 we present the algorithm for generating random logical 2-d range queries. We also provide analytical results about expected running time over any data set, and expected running time over uniformly distributed data. In Section 3 we present results of a performance study over other data distributions, which produces average running times within a factor of 2 of the expected time over uniform data. Section 4 considers the spatial properties of randomly chosen range queries, and in Section 5 we discuss the properties of rectangles generated by prior algorithms that explicitly considered spatial properties. Section 6 reflects on these results and considers their implications for the practical task of empirically analyzing index performance.

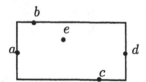

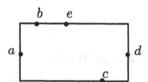

Fig. 2. The minimal bounding rectangle containing points a, b, c, d and e is shown.

Fig. 3.   Both $\{a, b, c, d\}$ and $\{a, e, c, d\}$ represent this rectangle

2   An Algorithm for Generating Random 2-d Range Queries

2.1   Preliminaries

Definition 1. *Let $S = \{(x_1, y_1), \ldots, (x_n, y_n)\}$ be a set of points in the plane. The* minimal bounding rectangle (MBR) *containing S is*

$$[\min\{x_1, \ldots, x_n\}, \max\{x_1, \ldots, x_n\}] \times [\min\{y_1, \ldots, y_n\}, \max\{y_1, \ldots, y_n\}]$$

The rectangle represented by S is the MBR containing S. A query rectangle, with respect to a data set I, is a rectangle that is represented by a set $S \subseteq I$.

The set of all distinct query rectangles corresponds precisely to the set of logically distinct rectangular region queries.

Although distinct sets of points can represent the same rectangle, we define the canonical set of points representing a rectangle (with respect to a data set) as follows.

Definition 2. *Let I be a data set and let q be a rectangle represented by a subset of I. The* canonical top point *of q (with respect to I) is the leftmost point in I lying on the top boundary of q. Similarly, the* canonical bottom point *is the leftmost point lying on the bottom boundary. The* canonical left *and* right *points of q are the topmost points lying respectively on the left and right and right boundaries of q.*

S is the canonical set of points *representing q if S consists of the canonical bottom, top, left, and right points of q.*

Definition 3. *There are four types of query rectangles: 1-point, 2-point, 3-point, and 4-point. An i-point query rectangle* is one whose canonical set consists of i distinct points.

A 4-point rectangle has one data point on each of its boundaries. A 3-point rectangle has one data point on a corner of the rectangle, and one point on each of the two sides that do not meet at this corner. A 2-point rectangle is either a line segment (a degenerate rectangle with zero height or width) with a data point on each end, or a non-degenerate rectangle with data points on 2 opposite corners. A 1-point rectangle is a single point (a degenerate rectangle, with no height or width).

Definition 4. *For data set I, the* logical distribution on rectangular queries *is the uniform distribution on the set of all distinct query rectangles represented by subsets of I. A* random query rectangle *is a query rectangle that is generated according to the logical distribution on rectangular queries.*

2.2   Approaches to Generating Random Query Rectangles

We consider the problem of generating random query rectangles. It is easy to generate a random rectangular region $[x_1, x_2] \times [y_1, y_2]$, chosen uniformly from the space of all such regions. Generating a random query rectangle is not as easy. Some of the most natural approaches to generating random query rectangles do not work, or are impractical. Consider for example the idea of generating query rectangles by choosing four data points at random, and taking the minimal bounding rectangle containing those points. Under this scheme, a rectangle which has one data point on each of its four sides could only be generated by choosing precisely those four points. In contrast, a rectangle with two data points at opposite corners, and many data points in its interior, could be generated by choosing the two corner points, and any two points from its interior. As a result, this scheme will be biased towards the latter type of rectangle. Other techniques, such as "growing" or "shrinking" random rectangles until a query rectangle is achieved, have similar biases.

A naive approach to avoiding such bias is to generate all query rectangles and pick one uniformly from among them. However, since there can be $\theta(n^4)$ query rectangles, this approach is grossly impractical for sizable databases. A somewhat less naive method, which uses a range tree, correctly generates random query rectangles, but requires $\theta(n^2 \log n)$ preprocessing time for a preprocessing stage, and $\theta(\log n)$ time to generate each query following the preprocessing stage. The method uses $\theta(n^2 \log n)$ storage (we omit the details of this method due to space limitations). Since n is typically large this is still impractical, and we omit the details of this method here. It is an interesting open question whether there is a scheme for generating random query rectangles that in the worst case uses $O(n \log n)$ space, preprocessing time $O(n \log n)$, and time $O(\log n)$ to generate each random query rectangle following the preprocessing stage. The method we present in the next section does not achieve these bounds in the worst case, but it does work quite well in practice.

2.3 The Algorithm

We present a simple Las Vegas algorithm for generating random query rectangles. The amount of time it takes to run can vary (because of randomness in the algorithm), but when it terminates it produces a correct output—a random query rectangle.

Our algorithm for generating a random query rectangle first chooses, with an appropriate bias, whether to generate a random 1-point, 2-point, 3-point, or 4-point rectangle. It then generates a rectangle of the appropriate type, chosen uniformly from all query rectangles of that type. We present the pseudocode in Figure 4. We call an iteration of the repeat loop in the algorithm a *trial*. We say that a trial is *successful* if the set Z generated in that trial is output.

Repeat until halted:

1. Generate a number i between 1 and 4, according to the following probability distribution:
   (a) Let $t = \binom{n}{1} + \binom{n}{2} + \binom{n}{3} + \binom{n}{4}$. For $j \in \{1, \ldots, 4\}$, $\text{Prob}[i = j] = \frac{\binom{n}{j}}{t}$.
2. (a) Generate a set Z containing i points of I uniformly at random from among all i-point sets in Z
   (b) If $i = 1$ or $i = 2$ output Z.
   (c) If $i = 3$ or $i = 4$, compute the MBR R containing Z, and check whether Z is the canonical set of points for R. If so, output Z.

Fig. 4. Las Vegas Algorithm for Generating Queries from the Logical Distribution

Proposition 1. *On any input data set I, the Las Vegas algorithm in Figure 4 outputs a random query rectangle.*

Proof. We consider the query rectangle output by the algorithm to be the rectangle represented by the set Z output by the algorithm.

Consider a single trial. If the set Z generated during the trial is a 1-point set or a 2-point set, then Z must be the canonical set of points representing the MBR containing Z. If Z is a 3-point set or a 4-point set, then Z is output iff it is the canonical set of points representing the MBR R containing Z. Thus Z is output iff it is the canonical set of points for the query rectangle it represents.

We need to show that the algorithm outputs each possible query rectangle with equal probability. Let R be a j-point query rectangle for some j between 1 and 4. Let Q be the canonical set of points for R. In any trial, the set Z will be equal to Q iff i is chosen to be equal to j in line 1, and Z is chosen to be equal to Q in line 2. Thus the probability that, in a given trial, Z is the canonical set of points for R is $\frac{\binom{n}{i}}{t} * \frac{1}{\binom{n}{i}} = \frac{1}{t}$.

The probability that a trial is successful is therefore $\frac{r}{t}$, where r is the number of distinct query rectangles R. The conditional probability of generating a particular query rectangle R in a trial, given that the trial is successful, is $\frac{1}{t}/\frac{r}{t} = \frac{1}{r}$. Since the algorithm outputs a query rectangle as soon as it has a successful trial, each distinct query rectangle R is output by the algorithm with the same probability of $\frac{1}{r}$. $\qquad\square$

Proposition 2. *On any input data set I consisting of n points, the expected number of trials of the Las Vegas algorithm in Figure 4 is $\frac{t}{r}$, where r is the number of distinct query rectangles represented by subsets of I, and $t = \binom{n}{1} + \binom{n}{2} + \binom{n}{3} + \binom{n}{4}$.*

Proof. This follows immediately from the proof of Proposition 1, in which it is shown that the probability that a given trial is successful is $\frac{r}{t}$. $\qquad\square$

2.4   Expected Performance over Worst-Case Data Sets

We now do a worst-case analysis of the expected running time of the algorithm. Our analysis will assume that the actual data are stored in the leaves of the index. When this is not the case (i.e. for "secondary" indexes), an additional random I/O is required for each item in the output set.

Proposition 3. *The expected number of trials of the Las Vegas algorithm of Figure 4 (on the worst-case input) is $\theta(n^2)$.*

Proof. By Proposition 2, the expected number of trials is $\frac{t}{r}$. This quantity depends on r, which can vary according to the configuration of the points in the data set. We now bound r. On any n-point data set, the number of 1-point query rectangles is n and the number of 2-point query rectangles is $\binom{n}{2}$. Therefore, on any data set, r is at least $n + \binom{n}{2}$. This bound is achieved by data sets in which all points fall on a line because such data sets define no 3-point and 4-point rectangles. Since $t = \theta(n^4)$, the proposition follows. $\qquad\square$

Proposition 4. *There is an implementation of the Las Vegas algorithm of Figure 4 that runs in expected time* $\theta(n^2)$ *(on the worst-case input) with* $\theta(n \log n)$ *preprocessing.*

Proof. Consider the following implementation of the algorithm. It requires that the data set be preprocessed. The preprocessing can be done as follows. Form two sorted arrays, the first containing the data set sorted by x coordinate (with ties broken by sorting on the y coordinate), and the second containing the data set sorted by y coordinate (with ties broken on the x coordinate). With each data point p in the first array, store a link to the corresponding point in the second array. This preprocessing can easily be implemented to run in time $O(n \log n)$.

The implementation of a trial is as follows. Generate the points Z using the first sorted array and calculate the MBR R containing them. If Z contains 1 or 2 points, then output Z and end the trial.

Otherwise, begin checking whether Z is the canonical set of points for R by first checking whether all points in Z lie on the boundary of R and whether each boundary of R contains exactly one point of Z. If not, end the trial without outputting Z.

If Z passes the above tests, it is sufficient to check, for each boundary of R, whether Z contains the canonical point on that boundary. To check a boundary of R, find the point p in Z lying on that boundary. Then access the point p' immediately preceding p in the first array (for the left and right boundaries) or immediately following p in the second array (for the top and bottom boundaries). Because of the links from p in the first to p in the second array, p' can be accessed in constant time for each of the boundaries. Check whether p' lies on the same boundary of R as p. If not, p is the canonical point on the relevant boundary of R, otherwise it is. If Z contains the canonical point for each boundary of R, then output Z. Otherwise, end the trial without outputting Z.

Since each of the steps in the above implementation of a trial takes constant time, each trial takes constant time. By the previous proposition, the expected number of trials is $\theta(n^2)$, and thus the expected running time is $\theta(n^2)$.   □

Fortunately, the expected number of trials is significantly lower than $\theta(n^2)$ for many data sets. For example consider the "plus" data set, where the data points lie on two line segments, a horizontal and a vertical, intersecting each other in the middle. Thus, the data set is divided into four partitions (up, down, left, right) of approximately the same size. For this data set it can be shown that a set Z generated in Step 2(a) of the above algorithm is a canonical set with significant probability. In particular, if Z is a 4-point set, the probability that Z is a canonical set is equal to the probability that the four points belong to different partitions. Hence:

$$P(Z \ is \ a \ 4-pt \ canonical \ set) = 1 \cdot \frac{3}{4} \cdot \frac{2}{4} \cdot \frac{1}{4} = \frac{3}{32} > \frac{1}{11}$$

Since for the other query types (eg. 1-,2- or 3-point) the above probability is even higher, it follows that the expected number of trials per query rectangle for this data set is most 11.

In the following section, we prove that on a uniform data set, the expected number of trials before the algorithm outputs a query rectangle is less than 6, independent of the number of points in the data set. In Section 3 we present empirical results on both artificial and real data sets, showing that the average number of trials is similarly small.

2.5   Algorithm Analysis: Uniform Data Sets

Definition 5. *A uniform data set is a set of points drawn independently from the uniform distribution on the points in the unit square.*

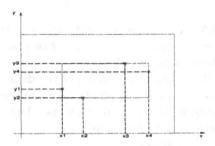

Fig. 5.   Query Rectangle

Proposition 5. *Let I be a uniform dataset of size n. The expected number of trials of the Las Vegas algorithm in Figure 4 on data set I is less than 6. As n increases, the expected number of trials approaches 6. (The expectation is over the choice of points in I.)*

Proof. Let $\{p_1, p_2, p_3, p_4\}$ be a set of four distinct random points chosen from I ($p_i = (x_i, y_i)$). Since the points in I are chosen from the uniform distribution on the unit square, the probability that any two have a common x or y coordinate is 0. Therefore, we assume without loss of generality that all four points have distinct x coordinates and all have distinct y coordinates.[1]

Let S_4 be the set of permutations of 4 elements x_1, x_2, x_3, x_4. We associate with the permutation $\sigma = (x_i, x_j, x_k, x_l)$ the event $A_\sigma = \{x_i < x_j < x_k < x_l\}$. Clearly the A_σ's partition the sample space, so if B is the event that $\{p_1, \ldots, p_4\}$ are the canonical set of points of a query rectangle, then by Bayes' formula

$$P(B) = \sum_{\sigma \in S_4} P(B|A_\sigma)P(A_\sigma)$$

---

[1]   In practice, the probability will not be zero because of finite precision in the representation of points on the unit squre, but it will usually be small enough so that its effect on the expected number of trials will be negligible.

By symmetry $P(A_\sigma) = \frac{1}{4!}$ for every $\sigma \in S_4$ and $P(B|A_\sigma)$ is the same for any $\sigma \in S_4$, so $P(B)$ is actually $P(B|A_\sigma)$ where σ is any permutation. Taken in particular $\sigma_0 = (x_1, x_2, x_3, x_4)$ (see Figure 5), then

$$
\begin{aligned}
P(B|A_\sigma) &= P(y_1, y_4 \; between \; y_2, y_3) \qquad by \; symmetry \\
&= 2P(y_2 < y_1, y_4 < y_3) \\
&= 2 \int_0^1 dy_3 \int_0^{y_3} dy_2 \int_{y_2}^{y_3} dy_1 \int_{y_2}^{y_3} dy_4 \\
&= 2 \int_0^1 dy_3 \int_0^{y_3} dy_2 (y_3 - y_2)^2 \\
&= \frac{1}{6}
\end{aligned}
$$

A similar argument shows that three distinct randomly selected points from I have probability $\frac{2}{3}$ of being a canonical set. One or two randomly selected points have probability 1 of being a canonical set.

Let I_j denote the set of all subsets of size j of the data set I, for $j = 1, 2, 3, 4$. For all sets S in I_j, let $\chi_S = 1$ if the points in S are the canonical points for the rectangle they represent, and $\chi_S = 0$ otherwise. The expected number r of query rectangles in I can be bounded as follows:

$$
\begin{aligned}
E[\text{Number of Query Rectangles}] \\
&= \sum_{j=1}^4 E[\text{Number of j-point Query Rectangles}] \\
&= \sum_{j=1}^4 E[\sum_{S \in I_j} \chi_S] \\
&= \sum_{j=1}^4 \sum_{S \in I_j} E[\chi_S] \\
&> \sum_{j=1}^4 \sum_{S \in I_j} (1/6) \\
&= \sum_{j=1}^4 \frac{1}{6} \binom{n}{j}.
\end{aligned}
$$

Since the expected number of trials of the Las Vegas algorithm is $\frac{t}{r}$, where $t = \sum_{j=1}^4 \binom{n}{j}$, the expected number of trials on data set I is less than 6. As n increases, the expected number of trials approaches 6, because for large n, $\binom{n}{4} \gg \binom{n}{j}$ for $j = 1, 2, 3$. $\qquad\qquad\qquad\square$

3   Empirical Performance

In order to validate the efficiency of the Las Vegas algorithm in practice, we conducted several experiments over standard synthetic and geographic data sets. We also used a technique called Lévy flights [21] to generate sets of points with fractal dimension similar to those found in real-life data [4,1]. All data sets were normalized to the unit square. In particular, we used the following 2-dimensional data sets:

- Uniform: In this data set 100000 points are uniformly distributed in the unit square.
- Double Cluster: This data set contains two clusters of approximately 50000 points each, one centered near the origin, and the other close to the point

Data Sets	Algorithm Performance		Query Properties (average over 1000 queries)		
	Average #Trials per Query Rectangle	Seconds for 1000 Queries	Mean Area	Mean Cardinality	Mean Aspect Ratio
Uniform	6.033	3.61	0.36475	35.67%	1.170289
Double Cluster	9.530	4.04	0.3015	39.28%	1.124432
LBCounty	8.640	3.25	0.17285	36.62%	1.138304
MGCounty	6.950	2.95	0.1351	37.19%	1.234010
Lévy 1.46	12.92	4.64	0.06955	33.60%	4.993343
Lévy 1.68	8.741	3.87	0.08729	35.11%	0.360295

Table 1. Performance of the Randomized Algorithm, and Properties of the Random Range Queries

$(1,1)$. The points in each cluster follow a 2-dimensional independent Gaussian distribution with $\sigma^2 = 0.1$.

- LBCounty: This data set is part of the TIGER database [22] and contains 53145 road intersections from Long Beach County, CA.
- MGCounty: The same as above from Montgomery County, MD containing 39231 points.
- Lévy 1.46: This is a data set of 100000 points generated by the Lévy flight generator, with fractal dimension approximately 1.46.
- Lévy 1.68: The fractal dimension here was close to 1.68 with the same number of points as above.

We used a main memory implementation of the algorithm to generate 1000 random range queries for each data set and the results are shown in Table 1. The cost of the algorithm is expressed both as the number of trials per random range query, and the elapsed time. Recall that all datasets are the same size except for the two real datasets. For the Uniform data set the cost was very close to 6 trials, as anticipated. For the Double Cluster data set the cost was a little higher but remained small. The algorithm performed very well for the real-life data sets even though these data sets are clearly non-uniform. Finally, for the Lévy Flights data sets, the one with fractal dimension 1.46 had the higher cost[2]. The results of the experiments indicate that our randomized algorithm is quite efficient in practice, and robust across a variety of distributions.

---

[2] This matches the intuition behind the use of fractal dimension in [4]: as discussed in Section 2.4, data laid out on a line (fractal dimension 1) results in more trials than data laid out uniformly in 2-space (fractal dimension 2), hence one should expect worse performance with lower fractal dimension. Unfortunately in further experiments we found counter-examples to this trend; additional study of fractal dimension and query generation seems interesting, but is beyond the scope of this paper.

4   Properties of Random Range Queries

In this section we consider various properties of the random range queries generated by our algorithm; in particular we consider the area, cardinality and aspect ratio of the query rectangles. Note that, given a data set, the areas of the query rectangles defined by that data set may not be uniformly distributed. In fact, as we show here, the contrary is often true.

We first prove a result concerning uniform datasets.

Proposition 6. *Let I be a uniform dataset of size $n \geq 4$. Let $z = (p_1, \ldots, p_4)$ be four distinct random points chosen from I. The expected area of the rectangle defined by z, given that z is the set of canonical set of points of a rectangle, is $\eta = 0.36$, and the variance is $\sigma^2 = 0.03$*

Proof. Let B be the event that z is the canonical set of points for a query rectangle, and let A_σ be the event associated with the permutation σ as above (Proposition 5). Then for $\sigma_0 = (x_1, x_2, x_3, x_4)$ the area of the generated rectangle is $g(z) = |x_4 - x_1||y_3 - y_2|$. Hence, the expected area is:

$$Expected\ Area = E\{g(z)|B\} = \int_B \frac{g(z)dz}{P(B)} = 6 \times \int_B g(z)dz$$

$$= 6 \times \sum_\sigma \int_{B \cap A_\sigma} g(z)dz$$

$$= 6 \times 4! \times \int_{B \cap A_\sigma} g(z)dz$$

$$= 6 \times 4! \times 2 \times \int_0^1 dx_4 \int_0^{x_4} dx_1 \int_{x_1}^{x_4} dx_2 \int_{x_2}^{x_4} dx_3 (x_4 - x_1)$$

$$\int_0^1 dy_3 \int_0^{y_3} dy_2 \int_{y_2}^{y_3} dy_1 \int_{y_2}^{y_3} dy_4 (y_3 - y_2)$$

$$= \frac{36}{100}$$

Similarly, the variance is computed equal to $\sigma^2 = 0.03$.   □

If we run our algorithm on a uniform dataset of any reasonably large size, then with high probability, the rectangle returned by the algorithm will be a 4-point query rectangle (because in each trial, the probability that the algorithm generates a 4-point set is very high, and on a uniform dataset, the probability that a 4-point trial is successful is $1/6$). Thus, by Proposition 6, the expected area of a rectangle generated by running our algorithm on a reasonably large uniform dataset is approximately .36, with variance approximately .03. A similar analysis shows that the expected aspect ratio of the generated rectangle (defined as the ratio of x-side over y-side) will be approximately 1.2 with variance approximately 0.96.

In light of the above results, we were interested in the spatial properties (namely area and aspect ratio) for all of our data sets. Table 1 shows the mean

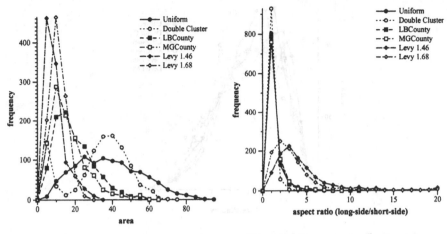

Fig. 6. Frequencies of query-area for various distributions.

Fig. 7. Frequencies of query-aspect-ratio for various distributions.

values of the three spatial properties in experiments of 1000 random range queries over each of the various data sets. Figure 6 shows the frequency graphs of the areas of the queries for each data set. From Figure 6 is clear that the distribution of the area of the generated random range queries is highly dependent on the underlying data set. The Uniform data set gives a variety of large-area range queries, whereas for the fractal data sets most of the query rectangles are smaller than 10% of the total area. In Figure 7 we present the frequencies of the aspect ratio (long-side/short-side) for the same set of range queries, and in Figure 8 we present the frequencies of cardinalities. Note that cardinality seems to be less sensitive to data distribution than the spatial properties.

One conclusion of this analysis is that a domain-independent "logical" query generator may have unusual properties, and those properties may vary widely in data-dependent ways. This is a cautionary lesson about generating test queries in a domain-independent fashion, which undoubtedly applies to the generation of queries over indexes in domains other than spatial range queries. A natural alternative is to consider using domain-specific query generators when possible. To explore this idea further, we proceed to examine domain-specific spatial query generation techniques from the literature, and demonstrate that they raise complementary and potentially problematic issues of their own.

5 Alternative Techniques for Query Generation

As remarked above, other authors have considered domain-dependent query distributions. The most extensive exploration of such distributions is due to Pagel et al. [17]. They considered the expected cost of 2-d range queries over distributions other than the logical distribution; in particular they proposed four specific classes of distributions.

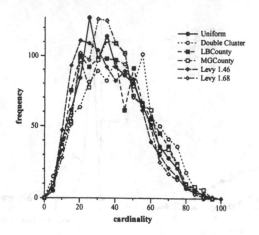

Fig. 8. Frequencies of query-cardinality for various distributions.

The first class, called QM_1, consists of distributions that are uniform over the space of all squares of area k (for some fixed k) whose centers fall "within the data space", i.e., within the spatial boundaries of the existing data set. This is a natural scheme with clear domain-specific properties. However, using a distribution from this class to test the performance of an index has notable drawbacks. The workloads generated from this distribution are very sensitive to the data distribution, and may not be statistically sound in *covering* the possible behaviors of the index. For example, if the area k is a relatively small fraction of the data space (as is common in many previous studies), and if the data is clustered in a small region of the data space, then random squares chosen from QM_1 are likely to be empty. Repeatedly testing an index on empty queries may not yield the kind of information desired in experiments.

The other classes of distributions proposed by Pagel et al. attempt to overcome such drawbacks. Each of these classes is defined in terms of a density function D on the data space. One, called QM_2, is like QM_1 in that it consists of distributions over the space of squares of area k, for some fixed k, whose centers are within the the data space. In QM_2 distributions, though, the probability of each square is weighted according to the value of D at the square's center. The remaining two classes of distributions, QM_3 and QM_4 are over the space of squares that enclose a fixed fraction s of the total probability mass (as defined by D), for some s, whose centers are within the data space. Distributions in QM_3 are uniform over such squares, and distributions in QM_4 weight each square according to the value of D at its center.

Pagel et al. point out that the expected cost of performing a random rectangular query in a particular LSD-tree (or R-tree, or similar data structure) is equal to the sum, over all leaves in the tree, of the probability that a random rectangle intersects the rectangular region defined by the points stored in that leaf [17]. They use this fact to compute analytically, for particular trees, the expected cost of a random rectangular query drawn from a distribution in QM_1. In contrast, to compute the expected cost of a rectangular query drawn from the logical distribution on rectangular queries, we would use an empirical approach; we would generate random queries, determine the cost of each, and take an average. The logical distribution is a difficult one to work with analytically; unlike distributions in QM_1, it is a discrete distribution defined by a data set.

In later experimental work [18,16], Pagel et al. use only distributions in QM_1. As they point out, exactly computing expected query cost with respect to distributions in QM_3 and QM_4 can be difficult [17]. In addition, distributions in QM_2, QM_3, and QM_4 are defined in terms of a distribution D on the data space. Since a real data set does not directly provide a distribution D on the data space, the last three query distributions are not well-defined "in the field," that is, for real data sets (although in some cases it may be feasible to model the distribution D).

In short, the Pagel query distributions present a mirror image of our logical query distribution. The Pagel distributions' domain-specific properties are easily controlled, and they are amenable to analytic analyses – they appeal to the intuitive properties of 2-space. By contrast, the logical properties of these distributions (e.g. query cardinality) are sensitive to data-distribution and often wildly skewed, and some of the available techniques are inapplicable to real data sets. The domain-specific and logical distributions have very different strengths and weaknesses for studying indexes, and we elaborate on this in the next section.

6   On Randomization, Benchmarks, and Performance Studies

One advantage of domain-dependent distributions like QM_1 is that they attempt to model a class of user behavior. This is the goal of so-called *Domain-Specific Benchmarking* [7], and is clearly a good idea: one main motivation for benchmarking is to analyze how well a technique works overall for an important class of users. In the case of spatial queries it makes sense to choose square queries of small area, for example, since users with graphical user interfaces are likely to "drag" such squares with their mouse. This is natural when trying to get detail about a small portion of a larger space shown on screen – e.g., given a map of the world one might drag a square around Wisconsin.

But random workloads can also be used to learn more about a technique – in particular to "stress test" it. To do this, one wants to provide a diversity of inputs to the technique, in order to identify the inputs it handles gracefully, and those it handles poorly. For indexes, a workload is described logically as a set of queries (subsets of the data), and the indexing problem can be set up as a logical optimization problem: an indexing scheme [10] should cluster items into fixed-size buckets to optimize some metric on bucket-fetches over the workload (e.g. minimize the total number of bucket fetches for a set of queries run in sequence). It is by no means clear that domain-specific considerations help set up these stress tests – logical workloads seem more natural for this task.

One can easily quibble with both of these characterizations, however. Clearly the (domain-dependent) $\mathcal{QM}_1$ workloads do a bad job of modeling user behavior when they generate many empty queries – in essence, they ignore the fact that users often do care about logical properties like cardinality. Conversely, the stress imposed by the logical workload on a 2-d index is questionable if most of the queries are actually large and squarish as in Table 1: evidence suggests that long, skinny queries are the real nemesis of spatial indexes like R-trees, which usuall try to cluster points into squarish regions [17,12][3].

What then can one conclude about the pros and cons of logical and domain-specific query generation? In short, that regardless of the technique an experimentalist uses to generate queries, she needs to understand and be able to control the distribution of a workload over domain-specific and logical properties of relevance. Identifying these properties is not a simple problem, and understanding how to generate queries that are well distributed over them is a further challenge. One strong conclusion of our work is that this process has been little explored in index experiments to date, and is in fact fairly complex.

Two-dimensional range queries are probably the best-understood, non-trivial indexing challenge. Thus a natural direction for future work is to attempt and merge the insights from the previous sections to develop a malleable, well-understood toolkit for experimenting with 2-d indexes. We conclude by exploring some ideas in this direction, and raising questions for generating queries in other domains.

7   Conclusion and Future Directions

In this paper we highlight a new approach to generating random queries for index experimentation, which uses a logical distribution on queries. We present an algorithm to generate queries from this distribution, showing that it has good expected performance for some distributions, and good measured performance over a variety of real and synthetic data. A remaining open problem is to devise an algorithm for this task with good guaranteed time- and space-efficiency over all point distributions.

The very different properties of this distribution and previously proposed distributions suggest a new line of research: developing techniques to allow experimentalists to easily understand and control various properties of their workload. A direct attack on this problem is to first map desired domain-dependent properties into a distribution over the space of logical queries, and then devise an efficient algorithm for choosing from that distribution. In general this seems quite difficult, but the original problem tackled in this paper is a simple instance of this approach: it specifies a distribution over all queries $P(D)$, with 100% of the distribution falling into the (domain-specific) category of query rectangles. Perhaps this direct approach will prove tractable for other simple spatial distributions as well.

---

[3] In fact our interest in the subject of random 2-d range queries was sparked by an attempt to experimentally validate this hypothesis for a variety of spatial indexes!

In addition to this direct theoretical challenge, a variety of potentially useful heuristics suggest themselves as well. Rather than map spatial properties to a distribution over the logical queries, one can simply partition the data set on spatial properties, and use the uniform logical distribution over the partitions. For example, to generate a distribution with smaller average query area, one can tile the data space and run our Las Vegas algorithm over data partitions that correspond to tiles. This seems rather *ad hoc*, but is perhaps easier to reason about logically than the totally domain-specific techniques of Pagel, et al. It is also applicable to extant "real-world" data sets.

Another heuristic is to introduce new points into the query generator's data set in order to achieve biases on spatial properties. For example, to increase the variance in aspect ratio of a uniformly distributed point set, one can insert clusters of points along the extremes of one axis or the other. One can then run the resulting queries over the original data set. This may allow for a better control over the resulting query mix than a domain specific spatial technique. The goal of the future research should be the creation of a domain-independed framework for index benchmarking and testing.

Acknowledgments

We thank Dina Kravets, Joe Kilian, and Boris Aronov for useful discussions, and Jeff Sidell for his Lévy flight generator.

References

1. Alberto Belussi and Christos Faloutsos. Estimating the Selectivity of Spatial Queries Using the 'Correlation' Fractal Dimension. In *Proc. 21st International Conference on Very Large Data Bases*, Zurich, September 1995, pages 299–310.
2. Norbert Beckmann, Hans-Peter Kriegel, Ralf Schneider, and Bernhard Seeger. The R*-tree: An Efficient and Robust Access Method For Points and Rectangles. In *Proc. ACM-SIGMOD International Conference on Management of Data*, pages 322–331, Atlantic City, May 1990.
3. Georgios Evangelidis, David B. Lomet, and Betty Salzberg. The hBΠ-tree: A Modified hB-tree Supporting Concurrency, Recovery and Node Consolidation. In *Proc. 21st International Conference on Very Large Data Bases*, Zurich, September 1995, pages 551–561.
4. Christos Faloutsos and Ibrahim Kamel. Beyond Uniformity and Independence: Analysis of R-trees Using the Concept of Fractal Dimension. In *Proc. 13th ACM SIGACT-SIGMOD-SIGART Symposium on Principles of Database Systems*, pages 4–13, Minneapolis, May 1994.
5. V. Gaede and O. Gunther. Multidimensional Access Methods. *ACM Computing Surveys*, 1997. To appear.
6. O. Gunther, V. Oria, P. Picouet, J.-M. Saglio, and M. Scholl. Benchmarking Spatial Joins A la Carte. In J. Ferriee (ed.), *Proc. 13e Journees Bases de Donnees Avancees*, Grenoble, 1997.
7. Jim Gray. *The Benchmark Handbook for Database and Transaction Processing Systems, Second Edition*. Morgan Kauffman, San Francisco, 1993.

8. Diane Greene. An Implementation and Performance Analysis of Spatial Data Access Methods. In *Proc. 5th IEEE International Conference on Data Engineering*, pages 606–615, 1989.

9. Antonin Guttman. R-Trees: A Dynamic Index Structure For Spatial Searching. In *Proc. ACM-SIGMOD International Conference on Management of Data*, pages 47–57, Boston, June 1984.

10. Joseph M. Hellerstein, Elias Koutsoupias, and Christos H. Papadimitriou. On the Analysis of Indexing Schemes. In *Proc. 16th ACM SIGACT-SIGMOD-SIGART Symposium on Principles of Database Systems*, pages 249–256, Tucson, May 1997.

11. Joseph M. Hellerstein, Jeffrey F. Naughton, and Avi Pfeffer. Generalized Search Trees for Database Systems. In *Proc. 21st International Conference on Very Large Data Bases*, Zurich, September 1995.

12. Ibrahim Kamel and Christos Faloutsos. On Packing R-trees. In *Proc. Second Int. Conference on Information and Knowledge Management (CIKM)*, Washington, DC, Nov. 1-5, 1993.

13. Curtis P. Kolovson and Michael Stonebraker. Segment Indexes: Dynamic Indexing Techniques for Multi-Dimensional Interval Data. In *Proc. ACM-SIGMOD International Conference on Management of Data*, pages 138–147, Denver, June 1991.

14. Marcel Kornacker, Mehul Shah, and Joseph M. Hellerstein. amdb: An Access Method Debugging Toolkit. In *Proc. ACM-SIGMOD International Conference on Management of Data*, Seattle, June 1998.

15. Elias Koutsoupias and David Scot Taylor. Tight bounds for 2-dimensional Indexing Schemes. In *Proc. 17th ACM PODS Symposium on Principles of Database Systems*, Seattle, 1998.

16. Bernd-Uwe Pagel and Hans-Werner Six. Are Window Queries Represesntative for Arbitrary Range Queries? In *Proc. 15th ACM PODS Symposium on Principles of Database Systems*, pages 151–160, 1996.

17. Bernd-Uwe Pagel, Hans-Werner Six, Heinrich Toben, and Peter Widmayer. Towards an Analysis of Range Query Performance in Spatial Data Structures. In *Proc. 12th ACM SIGACT-SIGMOD-SIGART Symposium on Principles of Database Systems*, pages 214–221, Washington, D. C., May 1993.

18. Bernd-Uwe Pagel, Hans-Werner Six, and Mario Winter. Window Query-Optimal Clustering of Spatial Objects In *Proc. 14th ACM PODS Symposium on Principles of Database Systems*, pages 86–94, 1995.

19. Vasilis Samoladas and Daniel P. Miranker. A Lower Bound Theorem for Indexing Schemes and its Application to Multidimensional Range Queries In *Proc. 17th ACM PODS Symposium on Principles of Database Systems*, Seattle, 1998.

20. Timos K. Sellis, Nick Roussopoulos, and Christos Faloutsos. Multidimensional Access Methods: Trees Have Grown Everywhere. In *Proc. 23rd International Conference on Very Large Data Bases*, Athens, August 1997.

21. Shlesinger, Zaslavsky, and Frisch (Eds.), editors. *Levy Flights and Related Topics in Physics*. Springer-Verlag, 1995.

22. U.S. Bureau of the Census. TiGER Files(TM), 1992 Technical Documentation, 1992.

Increasing the Expressiveness of Analytical Performance Models for Replicated Databases

Matthias Nicola   Matthias Jarke

Technical University of Aachen, Informatik V (Information Systems)
Ahornstr. 55, 52056 Aachen, Germany
nicola@informatik.rwth-aachen.de

Abstract. The vast number of design options in replicated databases requires efficient analytical performance evaluations so that the considerable overhead of simulations or measurements can be focused on a few promising options. A review of existing analytical models in terms of their modeling assumptions, replication schemata considered, and network properties captured, shows that data replication and intersite communication as well as workload patterns should be modeled more accurately. Based on this analysis, we define a new modeling approach named 2RC (2-dimensional replication model with integrated communication). We derive a complete analytical queueing model for 2RC and demonstrate that it is of higher expressiveness than existing models. 2RC also yields a novel bottleneck analysis and permits to evaluate the trade-off between throughput and availability.

1 Introduction

Replication management in distributed databases concerns the decision when and where to allocate physical copies of logical data fragments (replica placement), and when and how to update them to maintain an acceptable degree of mutual consistency (replica control). Replication intends to increase data availability in the presence of site or communication failures, and to decrease retrieval costs by local access if possible. The maintenance of replicated data is therefore closely related to intersite communication, and replication management has significant impact on the overall system performance.

The literature offers several algorithms for replica placement [32,22] as well as for replica control [8,9,15]. However, the sophistication of such methods is not matched by today's analytical models for performance evaluation. Considering the vast number of alternatives in the design of a replication schema, it becomes apparent that existing analytical models only consider very extreme replication schemata, e.g. no replication or full replication. Furthermore, the important role of intersite communication in replica management is not sufficiently taken into account. While the evolution and symbiosis of distributed database and modern communication systems is progressing, theoretical performance models to evaluate such systems lag

Catriel Beeri, Peter Buneman (Eds.): ICDT'99, LNCS 1540, pp. 131-149, 1998.
© Springer-Verlag Berlin Heidelberg 1998

behind. Our aim is to identify and remedy such flaws in the performance evaluations and to derive an analytical modeling approach that describes real-world replicated databases more accurately so that new and more expressive results are obtained.

In section 2 we present a critical review of existing performance models including a formal classification of how replication can be modeled. Section 3 presents the requirements for a new comprehensive performance model (2RC) to overcome the deficiencies of existing approaches. A new 2-dimensional model of replication and the dependency structure captured in 2RC is described. Section 4 develops an analytical queueing model that implements 2RC. It is based on the 2D-replication model and a detailed communication model. Section 5 presents results derived from our model, including a bottleneck analysis which is the critical part of any analytical throughput estimation [33].

2   Shortcomings in Existing Performance Models

In this section we analyze alternatives in performance modeling of distributed databases which reveals drawbacks in existing studies and motivates 2RC.

2.1   General Modeling Concepts and Communication

Performance studies of distributed databases employed analytical methods [20,26,27, 16,13,2], as well as simulations [3,17,25,31,18,29,10,7]. Simulations can evaluate complex system models whose level of detail precludes analytical solutions. However, simulations are costly in terms of programming and computing time. Thus, simulations often fail to cover the parameter space and to carry out a sensitivity analysis as thoroughly as desired.

Simulation and analytical studies often use queueing systems as the underlying models. Early queueing models of distributed databases model a fully replicated database of m local sites by a M/M/m/FCFS system with blocking [4,11,24]. Read transactions are processed by the m servers in parallel, while write transactions block all m servers. This models shared reads and exclusive writes. Major drawbacks of these models are that intersite communication is neglected and all sites share a single queue of incoming transactions.

To remedy these flaws, distributed databases can be modeled by *queueing networks*. [10, 23] use networks of M/M/1 queues, i.e. each local database is modeled as an M/M/1 system. However, this still restricts all transactions to have the same exponentially distributed service times. More general, [5,16] model the local databases as M/G/1 queues with arbitrarily distributed service times, while [13,20] use networks of $M/H_2/1$ systems with 2-phase hyper-exponentially distributed service times to assign different exponentially distributed service times to read-only transactions and updates. Nevertheless, such models do not allow to evaluate real-world systems with more than two transaction types.

Most analytical performance studies model the communication network by an infinite server that introduces a constant delay for each message, regardless of message size or network load [14,23,13,21,16,20]. "Infinite" means unlimited transmission capacity, no queueing of messages, and the network is never considered to be the bottleneck. Such models would predict that replication always deteriorates throughput but never increases it, which we will disprove in section 5. In modern, large wide area applications and in wireless and mobile information systems that suffer from low bandwidth, the communication links may indeed become a bottleneck. However, very few analytical studies tried to combine a detailed database model with a detailed communication model [2,26]. Most authors also assume uniformly distributed data access, i.e. each data item is accessed with equal probability [14,28,10,5,23,18, 29,21,20,3]. Non-uniform data access is more realistic but modeled in very few analytical studies [31,16]. Lock conflicts and blocking of transactions are usually only modeled to compare concurrency control algorithms [14,7,10,18,21]. Such models are of considerable complexity. They typically have to use simulations and simplified modeling assumptions concerning replication and communication.

2.2   Classification of Replication Models

Some performance studies of distributed databases simply assume *no replication*, i.e. each logical data item is represented by exactly one physical copy, [28,21]. Other models consider full or 1-dimensional partial replication:

(1) All objects to all sites (full replication)
Most performance evaluations assume full replication [11,14,4,24,23,18,29,27,3,17] i.e. all data objects are replicated to all sites so that each site holds a complete copy of the distributed database. This is an extreme case of replication and it has been recognized that for most applications neither full nor no replication is the optimal configuration [10,13,1].

(2) All objects to some sites (1-dimensional partial replication)
Several studies modeled partial replication in the way that each data object is replicated to some of the sites [7,10,16,31,20]. Formally, the degree of replication can be denoted by a parameter $r \in \{1,2,...,n\}$, describing that each logical data item is represented by r physical copies, where n is the number of sites. $r = 1$ expresses no replication, $r = n$ means full replication, and if $r > 1$, every data item is replicated. Consequently, either no or all data items are replicated. In many applications there is update-intensive data which should be replicated to very few sites while read intensive data should be replicated to many sites. This common situation cannot be modeled with the all-objects-to-some-sites scheme.

(3) Some objects to all sites (1-dimensional partial replication)
Alternatively, the degree of replication can be denoted by $r \in [0;1]$ describing the percentage of logical data items that are fully replicated to all sites. A data item is either fully replicated or not replicated at all. $r = 0$ expresses no replication, $r = 1$ means full replication. To the best of our knowledge, this model of partial replication

has only been considered in [2,13,1]. The some-objects-to-all-sites scheme is orthogonal to the all-objects-to-some-sites approach since the degree of replication is defined along the percentage of data items as opposed to the number of copies. However, in large wide area distributed databases it is hardly affordable to replicate some data items to all sites (causing considerable update propagation overhead) and others to none (reducing their availability severely). Thus, the some-objects-to-all-sites scheme is not realistic.

3 A 2D-Replication Model with Integrated Communication (2RC)

Learning from the existing models, we define the requirements for an improved modeling approach:

A more expressive model of replication is needed to represent and evaluate realistic replication schemata. Not only response time but also throughput and bottlenecks must be computable as important performance criteria. This requires to capture load dependent communication delay, network limited transaction throughput, and the interplay between replication and communication. Detailed transaction and communication patterns must be describable, so that real-world applications can be modeled. Non-uniform data access, the quality of replication schemata and relaxed coherency must also be considered.

All these requirements are met by 2RC. Additionally, the model of transaction processing in 2RC follows the primary copy approach [30], since it has been judged advantageous over other replica control concepts [15,18] and is implemented in commercial systems like Sybase and Oracle. In 2RC, asynchronous update propagation to the secondary copies is modeled, i.e. 2-phase-commit processing of updates is not considered, and transactions are assumed to be executed at a single site, either the local or a remote site. Since 2RC is not primarily intended to compare concurrency control algorithms, it refrains from modeling lock conflicts to allow for more details in the replication and communication submodels.

3.1 The 2-Dimensional Model of Replication

Based on the classification of section 2.2, the two orthogonal 1-dimensional concepts are combined to a new 2-dimensional scheme called "*Some objects to some sites*". In this, replication is modeled by a pair $(r_1, r_2) \in [0;1] \times \{2,...,n\}$ such that $r_1 \in [0;1]$ describes the percentage of logical data items which are represented by r_2 physical copies each, i.e. they are replicated to r_2 of the n sites. A share of $1 - r_1$ logical data items remain unreplicated. $r_1 = 0$ expresses no replication, $(r_1 = 1, r_2 = n)$ means full replication.

For d logical data items, a replication schema (r_1, r_2) increases the number of physical copies from d (no replication) to $(r_1 \cdot d \cdot r_2) + (d \cdot (1 - r_1))$. Viewing the number of copies of replicated objects $(r_1 \cdot d \cdot r_2)$ as the actual extent of replication, we express it (for visualization and further calculations) independently from d and normalized to the interval [0;1] as an overall level of replication, yielding $(r_1 \cdot r_2)/n$. This characteristic of the 2D-approach is depicted in Fig. 1 for $n = 50$ sites. Performance models which assume full replication only consider the point $(1,n)$ as the possible replication schema. The all-objects-to-some-sites scheme analyses replication along the bold line from point (1,50) to (1,0) only. The orthogonal some-objects-to-all-sites scheme studies replication along the line from (1,50) to (0,50) only. However, the 2D-scheme considers any point in Fig. 1 a possible replication schema so that real-world replication strategies can be captured more accurately. Thus, we believe that the 2D-model is a profitable contribution towards a better understanding of how replication affects distributed system performance.

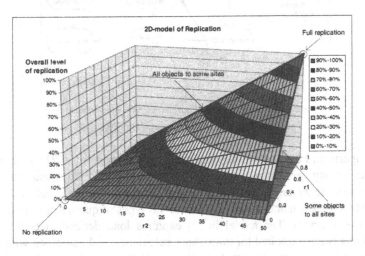

Fig. 1. The 2-dimensional model of replication

3.2   Dependency Structure

Apart from *how* the various aspects of a real system are modeled, it also matters which *dependencies* between them are considered in the model. Fig. 2 sketches the structure of dependencies we consider in 2RC. Rectangular nodes represent input parameters and modeling assumptions, oval nodes stand for intermediate or final results, the latter in bold. An arrow from a node A to a node B indicates that B depends directly on A. The 2D-replication scheme is a core part of our model and has direct impact on the quality of replication, the arrival rates and the network traffic, and thus substantial influence on all further results. τ transaction types (with different arrival rates and service time distributions) and 2 message types per transaction (with individually distributed transmission times depending on the message size) allow to model a wide range of different applications and workload patterns. The two bold arrows highlight the important dependencies through which load dependent communication delay and network limited throughput are captured. The overall throughput depends on both the network and the local database throughput, which allows a bottleneck analysis.

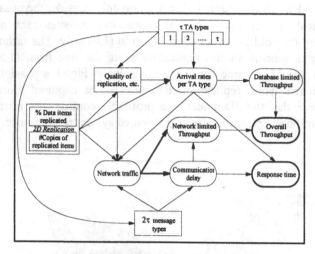

Fig. 2. Dependency structure of 2RC

For comparison, Fig. 3 shows the dependencies captured in [16,2] which we found typical for many analytical models. The model in [16] assumes constant communication delay and unlimited network capacity. On the database side, they consider 1D-replication and do not allow different types of queries or updates (like all models we examined). The model in [2] captures load dependent communication delay, but this is not exploited for throughput calculation and combined with a simple replication and transaction model. In [16] and [2] the arrival rates depend on non-uniform data access, modeled by a factor for access locality and hot spot access respectively, while such dependencies are neglected in most other studies. Almost all analytical studies fail to cover sufficient dependencies between transaction processing and communication, so that they do not calculate throughput as a performance criterion. In conclusion, 2RC combines a comprehensive database and replication model with a detailed communication model, and covers more interdependencies between the two than previous studies.

4   Analytical Queueing Model for 2RC

This section presents the mathematical implementation of a queueing model of a replicated database according to the 2RC approach. Table 1 shows the model parameters.

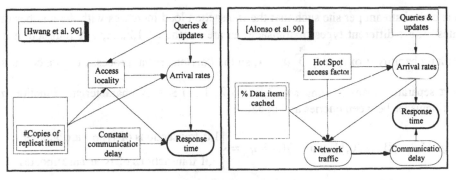

Fig. 3. Dependencies in Hwang et al. 96 [16] and Alonso et al. 90 [2].

Parameter	Meaning
n	Number of sites
τ	Number of transaction types
a_i	Percentage of transactions of type i
q_i	Function to distinguish between queries and updates
λ_i	Transaction arrival rate per site (TPS) of TA type i
r_1	Percentage of data items replicated
r_2	No. of copies of replicated data items
t_i	Mean service time for a transaction of type i (sec)
k	Coherency index
$baud$	Communication bandwidth (bps)
loc_i	Transactions' locality without replication
$plcmt_i$	Quality of replica placement
sel_i	Quality of replica selection
f_plcmt_i	Fine tuning replica placement
f_sel_i	Fine tuning replica selection
ℓ_i	Probability of local transaction execution
$size_c^{send-i}$	Message size for a send of a transaction of type i.
$size_c^{return-i}$	Message size of returned query results (byte)
t_c^{send-i}	Mean time to send a transaction of type (sec)
$t_c^{return-i}$	Mean time to return query results (sec)

Table 1. Model parameters.

4.1 Workload

We model a replicated database by an open queueing network in which each of the n identical sites is represented by a $M/H_\tau/1$ system. Transaction arrivals to the distributed system are modeled by n identical Poisson processes with parameter λ, i.e.

one arrival stream per site such that the transaction load increases with the number of sites. The τ different types of transactions are numbered $1,2,.....,\tau$. A transaction is with probability a_i of type i, $\sum_{i=1}^{\tau} a_i = 1$, so the Poisson arrival process at a site consists of τ separate streams having rate $\lambda_i = a_i \cdot \lambda$, $1 \leq i \leq \tau$. A characteristic function q distinguishes between queries and updates:

$$q: \{1,2,...,\tau\} \rightarrow \{0,1\} \text{ with } q(i) = q_i = \begin{cases} 1, \text{if transactions of type } i \text{ are queries} \\ 0, \text{if transactions of type } i \text{ are updates} \end{cases}$$

The number of data objects accessed per transaction is assumed to be geometrically distributed, so the service time for a transaction of type i at a local database is modeled as exponentially distributed with mean t_i (seconds) [28]. Thus, the service time for the combined arrival process of all τ transaction types follows a τ-phase hyperexponential distribution.

4.2   Locality and Quality of Replication

Without replication but due to skillful data allocation transactions exhibit a behaviour of locality, i.e. they tend to access data items locally available at their site of submission. This is modeled by the probability $loc_i \in [0;1]$ $(1 \leq i \leq \tau)$ that a transaction of type i can be executed at the local site, while it has to be forwarded to a remote site with probability $1 - loc_i$. Introducing partial replication (r_1, r_2) then increases the probability that a query can be answered locally by $(r_1 \cdot r_2)/n$. Due to the primary copy approach, the write availability does not increase.

The *selection* of data items to replicate and the decision where to *place* them can have significant impact on the overall system performance [32]. Thus, we consider this quality of a replication design in the performance evaluation. We find that *replica selection* has major impact on updates, while *replica placement* is more significant for query processing:

Updates: Selecting many update intensive data items for replication causes high update propagation overhead. Therefore we introduce a "selection parameter" $sel_i \in [0;1/r_i]$ for $1 \leq i \leq \tau$ and $q(i) = 0$, expressing to which extent updates of type i tend to access data items that were selected for replication. $sel_i = 0$ means that the replicated data items are never changed by updates of type i. $sel_i = 1$ signals no preferences towards replicated or unreplicated data, and $sel_i = 1/r_i$ declares that replica selection is so unfortunate that updates of type i always access replicated data.

Queries: Even if all read intensive data items are replicated, performance gains are quite low as long as these replicas are not available locally to the queries. Thus, a "placement parameter" $plcmt_i \in [1; n/(r_1 \cdot r_2)]$ for $1 \leq i \leq \tau$ and $q(i) = 1$ expresses to which extent replica placement is increasing the probability that a query of type i can be executed locally. $plcmt_i = 1$ means that replica placement does not necessarily increase the queries' locality, and $plcmt_i = n/(r_i \cdot r_2)$ declares that queries of type i can always run at their home sites.

The higher the degree of replication the more likely it is that not only update intensive data items are selected for replication, and the more likely it is that replication increases the local read probability. Therefore, the parameters sel_i and $plcmt_i$ have to depend on the degree of replication and are defined as

$$plcmt_i = \frac{1}{\left(\dfrac{r_1 \cdot r_2}{n}\right)^{f\_plcmt_i}} \quad \text{and} \quad sel_i = \frac{1}{(r_1)^{f\_sel_i}}$$

so that the parameters $f\_plcmt_i \in [0,1]$ and $f\_sel_i \in [-\infty,1]$ can „fine-tune" how far or close $plcmt_i$ and sel_i follow their optimum values $n/(r_i \cdot r_2)$ and $1/r_i$ respectively.

We assume that the replicas are distributed evenly across the sites, so that each site receives an equal share of forwarded transactions and propagated updates. Thus, the overall probability ℓ_i that a transaction of type i ($1 \leq i \leq \tau$) can be executed at its local site amounts to

$$\ell_i = loc_i + q_i \cdot (1 - loc_i) \cdot \frac{r_1 \cdot r_2}{n} \cdot plcmt_i$$

because without replication a transaction is processed locally with probability loc_i (first term). With probability $1 - loc_i$ queries ($q_i = 1$) cannot be executed locally, but replication increases the local read availability by $(r_i \cdot r_2)/n$ or higher, depending on the replica placement (second term). Note, that loc_i, sel_i and $plcmt_i$ model non-uniform data access.

4.3 Transaction Processing and Arrival Rates

The performance of replicated databases can be improved if the requirement of mutual consistency among the replicas of a logical data item is relaxed. Various concepts of relaxed coherency can be denoted by coherency conditions which allow to calculate a coherency index $k \in [0;1]$ as a measure of the degree of allowed divergence [13]. Small values of k express high relaxation, $k = 0$ models suspended update propagation, and for $k = 1$ updates are propagated immediately.

For $1 \leq i \leq \tau$, the total arrival rate λ_i^{total} of transactions of type i at a single site amounts to

$$\lambda_i^{total} = \ell_i \cdot \lambda_i + (n-1) \cdot (1 - \ell_i) \cdot \lambda_i \cdot \frac{1}{n-1} + (1 - q_i) \cdot (n-1) \cdot (r_1 \cdot sel_i) \cdot \frac{r_2 - 1}{n-1} \cdot k \cdot \lambda_i$$

because a share of ℓ_i of the incoming λ_i transactions can be executed locally (first term) whereas the remaining $(1 - \ell_i) \cdot \lambda_i$ transactions are forwarded to sites where appropriate data is available. The other $n-1$ sites also forward $1-\ell_i$ of their λ_i transactions which are received by each of the remaining databases with equal probability $1/(n-1)$. This explains the second term. The third term covers update propagation and its possible reduction through relaxed coherency: If transactions of type i are updates (i.e. $1 - q(i) = 1$) the local load λ_i^{total} is increased by update propagation from the $n-1$ remote sites. The probability that an update at one of the $n-1$ remote sites hits a primary copy which is replicated, is $r_1 \cdot sel_i$. The probability, that one of the corresponding secondary copies resides at the local database is $(r_2-1)/(n-1)$ because the $r_2 - 1$ secondary copies are distributed evenly over $n-1$ sites. Finally, update propagation may be reduced by relaxed coherency, i.e. if $k < 1$. The above formula simplifies to

$$\lambda_i^{total} = \lambda_i + (1 - q_i) \cdot (r_1 \cdot sel_i) \cdot (r_2 - 1) \cdot k \cdot \lambda_i \quad \text{and we define} \quad \lambda^{total} := \sum_{i=1}^{\tau} \lambda_i^{total} .$$

4.4   Intersite Communication

Two messages are required to execute a transaction at a remote site: a *send* and a *return*, e.g. a query is sent to a site and the result is returned. For each transaction type i the communication delay for a *send* (*return*) is modeled to be exponentially distributed with mean t_c^{send-i} ($t_c^{return-i}$) seconds ($1 \leq i \leq \tau$). These values mainly depend on the bandwidth and the message size. Therefore, the parameter *baud* represents the network's bandwidth in bps, and $size_c^{send-i}$ ($size_c^{return-i}$) denotes the message size in bytes for a *send* (*return*) of a transaction of type i. The means t_c^{send-i} and $t_c^{return-i}$ characterizing the exponentially distributed service times are hence defined as

$$t_c^{send-i} = \frac{8 \cdot size_c^{send-i}}{baud} \quad \text{and} \quad t_c^{return-i} = \frac{8 \cdot size_c^{return-i}}{baud}$$

The average number of messages per second in the distributed system amounts to

$$\overline{N} = \sum_{i=1}^{\tau} n \cdot (1-\ell_i) \cdot \lambda_i + (1-q_i) \cdot n \cdot (r_1 \cdot sel_i) \cdot (r_2 - 1) \cdot k \cdot \lambda_i + \sum_{i=1}^{\tau} q_i \cdot n \cdot (1-\ell_i) \cdot \lambda_i \quad (*)$$

The first sum covers messages of type *send* (transactions forwarded to remote sites due to a lack of appropriate local data and update propagation), the second sum are returned query results. Remote updates are assumed not to be acknowledged and thus do not cause return messages. To model limited network capacity, the local databases are considered to be connected to the network via local communication servers modeled as $M/H_\pi/1$ systems. The arrival rate at any such server is $\overline{N}/n$ messages per second because each site sends and receives the same number of messages due to the sites' identical layout and symmetrical behaviour. The service time follows an

$H_{2\tau}$ distribution, because τ transaction types imply 2τ different message types: τ message types have an exponentially distributed service time with mean t_c^{send-i}, and τ message types with mean $t_c^{return-i}$ ($1 \leq i \leq \tau$.). The expression (*) implies, that a share of $(n \cdot (1-\ell_i) \cdot \lambda_i + (1-q_i) \cdot n \cdot (r_1 \cdot sel_i) \cdot (r_2 -1) \cdot k \cdot \lambda_i)/\overline{N}$ of the $\overline{N}$ messages has a mean service time t_c^{send-i} (for $1 \leq i \leq \tau$) and a share of $(q_i \cdot n \cdot (1-\ell_i) \cdot \lambda_i)/\overline{N}$ of the messages has a mean service time $t_c^{return-i}$ (for $1 \leq i \leq \tau$). Hence, the first and second moment of the $H_{2\tau}$ service time distribution can be derived following [19]. Subsequently, the average waiting time $\overline{W}_c$ at a local communication server can be obtained using the *Pollaczek-Khinchin formula* for general M/G/1 systems [19] and results in

$$\overline{W}_c = \frac{\sum_{i=1}^{\tau} \left((1-\ell_i) \cdot \lambda_i + (1-q_i) \cdot (r_1 \cdot sel_i) \cdot (r_2 -1) \cdot k \cdot \lambda_i\right) \cdot \left(t_c^{send-i}\right)^2 + q_i \cdot (1-\ell_i) \cdot \lambda_i (t_c^{return-i})^2}{1 - \sum_{i=1}^{\tau} \left((1-\ell_i) \cdot \lambda_i + (1-q_i) \cdot (r_1 \cdot sel_i) \cdot (r_2 -1) \cdot k \cdot \lambda_i\right) \cdot t_c^{send-i} + q_i \cdot (1-\ell_i) \cdot \lambda_i \cdot t_c^{return-i}}$$

4.5   Performance Criteria

Similar to the calculation of $\overline{W}_c$, the mean waiting time $\overline{W}$ at a local database is found to be

$$\overline{W} = \frac{\lambda^{total} \cdot \sum_{i=1}^{\tau} \frac{2 \cdot \lambda_i^{total}}{\lambda^{total}} \cdot t_i^2}{2 \cdot \left(1 - \lambda^{total} \cdot \sum_{i=1}^{\tau} \frac{\lambda_i^{total}}{\lambda^{total}} \cdot t_i\right)} = \frac{\sum_{i=1}^{\tau} \lambda_i^{total} \cdot t_i^2}{1 - \sum_{i=1}^{\tau} \lambda_i^{total} \cdot t_i}$$

so that the combined average response time over all transaction types results in

$$\overline{R} = \sum_{i=1}^{\tau} a_i \cdot \overline{R}_i \quad , \quad \text{where} \quad \overline{R}_i = \overline{W} + t_i + (1-\ell_i) \cdot (\overline{W}_c + t_c^{send-i} + t_c^{return-i})$$

is the response time for transactions of type i. On average a transaction (of type i) needs to wait for $\overline{W}$ seconds at a database to receive a service of t_i seconds. Additionally, with probability $(1-\ell_i)$ a transaction needs to be forwarded to a remote site which takes $\overline{W}_c$ seconds to wait for plus the time to be sent and returned. Note, th we assume $t_c^{return-i} = 0$ if $q(i) = 0$, i.e. no return messages for updates.

In steady state, the throughput of the local databases equals the arrival rate λ but is bound by the limited system capacity. Specifically, the throughput can grow until either a local database server or a communication server (the network) is saturated, i.e. its utilization (ρ_D or ρ_c respectively) reaches 1. Solving the equations $\rho_D = 1$ and

$\rho_c = 1$ for the arrival rate λ yields the maximum database limited throughput T_D and the maximum communication/network limited throughput T_C as

$$T_D = \lambda = \left(\sum_{i=1}^{\tau} a_i \cdot \left(1 + (1-q_i) \cdot (r_1 \cdot sel_i) \cdot (r_2 - 1) \cdot k\right) \cdot t_i \right)^{-1} \quad \text{and}$$

$$T_C = \left(\sum_{i=1}^{\tau} \left((1-\ell_i) \cdot a_i + (1-q_i) \cdot (r_1 \cdot sel_i) \cdot (r_2 - 1) \cdot k \cdot a_i\right) \cdot t_c^{send\_i} + q_i \cdot (1-\ell_i) \cdot a_i \cdot t_c^{return\_i} \right)^{-1}$$

respectively. The maximum throughput at a database site is $T = min(T_D, T_C)$ because whatever server is saturated first (either the database or the communication server) is the bottleneck and limits throughput. The overall system throughput amounts to $n \cdot T$.

5   Results and Expressiveness of the 2RC-Approach

The results we present are based on parameter values which are carefully chosen after measurements in database systems for telecom applications [12]. The values also agree with [2,10]. For ease of presentation, we consider only 3 transaction types: short queries, updates, and long queries (e.g. statistical evaluations).

The sensitivity analysis (omitted here for brevity) showed that parameter variations affect the performance values in a reasonable way, i.e. the model is stable. Although we will mention absolute values to refer to characteristics in the diagrams below, we consider the general trends, shapes and expressiveness of the graphs as the primary results. Naturally, the graphs depend on input values like the

Parameter	Base setting
n	50
τ	3
q_i	$q_1 = 1, q_2 = 0, q_3 = 1$
a_i	$a_1 = 0.85,\ a_2 = 0.1,\ a_3 = 0.05$
loc_i	0.04
f_plcmt_i	0.55
f_sel_i	-0.8
k	1
t_i	$t_1 = 0.06, t_2 = 0.125, t_3 = 0.5$
$baud$	64000 (e.g. ISDN)
$size_c^{send\_i}$	400 byte each
$size_c^{return\_1}$	2000
$size_c^{return\_3}$	3500

number of updates etc. However, here we do not intend to compare results for many different parameter combinations rather than to show that the 2RC approach allows a more expressive analysis for *any* set of parameters.

Fig. 4 shows the maximum *throughput* $T(r_1, r_2) = min(T_D, T_C)$ over the r_1-r_2-space. A 1D-replication model considers either the „$r_1 = 1$ -edge" of the graph, or the „$r_2 = 50$ -edge". Either case merely expresses that the throughput increases with a moderate degree of replication ($r_1 = 0.3$ or $r_2 = 10$) but decreases remarkably when replication is medium or high. (Note: Models which assume unlimited network capacity cannot foresee this increase, e.g. [13,16,30].) However, the 2D-model tells us more: As long as less than 35% of the data items are replicated ($r_1 < 0.35$) throughput can be maximized by placing copies on all sites ($r_2 = 50$), reaching its highest peak of 320 TPS for $r_1 = 0.3$. If availability considerations require more data items to be replicated (e.g. 50%), a medium number of copies yields the maximum throughput (e.g. $r_2 = 30$ for $r_1 = 0.5$). When striving for very high availability, it is worthwhile to consider that replicating 75% of the data items to 40 sites allows a twice as high throughput as full replication. These results show the increased expressiveness of the 2D-model over 1-dimensional approaches.

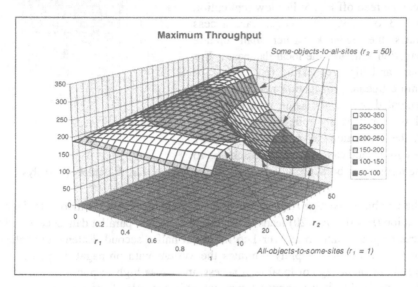

Fig. 4. Maximum Overall System throughput in TPS

The result that throughput can be maximized by placing copies at all sites for $r_1 < 0.35$ depends on the quality of replication. The input value $f\_sel_i = -0.8$ models a fairly good replication schema in which mainly read intensive but very little update intensive data items are selected for replication. With such a careful replica selection the update propagation overhead does not increase dramatically as the number of copies (r_2) is maximized to enhance local read availability. This relieves communication and increases the overall throughput. For larger values of r_1 $(r_1 \rightarrow 1)$ it becomes increasingly difficult to avoid replication of update intensive data items such that placing copies at all sites is not affordable anymore (cf. Fig. 5). Consequently, Fig. 4 looks different for a *bad* replica selection $(f\_sel_i > 0)$, i.e. the throughput peak is found at $r_1 = 1$ for a low number of copies $(r_2 \leq 12)$. The more data items are replicated $(r_1 \rightarrow 1)$ the more difficult it is to pick *only* update intensive objects for replication such that the read availability increases. This is captured in the model because sel_i converges towards 1 (i.e. unbiased replica selection) for $r_1 \rightarrow 1$ even for *bad* settings of f_sel_i.

The results presented throughout this section and the benefits of replication also depend on the percentage of updates in the overall workload. With an increasing percentage of updates the benefits of replication are gradually reduced and eventually outweighed by its drawbacks (update propagation cost vs. local and parallel read access) such that no replication ($r_1 = 0$ / $r_2 = 1$) yields the best performance.

Since the throughput calculation considered limited network capacity, a *bottleneck analysis* is possible for any replication schema and can be read off Fig. 5: For low replication ($r_1 < 0.3$ or $r_2 < 10$), remote data access saturates the network earlier than update propagation saturates the local databases. For medium and high replication ($r_1 > 0.5$, $r_2 > 25$) more update propagation network traffic is generated, but at the same time increased local data availability relieves the network, while the transaction load to update secondary copies grows and causes the local databases to be the throughput bottleneck.

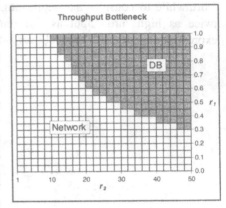

Fig. 5. Bottleneck Analysis

The combined average *response time* $\overline{R}$ is shown in Fig. 6. A moderate degree of replication ($r_1 < 0.5$, $r_2 < 20$) leads to increased local and parallel data access and thus reduces response time from over 1 to less than half a second. Extending replication along *both* dimensions rapidly saturates the system with propagated updates which outweigh the advantage of local read access and cause high response times. The 2D-model reveals that low response times are still possible if replication is extended along one dimension but kept moderate in the other. Replication schemata as different as ($r_1 = 1$, $r_2 = 10$), ($r_1 = 0.3$, $r_2 = 50$) or ($r_1 = 0.5$, $r_2 = 30$) could be chosen to satisfy an application's individual requirements regarding reliability and availability, while retaining similarly low response times. 1-dimensional models of replication did not allow this kind of examinations.

To address *scalability* issues, Fig. 7 depicts the throughput as a function of r_1 and the system size n. Note that the model considers one transaction arrival stream per site such that the overall transaction load increases as the number of sites increases. Furthermore, the number of logical data objects increases with the number of sites. As an example, r_2 is set to $2n/3$ for any value of n, i.e. r_1% of the logical data items are replicated to 2/3 of the n sites. If 100% of the data items are replicated, the throughput grows to about 100 TPS as the number of sites is increased to 30. Larger systems do not achieve a significantly higher throughput because without relaxed coherency high replication in large systems causes considerable update propagation overhead which hinders scalability [15]. Reducing replication ($r_1 < 1$) gradually improves scalability. If less than 40% of the data objects are replicated, far fewer update propagation transactions have to be processed so that the databases are not the bottleneck anymore (see Fig. 7) and throughput can grow to over 500 TPS for $r_1 = 0.25$.

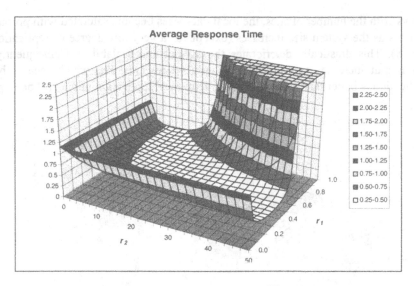

Fig. 6. Average overall response time $\overline{R}(r_1, r_2)$

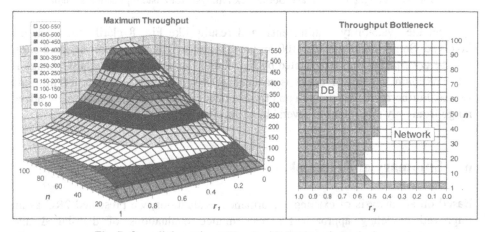

Fig. 7. Overall throughput $T(r_1, n)$ with Bottleneck Analysis

As indicated in the discussion for Fig. 4, the way throughput and scalability can be improved by means of replication depends critically on the selection of data items for replication and the placement of their copies. In Fig. 8 we examine the impact of the quality of replication on the scalability by considering a bad replication schema, i.e. one in which (a) not only read intensive but also a considerable amount of update intensive data items are replicated and (b) the copies are placed at randomly chosen sites rather than at remote sites where they are read particularly often. This can be modeled by the parameter settings $f\_plcmt_i = 0$ and $f\_sel_i = 0.6$. Such a replication schema causes more replica maintenance overhead than benefits through local and parallel read access. Since the transaction load and the number of secondary copies grows with the number of sites, the local databases become saturated with propagated updates as the system size increases (except for a very low degree of replication, cf. Fig. 8). This drastically deteriorates throughput and scalability. Consequently, the throughput increases as replication is reduced towards 0%, which means that *no* replication is better than *bad* replication. However, replication might still be required

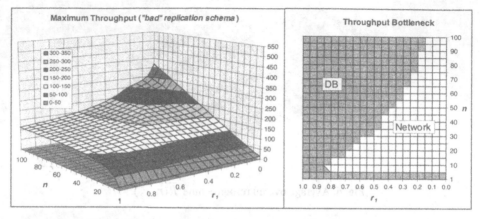

Fig. 8. Throughput $T(r_i, n)$ and Bottleneck Analysis for a bad replication schema

to meet the availability requirements, and results like Fig. 8 clarify the trade-off involved. Some might consider 100 an unreasonably high number of database sites, but the *general* findings represented by Fig. 7 and Fig. 8 do not drastically change if the maximum number of nodes is reduced to 40 or 20 sites, except for absolute values. Furthermore, depending upon the application, the number of sites may indeed range from only a few sites to several hundred sites [3].

6   Summary and Outlook

Based on an analysis of existing performance evaluations, we presented 2RC as an improved modeling approach for performance evaluations of distributed and replicated database systems. 2RC is of increased expressiveness through a new 2-dimensional replication model, an advanced database communication model, the possibility to model the quality of a replication schema, and the ability to consider arbitrary transaction and communication patterns of real-world applications. Particularly, 2RC reflects the close interplay between replica management and intersite communication, and allows for bottleneck considerations. The findings show how partial 2D-replication schemata, which have not been evaluated previously, affect response time, throughput and scalability. Although the results presented here illustrate only a limited number of the possible parameter variations, they demonstrate that 2RC allows more expressive performance evaluations than 1-dimensional approaches with simplifying communication models.

Numerous parameter variations can be investigated in an analytical model as opposed to simulations or measurements, making full validation virtually impossible [2,16,26,6,20]. However, a partial validation of our model has been conducted by matching the results against extensive measurement data gathered in a telecom database prototype [12]. Additionally, we are currently implementing a distributed database testbed to validate the analytical results more thoroughly.

References

[1] G. Alonso: *Partial Database Replication and Group Communication Primitives*, Proceedings of the 2nd European Research Seminar on Advances in Distributed Systems (ERSADS'97), March 1997.

[2] R. Alonso, D. Barbara, H. Garcia-Molina: *Data Caching Issues in an Information Retrieval System*, ACM Transactions on Database Systems, Vol. 15, No. 3, pp. 359-384, 1990.

[3] T. Anderson, Y. Breitbart, H. Korth, A. Wool: *Replication, Consistency, and Practicality: Are These Mutually Exclusive ?*, ACM SIGMOD International Conference on Management of Data, pp. 484-495, June 1998.

[4] F. Bacelli, E.G. Coffmann Jr.: *A database replication analysis using an M/M/m queue with service interruptions*, Performance Evaluation Review, Vol. 11, No. 4, pp. 102-107, 1983.

[5] Sujata Banerjee, Victor O K Li, Chihping Wang: *Performance analysis of the send-on-demand: A distributed database concurrency control protocol for high-speed networks*, Computer Communications, Vol. 17, No. 3, pp. 189-204, March 1994.

[6] A.B. Bondi, V. Jin: *A performance model of a design for a minimally replicated distributed database for database driven telecommunication services*, Journal on Distributed and Parallel Databases, Vol. 4, No. 4, pp. 295-317, October 1996.

[7] Michael J. Carey, Miron Livny: *Distributed Concurrency Control Performance: A Study of Algorithms, Distribution, and Replication*, Proceedings of the 14th International Conference on Very Large Databases, pp. 13-25, 1988.

[8] S. Ceri, M.A.H. Houtsma, A.M.Keller, P.Samarati: *A Classification of Update Methods for Replicated Databases*, Technical Report STAN-CS-91-1392, Stanford University, October 1991.

[9] Shu-Wie Chen, Calton Pu: *A Structural Classification of Integrated Replica Control Mechanisms*, Technical Report CUCS-006-92, Columbia University, NY, 1992.

[10] B. Ciciani, D.M. Dias, P.S. Yu: *Analysis of Replication in Distributed Database Systems*, IEEE Transactions on Knowledge and Data Engineering, Vol. 2, No. 2, pp. 247-261, June 1990.

[11] E.G. Coffmann, Erol Gelenbe, Brigitte Plateau: *Optimization of the number of copies in a distributed system*, IEEE Transactions on Software Engineering, Vol. 7, pp. 78-84, January 1981.

[12] R. Gallersdorfer, K. Klabunde, A. Stolz, M. Essmajor: *Intelligent Networks as a Data Intensive Application - Final Project Report*, Technical Report AIB-96-14, University of Aachen, 1996.

148   Matthias Nicola and Matthias Jarke

[13] Rainer Gallersdorfer, Matthias Nicola: *Improving Performance in Replicated Databases through Relaxed Coherency*, Proceedings of the 21th International Conference on Very Large Databases, pp. 445-456, Sept. 1995.

[14] H. Garcia-Molina: *Performance of the Update Algorithms for Replicated Data in a Distributed Database*, Ph.D. Dissertation, revised version, Computer Science Department, Stanford University, North Holland, 1982.

[15] Jim Gray, P. Helland, P. O'Neil, D. Shasha: *The dangers of replication and a solution*, SIGMOD Record, Vol. 25, No. 2, pp. 173-182, June 1996.

[16] S.Y. Hwang, K.S. Lee, Y.H. Chin: *Data Replication in a Distributed System: A Performance Study*, 7th International Conference on Database and Expert Systems Applications, pp. 708-717, 1996.

[17] B. Kemme, G. Alonso: *A Suite of Database Replication Protocols based on Group Communication Primitives*, Proceedings of the 18th International Conference on Distributed Computing Systems, May 1998.

[18] C.S. Keum, E.K. Hong, W.Y. Kim, K.Y. Whang: *Performance Evaluation of Replica Control Algorithms in a Locally Distributed Database System*, Proceedings of the 4th International Conference on Database Systems for Advanced Database Applications, pp. 388-396, April 1995.

[19] L. Kleinrock: *Queueing Systems, Volume I: Theory*, John Wiley & Sons, 1975.

[20] Kin K. Leung: *An Update Algorithm for Replicated Signalling Databases in Wireless and Advanced Intelligent Networks*, IEEE Transactions on Computers, Vol. 46, No. 3, pp. 362-367, March 1997.

[21] D. Liang, S. K. Tripathi: *Performance Analysis of Long-Lived Transaction Processing Systems with Rollbacks and Aborts*, IEEE Transactions on Knowledge and Data Engineering, Vol. 8, No. 5, pp. 802-815, 1996.

[22] M.C. Little, D.L. McCue: *The Replica Management System: A Scheme for Flexible and Dynamic Replication*, Proceedings of the 2nd Workshop on Configurable Distributed Systems, 1994.

[23] J. Mc Dermott, R. Mukkamala: *Performance Analysis of Transaction Management Algorithms for the SINTRA Replicated Architecture Database Systems*, IFIP Transactions (Comp. Science & Technology), Vol. A-47, pp. 215-234, 1994.

[24] Randolph D. Nelson, Balakrishna R. Iyer: *Analysis of a Replicated Database"*, Performance Evaluation, Vol. 5, pp. 133-148, 1985.

[25] Esther Pacitti, Erics Simon: *Update Propagation Strategies to Improve Freshness of* Data in Lazy Master Schemes, Technical Report No. 3233, INRIA Rocquencourt, France, August 1997.

[26] J.F. Ren, Y. Takahashi, T. Hasegawa: *Analysis of impact of network delay on multiversion timestamp algorithms in DDBS*, Performance Evaluation, pp. 21-50, July 1996.

[27] D. Saha, S. Rangarajan, S. K. Tripathi: *An Analysis of the Average Message Overhead in Replica Control Protocols*, IEEE Transactions on Parallel and Distributed Systems, Vol. 7, No. 10, pp. 1026-1034, Oct. 1996.

[28] S.H. Son, N. Haghighi: *Performance Evaluation of Multiversion Database Systems*, Proceedings of the 6th International Conference on Data Engineering, pp. 129-136, 1990.

[29] S.H. Son, F. Zhang: *Real-Time Replication Control for Distributed Database Systems: Algorithms and Their Performance"* 4th International Conference on Database Systems for Advanced Database Applications, pp. 214-221, 1995.

[30] M. Stonebraker. *Concurrency Control and Consistency of Multiple Copies of Data in Distributed Ingres*, IEEE Transactions on Software Engineering, 5(3):188-194, 1979.

[31] P. Triantafillou: *Independent Recovery in Large-Scale Distributed Systems*, IEEE Transactions on Software Engineering, Vol. 22, No. 11, pp. 812-826, November 1996.
[32] O. Wolfson, S. Jajodia, Y. Huang: *An Adaptive Data Replication Algorithm*, ACM Transactions on Database Systems, Vol. 22, No. 2, pp. 255-314, 1997.
[33] Shaoyu Zhou, M.H. Williams, H. Taylor: *Practical Throughput Estimation for Parallel Databases*, Software Engineering Journal, Vol. 11, No. 4, pp. 255-263, July 1996.

Transactions in Stack, Fork, and Join Composite Systems

Gustavo Alonso, Armin Feßler, Guy Pardon, and Hans-Jörg Schek

Institute of Information Systems
ETH Zentrum, CH-8092 Zürich, Switzerland
{alonso,fessler,pardon,schek}@inf.ethz.ch

Abstract. Middleware tools are generally used to glue together distributed, heterogeneous systems into a coherent composite whole. Unfortunately, there is no clear conceptual framework in which to reason about transactional correctness in such an environment. This paper is a first attempt at developing such framework. Unlike most existing systems, where concurrent executions are controlled by a centralized scheduler, we will assume that each element in the system has its own independent scheduler receiving input from the schedulers of other elements and producing output for the schedules of yet other elements in the system. In this paper we analyze basic configurations of such composite systems and develop correctness criteria for each case. Moreover, we also show how these ideas can be used to characterize and improve different transaction models such as distributed transactions, sagas, and federated database transactions.

1 Introduction

Composite systems consist of several components interconnected by middleware. Components provide services which are used as building blocks to define the services of other components as shown in fig. 1. This mode of operation is widely used, for instance, in TP-Monitors or CORBA based systems. To achieve true plug and play functionality, each component should have its own scheduler for concurrency control and recovery purposes. Unfortunately, most existing theory addresses only the case of schedulers with a single level of abstraction [6]. This is unnecessarily narrow: it hinders the autonomy of components and, by neglecting to take advantage of the available semantic information, also restricts the degree of parallelism. Except for open nested, multi-level transactions [14], almost no attention has been devoted to the case were several schedulers are interconnected with the output of one scheduler being used as the input to the next. In this paper, we address this problem by determining what information a scheduler must provide to another to guarantee global correctness while still preserving the autonomy of each scheduler. Based on multilevel [4,14], nested [9], and stack-composite [1] transactions we develop a theory that allows composite systems to be understood w.r.t. correct concurrent access. Of all possible configurations, we consider here only a few important cases: stacks, forks, and joins

Catriel Beeri, Peter Buneman (Eds.): ICDT'99, LNCS 1540, pp. 150–168, 1998.
© Springer-Verlag Berlin Heidelberg 1998

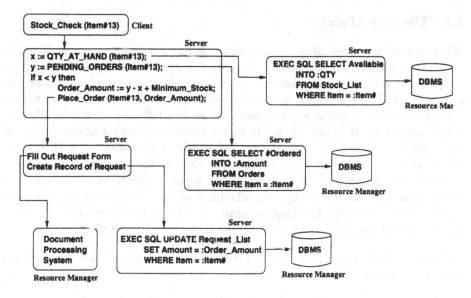

Fig. 1. An example transaction in a composite system

(see fig. 2) and simple combinations of them. The idea is to use these as building blocks that can later help us to understand and model more complex cases. We see the contribution of our paper in providing a formal basis for correctness in these architectures. In addition, we show how several classical problems of transaction management can be expressed and explained in a coherent manner using the proposed framework, without having to resort to separate models for each case. In particular, we prove this by showing that traditional distributed transactions, sagas, and federated databases (global and local transactions) are special cases of our model. The paper is organized as follows. Section 2 presents the transaction model and introduces conflict consistency as our basic correctness criterion. Section 3 discusses correct concurrent executions in stacks, forks, and join schedules and introduces a simple combination of forks and joins. Section 4 discusses distributed transactions, sagas and federated transactions within the framework of composite schedulers. Finally, section 5 concludes the paper with a brief summary of the results and future work.

2 Conflict Consistency

In this section, we present our basic correctness criteria. These serve as a necessary preparation for the rest of the paper, where it becomes obvious how operations of a scheduler act as transactions in other schedulers. In what follows, we assume familiarity with concurrency control theory [5].

2.1 The New Model

When executing transactions, a scheduler restricts parallelism because it must, first, observe the order constraints between the operations of each transaction and, second, impose order constraints between conflicting operations of different transactions. The restriction in parallelism occurs because, in a conventional scheduler, ordered operations are executed sequentially. As shown in [1], this is too restrictive. It is often possible to parallelize concurrent operations even when they conflict as long as the overall result is the same as if they were executed sequentially. This requires to relax some of the ordering requirements of traditional schedulers. In addition, when several schedulers are involved, a mechanism is needed to specify to a scheduler what is a correct execution from the point of view of the invoking scheduler. For these two purposes we use the notion of *weak* and *strong* orders (assumed to be transitively closed):

Definition 1 (Strong and Weak Order:). *Let A and B denote any tasks (actions, transactions).*

- *Sequential (strong) order: $A \ll B$, A has to complete before B starts.*
- *Unrestricted parallel execution: $A \| B$, A and B can execute concurrently equivalent to any order, i.e., $A \ll B$ or $B \ll A$.*
- *Restricted parallel (weak) order: $A < B$, A and B can be executed concurrently but the net effect must be equivalent to executing $A \ll B$.*   □

From here, and independently of the notion of equivalence used, it follows that turning a weak order into a strong one leads to correct execution since this implies sequential execution. In fact, traditional flat schedulers with only one level of abstraction, do just this, if two tasks conflict they impose a strong order between them. When moving to a composite system with several schedulers, it is often possible to impose a weak order instead of a strong one, thereby increasing the possibility of parallelizing operations. Thus, the aim will be to impose either no orders or only weak orders while still preserving global correctness and characterize the exchange of information between schedulers in terms of these orders. Note that in our model, weak and strong orders are *requirements and not observed (temporal) orders*. A strong order implies a temporal one, but not the other way round. In figure 3, t_3 is weakly input-ordered before t_1, and the serialisation order is according to it. Therefore, the execution is correct. However, t_1 is temporally ordered before t_3 (the execution order is indicated by the position: left comes first). This shows that the temporal order may be irrelevant. In other words, order preservation as postulated in [3] is not required in our model. With these ideas, a transaction is now defined as follows. Let $\hat{O}$ be the set of all operations of a scheduler with which transactions can be formed.

Definition 2 (Transaction). *A transaction, t, is a triple $(O_t, <_t, \ll_t)$, where O_t is a set of operations taken from $\hat{O}$, $<_t$ is a partial order on O_t termed the weak (intra-)transaction order, and $\ll_t$ is a partial order on O_t termed the strong (intra-)transaction order. For consistency we require $\ll_t \subseteq <_t$.*   □

Since now we have operations being executed at different schedulers, a modified notion of conflict is needed. Let $CON \subseteq \hat{O} \times \hat{O}$ be a conflict predicate that expresses whether two operation invocations commute. We say that two operations, o and o', commute if there is no difference in return values of the sequence $\alpha \, o \, o' \, \beta$ compared to $\alpha \, o' \, o \, \beta$ for all sequences α and β with elements from $\hat{O}$ [13]. Therefore, commutativity is not an absolute property but is relative to the given set of (allowed) operation invocations. From here, we say that two operations conflict if they do not commute, which also includes the case when it is unknown whether they commute or not. In practice, in a composite system, two operations conflict if there is a potential flow of information between them. With this, now we have all the necessary elements to formally define a scheduler:

Definition 3 (Schedule). *A schedule S is a five-tuple* $(T, \rightarrow, \mapsto, <, \ll)$, *where:*

- *T is a set of transactions.*
  Let O denote the set of all operations of T's transactions, i.e., $O = \bigcup_{t \in T} O_t$.
- *$\rightarrow$ and $\mapsto$ are the weak and strong input orders, partial orders over T with $\mapsto \; \subseteq \; \rightarrow$.*
- *$<$ and $\ll$ are the weak and strong output orders, partial orders over O such that:*
  1. *$\forall t, t' \in T, t \neq t', \forall o \in O_t, \forall o' \in O_{t'}, CON(o, o'):$*
     (a) $(t \rightarrow t') \Rightarrow (o < o')$
     (b) $(t' \rightarrow t) \Rightarrow (o' < o)$
     (c) otherwise: $(o < o') \vee (o' < o)$
  2. *(a) $\forall t \in T, \forall o, o' \in O_t : (o <_t o') \Rightarrow (o < o'),$*
     (b) $\forall t \in T, \forall o, o' \in O_t : (o \ll_t o') \Rightarrow (o \ll o'),$
  3. *Whenever $t \mapsto t'$, then $\forall o \in O_t, \forall o' \in O_{t'} : o \ll o',$*
  4. *$\ll \; \subseteq \; <.$*   □

According to point 1, a scheduler must weakly order every pair of conflicting operations without contradicting the weak input order, if any, between the parent transactions (otherwise, as we will see below, a cycle would immediately appear). Point 2 ensures well-formedness, that is, all weak and strong transaction orders are contained in the weak and strong output orders, respectively. Point 3 propagates the strong input order from the transactions to their operations, thereby separating the execution tree of strongly ordered transactions. Point 4 guarantees that the output orders of a scheduler are consistent between them. It is not stated explicitly that if at least one of two weakly output ordered operations is a leaf, then they are also strongly ordered. This is an evident requirement.

2.2 Conflict Consistency

The distinction between the two orderings requires to modify the traditional notion of correctness. We will assume, as usual, that a transaction executed in isolation is correct.

Definition 4 (Serial Schedule).
A schedule S is serial if $\mapsto_S$ is a total order, i.e., $\forall t, t' \in T : (t \mapsto t') \vee (t' \mapsto t)$. □

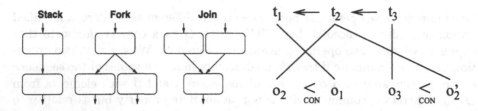

Fig. 2. Coupling modes between schedulers **Fig. 3.** Example for non-relevant temporal execution order

Note that serial schedule does not mean that all operations are executed serially. Operations within one transaction can be executed in parallel. In a serial schedule we have $\mapsto\ =\ \to$. Following the classical approach, we can now define the new correctness criterion, called *conflict consistency*.

Definition 5 (Conflict Consistency (CC)).
A schedule S is conflict consistent *if there is a serial schedule S_{ser}, whose strong input and weak output order contain the weak input and output order of S, resp., i.e., $(\to_S\ \subseteq\ \mapsto_{S_{ser}}) \wedge (<_S\ \subseteq\ <_{S_{ser}})$.* □

The name *conflict consistency* expresses that the order of all *conflicting* operations must be consistent with the weak input order, i.e., the serialisation order must not contradict the weak input order. This can be further formalized as follows:

Definition 6 (Serialisation Graph $\hookrightarrow$). *Given a schedule S, its* serialisation graph, *denoted $\hookrightarrow$, is a transitive irreflexive binary relation on $T \times T$, in which $t \hookrightarrow t'$ is contained if $t \neq t'$ and $\exists o \in O_t,\ \exists o' \in O_{t'} : CON(o, o') \wedge (o < o')$* □

Theorem 1. *A schedule S is conflict consistent iff the union of its weak input order and its serialisation graph $(\hookrightarrow_S \cup \to_S)$ is acyclic.* □

This can be proven by constructing a total order containing the union of weak order and serialisation graph, thereby defining a serial schedule with the same weak output order (see appendix). This theorem does not take explicitly into account the strong input order since it is contained in the weak one (see def. 3).

Compared to [1] we simplified the definitions: we dropped the notion of equivalent schedules and we included a clearer presentation of order constraints.

2.3   Recovery

For a formal treatment of recovery, we use the unified theory for concurrency control and recovery [2,13]. This theory is based on an expanded schedule which is used to represent the transaction's recovery operations explicitly, i.e., in every schedule each abort is replaced by the corresponding inverse operations ("undos") in the appropriate order. It has been shown that ordering commits in

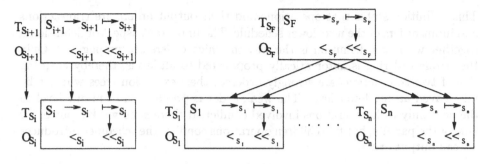

Fig. 4. Stack.   **Fig. 5.** Fork.

the order of conflicting operations and aborts in the opposite direction (SOT in [13]) leads to correct concurrency control and recovery. In order to achieve this, every scheduler must automatically generate the appropriate invocations of inverse operations properly ordered in case of a failure. If inverse operations are not available we will assume that a scheduler defers the commit of all operations that do not have inverses. A more comprehensive treatment of recovery is beyond the scope of this paper. We will concentrate here on concurrency control.

3 Composite Systems

In a composite system, every server has a scheduler S and provides a set $\hat{O}_S$ of operation invocations to be used to build transactions (the server's services), i.e., an operation of a scheduler can be and often will be a transaction of another one. Every scheduler S has a commutativity specification expressed by the conflict predicate CON_S. Every scheduler works locally ensuring correctness with respect to its (local) CON_S. The question to address is how to guarantee global correctness in such a scenario and what information is needed at each scheduler to guarantee global correctness.

3.1 Stack Schedules

Stack schedulers take the output of one scheduler and use it directly as input to the next (see fig. 4). Transactions can have different depths, but operations at the same level are always processed by the same scheduler. This structure is a generalization of multi-level and nested transactions [10,4,3,14] and it can be found in the internal structure of many systems. The notion of stack used in this paper is taken from [1]. Here, in addition, we prove correctness of stack schedules.

Definition 7 (Stack Schedule (SS)).
SS, an n-level stack schedule, consists of n schedules $S_1, \ldots, S_n$, *such that, for* $1 < i \leq n$:
- $T_{S_{i-1}} = O_{S_i}$ • $\rightarrow_{S_{i-1}} = <_{S_i}$ • $\mapsto_{S_{i-1}} = \ll_{S_i}$ □

This definition states that operations and their output orders are transactions and input orders of the next lower schedule. The important aspect of definition 3 together with this definition is the way in which orders are propagated. Only the strong ordering is automatically propagated to all levels, thereby ensuring that if two transactions are strongly ordered, their execution trees will not be interleaved at any lower level. The weak order is propagated from one level to the next only if the operations involved conflict. If there is no weak input order among the parents, but two children operations conflict, the scheduler introduces a weak output order.

Definition 8 (Stack Conflict Consistency (SCC)). *An n-level stack schedule SS is stack conflict consistent iff each individual schedule S_i in SS is conflict consistent, for $1 \leq i \leq n$.*   □

Theorem 2. *A stack schedule is correct if it is SCC.*   □

We prove this theorem by constructing a serial execution of all transactions of all levels, i.e., on all levels all transactions are strongly ordered (see appendix).

Notice that conflict consistency requires the existence of a serial schedule, where each transaction is executed serially, but not necessarily its operations. The advantage of SCC is that as long as each level independently enforces CC, the overall execution is correct. The weak order constraint and its careful propagation through the stack is important because often we do not know whether operations conflict or not. In these cases, one has to be careful and assume that they conflict. In contrast to existing multilevel transaction models [3,14], such a weak order constraint is irrelevant if there is no actual conflict at the next level. In [1], it is shown that SCC is a larger class than *order preserving serialisability* [3] and *level-by-level serialisability* [14], the two existing comparable criteria. Because we allow weak orders within transactions, SCC is also larger than multi-level-serialisability (MLSR in [14]).

3.2 Fork Schedules

In a fork (fig. 5), the output of a schedule is used as input to several other schedulers. Each pair top-level/lower-level scheduler can be seen as a stack and, indeed, it will follow the rules defined for stack schedulers. More formally:

Definition 9 (Fork Schedule (FS)). *A fork schedule FS consists of $(n+1)$ schedules $S_F, S_1, \ldots, S_n$, such that:*

1. $O_{S_F} = \bigcup_{i=1}^{n} T_{S_i}$

2. $\forall i \in \{1, \ldots, n\} : \forall t, t' \in T_{S_i} : \begin{cases} t <_{S_F} t' \Rightarrow t \rightarrow_{S_i} t' \\ t \ll_{S_F} t' \Rightarrow t \mapsto_{S_i} t' \end{cases}$

3. $\forall (o_i, o_j), o_i \in O_{S_i}, o_j \in O_{S_j}, i \neq j$, *we assume o_i and o_j commute.*   □

The output orders $<_{S_F}$ and $\ll_{S_F}$ of S_F are passed to the related component S_i as input orders. Note that every operation in S_F is sent to only one scheduler

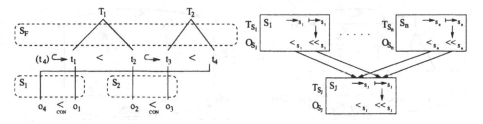

Fig. 6. Pure fork.   **Fig. 7.** Join.

S_i as a transaction. In "pure" forks we assume that invocation hierarchies are completely separated. No information flows from S_i to S_j or vice versa. This is why we assume that operations commute (point 3). Therefore, every weak order between two operations going to different schedulers S_i and S_J disappears. However, every weak order between two operations going to the same scheduler S_i is transformed to an input order in S_i, so this scheduler takes care of it. For instance, the execution in figure 6 is a correct pure fork. Pure forks are very common in practice, as shown in figure 1.

Definition 10 (Fork Conflict Consistency (FCC)). *A fork schedule FS is fork conflict consistent (FCC), if the schedule S_F is conflict consistent and* $\bigcup_{i=1}^{n} (\hookrightarrow_{S_i} \cup \rightarrow_{S_i})$ *is acyclic.*   □

Theorem 3. *An execution in a fork schedule is correct iff it is FCC.*   □

This can be proven by constructing an equivalent stack schedule (see appendix). FCC is a global criterion. Since we want to check for correctness locally, each scheduler should be able to decide independently if the schedule is correct or not. This can be done as follows:

Theorem 4 (Criterion for Fork Conflict Consistency). *A fork schedule FS is fork conflict consistent, iff each of the schedules $S_F, S_1, \ldots, S_n$ is conflict consistent.*   □

This can be proven by dividing $(\hookrightarrow_{S_i} \cup \rightarrow_{S_i})$ into subgraphs of the different schedules and considering their connections to each other (see appendix).

Forks (fig. 6) are a straightforward extension of stacks. The criterion for forks becomes more complicated when we allow that operation invocation hierarchies are not separated, i.e., when after the fork, it is possible to have a join schedule. This case is discussed in the next section.

3.3   Join Schedules

Join schedulers[1] entail several top schedulers whose outputs go to a common, single low-level scheduler (figure 7), called S_J. Joins are common at the resource

---

[1] Join schedules are not to be confused with join-transactions introduced in [11]

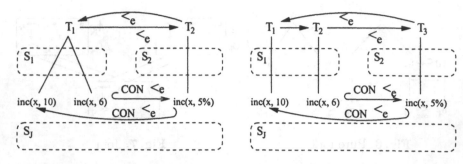

Fig. 8. Join with two transactions.   **Fig. 9.** Join with three transactions.

manager level, where a single resource manager is being accessed by several servers simultaneously. Again, each pair top-level/low-level schedule behaves like a stack, but care must be taken to avoid inconsistencies. For this purpose, conflicts must be assumed between operations of different higher level schedulers. The formal definition of join schedule is a straightforward extension of that of stacks: the output of the top-level schedulers (operations, and weak and strong orders) is used as the input to the lower-level scheduler (abusing notation, also called *join* schedule). Thus,

Definition 11 (Join Schedule (JS)). *A* join schedule JS *consists of (n+1) schedules* $S_J, S_1, \ldots, S_n$, *such that:*

- $\bigcup_{i=1}^{n} O_{S_i} = T_{S_J}$ $\bullet\ \forall i \in \{1, \ldots, n\} : \forall t, t' \in O_{S_i} : \begin{cases} t <_{S_i} t' \Rightarrow t \to_{S_J} t' \\ t \ll_{S_i} t' \Rightarrow t \mapsto_{S_J} t' \end{cases}$ □

Intuitively, since the lower level schedule follows the input orders provided, each pair top-level/lower-level scheduler behaves like a stack. From a correctness point of view, it remains to be determined whether and how to interleave transactions from different schedulers. The problems to avoid are illustrated in figures 8 and 9.

Assume two users, each one operating on one of two top-level schedulers in a join. In figure 8 the information flow from T_1 to T_2 and back can be detected neither by S_J nor S_1 nor S_2. This problem could be solved if, for instance, S_J would build the serialisation graph based on the root transactions, which would result in a cycle. In figure 9, however, this does not help because the information flows from T_2 to T_3 to T_1. The cycle can only be detected when considering the weak input order between T_1 and T_2.

In other words, assume T_1 and T_2 were directly given to S_J and not to S_1 and S_2 as before. Then S_J would directly reject the execution because it is not CC. To capture these situations we introduce the *ghost-graph*. Let $Act(T)$ represent the children of transaction T at all levels below that in which T appears.

Definition 12 (Ghost-Graph for Join Schedules($\lesssim_{JS}$)).
$\forall (T, T')$ *with* $T \in T_{S_i}, T' \in T_{S_j}, i \neq j$ *the ghost-graph* $\lesssim_{JS}$ *is defined as:*
$T \lesssim_{JS} T'$ *if there are children* t, t' *of* T, T', *resp., with* $t, t' \in T_{S_J}$ *and* $t \mapsto_{S_J} t'$. □

Definition 13 (Join Conflict Consistency (JCC)). *A join schedule JS is join conflict consistent, if the schedule S_J is conflict consistent and $\lesssim_{JS} \cup \bigcup_{i=1}^{n} (\hookrightarrow_{S_i} \cup \to_{S_i})$ is acyclic.* □

This definition matches the intuition that a join schedule should be considered correct if the whole stack schedule built from all partial schedules – together with the implicit (ghost) orderings between different schedules – is SCC.

Theorem 5. *An execution in a join schedule is correct iff it is JCC.* □

This can be proven by constructing an equivalent stack schedule that is SCC (see appendix). As pointed out above, the idea is that each scheduler will be able to make decisions locally. The criterion JCC, however, is a global property that cannot be enforced locally. Fortunately we can artificially generate weak input orders between all sub-transactions of transactions that come from different schedulers. The weak input order expresses the fact that we must assume a conflict between operations of such transactions. Remember that the weak input order generally stems from output orderings of conflicting operations at a level above. Since there is no common level above, we do not know about the commutativity of such operations and, therefore, must assume a conflict. This idea is formalized as follows:

Definition 14 (Completed Join Schedule (CJS)). *A completed join schedule CJS is a JS with additional input order compatible with:*
$$\forall S_i, S_j, i \neq j : (\forall t \in T_{S_i}, \forall t' \in T_{S_j} : t \to t') \vee (\forall t \in T_{S_i}, \forall t' \in T_{S_j} : t' \to t)$$ □

Theorem 6 (Criterion for JCC). *A completed join schedule CJS is JCC, if each of the schedules $S_J, S_1, \ldots, S_n$ is conflict consistent.* □

This locally testable criterion for JCC can be proven by reducing the ghost-graph to weak input orders between transactions of different schedules (see appendix).

From here, if each transaction that arrives at S_J contains the information about its parent scheduler, S_J can impose the additional weak input orderings. Then S_J can decide locally about correctness of the join schedule. In figures 8 and 9, S_J would impose an order from inc(x,10) and inc(x,6) to inc(x,5%) or vice versa. So, a cycle in the union of weak input order and serialisation graph of S_J would be detected.

Note that there exist JCC join schedules that cannot be transformed into a correct CJS. Counterexamples are join schedules whose ghost-graph builds a cycle "between schedules" but not between transactions. CJS is a purely static notion and cannot be used in practice for dynamic scheduling. Dynamic scheduling in these scenarios is a complex problem which can be addressed by adding further restrictions to the execution but which is beyond the scope of this paper.

3.4 FDBS-Schedules

The FDBS-schedule will be used later to describe federated databases. A federated database can be described by a fork schedule with additional schedules at the same level as S_F, one virtual schedule S_{Li} for each local transaction t_{Li} (see figure 11):

Definition 15 (FDBS-Schedule (FDS)). *An FDBS-schedule FDS consists of $(n+l+1)$ schedules $S_F, S_{L1}, \ldots, S_{Ll}, S_{J1}, \ldots, S_{Jn}$, such that:*

1. $O_{S_F} \cup \bigcup_{i=1}^{l} O_{S_{Li}} = \bigcup_{i=1}^{n} T_{S_{Ji}}$
2. $\forall i \in \{1, \ldots, l\} : T_{S_{Li}} = \{t_{Li}\}, O_{T_{Li}} = \{o_{Li}\}$
3. $\forall i \in \{1, \ldots, n\} : \forall t, t' \in T_{S_{Ji}} : \begin{cases} t <_{S_F} t' \Rightarrow t \to_{S_{Ji}} t' \\ t \ll_{S_F} t' \Rightarrow t \mapsto_{S_{Ji}} t' \end{cases}$ □

FDBS-schedules have the same problems as a join. Thus, to define correctness, we use a similar notion:

Definition 16 (Ghost-Graph for FDBS-Schedules($\lesssim_{FDS}$)).
$\forall (T, T')$ with $T \in T_S, T' \in T_{S'}, S, S' \in \{S_F, S_{L1}, \ldots, S_{Ll}\}, S \neq S'$ the ghost-graph $\lesssim_{FDS}$ is defined as:
$T \lesssim_{FDS} T'$ if there are children t, t' of T, T', resp., with $t, t' \in T_{S_{Ji}} (i \in \{1, \ldots, l\})$ and $t \mapsto_{S_{Ji}} t'$.   □

Not surprisingly, FDBS conflict consistency can be defined as join conflict consistency.

Definition 17 (FDBS Conflict Consistency (FDCC)). *An FDBS-schedule FDS is FDBS conflict consistent, if the schedules $S_{J1} \ldots S_{Jn}$ are conflict consistent and $\lesssim \cup (\hookrightarrow_{S_F} \cup \to_{S_F})$ is acyclic.*   □

Theorem 7. *An execution in an FDBS-schedule is correct iff it is FDCC.*   □

This can be proven by constructing an equivalent stack schedule (see appendix). Note that serialisation graphs and weak input orders can not appear in the "local schedules" S_{Li} since they are only virtual schedules. Thus, since FDCC cannot be applied locally we have to seek another criterion. For this, we define:

Definition 18 (Completed FDBS-Schedule (CFDS)). *A completed FDBS-schedule CFDS is an FDS with additional conflicts: $CON_{S_F} := CON_{S_F} \cup \{(o, o') \mid o \in O_t, o' \in O_{t'}, t \neq t', t, t' \in T_{S_F}, \exists i : (o, o' \in T_{S_{Ji}})\}$*
Note that this implies that S_F has to weakly order these extra conflicts, as required by its CC property.   □

Now, a CFDS is correct (FDCC), if the following holds:

Theorem 8 (Criterion for FDCC). *A completed FDBS-schedule CFDS is FDCC, if*
(1) each of the schedules $S_F, S_{L1} \ldots S_{Ll}, S_{J1} \ldots S_{Jn}$ is conflict consistent and
(2) if $\nexists t, t' \in O_T, T \in T_{S_F} : (t, t' \in T_{S_{Jj}} (j \in \{1 \ldots n\}, \exists t_{L1} \ldots t_{Lk} \in \bigcup_{i=1}^{l} O_{S_{Li}} : (t \mapsto_{S_{Jj}} t_{L1} \mapsto_{S_{Jj}} \ldots \mapsto_{S_{Jj}} t_{Lk} \mapsto_{S_{Jj}} t'))$.   □

The last condition means that in any S_{Jj} no local transactions must be serialised between global (sub-)transactions of the same parent (=transaction in S_F). We prove this theorem by assuming a cycle in the union of input, serialisation and ghost-order and showing a contradiction to CC of S_F (see appendix).

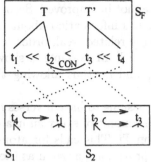

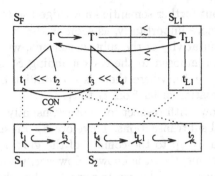

Fig. 10. An MDBS with partially non-conflicting subtransactions.

Fig. 11. FDBS: example.

4   Existing Composite Transaction Models

In this section we describe several transaction models using the ideas above. In
particular, we consider distributed transactions, sagas, and federated database
transactions. These models are two-level models: transactions consist of subtransactions considered as operations at the top-level, and executed as transactions at the lowest level. Top-level transactions are called global transactions,
operations in global transactions are global subtransactions and transactions
circumventing the global layer are called local transactions.

4.1   Distributed (Multi-database) Transactions

The model of interest here is often referred to as multidatabase system (MDBS).
Following the usual terminology, $T_i(i = 1, 2, ..., n)$ are global transactions. Each
global transaction is decomposed into global subtransactions, t_{ij}, encompassing
all operations to be executed at the component databases, $S_j(j = 1, ..., m)$.
For FS, the set T_{S_F} is the set of global transactions and O_{S_F} is the union of all
subtransactions t_{ij}. For the weak and strong input order we set $\to_{S_F} = \mapsto_{S_F} = \emptyset$.
For the bottom schedulers S_j, the set T_{S_j} of transactions are the subtransactions
t_{ij}. O_{S_j} is the set of operations at S_j to be executed for all t_{ij}. In the classical
treatment of distributed transactions nothing is known about the commutativity
of subtransactions. This is expressed in the scheduler S_F by assuming a conflict
between every pair of subtransactions: t_{ij} conflicts with $t_{rs} \Leftrightarrow i \neq r \wedge j = s$.
Therefore S_F orders all such pairs the same way: For all $i_1, i_2 \in \{1, 2, ...n\}$:
If $t_{i_1 j_1} < t_{i_2 j_1} \Rightarrow t_{i_1 j_2} < t_{i_2 j_2}$. Otherwise $\mapsto_{S_F}$ would by cyclic. Therefore the
weak input order imposed to all component schedulers is the same for all S_j.
According to FCC all S_j are CC. From there FCC - in this special MDB setting
- requires that all serialisation orders be the same.

    This result clearly is not surprising and corresponds to the usual understand-
ing. The advantage of our treatment is that several points become clear. First,

without further semantic knowledge the technique cannot be improved. Second, and more importantly, as soon as the S_F scheduler has information about the commutativity of the subtransactions, we can drop the related weak order constraint imposed to the corresponding S_j scheduler. Such an example is shown in figure 10, where there is no conflict between t_1 and t_4, thus allowing the serialisation order from t_4 to t_1.

Now, with respect to recovery, usually we do not assume to have inverses for global subtransactions. Therefore S_F must defer the commit of every subtransaction t_{ij} up to the commit of the global transaction Ti. This calls for atomic commitment as it is known. However, we can easily prove that, as soon as there are inverses t_{ij}^{-1} known to some t_{ij}, the scheduler can early commit such t_{ij} and, in case of failure, do recovery at the S_F level.

4.2 Sagas

A saga [7] T_i is a logical unit of work and shall be executed as a whole or not at all. It consists of a (partially) strongly ordered set of (sub-)transactions t_{ij}. Each transaction has an inverse t_{ij}^{-1} for compensation in case of recovery. With respect to concurrency, a saga does allow any kind of interleaving w.r.t. other concurrent sagas.

Let us describe sagas in a two-level stack or fork schedule consisting of a top-level schedule and one or more bottom-level schedules. The top-level scheduler assumes commutativity of all transaction pairs $(t_{ij}, t_{rs}), i \neq r$. Therefore no weak output order is generated and imposed as input to the bottom schedulers. No constraints are imposed over the serialisation orders of the subtransactions executed in S_j.

Again, this result is not surprising. However, as before we can easily incorporate the fact that not all transactions commute and not all transactions have inverses.

In comparison with distributed transactions and in summing up we have the following observation: *Distributed transactions correspond to a fork schedule where the transactions of different sagas conflict and no inverse transaction is known. Sagas correspond to the case where the transactions of different sagas commute and every transaction has an inverse.* From here, it is clear that our general fork schedule encompasses all cases "in between" these two extremes, i.e., if some transactions commute or if some transactions have inverses.

4.3 Federated Transactions

Federated transactions are a generalization of MDB transactions in that local transactions t_{Lk} circumvent the top-level scheduler and directly enter the bottom scheduler S_{Jj} (fig. 11). We have modelled this by a fork schedule with an (artificial) additional schedule S_{Lk} at the same level as S_F for every local transaction T_{Lk}, which we called an FDBS-Schedule (section 3.4). A correct FDBS is ensured by having the FDCC property, as mentioned earlier. Given this property, we easily relate special results obtained in the context of multi-level transactions [12]. There a "dynamic" conflict relation to be used by the top-level scheduler was introduced in order to capture indirect conflicts between local transactions and global subtransactions. This corresponds to the additional edges of the ghost-graph in S_F of definition 16.

As a practical method, [12] have proposed to introduce two kinds of commits: a commit with respect to other global subtransactions at the end of every subtransaction and a commit with respect to local transactions at the end of the global transaction. As a simple method for an implementation with locking, it was proposed to have "retained" locks, i.e. locks that are kept until the end of the global transaction to shield against local transactions. Such locks are not visible to other global subtransactions. The effect of this locking scheme is that no ghost order can arise between active transactions. As a result, the ghost order represents a temporal relationship reflecting the fact that two transactions were executed serially with respect to each other, making cycles impossible.

The FDCC property also allows a simple explanation of the ticket method for federated databases [8]. In this method, all global transactions have at most one operation at each local (join) site, hence there is no need for the join to check whether a local transaction is serialized between two global subtransactions of the same root. Furthermore, a global transaction must read and increase the value of a counter at each site. A global commit is done only if there is no cycle based on the ticket orders between different global transactions. Because there is no input order in traditional schedulers, this method has to rely on the ticket values to determine the serialization order at the local databases. The assumption that every pair of operations conflict (see definition 18) is translated here in the fact that a value has to be updated by each transaction, forcing all of them to conflict.

5   Conclusion

In this paper, we have developed a framework to reason about correctness in composite systems. Our main goal has been to allow individual components to decide locally while still ensuring global correctness and to determine what information needs to be provided to each scheduler in order to do so. We use the notion of conflict consistency to restrict correct executions to those consistent with the information passed to a scheduler (weak and strong input orders). Based on conflict consistency, correctness criteria for several configurations (stack, fork, and join) have been developed. These criteria characterize all correct and only correct executions. In particular, if the composite system has a tree configuration (no joins), it suffices to enforce conflict consistency locally to obtain global correctness. If joins are involved, however, additional restrictions are necessary since the criteria provided are based on non-local information (the ghost graph). As the example with federated transactions shows, it is still possible to design dynamic criteria for configurations containing joins in spite of the static nature of the criterion for joins. As an additional contribution, we have described known transaction mechanisms (distributed transactions, sagas, and federated transactions) as special cases of the composite framework and from there, we have demonstrated how more general mechanisms can be proven correct.

Future work involves dynamic schedulers including recovery within the composite framework and exploring more complex configurations, always with the trade-off in mind between passing global information and deciding locally.

References

1. G. Alonso, S. Blott, A. Fessler, and H.-J. Schek. Correctness and parallelism in composite systems. In *Proc. of the 16th Symp. on Principles of Database Systems (PODS'97)*, Tucson, Arizona, May 1997.
2. G. Alonso, R. Vingralek, D. Agrawal, Y. Breitbart, A. El Abbadi, H.-J. Schek, and G. Weikum. Unifying concurrency control and recovery of transactions. *Information Systems*, 19(1):101–115, Jan. 1994. An extended abstract of this paper appeared in the *Proceedings of the 4th International Conference on Extending Database Technology*, EDBT'94. March, 1994, pages 123-130.
3. C. Beeri, P. A. Bernstein, and N. Goodman. A model for concurrency in nested transactions systems. *Journal of the ACM*, 36(2):230–269, Apr. 1989.
4. C. Beeri, H.-J. Schek, and G. Weikum. Multilevel transaction management: Theoretical art or practical need? In *Proceedings of the International Conference on Extending Database Technology*, number 303 in Lecture Notes in Computer Science, pages 134–154, Venice, Italy, Mar. 1988. Springer-Verlag, New York.
5. P. A. Bernstein, V. Hadzilacos, and N. Goodman. *Concurrency Control and Recovery in Database Systems*. Addison Wesley, 1987.
6. Y. Breitbart, H. Garcia-Molina, and A. Silberschatz. Overview of multidatabase transaction management. *The VLDB Journal*, (1):181–239, 1992.
7. H. García-Molina and K. Salem. Sagas. In *Proc. 1987 SIGMOD International Conference on Management of Data*, pages 249–259, May 1987.
8. D. Georgakopoulos, M. Rusinkiewicz, and A. Sheth. Using tickets to enforce the serializability of multidabase transactions. *IEEE Knowl. and Data Engineering*, Feb. 1994.
9. J. Moss. *Nested Transactions: An Approach to Reliable Distributed Computing*. PhD thesis, M.I.T. Laboratory for Computer Science, Cambridge, Massachusetts, MIT Press, 1981.
10. J. E. B. Moss, N. D. Griffith, and M. H. Graham. Abstraction in recovery management. In *Proceedings of the ACM SIGMOD International Conference on Management of Data*, pages 72–83, 1986.
11. C. Pu, G. Kaiser, and N. Hutchinson. Split-Transactions for Open-Ended Activities. In *Proceedings of the 14th International Conference on Very Large Databases, Los Angeles*, pages 26–37, 1988.
12. H.-J. Schek, G. Weikum, and W. Schaad. A Multi-Level Transaction Approach to Federated Transaction Management. In *Proceedings of the International Workshop on Interoperability in Multi-database Systems, Research Issues in Data Engineering (IEEE-RIDE-IMS)*, Kyoto, Apr. 1991.
13. R. Vingralek, H. Hasse, Y. Breitbart, and H.-J. Schek. Unifying concurrency control and recovery of transactions with semantically rich operations. *Journal of Theoretical Computer Science*, 1998.
14. G. Weikum. Principles and Realisation Strategies of Multilevel Transaction Management. *ACM Transactions on Database Systems*, 16(1):132, March 1991.

6 Appendix

This section contains the proofs to the theorems in the paper.

Theorem 1. *A schedule S is conflict consistent iff the union of its weak input order and its serialisation graph* $(\hookrightarrow_S \cup \rightarrow_S)$ *is acyclic.*   □

This theorem was proven in [1] where we used slightly modified definitions. The idea is to construct a total order containing the union of weak order and serialisation graph, and to find a serial schedule with the same weak output order.

Theorem 2. *A stack schedule is correct if it is SCC.*

Proof. *We construct by induction a serial execution of all transactions of all levels, i.e., on all levels all transactions are strongly ordered:*

We can formulate the induction in two steps:

(1) Whenever a serial schedule S'_{i-1} *can be constructed which orders conflicting operations as* $<_{S_{i-1}}$ *and serialises the transactions in* T_{i-1} *as they are ordered in* $<_{S_i}$ *the following holds:*

(2) We can construct a serial schedule S'_i *which orders conflicting operations as* $<_{S_i}$ *and serialises the transactions in* T_i *as they are ordered in* $<_{S_{i+1}}$

Point (1) is true since:

$o <_{S_i} o' \Rightarrow o \rightarrow_{S_{i-1}} o' \Rightarrow \neg(o' \hookrightarrow_{S_{i-1}} o)$, *as otherwise there would be a cycle in* $(\hookrightarrow_{S_{i-1}} \cup \rightarrow_{S_{i-1}})$. *Thus, the transactions of* T_{i-1} *are serialised as* $<_{S_i}$.

Point (2) is true since:

S_i *is CC*

$\Rightarrow (\hookrightarrow_{S_i} \cup \rightarrow_{S_i})$ *is acyclic*

$\Rightarrow (\hookrightarrow_{S_i} \cup \rightarrow_{S_i})$ *can be completed to an acyclic total order which defines the order of the transactions of a serial schedule* S'_i *which orders conflicting operations as* $<_{S_i}$.

As (1) inductively implies (2), what remains is to show the induction hypothesis. There is a serial schedule S'_1 *which orders conflicting operations as* $<_{S_1}$ *since all its operations are executed sequentially. Therefore, (2) holds without (1) for* $i = 1$.   □

Theorem 3. *An execution in a fork schedule is correct iff it is FCC.*

Proof. *For every fork schedule FS a semantically equivalent stack schedule SS consisting of* SS_1 *and* SS_2 *can be constructed with:*

$SS_2 := S_F$; $T_{SS_1} := O_{S_F}$, $O_{SS_1} := \bigcup_{i=1}^{n} O_{S_i}$, $\rightarrow_{SS_1} := \bigcup_{i=1}^{n} \rightarrow_{S_i}$, $\hookrightarrow_{SS_1} :=$ $\bigcup_{i=1}^{n} \hookrightarrow_{S_i}$,

$CON_{SS_1} := \bigcup_{i=1}^{n} CON_{S_i}$, *(i.e.,* $\forall o \in t, o' \in t', t \in T_{S_i}, t' \in T_{S_j}, i \neq j :$ $\neg CON_{SS_1}(o, o'))$,

$<_{SS_1} := \bigcup_{i=1}^{n} <_{S_i}$, $\ll_{SS_1} := \bigcup_{i=1}^{n} \ll_{S_i}$.

Now, SS_2 *is CC iff* S_F *is, and* SS_1 *is CC iff* $\bigcup_{i=1}^{n} (\hookrightarrow_{S_i} \cup \rightarrow_{S_i})$ *is acyclic. Because the fork is FCC then the equivalent stack is SCC.*   □

The locally testable criterion for FCC can be proven by dividing $(\hookrightarrow_{S_i} \cup \rightarrow_{S_i})$ into subgraphs of the different schedules and considering their connections to each other:

Theorem 4 (Criterion for Fork Conflict Consistency). *A fork schedule FS is fork conflict consistent, iff each of the schedules $S_F, S_1, \ldots, S_n$ is conflict consistent.*

Proof. (Only if). *From FCC follows that $(\hookrightarrow_{S_i} \cup \to_{S_i})$ is acyclic $\forall i \in \{1, \ldots, n\}$. As all those partial graphs $(\hookrightarrow_{S_i} \cup \to_{S_i})$ are pairwise unconnected and therefore must also be acyclic, each one of the S_i schedules is CC.*

(If). *If each S_i is CC, all partial graphs $(\hookrightarrow_{S_i} \cup \to_{S_i})$ $(i \in \{1, \ldots, n\})$ are acyclic. Since there are no conflicts between operations in different S_i, no serialisation graph edge connects different S_i. Hence, all these subgraphs are unconnected and the union of all of all those graphs remains acyclic and, thus, FS is FCC.*   □

Theorem 5. *An execution in a join schedule is correct iff it is JCC.*

Proof. (If). *Let $:<:_{JS}$ be the transitive closure of $\lesssim_{JS} \cup \bigcup_{i=1}^{n} (\hookrightarrow_{S_i} \cup \to_{S_i})$. Then, for every JCC join schedule JS a semantically equivalent stack schedule SS consisting of SS_1 and SS_2 can be constructed with:*

$SS_1 := S_J$; $O_{SS_2} := T_{S_J}$, $T_{SS_2} := \bigcup_{i=1}^{n} T_{S_i}$, $\mapsto_{SS_2} := \bigcup_{i=1}^{n} \mapsto_{S_i}$, $\ll_{SS_2} := \bigcup_{i=1}^{n} \ll_{S_i}$

$CON_{SS_2} := \bigcup_{i=1}^{n} CON_{S_i} \cup \{(o,o') \mid o \in O_t, o' \in O_{t'}, t \in T_{S_i}, t' \in T_{S_j}, i \neq j\}$,

$\to_{SS_2} := \bigcup_{i=1}^{n} \to_{S_i} \cup \{(t,t') \mid (\exists o \in O_t, \exists o \in O_{t'} : CON_{SS_2}(o,o')) \wedge \neg(t' :<:_{JS} t)$, *such that $\to_{SS_2}$ is acyclic*$\}$.

Clearly, it is possible to construct an acyclic total order $\to_{SS_2}$ as it is not contradicting $:<:_{JS}$, which is acyclic, and every acyclic partial order can be completed to an acyclic total order. Note that SS_2 has an output order that directly follows from the definition of the new conflicts and its input order. As $\hookrightarrow_{SS_2}$ cannot contradict $\to_{SS_2}$, $(\hookrightarrow_{SS_2} \cup \to_{SS_2})$ is also acyclic and from SS_1 is CC follows that SS is SCC.

(Only if). *For a join schedule JS a semantically equivalent stack schedule SS consisting of SS_1 and SS_2 is constructed with:*

$SS_1 := S_J$; $O_{SS_2} := T_{S_J}$, $T_{SS_2} := \bigcup_{i=1}^{n} T_{S_i}$, $\mapsto_{SS_2} := \bigcup_{i=1}^{n} \mapsto_{S_i}$, $\to_{SS_2} := \bigcup_{i=1}^{n} \to_{S_i}$,

$CON_{SS_2} := \bigcup_{i=1}^{n} CON_{S_i} \cup \{(o,o') \mid o \in O_t, o' \in O_{t'}, t \in T_{S_i}, t' \in T_{S_j}, i \neq j\}$.

Be SS SCC and have $\lesssim_{JS} \cup \bigcup_{i=1}^{n} (\hookrightarrow_{S_i} \cup \to_{S_i})$ a cycle.

Case (1): From $T \lesssim_{JS} T'$ follows:

$\exists t \in O_T, \exists t' \in O_{T'} : t \to_{SS_1} t', CON_{SS_2}(t,t')$

$\Rightarrow t <_{SS_2} t', t \to_{SS_1} t'$, *as otherwise SS_1 not CC*

$\Rightarrow T \hookrightarrow_{SS_2} T'$.

Case (2): From $T \to_{S_i} T'$ follows: $T \to_{SS_2} T'$.

Case (3): From $T \hookrightarrow_{S_i} T'$ follows: $T \hookrightarrow_{SS_2} T'$.

Thus, there is a cycle in $(\hookrightarrow_{SS_2} \cup \to_{SS_2})$ which contradicts SCC. Note that in both directions CC of SS_1 is equivalent to CC of S_J.   □

Theorem 6 (Criterion for JCC). *A completed join schedule CJS is JCC, if each of the schedules $S_J, S_1, \ldots, S_n$ is conflict consistent.*

Proof. *Be $G := \lesssim_{JS} \cup \bigcup_{i=1}^{n} (\hookrightarrow_{S_i} \cup \to_{S_i})$. If all schedules are CC, all subgraphs $G|_{S_i}$ (= restriction of G on nodes of S_i)*

are acyclic as $\lesssim_{JS}$-edges exist only between subgraphs. Furthermore, every edge between subgraphs is a $\lesssim_{JS}$-edge.

Assume now a cycle in G. Then, because of the above reasons, there must be a cycle between subgraphs, in general:

$G|_{S_1} \lesssim_{JS} \cdots \lesssim_{JS} G|_{S_n} \lesssim_{JS} G|_{S_1}.$

Then there exist transactions in T_{S_J} with:

$t'_1 \hookrightarrow t_2, \ t'_2 \hookrightarrow t_3, \ \ldots, \ t'_{n-1} \hookrightarrow t_n, \ t'_n \hookrightarrow t_1.$

From definition 14 and CC follows that there exist weak input orders $t'_i \rightarrow t_{i+1}$ and also

$t_i \rightarrow t_{i+1}, \ t_i \rightarrow t'_{i+1}, \ t'_i \rightarrow t'_{i+1}.$

I.e., there is a cycle $t_1 \rightarrow t_2 \rightarrow \ldots \rightarrow t_n \rightarrow t_1$, which is a contradiction to CC of S_J. $\qquad\qquad\Box$

Theorem 7. *An execution in an FDBS-schedule is correct iff it is FDCC.*
Proof. (If). *Let $:<:_{JS}$ be the transitive closure of $\lesssim_{FDS} \cup \bigcup_{i=1}^{n} (\hookrightarrow_{S_i} \cup \rightarrow_{S_i})$. Then, for every FDCC join schedule FDS a semantically equivalent stack schedule SS consisting of SS_1 and SS_2 can be constructed, whereby SS_1 looks like:*

$T_{SS_1} := \bigcup_{i=1}^{n} T_{S_{Ji}}, \ O_{SS_1} := \{o \in O_t \mid t \in T_{SS_1}\}, \ \hookrightarrow_{SS_1} := \bigcup_{i=1}^{n} \hookrightarrow_{S_{Ji}},$
$CON_{SS_1} := \bigcup_{i=1}^{n} CON_{S_{Ji}}.$

Then SS_2 can be defined as:

$O_{SS_2} := \bigcup_{i=1}^{n} T_{S_{Ji}}, \ T_{SS_2} := \{t \mid \exists o \in O_{SS_2} : o \in O_t\}, \ \hookrightarrow_{SS_2} := \hookrightarrow_{S_F},$
$CON_{SS_2} := CON_{S_F} \cup \{(o,o') \mid o \in O_t, o' \in O_{t'}, t \in T_S, t' \in T_{S'}, S, S' \in \{S_F, S_{L1}, \ldots, S_{Ll}\}, S \neq S'\},$
$\rightarrow_{SS_2} := \rightarrow_{S_F} \cup \{(t,t') \mid (\exists o \in O_t, \exists o \in O_{t'} : CON_{SS_2}(o,o')) \wedge \neg(t' :<:_{FDS} t)\},$
such that $\rightarrow_{SS_2}$ is acyclic}.

Clearly, it is possible to construct an acyclic total order $\rightarrow_{SS_2}$ as it is not contradicting $:<:_{FDS}$, which is acyclic, and every acyclic partial order can be completed to an acyclic total order. Note that SS_2 has an output order that directly follows from the definition of the new conflicts and its input order. As $\hookrightarrow_{SS_2}$ cannot contradict $\rightarrow_{SS_2}$, $(\hookrightarrow_{SS_2} \cup \rightarrow_{SS_2})$ is also acyclic and from SS_1 is CC follows that SS is SCC.

(Only if). *For an FDBS-schedule FDS a semantically equivalent stack schedule SS consisting of SS_1 and SS_2 is constructed with SS_1 looking like:*

$T_{SS_1} := \bigcup_{i=1}^{n} T_{S_{Ji}}, \ O_{SS_1} := \{o \in O_t \mid t \in T_{SS_1}\}, \ \hookrightarrow_{SS_1} := \bigcup_{i=1}^{n} \hookrightarrow_{S_{Ji}},$
$CON_{SS_1} := \bigcup_{i=1}^{n} CON_{S_{Ji}}.$

Then SS_2 can be defined as:

$O_{SS_2} := \bigcup_{i=1}^{n} T_{S_{Ji}}, \ T_{SS_2} := \{t \mid \exists o \in O_{SS_2} : o \in O_t\}, \ \hookrightarrow_{SS_2} := \hookrightarrow_{S_F}, \ \rightarrow_{SS_2} := \rightarrow_{S_F},$
$CON_{SS_2} := CON_{S_F} \cup \{(o,o') \mid o \in O_t, o' \in O_{t'}, t \in T_S, t' \in T_{S'}, S, S' \in \{S_F, S_{L1}, \ldots, S_{Ll}\}, S \neq S'\}.$

Be SS SCC and have $\lesssim_{FDS} \cup (\hookrightarrow_{S_F} \cup \rightarrow_{S_F})$ a cycle.

Case (1): From $T \lesssim_{FDS} T'$ follows:

$\exists t \in O_T, \exists t' \in O_{T'} : t \hookrightarrow_{SS_1} t', CON_{SS_2}(t,t')$
$\Rightarrow t <_{SS_2} t', t \hookrightarrow_{SS_1} t',$ *as otherwise SS_1 not CC*
$\Rightarrow T \hookrightarrow_{SS_2} T'.$

Case (2): From $T \to_{S_F} T'$ follows: $T \to_{SS_2} T'$.
Case (3): From $T \hookrightarrow_{S_F} T'$ follows: $T \hookrightarrow_{SS_2} T'$.
Thus, there is a cycle in $(\hookrightarrow_{SS_2} \cup \to_{SS_2})$ which contradicts SCC.
Note that in both directions CC of SS_1 is equivalent to CC of $S_{J1} \ldots S_{Jn}$, as every S_{J1} is CC and there is neither an input order between $S_{J1} \ldots S_{Jn}$ nor an output order because there are no conflicts.   □

Theorem 8 (Criterion for FDCC). *A completed FDBS-schedule CFDS is FDCC, if*
(1) each of the schedules $S_F, S_{L1} \ldots S_{Ll}, S_{J1} \ldots S_{Jn}$ is conflict consistent and
(2) if $\nexists t, t' \in O_T, T \in T_{S_F} : (t, t' \in T_{S_{Jj}} (j \in \{1 \ldots n\}, \exists t_{L1} \ldots t_{Lk} \in \bigcup_{i=1}^{l} O_{S_{Li}} : (t \hookrightarrow_{S_{Jj}} t_{L1} \hookrightarrow_{S_{Jj}} \ldots \hookrightarrow_{S_{Jj}} t_{Lk} \hookrightarrow_{S_{Jj}} t'))$.
Proof. *Be $G := \lesssim_{FDS} \cup \bigcup_{i=1}^{n} (\hookrightarrow_{S_i} \cup \to_{S_i})$.*
If all schedules are CC, all subgraphs $G|_{S_i}$ are acyclic as $\lesssim_{FDS}$-edges exist only between subgraphs. Furthermore, every edge between subgraphs is a $\lesssim_{FDS}$-edge. Assume now a cycle in G. Then, because of the above reasons, there must be a cycle between subgraphs, in general (let $:<:_S := (\hookrightarrow_S \cup \to_S))$:

$T_{F11} :<:_{S_F} \ldots :<:_{S_F} T_{F1j_1} \lesssim_{FDS} T_{L11} \lesssim_{FDS} \ldots \lesssim_{FDS} T_{L1k_1} \lesssim_{FDS} T_{F21}$
$:<:_{S_F} \ldots :<:_{S_F} T_{F2j_2} \lesssim_{FDS} T_{L21} \lesssim_{FDS} \ldots \lesssim_{FDS} T_{Lmk_m} \lesssim_{FDS} T_{F11}$.

We know that all pairs of transactions in this cycle are different from each other, as otherwise the join schedule at which their subtransactions execute would detect a contradiction to condition (2) of this criterion.
Then there exist transactions $t_{F11} \in T_{F11}, \ldots$ with:
$(t_{F1j_1} \hookrightarrow_{S_{J1}} t_{L11} \hookrightarrow_{S_{J1}} \ldots \hookrightarrow_{S_{J1}} t_{L1k_1} \hookrightarrow_{S_{J1}} t_{F21}), \ldots,$
$(t_{Fm,j_m} \hookrightarrow_{S_{Jn}} t_{Lm1} \hookrightarrow_{S_{Jn}} \ldots \hookrightarrow_{S_{Jn}} t_{Lmk_m} \hookrightarrow_{S_{Jn}} t_{F11})$
There exist (a.o.) the following conflicts in S_F:
$(t_{F1j_1}, t_{F21}), \ldots, (t_{Fm-1,j_{m-1}}, t_{Fm1}), (t_{Fmj_m}, t_{F11})$.
Conflicting operations are weakly output ordered, and as they are transactions in one S_{Jj}, resp., also weakly input ordered.
$\Rightarrow T_{F11} :<:_{S_F} \ldots :<:_{S_F} T_{F1j_1} \hookrightarrow_{S_F} T_{F21} \ldots$.
This is a cycle in $(\hookrightarrow_{S_F} \cup \to_{S_F})$, hence, a contradiction to CC of S_F. Thus, G must be acyclic and CFDS is FDCC.   □

Databases for Tracking Mobile Units in Real Time

Ouri Wolfson[1], Liqin Jiang[1], A. Prasad Sistla[1], Sam Chamberlain[2], Naphtali Rishe[3], and Minglin Deng[1]

[1] University of Illinois,Chicago, IL 60607, USA
[2] Army Research Laboratory, Aberdeen Proving Ground, MD, USA
[3] Florida International University, University Park, Miami, FL 33199, USA

Abstract. In this paper we consider databases representing information about moving objects (e.g. vehicles), particularly their location. We address the problems of updating and querying such databases. Specifically, the update problem is to determine when the location of a moving object in the database (namely its database location) should be updated. We answer this question by proposing an information cost model that captures uncertainty, deviation, and communication. Then we analyze dead-reckoning policies, namely policies that update the database location whenever the distance between the actual location and the database location exceeds a given threshold, x. Dead-reckoning is the prevalent approach in military applications, and our cost model enables us to determine the threshold x. Then we consider the problem of processing range queries in the database, and we propose a probabilistic algorithm to solve the problem.

1 Introduction

1.1 Background

Consider a database that represents information about moving objects and their location. For example, for a database representing the location of taxi-cabs a typical query may be: retrieve the free cabs that are currently within 1 mile of 33 N. Michigan Ave., Chicago (to pick-up a customer); or for a trucking company database a typical query may be: retrieve the trucks that are currently within 1 mile of truck ABT312 (which needs assistance); or for a database representing the current location of objects in a battlefield a typical query may be: retrieve the friendly helicopters that are in a given region, or, retrieve the friendly helicopters that are expected to enter the region within the next 10 minutes. The queries may originate from the moving objects, or from stationary users. We will refer to the above applications as MOtion-Database (MOD) applications or moving-objects-database applications. In the military, MOD applications arise in the context of the digital battlefield (see [13,12]), and in the civilian industry they arise in transportation systems.

Catriel Beeri, Peter Buneman (Eds.): ICDT'99, LNCS 1540, pp. 169–186, 1998.

Currently, MOD applications are being developed in an ad hoc fashion. Database management system (DBMS) technology provides a potential foundation for MOD applications, however, DBMS's are currently not used for this purpose. The reason is that there is a critical set of capabilities that have to be integrated, adapted, and built on top of existing DBMS's in order to support moving objects databases. The added capabilities include, among other things, support for spatial and temporal information, support for rapidly changing real time data, new indexing methods, and imprecision management. The objective of our Databases fOr MovINg Objects (DOMINO) project is to build an envelope containing these capabilities on top of existing DBMS's.

In this paper we address the imprecision problem. The location of a moving object is inherently imprecise because, regardless of the policy used to update the database location of a moving object (i.e. the object-location stored in the database), the database location cannot always be identical to the actual location of the object. There may be several location update policies, for example, the location is updated every x time units. In this paper we address dead-reckoning policies, namely policies that update the database whenever the distance between the actual location of a moving object m and its database location exceeds a given threshold h, say 1 mile. This means that the DBMS will answer a query "what is the current location of m?" by an answer A: "the current location is (x,y) with a deviation of at most 1 mile". Dead-reckoning is the prevalent approach in military applications.

One of the main issues addressed in this paper is how to determine the update threshold h in dead-reckoning policies. This threshold determines the location imprecision, which encompasses two related but different concepts, namely deviation and uncertainty. The deviation of a moving object m at a particular point in time t is the distance between m's actual location at time t, and its database location at time t. For the answer A above, the deviation is the distance between the actual location of m and (x,y). On the other hand, the uncertainty of a moving object m at a particular point in time t is the size of the area in which the object can possibly be. For the answer A above, the uncertainty is the area of a circle with radius 1 mile. The deviation has a cost (or penalty) in terms of incorrect decision making, and so does the uncertainty. The deviation (resp. uncertainty) cost is proportional to the size of the deviation (resp. uncertainty). The ratio between the costs of an uncertainty unit and a deviation unit depends on the interpretation of an answer such as A above, as will be explained in section 3.

In MOD applications the database updates are usually generated by the moving objects themselves. Each moving object is equipped with a Geographic Positioning System (GPS), and it updates its database location using a wireless network (e.g ARDIS, RAM Mobile Data Co., IRIDIUM, etc.). This introduces a third information cost component, namely communication. For example, RAM Mobile Data Co. charges a minimum of 4 cents per message, with the exact cost depending on the size of the message. Furthermore, there is a tradeoff between communication and imprecision in the sense that the higher the communication cost the lower the imprecision and vice versa. In this paper we propose a model of the information cost in moving objects databases, which captures imprecision and communication. The tradeoff is captured in the model by the relative costs of an uncertainty unit, a deviation unit, and a communication unit.

1.2 Location Update Policies

Consider an object m moving along a prespecified route. We model the database location of m by storing in the database m's starting time, starting location, and a prediction of future locations of the object. In this paper the prediction is given as the speed v of the object. Thus the database location of m can be computed by the DBMS at any subsequent point in time. [1] This method of modeling the database location was originally introduced in [5,6] via the concept of a dynamic attribute; the method is modified here in order to handle uncertainty. The actual location of a moving object m deviates from its database location due to the fact that m does not travel at the constant speed v.

A *dead-reckoning update policy* for m dictates that there is a database-update threshold th, i.e. a deviation for which m should send a location/speed update to the database. (Note that at any point in time, since m knows its actual location and its database location, it can compute its current deviation.) *Speed dead-reckoning* [2] (sdr) is a dead-reckoning policy in which the threshold th is fixed for the duration of the trip.

In this paper we introduce another dead-reckoning update policy, called *adaptive dead reckoning(adr)*. Adr provides with each update a new threshold th that is computed using a cost based approach. th minimizes the total information cost per time unit until the next update. The total information cost consists of the update cost, the deviation cost, and the uncertainty cost. In order to minimize the total information cost per time unit between now and the next update, the moving object m has to estimate when the next update will occur, i.e. when the deviation will reach the threshold. Thus, at location update time, in order to compute the new threshold, adr predicts the future behavior of the deviation. The thresholds differ from update to update because the predicted behavior of the deviation is different.

A problem common to both sdr and adr is that the moving object may be disconnected from the network. In other words, although the DBMS "thinks" that updates are not generated since the deviation does not exceed the update threshold, the actual reason is that the moving object is disconnected. To cope with this problem we introduce a third policy, "disconnection detecting

---

[1] Our simulation experiments show that, even when the speed fluctuates sharply, this temporal technique reduces the number of updates to 15% of the number used by the traditional, nontemporal method in which the database simply stores the latest known location for each object; this saves 85% of the location-updates overhead.

[2] We use the term *speed* dead-reckoning to contrast it with the plain dead-reckoning (pdr) policy in which the database location is fixed until it is explicitly updated by the moving object; namely, pdr does not use dynamic attributes.

dead-reckoning (dtdr)". The policy avoids the regular process of checking for disconnection by trying to communicate with the moving object, thus increasing the load on the low bandwidth wireless channel. Instead, it uses a novel technique that decreases the uncertainty threshold for disconnection detection. Thus, in dtdr the threshold continuously decreases as the time interval since the last location update increases. It has a value K during the first time unit after the update, it has value $K/2$ during the second time unit after the update, it has value $K/3$ during the third time unit, etc. Thus, if the object is connected, it is increasingly likely that it will generate an update. Conversely, if the moving object does not generate an update, as the time interval since the last update increases it is increasingly likely that the moving object is disconnected. The dtdr policy computes the K that minimizes the total information cost, i.e. the sum of the update cost, the deviation cost, and the uncertainty cost.

To contrast the three policies, observe that for sdr the threshold is fixed for all location updates. For adr the threshold is fixed between each pair of consecutive updates, but it may change from pair to pair. For dtdr the threshold decreases as the period of time between a pair of consecutive updates increases.

We compared by simulation the three policies introduced in this paper. Our simulations indicate that adr is superior to sdr in the sense that it has a lower or equal information cost for every value of the update-unit cost, uncertainty-unit cost, and deviation-unit cost. Adr is superior to dtdr in the same sense; the difference between the costs of the two policies quantifies the cost of disconnection detection. For some parameters combinations the information cost of sdr is six times as high as that of adr.

Finally, an additional contribution of this paper is a probabilistic model and an algorithm for query processing in motion databases. In our model the location of the moving object is a random variable, and at any point in time the database location and the uncertainty are used to determine a density function for this variable. Based on this model we developed an algorithm that processes range queries such as Q='retrieve the moving objects that are currently inside a given region R'. The answer to Q is a set of objects, each of which is associated with the probability that currently the object is inside R.

The rest of this paper is organized as follows. In section 2 we introduce the data model and discuss location attributes of moving objects. In section 3 we discuss the information cost of a trip, and in section 4 we introduce our approach to cost optimization. In section 5 we describe the three location update policies. In section 6 we present our approach to probabilistic query processing. In section 7 we discuss relevant work, and in the last section we summarize our results.

2   The Data Model

In this section we define the main concepts used in this paper. A *database* is a set of object-classes. An *object-class* is a set of attributes. Some object-classes are designated as *spatial*. Each spatial object class is either a point-class, a line-class, or a polygon-class in two-dimensional space (all our concepts and results can be extended to three-dimensional space).

Point object classes are either mobile or stationary. A point object class O has a *location attribute L*. If the object class is *stationary*, its location attribute has two sub-attributes $L.x$, and $L.y$, representing the x and y coordinates of the object. If the object class is *mobile*, its location attribute has six sub-attributes, $L.route$, $L.startlocation$, $L.starttime$, $L.direction$, $L.speed$, and $L.uncertainty$.

The semantics of the sub-attributes are as follows. $L.route$ is (the pointer to) a line spatial object indicating the route on which an object in the class O is moving. Although we assume that the objects move along predefined routes, our results can be extended to free movement in space (e.g. by aircraft). We will comment on that option in the last paragraph of this section. $L.startlocation$ is a point on $L.route$; it is the location of the moving object at time $L.starttime$. In other words, $L.starttime$ is the time when the moving object was at location $L.startlocation$. We assume that whenever a moving object updates its L attribute it updates the $L.startlocation$ subattribute; thus at any point in time $L.starttime$ is also the time of the last location-update. We assume in this paper that the database updates are instantaneous, i.e. valid- and transaction- times (see [11]) are equal. Therefore, $L.starttime$ is the time at which the update occurred in the real world system being modeled, and also the time when the database installs the update. $L.direction$ is a binary indicator having a value 0 or 1 (these values may correspond to north-south, or east-west, or the two endpoints of the route). $L.speed$ is a function that represents the predicted future locations of the object. It gives the distance of the moving object from $L.startlocation$ as a function of the number t of time units elapsed since the last location-update, namely since $L.starttime$. The function has the value 0 when $t = 0$. In its simplest form (which is the only form we consider in this extended abstract) $L.speed$ represents a constant speed v, i.e. the distance is $v \cdot t$. [3] $L.uncertainty$ is either a constant, or a function of the number t of time units elapsed since $L.starttime$. It represents the threshold on the location deviation (the deviation is formally defined at the end of this section); when the deviation reaches the threshold, the moving object sends a location update message. Observe that the uncertainty may change automatically as the time elapsed since $L.starttime$ increases; this is indeed the case for the dtdr policy.

We define the *route-distance* between two points on a given route to be the distance along the route between the two points. We assume that it is straightforward to compute the route-distance between two points, and the point at a given route-distance from another point. The *database location* of a moving object at a given point in time is defined as follows. At time $L.starttime$ the database location is $L.startlocation$; the database location at time $A.starttime + t$ is the

---

[3] Another possibility for representing future locations is a sequence of speeds, i.e., the object will move at speed v_1 until time t_1, at speed v_2 until time t_2, etc. Such a future plan is typical of, for example, a vehicle that expects various traffic conditions; or a package that first travels by truck, then by plane, then waits (speed 0) for another truck loading, etc.

point (x,y) which is at route-distance $L.speed \cdot t$ from the point $L.startlocation$. Intuitively, the database location of a moving object m at a given time point t is the location of m as far as the DBMS knows; it is the location that is returned by the DBMS in response to a query entered at time t that retrieves m's location. Such a query also returns the uncertainty at time t, i.e. it returns an answer of the form: m is on $L.route$ at most $L.uncertainty$ ahead of or behind (x,y).

Since between two consecutive location updates the moving object does not travel at exactly the speed $L.speed$, the actual location of the moving object deviates from its database location. Formally, for a moving object, the *deviation* d at a point in time t, denoted $d(t)$, is the route-distance between the moving object's actual location at time t and its database location at time t. The deviation is always nonnegative. At any point in time the moving object knows its current location, and it also knows all the subattributes of its location attribute. Therefore at any point in time the (computer onboard the) moving object can compute the current deviation. Observe that at time $L.starttime$ the deviation is zero.

At the beginning of the trip the moving object updates all the sub-attributes of its location attribute. Subsequently, the moving object periodically updates its current location and speed stored in the database. Specifically, a *location update* is a message sent by the moving object to the database to update some or all the sub-attributes of its location attribute. The moving object sends the location update when the deviation exceeds the $L.uncertainty$ threshold, or when the moving object changes route or direction. The location update message contains at least the values for $L.speed$ and $L.startlocation$. Obviously, other subattributes can also be updated. The subattribute $L.starttime$ is written by the DBMS whenever it installs a location update; it denotes the time when the installation is done.

Before concluding this section we would like to point out that the results of this paper hold for free-movement modeling, i.e. for objects that move freely in space (e.g. aircraft) rather than on routes. In this case $L.route$ is an infinite straight line (e.g. 60 degrees from the starting point) rather than a line-object stored in the database. Then there are two possibilities of modeling the uncertainty. The first is identical to the one described above, i.e. the uncertainty is a segment on the infinite line representing the route. In this case every change of direction constitutes a change of route, thus necessitating a location update. The second possibility is to redefine the deviation to be the Euclidean distance between the database location and the actual location, and to remove the requirement that the object updates the database whenever it changes routes. In this case $L.uncertainty$ defines a circle around the database location, and a query that retrieves the location of a moving object m returns an answer of the form: m is within a circle having a radius of at most $L.uncertainty$ from (x,y). Observe that the second possibility of modeling uncertainty necessitates less location updates, but the answer to a query is less informative since the uncertainty is given in two dimensional space rather than one-dimensional.

3   The Information Cost of a Trip

In this section we define the information cost model for a trip taken by a moving object m, and we discuss information cost optimality.

At each point in time during the trip the moving object has a deviation and an uncertainty, each of which carries a penalty. Additionally the moving object sends location update messages. Thus the information cost of a trip consists of the cost of deviation, cost of communication, and cost of uncertainty.

Now we define the deviation cost. Observe first that the cost of the deviation depends both on the size of the deviation and on the length of time for which it persists. It depends on the size of the deviation since decision-making is clearly affected by it. To see that it depends on the length of time for which the deviation persists, suppose that there is one query per time unit that retrieves the location of a moving object m. Then, if the deviation persists for two time units its cost will be twice the cost of the deviation that persists for a single time unit; the reason is that two queries (instead of one) will pay the deviation penalty. Formally, for a moving object m the cost of the deviation between two time points t_1 and t_2 is given by the *deviation cost function*, denoted $COST_d(t_1, t_2)$; it is a function of two variables that maps the deviation between the time points t_1 and t_2 into a nonnegative number. In this paper we take the penalty for each unit of deviation during a unit of time to be one (1). Then, the cost of the deviation between two time points t_1 and t_2 is:

$$COST_d(t_1, t_2) = \int_{t_1}^{t_2} d(t)dt \qquad (1)$$

The *update cost*, denoted C_1, is a nonnegative number representing the cost of a location-update message sent from the moving object to the database. This is the cost of the resources (i.e. bandwidth and computation) consumed by the update. The update cost may differ from one moving object to another, and it may vary even for a single moving object during a trip, due for example, to changing availability of bandwidth. The update cost must be given in the same units as the deviation cost. In particular, if the update cost is C_1 it means the ratio between the update cost and the cost of a unit of deviation per unit of time (which is one) is C_1. It also means that the moving object (or the system) is willing to use $1/C_1$ messages in order to reduce the deviation by one during one unit of time.

Now we define the uncertainty cost. Observe that, as for the deviation, the cost of the uncertainty depends both, on the size of the uncertainty and on the length of time for which it persists. Formally, for a moving object m the cost of the uncertainty between two time points t_1 and t_2 is given by the *uncertainty cost function*, denoted $COST_u(t_1, t_2)$; it is a function of two variables that maps the uncertainty between the time points t_1 and t_2 into a nonnegative number. Define the *uncertainty unit cost* to be the penalty for each unit of uncertainty during a unit of time, and denote it by C_2. Then, the cost of the uncertainty of m between two time points t_1 and t_2 is:

$$COST_u(t_1, t_2) = \int_{t_1}^{t_2} C_2 u(t) dt \tag{2}$$

where $u(t)$ is the value of the $L.uncertainty$ subattribute as a function of time.

The uncertainty unit cost C_2 is the ratio between the cost of a unit of uncertainty and the cost of a unit of deviation. Consider an answer returned by the DBMS: "the current location of the moving object m is (x,y), with a deviation of at most u units". C_2 should be set higher than 1 if the uncertainty in such an answer is more important than the deviation, and lower than 1 otherwise. Observe that in a dead-reckoning update policy each update message establishes a new uncertainty which is not necessarily lower than the previous one. Thus communication reduces the deviation but not necessarily the uncertainty.

Now we are ready to define the information cost of a trip taken by a moving object m. Let t_1 and t_2 be the time-stamps of two consecutive location update messages. Then the *information cost* in the interval $[t_1, t_2)$ is:

$$COST_I[t_1, t_2) = C_1 + COST_d[t_1, t_2) + COST_u[t_1, t_2) \tag{3}$$

Observe that $COST_I[t_1, t_2)$ includes the message cost at time t_1 but not the cost of the one at time t_2. Observe also that each location update message writes the actual current location of m in the database, thus it reduces the deviation to zero. The total information cost of a trip is computed by summing up $COST_I[t_1, t_2)$ for every pair of consecutive update points t_1 and t_2. Formally, let the time points of the update messages sent by m be $t_1, t_2, ..., t_k$. Furthermore, let 0 be the time point when the trip started and t_{k+1} the time point when the trip ended. Then the *total information cost* of a trip is

$$COST_I = COST_d[0, t_1) + COST_u[0, t_1) + \sum_{i=1}^{k} COST_I[t_i, t_{i+1}) \tag{4}$$

4 Cost Based Optimization for Dead Reckoning Policies

As mentioned in the introduction, a dead-reckoning update policy for a moving object m dictates that at any point in time there is a database-update threshold th, of which both the DBMS and m are aware. When the deviation of m reaches th, m sends to the database an update consisting of the current location, the predicted speed, and the new deviation threshold K. The objective of the dead reckoning policies that we introduce in this paper is to set K (which the DBMS installs in the $L.uncertainty$ subattribute), such that the total information cost is minimized. Intuitively, this is done as follows. First, m predicts the future behavior of the deviation. Based on this prediction, the average cost per time time unit between now and the next update is obtained as a a function f of the new threshold K. Then K is set to minimize f [4]. It is important to observe that

---

[4] Let us observe that the proposed method of optimizing the new threshold K is not unique. We have devised other methods which are omitted from this extended abstract. A performance comparison among these methods is the subject of future work.

we optimize the average cost per time unit rather than simply the total cost between the two time points; clearly, the total cost increases as the time interval until the next update increases.

The next theorem establishes the optimal value K for $L.uncertainty$ under the assumption that the deviation between two consecutive updates is a linear function of time.

Theorem 1: Denote the update cost by C_1, and the uncertainty unit cost by C_2. Assume that for a moving object two consecutive location updates occur at time points t_1 and t_2. Assume further that between t_1 and t_2, the deviation $d(t)$ is given by the function $a(t - t_1)$ where $t_1 \leq t \leq t_2$ and a is some positive constant; and $L.uncertainty$ is fixed at K throughout the interval (t_1, t_2). Then the total information cost per time unit between t_1 and t_2 is minimized if $K = \sqrt{\frac{2aC_1}{2C_2+1}}$. □

The implication of theorem 1 is the following. Suppose that a moving object m is currently at time point t_1, i.e. its deviation has reached the uncertainty threshold $L.uncertainty$. Now m needs to compute a new value for $L.uncertainty$ and send it in the location update message. Suppose further that m predicts that following the update the deviation will behave as the linear function $a(t - t_1)$, and in the update message it has to set the uncertainty threshold $L.uncertainty$ to a value that will remain fixed until the next update. Then, in order to optimize the information cost, m should set the threshold to $K = \sqrt{\frac{2aC_1}{2C_2+1}}$.

Next assume that, in order to detect disconnection, one is interested in a dead-reckoning policy in which the uncertainty threshold $L.uncertainty$ continuously decreases between updates. Particularly, we consider a particular type of decrease, that we call fractional decrease; other types exist, but we found this one convenient. Let K be a constant. If the uncertainty threshold $L.uncertainty$ *decreases fractionally starting with* K, then during the first time unit after a location update u its value is K, during the second time unit after u its value is $K/2$, during the third time unit after u its value is $K/3$, etc., until the next update (which establishes a new K).

Theorem 2: Assume that for a moving object two consecutive location updates occur at time points t_1 and t_2. Assume further that between t_1 and t_2, the deviation $d(t)$ is given by the function $a(t - t_1)$ where $t_1 \leq t \leq t_2$ and a is some positive constant; and in the time interval (t_1, t_2) $L.uncertainty$ decreases fractionally starting with a constant K. Then the total information cost per time unit between t_1 and t_2 is given by the following function of K.

$$f(K) = \frac{C_1 + \frac{1}{2}K + C_2 K(1 + \frac{1}{2} + \frac{1}{3} + ... + \frac{1}{\sqrt{\frac{K}{a}}})}{\sqrt{\frac{K}{a}}}. \quad □$$

Similarly to theorem 1, the implication of theorem 2 is the following. Suppose that a moving object is currently at time point t_1, i.e. it is about to send a location update message, and it can predict that following the update the deviation will behave as the linear function $a(t - t_1)$, and in the update message it sets the uncertainty threshold $L.uncertainty$ to a fractionally decreasing value starting with K. Then in order to optimize the information cost it should set K to the value that minimizes the function of theorem 2.

5   The Location Update Policies and Their Performance

In this section we describe and motivate three location update policies. Then we report on their comparison by simulation.

The speed dead-reckoning (sdr) policy. At the beginning of the trip the moving object m sends to the DBMS an uncertainty threshold that is selected in an ad hoc fashion, it is stored in $L.uncertainty$, and it remains fixed for the duration of the trip. The object m updates the database whenever the deviation exceeds $L.uncertainty$; the update simply includes the current location and current speed. [5] $\Box$

The adaptive dead reckoning (adr) policy. At the beginning of the trip the moving object m sends to the DBMS an initial deviation threshold th_1 selected arbitrarily. Then m starts tracking the deviation. When the deviation reaches th_1, the moving object sends an update message to the database. The update consists of the current speed, current location, and a new threshold th_2 that the DBMS should install in the $L.uncertainty$ subattribute. th_2 is computed as follows. Denote by t_1 the number of time units from the beginning of the trip until the deviation reaches th_1 for the first time, by I_1 the cost of the deviation (which is computed using equation 1) during the same time interval, and let $a_1 = \frac{2I_1}{t_1^2}$. Then th_2 is $\sqrt{\frac{2a_1C_1}{1+2C_2}}$ (remember, C_1 is the update cost, C_2 is the unit-uncertainty cost). When the deviation reaches th_2, a similar update is sent, except that the new threshold th_3 is $\sqrt{\frac{2a_2C_1}{1+2C_2}}$, where $a_2 = \frac{2I_2}{t_2^2}$ (I_2 is the cost of the deviation from the first update to second update, t_2 is the number of time units elapsed since the first location update). Since a_2 may be different than a_1, th_2 may be different than th_3. When th_3 is reached the object will send another update containing th_4 (which is computed in a similar fashion), and so on. $\Box$

The mathematical motivation for adr is based on theorem 1 in a straightforward way. Namely, at each update time point p_i adr simply sets the next threshold in a way that optimizes the information cost per time unit (according to theorem 1), assuming that the deviation following time p_i will behave as the following linear function: $d(t) = \frac{2I_i}{t_i^2}t$, where t is the number of time units after p_i, and t_i is the number of time units between the immediately preceding update and the current one (at time p_i), and I_i the cost of the deviation during the same time interval. The reason for this prediction of the future deviation is as follows. Adr approximates the current deviation, i.e. the deviation from the time of the

---

[5] Sdr can also use another speed, for example, the average speed since the last update, or the average speed since the beginning of the trip, or a speed that is predicted based on knowledge of the terrain. This comment holds for the other policies discussed in this section.

immediately preceding update to time p_i, by a linear function[6] (see [14]) with slope $\frac{2I_i}{t_i^2}t$. Observe that at time p_i this linear function has the same deviation cost (namely I_i) as the actual current deviation [7]. Based on the locality principle, adr predicts that after the update at time p_i, the deviation will behave according to the same approximation function.

The disconnection detection dead reckoning (dtdr) policy. At the beginning of the trip the moving object m sends to the DBMS an initial deviation threshold th_1 selected arbitrarily. The moving objects sets the uncertainty threshold $L.uncertainty$ to a fractionally decreasing value starting with th_1. That is, during the first time unit the uncertainty threshold is th_1; during the second time unit period it is $\frac{th_1}{2}$, and so on. Then it starts tracking the deviation. At time t_1 when the deviation reaches the current uncertainty threshold, namely $\frac{th_1}{t_1}$, the moving object sends a location update message to the database. The update consists of the current speed, current location, and a new threshold th_2 to be installed in the $L.uncertainty$ subattribute.

th_2 is computed using the function $f(K)$ of theorem 2. Since $f(K)$ uses the slope a of the future deviation, we first estimate the future deviation as in the adr case, as follows. Denote by I_1 the cost of the deviation (which is computed using equation 1) since the beginning of the trip, and let $a_1 = \frac{2I_1}{t_1^2}$. Now, observe that $f(K)$ does not have a closed form formula. Thus we first approximate the sum $\frac{1}{2}+\frac{1}{3}+...+\frac{1}{\sqrt{\frac{K}{a_1}}}$ by $ln(\sqrt{\frac{K}{a_1}})$ (since $\ln n$ is an approximation for the nth harmonic number). Thus the approximation function for $f(K)$ is $g(K) = \frac{C_1+\frac{K}{2}+C_2K(ln(\sqrt{\frac{K}{a_1}})+1)}{\sqrt{\frac{K}{a_1}}}$. The derivative of $g(K)$ is zero when K is the solution to the following equation.

$$ln(K) = \frac{d_1}{K} - d_2 \qquad (5)$$

where in the equation, $d_1 = \frac{2C_1}{C_2}$ and $d_2 = \frac{1}{C_2} + 4 - ln(a_1)$. We find a numerical solution to this equation using the Newton Raphson method. The solution is the new threshold th_2, and the moving object sets the uncertainty threshold $L.uncertainty$ to a fractionally decreasing value starting with th_2.

After t_2 time units, when the deviation reaches the current uncertainty threshold, namely $\frac{th_2}{t_2}$, a location update containing th_3 is sent. th_3 is computed as above, except that a new slope (as in adr) a_2 is used; and I_2 is the cost of the deviation during the previous t_2 time units. The process continues until the end of the trip. That is, at each update time point, dtdr determines the next optimal threshold by the constants C_1, C_2, and the slope a_i of the current deviation approximation function. □

---

[6] More powerful, nonlinear approximation functions have been considered, but their discussion is omitted from this extended abstract.

[7] In this sense we are using a simple linear regression, but instead of the common least squares method we employ an equal sums method that is more appropriate for our cost function.

We compared by simulation the three policies introduced in this paper namely adr, dtdr, and sdr. The parameters of the simulation are the following. The update-unit cost, namely the cost of a location-update message; the uncertainty-unit cost, namely the cost of a unit of uncertainty; deviation-unit cost, namely the cost of a unit of deviation; a speed curve, namely a function that for a period of time gives the speed of the moving object at any point in time. The comparison is done by quantifying the total information cost of each policy for a large number of combinations of the parameters. For space considerations we omit the detailed results of the simulations. The main conclusions are: 1. adr is superior to sdr in the sense that it has a lower or equal information cost for every value of the update-unit cost, uncertainty-unit cost, and deviation-unit cost; for some parameter combinations the information cost of sdr is six times as high as that of adr. 2. adr is superior to dtdr in the same sense; the difference between the costs of the two policies quantifies the cost of disconnection detection.

6   Querying with Uncertainty

In this section we present a probabilistic method for specifying and processing range queries about motion databases. For example, a typical query might be "Retrieve all objects o which are within the region R". Since there is an uncertainty about the location of the various objects at any time, we may not be able to answer the above query with absolute certainty. Instead, our query processing algorithm outputs a set of pairs of the form (o, p) where o is an object and p is the probability that the object is in region R at time t; actually, the algorithm retrieves only those pairs for which p is greater than some minimum value. Note that here we are using probability as a measure of certainty.

As indicated, we assume that all the objects are traveling on routes. Since the actual location is not exactly known, we assume that the location of an object o on its route at time t is a random variable [3]. We let $f_o(x)$ denote the density function of this random variable. More specifically, for small values of dx, $f_o(x)dx$ denotes the probability that o is at some point in the interval $[x, x+dx]$ at time t (actually, f_o is a function of x and t; however we omit this as t is understood from the context). The mean m_o of the above random variable is given by the database location of o (this equals $o.L.startlocation + o.L.speed(t - o.L.starttime)$; see section 2).

Now we discuss some possible candidates for the density functions f_o. Many natural processes tend to behave according to the normal density function. Let $\mathcal{N}_{m,\sigma}(x)$ denote a normal density function with mean m and standard deviation σ. We can adopt the normal density functions follows. We take the mean m to be equal to m_o given in the previous paragraph. Next we relate the standard deviation to the uncertainty of the object location. We do this by setting $\sigma = \frac{1}{c}(o.L.uncertainty)$ where $c > 0$ is constant. In this case, the probability that the object is within a distance of $o.L.uncertainty$ (i.e. within a distance of $c\sigma$) from the location m_o will be higher for higher values of c; for example, this probability will be equal to .68,.95 and .997 for values of c equal to 1,2 and

3 respectively (see [3]). The value of c is a function of the update policy used, the reliability of the network, the time since the last update and the ratio between uncertainty and deviation unit costs. Whatever may be the value c, there is still a non-zero probability p that the object is at a distance greater than $o.L.uncertainty$ from the the mean m_o; we can interpret this probability to be the probability that there is a disconnection. An alternative is to make p zero. This can be done by modifying the normal distribution to be a bounded normal distribution. This is done by conditioning that the object is within distance $o.L.uncertainty$ from m_o. More specifically, we first use the normal distribution as above by choosing an appropriate c. Then we compute the probability q that the object is within a distance of $o.L.uncertainty$ from m_o. Define the density function $f_o(x)$ to be equal to $\frac{1}{q}\mathcal{N}_{m_o,\sigma}(x)$ for values of x within the interval $[(m_o - o.L.uncertainty), (m_o + o.L.uncertainty)]$ and to be zero for other values of x.

A range query on motion databases is of the following form:
RETRIEVE o FROM Moving-objects WHERE C.
Here the condition part C is a disjunction of clauses where each clause is a conjunction of two conditions C_1 and C_2; C_1 only refers to the static attributes of the objects (such as 'type', 'color' etc.) and is called the static part; C_2 depends upon the location attributes and is called the dynamic part of the condition (if C is not in this form then we can convert it into disjunctive normal form; in the resulting condition each disjunct can be separated into two parts— the static part and the dynamic part). To process such a query, we process each disjunct as a separate query and take the union. Now we describe a method to process query whose condition part is a conjunction of the static and dynamic parts C_1 and C_2 respectively (one can envision other possible methods). Using the underlying database management system we execute the query whose condition part is only C_1. The set of objects thus retrieved are processed against the condition C_2 and appropriate probability values are calculated as follows.

We assume that the dynamic part of the query condition is formed by using atomic predicates $inside(o, R)$, $within\_distance(o, R, d)$ and boolean connectives $\wedge$ ("and") and $\neg$ ("not")(note that $\vee$, i.e. the "or" operator, can be defined using $\wedge$ and $\neg$). In the atomic predicate $inside(o, R)$, o is an object variable and R is the name of a region. An object o_1 satisfies this predicate at time t if its location lies within the region R. The predicate $within\_distance(o, R, d)$ is satisfied by an object o_1 traveling on route r_1 if the location of o_1 is within distance d of the region R (here the distance is measured along the route, i.e. the route distance). The following is an example query.
RETRIEVE o FROM Moving-objects WHERE $o.type =$
$'ambulance' \wedge inside(o, R)$
Consider an object o_1 traveling on route r_1. We assume that the route r_1 intersects the region R at different places, and certain segments of the route are in the region R; each such segment is given by an interval $[u, v]$ (where $u \leq v$). For the route r_1, we let $Inside\_Int(r_1, R)$ denote the set of all such intervals. Clearly, object o_1 is in region R at time t, if its location at t lies within

any of the intervals belonging to $Inside\_Int(r_1, R)$. Using the set of intervals $Inside\_Int(r_1, R)$, we can easily compute another set of intervals on route r_1 , denoted by $Within\_Int(r_1, R, d)$, such that every point belonging to any of these intervals is within distance d of region R.

Now consider a condition q formed using the above atomic predicates and using the boolean connectives. We assume that q has only one free object variable o. Now we describe a procedure for evaluation of this condition against a set of objects. The satisfaction of this condition by an object o_1 traveling on route r_1 at time t only depends on the location of the object at time t. We first compute the set of all such points. We say that a point x on the route r_1 satisfies the query q, if an object o_1 at location x satisfies q. By a simple induction on the length of q, it is easily seen that the set of points on route r_1 that satisfy q is given by a collection of disjoint intervals (if q is an atomic predicate then this is trivially the case as indicated earlier; if q is a conjunction q_1 and q_2 the resulting set of intervals for q is obtained by taking pairwise intersection of an interval belonging to that of q_1 and another belonging to that of q_2 etc.). We let $Int(r_1, q)$ denote this set of intervals. A simple algorithm for computing this set is given below. The probability that o_1 satisfies q at time t equals the probability that the current location of o_1 lies within any of the intervals in $Int(r_1, q)$. Let $\{I_1, I_2, ..., I_k\}$ be all the intervals in $Int(r_1, q)$. Since all the intervals in $Int(r_1, q)$ are disjoint, it is the case that for any two distinct intervals I_i and I_j the events indicating that o_1 is inside the interval I_i (resp., inside I_j) are independent. Hence, the probability that o_1 satisfies q is equal to the sum, over all intervals I in $Int(r_1, q)$, of the probability that o_1 is in the interval I.

Theorem 3: For a query q and route r_1, let $\{I_1, ..., I_i, ..., I_k\}$ be all the intervals in $Int(r_1, q)$ where $I_i = [u_i, v_i]$. Then, the probability that object o_1 traveling on route r_1 satisfies q at time t is given by $\sum_{i=1}^{k} \int_{u_i}^{v_i} f_{o_1}(x)dx$. $\square$

For the route r_1, the set of intervals $Int(r_1, q)$ is computed inductively on the structure of q as follows.

q **is an atomic predicate:** If q is $inside(o, R)$, $Int(r_1, q)$ is the same as $Inside\_Int(r_1, R)$ and this is obtained directly from the database, possibly using a spatial indexing scheme. If q is $within\_distance(o, R, d)$ then $Int(r_1, q)$ is same as $Within\_Int(r_1, R, d)$, and this can be computed directly from $Inside\_Int(r_1, R)$. The list of intervals $Int(r_1, R)$ is output in sorted order.

$q = q_1 \wedge q_2$: First we compute the lists $Int(r_1, q_1)$ and $Int(r_1, q_2)$. After this, we take an interval I_1 from the first list and an interval I_2 from the second list, and output the interval $I_1 \cap I_2$ (if it is non-empty); the set of all such intervals will be the output. Since the original two lists are sorted, the above procedure can be implemented by a modified merge algorithm. The complexity of this procedure is proportional to the sum of the two input lists.

$q = \neg q_1$: First we compute $Int(r_1, q_1)$. We assume that the length of the route r_1 is l_1; thus the set of all points on r_1 is given by the single interval $[0, l_1]$. The set of all points on r_1 that satisfy q is the complement of the set of points that satisfy q_1 where this complement is taken with respect to all the points on the route; clearly, this set of points is a collection of disjoint intervals. Now, it is fairly straightforward to see how the sorted list of intervals in $Int(r_1, q)$ can be computed from $Int(r_1, q_1)$; the complexity of such a procedure is simply linear in the number of intervals in $Int(r_1, q_1)$.

If $L_1, L_2, ..., L_k$ are the lists of intervals corresponding to the atomic predicates appearing in q and l is the sum of the lengths of these lists, and m is the length of q then it can be shown that the complexity of the above procedure is $O(lm)$.

Now consider the query
RETRIEVE o FROM Moving-objects WHERE $C_1 \wedge C_2$
where C_1, C_2, respectively, are the static and the dynamic parts of the condition.

The overall algorithm for processing the query is as follows.

1. Using the underlying database process the following query.
   RETRIEVE o FROM Moving-objects WHERE C_1.
   Let O be the set of objects retrieved.
2. Using the underlying database retrieve the set of routes R on which the objects in O are traveling.
3. For each atomic predicate p appearing in C_2 and for each route r_1 in R, retrieve the list of intervals $Int(r_1, p)$. This is achieved by using any spatial indexing scheme.
4. Using the algorithm presented earlier, for each route r_1, compute the list of intervals $Int(r_1, q)$.
5. For each route r_1 and for each object o_1 traveling on r_1, compute the probability that it satisfies q using the formula given in theorem 3.

7 Relevant Work

One research area to which this paper is related is uncertainty and incomplete information in databases (see for example [9,1] for surveys). However, as far as we know this area has so far addressed complementary issues to the ones in this paper. Our current work on location update policies addresses the question: what uncertainty to initially associate with the location of each moving object. In contrast, existing works are concerned with management and reasoning with uncertainty, after such uncertainty is introduced in the database. Our probabilistic query processing approach is also concerned with this problem. However, our uncertainty processing problem is combined with a temporal-spatial aspect that has not been studied previously as far as we know.

Our problem is also related to mobile computing, particularly works on location management in the cellular architecture. These works address the following problem. When calling or sending a message to a mobile user, the network infrastructure must locate the cell in which the user is currently located. The network uses the location database that gives the current cell of each mobile user. The record is updated when the user moves from one cell to another, and it is read when the user is called. Existing works on location management (see, for example, [15,4,7]) address the problem of allocating and distributing the location database such that the lookup time and update overhead are minimized. Location management in the cellular architecture can be viewed as addressing the problem of providing uncertainty bounds for each mobile user. The geographic bounds of the cell constitute the uncertainty bounds for the user. Uncertainty at the cell-granularity is sufficient for the purpose of calling a mobile user or sending him/her a message. When it is also sufficient for MOD applications, the location database can be sold by wireless communication vendors to mobile fleet operators. However, often uncertainty at the cell granularity is insufficient. For example, in satellite networks the diameter of a cell ranges from hundreds to thousands of miles.

Another relevant research area is constraint databases (see [8] for a survey). In this sense, our location attributes can be viewed as a constraint, or a generalized tuple, such that the tuples satisfying the constraint are considered to be in the database. Constraint databases have been separately applied to the temporal (see [2]) domain, and to the spatial domain (see [10]). Constraint databases can be used as a framework in which to implement the proposed update policies and query processing algorithm.

Finally, the present paper extends the work on which we initially reported in [5,6] in two important ways. First, in this paper we introduce a quantitative new probabilistic model and method of processing range queries. In contrast, in previous works we took a qualitative approach in the form of "may" and "must" semantics of queries. Second, in this paper we introduce uncertainty as a separate concept from deviation. The previous work on update policies (i.e. [6]) is not equipped to distinguish between uncertainty and deviation. Consequently, The location update policies discussed in this paper are different in two respects from the update policies in [6]. First, they take uncertainty into consideration when determining when to send a location update message. Second they are dead reckoning policies; namely they provide the uncertainty, i.e. the bound on the deviation, with each location update message. In contrast, the [6] policies are not dead reckoning in the sense that the moving object does not update its location when the deviation reaches some threshold; the update time-point depends on the overall behavior of the deviation since the last update. Our simulation results indicate that the [6] policies are inferior to adr (and often to dtdr as well) when the uncertainty cost is taken into consideration, and this inferiority increases as the cost per unit of uncertainty increases.

8 Conclusion

In this paper we considered dead-reckoning policies for updating the database location of moving objects, and the processing of range queries for motion database. When using a dead-reckoning policy, a moving object equipped with a Geographic Positioning System periodically sends an update of its database location and provides an uncertainty threshold th. The threshold indicates that the object will send another update when the deviation, namely the distance between the database location and the actual location, exceeds th.

Dead-reckoning policies imply that the DBMS answers a query about the location of an object m by: "the current location of m is (x,y) with a deviation of at most th". When making decisions based on such an answer, there is a cost in terms of the deviation of m from (x,y), and in terms of the uncertainty about its location. These costs should be balanced against the cost (in terms of wireless bandwidth, and update processing) of sending location update messages. We introduced a cost model that captures the tradeoffs between communication, uncertainty and deviation by assigning costs to an uncertainty unit, a deviation unit, and a communication unit. We explained that these costs should be determined by answering questions such as: how many messages is the system willing to utilize in order to reduce the deviation by one unit during a unit of time? Is a unit of uncertainty more important than a unit of deviation, or vice versa?

Then we introduced two dead-reckoning policies, adaptive dead-reckoning (adr), and disconnection detection dead-reckoning (dtdr). Both adjust the uncertainty threshold at each update to the current motion (or speed) pattern. This pattern is captured by the concept of the predicted deviation. The difference between the two policies is that dtdr uses a novel technique for disconnection detection in mobile computing, namely decreasing uncertainty threshold. Intuitively, the technique postulates that the probability of communication should increase as the period of time since the last communication increases. Thus, the probability of the object being disconnected increases as the period of time since the last update increases. Dtdr demonstrates the use of this technique.

Then we reported on the development of a simulation testbed for evaluation of location update policies. We used it in order the compare the information cost of adr, dtdr, and speed dead-reckoning (sdr) in which the uncertainty threshold is arbitrary and fixed. The result of the comparison is that adr is superior to the other policies in the sense that it has a lower information cost. Actually, it may have an information cost which is six times lower than that of sdr. We quantified the disconnection detection cost as the difference between the cost of dtdr and that of adr. We also determined that when taking uncertainty into consideration, the information costs of adr and dtdr are lower than that of non-dead-reckoning policies which we developed previously.

Finally, an additional contribution of this paper is a probabilistic model and an algorithm for query processing in motion databases. In our model the location of the moving object is a random variable, and at any point in time the database location and the uncertainty are used to determine a density function for this variable. Then we developed an algorithm that processes range queries such as 'retrieve the moving objects that are currently inside a given polygon P'. The answer is a set of objects, each of which is associated with the probability that currently the object is inside P.

Now consider the following variant of the location update problem. In some cases MOD applications may not be interested in the *location* of moving objects at any point in time, but in their arrival time at the destination. Assume that the database arrival information is given by "The object is estimated to arrive at destination X at time t, with an uncertainty of U". In other words, t is the database estimated-arrival-time[8] (eat) and we assume that at any point in time before arrival at destination X, the moving object can compute the actual eat[9], t'. The difference between t and t' is the deviation, and the uncertainty U denotes the bound on the deviation of the eat; the object will send an eat update message when the deviation reaches U. In this variant, the motion database update problem is to determine when a moving object should update its database estimated-arrival-time. The results that we developed in this paper for the location update problem carry over verbatim to the eat update problem.

References

1. S. Abiteboul, R. Hull, V. Vianu : Foundations of Databases, Addison Wesley, 1995.
2. M. Baudinet, M. Niezette, P. Wolper : On the representation of infinite data and queries, ACM Symp. on Principles of Database Systems, May 1991.
3. W. Feller : An Introduction to Probability Theory, John Wiley and Sons, 1966
4. J. S. M. Ho, I. F. Akyildiz : Local Anchor Scheme for Reducing Location Tracking Costs in PCN, 1st ACM International Conference on Mobile Computing and Networking, Berkeley, California, Nov. 1995.
5. P. Sistla, O. Wolfson, S. Chamberlain, S. Dao : Modeling and Querying Moving Objects, Proceedings of the Thirteenth International Conference on Data Engineering (ICDE13), Birmingham, UK, Apr. 1997.
6. O. Wolfson, S. Chamberlain, S. Dao, L. Jiang, G. Mendez: Cost and Imprecision in Modeling the Position of Moving Objects, Proceedings of the Fourteenth International Conference on Data Engineering (ICDE14), 1998
7. T. Imielinski and H. Korth : Mobile Computing, Kluwer Academic Publishers, 1996.
8. P. Kanellakis : Constraint programming and database languages, ACM Symp. on Principles of Database Systems, May 1995.
9. A. Motro : Management of Uncertainty in Database Systems, In Modern Database Systems, Won Kim ed., Addison Wesley, 1995.
10. J. Paradaens, J. van den Bussche, D. Van Gucht : Towards a theory of spatial database queries, ACM Symp. on Principles of Database Systems, May 1994.
11. R. Snodgrass and I. Ahn : The temporal databases, IEEE Computer, Sept. 1986.

12. S. Chamberlain : Model-Based Battle Command: A Paradigm Whose Time Has Come, 1995 Symp. on C2 Research & Technology, June 1995
13. S. Chamberlain : Automated Information Distribution in Bandwidth-Constrained Environments MILCOM-94 conference, 1994.
14. S.D. Silvey : Statistical Inference, Chapman and Hall, 1975
15. N. Shivakumar, J. Jannink and J. Widom :Per-User Profile Replication in Mobile Environments: Algorithms, Analysis, and Simulation Results, ACM/Baltzer Journal on Special Topics in Mobile Networks and Applications, special issue on Data Management, 1997.

---

[8] equivalent to the database location
[9] equivalent to the actual location

On Capturing First-Order Topological Properties of Planar Spatial Databases

Bart Kuijpers[*][1] and Jan Van den Bussche[2]

[1] University of Antwerp (UIA), Dept. Math. & Computer Sci.,
Universiteitsplein 1, B-2610 Antwerp, Belgium
kuijpers@uia.ua.ac.be
[2] Limburgs Universitair Centrum, Dept. WNI,
B-3590 Diepenbeek, Belgium
vdbuss@luc.ac.be

Abstract. Spatial databases are modeled as closed semi-algebraic subsets of the real plane. First-order logic over the reals (expanded with a symbol to address the database) provides a natural language for expressing properties of such databases. Motivated by applications in geographical information systems, this paper investigates the question of which *topological* properties can be thus expressed. We introduce a novel, two-tiered logic for expressing topological properties, called $\mathcal{CL}$, which is subsumed by first-order logic over the reals. We put forward the question whether the two logics are actually equivalent (when restricting attention to topological properties). We answer this question affirmatively on the class of "region databases." We also prove a general result which further illustrates the power of the logic $\mathcal{CL}$.

1 Introduction and Summary

A simple yet powerful way of modeling spatial data is using *semi-algebraic sets*. A subset A of n-dimensional Euclidean space $\mathbf{R}^n$ is called semi-algebraic if it can be defined by a Boolean system of polynomial inequalities. First-order logic over the reals, denoted here by $FO[\mathbf{R}]$, then becomes a spatial query language, fitting in the (by now rather well known) framework of constraint query languages introduced by Kanellakis, Kuper and Revesz [12]. The goal of this paper is to understand the power of this formalism in expressing topological queries.[1]

We will work with *planar* spatial databases, whose content are described by semi-algebraic sets S in the plane $\mathbf{R}^2$. An example of a first-order query in this context is "is the database bounded?", which can be expressed in $FO[\mathbf{R}]$ as $(\exists b > 0)\forall x\forall y(S(x,y) \rightarrow (-b < x < b \wedge -b < y < b))$.[2] We will consider only sets

---

[*] Post-doctoral research fellow of the Fund for Scientific Research of Flanders (FWO-Vlaanderen).
[1] The work we will present is similar in spirit to work done in topological model theory [9,11,17], though the technical focus is quite different.
[2] The subformula $-b < x$ is, of course, a shorthand for $(\exists z)(z + b = 0 \wedge z < x)$. Note that formally, we work in an expansion of first-order logic over the reals with a binary

Catriel Beeri, Peter Buneman (Eds.): ICDT'99, LNCS 1540, pp. 187–198, 1998.
© Springer-Verlag Berlin Heidelberg 1998

that are closed in the ordinary topology on $\mathbf{R}^2$. This assumption is of great help from a technical point of view, and is harmless from a practical point of view.

Topological properties. A property of spatial databases is called *topological* if it is invariant under topological transformations of the plane. More precisely, whenever the property holds for some A, it must also hold for any other A' that is the image of A under a homeomorphism of the plane.[3] For example, the above-mentioned property "the database is bounded" is topological, as is the property "the database consists of (curved) lines only". In contrast, the property "the database contains a straight line" is not. Apart from our interest in topological properties as a natural and mathematically well-motivated class of properties, they are also practically motivated by geographical information systems [6,7,8,14,18].

So far there was not much understanding yet of the class of topological properties that are first-order (i.e., expressible in FO[$\mathbf{R}$]), except for the feeling that this class must be rather meager. Indeed, many topological properties are *not* first-order; for example, one cannot express in FO[$\mathbf{R}$] that the database is topologically connected.[4] But exactly which topological properties *are* first-order?

Cone Logic. What we do understand quite well is when two given sets A and A' are *topologically elementary equivalent*. This means that any FO[$\mathbf{R}$]-sentence that is topological will not distinguish between A and A'. Indeed, Paredaens and the present authors [15] discovered a characterization of topological elementary equivalence in terms of the *cone types* occurring in the two given databases. Semi-algebraic sets are topologically well-behaved in that locally around each point they are "conical" [4]. The cone of a point can either be completely filled (in case of points in the interior of the set), completely empty (in case of isolated points or points not in the set), or consisting of lines and regions arriving in the point. A database can be partitioned according to the cone types of its points. The characterization states that two databases are topologically elementary equivalent if and only if the cardinalities of the equivalence classes of their partitions match.

In this paper we introduce *Cone Logic* (*CL*), in which only topological properties can be expressed. The logic *CL* is two-tiered: at the bottom tier, there is a first-order logic for expressing properties of cones, which can talk about the lines and regions making up the cone, and their relative order in the cone. At the top tier, any sentence γ from the bottom tier can be used in an "atomic" formula of the form $[\gamma](p)$, where p is a point variable; this formula expresses that the cone of p satisfies property γ. The only other atomic predicate at the top tier is the

---

[3]   relation symbol S to address the content of the database. However, we will use the same notation FO[$\mathbf{R}$] to denote this first-order query language.

[3] A homeomorphism of the plane is a bijection $f : \mathbf{R}^2 \rightarrow \mathbf{R}^2$ such that both f and f^{-1} are continuous.

[4] This follows from the combined results of Benedikt, Dong, Libkin and Wong [2] and Grumbach and Su [10].

symbol S to address the database; the top tier is then closed under the standard first-order operations. An example of a sentence in $\mathcal{CL}$ is

$$\forall p[\exists x R(x) \rightarrow \exists! x L(x)](p),$$

which expresses that at every point bordering a region (R), there can be at most one line (L) entering that region. Another example is

$$\exists p[\exists x \exists y \exists z \exists u (R(x) \wedge L(y) \wedge R(z) \wedge L(u) \wedge B(x,y,z) \wedge B(z,u,x))](p),$$

which expresses that there is a point where two regions meet, and through which a line runs between the two regions. (The predicate $B(x,y,z)$ denotes that cone element y lies between cone elements x and z.)

Note that while FO[**R**] talks about points in terms of their coordinates, $\mathcal{CL}$ can only talk about points directly and does not even have access to their coordinates. Every property expressible in $\mathcal{CL}$ is also expressible in FO[**R**]. We investigate the question of the converse: *is $\mathcal{CL}$ first-order complete? That is, is every first-order topological property expressible in $\mathcal{CL}$?*

Circular languages. As a first illustration of the power of $\mathcal{CL}$, we show that *any* property of cones expressible in FO[**R**] can also be expressed in $\mathcal{CL}$. Since a non-trivial cone can be represented as a circular list of L's and R's, an arbitrary property of cones can be represented as a set of such circular lists; we call such a set a *circular language*. We prove for any circular language T that if "the cone of point (x,y) satisfies T" is expressible in FO[**R**], then "the cone of point p satisfies T" is expressible in $\mathcal{CL}$.

Region databases. A database is called a *region database* if, intuitively, it only contains "filled" figures. More precisely, the cone of every point in the database must either be completely full or consist exclusively of R's (regions). Region databases appear often in geographical information systems.

With each region database we can associate an abstract directed graph of a very simple form. For each singular point p in the database there is a "parent" node in the graph with outgoing edges to n "child" nodes, where n is the number of R's in the cone of p. The sets of child nodes for different parent nodes are disjoint. Importantly, by the above-mentioned characterization of topological elementary equivalence, any two topologically elementary equivalent region databases have the same associated abstract graph.

Our second main result is then that a topological property of region databases is expressible in FO[**R**] if and only if it is expressible in standard first-order logic when looking at the abstract graph of a database instead of at the database itself.[5] Using a quantifier elimination procedure, we obtain as a corollary the first-order completeness of $\mathcal{CL}$ on the class of region databases.

The general question of first-order completeness of $\mathcal{CL}$ the class of all planar spatial databases remains open. Other open questions are to extend our results

---

[5] With "standard" first-order logic of graphs we mean first-order logic over one binary relation E, used to address the edges of the graph.

to databases consisting of multiple semi-algebraic sets (rather than just one), or to non-planar (e.g., 3D) databases.

Lifting collapse theorems. In the proofs of our completeness results we make heavy use of a powerful tool: a "collapse theorem" by Benedikt, Dong, Libkin and Wong [2]. This theorem says that any FO[**R**]-definable property of *finite* databases that is invariant under monotone bijections from **R** to **R**, is already expressible by a sentence that uses no arithmetic, except for the order predicate. So, this sentence mentions only the predicate $<$ and the relation symbol S for the database content.

Now $\mathcal{CL}$ is subsumed by first-order logic over $(<, S)$. Hence, our first-order completeness result for $\mathcal{CL}$ "lifts" collapse to the level of infinite, semi-algebraic, sets, which are much more relevant in the spatial context than finite databases.

Acknowledgment. We thank Jan Paredaens for a number of inspiring discussions we had with him in the initial stage of this work.

2   Preliminaries

Spatial databases. We denote the real numbers by **R**, so $\mathbf{R}^2$ denotes the real plane. A *semi-algebraic set in* $\mathbf{R}^2$ is a set of points that can be defined as

$$\{(x, y) \in \mathbf{R}^2 \mid \varphi(x, y)\},$$

where $\varphi(x, y)$ is a formula built using the Boolean connectives $\wedge$, $\vee$, and $\neg$ from atoms of the form $P(x, y) > 0$, where $P(x, y)$ is a polynomial in the variables x and y with integer coefficients. Observe that $P = 0$ is equivalent to $\neg(P > 0) \wedge \neg(-P > 0)$, so equations can be used as well as inequalities.

In this paper, a *database* is defined as a semi-algebraic set in $\mathbf{R}^2$ that is closed in the ordinary topological sense. It is known [4] that these are precisely the finite unions of sets of points that can be defined as

$$\{(x, y) \in \mathbf{R}^2 \mid P_1(x, y) \geq 0 \wedge \ldots \wedge P_m(x, y) \geq 0\}.$$

In other words, we disallow the essential use of strict inequalities in the definition of a database.

First-order logic over the vocabulary $(0, 1, +, \times, <, S)$, with S a binary relation symbol, is denoted by FO[**R**]. An FO[**R**]-formula φ can be evaluated on a database A by letting variables range over **R**, interpreting the arithmetic symbols in the obvious way, and interpreting $S(x, y)$ to mean that the point (x, y) is in A.

To formalize what it means for two databases A and B to be topologically the same, we use the notion of *isotopy*. An isotopy is a continuous deformation of the plane;[6] A and B are called *isotopic* if there is an isotopy h such that $h(A) = B$.[7]

An FO[**R**]-sentence φ is called *topological* if whenever databases A and B are isotopic, then $A \models \varphi$ if and only if $B \models \varphi$. Finally, two databases A and B are called *topologically elementary equivalent* if for each topological sentence φ, $A \models \varphi$ if and only if $B \models \varphi$.

Cones. A known topological property of semi-algebraic sets [4] is that locally around each point they are conical. This is illustrated in Figure 1. For every point p of a semi-algebraic set A there exists an $\varepsilon > 0$ such that $D(p, \varepsilon) \cap A$ is isotopic to the planar cone with top p and base $C(p, \varepsilon) \cap A$.[8] We thus refer to *the cone of p in A*.

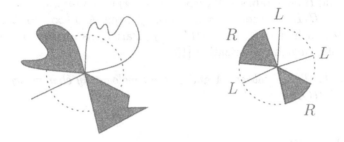

Fig. 1. A database and the cone of one of its points.

A database is also conical around the point at infinity.[9] More precisely, there exists an $\varepsilon > 0$ such that $\{(x, y) \mid x^2 + y^2 \geq \varepsilon^2\} \cap A$ is isotopic to $\{\lambda \cdot (x, y) \mid (x, y) \in C((0, 0), \varepsilon) \cap A \wedge \lambda \geq 1\}$. We can indeed view the latter set as the cone with top ∞ and base $C((0, 0), \varepsilon) \cap A$, and call it *the cone of ∞ in A*.

We use the following finite representation for cones. The cone having a full circle as its base (which appears around interior points) is represent by the letter F. Any other cone can be represented by a circular list of L's and R's (for "line"

---

[6] Formally, an isotopy is a homeomorphism of the plane that is isotopic to the identity. Two homeomorphisms f and g are isotopic if there is a continuous function $F :$ $\mathbf{R}^2 \times [0, 1] \rightarrow \mathbf{R}^2$ such that for each $t \in [0, 1]$, the function $F_t : \mathbf{R}^2 \rightarrow \mathbf{R}^2 : p \mapsto F(p, t)$ is a homeomorphism and F_0 is f and F_1 is g.

[7] A more relaxed notion of "being topologically the same" is to simply require that B is the image of A under a homeomorphism rather than an isotopy. The only difference between the two notions is that the latter considers mirror images to be the same, while the former does not. Indeed, every homeomorphism either is an isotopy itself, or is isotopic to a reflection [13]. All the results we will present under isotopies have close analogues under homeomorphisms.

[8] $D(p, \varepsilon)$ is the closed disk with center p and radius ε; $C(p, \varepsilon)$ is its bordering circle.

[9] If we project $\mathbf{R}^2$ stereographically onto a sphere, the point at infinity corresponds to the missing point on the sphere.

and "region") which describes the cone in a complete clockwise turn around the top. For example, the cone of Figure 1 is represented by $(LLRLR)$. The cone with empty base (which appears around isolated points) is represented by the empty list ( ). The set of all cones, represented in the way just explained, will be denoted by $\mathbf{C}$.

Let A be a database. The *point structure of A* is the function $\Pi(A)$ from $A \cup \{\infty\}$ to $\mathbf{C}$ that maps each point to its cone in A. It can be shown that $\Pi(A)^{-1}$ is empty on all but a finite number of cones. Moreover, there are only three cones where $\Pi(A)^{-1}$ can be infinite: F, (LL) (the cone around points on curves), and (R) (the cone around points on the smooth border of a region). It can indeed be shown that in each database, the points with a cone different from these three are finite in number. The points are called the *singular* points of the database.

Let A and B be databases. We say that $\Pi(A)$ is *isomorphic* to $\Pi(B)$, denoted by $\Pi(A) \cong \Pi(B)$, if there is a bijection f from $A \cup \{\infty\}$ to $B \cup \{\infty\}$ with $f(\infty) = \infty$, such that $\Pi(A) = \Pi(B) \circ f$. Paredaens and the present authors gave the following characterization [15]:

Theorem 1. *Two databases A and B are topologically elementary equivalent if and only if $\Pi(A) \cong \Pi(B)$.*

3   Cone Logic

In this section we introduce the logic $\mathcal{CL}$ (cone logic). This is a two-tiered logic. At the bottom tier we have a first-order logic for expressing properties of cones. At the top tier we can use sentences from the bottom tier to talk about points in the database and their cones.

Logical properties of cones. Consider the vocabulary $\mathcal{C}$ consisting of the propositional symbols F and E, the unary relation symbols L and R, and the ternary relation symbol B. First-order logic sentences over $\mathcal{C}$ will be called $\mathcal{C}$-*sentences*.

An arbitrary cone can be viewed as a finite $\mathcal{C}$-structure as follows. The full cone F is viewed as the empty structure where proposition F is true (and proposition E is false); the empty cone ( ) is viewed as the empty structure where E is true (and F false). A cone of the form $(c_0 \ldots c_{n-1})$, where each c_i is L or R, is viewed as the structure with domain $\{0, \ldots, n-1\}$ in which propositions F and E are false; relation L equals $\{i \mid c_i = L\}$; relation R equals $\{i \mid c_i = R\}$; and relation B equals $\{(i,j,k) \mid 0 \le (j-i) \bmod n < (k-i) \bmod n\}$. Relation B stands for "betweenness": $B(i,j,k)$ holds if when we walk around the cone in clockwise order starting from element nr. i, we meet element nr. j before we meet element nr. k.

Under the above view we can evaluate $\mathcal{C}$-sentences on cones. For example, the cone $(RLLRL)$ satisfies the $\mathcal{C}$-sentence

$$\exists x \exists y \exists z \exists u (R(x) \wedge L(y) \wedge R(z) \wedge L(u) \wedge B(x,y,z) \wedge B(z,u,x)).$$

The logic $\mathcal{CL}$. Cone logic is first-order logic over the infinite vocabulary consisting of the constant symbol ∞, the unary relation symbol S, and all unary relation symbols of the form $[\gamma]$, with γ a C-sentence.

A $\mathcal{CL}$-formula can be evaluated on a database A in the following way: ∞ is interpreted by the point at infinity; $S(p)$ means that p is a point belonging to A; and $[\gamma](p)$ means that the cone of p in A satisfies γ. Variables and quantifiers range over the points in the plane.

Since the cone structure of a database is left invariant by isotopies, we have:

Proposition 1. *Every property expressed by a $\mathcal{CL}$-sentence is topological.*

We also note: (proof delayed to the next section)

Proposition 2. *For every $\mathcal{CL}$-formula there is an equivalent FO[**R**]-formula.*

The natural question now arises: *is every topological property expressible in* FO[**R**] *also expressible in $\mathcal{CL}$?* We investigate this problem, which we call the *first-order completeness of $\mathcal{CL}$*, in the following sections.

4   Circular Languages

Let us call a *circular language* any cone property (i.e., a set of cones) that does not contain the two special cases of the full cone and the empty cone (these can be treated separately). So a circular language is a set of non-empty circular lists of L's and R's.

A circular language T is called FO[**R**]-*definable* if there is an FO[**R**]-formula $\varphi(x, y)$ such that for each database A and each point $(x_0, y_0) \in A$, $A \models \varphi[x_0, y_0]$ iff the cone of (x_0, y_0) in A belongs to T. We are going to show:

Theorem 2. *Every* FO[**R**]-*definable circular language T is definable by a C-sentence.*

Before we sketch the proof, we remark that it is easy to characterize the C-definable circular languages. Let T be an arbitrary set of words over the alphabet $\{L, R\}$. We can turn T into a circular language T^{circ} by circularizing every word in T. It is well known [19] how words over the alphabet $\{L, R\}$ can be viewed as finite structures over the vocabulary consisting of the unary relation symbols L and R, and the order predicate $<$. The first-order definable sets of words are then precisely the star-free regular languages. Using this fact, the following is not difficult to see:

Proposition 3. *The circular languages definable by C-sentences are precisely those of the form T^{circ}, with T a star-free regular language over $\{L, R\}$.*

Using this fact, we can prove Proposition 2 using induction on the star-free regular expressions. We omit the details.

We now present:

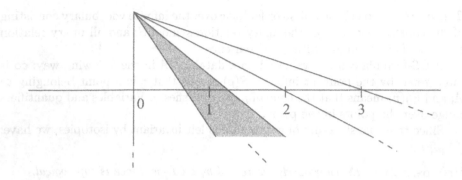

Fig. 2. Construction of $A(\Delta)$.

Proof of Theorem 2. (Sketch) Let φ be the FO[**R**]-formula defining T. Let T^{word} be the set of all words over $\{L, R\}$ that belong to T when viewed as circular lists.

Consider finite (L, R)-structures Δ over the reals, with L and R unary relation symbols. We first show that "$\Delta \in T^{\mathrm{word}}$" (meaning that the elements of L^Δ and R^Δ, when scanned from right to left, spell out a word in T^{word}) is expressible by a first-order sentence over the vocabulary $(L, R, <)$, where $<$ is the real ordering. Indeed, we can find an FO[**R**]-formula (over the vocabulary $(0, 1, +, \times, <, L, R)$) that defines, on any Δ, a database $A(\Delta)$ that is conical with top $(0, 1)$ and that contains through each element of L^Δ or R^Δ (embedded on the x-axis of $\mathbf{R}^2$) a line or triangular strip. This is illustrated in Figure 2 for $L^\Delta = \{0, 2, 3\}$ and $R^\Delta = \{1\}$.

Then "$\Delta \in T^{\mathrm{word}}$" is equivalent to $A(\Delta) \models \varphi[0, 1]$. The latter sentence is also invariant under monotone bijections from **R** to **R**. Hence, by a collapse theorem by Benedikt, Dong, Libkin and Wong [2], the sentence is equivalent to a sentence ψ over $(L, R, <)$. Moreover, we may assume without loss of generality that the quantifiers in ψ range only over the active domain of the given structure [16,3].

Consider now the $\mathcal{C}$-sentence $\gamma = \exists f \psi'$, where ψ' is obtained from ψ by replacing all occurrences of $x < y$ by $B(f, x, y)$. Then γ defines the circular language T.   □

5   Region Databases

In this section we focus on *region databases*, defined as databases in which the cone of every point is either F or consists exclusively of R's. Intuitively, such databases contain only "filled" figures. We are going to show:

Theorem 3. $\mathcal{CL}$ *is first-order complete on the class of region databases.*

We will prove Theorem 3 by establishing a connection between topological properties and logical properties of abstract graphs.

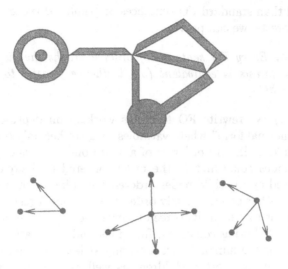

Fig. 3. At the top, a database A; at the bottom, graph(A).

Let A be a (fully two-dimensional) database, and let p be a singular singular point in A. The number of R's in the cone of p in A is called the *degree* of p in A and denoted by $\deg p$. We can now associate an abstract directed graph to A, denoted by graph(A), as follows (an illustration is given in Figure 3). The set of nodes of graph(A) equals the union of the set of singular points in A with the set $\{(p, i) \mid p$ a singular point in A and $1 \le i \le \deg p\}$.[10] The nodes in the first set are called *parent nodes*; the nodes in the second set are called *child nodes*. There is an edge from each node p to each node (p, i).

The graphs that equal graph(A) for some A are called the *depth-one forests*. Also note that, by Theorem 1, if graph(A) and graph(B) are isomorphic then A and B are topologically elementary equivalent.

We view directed graphs in the usual manner as structures over the vocabulary consisting of a single binary relation symbol E; the domain equals the set of nodes, and relation E equals the set of edges. We refer to first-order logic over this vocabulary $\{E\}$ as *FO of graphs*. To prove Theorem 3, we will also need to talk about ordered graphs. These are graphs with an additional order predicate $<$, which is an arbitrary linear order on all nodes. First-order logic over $(E, <)$ will be referred to as *FO of ordered graphs*.

Let $\mathbf{G}$ be some class of graphs. An FO sentence φ of ordered graphs is called *order-invariant over* $\mathbf{G}$ if it does not distinguish between different orderings of the same graph in $\mathbf{G}$. It is well known (e.g., [1, Exercise 17.27], [5, Proposition 2.5.6]) that in general, order-invariant FO sentences of ordered graphs are

---

[10] For simplicity of presentation in this section, we ignore the point at infinity. It can be accommodated for by adding a few technicalities.

more powerful than standard FO sentences of graphs. However, for **G** the class of depth-one forests, we can prove:

Proposition 4. *Every FO sentence of ordered graphs that is order-invariant over depth-one forests is equivalent (on depth-one forests) to a standard FO sentence of graphs.*

Proof. (Sketch) We rewrite FO formulas working on depth-one forests in a "many-sorted normal form" where variables range either only over parent nodes or only over child nodes. An ordering of a depth-one forest is called "canonical" if all parent nodes come first in the order, ordered by increasing number of children, followed by the child nodes ordered according to their parents.

We can show that on canonically ordered depth-one forests,[11] every FO formula is equivalent to a quantifier-free one over the expansion of the vocabulary $(E, <)$ with the following constants, functions and predicates. For each n, we have constants for the minimal parent having at least n children and the maximal parent having at most n children, as well as constants for the globally minimal and maximal parent. For each n, we have the binary predicate among parent nodes that the number of nodes between them in the order is at least n. We have functions giving the minimal and maximal child of a parent node. We have the sibling relation among child nodes. We have functions giving the minimal and maximal sibling of a child node. Finally, for each n, we have the binary predicate among child nodes that the number of nodes between them in the order is at least n.

The quantifier elimination procedure proceeds inductively as usual, distinguishing between parent variables and child variables in eliminating quantifiers, and adding the necessary extra predicates where needed to preserve equivalence. A quantifier-free sentence in this expanded logic can only talk about bounds on cardinalities of sets of parents defined by bounds on their number of children. Such properties are already expressible in standard FO of graphs.   □

Having Proposition 4 at our disposal, we can now establish the following upper bound on the topological properties expressible in FO[**R**]:

Lemma 1. *For every topological FO[**R**]-sentence φ there exists an FO sentence ψ of graphs such that for each database A, $A \models \varphi$ iff $\mathrm{graph}(A) \models \psi$.*

Proof. (Sketch) Given a depth-one forest G *embedded in the reals*, we can construct a database $A(G)$ topologically elementary equivalent to any database A for which $\mathrm{graph}(A)$ and G are isomorphic. This construction is illustrated in Figure 4. Actually, we can even find an FO[**R**]-formula θ (mentioning the relation symbol E) that performs this construction (i.e., that defines $A(G)$ given any G). Hence, the sentence ψ being the composition of θ with φ is the wanted sentence, if it were not for the fact that ψ is not in FO of graphs but rather

---

[11] Considering order-invariant sentences, it is sufficient to restrict attention to depth-one forests that are canonically ordered.

in the much richer logic FO[**R**]. However, ψ is order-generic, so by the collapse theorem already used in the proof of Theorem 2, we may assume it to be over the vocabulary $(E, <)$ only. Again, we may even assume that quantifiers in ψ range over the active domain only; hence ψ is an FO sentence of ordered graphs. Finally, since ψ is order-invariant, applying Proposition 4 yields the desired FO sentence of graphs.   □

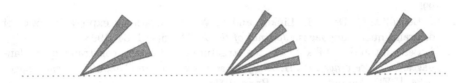

Fig. 4. The database $A(G)$ for some real embedding G of the graph of Figure 3. The parent nodes are placed on the real axis at the positions of their corresponding real numbers. The children are then drawn around the parents as regions, in the directions obtained from their corresponding real numbers (after a scaling from **R** to $\mathbf{R}^+$). Note that $A(G)$ is topologically elementary equivalent to the database of Figure 3; this is a crucial property of the construction.

Theorem 3 now follows immediately from Lemma 1 and the following counterpart to it:

Lemma 2. *For every FO sentence ψ of graphs there exists a $\mathcal{CL}$-sentence φ such that for each database A, graph$(A) \models \psi$ iff $A \models \varphi$.*

Proof. (Sketch) From the proof of Proposition 4 (which dealt with order-invariant FO sentences of ordered graphs and thus certainly applies to standard FO sentences of graphs), we may assume ψ to be quantifier-free, provided extra predicates are provided for talking about bounds on cardinalities of sets of parents defined by bounds on the number of their children. Translated from graph(A) to A this represents bounds on the cardinalities of sets of singular points defined by bounds on their degree. But such properties are expressible in $\mathcal{CL}$.   □

6   Discussion

The most obvious direction for further research is to extend our completeness result for $\mathcal{CL}$ from the class of region databases to the general class of all (closed) databases. The point where our proof fails for the general case is the construction illustrated in Figure 4, where we construct, in FO[**R**], from any real embedding of graph(A), for any region database A, a database topologically elementary equivalent to A. If A is not a region database, we cannot simply draw the children as regions emanating from their parents, as done in the figure; now some children have to be drawn as lines. The endpoints of these lines must be pairwise connected; they are unwanted extra singular points and cannot be left "dangling." The problem, however, is that this seems impossible to do in FO[**R**].

References

1. S. Abiteboul, R. Hull, and V. Vianu. *Foundations of Databases.* Addison-Wesley, 1995.
2. M. Benedikt, G. Dong, L. Libkin, and L. Wong. Relational expressive power of constraint query languages. *Journal of the ACM*, 45(1):1–34, 1998.
3. M. Benedikt and L. Libkin. On the structure of queries in constraint query languages. In *Proceedings 11th IEEE Symposium on Logic in Computer Science*, pages 25–34. IEEE Computer Society Press, 1996.
4. J. Bochnak, M. Coste, and M.-F. Roy. *Géométrie Algébrique Réelle.* Springer-Verlag, 1987.
5. H.-D. Ebbinghaus and J. Flum. *Finite Model Theory.* Springer, 1995.
6. M. Egenhofer and R. Franzosa. Point-set topological spatial relations. *Int. J. Geographical Information Systems*, 5(2):161–174, 1991.
7. M. Egenhofer and R. Franzosa. On the equivalence of topological relations. *Int. J. Geographical Information Systems*, 9(2):133–152, 1995.
8. M. Egenhofer and D. Mark. Modeling conceptual neighborhoods of topological line-region relations. *Int. J. Geographical Information Systems*, 9(5):555–565, 1995.
9. J. Flum and M. Ziegler. *Topological Model Theory*, volume 769 of *Lecture Notes in Mathematics.* Springer-Verlag, 1980.
10. S. Grumbach and J. Su. Queries with arithmetical constraints. *Theoretical Computer Science*, 173(1):151–181, 1997.
11. C.W. Henson, C.G. Jockusch, Jr., L.A. Rubel, and G. Takeuti. *First order topology*, volume CXLIII of *Dissertationes Mathematicae*. Polska Akademia Nauk, 1977.
12. P.C. Kanellakis, G.M. Kuper, and P.Z. Revesz. Constraint query languages. *Journal of Computer and System Sciences*, 51(1):26–52, August 1995.
13. E.E. Moise. *Geometric Topology in Dimensions 2 and 3*, volume 47 of *Graduate Texts in Mathematics.* Springer, 1977.
14. C.H. Papadimitriou, D. Suciu, and V. Vianu. Topological queries in spatial databases. In *Proceedings 15th ACM Symposium on Principles of Database Systems*, pages 81–92. ACM Press, 1996.
15. J. Paredaens, B. Kuijpers, and J. Van den Bussche. On topological elementary equivalence of spatial databases. In F. Afrati and Ph. Kolaitis, editors, *Database Theory—ICDT'97*, volume 1186 of *Lecture Notes in Computer Science*, pages 432–446. Springer, 1997.
16. J. Paredaens, J. Van den Bussche, and D. Van Gucht. First-order queries on finite structures over the reals. *SIAM Journal on Computing*, 27(6):1747–1763, 1998.
17. A. Pillay. First order topological structures and theories. *Journal of Symbolic Logic*, 52(3), September 1987.
18. D. Thompson R. Laurini. *Fundamentals of Spatial Information Systems.* Number 37 in APIC Series. Academic Press, 1992.
19. W. Thomas. Languages, automata, and logic. In G. Rozenberg and A. Salomaa, editors, *Handbook of Formal Language Theory*, volume III. Springer, 1997.

On the Orthographic Dimension of Constraint Databases*

Stéphane Grumbach[1], Philippe Rigaux[2], and Luc Segoufin[1]

[1] INRIA, Rocquencourt BP 105, F-78153 Le Chesnay, France
{Stephane.Grumbach,Luc.Segoufin}@inria.fr
[2] Cedric/CNAM, 292 rue St Martin, F-75141 Paris Cedex 03, France
rigaux@cnam.fr

Abstract. One of the most important advantages of constraint databases is their ability to represent and to manipulate data in arbitrary dimension within a uniform framework. Although the complexity of querying such databases by standard means such as first-order queries has been shown to be tractable for reasonable constraints (e.g. polynomial), it depends badly (roughly speaking exponentially) upon the dimension of the data. A precise analysis of the trade-off between the dimension of the input data and the complexity of the queries reveals that the complexity strongly depends upon the use the input makes of its dimensions. We introduce the concept of orthographic dimension, which, for a convex object O, corresponds to the dimension of the (component) objects $O_1, ..., O_n$, such that $O = O_1 \times \cdots \times O_n$. We study properties of databases with bounded orthographic dimension in a general setting of o-minimal structures, and provide a syntactic characterization of first-order orthographic dimension preserving queries.

The main result of the paper concerns linear constraint databases. We prove that orthographic dimension preserving Boolean combination of conjunctive queries can be evaluated independently of the global dimension, with operators limited to the orthographic dimension, in parallel on the components. This results in an extremely efficient optimization mechanism, very easy to use in practical applications.

1 Introduction

The recent field of constraint databases, initiated at the beginning of the decade [KKR90], has lead to sound data models and query languages for multi-dimensional data [PVV94,GST94,KG94,KPV95,GK97]. It allows to represent infinite relations of arbitrary dimension by quantifier-free formulae over some arithmetical domain, and to manipulate these relations in a symbolic way. There have been many theoretical studies on constraint databases, mostly focused on the

---

* Work supported in part by the ESPRIT TMR project Chorochronos and in part by the french CNRS GDR CASSINI. First author partly supported by IASI CNR in Rome.

Catriel Beeri, Peter Buneman (Eds.): ICDT'99, LNCS 1540, pp. 199–216, 1998.
© Springer-Verlag Berlin Heidelberg 1998

data model and on fundamental issues (expressive power and complexity) pertaining to the associated query languages. More recently, prototypes have started to emerge, showing the practical relevance of the constraint paradigm. Target applications are mainly spatial and temporal databases, where the expected improvement over traditional approaches follows from the formal framework which provides sound foundations for data modeling and query language design.

An important feature of constraint databases is their ability to handle in a uniform way pointsets in arbitrary dimension. The model is thus a natural candidate for applications which manipulate 3d objects (CAD), spatio-temporal data, or more generally for any scientific domain handling high dimensional pointsets. Although the complexity of querying such databases by standard means such as first-order queries has been shown to be tractable for reasonable constraints (e.g. polynomial constraints), it depends badly (roughly speaking exponentially) upon the dimension of the data. This seems to put a severe restriction on the ability of the forthcoming constraint database systems to handle efficiently high-dimensional relations.

In this paper we study techniques to overcome this problem which are based on restrictions of the geometry of the spatial objects allowed. They are expressible as conditions on the formulae representing the pointsets. We investigate how the query evaluation process can take advantage of these restrictions by manipulating the objects through their projections on lower dimensional subspaces, with a complexity which depends only linearly upon the dimension.

We first consider relations with *loose orthographic dimension* ℓ, as relations containing objects which are equal to the *join* of their projections on subspaces of dimension ℓ. They can be expressed by formulae over a first-order language with constraints, such that each atomic subformula involves at most ℓ variables. Unfortunately, this class is not closed under fundamental operations such as projection.

We thus investigate a more drastic restriction, the (strict) *orthographic dimension*, orthodim, of the data. A relation of dim d has orthodim bounded by ℓ if it can be represented by a formula with d variables, such that there is a partition of the set of variables into (say k) *components* of at most ℓ variables, such that each constraint in the formula can only involve variables from a single component. It is easy to see that a relation of orthodim bounded by ℓ is a finite collection of objects O, such that $O = \pi_{C_1} O \times \cdots \times \pi_{C_k} O$, where $\pi_{C_i} O$ is the projection of O on the ith component.

We consider the problem of deciding if a constraint relation has a given orthodim, or more generally, if it can be rotated to satisfy some given orthodim. We study the decidability of these problems in terms of the context structure, and prove that both problems are tractable for linear constraints.

We then consider first-order queries over databases of bounded orthodim. We first show that although it is undecidable in general if a query preserves the orthodim of its input, the class of preserving queries can be syntactically characterized. The characterization is rather ad hoc. We were able to define a natural class of *safe* queries that preserve the orthodim.

Finally, we focus on linear constraint databases. We consider the symbolic algebra, manipulating the generalized relations, and simulating operations of classical relational algebra over infinite relations. A detailed study of the complexity of the operations reveal that the evaluation of first-order queries depends exponentially upon the global dimension of the input data.

The main result of the paper shows that for safe Boolean Combination of Conjunctive Queries (BCCQ), the complexity of the evaluation depends exponentially upon the orthodim, and only linearly upon the global dimension.

The proof of this result is far from trivial. First note that among the operations of relational algebra, selection is the only one that does not preserve the orthodim since it might introduce a dependency between variables of different components. All other operations preserve the orthodim. We define ALG$^\ell$ as the set of queries which can be expressed with operations restricted to inputs of dimension at most the orthodim, including an approximated selection, which preserves the orthodim. We show that queries in ALG^ℓ capture at least the full expressive power of safe BCCQ.

The technique presented in this paper has been implemented in the DEDALE system [GRS98b] which can handle objects of orthodim 2 of any dimension d.

The paper is organized as follows. Section 2 introduces and studies the notion of orthographic dimension, Section 3 introduces a class of queries preserving the orthographic dimension of their inputs, and Section 4 focuses on the linear case.

2   Orthographic Dimension

We consider databases in the context of well-behaved infinite structures. We assume some first-order language $\mathcal{L}$, consisting of two interpreted *predicate* symbols, equality and order, and interpreted *function* and *constant* symbols. In the sequel, we consider an arbitrary $\mathcal{L}$-structure $\mathcal{A}$ with universe A. We will also make the assumptions that the structure $\mathcal{A}$ is *o-minimal* [VMM94] and admits *quantifier elimination*. A structure $\mathcal{A}$ is *o-minimal* if every definable set, $\{x|\varphi(x)\}$, with φ a first-order formula in $\mathcal{L}$, is a finite union of isolated points and open intervals. $\mathcal{A}$ admits *quantifier elimination* if for every first-order formula $\varphi(\bar{x})$, there exists an equivalent *quantifier free* formula $\psi(\bar{x})$ (i.e. $\mathcal{A} \models \forall \bar{x} \varphi(\bar{x}) \leftrightarrow \psi(\bar{x})$). Examples of structures of interest in the present context are: the rationals with addition, $(\mathbb{Q}, \leqslant, +, 0, 1)$, and the real polynomial arithmetic, $(\mathbb{R}, \leqslant, +, \times, 0, 1)$. Both structures are o-minimal, admit quantifier elimination, and have decidable first-order theories.

A *(database) schema* s is a finite set of relation symbols such that $s \cap \mathcal{L} = \emptyset$. We always assume that the schema is disjoint from the first-order language, and we distinguish between logical predicates (such as $=, \leqslant$) in $\mathcal{L}$, and relations in s.

We next define the finitely representable databases in the context of some $\mathcal{L}$-structure $\mathcal{A}$. Kanellakis, Kuper and Revesz [KKR95] introduced the concept of a d-ary *generalized tuple*, which is a conjunction of atomic formulas in $\mathcal{L}$ with d variables. For instance in the context of the real numbers, the expression

$(x^2 + y^2 = 1) \wedge (x \leqslant 0)$ is a binary generalized tuple representing a half circle in the real plane. A d-ary generalized relation is defined by a finite set of d-ary generalized tuples. In this framework, a tuple $[a, b]$ of the classical relational model [Ull88,Mai83] is an abbreviation of the formula $(x = a \wedge y = b)$ involving only the equality symbol and constants.

Definition 1 Let $\varphi(\bar{x})$ be a formula in $\mathcal{L}$ with d distinct variables $x_1, \ldots, x_d$. A d-ary relation $S \subseteq A^d$ is *represented by* φ over the $\mathcal{L}$-structure $\mathcal{A}$ if

$$\forall \bar{a} \in A, \mathcal{A} \models \varphi(\bar{a}) \quad \text{iff} \quad \bar{a} \in S$$

S is a finitely representable relation represented by φ over $\mathcal{A}$, and φ is a *finite representation of S over $\mathcal{A}$*. The attributes of S are denoted by the corresponding variables of φ.

Consider a d-ary relation R represented by a quantifier free formula in disjunctive normal form φ, of the form:

$$\varphi \equiv \bigvee_{i=1}^{n} \bigwedge_{j=1}^{\ell_i} \varphi_{i,j}$$

where the $\varphi_{i,j}$'s are atomic formulas in $\mathcal{L}$. Then, we also write the representation φ as a collection of generalized tuples t_i in the set notation:

$$\left\{ t_i \mid 1 \leqslant i \leqslant n, \ t_i = \bigwedge_{j=1}^{\ell_i} \varphi_{i,j} \right\}$$

A finitely representable database instance I over a schema s is a collection of finitely representable relations, each associated to a relation name in the schema. In the sequel, we often use the word "object" to denote finitely representable sets of points not associated to a relation name.

Because the structure $\mathcal{A}$ admits quantifier elimination, a relation is finitely representable iff it is finitely representable by a quantifier free formula. Therefore the restriction to quantifier free formula does not limit the definable relations. The use of quantifier free formula in DNF to represent relations, widely adopted in constraint databases, has a serious impact on the data complexity as was originally noticed in [KKR90]. In the present paper, we consider, in addition, the impact of the restrictions on the use of variables in the formulae on the complexity of query evaluation. Unless otherwise stated, we assume that all relations are finitely representable.

We introduce a first restriction based on the number of distinct variables in each atomic formula, and corresponding to the classical notion of orthographic projections.

Definition 2 A quantifier-free formula $\varphi(\bar{x})$ in $\mathcal{L}$ with d distinct variables $x_1, \ldots, x_d$ has *loose orthographic dimension* ℓ if each atom in $\varphi(\bar{x})$ involves at most ℓ distinct variables.

A relation S has *loose orthographic dimension* ℓ if there exists a representation of S with a formula of loose orthographic dimension ℓ. Note that ℓ is not unique, and if a relation has loose orthographic dimension ℓ, it has also loose orthographic dimension $(\ell + 1)$.

A convex d-dimensional object O with loose orthographic dimension ℓ can be seen as the join of all its projections on the $\binom{d}{\ell}$ ℓ-dimensional subspaces. For example, if O is a 3-dimensional object with loose orthographic dimension 2, then $O = \pi_{x,y}O \bowtie \pi_{x,z}O \bowtie \pi_{y,z}O$. That is the object O can be characterized by its orthographic projections. Figure 1.a shows an example of such an object.

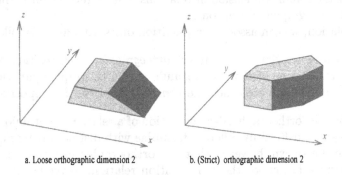

a. Loose orthographic dimension 2   b. (Strict) orthographic dimension 2

Fig. 1. 3-d objects with bounded orthographic dimension

Unfortunately, the class of relations with loose orthographic dimension ℓ is not closed under fundamental operations such as for instance the projection. Consider the relation S in $\mathbb{Q}^5$ defined by the formula $x - y - z = 0 \wedge x - t - u = 0$. S has loose orthographic dimension 3. Its projection on y, z, t, u is defined by the formula $y + z - t - u = 0$ which has loose orthographic dimension 4, but is not equivalent to a formula with loose orthographic dimension 3.

We therefore propose to consider a more drastic restriction which ensures better closure properties, and tighten the conditions on the use of the variables.

We first define the notion of *dependent* variables with respect to a formula. This notion was studied in [CGK96] in the context of linear constraint databases. Let $\varphi(x_1, \ldots, x_d)$ be a formula in $\mathcal{L}$ with d distinct free variables $x_1, \ldots, x_d$. Two distinct variables which occur in the same atom in $\varphi(x_1, \ldots, x_d)$ are said to be dependent in the same atom. The dependency relation between variables in φ is the reflexive symmetric transitive closure of the dependency in the same atom relation defined above. Variables which are not dependent are said to be independent. The *orthographic partition* of the set of variables of a formula is the partition in equivalence classes of the dependency relation. We can now introduce the concept of *orthographic dimension*.

Definition 3 A quantifier-free formula $\varphi(\bar{x})$ in $\mathcal{L}$ with d distinct variables $x_1, \ldots, x_d$ has *orthographic dimension* (orthodim) ℓ if each class of its orthographic partition has cardinality at most ℓ.

It is now possible to define the orthographic dimension of a relation.

Definition 4 A relation S is of *orthographic dimension* ℓ if there exists a representation of S with a quantifier-free formula φ of orthographic dimension ℓ.

Note that, as for the loose orthographicity, the orthographic dimension of a relation is not uniquely defined. We do not consider the intrinsic unique (e.g. minimal) orthographic dimension of relations, but merely, given ℓ, the relations that are of orthographic dimension ℓ.

To a relation, we can associate a partition of its attributes as follows.

Definition 5 A relation S admits an *orthographic decomposition* $\mathcal{P}$, if there exists a representation of S with a formula φ of orthographic partition $\mathcal{P}$. The subsets of the partition are called the *components* of the decomposition.

Note that the orthographic decomposition of a relation is not unique. Indeed, a relation can be defined by different formulae with distinct orthographic partitions. It can be shown, however, that the orthographic partitions of a set of k variables form a lattice for the sub-partition relation. Nevertheless, we do not consider a unique (e.g. thiner) decomposition associated to a relation, but conversely, given a fix decomposition, the relations that admit this decomposition.

A convex d-dimensional object O with orthographic decomposition $\mathcal{P}$ is equal to the Cartesian product of all its projections on the components of $\mathcal{P}$. Figure 1.b shows the example of such an object.

Note that for $\ell = 1$, the orthographic dimension 1 coincides with the loose orthographic dimension 1. In this case, we say that a relation is *rectangular*. It admits a definition φ with exclusively constraints of the form: $x\Theta a$, where a is a constant, and Θ is a predicate.

We can now prove the following proposition which relates the orthographic decomposition to the rectangularity.

Proposition 1 A relation R admits an orthographic decomposition $\mathcal{P} = (P_1, \ldots, P_n)$, iff for each pair of variables x, y, such that $x \in P_i$, and $y \in P_j$, with $i \neq j$, and all interpretation θ of the attributes of R distinct from x, y, the set $S_\theta = \{x, y \mid R(\cdots, x, \cdots, y, \cdots)\theta\}$ is a rectangular relation.

Therefore the orthographic decomposition can be reduced to the rectangularity of the projections on planes of independent axis. In the context of o-minimal structures, the boundary of a relation is definable in $FO(<)$. A binary relation is rectangular if each point in its boundary is either (i) an isolated point, (ii) a point inside a vertical or horizontal segment, or (iii) a point on the corner of a rectangle. Each of these properties can be expressed easily by a formula of $FO(<)$. The above development together with Proposition 1, lead to the following proposition.

Proposition 2 There is a $FO(<)$ formula $\mu_\mathcal{P}$ such that for all instance I, $\mu_\mathcal{P}(I)$ is true iff I admits the orthographic decomposition $\mathcal{P}$.

The relations of bounded orthographic dimension are very sensitive to various transformations. We consider the closure of the class of relations of some fixed orthographic dimension through algebraic operations such as set operations (union, intersection, set difference), projection, selection, and transformations, such as translation, rotation, etc. The selection operator can relate by a single constraint a group of independent variables, thus possibly modifying the orthographic dimension of the input. For instance, if x and y are two independent variables in a relation R, then in $\sigma_{x \leqslant y}(R)$, x and y are in general dependent.

Note that the class of relations of orthographic dimension ℓ, in the context of the real field, is closed under set operations, projection, translation, symmetries (axial), but not under rotations.

Although rotations do not preserve the orthographic dimension, there are relations originally not of orthodim ℓ, but which can be rotated adequately to become of orthodim ℓ, that is such that there exists a vector basis in which the relation has orthodim ℓ.

We consider the general problem of deciding if a relation is of orthodim ℓ. Finitely representable relations are defined and manipulated by means of quantifier-free formulae. In general these formulae need not be of orthodim ℓ even if the intended relation is. In such a case however, they are equivalent to some formula of orthographic dimension ℓ, defining the relation of corresponding orthographic dimension. It is important to determine if this is the case. We consider the two following problems.

1. **Explicit orthographic dimension** Given a quantifier-free formula in $\mathcal{L}$ with d distinct variables, is there an equivalent formula with orthodim $\ell \leqslant d$.
2. **Implicit orthographic dimension** Given a quantifier-free formula in $\mathcal{L}$ with d distinct variables, is there a linear transformation of the system of coordinates, in which an equivalent formula with orthodim $\ell \leqslant d$ can be found.

The decidability of these two fundamental problems is characterized in the sequel. The following result can be obtained using Proposition 2.

Theorem 3 Let $\mathcal{A}$ be an $\mathcal{L}$-structure which has a decidable first-order theory. Then it is decidable if a quantifier-free formula φ in $\mathcal{L}$ is equivalent to a formula ψ with orthographic dimension ℓ.

The following can be shown for the implicit orthographic dimension.

Theorem 4 Let $\mathcal{A}$ be an enumerable $\mathcal{L}$-structure which has a decidable first-order theory, and such that addition and multiplication are also decidable. Then it is decidable if a quantifier-free formula φ in $\mathcal{L}$ is equivalent, modulo a linear transformation of the system of coordinates, to a formula ψ with orthographic dimension ℓ.

More precise results can be obtained for specific choices of the language $\mathcal{L}$, and the structure $\mathcal{A}$. For instance in the case of linear constraints over rational numbers, a polynomial time bound can be obtained for both orthographic dimension problems. The following result generalizes the result of [CGK96].

Theorem 5 The problem of explicit and implicit orthographic dimension of a linear constraint relation defined by a linear formula φ can be solved in polynomial time.

3 Query Languages

We consider queries which can be expressed as first-order formulae in the language $\mathcal{L}$ in the context of $\mathcal{A}$. If s is a schema, each formula φ in $\mathcal{L} \cup s$ with free variables $x_1, \ldots, x_n$ $(n \geqslant 0)$ defines a *query over* s in the context of $\mathcal{A}$, mapping instances I of s to n-ary relations defined by $\{(a_1, \ldots, a_n) \mid \mathcal{A} \sqcup I \models \varphi(a_1, \ldots, a_n)\}$.

Suppose $q = \{(x_1, \ldots, x_n) \mid \varphi\}$ is a query over s, and I is an instance of s. Since each relation R in I can be defined by a quantifier-free formula in $\mathcal{L}$, and φ is a formula in $\mathcal{L} \cup s$, we can replace in φ each occurrence of the relation symbol $R \in s$ by a formula defining R. The resulting formula φ' is a formula in $\mathcal{L}$ with no reference to relation symbols in s, which defines the *answer to the query q on* I, denoted by $q(I)$.

For complexity reasons, we consider as usual answers defined by a quantifier-free formula ψ in $\mathcal{L}$ such that φ' and ψ are logically equivalent in $\mathcal{A}$. We assume in the sequel that the structure $\mathcal{A}$ admits effective quantifier elimination.

As mentioned in the previous section, there are queries manipulating data in dimension d with orthodim ℓ, which do not have an output of orthodim ℓ. This is the case for instance of $\sigma_{x \leqslant y}(R)$, where x and y are variables from two different components of the orthographic decomposition. We restrict our attention to queries preserving the orthographic decomposition.

Definition 6 Let s be a database schema, and $\mathcal{P}$ be an orthographic decomposition of the relations in s. A query Q over s *preserves the orthographic decomposition $\mathcal{P}$* if for each instance I of orthographic decomposition $\mathcal{P}$, $q(I)$ admits an orthographic decomposition which refines $\mathcal{P}$.

We consider also a generalization of the previous preservation property with no reference to a specific decomposition. A query Q over s *preserves the orthographic decomposition* if for each instance I of orthographic decomposition $\mathcal{P}$, $q(I)$ admits an orthographic decomposition which refines $\mathcal{P}$. It is clear that if a query preserves the orthographic decomposition, it also preserves a given orthographic decomposition $\mathcal{P}$.

As for many other preservation properties of queries [VGV96,BL98], we prove that the preservation of the orthographic decomposition is undecidable in a o-minimal context structure, and for a schema with at least a binary relation symbol.

Theorem 6 Let $\mathcal{A}$ be an o-minimal context $\mathcal{L}$ structure, and s be a schema with a relation symbol of arity at least 2. Then it is undecidable if a formula in $\mathcal{L} \cup s$ expresses a query over s which preserves the orthographic decomposition.

Proof : The proof is done by a reduction from the problem of satisfaction of a Boolean query, which was shown to be undecidable under the assumptions of the theorem [GS99]. Consider a schema with a single relation R of arity n with a non trivial orthographic decomposition. The formula:

$$\bigwedge_{0 < i < j < n} x_i \leqslant x_j \wedge \varphi(R)$$

defines a query which preserves the orthographic decomposition of the input iff $\varphi(R)$ is unsatisfiable. $\square$

If we restrict our attention to the class of conjunctive queries, then preserving the orthographic decomposition becomes decidable.

Proposition 7 It is decidable whether a conjunctive query preserves the orthographic decomposition.

Proof :(sketch) Let q be a conjunctive query. It can be recursively changed into an equivalent query of the form :

$$\pi_A \, \sigma_F \, R_1 \times \ldots \times R_n$$

where A is a set of attributes and F a conjunction of constraints.

Then it suffices to compute the non rectangular connections between pairs of variables from distinct components introduced by F. These are all pairs of variables dependent in F, but those introducing a rectangular connection. The connection between two variables x, y is said to be rectangular if the projection over the plane defined by x, y of $\sigma_F \, R_1 \times \ldots \times R_n$ is a rectangular relation. Since this property can be expressed in first-order logic and that the structure admits effective quantifier elimination, it is decidable.

We then check whether all connections between components added by F are *destroyed* by the projection on A. If this is the case, the query clearly preserves the orthographic decomposition. If this is not the case it is possible to construct an instance I such that $q(I)$ has an orthographic decomposition which does not refine the one of I. $\square$

We now provide a syntactic characterization of the set of orthographic decomposition preserving queries. Let μ_P be a Boolean formula (cf. Proposition 2) which holds if ϕ defines a relation that admits decomposition $\mathcal{P}$.

Let s be a schema, $\mathcal{P} = (P_1, ..., P_n)$ an orthographic decomposition, and I an instance of s, represented by a formula Φ_I, which satisfies the orthographic decomposition $\mathcal{P}$. Consider a formula $\varphi(y_1, \ldots, y_k)$ in $\mathcal{L} \cup s$, and assume wlog that $\{y_1, \ldots, y_k\} \subseteq \{x_1, \ldots, x_d\}$. A formula of the form

$$\varphi(y_1, \ldots, y_k) \wedge (\mu_P(\Phi_I) \rightarrow \mu_P(\varphi))$$

is called *decomposition $\mathcal{P}$ restricted.*

The following proposition follows easily from Proposition 2.

Theorem 8 The class of orthographic decomposition preserving queries and the class of decomposition restricted queries coincide.

The definition of decomposition restricted formulae is of little use in practice. It is not natural to write queries in this form. We therefore propose a second restriction which is intuitive and easy to check.

In order to give the next syntactic restriction, we consider an algebra, equivalent to first-order logic. The algebra consists of the following operations: Cartesian product, $\times$, projection, π, union, $\cup$, set difference, $-$. The algebra operations, whose effect is described below, are performed on sets of generalized tuples. Let R_1 and R_2 be two relations, and respectively e_1 and e_2 be sets of generalized tuples defining them.

1. $R_1 \times R_2 = \{t_1 \wedge t_2 \mid t_1 \in e_1, t_2 \in e_2\}$.
2. $\sigma_F(R_1) = \{t_1 \wedge F \mid t_1 \in e_1\}$ where F is any atom of $\mathcal{L}$.
3. $\pi_{\overline{x}} R_1$ is computed using the algorithm of quantifier elimination[1].
4. $R_1 \cup R_2 = e_1 \cup e_2$.
5. $R_1 - R_2 = \{t_1 \wedge t_2 \mid t_1 \in e_1, t_2 \in (e_2)^c\}$, where e^c is the set of tuples or disjuncts of a DNF formula corresponding to $\neg e$.
6. $simplify(R_1)$, eliminates redundancies and detects inconsistencies.

The symbolic operations above are well defined in the sense that their effect on the intensional definition of sets corresponds exactly to the semantics of the corresponding relational operators from the relational algebra over the possibly infinite extension of the sets. The relational intersection and join are definable with the symbolic Cartesian product. The sets of variables are different in these three operations. For the Cartesian product, the variables of the two relations are disjoint, they are similar in the case of the intersection, and with a non empty intersection in the case of the join and the selection. The *simplify* operator, given a conjunction of constraints, eliminates redundancies, and detects inconsistencies. Simplification is necessary for checking the satisfiability of formulae in $\mathcal{A}$.

All the logical operators, except selection, preserve the orthographic decomposition and can be carried out independently on each component of the input. For instance, the intersection of two objects can be processed by composing, at the tuple's level, the intersection of the corresponding components. Union, set difference and simplification can also be carried out independently on each component. Cartesian product does not affect the components, and projection applies to the appropriate components.

One way to be sure that a query preserves the orthographic dimension is to forbid selections introducing a binding between components. But this would limit in a drastic way the expressive power of the language. Some queries preserving the orthographic dimension might need intermediate result which have a higher dimension. Indeed queries like $\pi_x \, \sigma_{x<y}(R)$ where x and y are independent variables would not be expressible.

---

[1] In the linear case this is done by the Fourier-Motzkin elimination method [Sch86].

We now introduce a class of restricted algebraic expressions preserving an orthographic decomposition $\mathcal{P}$ which allows intermediate higher dimension. Basically, it consists in checking that when a selection introduces a binding between independent variables, this binding is further eliminated through a projection.

Let E be an algebraic expression. We recursively define the collection of bad bindings, as the set $BB(E)$ of pairs of components which are linked at each step of the computation process.

1. If E is a relation name or variable, $BB(E) = \emptyset$.
2. If $E = \sigma_F(E_1)$, then $BB(E)$ is the union of $BB(E_1)$ with the collection of pairs $< C_i, C_j >$ such that x is a variable of C_i, y is a variable of C_j and x and y are bound in F, where C_i and C_j are distinct components of $\mathcal{P}$.
3. If $E = \pi_{x_{i_1}, \ldots, x_{i_n}}(E_1)$, then $BB(E)$ is obtained by removing from $BB(E_1)$ all pairs p such that one of the components in p is only defined with variables that don't appear in $\{x_{i_1}, \ldots, x_{i_n}\}$.
4. If $E = E_1 \Theta E_2$ with Θ among $\{\cup, \cap, -, \times\}$, then $BB(E) = BB(E_1) \cup BB(E_2)$.

Now if E is an algebraic expression such that $BB(E) = \emptyset$, E is said to be bad-binding free.

Definition 7 $\mathcal{P}$-*Safe* queries are defined as the set of bad-binding free algebraic queries.

The following is immediate :

Proposition 9 Every $\mathcal{P}$-*safe* query preserves the orthographic decomposition.

The natural question is whether this restriction captures all the orthographic decomposition preserving queries. We can only give a partial answer to this question.

Theorem 10 Every conjunctive query which preserves the orthographic decomposition $\mathcal{P}$ is equivalent to a $\mathcal{P}$-*safe* query.

Proof :(sketch) Let φ be a conjunctive query preserving the orthographic dimension. It can be recursively transformed into a equivalent query ψ of the form $\pi_A \sigma_F(R)$ where R is a cross product. If $BB(\psi) = \emptyset$ we are done. If this is not the case, it means that there are variables which are connected by F but which have a *rectangular* connection. Let x and t be such variables. In ψ we replace equivalently the selection criteria F by F' which is the formula $\exists t \; F \wedge \exists x \; F$, after quantifier elimination. This can be done because F is a conjunction of constraints and represent a convex set. By repeating this process we get an equivalent conjunctive query with an empty BB.   □

It is possible to extend the above theorem to the disjunction of conjunctive queries. But it is not clear how to extend it to more general classes of queries like Boolean combination of conjunctive queries.

In the following section, we restrict our attention to a popular context structure of practical interest, and show the importance of the orthographic dimension for query evaluation.

4   Linear Constraint Databases

This section is limited to the case where the context structure is $\mathcal{A} = (\mathbb{Q}, \leqslant, +)$. The finitely representable relations are called linear constraint relations. We study the impact of the various parameters which characterize a linear instance (such as the number of variables, the orthographic dimension, the number of constraints, etc.) on the complexity of queries, and show that the evaluation process can take advantage of the orthographic dimension of an input. We exhibit queries on d-dimensional databases which can be solved using only manipulation of ℓ-dimensional pointsets.

We first consider the complexity of the algebraic operations. We consider an algebra, containing the operators, $\times$, π, $\cup$, $-$, σ and *simplify* presented above.

The DNF formulae representing pointsets are structured with the following constructs: (i) a top-level disjunction, (ii) conjunctions, (iii) predicates of the atomic constraints, and finally (iv) the parameters of the constraints.

The algebraic operations apply to different levels of the formulae. $\cup$, $\times$, and σ_F apply at the level of the logical connectives and can be evaluated in a purely symbolic way independently of the dimension. The other operations have an effect on lower levels. Their complexity depends strongly upon the dimension of the input.

- Set difference has an effect at all levels till the predicates of the constraints, which can be modified (e.g. $<$ replaced by $>$). It can be computed by first computing the cell decomposition of the space induced by all the constraints that occur in both relations, and then checking which cells are in the result. Cell decomposition can be computed in time complexity $O(n^{d+1})$ [GO97].
- Projection has an effect at all levels including the parameters, and implies numerical computation. The Fourier-Motzkin algorithm [Sch86] can be used to eliminate one variable of a convex set of n facets in dimension d in time complexity $O(n^2)$. If k variables need to be eliminated, the time complexity is then $O(n^{2^k})$. A more subtle algorithm would be to *simplify* after eliminating each variable, which reduces the output to a size linear in n. The overall complexity to eliminate k variables is then : $O((n^2 + 2^{2^k} n^4) + ... + (n^2 + 2^{2^k} n^4))$ which is $O(k 2^{2^k} n^4)$.
- The complexity of simplification (and therefore satisfaction) of n linear constraints in dimension d can be found in [Sch86,GO97]. It is essentially exponential in the dimension.

Figure 2 summarizes the costs of the algebraic operators in dimension 1, 2, 3 and d with respect to the following parameters: n is the total number of constraints in the relations, t is the number of tuples, and k the number of variables projected out. All complexities are upper-bounds given modulo a coefficient factor. The blow up in complexity comes from projection, set difference, and simplification.

In order to reduce the complexity, we consider input relations of orthodim bounded by a given ℓ. As mentioned in Section 3, queries over such relations can

Dimension → Operator ↓	1	2	3	d
×	t^2	t^2	t^2	t^2
∪	1	1	1	1
π_x	n	$n \log n$	n^4	$k2^{2^k} n^4$
σ_F	t	t	t	t
−	$n \log n$	n^2	n^4	n^{d+1}
$simplify$	n	$n \log n$	n^2	$(2^{2^d})n^2$

Fig. 2. Complexity of the operators in the dimension

be processed independently over each component except when a selection binds two components. In this later case, it seems necessary to use operators which operate on pointsets whose dimension is higher than ℓ.

We introduce a new selection operator which preserves the orthographic decomposition, and can be used in place of the classical selection. The new symbolic selection, denoted by $\tilde{\sigma}_F$, computes, for each generalized tuple t, the projection $\pi_{C_i}(F \wedge t)$ for each component C_i and returns $\tilde{\sigma}_F(t) = \pi_{C_1}(F \wedge t) \times \ldots \times \pi_{C_n}(F \wedge t)$. Note that $\tilde{\sigma}_F(t)$ is not equal to $\sigma_F(t)$. It defines an approximation of $\sigma_F(t)$, such that the two coincide on each component. We show how this new selection can be used in place of the traditional one.

To catch the intuition, consider a simple conjunctive $\mathcal{P}$-safe query $q(R) = \pi_z(\sigma_F(R))$, in the context of a relation of dimension 3 and orthodim 2, with decomposition $\mathcal{P} = (\{x, y\}, \{z\})$. We focus on the evaluation of q on a single tuple, O (see Figure 3.a).

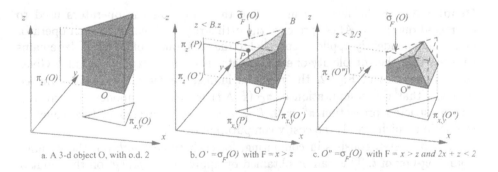

a. A 3-d object O, with o.d. 2   b. $O' = \sigma_F(O)$ with $F = x > z$ c. $O'' = \tilde{\sigma}_F(O)$ with $F = x > z$ and $2x + z < 2$

Fig. 3. Selection over a 3-d object of orthodim 2

In Figure 3.b: the selection $\sigma_F(O)$, with $F = x > z$, yields a polytope O'. The exact value of O' is not relevant for the final output of the query which is $\pi_z(O')$: O' can be approximated by $\tilde{\sigma}_F(O)$ (in dashed lines on Figure 3.b).

Two comments are noteworthy. First, the result features a new constraint $z < \alpha$ where α is the highest coordinate of O', $B.z$. Note that the point B can be simply computed using F and the bounding-box of O. Second, a point in $\tilde{\sigma}_F(O)$, P for instance, might not belong to O', but its projections on $\{x, y\}$ and $\{z\}$ belong to $\pi_{x,y}(O')$ and $\pi_z(O')$ respectively.

In Figure 3.c, $F = x > z \wedge 2x + z < 2$ consists of two constraints. The same technique applies: we approximate the result of $\sigma_F(O)$ by the cross-product of its components. The new constraint in the final result is here $z < 2/3$, a constant value which results from the intersection of the half-planes $x > z$ and $2x + z < 2$. Note that it depends upon the query *and not upon the database* and can thus be computed only once.

We now introduce ALG^ℓ as the set of queries expressed with the usual algebra where σ is replaced by $\tilde{\sigma}$.

Definition 8 ALG^ℓ is the class of queries which can be expressed by the following operations:

- $\cup, \times$
- $\pi^\ell, -^\ell$, and $simplify^\ell$ which are the usual projection, negation, and simplification but restricted to inputs of dimension at most ℓ.
- $\tilde{\sigma}_F$.

The main interest of ALG^ℓ is that the complexity of evaluating queries is linear in d and exponential in ℓ only.

Lemma 11 Let $\mathcal{I}$ be a class of instances of dimension d with orthodim ℓ. The complexity of evaluating queries in ALG^ℓ over $\mathcal{I}$ is exponential in ℓ, but only linear in d.

Proof : As for the linearity in d, note that since all the operators used to expressed queries in ALG^ℓ preserve the orthographic dimension, each operator can be independently applied in parallel to the component of its input. It remains to prove that the complexity of each operator is at most exponential in ℓ. Given the complexities of Fig. 2, the result is immediate for all, except $\tilde{\sigma}$. Indeed it seems that the computation of $\pi_{C_i}(F \wedge t)$ for each component C_i involves an unrestricted projection π^k with $\ell < k \leqslant d$. We develop in the sequel an evaluation which avoids the costly computation of π^k.

The first step consists in computing, for each tuple t, $mbb(t)$, the minimal bounding-box of t. This can be obtained by applying $simplify^\ell$ on the input of $\tilde{\sigma}$. Once $mbb(t)$ is known, $\tilde{\sigma}(t)$ is computed by:

$$E(t) \equiv t \wedge \pi_{C_1}(F \wedge mbb(t)) \wedge \ldots \wedge \pi_{C_n}(F \wedge mbb(t))$$

where the C_i's are the components. The operator π is introduced in a logical formula as an abreviation. We show that $E(t)$ is indeed equivalent to $\tilde{\sigma}(t)$:

1. ($\subseteq$) First, if $p \in E(t)$, then $p \in t$ and p satisfies $\pi_{C_1}(F \wedge mbb(t)) \wedge \ldots \wedge \pi_{C_n}(F \wedge mbb(t))$. Therefore each component C_i in p belongs to $\pi_{C_i}(F \wedge t \wedge mbb(t))$ which is $\pi_{C_i}(\sigma_F(t))$.

2. ($\supseteq$) If now $p \in \tilde{\sigma}_F(t) = \pi_{C_1}(F \wedge t) \times \ldots \times \pi_{C_n}(F \wedge t)$, then $p \in t$ since by hypothesis t is equivalent to the cross product of the projections on its components, and the projection of p on each component satisfies the projection of F. Hence p satisfies $E(t)$ which is equivalent to $\tilde{\sigma}_F(t)$

Finally, we show that $E(t)$ can be computed in constant time for each tuple as follows. Assume that $F = \{a^j \overline{x} + y \leqslant a_0^j, j = 1, \ldots, J\} \cup \{b^k \overline{x} - y \leqslant b_0^k, k = 1, \ldots, K\}$, where $\overline{x}$ ranges over $\mathbb{Q}^{d-1}$ and y ranges over $\mathbb{Q}$, and that $mbb(t)$ is defined by the couples $(x_{min}^l, x_{max}^l), l = 1, \ldots, d-1)$ and (y_{min}, y_{max}). Then the Fourier-Motzkin projection $\pi_{\overline{x}}(F \wedge mbb(t))$ is:

$$\begin{cases} b^k \overline{x} - b_0^k \leqslant a_0^j - a^j \overline{x} & \text{for } j = 1, \ldots, J, k = 1, \ldots, K & (1) \\ b^k \overline{x} - b_0^k \leqslant y_{max} & \text{for } k = 1, \ldots, K & (2) \\ a_0^j - a^i \overline{x} \geqslant y_{min} & \text{for } j = 1, \ldots, J & (3) \\ x_{min}^l \leqslant x^l \leqslant x_{max}^l & \text{for } l = 1, \ldots, d-1 & (4) \end{cases}$$

The set of constraints in (1) depends only upon F and can thus be computed only once. Constraints in (2), (3) and (4) depends upon the bounding box and must therefore be computed for each tuple, but their number is linear in the size of F. This means that, when evaluating $E(t)$, we can replace the costly computation of π by the computation of (2) and (3) in time $O(|F|)$.

The above algorithm illustrates the computation when a single variable is projected out. The generalized algorithm for computing $\tilde{\sigma}$ is given below.

1. **Step 1** Project F, using the Fourier-Motzkin algorithm, on each component. Note that this operation is done on the query and not on the database. For each component C, this gives a set of constraints similar to those of expression (1) above. See for instance the example of Figure 3.c, where $z < 2/3$ is obtained by applying Fourier-Motzkin on $F = x > z \wedge 2x + z < 2$.

2. **Step 2** For each tuple t,
   (a) **2.a** Simplify t with the $simplify^\ell$ operator. This yields as a side effect $mbb(t)$.
   (b) **2.b** Compute expressions (2) and (3) above for every component C_i. This can be done in time $O(|F|)$:
      i. For each constraint cst in F, put cst in the form $f(x_1^i, \ldots x_l^i) \Theta \Phi(x_1^j, \ldots x_m^j)$ where f and Φ are linear functions, the x^i are the variables of C_i and $\Theta \in \{\leqslant, \geqslant\}$.
      ii. If Θ is $\geqslant$ (resp. $\leqslant$), compute the local minimum (resp. maximum) L of Φ using the values of $mbb(t)$,
      iii. Output the constraint $f(x_1^i, \ldots x_l^i) \Theta L$.
   (c) **2.c** Finally, construct $E(t)$ using the conjunctions of constraints in (1, 2, 3, 4).

The operation $\tilde{\sigma}$ can be computed with $simplify^\ell$ and an $O(1)$ operation. This concludes the proof of Lemma 11.   □

Intuitively, queries in ALG^ℓ can be evaluated in parallel on each component. It remains to characterize the class of queries over databases with orthodim ℓ which can be equivalently rewritten as queries in ALG^ℓ. Note first that all first-order queries can be expressed in some ALG^ℓ. Indeed, it is easy to see that FO $= \cup_\ell ALG^\ell$. On the other hand, if P (and thus ℓ) is fixed, it is conjectured that not all first-order queries on databases of orthographic decomposition P can be expressed in ALG^ℓ, even if the query is supposed to be P-safe.

Consider the relation $R(x, y, z)$ with orthographic partition $(\{x, y\}, \{z\})$, the relation $S(y, z)$, and the P-safe query:

$$q = \pi_y(\underbrace{\pi_{y,z}(\sigma_{x<z}(R))}_{A} - S)$$

The subquery A is computed by $\pi^3_{y,z}(R \wedge x < z)$ which is in ALG^3. This suggests that the hierarchy of ALG^ℓ is strict.

However, if we restrict our attention to P-safe Boolean combinations of conjunctive queries (BCCQ) we can state the following fundamental result.

Theorem 12 Let s be a database schema of orthographic decomposition P of orthodim ℓ. Let q be a P-safe BCCQ over s. Then q can be easily rewritten in an equivalent query q' in ALG^ℓ.

Proof: We first prove the result in the conjunctive case. Let q be a P-safe conjunctive query, where $P = \{C_1, \ldots C_n\}$ is the orthographic decomposition of the schema s. As already mentioned, (see Proposition 7), it can be put into the form $\pi_A(\sigma_F(R_1 \times \ldots \times R_\ell))$, where A admits an orthographic decomposition $\{C'_1, \ldots C'_m\}$ which is a refinement of P.

Lemma For each instance I of s, $q(I) \equiv \pi_A(\sigma_F(R_1 \times \ldots \times R_\ell))$ is equivalent to $q'(I) \equiv \pi_A(\tilde{\sigma}_F(R_1 \times \ldots \times R_\ell))$.

Proof of Lemma: Let t be a tuple in $q(I)$, and t' be the tuple in $R_1 \times \ldots \times R_\ell$ such that $t = \pi_A(\sigma_F(t'))$. Since q is P-safe,

$$t \equiv \pi_{C'_1}(t) \times \ldots \times \pi_{C'_m}(t) \equiv \pi_{C'_1}(\sigma_F(t')) \times \ldots \times \pi_{C'_m}(\sigma_F(t'))$$

For each $C'_i \in A$, there exists some $C_{j_i} \in P$ such that (i) $C'_i \subseteq C_{j_i}$ and (ii) $\forall k \neq i, C'_k \cap C_{j_i} = \emptyset$. Therefore we have:

$$\pi_{C'_i}(t) \equiv \pi_{C'_i}(\pi_{C_{j_i}}(t)) \equiv \pi_A(\pi_{C_{j_i}}(t))$$

It follows that $t \equiv \pi_A(\pi_{C_{j_1}}(\sigma_F(t'))) \times \ldots \times \pi_A(\pi_{C_{j_m}}(\sigma_F(t')))$ which can be equivalently rewritten as $\pi_A(\pi_{C_{j_1}}(t') \times \ldots \times \pi_{C_{j_m}}(t'))$ because the set $\{C_{j_k}, k \in \{1, \ldots m\}\}$ is an orthographic partition. This proves that $t \equiv \pi_A(\tilde{\sigma}_F(t'))$, and thus that $q(I) \equiv q'(I)$. This concludes the proof of the Lemma.   □

Now, if q is a P-safe BCCQ query, is consists of a Boolean combination of conjunctive queries $\{q_1, \ldots q_n\}$. Since q is P-safe, we have $BB(q) = \emptyset = BB(q_1) \cup \ldots \cup BB(q_n)$. Hence $BB(q_i) = \emptyset$, for $i \in \{1, \ldots n\}$. Each q_i is safe, belongs to ALG^ℓ, and yields relations with orthodim ℓ. Finally q itself involves Boolean operations on relations with orthodim ℓ, and belongs to ALG^ℓ.   □

The new query q' can be obtained easily. Indeed, if q is a Boolean combination of conjunctive queries of the form $\pi\sigma$, then q' is obtained from q by simply replacing all the σ by $\tilde{\sigma}$. We can therefore conclude that there exists an evaluation of P-safe BCCQs such that each operator manipulates only pointsets of dimension ℓ. These results can be summarized as follows.

Corollary 13 Let s be a database schema of orthographic decomposition P. The complexity of evaluating P-safe BCCQs over s depends only linearly upon the global dimension.

This follows directly for Lemma 11 and Theorem 12. It is open whether the result extends to more general queries.

5 Conclusion

We have introduced restrictions on the geometry of the objects contained in a multidimensional databases, which (i) can be easily characterized by syntactic restrictions on the constraint formulae that represent the database, and (ii) ensure better performance for the evaluation of large classes of queries such as P-safe BCCQs. We have indeed demonstrated that the complexity of query evaluation depends linearly upon the global dimension.

We have thus restricted both the class of databases, and the class of queries of interest. Although both classes are of great practical interest, we can try to weaken the restrictions. The poor closure properties of the class of inputs with bounded loose orthographic dimension, lead us to consider strict orthographic dimension instead. Nevertheless, this class deserves more study in the case of relations of small dimension (e.g. $d \leqslant 3$). It can be shown that several results of the paper (Theorem 3, 4, etc.) extend to the case of such relations.

The class of queries can also be extended in various directions. For instance, the subclass of P-safe queries with projection limited to projection on variables of a same component, enjoys also a similar property. They can be rewritten in ALG^ℓ queries.

A spatio-temporal application runs on the DEDALE system with objects of orthodim 2 [GRS98a]. The restriction is transparent to the user, and the evaluation of P-safe BCCQs relies on 2d operations only. This allows the manipulation of multidimensional data at the cost of 2d data.

References

[BL98]   M. Benedikt and L. Libkin. Safe constraint queries. In *Proc. ACM Symp. on Principles of Database Systems*, 1998.

[CGK96]   J. Chomicki, D.Q. Goldin, and G. Kuper. Variable Independence and Aggregation Closure. In *Proc. ACM Symp. on Principles of Database Systems*, pages 40–48, 1996.

[GK97]   S. Grumbach and G. Kuper. Tractable recursion over geometric data. In *International Conference on Constraint Programming*, 1997.

[GO97]   Jacod E. Goodman and Joseph O'Rourke. *Handbook of Discrete and Computational Geometry*. CRC Press, 1997.

[GRS98a] S. Grumbach, P. Rigaux, and L. Segoufin. Spatio-Temporal Data Handling with Constraints. In *Proc. Intl. Symp. on Geographic Information Systems*, 1998.

[GRS98b] S. Grumbach, P. Rigaux, and L. Segoufin. The DEDALE System for Complex Spatial Queries. In *Proc. ACM SIGMOD Symp. on the Management of Data*, 1998.

[GS99]   S. Grumbach and J. Su. Finitely representable databases. *Journal of Computer and System Sciences*, Vol 55(2), pages 273-298, 1997.

[GST94]   S. Grumbach, J. Su, and C. Tollu. Linear constraint query languages: Expressive power and complexity. In D. Leivant, editor, *Logic and Computational Complexity*, Indianapolis, 1994. Springer Verlag. LNCS 960.

[KG94]   P. Kanellakis and D. Goldin. Constraint programming and database query languages. In *Manuscript*, 1994.

[KKR90]   P. Kanellakis, G Kuper, and P. Revesz. Constraint query languages. In *Proc. 9th ACM Symp. on Principles of Database Systems*, pages 299–313, Nashville, 1990.

[KKR95]   P.C. Kanellakis, G.M. Kuper, and P.Z. Revesz. Constraint query languages. *Journal of Computer and System Sciences*, 51:26–52, 1995.

[KPV95]   B. Kuijpers, J. Paredaens, and J. Van den Bussche. Lossless representation of topological spatial data. In M. J. Egenhofer and J. R. Herring, editors, *Advances in Spatial Databases, 4th Int. Symp., SSD'95*, pages 1–13. Springer, 1995.

[Mai83]   D. Maier. *The Theory of Relational Databases*. Computer Science Press, 1983.

[PVV94]   J. Paredaens, J. Van den Bussche, and D. Van Gucht. Towards a theory of spatial database queries. In *Proc. 13th ACM Symp. on Principles of Database Systems*, pages 279–288, 1994.

[Sch86]   A. Schrijver. *Theory of Linear and Integer Programming*. Wiley, 1986.

[Ull88]   J.D. Ullman. *Database and Knowledge Base Systems*. Computer Science Press, 1988.

[VGV96]   L. Vandeurzen, M. Gyssens, and D. Van Gucht. On query languages for linear queries definable with polynomial constraints. In *Proc. Second Int. Conf. on Principles and Practice of Constraint Programming*, pages 468–481. LNCS 1118, August 1996.

[VMM94]   L. Van den Dries, A. Macintyre, and D. Marker. The elementary theory of restricted analytic fields with exponentiation. *Annals of Mathematics*, 1994.

When Is "Nearest Neighbor" Meaningful?

Kevin Beyer, Jonathan Goldstein, Raghu Ramakrishnan, and Uri Shaft

CS Dept., University of Wisconsin-Madison
1210 W. Dayton St., Madison, WI 53706
{beyer, jgoldst, raghu, uri}@cs.wisc.edu

Abstract. We explore the effect of dimensionality on the "nearest neighbor" problem. We show that under a broad set of conditions (much broader than independent and identically distributed dimensions), as dimensionality increases, the distance to the nearest data point approaches the distance to the farthest data point. To provide a practical perspective, we present empirical results on both real and synthetic data sets that demonstrate that this effect can occur for as few as 10-15 dimensions.

These results should not be interpreted to mean that high-dimensional indexing is never meaningful; we illustrate this point by identifying some high-dimensional workloads for which this effect does not occur. However, our results *do* emphasize that the methodology used almost universally in the database literature to evaluate high-dimensional indexing techniques is flawed, and should be modified. In particular, most such techniques proposed in the literature are not evaluated versus simple linear scan, and are evaluated over workloads for which nearest neighbor is not meaningful. Often, even the reported experiments, when analyzed carefully, show that linear scan would outperform the techniques being proposed on the workloads studied in high (10-15) dimensionality!

1 Introduction

In recent years, many researchers have focused on finding efficient solutions to the *nearest neighbor (NN)* problem, defined as follows: *Given a collection of data points and a query point in an m-dimensional metric space, find the data point that is closest to the query point.* Particular interest has centered on solving this problem in high dimensional spaces, which arise from techniques that approximate (e.g., see [24]) complex data—such as images (e.g. [15,28,29,21,29,23,25,18,3]), sequences (e.g. [2,1]), video (e.g. [15]), and shapes (e.g. [15,30,25,22])—with long "feature" vectors. Similarity queries are performed by taking a given complex object, approximating it with a high dimensional vector to obtain the query point, and determining the data point closest to it in the underlying feature space.

This paper makes the following three contributions:
1) We show that under certain broad conditions (in terms of data and query distributions, or *workload*), as dimensionality increases, the distance to the nearest neighbor approaches the distance to the farthest neighbor. In other words, the

Catriel Beeri, Peter Buneman (Eds.): ICDT'99, LNCS 1540, pp. 217–235, 1998.
© Springer-Verlag Berlin Heidelberg 1998

contrast in distances to different data points becomes nonexistent. The conditions we have identified in which this happens are much broader than the independent and identically distributed (IID) dimensions assumption that other work assumes. Our result characterizes the problem itself, rather than specific algorithms that address the problem. In addition, our observations apply equally to the k-nearest neighbor variant of the problem. When one combines this result with the observation that most applications of high dimensional NN are heuristics for similarity in some domain (e.g. color histograms for image similarity), serious questions are raised as to the validity of many mappings of similarity problems to high dimensional NN problems. This problem can be further exacerbated by techniques that find approximate nearest neighbors, which are used in some cases to improve performance.

2) To provide a practical perspective, we present empirical results based on synthetic distributions showing that the distinction between nearest and farthest neighbors may blur with as few as 15 dimensions. In addition, we performed experiments on data from a real image database that indicate that these dimensionality effects occur in practice (see [13]). Our observations suggest that high-dimensional feature vector representations for multimedia similarity search must be used with caution. In particular, one must check that the workload yields a clear separation between nearest and farthest neighbors for typical queries (e.g., through sampling). We also identify special workloads for which the concept of nearest neighbor continues to be meaningful in high dimensionality, to emphasize that our observations should **not** be misinterpreted as saying that NN in high dimensionality is never meaningful.

3) We observe that the database literature on nearest neighbor processing techniques fails to compare new techniques to linear scans. Furthermore, we can infer from their data that a linear scan almost always out-performs their techniques in high dimensionality on the examined data sets. This is unsurprising as the workloads used to evaluate these techniques are in the class of "badly behaving" workloads identified by our results; the proposed methods may well be effective for appropriately chosen workloads, but this is not examined in their performance evaluation.

In summary, our results suggest that more care be taken when thinking of nearest neighbor approaches and high dimensional indexing algorithms; we supplement our theoretical results with experimental data and a careful discussion.

2 On the Significance of "Nearest Neighbor"

The NN problem involves determining the point in a data set that is nearest to a given query point (see Figure 1). It is frequently used in Geographical Information Systems (GIS), where points are associated with some geographical location (e.g., cities). A typical NN query is: "What city is closest to my current location?"

While it is natural to ask for the nearest neighbor, there is not always a meaningful answer. For instance, consider the scenario depicted in Figure 2.

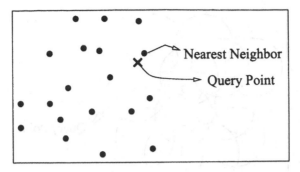

Fig. 1. Query point and its nearest neighbor.

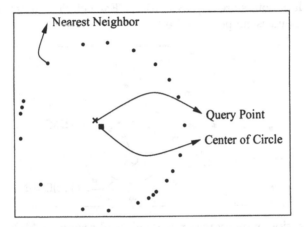

Fig. 2. Another query point and its nearest neighbor.

Even though there is a well-defined nearest neighbor, the difference in distance between the nearest neighbor and any other point in the data set is very small. Since the difference in distance is so small, the utility of the answer in solving concrete problems (e.g. minimizing travel cost) is very low. Furthermore, consider the scenario where the position of each point is thought to lie in some circle with high confidence (see Figure 3). Such a situation can come about either from numerical error in calculating the location, or "heuristic error", which derives from the algorithm used to deduce the point (e.g. if a flat rather than a spherical map were used to determine distance). In this scenario, the determination of a nearest neighbor is impossible with any reasonable degree of confidence!

While the scenario depicted in Figure 2 is very contrived for a geographical database (and for any practical two dimensional application of NN), we show that it is the norm for a broad class of data distributions in high dimensionality. To establish this, we will examine the number of points that fall into a query sphere enlarged by some factor ε (see Figure 4). If few points fall into this enlarged sphere, it means that the data point nearest to the query point is separated from the rest of the data in a meaningful way. On the other hand, if

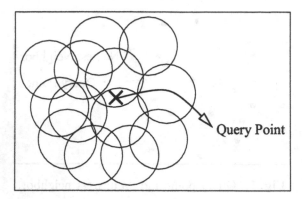

Fig. 3. The data points are approximations. Each circle denotes a region where the true data point is supposed to be.

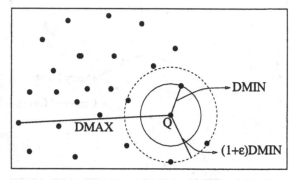

Fig. 4. Illustration of query region and enlarged region. (DMIN is the distance to the nearest neighbor, and DMAX to the farthest data point.)

many (let alone most!) data points fall into this enlarged sphere, differentiating the "nearest neighbor" from these other data points is meaningless if ε is small. We use the notion *instability* for describing this phenomenon.

Definition 1 *A nearest neighbor query is* **unstable** *for a given ε if the distance from the query point to most data points is less than $(1 + \varepsilon)$ times the distance from the query point to its nearest neighbor.*

We show that in many situations, for **any** fixed $\varepsilon > 0$, as dimensionality rises, the probability that a query is unstable converges to 1. Note that the points that fall in the enlarged query region are the valid answers to the approximate nearest neighbors problem (described in [6]).

3   NN in High-Dimensional Spaces

This section contains our formulation of the problem, our formal analysis of the effect of dimensionality on the meaning of the result, and some formal implications of the result that enhance understanding of our primary result.

3.1 Notational Conventions

We use the following notation in the rest of the paper:

A vector: x
Probability of an event e: $P[e]$.
Expectation of a random variable X: $\mathbf{E}[X]$.
Variance of a random variable X: $\text{var}(X)$.
IID: Independent and identically distributed.
  (This phrase is used with reference to the values assigned to a collection of random variables.)
$X \sim F$: A random variable X that takes on values following the distribution F.

3.2 Some Results from Probability Theory

Definition 2 *A sequence of random vectors (all vectors have the same arity) $A_1, A_2, \ldots$ converges in probability to a constant vector c if for all $\varepsilon > 0$ the probability of A_m being at most ε away from c converges to 1 as $m \to \infty$. In other words:*

$$\forall \varepsilon > 0 , \quad \lim_{m \to \infty} P[\|A_m - c\| \leq \varepsilon] = 1$$

We denote this property by $A_m \to_p c$. We also treat random variables that are not vectors as vectors with arity 1.

Lemma 1 *If $B_1, B_2, \ldots$ is a sequence of random variables with finite variance and $\lim_{m \to \infty} \mathbf{E}[B_m] = b$ and $\lim_{m \to \infty} \text{var}(B_m) = 0$ then $B_m \to_p b$.*

A version of Slutsky's theorem *Let $A_1, A_2, \ldots$ be random variables (or vectors) and g be a continuous function. If $A_m \to_p c$ and $g(c)$ is finite then $g(A_m) \to_p g(c)$.*

Corollary 1 (to Slutsky's theorem) *If $X_1, X_2, \ldots$ and $Y_1, Y_2, \ldots$ are sequences or random variables s.t. $X_m \to_p a$ and $Y_m \to_p b \neq 0$ then $X_m/Y_m \to_p a/b$.*

3.3 Nearest Neighbor Formulation

Given a data set and a query point, we want to analyze how much the distance to the nearest neighbor differs from the distance to other data points. We do this by evaluating the number of points that are no farther away than a factor ε larger than the distance between the query point and the NN, as illustrated in Figure 4. When examining this characteristic, we assume nothing about the structure of the distance calculation.

We will study this characteristic by examining the distribution of the distance between query points and data points as some variable m changes. Note that eventually, we will interpret m as dimensionality. However, nowhere in the following proof do we rely on that interpretation. One can view the proof as a convergence condition on a series of distributions (which we happen to call distance distributions) that provides us with a tool to talk formally about the "dimensionality curse".

We now introduce several terms used in stating our result formally.

Definition 3:
m *is the variable that our distance distributions may converge under (m ranges over all positive integers).*
$F_{data_1}, F_{data_2}, \ldots$ *is a sequence of data distributions.*
$F_{query_1}, F_{query_2}, \ldots$ *is a sequence of query distributions.*
n *is the (fixed) number of samples (data points) from each distribution.*
$\forall m \quad P_{m,1}, \ldots, P_{m,n}$ *are n independent data points per m such that $P_{m,i} \sim F_{data_m}$.*
$Q_m \sim F_{query_m}$ *is a query point chosen independently from all $P_{m,i}$.*
$0 < p < \infty$ *is a constant.*
$\forall m, d_m$ *is a function that takes a data point from the domain of F_{data_m} and a query point from the domain of F_{query_m} and returns a non-negative real number as a result.*
$DMIN_m = \min \{d_m(P_{m,i}, Q_m) \mid 1 \le i \le n\}.$
$DMAX_m = \max \{d_m(P_{m,i}, Q_m) \mid 1 \le i \le n\}.$

3.4   Instability Result

Our main theoretical tool is presented below. In essence, it states that assuming the distance distribution behaves a certain way as m increases, the difference in distance between the query point and all data points becomes negligible (i.e., the query becomes unstable). Future sections will show that the necessary behavior described in this section identifies a large class (larger than any other classes we are aware of for which the distance result is either known or can be readily inferred from known results) of workloads. More formally, we show:

Theorem 1 *Under the conditions in Definition 3, if*

$$\lim_{m \to \infty} var \left(\frac{(d_m(P_{m,1}, Q_m))^p}{\mathbf{E}\left[(d_m(P_{m,1}, Q_m))^p\right]} \right) = 0 \tag{1}$$

Then for every $\varepsilon > 0$

$$\lim_{m \to \infty} P\left[DMAX_m \le (1 + \varepsilon)DMIN_m\right] = 1$$

Proof Let $\mu_m = \mathbf{E}\left[(d_m(P_{m,i}, Q_m))^p\right]$. (Note that the value of this expectation is independent of i since all $P_{m,i}$ have the same distribution.)
Let $V_m = (d_m(P_{m,1}, Q_m))^p / \mu_m$.

Part 1: We'll show that $V_m \to_p 1$.

It follows that $\mathbf{E}\left[V_m\right] = 1$ (because V_m is a random variable divided by its expectation.)

Trivially, $\lim_{m \to \infty} \mathbf{E}\left[V_m\right] = 1$.

The condition of the theorem (Equation 1) means that $\lim_{m \to \infty} \mathrm{var}\left(V_m\right) = 0$. This, combined with $\lim_{m \to \infty} \mathbf{E}\left[V_m\right] = 1$, enables us to use Lemma 1 to conclude that $V_m \to_p 1$.

Part 2: We'll show that if $V_m \to_p 1$ then

$$\lim_{m \to \infty} P\left[\mathrm{DMAX}_m \leq (1 + \varepsilon)\mathrm{DMIN}_m\right] = 1.$$

Let $\boldsymbol{X}_m = (d_m(P_{m,1}, Q_m)/\mu_m, \ldots, d_m(P_{m,n}, Q_m)/\mu_m)$ (a vector of arity n). Since each part of the vector $\boldsymbol{X}_m$ has the same distribution as V_m, it follows that $\boldsymbol{X}_m \to_p (1, \ldots, 1)$.

Since min and max are continuous functions we can conclude from Slutsky's theorem that $\min(\boldsymbol{X}_m) \to_p \min(1, \ldots, 1) = 1$, and similarly, $\max(\boldsymbol{X}_m) \to_p 1$. Using Corollary 1 on $\max(\boldsymbol{X}_m)$ and $\min(\boldsymbol{X}_m)$ we get

$$\frac{\max(\boldsymbol{X}_m)}{\min(\boldsymbol{X}_m)} \to_p \frac{1}{1} = 1$$

Note that $\mathrm{DMIN}_m = \mu_m \min(\boldsymbol{X}_m)$ and $\mathrm{DMAX}_m = \mu_m \max(\boldsymbol{X}_m)$. So,

$$\frac{\mathrm{DMAX}_m}{\mathrm{DMIN}_m} = \frac{\mu_m \max(\boldsymbol{X}_m)}{\mu_m \min(\boldsymbol{X}_m)} = \frac{\max(\boldsymbol{X}_m)}{\min(\boldsymbol{X}_m)}$$

Therefore,

$$\frac{\mathrm{DMAX}_m}{\mathrm{DMIN}_m} \to_p 1$$

By definition of convergence in probability we have that for all $\varepsilon > 0$,

$$\lim_{m \to \infty} P\left[\left|\frac{\mathrm{DMAX}_m}{\mathrm{DMIN}_m} - 1\right| \leq \varepsilon\right] = 1$$

Also,

$$P\left[\mathrm{DMAX}_m \leq (1 + \varepsilon)\mathrm{DMIN}_m\right] = P\left[\frac{\mathrm{DMAX}_m}{\mathrm{DMIN}_m} - 1 \leq \varepsilon\right] = P\left[\left|\frac{\mathrm{DMAX}_m}{\mathrm{DMIN}_m} - 1\right| \leq \varepsilon\right]$$

($P\left[\mathrm{DMAX}_m \geq \mathrm{DMIN}_m\right] = 1$ so the absolute value in the last term has no effect.) Thus,

$$\lim_{m \to \infty} P\left[\mathrm{DMAX}_m \leq (1 + \varepsilon)\mathrm{DMIN}_m\right] = \lim_{m \to \infty} P\left[\left|\frac{\mathrm{DMAX}_m}{\mathrm{DMIN}_m} - 1\right| \leq \varepsilon\right] = 1$$

∎

In summary, the above theorem says that if the precondition holds (i.e., if the distance distribution behaves a certain way as m increases), all points converge to the same distance from the query point. Thus, under these conditions, the concept of nearest neighbor is no longer meaningful.

We may be able to use this result by directly showing that $V_m \rightarrow_p 1$ and using part 2 of the proof. (For example, for IID distributions, $V_m \rightarrow_p 1$ follows readily from the Weak Law of Large Numbers.) Later sections demonstrate that our result provides us with a handy tool for discussing scenarios resistant to analysis using law of large numbers arguments. From a more practical standpoint, there are two issues that must be addressed to determine the theorem's impact:

— How restrictive is the condition

$$\lim_{m \to \infty} \text{var} \left(\frac{(d_m(P_{m,1}, Q_m))^p}{\mathbf{E}\left[(d_m(P_{m,1}, Q_m))^p\right]} \right) =$$

$$= \lim_{m \to \infty} \frac{\text{var}\left((d_m(P_{m,1}, Q_m))^p\right)}{\left(\mathbf{E}\left[(d_m(P_{m,1}, Q_m))^p\right]\right)^2} = 0 \qquad (2)$$

which is necessary for our results to hold? In other words, it says that as we increase m and examine the resulting distribution of distances between queries and data, the variance of the distance distribution scaled by the overall magnitude of the distance converges to 0. To provide a better understanding of the restrictiveness of this condition, Sections 3.5 and 4 discuss scenarios that do and do not satisfy it.
— For situations in which the condition is satisfied, at what rate do distances between points become indistinct as dimensionality increases? In other words, at what dimensionality does the concept of "nearest neighbor" become meaningless? This issue is more difficult to tackle analytically. We therefore performed a set of simulations that examine the relationship between m and the ratio of minimum and maximum distances with respect to the query point. The results of these simulations are presented in Section 5 and in [13].

3.5   Application of Our Theoretical Result

This section analyses the applicability of Theorem 1 in formally defined situations. This is done by determining, for each scenario, whether the condition in Equation 2 is satisfied. Due to space considerations, we do not give a proof whether the condition in Equation 2 is satisfied or not. [13] contains a full analysis of each example.

All of these scenarios define a workload and use an L_p distance metric over multidimensional query and data points with dimensionality m. (This makes the data and query points vectors with arity m.) It is important to notice that this is the first section to assign a particular meaning to d_m (as an L_p distance metric), p (as the parameter to L_p), and m (as dimensionality). Theorem 1 did not make use of these particular meanings.

We explore some scenarios that satisfy Equation 2 and some that do not. We start with basic IID assumptions and then relax these assumptions in various ways. We start with two "sanity checks": we show that distances converge with

IID dimensions (Example 1), and we show that Equation 2 is not satisfied when the data and queries fall on a line (Example 2). We then discuss examples involving correlated attributes and differing variance between dimensions, to illustrate scenarios where the Weak Law of Large Numbers cannot be applied (Examples 3, 4, and 5).

Example 1 *IID Dimensions with Query and Data Independence.*

Assume the following:

- The data distribution and query distribution are IID in all dimensions.
- All the appropriate moments are finite (i.e., up to the $\lceil 2p \rceil$'th moment).
- The query point is chosen independently of the data points.

The conditions of Theorem 1 are satisfied under these assumptions. While this result is not original, it is a nice "sanity check." (In this very special case we can prove Part 1 of Theorem 1 by using the weak law of large numbers. However, this is not true in general.) The assumptions of this example are by no means necessary for Theorem 1 to be applicable. Throughout this section, there are examples of workloads which cannot be discussed using the Weak Law of Large Numbers. While there are innumerable slightly stronger versions of the Weak Law of Large Numbers, Example 5 contains an example which meets our condition, and for which the Weak Law of Large Numbers is inapplicable.

Example 2 *Identical Dimensions with no Independence.*

We use the same notation as in the previous example. In contrast to the previous case, consider the situation where all dimensions of both the query point and the data points follow identical distributions, but are completely dependent (i.e., value for dimension 1 = value for dimension 2 = ...). Conceptually, the result is a set of data points and a query point on a diagonal line. No matter how many dimensions are added, the underlying query can actually be converted to a one-dimensional nearest neighbor problem. It is not surprising to find that the condition of Theorem 1 is not satisfied.

Example 3 *Unique Dimensions with Correlation Between All Dimensions.*

In this example, we intentionally break many assumptions underlying the IID case. Not only is every dimension unique, but *all dimensions are correlated with all other dimensions* and the variance of each additional dimension increases. The following is a description of the problem.

We generate an m dimensional data point (or query point) $\boldsymbol{X}_m = (X_1, \ldots, X_m)$ as follows:

- First we take independent random variables
  $U_1, \ldots, U_m$ such that $U_i \sim \text{Uniform}(0, \sqrt{i})$.
- We define $X_1 = U_1$.
- For all $2 \leq i \leq m$ define $X_i = U_i + (X_{i-1}/2)$.

The condition of Theorem 1 is satisfied.

Example 4 *Variance Converging to 0.*

This example illustrates that there are workloads that meet the preconditions of Theorem 1, even though the variance of the distance in each added dimension converges to 0. One would expect that only some finite number of the earlier dimensions would dominate the distance. Again, this is not the case.

Suppose we choose a point $X_m = (X_1, \ldots, X_m)$ such that the X_i's are independent and $X_i \sim N(0, 1/i)$. Then the condition of Theorem 1 is satisfied.

Example 5 *Marginal Data and Query Distributions Change with Dimensionality.*

In this example, the marginal distributions of data and queries change with dimensionality. Thus, the distance distribution as dimensionality increases cannot be described as the distance in a lower dimensionality plus some new component from the new dimension. As a result, the weak law of large numbers, which implicitly is about sums of increasing size, cannot provide insight into the behavior of this scenario. The distance distributions must be treated, as our technique suggests, as a series of random variables whose variance and expectation can be calculated and examined in terms of dimensionality.

Let the m dimensional data space S_m be the boundary of an m dimensional unit hyper-cube. (i.e., $S_m = [0, 1]^m - (0, 1)^m$). In addition, let the distribution of data points be uniform over S_m. In other words, every point in S_m has equal probability of being sampled as a data point. Lastly, the distribution of query points is identical to the distribution of data points.

Note that the dimensions are not independent. Even in this case, the condition of Theorem 1 is satisfied.

4   Meaningful Applications of High Dimensional NN

In this section, we place Theorem 1 in perspective, and observe that it should *not* be interpreted to mean that high-dimensional NN is never meaningful. We do this by identifying scenarios that arise in practice and that are likely to have good separation between nearest and farthest neighbors.

4.1   Classification and Approximate Matching

To begin with, exact match and approximate match queries can be reasonable. For instance, if there is dependence between the query point and the data points such that there exists some data point that matches the query point exactly, then $DMIN_m = 0$. Thus, assuming that most of the data points aren't duplicates, a meaningful answer can be determined. Furthermore, if the problem statement is relaxed to require that the query point be within some small distance of a data point (instead of being required to be identical to a data point), we can still call the query meaningful. Note, however, that staying within the same small distance becomes more and more difficult as m increases since we are adding terms to the

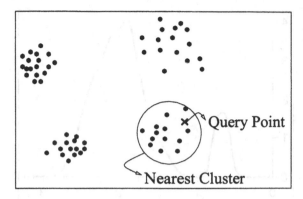

Fig. 5. Nearest neighbor query in clustered data.

sum in the distance metric. For this version of the problem to remain meaningful as dimensionality increases, the query point must be increasingly closer to some data point.

We can generalize the situation further as follows: The data consists of a set of randomly chosen points together with additional points distributed in clusters of some radius δ around one or more of the original points, and the query is required to fall within one of the data clusters (see Figure 5). This situation is the perfectly realized classification problem, where data naturally falls into discrete classes or clusters in some potentially high dimensional feature space. Figure 6 depicts a typical distance distribution in such a scenario. There is a cluster (the one into which the query point falls) that is closer than the others, which are all, more or less, indistinguishable in distance. Indeed, the proper response to such a query is to return all points within the closest cluster, not just the nearest point (which quickly becomes meaningless compared to other points in the cluster as dimensionality increases).

Observe however, that if we don't guarantee that the query point falls within some cluster, then the cluster from which the nearest neighbor is chosen is subject to the same meaningfulness limitations as the choice of nearest neighbor in the original version of the problem; Theorem 1 then applies to the choice of the "nearest cluster".

4.2   Implicitly Low Dimensionality

Another possible scenario where high dimensional nearest neighbor queries are meaningful occurs when the underlying dimensionality of the data is much lower than the actual dimensionality. There has been recent work on identifying these situations (e.g. [17,8,16]) and determining the useful dimensions (e.g. [20], which uses principal component analysis to identify meaningful dimensions). Of course, these techniques are only useful if NN in the underlying dimensionality is meaningful.

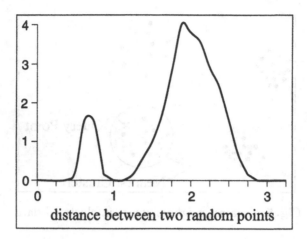

Fig. 6. Probability density function of distance between random clustered data and query points.

5   Experimental Studies of NN

Theorem 1 only tells us what happens when we take the dimensionality to infinity. In practice, at what dimensionality do we anticipate nearest neighbors to become unstable? In other words, Theorem 1 describes some convergence but does not tell us the rate of convergence. We addressed this issue through empirical studies. Due to lack of space, we present only three synthetic workloads and one real data set. [13] includes additional synthetic workloads along with workloads over a second real data set.

We ran experiments with one IID uniform(0,1) workload and two different correlated workloads. Figure 7 shows the average $\text{DMAX}_m/\text{DMIN}_m$ as dimensionality increases of 1000 query points on synthetic data sets of one million tuples. The workload for the "recursive" line (described in Example 3) has correlation between every pair of dimensions and every new dimension has a larger variance. The "two degrees of freedom" workload generates query and data points on a two dimensional plane, and was generated as follows:

- Let $a_1, a_2, \ldots$ and $b_1, b_2, \ldots$ be constants in (-1,1).
- Let U_1, U_2 be independent uniform(0,1).
- For all $1 \leq i \leq m$ let $X_i = a_i U_1 + b_i U_2$.

This last workload does not satisfy Equation 2. Figure 7 shows that the "two degrees of freedom" workload behaves similarly to the (one or) two dimensional uniform workload, regardless of the dimensionality. However, the recursive workload (as predicted by our theorem) was affected by dimensionality. More interestingly, even with all the correlation and changing variances, the recursive workload behaved almost the same as the IID uniform case!

This graph demonstrates that our geometric intuition for nearest neighbor, which is based on one, two, and three dimensions, fails us at an alarming rate as

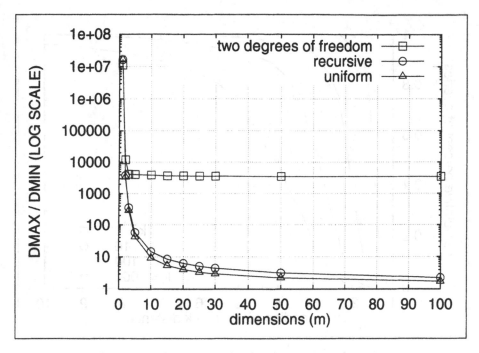

Fig. 7. Correlated distributions, one million tuples.

dimensionality increases. The distinction between nearest and farthest points, even at ten dimensions, is a tiny fraction of what it is in one, two, or three dimensions. For one dimension, $\text{DMAX}_m/\text{DMIN}_m$ for "uniform" is on the order of 10^7, providing plenty of contrast between the nearest object and the farthest object. At 10 dimensions, this contrast is already reduced by 6 orders of magnitude! By 20 dimensions, the farthest point is only 4 times the distance to the closest point. These empirical results suggest that NN can become unstable with as few as 10-20 dimensions.

Figure 8 shows results for experiments done on a real data set. The data set was a 256 dimensional color histogram data set (one tuple per image) that was reduced to 64 dimensions by principal components analysis. There were approximately 13,500 tuples in the data set. We examine k-NN rather than NN because this is the traditional application of image databases.

To determine the quality of answers for NN queries, we examined the percentage of queries in which at least half the data points were within some factor of the nearest neighbor. Examine the graph at *median distance/k distance* = 3. The graph says that for $k = 1$ (normal NN problem), 15% of the queries had at least half the data within a factor of 3 of the distance to the NN. For $k = 10$, 50% of the queries had at least half the data within a factor of 3 of the distance to the 10th nearest neighbor. It is easy to see that the effect of changing k on the quality of the answer is most significant for small values of k.

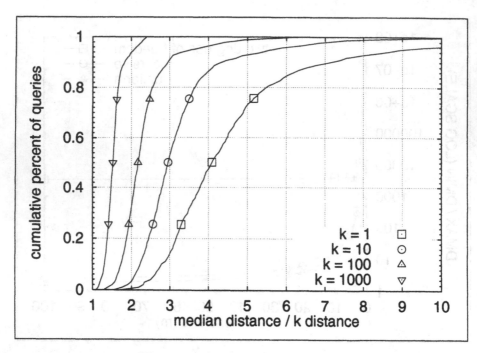

Fig. 8. 64-D color histogram data.

Does this data set provide meaningful answers to the 1-NN problem? the 10-NN problem? the 100-NN problem? Perhaps, but keep in mind that the data set was derived using a heuristic that approximates image similarity. Furthermore, the nearest neighbor contrast is much lower than our intuition suggests (i.e., 2 or 3 dimensions). A careful evaluation of the relevance of the results is definitely called for.

6   Analyzing the Performance of a NN Processing Technique

In this section, we discuss the ramifications of our results when evaluating techniques to solve the NN problem; in particular, many high-dimensional indexing techniques have been motivated by the NN problem. An important point that we make is that all future performance evaluations of high dimensional NN queries must include a comparison to linear scans as a sanity check.

First, our results indicate that while there exist situations in which high dimensional nearest neighbor queries are meaningful, they are very specific in nature and are quite different from the "independent dimensions" basis that most studies in the literature (e.g., [31,19,14,10,11]) use to evaluate techniques in a controlled manner. In the future, these NN technique evaluations should focus on those situations in which the results are meaningful. For instance, answers are meaningful when the data consists of small, well-formed clusters, and the query is guaranteed to land in or very near one of these clusters.

In terms of comparisons between NN techniques, most papers do not compare against the trivial linear scan algorithm. Given our results, which argue that in many cases, as dimensionality increases, all data becomes equidistant to all other data, it is not surprising that in as few as 10 dimensions, linear scan handily beats these complicated indexing structures. [1] We give a detailed and formal discussion of this phenomenon in [27].

For instance, the performance study of the parallel solution to the k-nearest neighbors problem presented in [10] indicates that their solution scales more poorly than a parallel scan of the data, and never beats a parallel scan in any of the presented data.

[31] provides us with information on the performance of both the SS tree and the R* tree in finding the 20 nearest neighbors. Conservatively assuming that linear scans cost 15% of a random examination of the data pages, linear scan outperforms both the SS tree and the R* tree at 10 dimensions in all cases. In [19], linear scan vastly outperforms the SR tree in all cases in this paper for the 16 dimensional synthetic data set. For a 16 dimensional real data set, the SR tree performs similarly to linear scan in a few experiments, but is usually beaten by linear scan. In [14], performance numbers are presented for NN queries where bounds are imposed on the radius used to find the NN. While the performance in high dimensionality looks good in some cases, in trying to duplicate their results we found that the radius was such that few, if any, queries returned an answer.

While performance of these structures in high dimensionality looks very poor, it is important to keep in mind that all the reported performance studies examined situations in which the distance between the query point and the nearest neighbor differed little from the distance to other data points. Ideally, they should be evaluated for meaningful workloads. These workloads include low dimensional spaces and clustered data/queries as described in Section 4. Some of the existing structures may, in fact, work well in appropriate situations.

7   Related Work

7.1   The Curse of Dimensionality

The term *dimensionality curse* is often used as a vague indication that high dimensionality causes problems in some situations. The term was first used by Bellman in 1961 [7] for combinatorial estimation of multivariate functions. An example from statistics: in [26] it is used to note that multivariate density estimation is very problematic in high dimensions.

---

[1] Linear scan of a set of sequentially arranged disk pages is much faster than unordered retrieval of the same pages; so much so that secondary indexes are ignored by query optimizers unless the query is estimated to fetch less than 10% of the data pages. Fetching a large number of data pages through a multi-dimensional index usually results in unordered retrieval.

In the area of *the nearest neighbors problem* it is used for indicating that a query processing technique performs worse as the dimensionality increases. In [11,5] it was observed that in some high dimensional cases, the estimate of NN query cost (using some index structure) can be very poor if "boundary effects" are not taken into account. The boundary effect is that the query region (i.e., a sphere whose center is the query point) is mainly outside the hyper-cubic data space. When one does not take into account the boundary effect, the query cost estimate can be much higher than the actual cost. The term *dimensionality curse* was also used to describe this phenomenon.

In this paper, we discuss the meaning of the nearest neighbor query and not how to process such a query. Therefore, the term *dimensionality curse* (as used by the NN research community) is only relevant to Section 6, and not to the main results in this paper.

7.2   Computational Geometry

The nearest neighbor problem has been studied in computational geometry (e.g., [4,5,6,9,12]). However, the usual approach is to take the number of dimensions as a constant and find algorithms that behave well when the number of points is large enough. They observe that the problem is hard and define the approximate nearest neighbor problem as a weaker problem. In [6] there is an algorithm that retrieves an approximate nearest neighbor in $\mathcal{O}(\log n)$ time for any data set. In [9] there is an algorithm that retrieves the true nearest neighbor in constant expected time under the IID dimensions assumption. However, the constants for those algorithms are exponential in dimensionality. In [6] they recommend not to use the algorithm in more than 12 dimensions. It is impractical to use the algorithm in [9] when the number of points is much lower than exponential in the number of dimensions.

7.3   Fractal Dimensions

In [17,8,16] it was suggested that real data sets usually have fractal properties (self-similarity, in particular) and that fractal dimensionality is a good tool in determining the performance of queries over the data set.

The following example illustrates that the fractal dimensionality of the data space from which we sample the data points may not always be a good indicator for the utility of nearest neighbor queries. Suppose the data points are sampled uniformly from the vertices of the unit hypercube. The data space is 2^m points (in m dimensions), so its fractal dimensionality is 0. However, this situation is one of the worst cases for nearest neighbor queries. (This is actually the IID Bernoulli(1/2) which is even worse than IID uniform.) When the number of data points in this scenario is close to 2^m, nearest neighbor queries become stable, but this is impractical for large m.

However, are there real data sets for which the (estimated) fractal dimensionality is low, yet there is no separation between nearest and farthest neighbors? This is an intriguing question that we intend to explore in future work.

We used the technique described in [8] on two real data sets (described in [13]). However, the fractal dimensionality of those data sets could not be estimated (when we divided the space once in each dimension, most of the data points occupied different cells). We used the same technique on an artificial 100 dimensional data set that has known fractal dimensionality 2 and about the same number of points as the real data sets (generated like the "two degrees of freedom" workload in Section 5, but with less data). The estimate we got for the fractal dimensionality is 1.6 (which is a good estimate). Our conclusion is that the real data sets we used are inherently high dimensional; another possible explanation is that they do not exhibit fractal behavior.

8 Conclusions

In this paper, we studied the effect of dimensionality on NN queries. In particular, we identified a broad class of workloads for which the difference in distance between the nearest neighbor and other points in the data set becomes negligible. This class of distributions includes distributions typically used to evaluate NN processing techniques. Many applications use NN as a heuristic (e.g., feature vectors that describe images). In such cases, query instability is an indication of a meaningless query. This problem is worsened by the use of techniques that provide an approximate nearest neighbor to improve performance.

To find the dimensionality at which NN breaks down, we performed extensive simulations. The results indicated that the distinction in distance decreases fastest in the first 20 dimensions, quickly reaching a point where the difference in distance between a query point and the nearest and farthest data points drops below a factor of four. In addition to simulated workloads, we also examined two real data sets that behaved similarly (see [13]).

In addition to providing intuition and examples of distributions in that class, we also discussed situations in which NN queries do not break down in high dimensionality. In particular, the ideal data sets and workloads for classification/clustering algorithms seem reasonable in high dimensionality. However, if the scenario is deviated from (for instance, if the query point does not lie in a cluster), the queries become meaningless.

The practical ramifications of this paper are for the following two scenarios:

Evaluating a NN workload. Make sure that the distance distribution (between a random query point and a random data point) allows for enough contrast for your application. If the distance to the nearest neighbor is not much different from the average distance, the nearest neighbor may not be useful (or the most "similar").

Evaluating a NN processing technique. When evaluating a NN processing technique, test it on meaningful workloads. Examples for such workloads are given in Section 4. In addition, the evaluation of the technique for a particular workload should take into account any approximations that the technique uses to improve performance. Also, one should ensure that a new processing technique outperforms the most trivial solutions (e.g., sequential scan).

9 Acknowledgements

This work was partially supported by a "David and Lucile Packard Foundation Fellowship in Science and Engineering", a "Presidential Young Investigator" award, NASA research grant NAGW-3921, ORD contract 144-ET33, and NSF grant 144-GN62.

We would also like to thank Prof. Robert Meyer for his time and valuable feedback. We would like to thank Prof. Rajeev Motwani for his helpful comments.

References

1. Agrawal, R., Faloutsos, C., Swami, A.: Efficient Similarity Search in Sequence Databases. In Proc. 4th Inter. Conf. on FODO (1993) 69–84
2. Altschul, S.F., Gish, W., Miller, W., Myers, E., Lipman, D.J.: Basic Local Alignment Search Tool. In Journal of Molecular Biology, Vol. 215 (1990) 403–410
3. Ang, Y.H., Li, Z., Ong, S.H.: Image retrieval based on multidimensional feature properties. In SPIE, Vol. 2420 (1995) 47–57
4. Arya, S.: Nearest Neighbor Searching and Applications. Ph.D. thesis, Univ. of Maryland at College Park (1995)
5. Arya, S., Mount, D.M., Narayan, O.: Accounting for Boundary Effects in Nearest Neighbors Searching. In Proc. 11th ACM Symposium on Computational Geometry (1995) 336–344
6. Arya, S., Mount, D.M., Netanyahu, N.S., Silverman, R., Wu, A.: An Optimal Algorithm for Nearest Neighbor Searching. In Proc. 5th ACM SIAM Symposium on Discrete Algorithms (1994) 573–582
7. Bellman, R.E.: Adaptive Control Processes. Princeton University Press (1961)
8. Belussi, A., Faloutsos, C.: Estimating the Selectivity of Spatial Queries Using the 'Correlation' Fractal Dimension. In Proc. VLDB (1995) 299–310
9. Bentley, J.L., Weide, B.W., Yao, A.C.: Optimal Expected-time Algorithms for Closest Point Problem", In ACM Transactions on Mathematical Software, Vol. 6, No. 4 (1980) 563–580
10. Berchtold, S., Böhm, C., Braunmüller, B., Keim, D.A., Kriegel, H.-P.: Fast Parallel Similarity Search in Multimedia Databases. In Proc. ACM SIGMOD Int. Conf. on Management of Data (1997) 1–12
11. Berchtold, S., Böhm, C., B., Keim, D.A., Kriegel, H.-P.: A Cost Model for Nearest Neighbor Search in High-Dimensional Data Space. In Proc. 16th ACM SIGACT-SIGMOD-SIGART Symposium on PODS (1997) 78–86
12. Bern, M.: Approximate Closest Point Queries in High Dimensions. In Information Processing Letters, Vol. 45 (1993) 95–99
13. Beyer, K., Goldstein, J., Ramakrishnan, R., Shaft, U.: When Is Nearest Neighbors Meaningful? Technical Report No. TR1377, Computer Sciences Dept., Univ. of Wisconsin-Madison, June 1998
14. Bozkaya, T., Ozsoyoglu, M.: Distance-Based Indexing for High-Dimensional Metric Spaces. In Proc. 16th ACM SIGACT-SIGMOD-SIGART Symposium on PODS (1997) 357–368
15. Faloutsos, C., et al: Efficient and Effective Querying by Image Content. In Journal of Intelligent Information Systems, Vol. 3, No. 3 (1994) 231–262

16. Faloutsos, C., Gaede, V.: Analysis of n-Dimensional Quadtrees Using the Housdorff Fractal Dimension. In Proc. ACM SIGMOD Int. Conf. of the Management of Data (1996)

17. Faloutsos, C., Kamel, I.: Beyond Uniformity and Independence: Analysis of R-trees Using the Concept of Fractal Dimension. In Proc. 13th ACM SIGACT-SIGMOD-SIGART Symposium on PODS (1994) 4–13

18. Fayyad, U.M., Smyth, P.: Automated Analysis and Exploration of Image Databases: Results, Progress and Challenges. In Journal of intelligent information systems, Vol. 4, No. 1 (1995) 7–25

19. Katayama, N., Satoh, S.: The SR-tree: An Index Structure for High-Dimensional Nearest Neighbor Queries. In Proc. 16th ACM SIGACT-SIGMOD-SIGART Symposium on PODS (1997) 369–380

20. Lin, K.-I., Jagadish, H.V., Faloutsos, C.: The TV-Tree: An Index Structure for High-Dimensional Data. In VLDB Journal, Vol. 3, No. 4 (1994) 517–542

21. Manjunath, B.S., Ma, W.Y.: Texture Features for Browsing and Retrieval of Image Data. In IEEE Trans. on Pattern Analysis and Machine Learning, Vol. 18, No. 8 (1996) 837–842

22. Mehrotra, R., Gary, J.E.: Feature-Based Retrieval of Similar Shapes. In 9th Data Engineering Conference (1992) 108–115

23. Murase, H., Nayar, S.K.: Visual Learning and Recognition of 3D Objects from Appearance. In Int. J. of Computer Vision, Vol. 14, No. 1 (1995) 5–24

24. Nene, S.A., Nayar, S.K.: A Simple Algorithm for Nearest Neighbor Search in High Dimensions. In IEEE Trans. on Pattern Analysis and Machine Learning, Vol. 18, No. 8 (1996) 989–1003

25. Pentland, A., Picard, R.W., Scalroff, S.: Photobook: Tools for Content Based Manipulation of Image Databases. In SPIE Vol. 2185 (1994) 34–47

26. Scott, D.W.: Multivariate Density Estimation. Wiley Interscience, Chapter 2 (1992)

27. Shaft, U., Goldstein, J., Beyer, K.: Nearest Neighbors Query Performance for Unstable Distributions. Technical Report No. TR1388, Computer Sciences Dept., Univ. of Wisconsin-Madison, October 1998

28. Swain, M.J., Ballard D.H.: Color Indexing. In Inter. Journal of Computer Vision, Vol. 7, No. 1 (1991) 11–32

29. Swets, D.L., Weng, J.: Using Discriminant Eigenfeatures for Image Retrieval. In IEEE Trans. on Pattern Analysis and Machine Learning, Vol. 18, No. 8 (1996) 831–836

30. Taubin, G., Cooper, D.B.: Recognition and Positioning of Rigid Objects Using Algebraic Moment Invariants. In SPIE, Vol. 1570 (1991) 318–327

31. White, D.A., Jain, R.: Similarity Indexing with the SS-Tree. In ICDE (1996) 516–523

On Rectangular Partitionings in Two Dimensions: Algorithms, Complexity, and Applications

S. Muthukrishnan[1], Viswanath Poosala[1], and Torsten Suel[*2]

[1] Bell Laboratories, 700 Mountain Avenue, Murray Hill, NJ 07974.
{muthu,poosala}@research.bell-labs.com
[2] Polytechnic University, Six MetroTech Center, Brooklyn, NY 11201.
suel@photon.poly.edu

Abstract. Partitioning a multi-dimensional data set into rectangular partitions subject to certain constraints is an important problem that arises in many database applications, including histogram-based selectivity estimation, load-balancing, and construction of index structures. While provably optimal and efficient algorithms exist for partitioning one-dimensional data, the multi-dimensional problem has received less attention, except for a few special cases. As a result, the heuristic partitioning techniques that are used in practice are not well understood, and come with no guarantees on the quality of the solution. In this paper, we present algorithmic and complexity-theoretic results for the fundamental problem of partitioning a two-dimensional array into rectangular tiles of arbitrary size in a way that minimizes the number of tiles required to satisfy a given constraint. Our main results are approximation algorithms for several partitioning problems that provably approximate the optimal solutions within small constant factors, and that run in linear or close to linear time. We also establish the NP-hardness of several partitioning problems, therefore it is unlikely that there are efficient, i.e., polynomial time, algorithms for solving these problems *exactly*.
We also discuss a few applications in which partitioning problems arise. One of the applications is the problem of constructing multi-dimensional histograms. Our results, for example, give an efficient algorithm to construct the *V-Optimal* histograms which are known to be the most accurate histograms in several selectivity estimation problems. Our algorithms are the first to provide guaranteed bounds on the quality of the solution.

1 Introduction

Many problems arising in databases and other areas require partitioning a multi-dimensional data set into rectangular partitions or tiles such that certain mathematical constraints are satisfied. Often these constraints take the form of minimizing (or maximizing) a metric using a fixed number of partitions or, conversely,

---

* This work was done while the author was at Bell Labs.

Catriel Beeri, Peter Buneman (Eds.): ICDT'99, LNCS 1540, pp. 236–256, 1998.
© Springer-Verlag Berlin Heidelberg 1998

minimizing the number of partitions while not exceeding (or falling below) a given value of that metric.

These problems are quite challenging for most interesting metrics and hence one usually resorts to heuristic approaches. Unfortunately, many of these approaches do not provide any guarantees on the quality of the solution and may thus adversely affect the application. In this paper we present algorithmic and complexity-theoretic results on the fundamental problem of partitioning two-dimensional arrays into rectangular partitions tiles[1] of arbitrary sizes. We develop solutions that offer guarantees on the quality of their solutions *and* that run in small polynomial time (near-linear in most cases). We start out with a few examples.

Example 1. Consider the 4×4 array in Fig. 1(a). A partitioning with 5 tiles is shown in Figure 1(b) such that the maximum sum of the elements that fall within any one tile is at most 57. There are many different ways to tile the array with 5 tiles with different maximum sums. There are also alternative ways to evaluate the partitioning, other than by considering the maximum sum of the elements. For instance, for each tile, we could sum up the squares of the difference between each element in the tile and the average of all the elements in that tile; we could then total all the values thus obtained for the tiles. This value is 204.7 as shown in Fig. 1(b). Again different partitions induce different values.   □

Example 2. Consider the 4×4 array in Fig. 1. A 3×3 tiling, namely one obtained by partitioning rows into 3 intervals and columns into 3 intervals, is presented in Fig. 1(c). For the partition presented there, the maximum sum of the elements that fall within any tile is at most 79. Again different partitions induce different values.   □

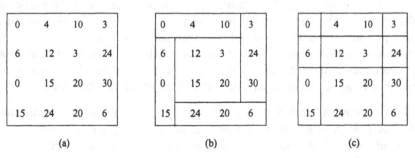

(a)   (b)   (c)

Fig. 1. Partitioning Examples

Example 1 arises in data partitioning for load balancing [23] and histogram-based selectivity estimation [31], while Example 2 arises in constructing grid-files which are well-known index structures [28]. We will list other application scenarios further below, but we briefly describe the histogram context here.

---

[1] We use the terms tile and partition interchangeably in the rest of the paper.

Example Application: *(Histograms)* Query optimizers require reasonably accurate estimates of query result sizes in order to estimate the costs of various execution plans. Most commercial database management systems use *histograms* to approximate the data in the database in order to perform these estimations. Histograms group attribute values into subsets (*buckets*) and approximate true attribute values and their frequencies based on summary statistics maintained in each bucket [20,31]. Researchers have proposed the use of *multi-dimensional histograms* for approximating distributions with multiple attributes [27,32]. This approach involves partitioning the multi-dimensional space of attribute values into rectangular buckets based on various partitioning constraints. This leads to partitioning problems of the sort we consider in this paper. In particular, the well-known V-optimal histogram in two dimensions, which has been shown to minimize selectivity estimation errors for estimating the result sizes of several classes of queries [14,30], corresponds to the alternative metric, and one of the partitions in Example 1.   □

There are many different types of partitions and many different metrics to evaluate the partitions. A generic optimization problem that arises in several application contexts is as follows.

The Partitioning Problem. We are given a two-dimensional array of elements, the type of partition sought, a metric to evaluate the partitions, and a bound δ. The problem is to produce a partitioning of the array of the type sought, with the minimal number of rectangular tiles such that the metric computed on the partition is at most δ.   □

The partitioning problem has been extensively studied in many application scenarios in the Database and Algorithms Research communities, in various specialized forms. However, most known results are either heuristics without provable guarantees, or provably efficient algorithms for simple, specific metrics and tilings. For example, little is known about the complexity of the partitioning problem with the alternative metric in Example 1 for different types of partitions, but this problem is fundamental in histogram construction.

Motivated by this state-of-the-art, we formulate the partitioning problem in its generality and study its difficulty for various types of partitions and metrics of relevance in application scenarios. Our contributions are two-fold.

1. *We show that the partitioning problem is NP-hard for many natural metrics and partitionings arising in database applications. Thus, efficient, i.e. polynomial time, algorithms exist if and only if $NP = P$, a central complexity question that remains unresolved.*
   The partitioning problem can be naturally defined on one-dimensional arrays too. These problems can be solved efficiently in small polynomial time [15], but our claim above implies that their natural two-dimensional variants are NP-Hard. Thus, the partitioning problem becomes fundamentally different as we go from one-dimensional to multidimensional arrays.
2. Our main technical results are a number of algorithms that complement the negative results above. *We present very efficient (near-linear time) algorithms for approximately solving the partitioning problem in two dimensions*

for fairly general metrics and different partitionings (including most that arise in our database applications); the approximation bounds are guaranteed, and they are small constants.

We define the partitioning problem and state our results more formally in Section 2. Here are a few high-level remarks on our results.

Remark 1. All of our algorithms extend to multiple dimensions with similar (i.e., near-linear) performance bounds. However, this may sound better than it actually is, because they will take time that is linear in the size of the underlying d-dimensional array. However, in many applications, this array may be very sparse, and an algorithm that works in time linear in the number of non-zero entries would be much preferable, while one that works in time linear in the size of the array can be prohibitively expensive. Some of our algorithms can likely be modified to exploit sparseness of the input domain, while for others this is more difficult.

Remark 2. There are other limitations to our framework of partitioning problems. For example, in some application scenarios, tiles may be allowed to overlap, i.e., the problem may be one of *covering* the array rather than partitioning it. This arises, for example, when building certain spatial indices such as R-trees. Our results do not directly apply to such covering problems. Also, there are application scenarios where one may be allowed to permute the rows and columns of the input array. All our results assume that some canonical ordering (such as that given by the natural order of numeric attributes in database applications) is fixed.

Remark 3. Despite the limitations above, the partitioning problems we study are very general, and they arise in a number of important application scenarios within databases. Besides the problems of histogram-based selectivity estimation, grid file construction, and load balancing mentioned earlier, there are applications in database compression, bulk-loading of hierarchical index structures, and partitioning of spatial data, as well as to problems outside databases such as domain partitioning in scientific computation, support of data partitioning in data-parallel languages, and image and video processing. In this paper, we clarify applications to histogram-based selectivity estimation only; discussions about other applications can be found in the full version of this paper.

□

Map. The rest of the paper is organized as follows. We formalize the partitioning problem and relate it to various application contexts in Section 2; we also state our results formally there. In Sections 4, 5, and 6, we present hardness and algorithmic results for different types of partitions with different metrics. In Section 7, we discuss the implications of our results for one applied area in databases, namely, histogram-based selectivity estimation. Section 8 has concluding remarks.

2 Problem Formulation and Overview of Results

2.1 The Partitioning Problem Definition

We are given an $n \times n$ array A containing $N = n^2$ real numbers. A *tile* is any rectangular subarray $A[i \dots j, k \dots l]$. A *partitioning* of array A is a partitioning of A into tiles; by definition of a partition, each element $A[i, j]$ lies within some tile and no two tiles overlap. As mentioned in the previous section, partitioning schemes can be classified based on the *type of partition* and the *metric functions* used within and outside the tiles to evaluate the partition. We define these criteria below and present interesting instantiations for each of them.

Type of Partitioning: There are many possible types of partitionings of a two-dimensional array. The ones we consider here are the common ones that arise in database applications:

1. *Arbitrary:* No restrictions on the arrangement of tiles within A (Figure 2.a).
2. *Hierarchical:* A hierarchical partition is one in which there exists a vertical or horizontal separation of array into two disjoint parts in each of which the partitioning is again hierarchical (Figure 2.b). A hierarchical partitioning is naturally represented by a *hierarchy tree* which is a binary tree in which a node represents a subarray of A and each of its children represent a partition of that subarray of A into two disjoint parts; the root represents A.
3. $p \times p$: Here, the rows and columns of A are partitioned into p disjoint intervals each; the induced p^2 tiles form the $p \times p$ partitioning. This can be thought of as a special case of hierarchical partitioning where the tiling in the subarrays of two sibling nodes of the hierarchy tree are the same along one dimension (Figure 2.c).

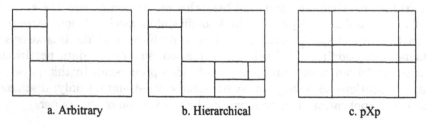

a. Arbitrary   b. Hierarchical   c. pXp

Fig. 2. Tilings

Quality Metrics: Metrics are defined on the tiling using the following three functions.

1. *Elementary Function:* An elementary function h maps the array elements of any tile to real numbers. Common functions include (*i*) ID, i.e., $h(A[i]) = A[i]$, (*ii*) AVG_DIFF, i.e., $h(A[i]) = |A[i] - \overline{A}|$ where $\overline{A}$ is the average of the elements in that tile, (*iii*) GEO_DIFF, i.e., $h(A[i]) = |A[i] - A'|$ where A' is

the geometric median of the elements in the tile, and (*iv*) SQR_DIFF which is the square of AVG_DIFF.

2. *Heft Function.* A heft function g is defined for a tile r and an elementary function h of the elements in that tile. The common heft functions are (*i*) SUM, i.e., $\sum_{A[i,j] \in r} h(A[i,j])$, (*ii*) MAX, i.e., $\max_{A[i,j] \in r} h(A[i,j])$, (*iii*) RATIO, i.e., $\frac{\max_{A[i,j] \in r} h(A[i,j])}{\min_{A[i,j] \in r} h(A[i,j])}$, etc. SUM and MAX are the common heft functions in our application scenarios. Notice that the heft is an "intra-tile" function. The value evaluated by the heft function in a tile is called its *heft*.

3. *Cumulative Function.* A cumulative function f is defined for the entire set of tiles, for combining heft function g. The common cumulative functions are SUM and MAX, representing the total and maximum heft value of tiles in the given tiling, respectively. Note that the cumulative function is an "inter-tile" function.

Any partition thus has a *metric* that is a combination of these three functions $f - g - h$. For example, the SUM-MAX-ID metric of a partition is the sum over the tiles of the maximum element in each tile. In Section 1, Example 1 has the MAX-SUM-ID metric with the alternative being the SUM-SUM-SQR_DIFF metric, and Example 2 has the MAX-SUM-ID metric. Some combination of the functions are trivial – for example, all partitions are identical under the MAX-MAX-ID and SUM-SUM-ID metrics – but most of the metrics are nontrivial. The value the metric evaluates to on a given array and a partition, is called its *metric value*, or where there is no ambiguity, the *heft* of the partition.

The Optimization Problem: The optimization problem we consider is as follows: *For the given type of partition, metric, and bound δ, determine the partitioning of that type that has the minimum number of tiles with the metric value of the partition being at most δ.* A related problem is one in which we are given a bound p on the number of tiles and the goal is to determine a tiling using at most p tiles with minimum metric value. As far as the NP-Hardness is concerned, these two optimization problems are identical, that is, if one is NP-hard, so is the other. However, this similarity does not extend to efficient approximability of these problems. In this paper, we only consider the first version.

Several partitioning problems arising in real applications mentioned in the Introduction fit naturally in our framework. We present one such application (histograms) in full detail in Section 7 and illustrate how our problem definition and results solve an important problem arising in that application.

2.2 Some Preliminaries

We state some properties of the metrics and hefts that will be used latter. We say that a heft function g is *monotonic* if $g(r) \leq g(R)$ for two tiles r and R, $r \in R$. For example, SUM-ID is monotonic provided the array elements are non-negative. Most of the heft functions that arise in our applications are monotonic. We say that a metric $f - g$ is *superadditive* if the following holds. $f(g(r \bigcup R)) \geq$

$f(g(r), g(R))$, where r and R are any two disjoint tiles. For example, SUM-SUM-SQR_DIFF is superadditive (this requires a nontrivial proof). Some of our results hold only for superadditive metrics.

Our algorithms often identify tiles and are required to compute their hefts. Say t_Q represents the time to determine the heft of any tile. The straightforward way would be to consider each element of the tile and this takes $t_Q = O(N)$ time in the worst case. However, there is a more efficient method in some cases. Consider the MAX heft function: after $O(N)$ time preprocessing, we can compute the heft of any tile in $t_Q = O(1)$ time. We omit the details of this procedure here. For SUM heft functions, the same holds for some elementary functions such as the SQR_DIFF and ID, and not for others, such as the AVG_DIFF, GEO_DIFF etc. There are still other examples of heft functions for which t_Q is $O(\log N)$. In what follows, we state all our bounds in terms of t_Q. For applications arising in databases, t_Q is often $O(1)$ since SUM-SQR_DIFF is the most common heft function (such as in V-optimal histograms).

3   Related Work

Partitioning problems have been studied extensively in various application areas including databases, parallel computing (e.g., load balancing), computational geometry (e.g., clustering), video compression (e.g., block matching) etc. Some related papers from a variety of application areas include [17,23,25,24,1,3,10]. Here we review a selection of related work most relevant to us.

Hardness Results. Hardness results exist only for a simple metric function, namely, MAX-SUM-ID – [18] proved it to be NP-hard for arbitrary partitions, and [11,6] proved it to be NP-hard for $p \times p$ partition. Our NP-hardness results are inspired by the abovementioned results. However, the basic gadgets in our reductions are different from the ones in [18,6] and we derive different non-approximability bounds for various metrics.

Algorithmic Results. Dynamic programming has been used to find optimal results for hierarchical partitions in several contexts [2,26,18]. However, our sparse hierarchy approach with provable guarantee appears to be new. For $p \times p$ partition MAX-SUM-ID, the best known approximation is by $O(\log n)$ factor [19]. We derived substantially improved bounds for this problem. Many heuristic algorithms have been proposed for this problem [23].

Applications: We focus on prior work in one database application, namely, histograms. Histograms have been studied quite extensively in the literature in the context of approximating single attributes [20,33,13,14,30,31,15]. On the other hand, these has been very little work on multi-dimensional histograms. Muralikrishna *et al* proposed a heuristic hierarchical algorithm for constructing multi-dimensional equidepth histograms [27]. Poosala *et al* extended the definition of multi-dimensional histograms to other bucketization techniques, such as V-Optimal, MaxDiff etc [32] and provided a more sophisticated and general hierarchical partitioning algorithm called *MHIST*. But, neither of these algorithms provide any guarantee on the quality of the partitioning.

4   Hierarchical Tilings

In this section, we consider the hierarchical partitioning problems. Recall that the problem is to produce a hierarchical partition of an $n \times n$ array A with metric value at most δ using the minimum number of tiles. We set $N = n^2$ throughout. Let t_Q be an upper bound on the time taken to calculate the heft value of any tile in A; all our bounds below will be in terms of t_Q. First we focus on exact algorithms, and then approximate ones. *We state our results for only SUM and MAX metrics, but they hold for any superadditive metric with time bound identical to that for the SUM metric.*

4.1   Exact Algorithms

Theorem 1. *For cumulative function MAX, there exists an $O(N^{2.5} + N^2 t_Q)$ time algorithm to solve the hierarchical partitioning problem exactly. For cumulative function SUM, there exists an $O(N^{2.5}(B^*)^2 t_Q)$ time algorithm to solve the hierarchical partitioning problem exactly; here, B^* is the number of tiles in the optimum solution.*

Proof. The proof uses dynamic programming; it is simple, and it has appeared, for example, in [18], for a special case of the heft function. We include it here since some of our algorithms will be derived by suitably modifying this solution. We consider the cumulative function MAX only; the SUM case is a simple modification. Define $E^*(i \cdots j, k \cdots \ell)$ to be smallest number of tiles needed to partition the region $A[i \cdots j, k \cdots \ell]$ with metric value at most δ. If the heft of the tile $A[i \ldots j, k \ldots \ell]$ is at most δ, we have $E^*(i \cdots j, k \cdots \ell) = 1$. Else, we have Equation (I) below:

$$E^*(i \cdots j, k \cdots \ell) = \min_{i \leq x < j, \, k \leq y < \ell} \left\{ \begin{array}{l} E^*(i \cdots x, k \cdots \ell) \\ +E^*(x+1 \cdots j, k \cdots \ell), \\ E^*(i \cdots j, k \cdots y) \\ +E^*(i \cdots j, y+1 \cdots \ell) \end{array} \right\}$$

We need to calculate $E^* = E^*(1 \cdots n, 1 \cdots n)$. We use the dynamic programming technique and calculate $E^*(i \cdots j, k \ldots \ell)$ for all $1 \leq i < j \leq n$ and $1 \leq k < \ell \leq n$. In all, there are $O(n^4)$ possible sub-rectangles and for each we calculate $O(n)$ values and the heft of a single tile. Thus we take $O(n^5 + n^4 t_Q)$ time which is $O(N^{2.5} + N^2 t_Q)$ time.   □

4.2   Approximate Algorithms

In this section, we present approximation algorithms for computing hierarchical partitions for the SUM and MAX metrics (as before, they can be modified to work for any superadditive metric); the algorithms in this section are faster than the exact ones in Section 4.1. Our algorithms rely on two natural, well-known ideas, namely, *rounding*, and *pruning*, which we informally describe below. These strategies "sparsify" the dynamic programming, that is, reduce the number of subproblems to be considered; this results in a speedier dynamic programming solution. They are easy to implement, and the technical crux is their analyses.

Rounding is a structured way to limit ourselves to only a subset of all possible tiles. This is achieved by considering only tiles with endpoints at multiples of a small number of parameters. However, there are many ways to perform rounding: round only along one of the dimensions, or possibly both; round so both the endpoints of tiles are multiples of the parameters, or just one of them; etc. Rounding can also be done hierarchically with choice of parameter values and rounding techniques at different levels. A general tradeoff for solving the partitioning problems in terms of all these combinations is difficult to state, but in our solutions, we employ interesting combinations and obtain our bounds.

Rounding to one grid pattern. We fix a parameter L and assume n is a multiple of L – the following description can be easily modified to handle other values of n. We define an L-*grid* as the subset of columns and rows numbered $1, L + 1, 2L + 1, \cdots$; thus there are n/L grid columns and rows in an L-grid. We refer to each such row (column) as the L-*row* (L-*column* respectively). We define the 1-hierarchical partition to be a hierarchical partition in which the tiles *additionally* satisfy the following two conditions. (1) At least one side has both its endpoints on L-rows on L-columns, that is, the side is of length a multiple of L, and (2) Both its sides have their endpoints *between* two consecutive L-rows or two consecutive L-columns; that is, they are each of length at most L. The 1-hierarchical partitioning problem is to produce a 1-hierarchical partition of an $n \times n$ array A with metric value at most δ using the minimum number of tiles. In what follows we will argue the following two points: (1) the optimal 1-hierarchical partition can be determined efficiently, and (2) the optimal 1-hierarchical partition approximates the hierarchical partition nicely.

Lemma 1. *For cumulative function MAX, there exists an $O(N^{1.6} t_Q)$ time algorithm to solve the 1-hierarchical partitioning problem exactly. For cumulative function SUM, there exists an $O(N^{1.6} (B^*)^2 t_Q)$ time algorithm to solve the 1-hierarchical partitioning problem exactly; here, B^* is the number of tiles in the optimum solution.*

Proof. We will only show the proof for the MAX function; the proof for the SUM function is similar. Define $E^*(i \cdots j - 1, k \cdots \ell - 1)$ to be smallest number of tiles in an 1-hierarchical partition of the region $A[i \cdots j - 1, k \cdots \ell - 1]$ with metric value at most δ. We employ the Equation (I) to compute $E^*(i \cdots j, k \cdots \ell)$, with some changes in the set of values taken by x and y in Equation (I). If $j - i > L$, then x takes *only* the values of L-rows in Equation (I) between i and j. otherwise, x takes all values between i and j; same holds for y values too. As before, the computation is done using the dynamic programming technique to calculate $E^* = E^*(1 \cdots n, 1 \cdots n)$. By choosing $L = n^{2/5}$ (optimized based on the running time calculations), the total running time of this algorithm turns out to be $O(N^{1.6}t_Q)$.   □

Lemma 2. *Consider any hierarchical partition of array A with B tiles and metric value at most δ, for an superadditive metric. There exists a 1-hierarchical partition using at most $9B$ tiles with metric value at most δ for any positive integer L.*

The proof of this lemma is omitted for space constraints. The two preceding lemmas together let us conclude that,

Theorem 2. *For cumulative function MAX, there exists an $O(N^{1.6}t_Q)$ time algorithm for solving the hierarchical partitioning problem that returns a hierarchical partition with at most $9B^*$ tiles and metric value at most δ; here, B^* is the minimum number of tiles in a hierarchical partition with metric value at most δ and the metric is superadditive. For the cumulative function SUM, the same holds with running time $O(N^{1.6}(B^*)^2 t_Q)$; here, B^* is the number of tiles in the optimum solution.*

This algorithm is faster than the one in Theorem 1, but produces a partitioning with a slightly larger number of tiles. We can improve the running time further by increasing the number of tiles in a structured manner as described below.

Rounding to several grid patterns. We are given a sequence of positive integers $L_0, L_1, L_2, \ldots L_k$ such that $L_0 = n$, $L_k = 1$ and L_{i+1} divides L_i for $i > 0$. We define a k-*hierarchical partition* as follows. It is a hierarchical partition in which there are k sets S_i of permissible intervals that can be the side lengths of the tiles. S_1 comprises of intervals $[jL_1, \ell L_1]$ for some integers $j < \ell$. In general, S_i for $1 \leq i < k$, comprises the set of intervals $[jL_i, \ell L_i]$ such that for some h, $hL_{i-1} \leq jL_i$ and $(h+1)L_{i-1} \geq \ell L_i$. The set S_k comprises intervals in S_i, for $i = k$, as defined above, but additionally, all subintervals thereof. The k-hierarchical partitioning problem is to find the k-hierarchical partition with metric value at most δ and minimum number of tiles. We can solve this problem again using dynamic programming, although the solution is somewhat more involved. The analysis of the running time of this algorithm follows the same line as in Lemma 1. We choose L_i's appropriately to minimize the running time; it turns out to be a geometric progression of values. Also, we claim: *Consider any hierarchical partition of array A with B tiles and cumulative metric value at most δ, for any superadditive metric. There exists a k-hierarchical partition using at most $(2k+1)^2 B$ tiles with cumulative metric value at most δ for any positive integer k.* The proof is similar to that of Lemma 2. This lets us conclude,

Theorem 3. *For cumulative function MAX, there exists an $O(N^{1+\epsilon}t_Q)$ time algorithm for solving the hierarchical partitioning problem with at most $B^*O(1/\epsilon^2)$ tiles with metric value at most δ; here, B^* is the the minimum number of tiles in a hierarchical partition with metric value at most δ, ϵ is any chosen positive fraction, and the cumulative metric is superadditive.*

By choosing ϵ appropriately, we can get the running time to be as close to $O(Nt_Q)$ as we desire (which is linear for our applications – See Section 2.2). This is achieved at the expense of more (though not a very large number of) tiles. A different result which may be of interest is the following: we can prove that there is an $O(N(B^*)^2)$ time algorithm that approximates the minimum number of buckets to $O((\log\log n)^2)$ factor, for any superadditive metric.

The other natural idea we explore for approximate algorithms is pruning. Pruning also limits the set of tiles that are examined in dynamic programming. However, this is data-dependent since, effectively, we do not examine those tiles for which the heft is beyond certain prune condition. There is no efficient pruning strategy without rounding, since there are many large tiles that cannot be pruned. We have different pruning conditions for MAX and SUM. Due to space constraints, we omit the description of these conditions which can be found in [29]. Two examples of the results we obtain for MAX metrics are: an $O(N^{1.25}(B^*)^3)$ time algorithm for factor 9 approximation, and $O(N(B^*)^3)$ time algorithm for factor 25 approximation. Further results for MAX, SUM and other superadditive metrics can be found in [29].

5   Arbitrary Partitionings

5.1   NP-Hardness Results

In this subsection, we prove NP-hardness results for several metrics that show that minimizing the partitioning with p tiles that minimizes the heft is NP-hard. In fact, the proof also implies limits on the approximability of the problem for some cases.

For the special case of the MAX-SUM-ID metric, it was shown in [18] that the minimum heft cannot be approximated to within a factor of 1.25. We establish similar results for a a different set of metrics that includes SUM-SUM-SQR_DIFF, MAX-MAX-AVG_DIFF, and MAX-MAX-GEO_DIFF. As in [18] and the earlier work in [9], the proof is based on a reduction from the *Planar 3SAT* problem (shown to be NP-complete in [21]), though a number of changes are needed to adapt the argument to our types of metrics. Similar results can also be shown for several other metrics, but we restrict ourselves to the most important ones (proofs are omitted here).

Theorem 4. *Given a data distribution A and an upper bound on p, it is NP-hard*

- *to find the minimum heft of any rectangular partitioning with p tiles under the SUM-SUM-SQR_DIFF metric, and*
- *to approximate the minimum heft of any rectangular partitioning with p tiles under the MAX-MAX-GEO_DIFF metric to any factor less than 2, and*
- *to approximate the minimum heft of any rectangular partitioning with p tiles under the MAX-MAX-AVG_DIFF metric to any factor less than 3/2.*

5.2 Approximate Algorithms

In view of the hardness results in Section 5.1, we can not anticipate efficient, that is, polynomial time algorithms for exactly solving the partitioning problems with arbitrary partitions for many natural metrics. In this section, we focus on developing efficient approximate algorithms instead. All our approximations are based on the following observation which was presented in [18] for a special metric.

Lemma 3. *Consider any arbitrary partitioning of a two dimensional array A with superadditive cumulative metric at most δ and B tiles. There exists a hierarchical partition of A with cumulative metric at most δ and at most $4B$ tiles.*

Proof. It is shown in [8] that any arbitrary rectangular partition can be converted into a hierarchical one by splitting each tile into at most 4 disjoint tiles. If we apply their procedure to the given arbitrary partition, the resulting hierarchical partition has at most $4B$ tiles; furthermore, the metric value of this hierarchical partition is at most δ by the superadditivity of the metric.   □

Using this observation with the results in Section 4, we get the following. (Similar results can be obtained for the SUM cumulative function as well.)

Theorem 5. *For cumulative function MAX, say B^* is the optimal solution to the arbitrary partitioning problem with metric value at most δ. There is an algorithm that finds a partition with metric value at most δ in*

1. $O(N^{2.5} + N^2 T)$ *time; the solution has at most $4B^*$ tiles.*
2. $O(N^{1+\epsilon}T)$ *time; the solution has at most $4B^* O(1/\epsilon^2)$ tiles.*

Again, by setting ϵ appropriately, we can obtain an algorithm with near linear running time.

Note. Using the ideas in [18], an $O(N^c)$ time algorithm can be obtained that approximates the arbitrary partition using at most twice as many buckets as the optimum; however, the c is rather large (at least 5), and the resulting algorithm is impractical for all but tiny values of N.

6 p×p Partitioning Schemes

In this section, we consider the $p \times p$-partitioning problem defined earlier. Thus, we are given a two-dimensional distribution A, a metric E and a value δ, and we are interested in finding a minimum p, and a $p \times p$ partitioning H, such that $E(H) \leq \delta$. Here, a $p \times p$ partitioning is determined by a set of horizontal dividers (rows) $h_0 = 0 \leq h_1 \leq \ldots \leq h_p = n$ and a set of vertical dividers (columns) $v_0 = 0 \leq v_1 \leq \ldots \leq v_p = n$, and tile $r_{i,j}$ of the partition consists of all entries $A[k, l]$ such that $h_{i-1} < k \leq h_i$ and $v_{j-1} < l \leq v_j$.

We describe algorithms that run in linear or nearly linear time and that compute solutions that are guaranteed to be within a small constant factor of optimal. The algorithms provide an interesting application of the framework for approximating Set Cover for set systems with bounded Vapnik-Chervonenkis (VC) dimension described by Brönnimann and Goodrich [4] (see also the discussion in Section 6.3.)

6.1   NP-Hardness Results

For the special case of the MAX-SUM-ID metric, Charikar, Chekuri, Feder, and Motwani [6] have shown that it is NP-hard to approximate the minimum heft of any $p \times p$ partitioning to within a factor of less than 2. This result can be extended to several other interesting metrics, including SUM-SUM-SQR_DIFF, MAX-MAX-AVG_DIFF, and MAX-MAX-GEO_DIFF. We point out that all the results are obtained by modifications of the hardness proof in [6], which uses a reduction from the k-Balanced Bipartite Vertex Cover (k-BBVC) problem. The results are summarized in the following theorem, the proof of which is omitted for space constraints.

Theorem 6. *Given a data distribution A and an upper bound on p, it is NP-hard*

- *to approximate the minimum heft of any $p \times p$ partitioning under the MAX-MAX-AVG_DIFF and MAX-MAX-GEO_DIFF metrics to any factor less than 2, and*
- *to find the minimum heft of any $p \times p$ partitioning under the SUM-SUM-SQR_DIFF metric.*

The proof of the first claim follows from some fairly simple modifications of the proof in [6], while the second claim requires an additional accounting argument. Of course, the result also implies the NP-hardness of the problem of minimizing p given an upper bound on the heft, though we do not have any inapproximability result for that case.

6.2   Preliminaries

We denote by X the set of n rows and n columns of the $n \times n$ distribution A. As before, we assume $N = n^2$. For each tile $r_{i,j}$ of a $p \times p$ partitioning H, we define a corresponding subset $R_{i,j}$ of X consisting of all rows and columns that intersect $r_{i,j}$, except for the last intersecting row and column. We also use a weight function w, to be defined later, that assigns a real-valued weight $w(x)$ to each $x \in X$, and define $w(Y) = \sum_{y \in Y} w(y)$ for any subset Y of X.

Definition 1. *Given a weight function w, we say that a $p \times p$ partitioning is α-good if every tile $r_{i,j}$ of H satisfies $w(R_{i,j}) \leq \alpha \cdot w(X)$.*

We remark that our α-good partitionings correspond to the ϵ-nets used in [4] and originally introduced in [12], which have found many applications in computational geometry.

6.3 Upper Bounds for MAX Metrics

We now present approximation results for the $p \times p$-partitioning problem where the cumulative metric is the MAX metric, i.e., the heft of a partition is the largest heft of any of the tiles. We also require that the heft function is monotonic, i.e., the heft of a tile does not decrease if we grow its size, which is true for most interesting cases[2].

The Algorithm Suppose that we are given a maximum value δ for the heft of the solution, and assume that there exists a $p_0 \times p_0$ partitioning H_0 with heft at most δ (the value of p_0 will be guessed using binary search). We will show that the following algorithm computes a $p \times p$ partitioning with heft at most δ and $p \leq (2 + \epsilon) \cdot p_0$, for any chosen $\epsilon > 0$.

Algorithm *MAX-pxp*.

(1) Set the weights of all elements of X to 1.
(2) Repeat the following three steps:
    (a) Compute an α-good partitioning H, for $\alpha = \frac{1}{(2+\epsilon)p_0}$.
    (b) Find a tile $r_{i,j}$ in H such that $w(R_{i,j}) > \delta$. If none exists, terminate and return H as solution.
    (c) Multiply the weights of all elements of X that are contained in $R_{i,j}$ by $\beta = (1 + \epsilon/2)$.

Analysis of the Algorithm. We now analyze the performance of the algorithm in three steps: (1) We show how Step (2a) can be implemented, and bound the size of the resulting α-good partitioning, (2) we bound the number of iterations in Step (2), and (3) we analyze the running time of each iteration. Theorem 7 then gives the main result of this subsection.

Lemma 4. *There exists an α-good $p \times p$ partitioning with $p = 1/\alpha$. It can be computed in time $O(n)$.*

Proof: Simply set $1/\alpha - 1$ horizontal dividers one after the other, starting at the top, and repeatedly choosing the next divider h_i as the first element where the sum of the weights of all rows encountered after h_{i-1} surpasses $\alpha \cdot w(X_h)$, where X_h is the set of all rows. Choose the vertical dividers v_i in an analogous fashion. □

Lemma 5. *The loop in Step (2) of MAX-pxp terminates after $O(p \log n)$ iterations.*

Proof: The proof is similar to that of Lemma 3.4 of [4], which itself follows the arguments in [7,22,34].
  Note that the weight $w(X)$ is initially $2n$, and that it increases by at most a factor of $\left(1 + \frac{\epsilon}{2 \cdot (2+\epsilon) \cdot p_0}\right)$ in each iteration, since in each iteration we multiply

---

[2] An exception is the MAX-MAX-AVG_DIFF metric.

the weights of exactly one of the sets $R_{i,j}$ by a factor of $(1 + \epsilon/2)$, and this set $R_{i,j}$ has a total weight of at most $\frac{1}{(2+\epsilon)\cdot p_0} \cdot w(X)$ due to the definition of α-goodness. Thus, after k iterations, we can upperbound $w(X)$ by

$$2n \left(1 + \frac{\epsilon}{2 \cdot (2 + \epsilon) \cdot p_0}\right)^k \leq 2n \cdot exp\left(\frac{\epsilon \cdot k}{2 \cdot (2 + \epsilon) \cdot p_0}\right) = exp\left(\frac{\epsilon k}{2 \cdot (2 + \epsilon) \cdot 0} + ln(2n)\right)$$

where $exp()$ denotes the exponential function with basis e. We now consider the weight $w(H_0)$ of the $p_0 \times p_0$ partitioning H_0 of heft at most δ that we assume to exist.[3] Note that any tile $r_{i,j}$ that is selected in Step (2b) has a heft larger than δ, and hence H_0 must cut $r_{i,j}$, due to the monotonicity of the heft function. This implies that at least one element of H_0 is also contained in $R_{i,j}$ and has its weight increased by a factor of $(1 + \epsilon/2)$. Thus, we have

$$w(H_0) = \sum_{x_i \in H_0} (1 + \epsilon/2)^{z_i}$$

with $\sum z_i >= k$, where z_i denotes the number of times the weight of the corresponding element $x_i \in H_0$ has been multiplied by $(1+\epsilon/2)$. Using the convexity of the exponential function with basis $(1 + \epsilon/2)$, we can lower-bound this as

$$w(H_0) \geq 2p_0 \cdot (1 + \epsilon/2)^{k/(2p_0)} = exp\left(\frac{ln(1 + \epsilon/2) \cdot k}{2p_0} + ln(2p_0)\right).$$

Since H_0 is a subset of X, we must have $w(H_0) \leq w(X)$, which implies that

$$\frac{ln(1 + \epsilon/2) \cdot k}{2p_0} + ln(2p_0) \leq \frac{\epsilon \cdot k}{2 \cdot (2 + \epsilon) \cdot p_0} + ln(2n),$$

which, using the inequality $ln(1 + \epsilon/2) \geq \frac{\epsilon}{2+\epsilon}$ for $0 < \epsilon < 1$, can be shown to imply that

$$k \leq p_0 \cdot \frac{ln(n/p_0)}{ln(1 + \epsilon/2) - \frac{\epsilon}{2+\epsilon}}.$$

$\square$

Lemma 6. *Each iteration in Step (2) runs in time $O(n + p^2 \cdot t_Q)$, where t_Q is the time needed to compute the heft of a tile.*

Proof: Steps (2a) and (2c) clearly run in time $O(n)$. In Step (2b), we have to compute the heft of at most p^2 tiles to find a tile with heft more than δ. $\square$

Theorem 7. *For any δ and any $\epsilon > 0$, a $p \times p$ partitioning H with heft at most δ and $p \leq (2 + \epsilon)p_0$ can be computed in time $O((n + p^2 \cdot t_Q) \cdot p \log n)$, where p_0 is the minimum number such that there exists a $p_0 \times p_0$ partitioning with heft at most δ, and t_Q is the time needed to compute the heft of any tile.*

---

[3] The weight of H_0 is the sum of the weights of the rows and columns that are horizontal dividers h_i or vertical dividers v_i, respectively, of H_0.

Proof: We perform binary search for the value of p_0, starting at $p_0 = 2$. We run algorithm *MAX-pxp* for each p_0 in the search. If the algorithm does not terminate after the number of iterations stated in Lemma 5, then we know that there is no $p_0 \times p_0$ partitioning with heft at most δ, and we increase p_0 by some small factor $(1 + \epsilon')$. The total running time is dominated by the time used to run *MAX-pxp* on the largest p_0; this implies the stated bound.   □

As explained before, in many cases the heft of each tile can be computed in $O(1)$ time, by performing $O(N)$ steps of preprocessing. In particular, this is true for the case of the MAX-SUM-ID metric, which is probably the most important of the metrics covered by Theorem 7, and we get the following corollary. Note that for the common case of $p \ll \sqrt{N}$, this gives a linear time bound.

Corollary 1. *For the MAX-SUM-ID metric, a $p \times p$ partitioning H with heft at most δ and $p \leq (2 + \epsilon)p_0$ can be computed in time $O(N + p^3 \log N)$, where p_0 is the minimum number such that there exists a $p_0 \times p_0$ partitioning with heft at most δ.*

Discussion. We now discuss the relation of our algorithm to the work in [19] and [4]. A simple reduction of the $p \times p$ partitioning problem to the Set Cover problem was given in [19], resulting in an approximation ratio of $O(\log N)$ using the well known greedy algorithm for Set Cover. This bound can be improved to $O(\log p)$ by using the algorithm for approximating Set Cover for the case of bounded VC-dimension in [4], and observing that the set system generated by the reduction in [19] has VC-dimension 4. By additionally using a construction of an ϵ-net for this set system along the lines of our Lemma 5, one can obtain an approximation ratio of 16 and a running time of $O(N^{3/2} \cdot p \log N)$. In order to get near-linear running time, we describe a modified algorithm that operates directly on the data distribution without materializing the set system used for the reduction to Set Cover, which could be of size $\Theta(N^{3/2})$ in the worst case. The approximation ratio of $(2 + \epsilon)$ is then obtained by tightening the analysis of [4] in several places.

Approximating the Error. For the important special case of the MAX-SUM-ID metric, which arises when partitioning data or work evenly among the tiles, we can also get significantly improved results for the problem of approximating the minimal heft of any $p \times p$ partitioning given an upper bound on p. The best previous result in [19] achieved a running time of $O(N^2)$ and an approximation ratio of around 120. We can show the following results.

Theorem 8. *Let δ_0 be the minimum heft of any $p_0 \times p_0$ partitioning. Then in time $O(N + p^3 \log N)$, we can compute*

(a) a $p \times p$ partitioning with heft $\delta \leq 4\delta_0$ and $p \leq (\frac{2}{3} + \epsilon)p_0$, and
(b) a $p \times p$ partitioning with heft $\delta \leq 2\delta_0$ and $p \leq (1 + \epsilon)p_0$,

for any chosen $\epsilon > 0$.

Note that these results come quite close to the lower bound of 2 on the approximability shown by Charikar, Chekuri, Feder, and Motwani [6]. These results are based on a fairly simple observation: If we modify Algorithm *MAX-pxp* such that in Step (2b) we search for a tile with heft at least $2\delta_0$ $(4\delta_0)$, then we can conclude that the optimum solution H_0 must cut this tile at least 2 (resp., 3) times in order to get a heft of at most δ_0. This means that Step (2c) guarantees a larger increase in the weight of H_0. We can then adjust the choice of the other parameters α and β appropriately to get the result.

Other Extensions. All results in this subsection can also be easily extended to $p \times q$ partitionings with $p \neq q$, and to non-square input distributions. In particular, in the case of a $p \times q$ partitioning of an $n \times m$ data distribution, the running time becomes $O(n + m + pq \cdot t_Q)(p + q)^2 \log(n + m))$, while the approximation ratio remains as before. It is also easy to extend the techniques to d dimensions, resulting in an approximation ratio of $d + \epsilon$ and a running time of $O((n + p^d \cdot t_Q)p \log N)$ for the result in Theorem 7.

Input data in higher dimensions is usually sparse, and thus efficiency crucially depends on exploiting this sparseness. For the algorithms in this subsection, the easiest solution would be to implement the computation of the heft of a tile (represented by the term t_Q) in a way that exploits sparseness; the details depend on the particular metric.

6.4   Upper Bounds for SUM Metrics

We now present approximation results for the case where the cumulative metric is the SUM metric. We again require that the heft function is monotonic. The algorithm follows the approach from the previous subsection. In contrast to the MAX case, we are not aware of any direct reduction of the SUM case to the Set Cover problem, and thus it is surprising that the same approach applies.

The Algorithm Suppose that we are given a maximum value δ_0 for the heft of the solution, and assume that there exists a $p_0 \times p_0$ partitioning H_0 with heft at most δ_0. Then the following algorithm computes a $p \times p$ partitioning with heft at most $2\delta_0$ and $p \leq (4 + \epsilon) \cdot p_0$, for any chosen $\epsilon > 0$.

Algorithm *SUM-pxp*.

(1) Set the weights of all elements of X to 1.
(2) Repeat the following three steps:
  (a) Compute an α-good partitioning H, for $\alpha = \frac{1}{(4+\epsilon)p_0}$.
  (b) If the heft of the partitioning is at most $2\delta_0$, terminate and return H as solution. Otherwise, select a tile $r_{i,j}$ at random such that the probability of picking a tile is proportional to its heft.
  (c) Multiply the weights of all elements of X that are contained in $R_{i,j}$ by $\beta = (1 + \epsilon/2)$.

Sketch of Analysis. The following lemma provides the main insight underlying the analysis.

Lemma 7. *With probability at most $\frac{1}{2}$, the tile chosen in Step (2b) is not cut by H_0.*

Proof: Let U be the set of tiles that are not cut by H_0. Then the hefts of the tiles in U sum up to at most δ_0, since otherwise the monotonicity of the heft function would imply that H_0 has a heft of more than δ_0. Since the sum of the hefts of all the tiles is at least $2\delta_0$, and each tile is chosen with probability proportional to its heft, the probability of choosing a tile from U is at most $\frac{1}{2}$.   □

The lemma directly implies that the weight of H_0 is increased in Step (2c) with probability at least $\frac{1}{2}$. This results in a slightly weaker lower bound for $w(H_0)$ as compared to the MAX case in the previous subsection. To deal with this weaker lower bound, we compute an α-good partitioning with $\alpha = \frac{1}{(4+\epsilon)p_0}$ instead of $\frac{1}{(2+\epsilon)p_0}$. The remainder of the analysis is then along the lines of the analysis for the MAX case, and we get the following result.

Theorem 9. *For any δ_0 and any $\epsilon > 0$, a $p \times p$ partitioning H with heft at most $2\delta_0$ and $p \leq (4+\epsilon)p_0$ can be computed in expected time $O((n + p^2 \cdot t_Q) \cdot p \log n)$, where p_0 is the minimum number such that there exists a $p_0 \times p_0$ partitioning with heft at most δ_0, and t_Q is the time needed to compute the heft of any tile.*

Discussion and Extensions. We point out that the algorithm can be easily made deterministic by modifying Steps (2b) and (2c) such that instead of choosing one particular tile at random, we take every tile $r_{i,j}$ and increase the weight of the elements in $R_{i,j}$ by a factor that is proportional to the heft of the tile. Also, the algorithm can be generalized to yield a trade-off between the approximation of the error and the approximation of the number of cuts.

As before, in many cases t_Q can be implemented in $O(1)$ steps by performing appropriate preprocessing. An interesting example is the SUM-SUM-SQR_DIFF metric, which models the case when we wish to form tiles containing similar values. Finally, the result can also be extended to $p \times q$ partitionings with $p \neq q$ and to higher dimensions, resulting in the same bounds as for the MAX case.

7   An Example Application of Results

We focus on one database application where partitioning problems arise; see [29] for the implications of our results in other applications.

Consider a database over relation R with n numerical attributes. This can be visualized as a multidimensional array A with one attribute along each dimension in which each array element contains the number of tuples in the database with the associated attribute values. This is the *joint frequency distribution* of the database. Histograms partition this distribution into rectangular regions (*buckets*) and approximate each region using a small amount of space. Typically, the frequencies in a bucket are approximated by their average.

Histograms are typically used to estimate the result sizes of relational queries. The errors in the estimation depend mainly on the bucketization. A theory of optimal histograms has been developed [31] in which a number of histograms have been identified as being optimal for various queries and operators. These histograms, such as Equidepth, Equiwidth etc can all be considered as special cases of our partitioning problems, and our results apply to them uniformly. Here, we focus on an important class of histograms, namely, the *V-Optimal histogram* which is provably the most accurate in several estimation problems [31].

Definition 2. V-Optimal Histogram *[14]: For a given number of buckets, a V-Optimal histogram is the one with the number of buckets bounded by the specified threshold, but having the least variance, where variance is the sum of squared differences between the actual and approximate frequencies. Alternately, for a given total variance, the V-Optimal histogram is one with the least number of buckets with total variance bounded by the specified threshold.*

Note that for joint distributions over two attributes, one version of the problem of constructing the optimal V-optimal histogram is identical to the partitioning problem with arbitrary partitions under the SUM-SUM-SQR_DIFF metric. By applying our general results to this partitioning problem, we derive the following results (further details are in [29].):

1. Identifying the optimal V-Optimal histogram with arbitrary buckets is NP-Hard.
2. The greedy MHIST algorithm presented in the literature [32] can result in *arbitrarily* poor histograms in terms of the buckets, as well as the total variance, whichever is being optimized; we can construct inputs to induce such worst case behavior. In fact, this applies to many other greedy solutions we can design for this problem.
3. We can approximate the minimum number of buckets needed to achieve the threshold variance in the *V*-Optimal histogram by using results in Section 5.2. The resulting algorithms work in near-linear time and produce small factor approximations.

8   Conclusions

We have considered the complexity of partitioning problems for different partitions and metrics. These problems are fundamental, and they arise in application scenarios such as histogram-based selectivity estimation, constructing grid files, load balancing, and many others. Very little is known about the complexity of these problems except for some special metrics, and heuristics with no proven guarantees on the quality of the solution are used.

In this paper, we show that many natural versions of the partitioning problem are NP-hard and thus it is unlikely they have efficient (polynomial time) *exact* solutions in the worst case. Our main results, however, are positive ones. We present highly efficient (near-linear time) algorithms that approximate the solutions to within small constant factors, for different partitions and metrics.

We applied our general results to solving an important problem arising in query result size estimation: the identification of V-Optimal histograms in two dimensions. Existing greedy algorithms do not offer any quality guarantees for this NP-Hard problem; our approximate solutions to the partitioning problems imply the first known efficient algorithms for this problem with guarantees. We are investigating its impact in practice.

References

1. S. Anily and A. Federgruen. Structured partitioning problems. *Operations Research*, 13, 130–149, 1991.
2. S. Arora. Polynomial time approximation schemes for euclidean tsp and other geometric problems. *Proc 37th IEEE Symp. of Foundations of Computer Science (FOCS)*, pages 2–12, 1996.
3. S. Bokhari. Partitioning problems in parallel, pipelined, and distributed computing. *IEEE Transactions on Computers*, 37, 38–57, 1988.
4. Brönnimann and Goodrich. Almost optimal set covers in finite VC-dimension. In *Proceedings of the 10th Annual Symposium on Computational Geometry*, 1994.
5. B. Carpentieri and J. Storer. A split-merge parallel block matching algorithm
6. M. Charikar, C. Chekuri, T. Feder, and R. Motwani. Personal communication, 1996.
7. K. L. Clarkson. A Las Vegas algorithm for linear programming when the dimension is small. In *Proc. 29th Annual IEEE Symposium on Foundations of Computer Science*, pages 452–456, October 1988.
8. F. d'Amore and P. Franciosa. On the optimal binary plane partition for sets of isothetic rectangles. *Information Proc. Letters*, 44, 255–259, 1992.
9. R. Fowler, M. Paterson, and S. Tanimoto. Optimal packing and covering in the plane are np-complete. *Information Proc. Letters*, 12, 133–137, 1981.
10. G. Fox, M. Johnson, G. Lyzenga, S. Otto, J. Salmon, and D. Walker. *Solving Problems on Concurrent Processors*, volume 1. Prentice-Hall, Englewood Cliffs, New Jersey, 1988.
11. M. Grigni and F. Manne. On the complexity of the generalized block distribution. Proc. of 3rd international workshop on parallel algorithms for irregularly structured problems (IRREGULAR '96), Lecture notes in computer science 1117, Springer, 319-326, 1996.
12. D. Haussler and E. Welzl. Epsilon-nets and simplex range queries. *Discrete and Computational Geometry*, 2:127–151, 1987.
13. Y. Ioannidis. Universality of serial histograms. *Proc. of the 19th Int. Conf. on Very Large Databases*, pages 256–267, December 1993.
14. Y. Ioannidis and V. Poosala. Balancing histogram optimality and practicality for query result size estimation. *Proc. of ACM SIGMOD Conf*, pages 233–244, May 1995.
15. H. V. Jagadish, N. Koudas, S. Muthukrishnan, V. Poosala, K. Sevcik, and T. Suel. Optimal histograms with quality guarantees. *Proc. of the 24rd Int. Conf. on Very Large Databases*, pages 275–286, August 1998.
16. J. Jain and A. Jain. Displacement measurement and its application in interframe coding. *IEEE Transactions on communications*, 29, 1799–1808, 1981.
17. M. Kaddoura, S. Ranka and A. Wang. Array decomposition for nonuniform computational environments. *Technical Report*, Syracuse University, 1995.

18. S. Khanna, S. Muthukrishnan, and M. Paterson. Approximating rectangle tiling and packing. *Proc Symp. on Discrete Algorithms (SODA)*, pages 384–393, 1998.
19. S. Khanna, S. Muthukrishnan, and S. Skiena. Efficient array partitioning. *Proc. Intl. Colloq. on Automata, Languages, and Programming (ICALP)*, pages 616–626, 1997.
20. R. P. Kooi. *The optimization of queries in relational databases.* PhD thesis, Case Western Reserve University, Sept 1980.
21. D. Lichtenstein. Planar formulae and their uses. *SIAM J. Computing*, 11, 329–343, 1982.
22. N. Littlestone. Learning quickly when irrelevant attributes abound: A new linear-threshold algorithm. In *Proceedings of the 28th Annual Symposium on Foundations of Computer Science*, pages 68–77, October 1987.
23. F. Manne. *Load Balancing in Parallel Sparse Matrix Computations.* Ph.d. thesis, Department of Informatics, University of Bergen, Norway, 1993.
24. F. Manne and T. Sorevik. Partitioning an array onto a mesh of processors. *Proc. of Workshop on Applied Parallel Computing in Industrial Problems.* 1996.
25. C. Manning. *Introduction to Digital Video Coding and Block Matching Algorithms.* http://atlantis.ucc.ie/dvideo/dv.html.
26. J. Mitchell. Guillotine subdivisions approximate polygonal subdivisions: A simple method for geometric *k*-mst problem. *Proc. ACM-SIAM Symp. on Discrete Algorithms (SODA)*, pages 402–408, 1996.
27. M. Muralikrishna and David J Dewitt. Equi-depth histograms for estimating selectivity factors for multi-dimensional queries. *Proc. of ACM SIGMOD Conf*, pages 28–36, 1988.
28. J. Nievergelt, H. Hinterberger, and K. C. Sevcik. The grid file: An adaptable, symmetric multikey file structure. *ACM Transactions on Database Systems*, 9(1):38–71, March 1984.
29. S. Muthukrishnan, V. Poosala and T. Suel. On rectangular partitionings in two dimensions: algorithms, complexity and applications. *Manuscript*, 1998.
30. V. Poosala, Y. Ioannidis, P. Haas, and E. Shekita. Improved histograms for selectivity estimation of range predicates. *Proc. of ACM SIGMOD Conf*, pages 294–305, June 1996.
31. V. Poosala. *Histogram-based estimation techniques in databases.* PhD thesis, Univ. of Wisconsin-Madison, 1997.
32. V. Poosala and Y. Ioannidis. Selectivity estimation without the attribute value independence assumption. *Proc. of the 23rd Int. Conf. on Very Large Databases*, August 1997.
33. G. P. Shapiro and C. Connell. Accurate estimation of the number of tuples satisfying a condition. *Proc. of ACM SIGMOD Conf*, pages 256–276, 1984.
34. E. Welzl. Partition trees for triangle counting and other range searching problems. In *Proceedings of the 4th Annual Symposium on Computational Geometry*, pages 23–33, June 1988.

Optimal Dynamic Range Searching in Non-replicating Index Structures*

K. V. Ravi Kanth[1]** and Ambuj Singh[2]

[1] Oracle NEDC, Nashua, USA.
rkothuri@us.oracle.com
[2] Department of Computer Science,
University of California, Santa Barbara, USA.
ambuj@cs.ucsb.edu

Abstract. In this paper, we examine the complexity of multi-dimensional range searching in non-replicating index structures. Such non-replicating structures achieve low storage costs and fast update times due to lack of multiple copies. We first obtain a lower bound for range searching in non-replicating structures. Assuming a simple tree structure model of an index, we prove that the worst-case time for a query retrieving t out of n data items is $\Omega((n/b)^{(d-1)/d} + t/b)$, where d is the data dimensionality and b is the capacity of index nodes. We then propose a new index structure, called the O-tree, that achieves this query time in dynamic environments. Updates are supported in $O(\log_b n)$ amortized time and exact match queries in $O(\log_b n)$ worst-case time. This structure improves the query time of the best known non-replicating structure, the divided k-d tree, and is optimal for both queries and updates in non-replicating tree structures.

1 Introduction

Multi-dimensional range searching has important applications in geographic information systems, image databases, constraint databases, CAD, and computer graphics. Over the past few decades, researchers have developed several data structures that support range searching. However, experiments have shown that these structures seldom scale with data dimensionality in practice. This led to theoretical investigations and several results on lower bound characterizations of range searching in the past few years. These results can be grouped into two categories. The first category of results estimates the overhead of *retrieving* multi-dimensional data items in external memory environments without accounting for the overheads of *locating (or identifying)* the disk blocks where they reside. The second category of results assumes a specific model for the index structure and the query navigation process. These results estimate the complete overhead

---

* Work supported in part by research grants NSF/ARPA/NASA IRI-9411330 and NSF CCR-9505807.
** Work done when the author was at University of California, Santa Barbara.

Catriel Beeri, Peter Buneman (Eds.): ICDT'99, LNCS 1540, pp. 257–276, 1998.

for range searching within the assumed "index model". We describe some of the recent results in each class in turn and put our contributions in perspective.

Hellerstein, Koutsoupias, and Papadimitriou [HKP97] investigate the complexity of retrieving d-dimensional data items from secondary storage once the desired data items are identified by an index structure. Assuming that data items are stored and retrieved in blocks of b items each in external memory, they investigate the relationship between the storage redundancy (r) of an indexing scheme, and the worst-case access overhead (a) for a range query. The storage redundancy of an indexing scheme is measured as the ratio of the storage occupied to the minimum storage required. The access overhead for a range query that retrieves t data items is defined as the ratio of the number of blocks required to answer the query and the minimum number required (i.e., t/b). (Note that the overheads of locating the data items is not included). For the case of a 2-dimensional rectangular grid, they prove that $r = \Omega(\log b/a^2 \log a)$ and present a tight lower bound on the access overhead when $r = 1$. Recently, Samoladas and Miranker [SM98] extend these results and establish a nice lower bound of $r = \Omega(\log b/\log a)$ for a two-dimensional grid. Furthermore, for the d-dimensional case, they prove that $r = \Omega((\log b/\log a)^{d-1})$. In a different vein, Koutsoupias and Taylor [KT98], consider a different instance of input workload. Instead of a 2-d grid, they consider a 2-d grid rotated by the golden ratio; the resulting workload is termed the *fibonacci workload*. They show that for this particular workload, the access overhead must be b (highest possible) for any storage redundancy that is less than $c\log n$, c being a constant. Note that all the above bounds are concerned with the accessing of disk blocks. We concentrate on the indexing problem: how to locate the relevant disk blocks that contain the objects of interest.

Complexity results that include *locating* overheads assuming a specific index structure model also exist in the literature. By modeling index structures as DAGs, Chazelle showed that a storage space of $O(n(\frac{\log n}{\log\log n})^{d-1})$ is essential to achieve a query time of $O(\text{poly-log } n + t)$. Note that the poly-logarithmic factor in query time indicates the overhead of locating data items in the index structure. In the external-memory model (*i.e.*, $b >> 2$), Sairam and Subramanian [SR95] extend this result to 2-dimensions and propose the P-range tree, which achieves a query time of $O(\log_b^c n + t/b)$ query time for any constant $c > 0$ using $O(\frac{n}{b} \frac{\log n}{\log\log_b n})$ storage for n 2-dimensional data.

In this paper, we examine the worst-case overheads of locating and retrieving data items for range queries using non-replicating tree structures. This model requires low storage space and allows for efficient updates. It is representative of most existing database structures such as Quad trees [Sam89], R-trees [BKSS90,Gut84,BKK96], BANG files [Fre87,Fre95], K-D-B trees [Rob81], and hB-trees [LS90]. We prove that the worst-case range query overhead in such non-replicating tree structures is bounded below by $\Omega((n/b)^{(d-1)/d})$ for n d-dimensional data. This result extends Mehlhorn's result [Meh84] from a ternary decision-tree model to arbitrary b-ary trees. (Note that the results on retrieval overhead [HKP97,KT98,SM98] also yield a partial query overhead (assuming

$r = 1$); this needs to be added to the indexing overhead to obtain the total query overhead. In our model, we obtain a single term for the total query overhead.) Our lower bound result explains why popular database tree structures such as R*-trees [BKSS90], SS-trees [WJ96], and SR-trees [KS97] do not scale with data dimensionality.

After presenting our lower-bound results, we propose a new non-replicating tree structure, called the O-tree (O for optimal), that achieves the proposed lower bound in dynamic environments. Note that in static environments, this bound is met by Bentley's k-d trees [Ben75]. In dynamic environments, the O-tree removes a logarithmic factor from the overhead of the best known non-replicating tree structure, the divided k-d tree [vKO91]. In contrast, popular structures such as R-trees and Bang files have linear overheads (i.e., a query time of $O(n)$ for n data items) as shown in [Rav98].

2   Related Work on Non-replicating Structures

Table 1 describes the related work on replicating index structures and summarizes our contributions. The complexity results are expressed for n d-dimensional data items, assuming a node capacity of b for the data structures. Query complexities also indicate the impact of the number of data items retrieved, t. For non-replicating index structures, we first list the Pseudo Quad and k-d trees, which are defined using quad and balanced binary trees, (i.e., $b \leq 4$). They achieve a query time of $O(n^{(d-1)/d} + t)$ and update time of $O(\log^2 n)$. The divided k-d tree reduces the query time overhead to $O(n^{(d-1)/d} \log^{1/d} n)$ and update time overhead to $O(\log^2 n)$. The Pseudo Quad and k-d trees assume a Quad-tree or balanced binary tree representation for the data structures. Our results are more general and are defined for arbitrary node capacities. In particular, we prove that the query time in non-replicating structures is bounded below by $\Omega((n/b)^{(d-1)/d} + t/b)$. The O-tree presented in this paper achieves this query complexity while supporting updates in $O(\log_b n)$ time. This structure is optimal for both queries and updates in non-replicating tree structures. Note that when the node capacities in an O-tree are restricted to 3 (as in 2-3 trees), the query complexity of O-tree is better off by a factor of $O(\log^{1/d} n)$ with respect to the best known non-replicating structure – the divided k-d tree.

The rest of the paper is organized as follows: In Section 3, we describe our model for non-replicating data structures and obtain a lower bound for range query time complexity in these structures. In Section 4, we examine how to extend this result to dynamic environments. We propose a new structure, called the O-tree, for this purpose. This structure is optimal for both queries and updates in non-replicating tree structures. The final section summarizes these results. Appendix A gives details of the lower bound results.

3   Lower Bound for Range Query Time

In this section, we describe our model of external-memory non-replicating data structures. We then obtain a lower bound for answering range queries in such non-replicating structures.

Node Capacity b	Non-Replicating Structure	Query Time	Insert/Delete Time
$b \leq 4$	Lower Bound [Meh84]	$O(n^{\frac{(d-1)}{d}} + t)$	$O(\log n)$
	Pseudo k-d tree [OvL81]	$O(n^{\frac{(d-1)(1+\epsilon)}{d}} + t)$	$O(\log^2 n)$
	Divided k-d tree [OvL81]	$O(n^{\frac{(d-1)}{d}} \log^{1/d} n + t)$	$O(\log n)$
Arbitrary b	**Lower Bound** [this paper]	$O((n/b)^{\frac{(d-1)}{d}} + t/b)$	$O(\log_b n)$
	O-tree [this paper]	$O((n/b)^{\frac{(d-1)}{d}} + t/b)$	$O(\log_b n)$
	R-trees, Bang Files [Gut84,Fre87]	$O((n/b) + t/b)$	$O(\log_b n)$

Table 1. Comparison of index structures for dynamic range searching: The results of this paper are highlighted.

3.1   Model of a Non-replicating Index Structure

We model an index structure as a rooted tree, in which each node is of finite size, and is associated with a search predicate. The search predicate for d dimensions is assumed to be a conjunction of at most $2d$ binary comparisons. We denote the search predicate for a vertex v as *cond(v)*. Each comparison in the search predicate involves an endpoint of a query (i.e., the start or the end of a query along a specific dimension) and evaluates to *true* only if a specified query satisfies all the comparisons. For example, a 2-dimensional search predicate involving such comparisons may be specified as $(q_1^s > 1) \wedge ((q_1^e < 4) \wedge (q_2^s > 0) \wedge (q_2^e > 10)$. We refer to the conjunction of comparisons, which involve the query endpoints in a specific dimension i, by conjunct C_i. For instance, for the example predicate the conjunct C_1 refers to $(q_1^s > 1) \wedge ((q_1^e < 4)$ and the conjunct C_2 refers to $(q_2^s > 0) \wedge (q_2^e > 10)$. In addition to the search predicate, an index node also stores at most b data items, where b is a constant, and a finite number (also assumed to be b) of child pointers. Each data item is stored in exactly one node of the index (*non-replicating* property). When presented with a query, an index node returns a partial result set and forwards the query to a subset of all children, whose search predicates are satisfied by the query. At the leaf level, index nodes do not have any children; the response to a presented query is just a partial result set. The result of a query is obtained by the union of the result sets of all visited index nodes.

The above model for an index structure is similar to the tree model of Vaidya [Vai89]. However, there are two differences: (1) Search predicates are represented as a conjunction of comparisons rather than as a disjunction of comparisons. (2) The data associated with an index node is bounded. This simplifies the model, since the cost of accessing an index node is no longer proportional to the associated number of data items; instead, it is a constant. This model is a direct extension of Mehlhorn's decision tree model from ternary trees to arbitrary b-ary trees, assuming each node has at most b children. Note that this tree model is more restrictive than Chazelle's model [Cha90], where data structures are represented as DAGs, or the more general "pointer-machine" model of Tarjan [Tar79]. Non-replication is hard to enforce in a graph model since multiple paths to same data items are possible without actually replicating the data items themselves. Therefore, we focus on a tree structure model, which captures the basic limitations of external-memory data structures such as finite node sizes, and models most existing data structures. This model for non-replicating index structures excludes threaded search trees where data items can be reached via multiple paths in the tree, for instance the Cross tree of Grossi and Italiano [GI97].

Next, we describe complexity measures for comparing data structures in this model. The space complexity of a data structure is determined by the total size for leaf and non-leaf nodes in the index structure. Query and update time complexities are estimated using the number of nodes visited in the index during a query and an update respectively. For queries, we measure the worst-case complexity. For updates, which are much less frequent, we measure the amortized time complexity over a sequence of update operations.

3.2   Lower Bound

In this subsection, we obtain a lower bound on range query time complexity in non-replicating structures. Our lower bound extends the result of Mehlhorn [Meh84]. His proof does not consider b, the node capacity of index nodes. As a result, the ensuing lower bound is independent of b. For realistic external-memory devices, the value of b could be quite large and cannot be ignored in complexity analysis. Our lower bound captures the exact dependence of range query time complexity on node capacity of an index structure along with the number of points and their dimensionality. The proof proceeds by considering a specific data set and is straightforward.

Since a lower bound in a restricted domain also holds for much general ones, we restrict the data points to have only integer values for their coordinates. Without loss of generality, the constants in edge conditions are also assumed to be integer values. To obtain a lower bound for range query time complexity in non-replicating index structures, we work with the following layout of n d-dimensional points. For simplicity, let $n = k^d$.

$$S_d^n = \{(2a_1-1, 2a_2-1, \ldots, 2a_i-1, \ldots, 2a_d-1) \mid a_i \in \{1, \ldots, k\}, \forall i \in \{1, \ldots, d\}\}.$$

This set S_d^n forms a d-dimensional grid of length $k = n^{1/d}$ in each dimension with a 2-unit separation between every two adjacent vertices. We omit the superscript n, wherever possible, for clarity. For any subset S of S_d, we define an i-projection set $P_i(S)$ as the set of X_i-coordinates of all points in S, i.e., $P_i(S) = \{p_i \mid (p_1, \ldots, p_d) \in S\}$. Such a projection set has a *gap* at x if

- x lies in the range of $P_i(S)$ (i.e., $\exists a, b \in P_i(S) : a < x < b$), and,
- x is *even*.

We concentrate on the following set of queries $Q = \bigcup_{1 \le i \le d} Q_i$, where Q_i is the set of queries with the following specification:

- The interval along the ith dimension X_i is $[2c, 2c]$ for some c: $1 \le c \le k$, and,
- Intervals in all other dimensions are $[1, 2k + 1]$.

Note that none of the queries in Q retrieve any data from the set S_d. Hence, they are referred to as *hole* queries in general, and as *i-hole* queries if they are specifically from Q_i. Also note that the projection of an i-hole query to the dimension X_i corresponds to a gap. Since the number of gaps in each dimension is $n^{1/d} - 1$, the total number of holes in all the d dimensions is $d(n^{1/d} - 1)$ holes. Using these observations, we show that there exists a hole query in any non-replicating index structure for S_d that has a query complexity of $O(n^{(d-1)/d})$.

Theorem 1 The worst-case time complexity of a range query retrieving t out of n d-dimensional points in a non-replicating index structure is $\Omega((n/b)^{(d-1)/d} + t/b)$.

Proof: Let $n = k^d$. Let T be any non-replicating index structure for the set of points S_d^n. Then from Lemma 8 in Appendix A, the total query cost in T for all the holes is at least $(n - o(n))/(b^{(d-1)/d})$. Since the number of hole queries is at most $d(n^{1/d} - 1)$, by pigeonhole principle it follows that there is a hole whose query overhead is $O((n/b)^{(d-1)/d})$. Combining it with the minimum cost t/b for accessing t data items stored in b-ary nodes, we obtain the desired bound. $\square$

4   Optimal Non-replicating Structure for Dynamic Environments

In this section, we describe O-tree, an optimal non-replicating structure for dynamic environments. We first introduce some preliminary concepts for organizing 2-dimensional data in Section 4.1. We then describe an intermediate structure for 2-dimensional data, called the C-tree, that supports range queries in optimal time and insertions and deletions in $O(\log^2 n \log \log^2 n)$ time, in Section 4.2. In subsection 4.3, we refine the C-trees to O-trees to reduce insertion/deletion times to $O(\log n)$. These results are then extended to an arbitrary number of dimensions.

4.1   Basic Concepts

Notation A 1-dimensional interval I is specified by a starting point (denoted I^s) and an ending point (denoted I^e) in a linear domain. Interval I is *contained* in interval J if $((I^s \ge J^s) \wedge (I^e \le J^e))$. Interval I *intersects* interval J if $((I^s \le$

$J^e) \wedge (J^s \leq I^e))$. Note that containment is a special case of intersection. A 2-dimensional interval object I is specified by 2 1-dimensional intervals, one in the X-dimension and the other in the Y-dimension. This object I is *contained* in another 2-dimensional object J if the containment holds in each dimension. Similarly, it *intersects* J if the intersection holds in each dimension. We say a 2-dimensional interval object I is contained in another object J in a specific dimension if the interval of I in that dimension is contained in the corresponding interval of J. These definitions can be easily generalized to arbitrary dimensions.

Partitioning 2-dimensional Data Consider a set S of 2-dimensional points. These points can be ordered using their X-coordinates. If the X-coordinates match, the points can be ordered using their Y-coordinates. Alternately, they can be ordered using their Y-coordinates first, and then using their X-coordinates. Let the former ordering be referred to as the X-order and the latter as the Y-order. We denote that point p_1 precedes point p_2 in X-order by $p_1 \prec_X p_2$. Likewise, $p_1 \prec_Y p_2$ denotes the precedence of point p_1 over p_2 in Y-order. Let S_σ denote the sequence of points in S sorted using σ-order, where σ denotes either the X- or the Y-dimension. The extent of such a sequence can be represented by the first and last points in the sequence. This extent denotes the extent of the set S in σ-order. An alternative but not equivalent representation for the extent of the set S is by its *bounding rectangle*, denoted by $b(S)$. This bounding rectangle has an interval for each dimension. The interval in X-dimension is denoted by $b_X(S)$ and is obtained by taking the minimum and maximum values of the X-coordinates of the points in the set S. Likewise, the interval in Y-dimension is denoted as $b_Y(S)$ and is obtained using the Y-coordinates. To illustrate these concepts, consider an example: Let $S' = \{(1,1),(2,6),(2,4),(3,5),(5,1),(6,6),(6,4),(7,5)\}$. The X-order orders the points in S using the X-coordinates. Points that have same X-coordinates, for instance $(2,4)$ and $(2,6)$, are ordered using the Y-coordinates. The extent of the set S' is the first and last points in this sequence, which are $(1,1)$ and $(7,5)$. The minimum and maximum X-coordinates for points in S' are 1 and 7. Therefore, the X-interval of the bounding rectangle for S' is $b_X(S') = [1,7]$. Similarly, the minimum and maximum Y-coordinates are 1 and 6. Therefore, the Y-interval is $b_Y(S) = [1,6]$.

Total orders, such as $\prec_X$ and $\prec_Y$ above, can be used to partition a set S into smaller subsets that are disjoint and are of approximately same size. We refer to such subsets as partitions of S in the specified order. For example, the set S' can be divided into 4 partitions, $P_1, \ldots, P_4$ using X-order as:

$$P_1 = \{(1,1),(2,4)\}, P_2 = \{(2,6),(3,5)\};$$

$$P_3 = \{(5,1),(6,4)\}, P_4 = \{(6,6),(7,5)\}.$$

A total order on individual points can be extended to the extents of partitions of a set S. Partition extent $\langle a,b \rangle$ precedes another partition extent $\langle c,d \rangle$ in σ-order if b precedes c in σ-order.

B-tree for Partitions of 2-dimensional Data Let P denote the set of partitions for a set of 2-dimensional points obtained using σ-order. Since the extents of the partitions in P can be totally ordered using σ-order, a B-tree (the variant that stores data in the leaves) can be constructed over the partitions using these extents. We refer to this tree as a B-tree for the partitions in σ-order, and denote it by $B(|P|, \langle \sigma \rangle)$. Figure 1 shows such a tree for the partitions of S'. Such a tree facilitates efficient location of necessary partitions. For instance, identifying a partition in which a new point s is to be stored can be accomplished as follows. We start at the root of the B-tree and traverse down the tree by choosing the ith entry (corresponding subtree) such that $p_1^i \prec_\sigma s \prec_\sigma p_1^{i+1}$, where $\langle p_1^i, p_2^i \rangle$ and $\langle p_1^{i+1}, p_2^{i+1} \rangle$ are the extents associated with the ith and $(i+1)^{st}$ entries. For example, for inserting a new point $(4, 1)$, we choose the left subtree at the root and then the partition P_2 at vertex v. In general, for a tree of k partitions, this procedure takes $\log k$ time.

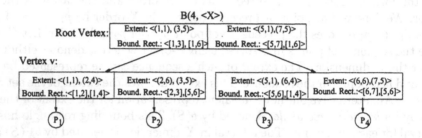

Fig. 1. B-tree for 4 partitions of S' using X-order.

In addition to the partition extent information used during updates, each index entry is associated with a bounding rectangle to aid in the navigation of queries. The intersection of an arbitrary query with the bounding rectangle represents the edge condition associated with an index entry. Given this structure, a query $q = \langle q_X, q_Y \rangle$ at vertex u accesses a child vertex v only if it intersects the bounding rectangle, denoted by $[l_i, m_i]$ for dimension i, for vertex v (i.e., if the query satisfies the condition $(q_i^s <= m_i) \wedge (l_i <= q_i^e)$ for each dimension $i \in \{X, Y\}$ associated with the edge $\langle u, v \rangle$). For example, in Figure 1(a) a query at the root vertex accesses vertex v only if it intersects the bounding rectangle $\langle [1, 3], [1, 6] \rangle$ associated with the entry for v in the root vertex. Since checking for intersection involves a conjunction of binary comparisons, this structure satisfies the model of Section 3. Before proceeding further, we state the following property for a B-tree on partitions constructed as above.

Lemma 1 *For any query q and any dimension σ at most 2 partitions that intersect the query are not contained in the query in dimension σ.*

4.2 C-tree: An Optimal Structure for Queries

Let us now examine how best to organize an arbitrary 2-dimensional data set S while achieving good update times. Assume the data set is partitioned into k

subsets using Y-order. (The best value of k for a set S of n points will be determined during the course of the discussion). Figure 2(a) shows the partitions $P_1, \ldots, P_k$ for the 2-dimensional set S. By maintaining a B-tree for these partitions, we can locate partitions intersecting a query $q = \langle q_X, q_Y \rangle$ efficiently. Of these intersecting partitions, there are at most two *extreme* partitions which are not contained in q in the Y-dimension. Partitions P_i and P_j are such extreme partitions in Figure 2(a) for the query q. All other intersecting partitions are contained in the query interval q_Y and hence are referred to as *interior* partitions. In Figure 2(a), partitions P_{i+1} to P_{j-1} are interior partitions. In these partitions, we have to search using the query interval q_X. This search can be accomplished efficiently if the data in these partitions is ordered according to their X-coordinates. Hence, each partition is subdivided into m sub-partitions using X-order. The sub-partitions for each partition are organized as a B-tree. Figure 2(b) shows the resulting organization. We have two layers of B-trees. The top layer (referred to as layer-2 tree) has k partitions using Y-order. Each partition of this tree is organized as a layer-1 B-tree of m partitions using X-order.

Range Queries Let us examine how range queries are processed in the above organization. As specified in the model of Section 3, a query $q = \langle q_X, q_Y \rangle$ starts at the root of the layer-2 B-tree and accesses a vertex v only if q intersects the associated bounding rectangle (i.e., satisfies the corresponding edge condition). We trace the worst-case time complexity t for the query as follows:

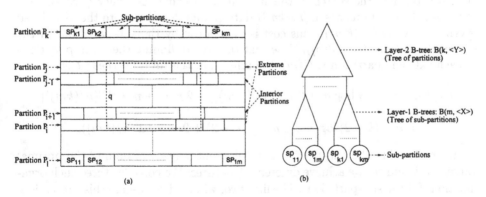

(a)   (b)

Fig. 2. (a) Partitions and sub-partitions for 2-dimensional data. (b) 2-layered tree over the sub-partitions.

1. Find all the partitions intersecting query q in the layer-2 B-tree.
2. For each interior partition (the Y-interval is contained in q_Y), such as $P_{i+1}, \ldots, P_{j-1}$ in Figure 2(a), search in the layer-1 B-tree as follows:
   (a) Find all sub-partitions that intersect q in the corresponding B-tree.
   (b) For the interior sub-partitions (i.e., for the sub-partitions with X-intervals contained in q_X), retrieve all associated data. All such data form part of the query result.
   (c) For the extreme sub-partitions, search in the sub-partitions.

3. For the extreme partitions, such as P_i and P_j in Figure 2(a),
   (a) Find all sub-partitions that intersect q in the corresponding B-tree.
   (b) Search in these sub-partitions.

Step 1 of the algorithm takes $O(k)$ time, since the B-tree has at most k partitions. This is because some partitions may intersect the query in the Y-dimension and not in the X-dimension. Let $n_p \leq k$ partitions intersect the query in both dimensions. Of these at most two of them can be extreme partitions, i.e., the Y-intervals of their bounding rectangles are not contained in the corresponding query interval. Consequently, step 2 is executed $(n_p - 2)$ times, whereas step 3 is executed at most 2 times. For each of the $(n_p - 2)$ interior partitions, step 2(a) has overheads of $\log m$ in the corresponding layer-1 B-tree. Note that in this case, logarithmic overheads are achieved as opposed to the linear overheads in Step 1 for the following reasons: First, all sub-partitions intersecting q are stored as a linear sequence using the X-order. Second, all of these sub-partitions, being parts of an interior partition, are contained in the query in the Y-dimension (i.e., q_Y contains their corresponding Y-intervals). Next, note that the interior sub-partitions are contained in the query in both X- and Y-dimensions. Hence, all data points in such sub-partitions are part of the query result. Assuming they are organized using space linear in the number of points, the retrieval cost in these sub-partitions is directly proportional to the query result. Hence, they do not contribute to the query overheads. For the extreme sub-partitions in step 2(c), we continue the search in the sub-partition using the query q. Since each of these sub-partitions has $O(n/(km))$ data points, let us denote the associated overheads by $ST(n/(km))$. This cost is also borne by the sub-partitions of the extreme partitions (step 3(b)). Note that the cost of finding these sub-partitions in each extreme partition is $O(m)$. Summing up, the total overhead t is:

$$t = k + (k - 2) * [\log m + 2 * ST(n/(km))] + 2 * [m + m * ST(n/(km))]$$

$$= k + (k - 2) \log m + 2m + [2(k - 2) + 2m] * ST(n/(km)).$$

By organizing the sub-partitions in different ways and finding the optimal values for k and m, we achieve different structures. We consider three such organizations for the sub-partitions. The first two, will be discussed in this subsection. The third yields the O-tree and is described in the Section 4.3.

Assuming that the search in the sub-partitions involves a linear scan of all the data points (i.e., $ST(l) = l$), the above equation yields a minimum value of $O(\sqrt{(n \log n)})$ for t, when $k = m = O(\sqrt{(n/\log n)})$. The same overhead is also obtained when $k = O(\sqrt{(n/\log n)})$ and $m = O(\sqrt{(n \log n)})$. This latter organization corresponds to the divided k-d tree of Kreveld and Overmars [vKO91].

Consider an alternative organization for the data in sub-partitions of Figure 2(b) to reduce the search costs. Assume each sub-partition is organized as a static k-d tree [Rav98]. Then the search cost in a sub-partition of size $c = O(n/(km))$ reduces from c in the divided k-d tree to $\sqrt{c}$. Consequently, the query overhead becomes

$$t = k + (k - 2)\log m + 2m + [2(k - 2) + 2m] * O(\sqrt{(n/(km))})$$

This equation has minimum value of $O(\sqrt{n})$ when $k = m = O(\sqrt{n}/\log n)$. Note that this query overhead corresponds to the lower bound (for 2-dimensional data) obtained in Section 3. Hence, this structure is optimal for range queries. We refer to this structure as the combined k-d tree, C-tree for short, since it combines the divided k-d tree with the static k-d trees. As in the divided k-d tree [vKO91], the C-tree has 2-layers of B-trees, each organized on a different dimension. However, at both the layers, every B-tree has $k = O(\sqrt{n}/\log n)$ partitions. The exact value of k will be specified later. We refer to these two layers as a 2-layered B-tree of k partitions. In addition, the C-tree has a third layer that is organized as static k-d trees. We refer to the trees in the third layer as the *leaf partitions of the 2-layered B-tree.*

C-tree for n 2-dimensional points
    = 2-layered B-tree of $O(\sqrt{n}/\log n)$ partitions
    + 2-dimensional k-d tree of $O(\log^2 n)$ points.

Generalizing to d dimensions, a C-tree contains d-layers of B-trees followed by a static k-d tree. Each layer-i B-tree contains $O(\sqrt{n}/\log n)$ partitions and is constructed using the coordinates in dimension X_i (X_i-order to be precise). The static k-d trees at the leaves of these d-layers are constructed for $O(\log^2 n)$ points each. Note that the above organization yields a tree height of $d*\lceil\log(n^{1/d}/\log n)\rceil$ in the d-layered tree and $\lceil\log(\log^d n)\rceil$ for the static k-d tree. Due to the ceiling factors in the equation, the resulting height is $O(\lfloor\log n\rfloor + d)$ in the worst-case.

Exact-Match Queries Next, let us analyze the complexity of exact-match queries in a C-tree. This is useful for describing and analyzing insertions and deletions later. Given a specific location p, an exact match query retrieves all data points in the C-tree located at p. This can be accomplished by first identifying a sub-partition in which p may be stored and then searching in that sub-partition, which is organized as a static k-d tree. Since each sub-partition has $O(n/(km)) = O(\log^2 n)$ points, the latter part of the search can be accomplished using the corresponding algorithm for a static k-d tree in $O(\log\log^2 n)$ time. Next, we describe the time for locating a sub-partition in which p could be stored.

1. Start with the root v of the layer-2 B-tree.
2. Search in the tree rooted at v using p as follows:
   (a) Let v have m entries $\langle[e_1, c_1], \ldots, [e_m, c_m]\rangle$ ordered using Y-order. Then, choose the ith entry $([e_i, c_i])$ such that the extent $e_i \prec_Y p \prec_Y e_{i+1}$ (i.e., e_i precedes p and p precedes e_{i+1} in Y-order). If no such entry exists, then choose the first entry.
   (b) Repeat the above step for the corresponding child c till we reach a partition P of the B-tree.
3. The partition P is organized as a layer-1 B-tree. Repeat Step 2 using this tree to identify the sub-partition in which the insertion/deletion has to occur. Since the layer-1 B-tree uses X-order, the search criterion in Step 2(a) uses X-order.

Unlike range queries, the above algorithm for sub-partition identification uses the extents in the B-tree. Since the disjointness of the partitions is reflected in their extents, only one entry is chosen in Step 2(a). These extents are stored in sorted order and each B-tree has at most $O(\sqrt{n}/\log n)$ partitions. Therefore, Step 2 costs $O(\log n)$ time. The same process is also repeated in Step 3. The total time complexity of this algorithm is $O(\log n)$. Hence, sub-partition identification and subsequently exact match queries are answered in the C-tree in logarithmic time.

Insertions and Deletions Let us now analyze the impact of organizing each sub-partition as a static k-d tree on the complexity of insertions and deletions. Insertions and deletions are performed as follows:

1. Identify the sub-partition in which the insertion/deletion has to occur.
2. Perform the insertion/deletion in the static k-d tree corresponding to the identified sub-partition.
3. Re-balance the trees, as necessary.

From Section 4.2, we know that the first step takes $O(\log n)$ time. Next, we analyze the complexity of Step 2. As mentioned earlier, the static k-d tree can support insertions and deletions without degrading query performance only if it is reconstructed after each insertion/deletion. Consequently, insertion in each sub-partition takes $O(c \log c)$ time, where c is the number of points in the static k-d tree. Since this number is $O(n/(km)) = O(\log^2 n)$, each insertion/deletion takes at least $O((\log^2 n) \log(\log^2 n))$ time in Step 2. In Step 3, re-balancing of the trees can be accomplished using the technique of *partial rebuilding* [Ove83]. Here, each B-tree of n partitions is reconstructed after αn more partitions are created or deleted, where α is a small fraction. Since there are at most $O(\log n)$ levels in a tree of n points, the time for such reconstruction is $O(n \log n)$. The number of insertions, deletions that trigger such reconstruction is proportional to the number, n, of data points in the tree. Consequently, the reconstruction time for each layer B-tree is amortized over the number of updates that occur in it. This adds a logarithmic amortized cost to each update due to reconstruction of each layer B-tree. Since the number of such layers is $2 * d = 4$ for $d = 2$ (i.e., for 2-dimensions), the total accrued cost for an update is $O(d * \log n) = O(\log n)$.

Combining the above three costs, a C-tree for n points supports range queries in optimal time and insertions/deletions in $O(\log n + (\log^2 n) \log(\log^2 n))$ time.

Theorem 2 *There exists a non-replicating data structure that supports range queries on n d-dimensional points in $O(n^{(d-1)/d})$ overheads. Insertions and deletions are supported in $O(\log^2 n \log \log^2 n)$ amortized time.*

4.3   O-tree: An Optimal Structure for Queries, Insertions, and Deletions

Consider the C-tree for n points. Range queries are answered in optimal time in this structure. The insertion/deletion time, however, is non-optimal and has two principal components – $O(\log n)$ complexity in the 2-layered B-tree and $O((\log^2 n) \log(\log^2 n))$ complexity in the static k-d trees. If we used only a static k-d tree, it would have an optimal query complexity and $O(n \log n)$ insertion/deletion time. Note that by going from a static k-d tree to a C-tree, we have successfully reduced the insertion/deletion time from $O(n \log n)$ to $O((\log^2 n) \log(\log^2 n))$ without affecting the query time. Hence, a C-tree can modularly replace a static k-d tree to reduce the insertion/deletion time. Based on this observation, we organize the leaf partitions of a C-tree not as static k-d trees but as C-trees. This reduces the insertion/deletion time from $O(\log n + (\log^2 n) \log(\log^2 n))$ to $O(\log n + (\log^2 \log^2 n) \log(\log^2 \log^2 n))$. This yields a total time of $O(\log n)$ for insertions and deletions. Since this organization has optimal query and insertion/deletion times, we call it the O-tree. To summarize, the O-tree has the following structure.

O-tree(2,n) =   2-layered B-tree of $O(\sqrt{n}/\log n)$ partitions
                 + C-tree of $O(\log^2 n)$ points.
Since a C-tree is a 2-layered B-tree followed by static k-d trees, we have
O-tree(2,n) =   2-layered B-tree of $O(\sqrt{n}/\log n)$ partitions
                 + 2-layered B-tree of $O(\log n/\log \log n)$ partitions
                 + 2-dimensional static k-d tree of $O(\log^2 \log^2 n)$ points.

This organization for the O-tree is shown in Figure 3. At the first level, we have a 2-layered B-tree of $O(\sqrt{n}/\log n)$ partitions. The leaf partitions of this 2-layered B-tree have $O(\log^2 n)$ points and are organized as second-level structures. Each second-level structure is a 2-layered B-tree of $O(\log n/\log \log n)$ partitions. The leaf partitions of these second-level 2-layered B-trees are organized as static k-d trees of $O(\log^2 \log^2 n)$ points at the third level.

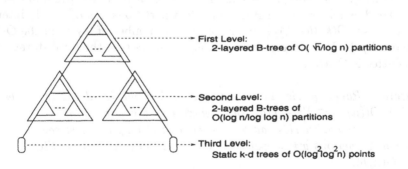

First Level:
2-layered B-tree of $O(\sqrt{n}/\log n)$ partitions

Second Level:
2-layered B-trees of
$O(\log n/\log \log n)$ partitions

Third Level:
Static k-d trees of $O(\log^2 \log^2 n)$ points

Fig. 3. O-tree for n 2-dimensional points.

The above arguments show that this organization achieves optimal range query time and logarithmic update time. The update times are amortized bounds. Note that in the above description, we assumed a 2-3 tree as the basic building structure. By appropriately modifying it with an arbitrary b-ary tree, we obtain the following result.

Theorem 3 *There exists a non-replicating data structure that supports range queries on n 2-dimensional points in $O(\sqrt{(n/b)}+t/b)$ overheads, where t denotes the size of the query result. Insertions and deletions are supported in $O(\log_b n)$ amortized time.*

The 2-dimensional O-tree can be generalized to d-dimensions by making the following changes:

1. Replace the first-level 2-layered B-tree by a d-layered B-tree of $O(n^{1/d}/\log n)$ partitions.
2. Replace the second-level 2-layered B-trees by d-layered B-trees of $O(\log n/\log\log n)$ partitions.
3. At the third level, replace each 2-dimensional static k-d tree by a d-dimensional static k-d tree of $O(\log^d \log^d n)$ points.

In summary, an O-tree for n d-dimensional points is organized as:

$$
\begin{aligned}
\text{O-tree(d,n)} = \quad & d\text{-layered B-tree of } O(n^{1/d}/\log n) \text{ partitions}\\
& + d\text{-layered B-tree of } O(\log n/\log\log n) \text{ partitions}\\
& + d\text{-dimensional static k-d tree of } O(\log^d \log^d n) \text{ points.}
\end{aligned}
$$

Note that each C-tree of m points is of height $O(d*\lceil\log_b m\rceil)$, and the O-tree of n points is of height of $O(2d*\lceil\log_b n\rceil) = O(\log_b n)$ in the worst-case. This leads to $O(d*\log_b n)$ update and exact match query time complexities. The analysis of the query time complexity directly extends from the 2-dimensional case. This leads us to the following result.

Let us examine the storage cost next. Data in the static k-d trees of an O-tree are stored in blocks of size b. Therefore, the storage cost in the static k-d trees is $O(n/b)$. The storage costs for B-trees at each of the layers above can be calculated as follows. Each B-tree of k leaf partitions has $k/(b-1)$ internal nodes; i.e., uses $O(k/(b-1))$ storage space. The number of layers in the O-tree is bounded by $2d$. Using these observations, it follows that the total storage cost for an O-tree is $O(n/b)$.

Theorem 4 *Range queries in an O-tree of n d-dimensional points can be answered in $O((n/b)^{(d-1)/d} + t/b)$ time, where t is the number of retrieved data points. Exact match queries can be answered in $O(\log_b n)$ worst-case time. Insertions and deletions are supported in $O(\log_b n)$ amortized time. Storage space used is $O(n/b)$.*

5 Conclusions

In this paper, we examined the complexity of range searching in non-replicating tree structures. We first proved that the time complexity of querying over n d-dimensional data using these structures is bounded below by $\Omega((n/b)^{(d-1)/d} + t/b)$, where t is the number of retrieved items, and b is the capacity of index nodes. We then proposed a new structure, called the O-tree, that achieves this lower bound in dynamic environments.

In future, we plan to investigate the experimental and average-case behavior of O-trees. A straightforward implementation of an O-tree would be to map each node of the internal trees of an O-tree to a disk page. However, this may lead to poor storage utilization since the trees could be small and may have low branching factor. In such cases, one could employ packing algorithms to combine under-filled root nodes of adjacent trees, or to store complete subtrees in few disk pages as in [DRSS96] without affecting the logical organization of the O-tree. Additionally, maintaining minimum bounding rectangles in index nodes may help in pruning irrelevant search paths.

References

[Ben75] J. L. Bentley. Multi-dimensional binary search trees used for associative searching. *Communications of the ACM*, 18:509–517, 1975.

[BKK96] S. Berchtold, D. A. Keim, and H. P. Kriegel. The X-tree: An index structure for high dimensional data. In *Proc. Int. Conf. on Very Large Data Bases*, pages 28–39, 1996.

[BKSS90] N. Beckmann, H. Kriegel, R. Schneider, and B. Seeger. The R* tree: An efficient and robust access method for points and rectangles. In *Proc. ACM SIGMOD Int. Conf. on Management of Data*, pages 322–331, May 23-25 1990.

[Cha90] B. Chazelle. Lower bounds for orthogonal range searching: I. The reporting case. *Journal of the ACM*, 37(2):200–212, April 1990.

[DRSS96] A. A. Diwan, S. Rane, S. Seshadri, and M. Sudarshan. Clustering techniques for minimizing external path length. *Proc. Int. Conf. on Very Large Data Bases*, pages 342–353, 1996.

[Fre87] M. W. Freeston. The BANG file: A new kind of grid file. In *Proc. ACM SIGMOD Int. Conf. on Management of Data*, pages 260–269, 1987.

[Fre95] M. W. Freeston. A general solution of the n-dimensional B-tree problem. *Proc. ACM SIGMOD Int. Conf. on Management of Data*, pages 80–92, May 1995.

[GI97] R. Grossi and F. Italiano. Efficient splitting and merging algorithms for order-decomposable searching problems. In *International Colloquium on Automata, Languages and Programming (ICALP '97)*, pages 605–615, July 1997.

[Gut84] A. Guttman. R-trees: A dynamic index structure for spatial searching. In *Proc. ACM SIGMOD Int. Conf. on Management of Data*, pages 47–57, June 1984.

[HKP97] J. M. Hellerstein, E. Koutsoupias, and C. H. Papadimitriou. On the analysis of indexing schemes. In *Proc. ACM Symp. on Principles of Database Systems*, pages 249–256, Tucson, Arizona, May 1997.

[KS97] N. Katayama and S. Satoh. The SR-tree: An index structure for high-dimensional nearest-neighbor queries. In *Proc. ACM SIGMOD Int. Conf. on Management of Data*, pages 369–380, May 1997.

[KT98] E. Koutsoupias and D. S. Taylor. Tight bounds for 2-dimensional indexing schemes. In *Proc. ACM Symp. on Principles of Database Systems*, pages 52–58, Seattle, Washington, June 1998.

[LS90] D. B. Lomet and B. Salzberg. The hB-tree: A multiattribute indexing method with good guaranteed performance. *Proc. ACM Transactions on Database Systems*, 15(4):625–658, 1990.

[Meh84] K. Mehlhorn. *Data Structures and Algorithms 3: Multidimensional Searching and Computational Geometry*. Springer-Verlag, 1984.

[Ove83] M. Overmars. The design of dynamic data structures. *Lecture Notes in Computer Science 156*, 1983.

[OvL81] M. Overmars and J. van Leeuwen. Worst-case optimal insertion and deletion methods for decomposable searching problems. *Information Processing Letters*, 12(4):168–172, 1981.

[Rav98] K. V. Ravi Kanth. Indexing multi-dimensional data. In *Ph.D. thesis, University of California, Santa Barbara*, April 1998.

[Rob81] J. T. Robinson. The kdb-tree: A search structure for large multi-dimensional dynamic indexes. In *Proc. ACM SIGMOD Int. Conf. on Management of Data*, pages 10–18, 1981.

[Sam89] H. Samet. *The design and analysis of spatial data structures*. Addison-Wesley, 1989.

[SM98] V. Samoladas and D. P. Miranker. A lower bound theorem for indexing schemes and its application to multidimensional range queries. In *Proc. ACM Symp. on Principles of Database Systems*, pages 44–51, Seattle, Washington, June 1998.

[SR95] S. Subramanian and S. Ramaswamy. The P-range tree: A new data structure for range searching in secondary memory. In *Proc. ACM-SIAM Symposium on Discrete Algorithms*, pages 378–387, 1995.

[Tar79] R. E. Tarjan. A class of algorithms which require non-linear time to maintain disjoint sets. *Journal of Computer and System Sciences*, 18:110–127, 1979.

[Vai89] P. M. Vaidya. Space-time tradeoffs for orthogonal range queries. *SIAM Journal of Computing*, 18(4):748–758, 1989.

[vKO91] M. van Kreveld and M. Overmars. The divided k-d tree. *Algorithmica*, 6:840–858, 1991.

[WJ96] D. White and R. Jain. Similarity indexing with the SS-tree. In *Proc. Int. Conf. on Data Engineering*, pages 516–523, 1996.

Appendix A: Lower Bound Proofs

Let T denote a non-replicating index structure. Let $D(v)$ denote the set of data points in the subtree rooted at a vertex v in T. Let the cardinality of this set be denoted by $n_D(v)$. Define a point query at $l = (l_1, \ldots, l_d)$ to be a restricted range query $\Psi_d(l) = \langle [l_1, l_1], \ldots [l_d, l_d] \rangle$. The subscript d indicates the dimensionality of the query. All these symbols used in the lower bound proofs are enumerated in Table 2 for reference. Next, we prove several lemmata leading to Lemma 8.

Lemma 2 *For a vertex v, the point query $\Psi_d(p)$ satisfies cond(v) if $p \in D(v)$.*

Proof: Consider a point $p \in D(v)$. Since the index is non-replicating, point p is stored in only one vertex, say vertex u. In addition, $p \in D(v)$ implies vertex u is either the same as vertex v, or is a descendant of v. In either case, since the index is a tree, the path from the root to vertex u goes through vertex v. Next, by definition of a range query, $\Psi_d(p)$ retrieves point p. This implies $\Psi_d(p)$ satisfies the conditions associated with vertices on the path from the root to vertex u. Since v is on this path, $\Psi_d(p)$ satisfies cond(v). □

Symbol	Explanation
C_i	Conjunction of comparisons involving query endpoints in the X_i-dimension.
$cond(v)$	Edge condition associated with vertex v.
$D(v)$	Set of data points in subtree rooted at vertex v.
$n_D(v)$	Cardinality of the set $D(v)$.
S_d^n	Set of n data points in a d-dimensional grid.
$P_i(S)$	Set of X_i-coordinates of the points in S.
gap	Gap exists at x in $P_i(S)$ if $\exists a, b \in P_i(S) : a < x < b$ and x is *even*.
$\Psi_d(l)$	Point-query at location l.
Q_i	Set of queries whose intervals in dimension i corresponds to gaps. Intervals in other dimensions span entire data space.

Table 2. Symbols used in the lower bound proof.

Lemma 3 *For any vertex v in a non-replicating index, if $p = (p_1, p_2, \ldots, p_d) \in D(v)$, then the interval $[s_i, e_i]$ along dimension X_i, where $s_i \leq p_i \leq e_i$, satisfies the conjunct C_i of $cond(v)$.*

Proof: By contradiction. Consider a query $q = \langle [a_1, b_1], \ldots, [a_d, b_d] \rangle$, where $a_i = s_i$, $b_i = e_i$ and $a_j = b_j = p_j$ for all $j \neq i$. Then, by assumption, q does not satisfy the conjunct C_i of $cond(v)$ and therefore $cond(v)$. Consequently, the point p, which falls in the query range of q is not retrieved by q. This contradicts the range query semantics. $\square$

The following property holds for any subset U of S_d.

Lemma 4 *For any set $U \subseteq S_d$, $\Sigma_{1 \leq i \leq d} |P_i(U)| \geq d|U|^{1/d}$.*

Proof: By induction on d.
Basis: Let $d = 1$. Since $P_1(U) = U$, the lemma trivially holds.
Hypothesis: Assume the lemma holds for $d = l$.
Let $U \subseteq S_{l+1}$. Consider the l-dimensional set U' obtained by deleting the X_{l+1}-coordinate for each point $p \in U$, i.e.,

$$U' = \{(p_1, \ldots, p_l) \mid (p_1, \ldots, p_l, p_{l+1}) \in U\}.$$

Clearly, $U' \subseteq S_l$. Hence, by induction hypothesis,

$$\sum_{1 \leq i \leq l} |P_i(U')| \geq l|U'|^{1/l}. \tag{1}$$

The number of points in U is at most a product of those in U' and the number of distinct X_{l+1}-coordinates (given by $|P_{l+1}(U)|$). Hence,

$$|P_{l+1}(U)| * |U'| \geq |U|. \tag{2}$$

Since U' and S_{l+1} have the same projection-sets in the dimensions X_1 to X_l (i.e, $\forall i : (1 \leq i \leq l) : |P_i(U')| = |P_i(U)|$), the required summation can be computed as

$$\sum_{1 \leq i \leq l+1} |P_i(U)| = \sum_{1 \leq i \leq l} |P_i(U')| + |P_{l+1}(U)|. \tag{3}$$

Using equations 1, 2 and 3, we obtain

$$\sum_{1 \leq i \leq l+1} |P_i(U)| \geq l * |U'|^{1/l} + \frac{|U|}{|U'|}.$$

The above sum is minimum when $|U'| = |U|^{l/(l+1)}$, the minimum value being $(l+1)|S|^{1/(l+1)}$. Hence, the lemma holds. $\square$

Lemma 5 *Let C be a conjunction of binary comparisons, each involving an endpoint of an arbitrary 1-dimensional interval x and a constant. Let G be a subset of S_1 such that for each $p \in G$, $\Psi_1(p)$ satisfies C. Then, there are at least $(|G| - 1)$ point queries corresponding to gaps in G that also satisfy C.*

Proof: If G has less than 2 elements, then the lemma is trivially true. Assume G has at least 2 elements. Let $C = C^s \wedge C^e$, where C^s involves only the left endpoint x^s and C^e involves only the right endpoint x^e.

Consider the conjunction of comparisons C^s. Each comparison is of the form $(x^s \ op \ c)$, where op is one of the three relational operators, $<, >$, or $=$. The $\leq$ and $\geq$ operators can be rewritten using $<$ and $>$ respectively by modifying the constants appropriately. Since G has at least two elements, an equality comparison is not permissible in C^s. Let $C^s = C_g^s \wedge C_l^s$, where the comparisons in C_g^s involve only the *greater than* ($>$) operator and those in C_l^s involve only the *less than* ($<$) operator. The conjunction C_g^s can be reduced to one comparison between x^s and the maximum value of all the constants in its comparisons. C_l^s can be similarly reduced by taking the minimum value of its constants. Let $C^s = (x^s > c_1^s) \wedge (x^s < c_2^s)$. (If C^s does not have a comparison of the form $(x^s > c_1^s)$, then c_1^s can be set to $-\infty$; similarly, if the comparison $(x^s < c_s^2)$ is missing, then c_2^s can be set to ∞).

Now consider the set of points in G. Sort them in ascending order. Consider any pair of consecutive points a and b in this sorted sequence. Since G is a subset of S_1, a and b are odd values. Therefore, there exists a gap g such that $a < g < b$. Next, note that the point queries for a and b satisfy the conjunct C and therefore, the conjuncts C^s and C^e. Consider the conjunct C^s. Since $\Psi_1(a)$ satisfies C^s, we have $(a > c_1^s) \wedge (a < c_2^s)$, i.e., $c_1^s < a < c_2^s$. Likewise, for b we have $c_1^s < b < c_2^s$. Since $a < g < b$, it follows that $c_1^s < g < c_2^s$, i.e., $\Psi_1(g)$ satisfies C^s. A similar argument establishes that $\Psi_1(g)$ also satisfies C^e. Therefore, the query $\Psi_1(g)$ satisfies the conjunct C. Next, let us count the number of gaps that satisfy C. The number of consecutive pairs in the sorted sequence of G is $(|G|-1)$. Since each such pair is separated by at least one gap, we have at least $(|G| - 1)$ point queries corresponding to gaps that satisfy the conjunct C. $\square$

Next, we estimate the number of holes that satisfy $cond(v)$ for any vertex $v \in T$. We restrict ourselves to vertices that have at least one data point in their subtrees (i.e., $D(v) \neq \phi$).

Lemma 6 *For any vertex $v \in T$, the number of hole queries that satisfy $cond(v)$ is at least $d(n_D(v)^{1/d} - 1)$.*

Proof: First, we estimate the number of i-hole queries that satisfy $cond(v)$. Each i-hole query corresponds to a gap in the ith dimension and has an interval $[1, 2k + 1]$ in all other dimensions. Now, consider $cond(v)$. Since it is expressed as $cond(v) = C_1 \wedge C_{=2} \wedge \ldots, C_d$, the i-hole query satisfies $cond(v)$ if its interval in the jth dimension satisfies the conjunct $C_j, \forall j$.

First, we show that, when $j \neq i$, the conjunct C_j is satisfied by the corresponding interval of every i-hole query. Consider any i-hole query. It has a query interval of $[1, 2k + 1]$ in dimension X_j. Since $D(v) \neq \phi$, there exists a point $p \in D(v)$ and since $D(v) \subseteq S_d$, the X_j-coordinate of the point p, p_j, satisfies: $1 \leq p_j \leq 2k+1$. Then, from Lemma 3 it follows that the conjunct C_j is satisfied by an interval $[1, 2k + 1]$, i.e., by the jth interval of any i-hole query.

Given the above argument, the total number of i-holes that satisfy $cond(v)$ is given by the number of them satisfying the conjunct C_i of $cond(v)$. To estimate this, we first note that an i-hole corresponds to a gap in $P_i(D(v))$, the i-projection set of $D(v)$. Hence, the number of i-holes satisfying $cond(v)$ is given by the number of gaps of $P_i(D(v))$ satisfying C_i. From Lemma 5, this number is at least $(|P_i(D(v))| - 1)$. This gives a lower bound on the number of i-holes that satisfy $cond(v)$. By summing the number of i-holes that satisfy the condition $cond(v)$ for all i, the total number of holes that satisfy $cond(v)$ is at least $\Sigma_{1 \leq i \leq d}(|P_i(D(v))| - 1)$. From Lemma 4, this number is $\geq d(|D(v)|^{1/d} - 1)$. $\square$

Lemma 7 *A vertex v in a non-replicating index for S_d^n is accessed by at least $(d((n_D(v))^{1/d} - 1)$ hole queries.*

Proof: Let vertex u be a parent of vertex v. Then, $D(v) \subseteq D(u)$. Since each of these sets is a subset of S_d^n that has all data coordinates at *odd* values (and none at *even* values), every gap (which as at an *even* value by definition) in a $P_i(D_v)$) is also a gap in $P_i(D_u)$) for all dimensions i. Therefore, it follows that every hole-query that satisfies the edge condition of vertex v ($cond(v)$) also satisfies the edge condition of u, vertex v's parent. Extending this argument, it follows that every hole query that satisfies $cond(v)$ also satisfies the edge conditions of all the vertices from the root to vertex v. The semantics of query processing ensures that these hole-queries access vertex v. Since the number of these hole-queries is $d((n_D(v))^{1/d} - 1)$ (from Lemma 6), the result follows. $\square$

Next, we estimate the total complexity of all the hole queries in any non-replicating index for the set of points S_d^n.

Lemma 8 *Let T be a non-replicating index for the set of points S_d^n. Then, the total access cost for all the hole queries in T is $O((n - o(n))/(b^{(d-1)/d}))$.*

Proof: We prove this by induction on the height h of the tree T.

Basis: h=0. Then, the tree consists of one single node – the root with all the data in it. Since the capacity of a node is at most b, the number of points n is at most b. From Lemma 6, there are at least $d(n^{1/d} - 1)$ hole queries that access this node, the access cost being 1. Since n is $O(b)$, the cost for all these queries is:

$$dn^{1/d} - d = d(n - 1) = d((n - o(n))/n^{(d-1)/d}) = O((n - o(n))/(b^{(d-1)/d})).$$

Hypothesis: Assume that the lemma is true for all trees of height $\leq l$.

Consider a tree T of height $l+1$. Then, the total access cost for all the hole queries is given by the cost at the root followed by the cost at the subtrees corresponding to its children. Each hole query that accesses the root incurs a unit cost for the access. The number of such hole queries is obtained from Lemma 7. Hence, the total access cost for all hole queries on tree T rooted at R (denoted by $c(R)$) is:

$$c(R) = d(n_D(R)^{1/d} - 1) + \sum_{v \in children(R)} c(v).$$

Since $n_D(R) = n$, we have

$$c(R) = d(n^{1/d} - 1) + \sum_{v \in children(R)} c(v).$$

Note that each subtree rooted at any child of R is of height at most l. Then, by induction hypothesis, we have for each child v of R, $c(v) \geq O((n_D(v) - o(n_D(v)))/(b^{(d-1)/d})$. Since $\sum_{v \in children(R)} n_D(v) = n - |data(R)|$, we have for some constant m

$$c(R) = d(n^{1/d} - 1) + m * [(n - |data(R)|) - \sum_{v \in children(R)} o(n_D(v))]/(b^{(d-1)/d}).$$

Since the size of the data set $data(R)$ stored at the root is at most b and each node in the tree has at most a constant number, r, of children, it follows that

$$c(R) \geq d(n^{1/d} - 1) + m(n - b - r * o(n))/(b^{(d-1)/d}) = O((n - o(n))/(b^{(d-1)/d})).$$

Hence, the total access cost is $O((n - o(n))/(b^{(d-1)/d}))$. $\square$

Index Structures for Path Expressions

Tova Milo[1] and Dan Suciu[2]

[1] Tel Aviv University milo@math.tau.ac.il
[2] AT&T Labs suciu@research.att.com

1 Introduction

In recent years there has been an increased interest in managing data that does not conform to traditional data models, like the relational or object oriented model. The reasons for this non-conformance are diverse. On the one hand, data may not conform to such models at the physical level: it may be stored in data exchange formats, fetched from the Web, or stored as structured files. One the other hand, it may not conform at the logical level: data may have missing attributes, some attributes may be of different types in different data items, there may be heterogeneous collections, or the schema may be too complex or changes too often. The term *semistructured* data has been used to refer to such data. The semistructured data model consists of an edge-labeled graph, in which nodes correspond to objects and edges to attributes or values. Figure 1 illustrates a semistructured database providing information about a city.

Relational databases are traditionally queried with associative queries, retrieving tuples based on the value of some attributes. To answer such queries efficiently, database management systems support indexes for translating attribute values into tuple ids (e.g. B-trees or hash tables). In object-oriented databases, *path queries* replace the simpler associative queries. Several data structures have been proposed for answering path queries efficiently: e.g., access support relations [14] and path indexes [4].

In the case of semistructured data, queries are even more complex, because they may contain *regular* path expressions [1,7,8,16]. The additional flexibility is needed in order to traverse data whose structure is irregular, or partially unknown to the user. For example the following query retrieves all restaurants serving *lasagna* for dinner:

select x from ($*.Restaurant$) x ($Menu.*.Dinner.*.Lasagna$) y

Starting at the root of the database DB, the query searches for paths satisfying the regular expression $*.Restaurant$ and, from the retrieved nodes x, searches for another regular expression, $Menu.*.Dinner.*.Lasagna$.

How are such queries evaluated? A naive evaluation that scans the whole database is obviously very expensive. As in the case of relational and oo databases, we would like to use some indexes to speed up the evaluation. Index structures developed for traditional data models are tied to a pre-defined schema: e.g. relational databases index on a specific attribute of a specific relation, while object-oriented databases index on a specific path in the object-oriented schema [4,14],

Catriel Beeri, Peter Buneman (Eds.): ICDT'99, LNCS 1540, pp. 277–295, 1998.
© Springer-Verlag Berlin Heidelberg 1998

e.g. *document.section.title*. Hence, these index structures are not applicable to semistructured data, because here the schema is unavailable. Full text indexing systems take an opposite approach: given no knowledge on the structure of information, they index *all* the data. But this is of limited use for semistructured data, where some (perhaps very partial) knowledge on the structure may be available and exploited in path expressions: e.g. the query above insists that a *Dinner* item appears inside a *Menu*.

Recent work has addressed the problem of path expressions evaluation in semistructured databases [2,19,18,11]. But they focused mainly on deriving and using schema information to rewrite queries and guide the search. The issue of indexing was almost ignored. An exception are the *dataguides* of [11] which record information on the existing paths in a database, using this as an index. Dataguides are restricted to a single regular expression and are not useful in more complex queries with several regular expressions, like the one above.

In this paper we propose a novel, general index structure for semistructured databases, called *template index*, or T-index. It improves over the previous approaches in several ways. First, T-indexes allow us to trade space for generality. The class of paths associated with a given T-index is specified by a *path template*. For example, we can build a T-index to evaluate paths described by the template $\boxed{P}$ x $\boxed{P}$ y: here $\boxed{P}$ can be replaced by any regular expression (P stands for "path expression"). The query above is of this form. Another example is $(*.Restaurant)$ x $\boxed{P}$ y, in which the first regular expression is fixed to $*.Restaurant$: this T-index takes less space but is less general. Second, T-indexes can be efficiently constructed. Dataguides [11] require a powerset construct over the underlying database, which in the worst case can be of exponential cost: by contrast, T-indexes rely on the computation of a simulation or a bisimulation relation, for which efficient algorithms exists. Third, we offer guarantees for the size of a T-index. For example the size of a T-index associated to a single regular expression is at most linear in that of the database, (again, we contrast this to dataguides which, in the worst case, are exponential), and often, as our experiments show, it is much less. Forth, we show that T-indexes turn out to be an elegant generalizations of index structures considered previously in various contexts: dataguides for semistructured data, Pat trees for full text indexes [12,21], and Access Support Relations for OODBs [14].

Our technique consists in grouping database objects into equivalence classes containing objects that are indistinguishable w.r.t to a class of paths defined by a path template as described above. Computing this equivalence relation may be expensive (PSPACE complete), so we consider finer equivalence classes defined by bisimulation or simulation, which are efficiently computable [6]. A T-index is built from these equivalence classes, by constructing a non-deterministic automaton whose states represent the equivalence classes and whose transitions correspond to edges between objects in those classes.

While each T-index is designed for a particular class of queries (given by one template), it can be *used* to answer queries of more general forms. We address the problem of deciding whether a given query with regular path expressions can be rewritten to take advantage of a given T-index. In this formulation the problem generalizes the query rewriting problem [15] to the case of queries with regular path expressions which, to the best of our knowledge, is still open. Here we have a more modest goal: we show that a certain restriction of this query rewriting problem is decidable, and, moreover, it is in PTIME for a specific class of queries, which is of interest in practice. Even in this restricted form, our result has an interesting corollary: the fact that containment of regular expressions consisting of concatenations of constants and wildcards is decidable in PTIME. This is non obvious, because the associated deterministic automaton in this case is still exponential in the size of the regular expression.

In section 2 we review the data model and query language for semi-structured data and introduce the notion of *path templates*. We first consider two specific templates in Sections 3 and 4 whose corresponding indexes we call 1 and 2-index respectively: we illustrate details of our techniques on these simpler cases. General T-indexes are presented in Section 5. We conclude in section 6.

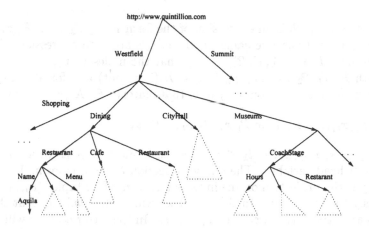

Fig. 1. Example of a semistructured database with small towns in New Jersey.

2   Review: Data Model and Query Languages

We review here the basic framework on semistructured databases and queries.

The data model: Semistructured data is modeled as a labeled graph, in which nodes correspond to the objects in the database, and edges to their attributes. We assume an infinite set $\mathcal{D}$ of *data values* and an infinite set $\mathcal{N}$ of *Nodes*.

Definition 1. *A data graph* $DB = (V, E, R)$ *is a labeled rooted graph, where* $V \subset \mathcal{N}$ *is a finite set of nodes;* $E \subseteq V \times \mathcal{D} \times V$ *is a set of labeled edges, and* $R \subseteq V$ *is a set of root nodes. W.l.o.g. we assume that all the nodes in V are reachable from some root in R. We will often refer to such a data graph as a database.*

Path expressions: We assume a set of base predicates $p_1, p_2 \ldots$, over the domain of values $\mathcal{D}$, and denote with $\mathcal{F}$ the set of boolean combinations of such predicates. We assume that we have effective procedures for evaluating the truth values of sentences $f(d)$ and $\exists x. f(x)$, for $f \in \mathcal{F}$ and $d \in \mathcal{D}$.

We define *regular path expressions*, or *path expressions*, P, over formulas in $\mathcal{F}$: $P ::= \emptyset \mid \epsilon \mid f \mid (P|P) \mid (P.P) \mid P*$. We denote with $L(P)$ the regular language defined by P, and with $W(P)$ the set of all words $w = a_1 \ldots a_n$ in $\mathcal{D}^*$, s.t. there exists a word $w' = f_1 \ldots f_n \in L(P)$ and $f_i(a_i)$ holds for all $i = 1 \ldots n$ (i.e. the set of words obtained by replacing each formula by some value that satisfies it). It is easy to see that the languages defined by path expressions are closed under intersection and that the emptiness problem for $W(P)$ is decidable.

Given a data graph DB and a path $p = v_0 \overset{a_1}{\to} v_1 \overset{a_2}{\to} v_2 \ldots v_{n-1} \overset{a_n}{\to} v_n$ in DB, we say that p *matches* the path expression P iff the word $a_1 \ldots a_n$ is in $W(P)$.

We denote with _ the predicate $True$, and abbreviate _* with *. Each constant $d \in D$ also denotes a predicate d s.t. $\forall x \in D$, $d(x)$ is true iff $x = d$. For example $*.Restaurant. * .Name._Fridays$ is a path expression.

Queries: A *query path* is an expression of the form $P_1 \ x_1 \ P_2 \ x_2 \ldots P_n \ x_n$ where the x_i's are distinct variable names, and the P_i's are path expressions. Given a graph database $DB = (V, E, R)$, we say that the nodes $v_0, v_1, \ldots, v_n$ *satisfy* a query path $P_1 \ x_1 \ P_2 \ x_2 \ldots P_n \ x_n$ if $v_0 \in R$ (is a root) and for all $v_{i-1}, v_i, i = 1 \ldots n$, there exist a path from v_{i-1} to v_i that matches P_i. A *query* has the form:

select $x_{i_1}, x_{i_2}, \ldots, x_{i_k}$ from $P_1 \ x_1 \ P_2 \ x_2 \ldots P_n \ x_n$

where $1 \leq i_1 < i_2 < \ldots < i_k \leq n$. That is, a query consists of a query path and a set of head variables. The query in Section 1 has this form. The *answer* of a query is the projection on the indexes $i_1, \ldots, i_k$ of all tuples $(v_0, v_1, \ldots, v_n)$ that satisfy the query path. In the sequel we will assume w.l.o.g. that the head variables are either $x_1, \ldots, x_{n-1}$ or $x_1, \ldots, x_n$. In the latter case we will refer to the query by giving only the query path.

Path Templates: A *path template* t has the form $T_1 \ x_1 \ T_2 \ x_2 \ldots T_n \ x_n$ where each T_i is either a regular path expression, or one of the following two place holders: $\boxed{P}$ and $\boxed{F}$. A query path q is obtained from t by instantiating each of the $\boxed{P}$ place holders by some regular path expressions, and each of the $\boxed{F}$ place holders by some formula. The query path thus obtained is called an *instantiation* of the path template t. The set of all such instantiations is denoted $inst(t)$.

For example, consider the path template $(*.Restaurant) \ x_1 \ \boxed{P} \ x_2 \ Name \ x_3 \ \boxed{F} \ x_4$. The following three query paths are possible instantiations:

$$q_1 = (*.Restaurant) \ x_1 \ * \ x_2 \ Name \ x_3 \ Fridays \ x_4$$
$$q_2 = (*.Restaurant) \ x_1 \ * \ x_2 \ name \ x_3 \ \_ \ x_4$$
$$q_3 = (*.Restaurant) \ x_1 \ (\epsilon \mid \_) \ x_2 \ Name \ x_3 \ Fridays \ x_4$$

Given a path template t, our goal is to construct an index structure that will enable an efficient evaluation of queries in $inst(t)$. (In fact, as we shall see later, it will also assist in answering other queries as well). The templates are used to guide the indexing mechanism to concentrate on the more interesting (or frequently queried) parts of the data graph. For example, if we know that the database contains a restaurants directory and that most common queries refer to the restaurant and its name, we may use a path template such as the one above. As another example, assume we know nothing about the database, but users never ask for more than k objects on a path. Then we may take $t = \boxed{P}\, x_1\, \boxed{P}\, x_2 \ldots \boxed{P}\, x_k$, and build the corresponding index.

In the next two sections we focus on two particular templates $t_1 = \boxed{P}\, x$ and $t_2 = *\, x_1\, \boxed{P}\, x_2$, and illustrate most technical details on these simpler indexes, called 1- and 2-indexes. We present the general case in Sec. 5.

3   1-Indexes

Our goal here is to compute efficiently queries $q \in inst(\boxed{P}\, x)$.

A First attempt: A naive way (which we will soon refine) is the following. For each node v in DB, let $L_v(DB)$, or L_v in short, be the set of words on paths from some root node to v:

$$L_v(DB) \stackrel{\text{def}}{=} \{w \mid w = a_1 \ldots a_n, \exists \text{ a path } v_0 \stackrel{a_1}{\to} \ldots \stackrel{a_n}{\to} v, \text{ with } v_0 \text{ a root node}\}$$

Next, define the *language equivalence relation*, $v \equiv u$ on nodes in DB to be:

$$v \equiv u \Longleftrightarrow L_v = L_u$$

We denote with $[v]$ the equivalence class of v. Clearly, there are no more equivalence classes than nodes in DB. Language equivalence is important because two nodes v, u in DB can be distinguished[1] by a query path in $inst(\boxed{P}\, x)$ iff $u \not\equiv v$.

A naive index can be constructed as follows: it consists of the collection of all equivalence classes $s_1, s_2, \ldots$, each accompanied by (1) an automaton/regular expression describing the corresponding language, and (2) the set of nodes in the equivalence class. We call this set the *extent* of s_i, and denote it by $\text{extent}(s_i)$. Given the naive index, a query path of the form $P\, x$ can be can be evaluated by iterating over all the classes s_i, and for each class testing if the language of that class has a nonempty intersection with $W(P)$. The answer of the query is the union of all $\text{extent}(s_i)$ for which this intersection is not empty.

This naive approach is inefficient, for two reasons.

- *Construction Cost:* the construction of the index is very expensive since computing the equivalence classes for a given data graph is a PSPACE-complete problem [22].

---

[1] *Distinguished* means that one node is in the query's answer while the other is not.

— *Index Size:* the automaton/regular expressions associated with different equivalence classes have overlapping parts which are stored redundantly. This also results in inefficient query evaluation, since we have to intersect $W(P)$ with each regular language.

We next address these problems. To tackle the construction cost we consider refinements. An equivalence relation $\approx$ is called a *refinement* if:

$$v \approx u \Longrightarrow v \equiv u \qquad (1)$$

As we shall see, any refinement is fine for constructing 1-indexes, as long as it is efficiently computable: we illustrate below two examples. The basic idea to tackle the index size was introduced in [19], and consists in a more concise representation of the languages of $s_1, s_2, \ldots$, based on finite state automata. A novelty here over [19] is the use of a *non deterministic* automaton to get an even more compact structure.

Refinements: We discuss here two choices for refinements: *bisimulation*, $\approx_b$, and *simulation*, $\approx_s$. Both are discussed extensively in the literature [17,20,13]. The idea that these can be used to approximate the language equivalence dates back to the modeling of reactive systems and process algebras [13]. For completeness, we revise their definitions here. Unlike standard definitions in the literature we need to traverse edges "backwards", because L_v refers to the set of paths leading *into* v.

Definition 2. *Let DB be a data graph. A binary relation $\sim$ on its nodes is a* backwards bisimulation *if:*

1. *If $v \sim v'$ and v is a root, then so is v'.*
2. *Conversely, if $v \sim v'$ and v' is a root, then so is v.*
3. *If $v \sim v'$, then for any edge $u \xrightarrow{a} v$ there exists an edge $u' \xrightarrow{a} v'$, s.t. $u \sim u'$.*
4. *Conversely, if $v \sim v'$, then for any edge $u' \xrightarrow{a} v'$ there exists an edge $u \xrightarrow{a} v$, s.t. $u \sim u'$.*

A binary relation $\preceq$ is a backwards simulation, *if it satisfies conditions 1 and 3.*

Since we consider only backwards simulations and bisimulations in this paper we safely refer to them as *simulation* and *bisimulation*.

Two nodes v, u are *bisimilar*, in notation $v \approx_b u$, iff there exists a bisimulation $\sim$ s.t. $v \sim u$. Paige and Tarjan [20] describe an $O(m \log n)$ time algorithm for computing $\approx_b$ on a unlabeled graph with n nodes and m edges, which can be easily adapted to a $O(m \log m)$ algorithm for labeled graphs [6].

Two nodes v, u are *similar*, in notation $v \approx_s u$, if there exists two simulations $\preceq, \preceq'$ s.t. $v \preceq u$ and $u \preceq' v$. Henzinger, Henzinger, and Kopke[13] give an $O(mn)$ algorithm for computing $\approx_s$ on an unlabeled graph with n nodes and m edges, which can be easily adapted to an $O(m^2)$ algorithm for labeled graphs [6].

We have: $v \approx_b u \Longrightarrow v \approx_s u \Longrightarrow v \equiv u$, hence both $\approx_b$ and $\approx_s$ are refinements, i.e. satisfy Equation 1. The implications are strict as illustrated in Figure 2, where $x \equiv y \equiv z$, $x \not\approx_s y \approx_s z$, and $x \not\approx_b y \not\approx_b z$.

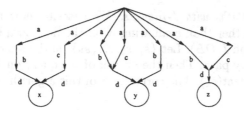

Fig. 2. A data graph on which the relations $\equiv$, $\approx_s$, and $\approx_b$ differ.

In constructing our indexes we will use either a bisimulation or a simulation. The reader may wonder how much we loose in practice by using a refinement instead of $\equiv$. The answer is: not much. In fact, for tree data graphs the three coincide. We prove a slightly more general statement. Let us say that a database DB has *unique incoming labels* if for any node x, whenever a, b are labels of two distinct edges entering x, then $a \neq b$. In particular, tree databases have unique incoming labels.

Proposition 1. *If DB is a graph database with unique incoming labels, then $\equiv$, $\approx_s$, and $\approx_b$ coincide.*

Proof. Recall that we only consider *accessible* graph databases, i.e. in which every node is accessible from some root. We will show that $\equiv$ is a bisimulation: this proves that $v \equiv u \implies v \approx_b u$, and the proposition follows. We check the four conditions in Definition 2. If $v \equiv u$ and v is a root, then $\varepsilon \in L_v$, hence $\varepsilon \in L_u$, so u is a root too. This proves items 1 and 2. Let $v \equiv u$ and let $v' \xrightarrow{a} v$ be some edge. Hence $L_v = L_1.a \cup L_2$, where $L_1 = L_{v'}$, while L_2 is a language which does not contain any words ending in a (because DB has unique incoming labels). It follows that $L_u = L_1.a \cup L_2$. Since v' is an accessible node in DB, we have $L_1 \neq \emptyset$, hence there exists some edge $u' \xrightarrow{a} u$ entering u, and it also follows that $L_{v'} = L_{u'}$.

1-Indexes: We can now define 1-indexes. Given a database DB and a refinement $\approx$, the 1-index $I(DB)$ is a rooted, labeled graph defined as follows. Its nodes are equivalence classes $[v]$ of $\approx$; for each edge $v \xrightarrow{a} v'$ in DB there exists an edge $[v] \xrightarrow{a} [v']$ in $I(DB)$; the roots are $[r]$ for each root r in DB. When DB is clear from the context we omit it and simply write I.

We store I as follows. First we associate an oid s to each node in I, and store I's graph structure in a standard fashion. Second, we record for each node s the nodes in DB belonging to that equivalence class, which we denote **extent**(s). That is, if s is an oid for $[v]$, then **extent**$(s) = [v]$. The space for I incurs two costs: the space for the graph I, and that for the extents. The graph is at most as large as the data graph DB, but we will argue that in practice it may be much less. The extents contain each node in DB exactly once. This is similar to an unclustered index in a relational databases, where each tuple id occurs exactly once in the index.

Evaluating Query Paths with 1-Indexes: We describe now how to evaluate a query path P x. Rather than evaluating it on the data graph DB we evaluate it on the index graph $I(DB)$. Let $\{s_1, s_2, \ldots, s_k\}$ be the set of nodes in $I(DB)$ that satisfy the query path. Then the answer of the query on DB is extent$(s_1) \cup$ extent$(s_2) \cup \ldots \cup$ extent(s_k). The correctness of this algorithms follows from the following proposition:

Proposition 2. *Let $\approx$ be a refinement (i.e. satisfies Equation (1)) on DB. Then, for any node v in DB, $L_v(DB) = L_{[v]}(I(DB))$.*

Proof. The inclusion $L_v \subseteq L_{[v]}$ holds for any equivalence relation $\approx$, not only refinements: this is because any path $v_0 \overset{a_1}{\to} v_1 \overset{a_3}{\to} v_2 \ldots$ in DB, with v_0 a root node, has a corresponding path $[v_0] \overset{a_1}{\to} [v_1] \overset{a_3}{\to} [v_2] \ldots$ in I. For the converse, we prove by induction on the length of a word w that, if $w \in L_{[v]}$, then $w \in L_v$. When $w = \varepsilon$ (the empty word), then $[v]$ is a root of I: hence $v \approx r$ for some root r. This implies $L_v = L_r$, so $\varepsilon \in L_v$. When $w = w_1.a$, then we consider the last edge in I: $s \overset{a}{\to} [v]$, with $w_1 \in L_s$. By definition there exists nodes $v_1 \in [s]$ and $v' \in [v]$ and an edge $v_1 \overset{a}{\to} v'$ and, by induction, $w_1 \in L_{v_1}$. This implies $w \in L_{v'}$. Now we use the fact that $\approx$ is a refinement, to conclude that $w \in L_v$.

The cost of evaluating a query P x on a graph is polynomial in the size of the graph and that of the query path[2]. Since $I(DB)$ is likely to be smaller than DB, evaluating a query on $I(DB)$ rather than DB is faster. Note that nodes in the index graph may have many outgoing edges. This is because an equivalence class may contain many nodes, and the outgoing edges of the class node is the union of all their outgoing edges. To make the computation faster, these edges can be further indexed (e.g. by hashing or using B-tree on the labels) so that the selection of edges with specific labels is faster.

Example 1. Fig. 3 (a) illustrates a graph data DB and Fig. 3 (b) its 1-index I. Considering the query $q = t.a$ x, its evaluation follows the two paths $t.a$ in I (rather than the 5 in DB), and unions their extents: $\{7, 13\} \cup \{8, 10, 12\}$.

The Size of a 1-Index: The storage of a 1-index consists of the graph I and the sum of all extents. Query performance is dictated by the former, which we discuss here. On the experimental side we computed $I(DB)$ for a variety of databases, obtaining results which show that in common scenarios I is significantly smaller than DB. A brief discussion of the experiments is given in the Appendix. On the theoretical side we identified two parameters which alone control the size of I. These are: (1) the number of distinct labels in DB, and (2) the longest simple path[3]. We show here that there exists an upper bound for the size of I

---

[2] We assume here that each predicate $p(d)$ can be computed in $O(1)$, for each $d \in \mathcal{D}$.
[3] A simple path is a path which does not go twice through the same node.

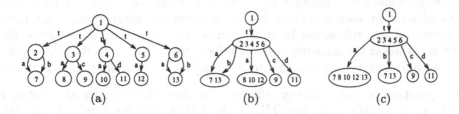

Fig. 3. A data graph (a), its 1-index (b), and its strong dataguide (c)

which depends only on these two parameters and is otherwise independent on
DB. Technically this is one of the hardest results in this paper, whose proof will
be included in the full version (omitted here for lack of space), and we believe it
is valuable in focusing future research aimed at reducing the index size.

Formally, for a database DB and number k, we say that DB is "k-short"
if there are no simple paths of length $> k$. For example trees of depth $\leq k$ are
k-short. Some important instances of semistructured databases are in practice
k-short, for some small k. Namely many web sites have the following structure:
they start as a tree of depth d, then add a *navigation bar*, consisting of p links to p
distinguished pages in the web site: importantly, every page having a navigation
bar refers to the same set of p distinguished pages. It is easy to see that such a
database is $d + p(d - 1)$ short. In practice, both d and p are very small, even if
the web site itself is large.

Theorem 1. *Let DB be a k-short database having at most p distinct labels,
and let $\approx$ be any refinement which is at least as coarse as a bisimulation[4]. Then
the size of I is bounded by some number depending only on k and p, and is
independent on the size of DB.*

Connection to Related Work: Data Guides – In [19] and [11], the authors proposed for the first time a method for extracting all the possible path information
from a given database DB, and describe it as a concise labeled graph called a
dataguide. In their approach each path in the data is represented exactly once
in the dataguide. If we view DB as an automaton by making each each node a
terminal state and each root an initial state, then a dataguide is by definition a
deterministic automaton equivalent to DB. Among all dataguides only one has
states which are related to sets of nodes in DB (what we call here *extents*): this
is called a *strong dataguide*, and is precisely the standard powerset automaton
of DB. Unlike 1-indexes, the extents in a strong dataguide may overlap. Hence,
the storage for dataguides can be larger than for 1-indexes for two reasons: (1)
the size of the dataguide graph may be as large as exponential in that of the
database, while the 1-index is at most linear, and (2) the total size of all extents
in a dataguide may be as large as exponential in that of the database, due to

---

[4] That is $u \approx_b v \implies u \approx v$.

overlaps, while for 1-indexes it is exactly the number of nodes in DB. A contribution of our work is to show that, by relaxing the determinism requirement imposed on dataguides, the 1-indexes can be constructed and stored more efficiently, while at the same time serve similar goals. We pinpoint the relationship between dataguides and 1-indexes in the following proposition. (Proof omitted.)

Proposition 3. *Let $\approx$ be any refinement relation on the nodes of a database DB (i.e. $\approx$ satisfies Equation (1)), and let I be the 1-index constructed on DB using $\approx$. Then the deterministic automaton built from I by the standard powerset construct coincides with the strong dataguide.*

Referring to the data graph DB in Fig. 3 (a) and index I in Fig. 3 (b), the strong dataguide is shown in Fig. 3 (c): it is the powerset construct of both DB and I. On tree databases however, 1-indexes coincide with strong dataguides (because here I is deterministic).

4   2-Indexes

In this section we describe index structures for answering queries of the form select x_1, x_2 from $* \; x_1 \; P \; x_2$, with P a regular path expression: the template is $* \; x_1 \boxed{P} \; x_2$. We are interested in pairs of nodes (x_1, x_2), so we define:

$$L_{(v,u)}(DB) \stackrel{\text{def}}{=} \{w \mid w = a_1 \ldots a_n, \text{and there exists a path } v \stackrel{a_1}{\rightarrow} \ldots \stackrel{a_n}{\rightarrow} u \text{ in } DB\}$$

We write $L_{(v,u)}$ when DB is clear from the context. Now, define two pairs to be equivalent, $(v, u) \equiv (v', u')$, iff $L_{(v,u)} = L_{(v',u')}$, and let $[(v, u)]$ denote the equivalence class of (v, u). As before, computing $\equiv$ is expensive, so we consider (efficiently computable) refinements, $\approx$, satisfying:

$$(y, u) \approx (v', u') \Longrightarrow (v, u) \equiv (v', u') \qquad (2)$$

As before, there exist efficient refinements based in simulation and bisimulation. (Details are omitted for lack of space). We define the 2-index $I^2(DB)$ of DB to be the following rooted graph. Its nodes are equivalence classes, $[(v, u)]$, of $\approx$; the roots are all the equivalence classes of the form $[(x, x)]$; finally, for each edge $u \stackrel{a}{\rightarrow} u'$ and each node v in DB there is an edge $[(v, u)] \stackrel{a}{\rightarrow} [(v, u')]$. We store I^2 as two logical components: the graph itself and the extent $\text{extent}(s) \stackrel{\text{def}}{=} [(v, u)]$, for each node s representing the equivalence class $[(v, u)]$.

Proposition 2 now becomes: $L_{(v,u)}(DB) = L_{[(v,u)]}(I^2(DB))$. Node that the $L_{(v,u)}(DB)$ on the left represent the paths between v and u in DB, while the $L_{[(v,u)]}(I^2(DB))$ on the right represents the paths, in the 2-index $I^2(DB)$, between some *root* of the index and $[(v, u)]$.

Query evaluation with 2-indexes proceeds similarly to that with 1-indexes, with small modification: To compute select x, y from $* \; x \; P \; y$, we compute the query path $P \; y$ on I^2 and take the union of the extents. Note that this saves the $*$ search: but we may have to start at several roots in I^2. Often, these are only a few. For example, in acyclic databases, I^2 has a single root, because[5] $(u, u) \equiv (v, v)$ for every nodes $u, v \in DB$. Figure 4 shows the 2-Index (without extents) for the database in Figure 3 (a). It has a single root: the top node. The query select x, y from $* \ x \ a \ y$ is evaluated by traversing the outgoing a edges of that root.

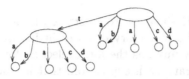

Fig. 4. A 2-index for the data graph

As for 1-indexes, the storage of a 2-index consists of two parts: the graph and the extents. Both are now (at worst) quadratic in the size of DB. Again, while this guarantees that querying the index is no more expensive than querying the database, we would like to keep the index as small as possible. Our experiments (described briefly in the Appendix) indicate that in practice the index size is smaller than this upper bound, thus providing a significant improvement in query evaluation. A number of implementation techniques for further reducing the size of 2-indexes are also available, but they are beyond the scope of this paper. On the theoretical side, Theorem 1 can be extended to 2-indexes for obtaining upper bounds on the size of the graph of I^2 which are independent on the size of DB: we omit this for lack of space.

Connection to Related Work: Patricia Trees – We conclude this section by mentioning the relationship to full-text indexing mechanisms and in particular to Pat trees [12,21]. Its purpose is to assist in computing regular expressions over large text files. A Pat tree is a Patricia tree [9,12] constructed over all the possible suffixes of a text (viewing the text as infinitely long), as follows. The root node will have one outgoing edge for each character in the file. Each of its children, say that corresponding to the letter k, will have one child for each character following that letter, e.g. the children may correspond to $ka, kb, kc, \ldots$ These nodes in turn will have one child for each continuation of that group of two characters, etc. If a node has only one child, that child is deleted, and the node is annotated with the number of descendents being omitted. The leaves of the tree point back into the data, to the beginning of the corresponding strings.

There exists a close relationship between Pat trees and 2-indexes. To a sequence of characters $a_1, a_2, \ldots$ associate a data graph DB with a single long chain: $v_1 \xrightarrow{a_1} v_2 \xrightarrow{a_1} \ldots$ Then the 2-index I^2 for DB is a tree, and the Pat tree can be obtained from I^2 by performing some simple optimizations: (1) keeping only the x values in the extents, (2) skipping nodes and pointing back to the

---

[5] This statement applies also to $\approx_b$ and $\approx_s$.

data whenever the descendents form a long chain, and (3) keeping extents only in leaf nodes. These and other optimizations will be described in the full version of the paper.

5   T-Indexes

We now turn to general T-indexes. To illustrate with an example from semistructured data, consider the repository of cities in Figure 1. Assume that a high percentage of the query mix has the form select x_2 from $*.Restaurant$ x_1 R x_2, where R is some arbitrary path expression: that is, the query conforms to the template $*.Restaurant$ x_1 $\boxed{P}$ x_2. Rather than indexing all the paths, it is more convenient to index only those having a $Restaurant$ incoming edge. Another example is the case where most of the information in the database has a fixed, pre-defined structure, and only certain components are irregular. For example, consider the relation $Restaurants(Name, Phone, Menu)$: $Name$ and $Phone$ have a fixed structure while the $Menu$ attribute has a complex structure that differs from one restaurant to the other. We want to use standard optimization and indexing techniques for the structured parts, and focus our novel indexing mechanisms to the $Menu$ part, where the standard ones do not apply.

For the remainder of this section we fix a template $t = T_1$ x_1 T_2 $x_2 \ldots T_n$ x_n, where each of the T_i's is either a path expression or a place holder $\boxed{P}$ or $\boxed{F}$. We build an index structure, called a T-index, to assist in answering queries $q \in inst(t)$. Before going into the definition of the index, we would like to point out that T-index both generalize and specialize 1 and 2-indexes, in certain ways. The generalization comes from the fact that both 1 and 2-indexes are particular cases of T-indexes (see below). But T-indexes also specialize 1 and 2-indexes, because of the following intuition. Suppose we built a T-index for a template t, and then want to evaluate a query $Q =$ select x from P x. We can always use a 1-index to evaluate Q, but we can use the T-index only if the path expression P is in some sense "compatible" with the $T_1.T_2 \ldots T_n$ path in t: thus T-indexes reduce the class of path expressions that can be evaluated. We will discuss below how to test whether a given query can be evaluated using a T-index.

Definitions: We assume that the query binds the n variables $x_1, \ldots, x_n$ in that order. A partial binding will correspond then to an i-tuple $(v_1, \ldots, v_i)$ of nodes in DB, for some $i = 1, n$. For each such i-tuple we will consider the languages $L_{(v_{j-1}, v_j)}$ for $j = 1, i$ defined in Sec. 4. (by convention $L_{(v_0, v_1)} \overset{\text{def}}{=} L_{v_1}$, defined in Sec. 3). We fix $n + 1$ fresh symbols \$$, S_1, \ldots, S_n$ not occurring in $\mathcal{D}$. ($\mathcal{D}$ is the domain of data values from Definition 1.)

Definition 3. *Let* $t = T_1$ $x_1 \ldots T_n$ x_n *be a path template and* $(v_1, \ldots, v_i)$ *an* i-*tuple of nodes in* DB, $i = 1 \ldots n$. $T_{(v_1, \ldots, v_i)}(DB)$ *is the language over the alphabet* $\mathcal{D} \cup \{\$, S_1, \ldots, S_n\}$ *generated by the regular expression* $R_1.\$.R_2.\$ \ldots \$.R_i$, *where the* R_j's *,* $j = 1 \ldots i$ *are the regular expression below:*

- If $T_j = \boxed{P}$ *(path)*, then $R_j \overset{\text{def}}{=} L_{(v_{j-1}, v_j)}$.
- If $T_j = \boxed{F}$ *(formula)*, then $R_j \overset{\text{def}}{=} L_{(v_{j-1}, v_j)} \cap \mathcal{D}$.
- If $T_j = P_j$ *(constant)*, if $L_{(v_{j-1}, v_j)} \cap W(P_j) \neq \emptyset$ then $R_j \overset{\text{def}}{=} S_j$, otherwise $R_j \overset{\text{def}}{=} \emptyset$.

For two i-tuples $(v_1, \ldots, v_i)$ and $(u_1, \ldots, u_i)$ we define the language-equivalence relation, $(u_1, \ldots, v_i) \equiv (u_1, \ldots, u_i)$, iff $T_{(v_1, \ldots, v_i)}(DB) = T_{(u_1, \ldots, u_i)}(DB)$. The equivalence class of $(v_1, \ldots, v_i)$ is denoted $[(v_1, \ldots, v_i)]$

As before two tuples $(v_1 \ldots v_n)$, $(u_1 \ldots u_n)$ in DB can be distinguished by a query path $P_1 \, x_1 \ldots P_n \, x_n$ in $inst(t)$ iff $(v_1, \ldots, v_n) \not\equiv (u_1, \ldots, u_n)$. The goal of the the \$ and the new S_i symbols is to pinpoint the range of each of the path term in the query, (and in particular those that match the constant path expressions in the template), and thus determine the assignments of nodes to the query variables. This issue will be further clarified below.

Computing $\equiv$ is expensive, so we consider refinements, $\approx$, satisfying:

$$(v_1, \ldots, v_i) \approx (u_1, \ldots, u_i) \implies (v_1, \ldots, v_i) \equiv (u_1, \ldots, u_i) \qquad (3)$$

and that can be computed efficiently. As for the case of 1 and 2-index, it is possible to define efficient refinements using variants of the traditional simulation and bisimulation relations. (Details omitted).

Given $\approx$, the T-index $I^t(DB)$ for t is the following rooted, labeled graph:
Nodes - The nodes include all the equivalence classes (w.r.t $\approx$) $[(v_1, \ldots, v_i)]$, $i = 1, n$. Also, for each such class we introduce an additional new node which we denote $[(v_1, \ldots, v_i)]^\$$.
Edges - For each i-tuple there is an edge labeled \$ from $[(v_1 \ldots v_{i-1}, v_i)]^\$$ to $[(v_1 \ldots v_{i-1}, v_i, v_i)]$, $1 \leq i < n$. Additionally, each T_i in the template $t = T_1 \, x_1 \ldots T_n \, x_n$ introduces some edges, depending on its structure:

1. If $T_i = \boxed{P}$, then for each edge $v_i \overset{a}{\to} v_i'$ is in DB, I^t has an edge $[(v_1 \ldots v_{i-1}, v_i)] \overset{a}{\to} [(v_1 \ldots v_{i-1}, v_i')]$. Additionally, each $[(u_1 \ldots u_i)]$ has an edge to $[(u_1 \ldots u_i)]^\$$ labeled by a special ϵ symbol.
2. If $T_i = \boxed{F}$, then for each edge $v_i \overset{a}{\to} v_i'$ is in DB, I^t has an edge $[(v_1 \ldots v_{i-1}, v_i)] \overset{a}{\to} [(v_1 \ldots v_{i-1}, v_i')]^\$$.
3. If $T_i = P_i$, then for each node $[(v_1 \ldots v_{i-1}, v_i)]$ and every v_i' s.t. $L_{(v_i, v_i')} \cap W(P_i) \neq \emptyset$, I^t contains an edge $[(v_1 \ldots v_{i-1}, v_i)] \overset{S_i}{\to} [(v_1 \ldots v_{i-1}, v_i')]^\$$, where S_i is a new symbol.

Root nodes - The roots are all the nodes $[(v)]$ where v is a root of DB.
Terminal nodes - Unlike graph databases and 1 and 2-indexes, here we distinguish terminal nodes: these are all nodes of the form $[(v_1, \ldots, v_n)]^\$$.

Finally, we remove all nodes not reachable from a root or not having an outgoing path to a terminal node, and associate with each terminal node $[(v_1, \ldots, v_n)]^\$$ the extent containing all tuples in $[(v_1, \ldots, v_n)]$.[6]

---

[6] As in the case of 1 and 2-indexes, when nodes in I^t have many outgoing edges, we can further index their labels.

Example 2. Consider the template $t = (*.Restaurant.*.Menu)$ x $\boxed{P}$ y. The equivalence classes are the following. For single nodes, u, there are exactly two classes $[(u)]$: the first, s_1, contains all nodes u reachable from a root via a path matching $*.Restaurant.*.Menu$, and the second, s_2, contains all the other nodes. Considering pairs next, the equivalence classes are now sets of pairs (u, v) for which $u \in s_1$ and which have the same language $L_{(u,v)}$; in addition there are similar equivalence classes for pairs (u, v) with $u \in s_2$.

I^t has one edge $s_1 \xrightarrow{S_1} s_1^\$$, continued with $s_1^\$ \xrightarrow{\$} [(u, u)]$, for $u \in s_1$, has edges $[(u, v)] \xrightarrow{a} [(u, v')]$ for edges $v \xrightarrow{a} v'$ in DB and $u \in s_1$, and finally has edges $[(u, v)] \xrightarrow{\epsilon} [(u, v)]^\$$, ending in a terminal state. Note that s_2 has no outgoing edges, hence all nodes $[u], [(u, v)]$ with $u \in s_2$ are removed from the graph. The resulting T-index looks like a 2-index that considers only the data reachable by a $*.Restaurant.*.Menu$ path.

Observe that every path from a root to a terminal node traverses exactly $n - 1$ \$-edges. We define $L_{[(u_1,...,u_i)]}$ to be the language describing paths from the root to $[(u_1, ..., u_i)]$, with the slight modification that the ϵ symbols are interpreted as the epsilon moves (i.e. they are omitted from the strings).

Evaluating Query Paths with T-Indexes: In the simplest scenario the query matches the template completely, i.e. $q = P_1 x_1 \ldots P_n x_n \in inst(t)$: we assume that each wildcard $\_$ is replaced with $(not (\$) \wedge not (S_1) \wedge \ldots \wedge not (S_n))$, since our alphabet becomes now $\mathcal{D} \cup \{\$, S_1, \ldots, S_n\}$. First, let $P_q \stackrel{def}{=} P_1'.\$ \ldots \$.P_n'$, where:

$$P_i' \stackrel{def}{=} \begin{cases} S_i \text{ when } T_i \text{ is a constant} \\ P_i \text{ when } T_i \text{ is } \boxed{P} \text{ or } \boxed{F} \end{cases}$$

Then evaluate the query path P_q x on I^t, interpreting the ϵ edges as epsilon moves. Since P_q has exactly $n - 1$ \$-signs, all the retrieved nodes are of the form $[(v_1, \ldots, v_n)]^\$$. The answer to the query is the union of the extents of the retrieved nodes. The following guarantees the correctness of this algorithm.

Proposition 4. *(1) Let $\approx$ be a refinement on DB. Then, for every $i = 1 \ldots n$ and every i-tuple $(v_1 \ldots v_i)$, we have $T_{(v_1,...,v_i)}(DB) = L_{[(v_1,...,v_i)]\$}(I^t(DB))$. (2) a tuple $(v_1, \ldots, v_n)$ satisfies a query q iff $W(P_q) \cap T_{(v_1,...,v_n)}(DB) \neq \emptyset$.*

Evaluating More Complex Queries: Sometimes we can use a T-index to evaluate queries $q \notin inst(t)$. We illustrate first with two examples.

Example 3. Let $t = \boxed{P}$ x $((B.A)*)$ y C z and $q = ((A.B)*).A$ y C z. Obviously $q \notin inst(t)$, but we can still use I^t as follows. First instantiate t to $p = A$ x $((B.A)*)$ y C $z \in inst(t)$ (we have instantiated $\boxed{P}$ with A). Then q can be expressed as a projection from p, namely as select y, z from p, because $A.(B.A)* = (A.B)*.A$.

Example 4. Let $t = A\,x\,B\,y\,C\,z$ and $q = A\,x\,B\,y\,(C.D)\,u\,E\,v$. Again $q \notin inst(t)$. Here t has a single instance, $p = A\,x\,B\,y\,C\,z$. We can use it to compute a prefix of q, namely the variables x and y, then continue to compute u, v with a search in the data graph. That is, we rewrite q as: select (x, y, u, v) from $p, y\,(C.D)\,u\,E\,v$. A subtle point here is that the unused "side branch" of p, namely $C\,z$ is not harmful (it is implied by $y\,(C.D)\,u$). In effect we have replaced some prefix of q with an instance of t: we call this *prefix replacement*.

The general problem of deciding whether a path query q can be rewritten in terms of one or more T-indexes generalizes the *query rewriting problem* [15] to regular path expressions. We do not attempt to solve the general problem (for regular expressions it is still open) but restrict ourselves to prefix replacement.

Given a template t and query path q with variables $x_1, \ldots, x_n$, we define a *prefix replacement* of q w.r.t. t to consists of (1) an instance $p \in inst(t)$ whose variables are renamed to include a prefix $x_1, \ldots, x_i$ of q's variables, in that order, and (2) a postfix q' of q containing the variables $x_i, \ldots, x_n$, such that the query select $(x_1, \ldots, x_n)$ from p, q' is equivalent to q. Note that the new query consists of a query paths which includes the variables $x_1, \ldots, x_n$, and a possible side branch (everything after x_i in p; see Example 4). Checking whether a query path q admits a prefix replacement is PSPACE-hard, by reduction to the equivalence problem for regular expressions (which is PSPACE-complete [22]): R, R' are equivalent iff the query path $q = R\,x$ has a prefix replacement w.r.t. the template $t = R'\,y$. In the full version of the paper we prove that one can check in PSPACE whether there exists a prefix replacement (and find one, when it exists).

Finally, we consider a particular case of templates and queries which we believe to be more frequent in practice. Define a regular path expression to be *simple* if it consists of a concatenation of (1) constants from $\mathcal{D}$, (2) _, and (3) *. For example $*.A. * .B.\_\_.C$ is a simple regular path expression. Similarly, define a template to be *simple* if all its constant regular expressions (if it has any) are simple. We prove in the full version of the paper that checking/finding a prefix replacement for a simple query w.r.t. a simple template is in PTIME. At the core of this result lies a Lemma stating that containment of simple path expressions can be tested in PTIME. This may come at a surprise, since the deterministic automata associated to a simple regular path expression may have exponentially many states (proof omitted), hence the traditional containment test of regular languages would be much more expensive. Summarizing:

Proposition 5. *Given a template t and a query path Q, the problem whether there exists a prefix replacement of Q w.r.t. t is PSPACE complete. When both Q and t are simple, then the problem is in PTIME.*

Connection to Related Work: T-indexes are flexible structures which can be fine-tuned to trade-off space for generality. They capture 1- and 2-indexes, by taking the templates $\boxed{P}\,x$ and $*\,x\,\boxed{P}\,y$ respectively. They also generalize traditional relational indexes: assuming the encoding of relational databases as in [7], an index on attribute A of the relation $R1$ can be captured with the template $(R1.tup)\ x\ A\ y\ \boxed{F}\ z$. Finally, they generalize path indexes in OODBs. For example Kemper and Moerkotte describe in [14] *access support relation* (ASR), an index structure for query paths in OODBs. ASR's are designed to evaluate efficiently paths of the form $o.A_1.A_2 \ldots A_n$, where o is an object and $A_1, \ldots, A_n$ are attribute names. They define an *access support relation*, ASR, to be an $n + 1$-ary relation R such that $(u, u_1, u_2, \ldots, u_n) \in R$ iff there exists a path $u \xrightarrow{A_1} u_1 \xrightarrow{A_2} u_2 \ldots u_n$ in the database. Ignoring the mismatch between the object-oriented and the semistructured data model, there exists a close relationship between an ASR and the T-index for the template $*\ x\ A_1\ x_1\ A_2\ x_2\ \ldots\ A_n\ x_n$. The graph structure of the T-index would be a chain of $2n$ nodes $[(r)] \to [(r)]^\$ \to [(u, u_1)] \to [(u, u_1)]^\$ \to [(u, u_1, u_2)] \to \ldots \to [(u, u_1, u_2, \ldots, u_n)]^\$$, where the last (terminal) node has an associated extension: this extension is precisely the ASR.

6   Conclusions

We presented an indexing mechanism, called T-index, aimed to assist in evaluating query paths in semi-structured data. A T-index captures the (possibly partial) knowledge about the structure of data and the type of queries in the query mix, as described by a *path templates*.

Abiteboul and Vianu consider in [3] First-Order equivalence classes over tuples of values in the database. Two tuples $(x_1, \ldots, x_n)$ and $(y_1, \ldots, y_n)$ are equivalent if they are indistinguishable by any FO formula. The language equivalences on which we base our index constructs are only superficially related to the FO equivalence classes: in our setting equivalence classes are distinguished by path queries, while in their setting they are distinguished by first order formulas. Hence the language equivalences are coarser than FO equivalences, and result in fewer equivalence classes. Buchsbaum, Kanellakis, and Vitter consider in [5] the problem of incrementally maintaining query paths given by a fixed regular expression under either database insertions or deletions (but not both). They describe an efficient method for incremental updates. Since their method refers to a fixed regular expression, it could be used in incremental updates of T-indexes but only when the template is restricted to constant regular expressions. We do not address index maintenance here, but note that a possible alternative to incremental maintenance can be based on an optimization technique, presented in the full version of the paper, of pointing back to the data, doing so whenever a portion of the index graph is invalidated by an update.

Acknowledgment: We thank Micky Frankel for the implementation of the 1-, 2- and T-indexes.

References

1. S. Abiteboul, D. Quass, J. McHugh, J. Widom, and J. Wiener. The Lorel query language for semistructured data. *International Journal on Digital Libraries*, 1(1):68–88, April 1997.
2. Serge Abiteboul. Querying semi-structured data. In *ICDT*, 1997.
3. Serge Abiteboul and Victor Vianu. Generic computation and its complexity. In *Proceedings of 23rd ACM Symposium on the Theory of Computing*, 1991.
4. Elisa Bertion and Won Kim. Indexing techniques for queries on nested objects. *IEEE Transactions on Knowledge and Data Engineering*, 1(2):196–214, June 1989.
5. Adam Buchsbaum, Paris Kanellakis, and Jeffrey Scott Vitter. A data structure for arc insertion and regular path finding. *Annals of Mathematics and Artificial Intelligence*, 3:187–210, 1991.
6. Peter Buneman, Susan Davidson, Mary Fernandez, and Dan Suciu. Adding structure to unstructured data. In *Proceedings of the International Conference on Database Theory*, pages 336–350, Deplhi, Greece, 1997. Springer Verlag.
7. Peter Buneman, Susan Davidson, Gerd Hillebrand, and Dan Suciu. A query language and optimization techniques for unstructured data. In *Proceedings of ACM-SIGMOD International Conference on Management of Data*, 1996.
8. V. Christophides, S. Abiteboul, S. Cluet, and M. Scholl. From structured documents to novel query facilities. In Richard Snodgrass and Marianne Winslett, editors, *Proceedings of 1994 ACM SIGMOD International Conference on Management of Data*, Minneapolis, Minnesota, May 1994.
9. P. Flajolet and R. Sedgewick. Digital search trees revisited. *SIAM Journal on Computing*, 15:748–767, 1986.
10. Harold Gabow and Robert Tarjan. Faster scaling algorithms for network problems. *SIAM Journal of Computing*, 18(5):1013–1036, 1989.
11. Roy Goldman and Jennifer Widom. DataGuides: enabling query formulation and optimization in semistructured databases. In *VLDB*, September 1997.
12. G. Gonnet. Efficient searching of text and pictures (extended abstract). Technical Report OED-88-02, University of Waterloo, 1988.
13. Monika Henzinger, Thomas Henzinger, and Peter Kopke. Computing simulations on finite and infinite graphs. In *Proceedings of 20th Symposium on Foundations of Computer Science*, pages 453–462, 1995.
14. Alfons Kemper and Guido Moerkkotte. Access support relations: an indexing method for object bases. *Information Systems*, 17(2):117–145, 1992.
15. Alon Levy, Alberto Mendelzon, Yehoshua Sagiv, and Divesh Srivastava. Answering queries using views. In *Proceedings of the 14th Symposium on Principles of Database Systems*, San Jose, CA, June 1995.
16. A. Mendelzon, G. Mihaila, and T. Milo. Querying the world wide web. In *Proceedings of the Fourth Conference on Parallel and Distributed Information Systems*, Miami, Florida, December 1996.
17. Robin Milner. *Communication and concurrency*. Prentice Hall, 1989.
18. S. Nestorov, S. Abiteboul, and R. Motwani. Inferring structure in semistructured data. In *Proceedings of the Workshop on Management of Semi-structured Data*, 1997.
19. S. Nestorov, J. Ullman, J. Wiener, and S. Chawathe. Representative objects: concise representation of semistructured, hierarchical data. In *ICDE*, 1997.
20. Robert Paige and Robert Tarjan. Three partition refinement algorithms. *SIAM Journal of Computing*, 16:973–988, 1987.

21. A. Salminen and F. W. Tompa. Pat expressions: an algebra for text search. In *Papers in Computational Lexicography: COMPLEX'92*, pages 309–332, 1992.
22. L. J. Stockmeyer and A.R. Meyer. Word problems requiring exponential time. In *5th STOC*, pages 1–9. ACM, 1973.

A   Appendix

Experiments: Recall that index storage consists of two parts: the graph and the extents. We argued that the graph size is critical for query performance, and we are currently conducting a series of experiments to asses its size. Some of the results are reported in Table 1. The Bibtex data is a relatively structured one, while the Web site (of the CS department of Tel-Aviv University) is far less structured. We also considered randomly generated graphs, and mixed graphs composed of both structured and unstructured components. We briefly describe these experiments here. In order to asses the schematic information we measure only the the number of non-leaf nodes in the graphs.

Data	Graph Size	1-index	2-index
Bibtex	150	40	50
Web site	1521	198	1100

Table 1. Experiments showing index size

We started by considering 1 and 2-indices. Not surprisingly, the smallest indices were obtained for the BibTex data: although the structure of BibTex items may vary (hence a collection of such items is naturally modeled by the semi-structured data model), the number of possible paths between nodes is rather limited. We considered increasingly growing files and their corresponding graph representation. Already at 150 nodes the size of the 1 and 2-indices almost stabilized having about 40 and 50 vertices resp., staying at about the same size regardless of the growth of the data, and thus providing significant performance improvement when querying large files. Observe that the independence of the index size from the data size is also implied here from Theorem 1, but the experimental results show that in practice the index size is much smaller than the theoretical upper bound induced by the proof of the theorem.

The Web example is far less structured: many pages at the site are each built and maintained individually by distinct people without coordinating the structure. Hence the structure is rather loose and makes the site a typical example for semi-structured information. For a graph of about 1500 nodes, the size of the 1-index amounts to about 13% of the original size, and that of the 2-index to about 72%. Observe that the later is only 0.0475% of the potential upper bound on the size of the 2-index, which is the square of the number of nodes in the graph ! This also implies that the effort in evaluation of queries of the form $* x_1 \ P \ x_2$ on the original data can potentially be as much as square of that needed when using the 2-index. (Since on DB we need to evaluate the query from each node, while on I we just evaluate $P \ x_2$ from the I's root.)

The usage of T-indices for focusing on specific, more interesting, parts of the data was tested on mixed graphs combining randomly generated subgraphs with BibTex or Web site-like data, and using templates focusing on the Bib-Tex/Web parts. The reduction is size was similar to the one reported above and more, depending on the size of the random-generated parts being ignored in the construction due to the given template.

Schemas for Integration and Translation of Structured and Semi-structured Data *

Catriel Beeri[1] and Tova Milo[2]

[1] Hebrew University `beeri@cs.huji.ac.il`
[2] Tel Aviv University `milo@math.tau.ac.il`

Abstract. With the emergence of the Web as a universal data repository, research has recently focused on data integration and data translation, and a common *data model* of semistructured data has been established. It is being realized, however, that having a common *schema model* is also necessary, to support tasks such as query formulation, decomposition and optimization, or declarative specification of data translation. In this paper we elaborate on the theoretical foundations of a middleware schema model. We present expressive and flexible schema definition languages, and investigate properties such as expressive power and the complexity of decision problems that are significant in the context of data translation and integration.

1 Introduction

The Web is emerging as a universal data repository, offering access to sources whose data organization varies from strictly structured databases to almost completely unstructured pages, and everything in between. Consequently, much research has recently focused on data integration and data translation systems [10, 6, 9, 8, 17, 13, 2, 19], whose goals are to allow applications to utilize data from many sources, with possibly widely varying formats. These research efforts have established a common *data model* of semistructured data, for uniformly representing data from any source. Recently, however, it is being realized that having a common *schema model* is also beneficial, and even necessary, in translation and integration systems to support tasks such as query formulation, decomposition and optimization, or declarative specification of data translation.

As an example, which we use for motivation throughout the paper, recently suggested tools for data translation [2, 11, 19] use the semistructured data model as a common middleware data model to which data sources are mapped. Translation from source to target formats is achieved by (1) importing data from the source to the middleware model, (2) translating it to another middleware representation that better fits the target structure, and then (3) exporting the translated data to the target system. In [11, 19], *schema* information is extensively utilized in this process. Source and target formats are each represented

---

* The work is supported by the Israeli Ministry of Science and by the Academy of Arts and Sciences

Catriel Beeri, Peter Buneman (Eds.): ICDT'99, LNCS 1540, pp. 296–313, 1998.

in a common schema language; then a correspondence between the source and target schemas can be specified in the middleware model. In many cases, the two schemas are rather similar, with differences mostly due to variations in their data models; after all, they both represent the same data. Consequently, most of the correspondence between the two schemas can be determined *automatically*, with user intervention required only for endorsement or for dealing with difficult cases. Once such a correspondence is established, translation becomes an automatic process: Data from the source is imported to the common data model and is "typed", i.e. matched to its schema, thus its components are associated with appropriate schema elements. Next, the schema correspondence is used for a translation of the data to the target structure, where each component is translated according to its type. Then data is exported to the target

The above idea was in fact implemented in the TRANSCM translation system, whose the architecture and functionalities are described in [19]. In the present paper we elaborate on the theoretical foundations of the middleware schema model. (The model has only been informally sketched in [19] and its properties have not be investigated there.) While we refer to the TRANSCM system for motivation, our results are relevant to other translation systems (e.g. YAT [11]), and to other applications of semi-structured data such as data integration. Our main contribution is the presentation of schema definition languages that are both expressive and flexible, and an investigation of properties such as expressive power and the complexity of significant decision problems for the context of data translation and integration. Our schema languages are considerably more expressive than those found in recent work on schematic constraints for semi-structured data (e.g. [5, 16]), providing a combination of expressibility and tractability. Another contribution here is the extension of the data model to support order in data, not supported by the common semistructured data model, both in the data and in the schema level. The closest to our model is YAT [11], supporting order and an expressive schema language, but lacking some of the features described here. (They also do not mention expressiveness and complexity results.) Further comparison is presented in the last section.

The paper is organized as follows. In Section 2 we present our data model and two schema specification languages. We first introduce a basic schema specification language and illustrate its flexibility and expressive power, then we discuss an extension that is useful for data translation, and show it increases the expressive power. Relationships between the languages and context-free/regular grammars are established. Detection and removal of redundancy from schemas is discussed in Section 3, the closure of schemas under operations in Section 4, and the complexity of matching of data to schemas and related problems in Section 5. In Section 6 we present a preliminary study of the computation of schema information for queries and its use for optimization. Section 7 summarizes the results. All figures appear in the Appendix.

2 Data and Schemas

We define here the middleware data model, introduce our first schema specification language and illustrate its capabilities. Then we explain an extension
useful in data translation. Close relationships between the languages and context-
free/regular grammars are established; these are extensively used in the sequel.

2.1 The Data Model

The common model for semi-structured data [20, 6, 2] represents data by trees
or forests, augmented with references to nodes. Thus, it is essentially that of
labeled directed graphs. This, with the significant addition of order, is also our
model. More differences and extensions are explained below.

Definition 1. *Let $\mathcal{D}$ be an infinite set of* **label values**. *A* **data graph** $G =
(V, E, L, O, \omega)$ *is a finite directed node-labeled graph, where V and $E \subseteq V \times V$
are finite sets of nodes and edges, respectively; $L : V \to \mathcal{D}$ is the labeling function
for the nodes; $O \subseteq V$ is the set of* **ordered** *nodes; and ω associates with each
node in O a total order relation on its outgoing edges.*

A **rooted** *data graph is a graph as above, with a designated* **root** *node,
denoted v_0, and where each node in the graph is reachable from v_0.*

Like in all models in the literature, node labels in our model can be used both to
represent data such as integers and strings, and to represent schematic information, such as relation, class, and attribute names. While it might seem natural
to represent schematic data as edge labels, and 'real' data as node labels, for
convenience usually only one of the two kinds of labels is used. For our work,
node labels seem to have an advantage. It is easy to convert edge labels to node
labels: create a node to represent the edge, and move the label to it. Thus, our
results apply to edge-labeled graphs as well.

Allowing an order to be defined on the children of some of the nodes is a
significant extension, missing in most previous models. Order is inherent in data
structures such as tuples and lists, and is essential for representing textual data,
either as sequences of characters or words, or on a higher level by parse trees. As
shown in [2], supporting order in the data model enables a natural representation
of such data. By allowing order to be defined for *part of the nodes* we are able
to naturally describe data containing both ordered and unordered components.

Reachability of data from one or more roots is a de-facto standard in essentially all data sources, from database systems to Web sites. In the sequel, we
are mainly interested in rooted graphs; non-rooted graphs are used mainly for
technical reasons. For brevity in the sequel a *data graph* will mean a rooted one
(unless explicitly stated otherwise). For simplicity we assume here a single root,
but all subsequent results can be naturally extended for the case of multiple
roots.

2.2 Schemas

We now present the basic Schema Definition Language, SCMDL. A schema is a set of type definitions. Following the SGML/XML syntax for element definition[15, 1], the definition of a type (schema element) has two parts. The first is a regular expression describing the possible sequences of children that a node can have. We use common notation for regular expressions: ϵ denotes the empty language, and · and | denote concatenation and alternation resp. The second part contains attributes that describe properties of a node. Three of these are boolean flags, that determine if instance data nodes of this type (i) are ordered, (ii) can be referenced from other nodes; only such nodes can have more than one incoming edge, (iii) can be roots of the data graph. The fourth attribute is a unary predicate, that determines the possible labels of data nodes of this type. We do not use any specific predicate language. We assume given some collection $\mathcal{P}$ of predicates over $\mathcal{D}$, the domain of label values, that is closed under the boolean operations, and such that satisfiability of a predicate, and whether $p(d)$ holds, for a predicate p and a label d, can be decided in time polynomial in d and p's definition.[1] We also assume that: (a) For base types such as *Int*, *String*, $\mathcal{P}$ contains a corresponding base predicate satisfied by the relevant subset of $\mathcal{D}$ (b) For each constant $d \in \mathcal{D}$ there is a predicate satisfied only by d (i.e. $\lambda x.x = d$), denoted by *is-d*, where in the case of strings, the quotes are omitted: e.g. *is-foo* denotes the predicate satisfied only by "foo". (c) Finally, to capture cases where no restrictions are imposed on the labels, we assume that $\mathcal{P}$ also contains a predicate, denoted *Dom*, that is satisfied by all the elements in $\mathcal{D}$ (i.e. $\lambda x.true$).

Definition 2. *Let $\mathcal{T}$ be an infinite set of type names. A* **type definition** *has the form*

$$t = R_t \, (label = t_{label}, ord = t_{ord}, ref = t_{ref}, root = t_{root})$$

where $t \in \mathcal{T}, R_t$ is a regular expression over $\mathcal{T}$, t_{label} is a predicate name in $\mathcal{P}$, and $t_{ord}, t_{ref}, t_{root}$ are boolean values. (For additional conventions and abbreviations, see below.)

A SCMDL **schema** *is a pair $S = (T, Def)$, where $T \subset \mathcal{T}$ is a finite set of type names, and Def is a set of type definitions containing precisely one definition for each of the type names in T and using only type names in T.* [2]

We use $Lang(t)$ to denote the regular language defined by R_t, and we use $t.a$, for $a \in \{label, ord, root, ref\}$, to denote the value of the attribute a in t's definition. We say that a type t is **ordered** (is **a root**, is **referencable**) iff $t.ord$ ($t.root$,$t.ref$, resp.) is true.

It can be seen that we follow the SGML/XML style of definition [15, 1], as shown in Figure 1, in that a type definition describe both the attributes of nodes, and their children. We chose a less verbose style, for brevity.

---

[1] This assumption is used in deriving some of our complexity results; the consequences of dropping it on these results are quite obvious.

[2] In [19] schemas are presented graphically, as the system is oriented towards a graphical interface for defining schemas and representing schemas and data.

$$<!ELEMENT\ t \quad (R_t)>$$
$$<!ATTLIST \quad t$$
$$label\ t_{label} \qquad \#Required$$
$$ord\ Boolean\ t_{ord}$$
$$ref\ Boolean\ t_{ref}$$
$$root\ Boolean\ t_{root}>$$

Fig. 1. SGML/XML-style type definition

A SCMDL schema defines a set of data instances. Intuitively a data graph G **conforms** to a schema S if each of the nodes $v \in G$ can be assigned a type t s.t. v satisfies the requirements of t, as described in t's definition. This is formally defined below.

Definition 3. *Let G be a data graph and S be a schema. We say that G **conforms** to S (or is an **instance** of S), if there is a type assignment on its nodes, i.e. a total mapping h from the nodes in G to types in S s.t. for each node $v \in G$ the following holds:*

1. *v's label satisfies $h(v).label$,*
2. *v is ordered iff $h(v)$ is ordered,*
3. *If v is a root node then $h(v)$ is a root type,*
4. *If v has more than one incoming edge then $h(v)$ is referencable,*
5. *Finally, if v is ordered and its children are $v_1, \ldots, v_n$ (in that order) then the sequence $h(v_1), \ldots, h(v_n)$ is a word in $Lang(t)$, and if v is unordered then there exists some order on its children for which the above holds.*

*The set of all data graph instances of a schema S is denoted $inst(S)$, and we say that two schemas S, S' are **equivalent** if $inst(S) = inst(S')$.*

Notational conventions: To further simplify type definitions, we assume the convention that flags whose value is false are omitted, while those that are true are represented by their name. Thus

$$t = R_t\ (label = t_{label}, ord)$$

represents a type for which $ord = true, ref = false, root = false$. Another convention is used for types of leaf node, i.e. nodes that have no outgoing edges, hence their regular expression is ϵ. Almost always, for leaves all three flags are false. Further, in essentially all cases, the labels of such nodes are values of base types, such as $Int, String$, that have a corresponding predicate. Hence, from now we consider type definitions for such leaves as given, as in the following definition,

$$Int = \epsilon\ (label = Int, ord = false, ref = false, root = false)$$

and freely use $Int, String$, as type names in schemes without defining them.

2.3   Examples

Descriptive power is an obvious requirement from a middleware schema language. One should be able to describe the strict and precise formats of database sources, the variety of formats used in scientific disciplines, the very loose formats of Web pages, and also cases where the data has parts that are precisely specified, and other parts that are allowed to vary. We now illustrate the expressiveness and flexibility of the language in describing possible structures of data.

An OODB schema and its instance database are shown in Figures 2 and 3, respectively. The corresponding SCMDL schema and data graph are shown in Figures 4 and 5. Note that *article* is the root, *authors* is the only ordered node, and that the data graph conforms to the schema, with the natural type assignment.

$$
\begin{aligned}
&\textit{class article public type}\\
&\qquad \textit{tuple (title} \quad : \ \textit{string,}\\
&\qquad\qquad \textit{authors} \ : \ \textit{list(author),}\\
&\qquad\qquad \textit{contact\_author} \ : \ \textit{author,}\\
&\qquad\qquad \textit{sections} \ : \ \textit{set(string))}\\
\\
&\textit{class author} \ : \ \textit{string;}
\end{aligned}
$$

Fig. 2. OODB Schema

class name	oid	value
article	o_0	tuple(title : "From Structured Documents to Novel Query Facilities", authors : list(o_1, o_2, o_3), contact_author : o_1, sections : set("Structured documents ...",...))
author	o_1	V. Christophides
author	o_2	S. Abiteboul
author	o_3	S. Cluet

Fig. 3. An OODB Instance

A DTD for an SGML document and its instance document are presented in Figures 6 and 7 respectively. The corresponding SCMDL schema and data graph are presented in Figures 8 and 9. All the internal nodes are ordered, with *article* being the root.

The above were examples for homogeneous, strictly structured data. The schema in Figure 10 illustrates the opposite case, where no constraints at all

$$
\begin{array}{llll}
article & = & title \cdot authors \cdot contact\_author \cdot sections & (label = is\text{-}article, root, ref) \\
title & = & String & (label = is\text{-}title) \\
authors & = & author^* & (label = is\text{-}authors, ord) \\
author & = & String & (label = is\text{-}author, ref) \\
contact\_author & = & String & (label = is\text{-}contact\_author) \\
sections & = & String^* & (label = is\text{-}sections)
\end{array}
$$

Fig. 4. SCMDLschema for the OO data graph

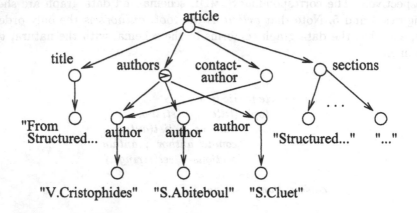

Fig. 5. Data graph of an OODB article

```
<!DOCTYPE article [
<!ELEMENT article          (title, author*, contact_author, section*) >
<!ELEMENT title            (#PCDATA) >
<!ELEMENT author           (#PCDATA) >
<!ELEMENT contact_author   (#PCDATA) >
<!ELEMENT section          (#PCDATA) >
```

Fig. 6. SGML DTD

```
< article >
< title > From structured Documents to Novel Query Facilities  < /title >
< author > V. Christophides  < /author >
< author > S. Abiteboul  < /author >
< author > S. Cluet  < /author >
< contact_author > V. Christophides  < /contact_author >
< section > Structured documents are central...  < /section >
... < /article >
```

Fig. 7. SGML Document

$$
\begin{array}{llll}
article & = & title \cdot author^* \cdot contact\_author \cdot section^* & (label = is\text{-}article, ord, root) \\
title & = & String & (label = is\text{-}title, ord) \\
author & = & String & (label = is\text{-}author, ord) \\
contact\_author & = & String & (label = is\text{-}contact\_author, \\
& & & \qquad ord) \\
section & = & String & (label = is\text{-}section, ord)
\end{array}
$$

Fig. 8. SCMDLschema of an SGML article

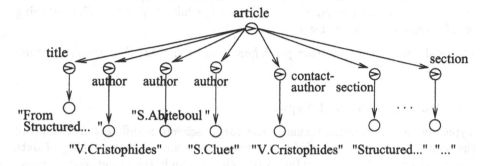

Fig. 9. Data graph of an SGML article

are imposed on data graphs. (Recall that Dom is the label predicate $\lambda x.true.$)
It is easy to see that all data graphs conform to the above schema with a type
assignment h assigning any_{ord} to all the ordered vertices and any_{unord} to the
unordered ones.

$$
\begin{array}{lll}
any_{ord} & = & (any_{ord} \mid any_{unord})^* \ (label = Dom, ord, root, ref) \\
any_{unord} & = & (any_{ord} \mid any_{unord})^* \ (label = Dom, root, ref)
\end{array}
$$

Fig. 10. Schema for arbitrary graphs

Finally, we present an example for the modeling of partial constraints. Assume that we are modeling a web site with arbitrary structure, but where one
of the links leads to an OODB describing articles, with structure as described
above. The schema for such mixed data is presented in Figure 11. (W.l.o.g. we
assume that all the nodes representing Web pages are ordered, reflecting the
order of elements in the page.)

Note that in [5], schema information was captured using *schema-graphs*, i.e,
graphs whose nodes represent types and whose edges describe the possible children that a node of a certain type may have. We argue that SCMDL is powerful
enough to express all the schema constraints expressible by the *schema-graphs*

$$
\begin{aligned}
mixed &= any^*.(db \mid mixed).any^*. & (label = Dom, ord, root, ref) \\
any &= any^* & (label = Dom, ord, ref) \\
db &= article^* & (label = Dom) \\
article &= defined\ as\ in\ Figure\ 4 & (\ldots)
\end{aligned}
$$

Fig. 11. Schema for a Web site containing an articles OODB

of [5] and **much more:**[3] We can *require* a node to have a certain outgoing edge, while schema-graphs only allows to state that such an edge is *possible*. We also deal with order and referencebility constrains, while they don't. The following proof is omitted for space reasons.

Proposition 1. *Every schema-graph has an equivalent* SCMDL *schema, but not vice versa.*

2.4   Virtual Nodes and Types

Typically, in a translation scenario, the target schema is different from that of the source. One common difference is that in the source the grouping of data into subtrees/subgraphs is less (or more) refined than in the target. For example, assume we want to convert the SGML document in Figure 7 into an OO format, as in Figure 3. In both formats an article consists of four logical components, namely the title, the authors list, the contact author, and the sections. However, while in the OO data graph (Figure 5) each of these parts occurs in a subtree under an appropriately named node, this does not hold in the data graph of the SGML document (Figure 9), which is just a sequence of elements. Note that the refined structure (implicitly) exists in the parse tree of the document, relative to the regular expression defining it. For facilitating the translation, it is convenient to make the logical structure explicit and split the sequence into its logical sub-components. That is, rather than looking at the "real" SGML instance in Figure 9, it is convenient to use a "virtual" graph with structure as in Figure 12, remembering that the *authors* and *sections* are "virtual" vertices that do not really occur in given the data.

The first step is to define *virtual* graphs and schemas, and extend the notion of conformity accordingly. Observe that, since virtual nodes represent logical components that do not actually occur in the data, they cannot be serve as roots or be referenced (i.e. have more than one incoming edge). Also, since virtual nodes are introduced to represent subsets or subsequences of the children of a given node, if the node is (un)ordered so should be the virtual types used in its definition.

Definition 4. *A* **virtual** *data graph is a data graph with some nodes marked as virtual. A* **virtual** *schema is a schema as in Def 2, with one more boolean attribute,* virtual, *in the type definitions, such that:*

---

[3] As already mentioned, the fact that they use edge labels while we use node labels does not prevent a meaningful comparison.

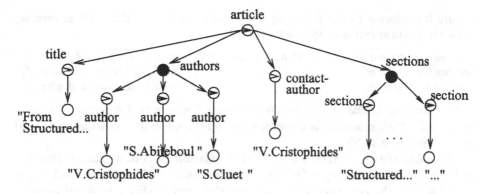

Fig. 12. Virtual version of the data graph of an SGML article

(i) a virtual type is neither referencable nor a root,
(ii) if a virtual type t_v occurs in the regular expression associated with a type t, then t, t_v are both ordered or both unordered.
The extended schema definition language is denoted VSCMDL. *A virtual graph G_V* **v-conforms** *to a* VSCMDL *schema S if there exists a type assignment h satisfying all the conditions in Definition 3, and additionally v is virtual, iff so is $h(v)$.*

Note that by the definition, a virtual node in an instance data graph is not the root, is not referencable, and is ordered iff its parent (if one exists) is. Hence we will consider in the sequel only virtual graphs where all the virtual nodes have this property. We refer to data graphs without virtual nodes, to types whose *virtual* flag is false, and to schemas that contain only such types (equivalently SCMDL schemas) as **real**.

We can now state the relationship between real data graphs and virtual graphs and schemas.

Definition 5. *Let G and G_v be a real and a virtual data graphs, resp. We say that G_V is a (possible)* **virtual** *version of G if G can be obtained from G_v by identifying each virtual node with its closest non-virtual ancestor, gluing its children directly to this ancestor, preserving the order of the children, and using the label of the ancestor for the resulting node.*

Definition 6 (conformity - revisited). *A real data graph G* **conforms** *to a* VSCMDL *schema S if some virtual version G_V of G v-conforms to S by some type assignment h. This h is called a* **virtual type assignment** *for G; its restriction to nodes of G is called a* **type assignment** *for G.*

The set of virtual graphs that v-conform to S is denoted $v\_inst(S)$, the set of real graphs that conform to it is denoted $inst(S)$; two schemas S, S' are (v-) equivalent if $inst(S) = inst(S')$ (resp. $v\text{-}inst(S) = v\text{-}inst(S')$).

Continuing with the above example, the virtual graph in Figure 12 is a possible virtual version of the data graph in Figure 9. Thus the SGML article of

Figure 9 conforms to the following virtual schema due to this virtual version, with the natural (virtual) type assignment.

$article$ = $title \cdot authors \cdot contact\_author \cdot sections$ $(label = is\text{-}article, ord, root)$
$authors$ = $author^*$ $(label = is\text{-}authors, ord, virtual)$
$sections$ = $section^*$ $(label = is\text{-}sections, ord, virtual)$

Note that if a VScMDL has no virtual types (i.e. is a real schema, or equivalently, a ScMDL schema) then conformity and v-conformity coincide, and so do $inst(S)$ and $v\text{-}inst(S)$.

Recalling the above SGML-to-OODB translation process, we can see that the introduction of virtual types facilitates the comparison of the source and target schemas, and the correspondence between their types. (For additional illustrations and translation examples see [19].) Similarly, the introduction of virtual nodes into the source data facilitates its matching to its schema augmented with these virtual types, and hence the translation of the data. Finding where such virtual nodes are needed is part of the conformity test. The complexity of this and related problems are discussed in the following sections. Observe that, in general, a data graph may have more than one possible virtual version and (virtual) type assignment. We shall also consider this issue in the sequel and present conditions under which a unique type assignment is guaranteed.

2.5 Schemas and Grammars

Real schemas associate types with regular grammars. It turns out that the extension of schemas to include virtual types, with the refined notion of conformity, extend the expressive power of the language. Denote by CF-ScMDL a variant of ScMDL, also without virtual types, where types can be described by context free grammars, rather than by regular expressions, and similarly use VCF-ScMDL for such schemas with virtual types. The semantics is defined exactly as in Definitions 3 and 6, except that now $Lang(t)$ is in general a context free language.

Proposition 2. *Every* VScMDL *schema has an equivalent* CF-ScMDL *schema. Conversely, every* CF-ScMDL *schema has an equivalent* VScMDL *schema, but not necessarily an equivalent* ScMDL *schema.*

The intuition here is based on the analogy between virtual nodes of a graph and internal nodes of derivation trees for CF grammars. Thus the extension of ScMDL to VScMDL adds expressive power. In contrast, enriching CF-ScMDL with virtual types does not extend the expressive power.

Proposition 3. *Every* VCF-ScMDL *schema has an equivalent* CF-ScMDL *schema. Moreover, every* (V)CF-ScMDL *schema has an equivalent* CF-ScMDL *Schema where all unordered types are associated with regular expressions.*

An immediate consequence of the second part of the Proposition (proved using Parikh's theorem[14]) is that Proposition 2 can now be refined: *"Every* VScMDL *schema has an equivalent* CF-ScMDL *where all unordered types are associated with regular expressions"*. Thus the use of virtual types adds expressive power only in describing ordered types.

3   Redundant Types

Since schemas allow the description of optional data, a type assignment for a given data graph may not use all types in a schema, and type assignments to different graphs may use distinct types. However, it may be the case that a schema contains some types that are redundant — they are not used by any type assignment. For example, consider the following schema.

$$r = \ t \mid q \ (label = Dom, root)$$
$$q = \ \ \epsilon \ \ \ \ (label = Dom)$$
$$t = \ t \ \ \ \ (label = Dom)$$

It is easy to see that it has only one possible instance having a root of type r with one child of type q. The other alternative, namely having a child of type t, is impossible since t requires a child of type t, and so on till infinitum. Such an infinite chain of nodes of type t can exist in a finite graph only in a cycle in which an edge points back to a previous t node in the chain. But nodes of type t are not referencable, hence this is not allowed. It follows that t is redundant.

Formally, a type t is *redundant* in a schema S if there is no instance G of S having a virtual type assignment that uses t. Clearly one would like to avoid having redundant types in a schema - they make the schema larger than necessary, hence more complex to understand and handle. We prove that type redundancy can be treated and eliminated efficiently, hence from now we assume that schemas contain no redundant types.

Theorem 1. *Every* (V)SCMDL *schema S can be transformed to an equivalent* (V)SCMDL *schema S' with no redundant types, in time polynomial in the size of S.*

Corollary 1. *Given a schema S, it is possible to decide if $inst(S)$ is empty, in time polynomial in the size of S.*

4   Closure Properties

In data integration one imports data from multiple sources, each described by its own schema, and it is often desirable to describe all data using a single schema. For simple scenarios, this requires performing on schemas operations that reflect the basic set theoretic operations on the data. We consider the following two questions: Given two VSCMDL schemas S_1, S_2, does there always exist a VSCMDL schema S_{op}, such that

1. $inst(S_{op}) = inst(S_1)$ **op** $inst(S_2)$, where **op** is one of $\cup, \cap, -$?
2. $v\_inst(S_{op}^v) = v\_inst(S_1)$ **op** $v\_inst(S_2)$, for **op** in $\cup, \cap, -$?

We will refer to the first as closure under *op* and to the later as closure under *virtual op*. We note that closure under (virtual) difference implies closure under (virtual) complement since we have shown that SCMDL can define a schema with all data graphs as its instances (and a similar VScMDL schema can be defined for virtual instances). Also, since by Proposition 1 one can test emptiness of schemas, computable closure under difference implies that testing for the equivalence and the containment of schemas (hence schema subsumption) is possible.

Proposition 4. .
(1) VScMDL schemas are closed under union, but not under intersection, subtraction and complement. If one of them is real, then they are closed under intersection.
(2) ScMDL schemas (i.e. schemas with no virtual types) are closed under all these operations.
(3) Finally, all schemas are closed under virtual union, intersection, subtraction and complement.

Note that in here we need our predicate language to be closed under boolean operations. Also, observe that for ordered types the results follow from closure properties of context-free and regular languages, but for unordered types we use the theory of semi-linear sets [14].

Initial results regarding schema closure under more general query operations are presented below.

5   Matching Data and Schema

Given a (V)ScMDL schema S, we call the problem of testing if a data graph G conforms to it the *(v-)matching problem*. Finding a corresponding virtual version (for the case of VScMDL schemas) and the (virtual) type assignment, if one exists, is called the *type derivation* problem. We are interested in the complexity of the problems as a function of the size of the input data graph G.

Theorem 2. *The matching, v-matching and type derivation problems are NP-complete. The problems remain NP-complete even if the nodes in the graph are all ordered (or all unordered).*

Proof. (sketch) For the upper bound, guess a type assignment for the nodes. Testing the local properties for each node is easy. For the relationship with its children, convert a VScMDL into a CF-ScMDL schema. Then, for each node, use the parse tree of the word for deriving the virtual nodes and their assigned types. (For real schemas, this step is simpler). Completeness is proved via reduction to satisfiability of 3NF formulas.

Despite this result, in many practical cases the above problems can be solved in polynomial time. We present some examples below.

Proposition 5. *If the data graph is a tree then the (v-)matching and type derivation problems for it can be solved in a polynomial time.*

Proof. (sketch) We determine all possible type assignments for each node, going up from the leaves. For unordered nodes we use dynamic programming to avoid considering all the possible orders of the edges.

Non-tree data can also be handled efficiently in some cases. One case is the class of schema-graphs of [5], which, as shown in the proof of Proposition 1, have very simple syntactic characterization in SCMDL. Following [5] we have that the matching and the type derivation problems for this class can be solved in polynomial time (details omitted). Next, we consider in more detail another case:

Definition 7. *We say that an CF-SCMDL schema S is* **tagged** *if for every type name t in S, for any two types t_1, t_2 in $Lang(t)$, their label predicates are disjoint (i.e. cannot be satisfied by the same label value).*

A VSCMDL schema is **tagged**, *if its equivalent CF-SCMDL schema S', as constructed in the proof of Proposition 2, is tagged.*

Observe that relational and object oriented databases, and in general strongly typed databases, with homogeneous bulk types and tagged union are all naturally described by tagged (real) schemas.

Proposition 6. *For tagged schemas the (v-)matching and the type inference problems can be solved in polynomial time.*

Proof. (sketch) Here the algorithm works from the root down to the leaves. Again, unordered nodes pose a difficulty, since one needs to avoid considering all the possible orders for the set of children, which is addressed using dynamic programming.

Conformity of a data graph to a schema implies there is at least one type assignment h for its nodes, but there may exist more than one assignment. From the proof of Proposition 6 we have:

Proposition 7. *Instances of tagged real schemas have a single type assignment.*

Given a VSCMDLschema S, we call the problem of testing if every instance of S has a unique (virtual) type assignment, the *unique (virtual) assignment* problem. Observe that having a unique virtual assignment always implies having a unique type assignment, but not vice versa.

Theorem 3.
(1) The unique (virtual) assignment problem is in general undecidable.
(2) The problem is decidable for real schemas.

Proof. (sketch) We prove (1) by reductions to the problem of deciding the emptiness of the intersection of two context free languages (for unique assignment), and of testing ambiguity of context-free languages (for unique virtual assignment). The proof for (2) involves intricate analysis of the possible causes for non unique typing in real schemas.

6   Schemas and Queries

Often in data integration or translation one may be interested in only a part of the data in a source, defined by a query. For example, a query in an integration system is broken into components that are pushed to the sources; only the corresponding results are translated and integrated. A natural issue that arises here is to derive the schema of a query result. This can, e.g., facilitate the translation of the retrieved data. In the opposite direction, query evaluation on a source can benefit by using schema information to prune the search. This well known idea of classical database systems is attracting attention in systems that manipulate heterogeneous and semi-structured data [16, 5, 11]. In this direction, one would like to derive schema information for node variables in a query, and use it to restrict the search.

Query languages for semi-structured data, like their classical ancestors, have a body and a head [18, 12, 11]. In the body, node variables are introduced, operated upon by predicates, and related by edges and paths. We consider here the component that seems to be the more difficult to treat, for deriving schema information, namely generalized path expressions [10, 18, 3, 6, 12], of the form $x_0 \; P_1 \; x_1 \; P_2 \; x_2 \ldots P_n \; x_n$ where the x_i's are variable names, and the P_i's are regular expressions or path variables. Intuitively, given a data graph G, such expressions search for nodes $v_0, \ldots, v_n$ s.t. the path between v_{i-1} and $v_i, i = 1 \ldots n$, matches P_i, (and v_0 is a root node). Determining the possible types for the v_i's can help both in determining the schema of the query result and in pruning the search.

Formally, we consider path expressions of the form $P = x_0 \; R_1 \; x_1 \; \ldots R_n \; x_n$ where the x_i's are *distinct* variable names, and the R_i's are regular expressions over predicates in $\mathcal{P}$.[4] (The case where some of the variables may be identical will be considered later). Given a data graph G and a path $p = u_0 \rightarrow u_1 \rightarrow \ldots \rightarrow u_k$ in G, where the label of u_i is l_i, for $i = 0, \ldots, k$, we say that p **matches** R_i iff the language defined by R_i contains a word $w = p_0 \ldots p_k$ s.t. $p_i(l_i)$ holds, for all $i = 0, \ldots, k$. We say that the nodes $v_0, v_1, \ldots, v_n$ that lie on a path in a data graph G **satisfy** the generalized path expression $P = x_0 \; R_1 \; x_1 \; \ldots R_n \; x_n$, if v_0 is a root node, and for all $i = 1 \ldots n$, there exist a path from v_{i-1} to v_i that matches R_i.

Now, we say that the vector of types $t_0, t_1, \ldots, t_n$ in a VScMDL schema S is a **possible type assignment** for $x_0, \ldots, x_n$, respectively, if there exists a data graph G that conforms to S w.r.t a type assignment h, and nodes $v_0, v_1, \ldots, v_n \in G$ satisfying P, s.t. $h(v_i) = t_i$, $i = 0 \ldots n$. Each such possible type assignment describes the types of objects in some occurrence of the path expression. Given a schema S and a generalized path expression P, our goal is to find the set of all possible type assignments for the variables in P. We note that the size of the answer may be large, compared to the schema: if the schema is very loose, it may be the case that each of the variables can be associated with most of the types

---

[4] Note that these regular expressions are different than the ones used in our schema language and which are defined over types in $\mathcal{T}$ and not over predicates.

in the schema, so the size of the answer can be up to $O(|P|^{|S|})$, i.e. exponential in the size of the schema. So rather than measuring the complexity of the type computation only in terms of the size of the schema and the query, it is useful to also take the size of the answer into consideration.

Theorem 4. *Given a schema S and a path expression P, the possible type assignments for the variables in P can be computed in time polynomial in the size of S, P, and the number of possible type assignments $+1$.*[5]

Proof. (sketch) To prove the theorem we first show that for every two types t', t'' in S and every regular expression R_i, it is possible to define (in polynomial time) a regular language describing all the possible paths that start at a node of type t', end at a node of type t'', and match R_i. Then we use these languages to compute the possible type assignments.

Next, we consider how computing the possible types of query variables may be useful for optimizing the query evaluation, by allowing to prune the search space.

Definition 8. *Given a schema S, two types t', t'' in S, and a regular expression R over $\mathcal{P}$, we say that a type t in S is* **useful** *w.r.t t', t'', R, if there exists a data graph G that conforms to S with a type assignment h, and a path $p = v_0 \rightarrow v_1 \rightarrow \ldots \rightarrow v_n$ in G that matches R, s.t. $h(v_0) = t'$, $h(v_n) = t''$, and $h(v_i) = t$ for some $0 < i < n$.*

Theorem 5. *For every t', t'', R, the set of useful types w.r.t t', t'', P can be computed in time polynomial in the size S and R.*

At each step in the computation of a generalized path expression P, one holds some node v_i (initially the root node v_0) and searches for paths that match a path expression R_{i+1}, looking for the nodes v_{i+i} at the end of such a path. If we know the type assignment for nodes, and in particular the type t' of v_i, then we can prune the search whenever we run into a node of type t that is not useful w.r.t t', R_{i+1}, and any of the types t'' in S.

Moreover, if we pre-compute the possibly type assignments for P, then we can do even better: Given the type of a current node (and the types of the nodes assigned to previous variables in P), we can check what are the possible type assignments for the next variable, and prune all paths going through non-useful types w.r.t these possible assignments.

Remark: When variables may occur several times in a path, we can remove from the type assignments all those vectors in which different occurrences of the same variable have been assigned distinct types. Note however that this still does not guarantee that all the remaining vectors are actually possible assignments, i.e. that there exists an instance with a path where the two occurrences of the variable have been assigned the same *node*, and not just the same *type*. Selecting the appropriate vectors in this case is still an open problem.

---

[5] The "+1" is for the extreme case where there aren't any.

7   Conclusion

We have presented two schema definition languages, and illustrated their expressive power. In particular, we presented motivation for augmenting the basic language with the notions of virtual nodes and types, and showed these extend the expressive power. We also investigated the complexity of significant problems regarding schemas and instances, showing that in many cases they can be solved efficiently. Hence, we believe that our schema languages, particularly SCMDL, present a good combination of expressibility and tractability, and that our approach and results can be used to enhance the usability of data translation and integration systems, as illustrated in the TRANSCM system.

As we mentioned, there has been recent work on schematic description of semistructured data [5, 16, 4, 7]. However, these works focus more on describing patterns of paths in the data than on precisely describing its structure. For example, they can specify that edges with a given property going out of a node may exist, but they cannot *require* their occurrence, which can easily be done in our language. Thus, our work is much closer to classical approaches to schemas and types.

A significant recent work that presents a comparable approach is YAT [11]. They have order in their data and schemas, (but there *all* the nodes are ordered, which is less natural when modeling unordered components like sets). More importantly, it can be seen that their schema language essentially uses regular expressions, and is thus similar to SCMDL, but they do not support virtual types. While their *instantiation* mechanism provides a notion matching of data to a schema, it does not provide an explicit type assignment to instance nodes as our formalism does. But it offers subtyping that we do not treat here. Their notion seems to differ from ours in some subtle points, e.g., in the treatment of the combination of *, | in regular expressions. Such differences may impact some of the complexity results we have obtained for our model. While they mention matching of data to schemas, and inferring the schemas for queries (although without regular paths), they do not mention complexity results. Further study is needed to clarify the differences, and to investigate the impact on the complexity of significant problems.

References

[1] Extensible markup language, 1998. Available by from http://www.w3.org/XML/.

[2] S. Abiteboul, S. Cluet, and T. Milo. Correspondence and translation for heterogeneous data. In *Proc. ICDT 97*, pages 351–363, 1997.

[3] S. Abiteboul, D. Quass, J. McHugh, J. Widom, and J.L. Wiener. The lorel query language for semistructured data. *Journal on Digital Libraries*, 1(1), 1997.

[4] S. Abiteboul and V. Vianu. Regular path queries with constraints. In *Proc. Symp. on Principles of Database Systems - PODS 97*, 1997.

[5] P. Buneman, S. Davidson, M. Fernandez, and D. Suciu. Adding structure to unstructured data. In *Proc. Int. Conf. on Database Theory ICDT 97*, 1997.

[6] P. Buneman, S. Davidson, G. Hillebrand, and D. Suciu. A query language and optimization techniques for unstructured data. In *Proceedings of SIGMOD '96*, pages 505–516, 1996.

[7] P. Buneman, W. Fan, and S. Weinstein. Path constraints on semistructured and structured data. In *Proceedings of PODS '98*, pages 129–138, 1998.

[8] M.J. Carey et al. Towards heterogeneous multimedia information systems : The Garlic approach. Technical Report RJ 9911, IBM Almaden Research Center, 1994.

[9] T.-P. Chang and R. Hull. Using witness generators to support bi-directional update between object-based databases. In *Proc. Symp. on Principles of Database Systems – PODS 95*, San Jose, California, May 1995.

[10] V. Christophides, S. Abiteboul, S. Cluet, and M. Scholl. From structured documents to novel query facilities. In *Proc. ACM SIGMOD Symp. on the Management of Data, 94*, pages 313–324, 1994.

[11] S. Cluet, C. Delobel, J. Simeon, and K. Smaga. Your mediators need data conversion! In *SIGMOD '98, to appear*, 1998.

[12] M. Fernandez, D. Florescu, A. Levy, and D. Suciu. A query language for a web-site management system. *SIGMOD Record*, 6(3):4–11, 1997.

[13] H. Garcia-Molina, Y. Papakonstantinou, D. Quass, A. Rajaraman, Y. Sagiv, J. Ullman, V. Vassalos, and J. Widom. The tsimmis approach to mediation: Data models and languages. In *Journal of Intelligent Information Systems*, 1997.

[14] S. Ginsburg. *The Mathematical Theory of Context-Free Languages*. McGraw-Hill, 1966.

[15] C.F. Goldfarb. *The SGML Handbook*. Calendon Press, Oxford, 1990.

[16] R. Goldman and J. Widom. Dataguides: Enabling query formulation and optimization in semistructured databases. In *Proceedings of Conf. on Very Large Data Bases, VLDB '97*, 1997.

[17] A. Levy, A. Rajaraman, and J. Ordille. Querying heterogeneous information sources using source descriptions. In *Proceedings of Conf. on Very Large Data Bases, VLDB '96*, 1996.

[18] A. Mendelzon, G. Michaila, and T. Milo. Querying the world wide web. *Int. Journal of Digital Libraries*, 1(1), 1997.

[19] T. Milo and S. Zohar. Using schema matching to simplify heterogeneous data translation. In *To appear in VLDB '98*, 1998.

[20] Y. Papakonstantinou, H. Garcia-Molina, and J. Widom. Object exchange across heterogeneous information sources. In *Proc. IEEE International Conference on Data Engineering 95*, 1995.

In Search of the Lost Schema *

Stéphane Grumbach[1] and Giansalvatore Mecca[2]

[1] IASI and INRIA
Rocquencourt BP 105
78153 Le Chesnay, France
stephane.grumbach@inria.fr

[2] DIFA – Università della Basilicata
via della Tecnica, 3
85100 Potenza, Italy
mecca@dia.uniroma3.it

Abstract. We study the problem of rediscovering the schema of nested relations that have been encoded as strings for storage purposes. We consider various classes of encoding functions, and consider the mark-up encodings, which allow to find the schema without knowledge of the encoding function, under reasonable assumptions on the input data. Depending upon the encoding of empty sets, we propose two polynomial on-line algorithms (with different buffer size) solving the schema finding problem. We also prove that with a high probability, both algorithms find the schema after examining a fixed number of tuples, thus leading in practice to a linear time behavior with respect to the database size for wrapping the data. Finally, we show that the proposed techniques are well-suited for practical applications, such as structuring and wrapping HTML pages and Web sites.

1 Introduction

Databases traditionally provide consolidated technologies for organizing and manipulating structured data. However, in recent years, alternative approaches to data organization have imposed themselves as *de facto* standards. A prominent driving force behind this has been the World Wide Web, which delivers information in less structured form, essentially as hypertextual documents.

It has been argued in several contexts that document management still lacks the flexibility offered by database systems. Therefore, a number of recent proposals aim at extending database-like techniques to textual data coming from the Web. In most cases, in fact, Web documents have a rather tight structure that can be assimilated to a database type. For example, a large number of organizations are now providing a Web access to their information systems and databases. Several commercial packages now support the activity of publishing in HTML format data coming from a DBMS. In this process, a collection of

---

* Work supported by Università di Roma Tre, MURST and Consiglio Nazionale delle Ricerche.

Catriel Beeri, Peter Buneman (Eds.): ICDT'99, LNCS 1540, pp. 314–331, 1998.

database objects — such as for example tuples corresponding to employees — are somehow "encoded" into HTML pages, to be browsed by users. Of course, these generated pages clearly reflect the regularities of the initial database.

In many cases, users do not have access to the original database: All they can access are the HTML files on the site. Therefore, in order to be able to apply database-like query techniques to Web pages, a key problem is to identify relevant pieces of information inside text, and to extract them in order to build an internal representation in some data model, which can then be manipulated by a query language. This process, which is usually referred to as a *wrapping* of a data source, can be seen as an attempt to "decode" the original database objects that have been encoded as HTML files for publishing purposes.

In this paper, we formally investigate exact methods for this *Schema Finding Problem* (SFP), which can be informally stated as follows: *Given a collection of strings encoding instances of some database type, derive the type and a database representation of the original instances.*

1.1 The Framework

To show a practical example of a schema finding problem, consider the Nagano Winter Olympics Web site [Nag]: The site contains data about athletes and events at the last Winter Olympics, and has been implemented using an object-relational database as a back-end [Las98].

Fig. 1. Athletes at the Winter Olympics

Coming from a database, pages in the site have a rather tight structure. For example, two pages from the site are shown in Figure 1; they report data about two athletes, Manuela di Centa and Ian Piccard. For each athlete, the name, the country, and a list of performances are reported[1]. Note that the site contains

---

[1] The page also contains several links, like, for example, a link to a biography, to the country page, and to each competition page. To simplify the discussion, we ignore

a page of this kind for each competing athlete. We can abstract the content of such pages as a counterpart to database objects of a nested type *athlete*, with attributes *name* and *country* of type *string*, plus an attribute *performances*, a collection of tuples, each reporting the *event*, *placement* and *performance*, as follows:

```
type athlete ( name:          string;
               country:       string;
               performances:  set ( event:       string;
                                    placement:   string;
                                    performance: string; ) )
```

Given such a precise structure, it would be reasonable to think of using some high-level tool to ask complex queries, like *"Find all athletes in the site that won at least two medals"*. Unfortunately, we can't directly query the underlying database: the only way of accessing the site is by downloading raw-text HTML pages through the network and inspecting their content. We have no access to the original objects in the database, but rather to their *HTML-encoded versions*. This, of course, complicates the query process.

Note, in fact that whenever we download a page corresponding to a database object, the underlying structure is completely lost in favor of some HTML tagging. Before actually being able to query the site, we have somehow to re-discover the lost database schema, and, based on that, *decode* the original objects from the HTML strings, i.e., we face an instance of what we call the *Schema Finding Problem*.

1.2   Related Work

The early approaches to structuring and wrapping Web sites were essentially based on manual techniques [AM97,HGMC+97,CM98]; these proposals assume that a human programmer examines a site and manually codes wrappers that abstract the logical features of HTML pages and store them in a local database. The focus, here, is on the development of languages and tools to support this wrapping process.

A number of other approaches have studied the problem of (semi-) automatically inferring the schema of a collection of fairly well structured Web pages. We briefly mention some in the following. Most of these approaches heavily rely on the use of heuristics. For example, in [AK97], the authors develop a practical approach to identify attributes in a HTML page; the technique is based on the identification of specific formatting tags (like the ones for headings, boldface, italics etc.) in order to recognize semantically relevant portions of a page.

An alternative approach is the one developed in [KWD97] and [Ade98]. In these cases, it is assumed that the wrapper generator has some a-priori knowledge about the semantics of a page. In [KWD97], *oracles* are used to this end.

---

the links here. In Section 4, we will discuss how to deal with attributes that are links to other pages.

They are software modules embedding lexical knowledge about a particular application domain, used to recognize all occurrences of a relevant attribute in a page. In [Ade98] the user itself manually starts the semi-automatic structuring phase, by interactively labeling some example files, that is, by showing to the system some example attributes and their semantics. Then, based on this accumulated knowledge, in both cases a wrapper generator tries to infer the patterns according to which data items are organized in the target pages. This is accomplished by examining one page at a time, and progressively refining a grammar for the pages.

Similar problems have also been studied in other frameworks. For example, the work in [Bri98] aims at extracting sets of tuples of a pre-determined type (pairs of book titles and author names) not from a set of homogeneous pages in a site, but from possibly heterogeneous pages in the whole Web. In [NAM98] the authors address the problem of clustering similar objects in a semistructured Lore [ACC+97] database, i.e., inferring some form of common schema starting from schemaless data.

More generally, the problem of identifying the common structure (in 2 dimensions) of a collection of objects that are available only as one-dimensional sequences has gained a lot of attention recently for its applications in molecular biology [Wat89,HK93].

1.3   Contributions of the Paper

In this paper, we develop a formal framework for studying the Schema Finding Problem. Our approach departs from all the ones discussed above, in several respects. In fact, we aim at studying how far a completely automatic approach can be pushed in order to solve the schema finding problem; therefore, differently from [AK97], our approach makes very little use of heuristics; also, we do not assume any prior knowledge about the input data, as opposed to [KWD97,Ade98]. In fact, we are not primarily concerned with identifying the *semantics* of data in a page (i.e., the fact that a given string is the name of an athlete), but rather focus on the problem of recovering *types*. More specifically, given a set of encoded instances of a type T, we concentrate on the task of re-discovering the structure of type T. In this framework, a critical issue in recovering the scheme from a set of encoded instances is the ability of detecting collection (i.e., set) types from aggregation (i.e., tuple) types. Studying this relationship is a primary goal of the paper.

The techniques we use are also different from other proposals in the literature. In fact, given a collection of pages of a given logical type, instead of working on one page at a time, we try to infer the type by comparing different pages and looking at textual similarities between them. We formalize this process as a *decoding process*.

We identify nested relations as a natural abstraction for Web pages. This is motivated by several observations. First, HTML pages often have a nested structure, due to the presence of collections of items (like lists or tables); also, many Web sites are now built starting from relational and object-relational databases, and in some sense reflect the (possibly) nested structure of the underlying database. In fact, it has been shown in [AMM97,MMM98] that a data model based on nested relations is a promising abstraction for describing the structure of a large number of actual Web sites. Of course, this choice is by no means the most general one, and probably cannot capture all of the richness present in HTML pages. However, we feel it to be a good starting point for studying the schema finding problem.

To settle the background, in Section 2 we formalize the notion of encoding of database instances into sequences, and introduce various classes of encodings. We first consider a general version of the schema finding problem (SFP), where the encoding function is part of the input. In the general case, we show that the SFP is partial recursive if the encoding function is recursive. We then refine the class of encoding functions and relate the space complexity of the SFP to the time complexity of the encoding.

In practice, the encoding function is not given with the encoded data. It is therefore desirable to be able to solve the SFP without knowledge of the encoding function. We further restrict the encoding functions, and introduce the *mark-up encodings*, which satisfy the previous requirement, and, at the same time, nicely abstract SGML-like languages [ISO86] – like HTML – which are used in practice to encode information. Essentially, the mark-up encodings map database objects into strings in which the constants are encoded as strings over some alphabet, Δ, and the structure is encoded by arbitrary tags in some other alphabet, Σ. We distinguish between strict and loose mark-up, depending upon the encoding of empty sets. In the strict case, the structure of empty sets is maintained in the encoding, while it is lost in the loose case.

Then, in Section 3 we restrict our study to data that can be represented as nested relations and develop an algorithm that takes as input a set of strings and, by successive alignments, progressively refine their type. Our approach relies on a close correspondence between nested objects and regular expressions. In fact, we show that, given a collection of encoded tuples, finding a database type that subsumes them is reducible to finding a regular expression defining a language containing the input strings. Note that the containment problem for regular expressions is known to be PSPACE complete [Pap94]. However, dealing with restricted classes of expressions, our algorithms run in polynomial time.

The main contribution of the paper is the definition of two on-line algorithms for solving the schema finding problem in the case of mark-up encodings. The first algorithm works on strict mark-up, and uses a buffer of size linear in the size of an object (e.g. a tuple of a relation). The second algorithm works in the loose case and uses a buffer whose size is linear in the size of the loaded data. Both algorithms are shown to work in polynomial time.

Finally, in Section 4, we show how in practice, these algorithms can be used to load data from the Web into a database by first extracting the schema, and then wrapping HTML pages according to the schema. We also exhibit examples of HTML documents on which we illustrate the use of the proposed techniques. The algorithms are under implementation as part of a system for schema-finding on the Web. For space reasons, proofs of the theorems and code of the algorithms are omitted.

2 The Encoding of Data

In this section, we describe the abstract data to which we restrict our attention, and introduce formal methods for encoding it into sequences of characters. We also define our fundamental problem.

2.1 Abstract Data

The abstract data we consider are nested relations [AB95,Hul88], that is typed objects allowing nested sets and tuples. The types are defined as follows. We assume the existence of an atomic type U, called the *basic type*, whose domain, denoted by $dom(U)$ is a countable set of constants. Other *types* (and their respective domains) can be recursively defined as follows: (*i*) If $T_1, \ldots, T_n$ are basic or set types, then $[T_1, \ldots, T_n]$ is a *tuple* type, with domain $dom([T_1, \ldots, T_n]) = \{[a_1, \ldots, a_n] \mid a_i \in dom(T_i)\}$; (*ii*) If T is a tuple type, then $\{T\}$ is a *set* type, with domain $dom(\{T\}) = \mathcal{P}_f(dom(T))$ (where $\mathcal{P}_f(S)$ denotes the collection of finite subsets of S).

Given a type T, an *instance* of T is an element of $dom(T)$. Let $\mathcal{I}$ be the set of all instances. A *relational instance* is an instance of a set type. Classical (flat) relations are instances of unnested set types, and nested relations are instances of arbitrary set types. Types can be conveniently represented as trees [Hul88], which can be constructed recursively as follows. (*i*) The basic type, U, is a leaf tree, U. (*ii*) A tuple type $[T_1, \ldots, T_n]$ corresponds to a tree rooted at a *tuple node*, with n subtrees, one for each T_i. (*iii*) A set type $\{T\}$ corresponds to a tree rooted at a *set node*, with one subtree. Similarly, instances can also be represented as trees, with constant instances, c, represented as a leaf tree c; tuple instances, $[t_1, \ldots, t_n]$, represented as a tree rooted at a *tuple node*, with n subtrees, one for each t_i; and set instances $\{t_1; \ldots; t_k\}$ represented as a tree rooted at a *set instance node*, with k subtrees, corresponding to the elements $t_1, \ldots, t_k$. If I is an instance, any subtree of I is a *subinstance* of I.

We introduce a labeling of type trees, recursively defined as follows. The root is labeled by the empty string ϵ. If a set node is labeled α, then its child is labeled $\alpha.0$; and if a tuple node with n children is labeled α, then its children are labeled $\alpha.1, \ldots, \alpha.n$. Instances are labeled similarly, with the children of a set node labeled α, all labeled $\alpha.0$. So an instance and its type have the same set of labels.

Instances can sometimes underuse their type. It has been shown in [GV95], that it has a strong impact on the expressive power of query languages. In the present context, we show that it is fundamental for finding the schema. An instance underuses its type for example when set types are used to model objects that always have the same cardinality (and would have been more accurately typed with a tuple), or when the attribute of a tuple always has the same value (and could have been omitted). We define this notion formally.

Definition 1. *A collection of instances I is* rich *with respect to a type σ if it satisfies the following two properties: (i)* set richness: *for each label α of a set node, there are sets of distinct cardinalities labeled α, and (ii)* tuple richness: *for each label α of a tuple node of arity k, and each $i \leq k$, there are distinct objects labeled $\alpha.i$*

Intuitively, if a collection of instances is rich with respect to a type, it makes full use of this type, and we will see in the sequel that it then contains enough information to recover the type.

2.2   Encoding of Abstract Data

We next study the encoding of instances into sequences of characters over a finite alphabet Σ. We define an *abstract encoding function*, *enc*, as a 1-1 mapping from the set of all instances $\mathcal{I}$ to Σ^*. We consider the problem of reversing an encoding, that is given a string in Σ^*, find the abstract data that it represents and its type.

For computation purposes, the abstract data is manipulated as strings obtained by a simple *standard encoding* based on a parenthetical representation, which is essentially the one used in the paper to "write" abstract objects. We consider an ordered alphabet Δ. The order on Δ induces a (lexicographic) order on Δ^*, which in turn induces an order on the set of all instances $\mathcal{I}$ ($I \leq J$ if $enc(I) \leq enc(J)$), and in particular on U. The standard encoding ξ of an instance I is defined recursively as follows. Constants are encoded by words in Δ^*. Tuples $[a_1, \ldots, a_n]$ by the string $[\xi(a_1), \ldots, \xi(a_n)]$, and sets $\{a_1, \ldots, a_n\}$, by the string $\{\xi(a_{i_1}), \ldots, \xi(a_{i_n})\}$, where $\xi(a_{i_1}) < \ldots < \xi(a_{i_n})$. Let $\bar{\mathcal{I}} \subset (\Delta \cup \{"\{", ",", "\}", "[", "]"\})^*$ be the set of standard representation of instances.

Concrete encoding functions are 1-1 mapping from $\bar{\mathcal{I}}$ to Σ^*. When it is clear from the context we simply say instance for either the abstract instance or its standard representation, and, similarly, encoding function for abstract or concrete encoding function. Let us now define formally the problem.

Definition 2. *Schema Finding Problem (SFP)*
Input: *An encoding function enc, and a finite collection W of strings of Σ^*.*
Output: *A type σ, and a collection C of standard representation of instances of type σ, such that enc $: C \to W$ is a bijection.*

We can immediately make the following general observation. If *enc* is a recursive function, then the schema finding problem is partial recursive. Indeed, it suffices to enumerate all possible instances, $I \in \bar{\mathcal{I}}$, and check if $enc(I) = w$ for some $w \in W$. If W is a collection of strings corresponding to instances, then it halts when all such instances have been enumerated.

We now consider the complexity of the schema finding problem in the size of the collection W. The size $|w|$ of a sequence w is defined as usual as the length of w. The *size* $|I|$ of an instance I is defined as the size of its standard encoding as a sequence [AHV94]. The *domain* of an instance is the set of constants occurring in the instance, and for the standard encoding of the instance, the domain is the set of words in Δ^* encoding the constants.

It is not sufficient to restrict the complexity of encoding functions in order to bound the complexity of the schema finding problem. We next propose a sufficient restriction on the encodings to ensure a complexity bound on the SFP. We say that an encoding enc is *non-compacting*, if there exists a constant C such that for any instance I, $|I| \leq C|enc(I)|$. We can now give the correlation between the complexity of the encoding and the complexity of the SFP.

Theorem 1. *Let enc be a non-compacting encoding function having complexity* $\text{TIME}(f(n))$, *($f(n) \geq n$). Then the SFP can be solved in* $\text{SPACE}(f(n))$.

The previous result provides sufficient conditions for bounding the complexity of the schema finding problem. These conditions do not ensure tractability though. Moreover, we would like to restrict further the class of encodings, to obtain an encoding–invariant solution to the SFP. This is a desirable property, since in practice, encoding functions are not given, and only the encoded data can be found. So our approach is to find classes of encoding functions such that the SFP can be decided without the knowledge of the encoding function. Note that this is a strong assumption, which implies that the result does not depend upon the chosen encoding. For that purpose we introduce a restricted class of non-compacting encodings, namely *mark-up encodings*.

2.3 Mark-Up Encodings

In a mark-up encoding the schema and the data are encoded in disjoint finite alphabets, the *schema alphabet*, Σ, and the data alphabet, Δ. As for the standard encoding, constants are encoded as words in Δ^+, by some *data encoding*, δ, that is a 1-1 mapping from U to Δ^+.

Consider a type σ, and a corresponding labeled tree T_σ. We define a *tagging function* as a function that associates a pair of strings, called *start* and *end tags* to each label in $\mathcal{L}$, in such a way that respectively basic, set and tuple labels have different start and end tags. More formally, let Θ be a prefix subset[2] of Σ^*. Let $\Theta_1 \cup \Theta_2 \cup \Theta_3$ be a partition of Θ. A *tagging function* is a mapping from the set of labels $\mathcal{L}$ of T_σ to $\Theta \times \Theta$, which associates to each basic (resp. tuple, set) label $\alpha \in \mathcal{L}$ a pair of strings in Θ_1 (resp. Θ_2, Θ_3), denoted by $start(\alpha)$ and $end(\alpha)$, with $start(\alpha) \neq end(\alpha)$.

Definition 3. *A (loose) mark-up encoding enc based on a structure $(\Sigma, \Delta, <_\Delta , \delta, tag)$ — where Σ and Δ are two disjoint finite alphabets, $<_\Delta$ is an order on Δ, δ a data encoding, and tag a tagging function — is a function recursively defined on the tree of an instance as follows:*

- *for a leaf node $u \in U$ with label α, $enc(u) = start(\alpha) \cdot \delta(u) \cdot end(\alpha)$;*
- *for a tuple node $[T_1, \ldots, T_n]$ with label α, $enc([T_1, \ldots, T_n]) = start(\alpha) \cdot enc(T_1) \cdot \ldots \cdot enc(T_n) \cdot end(\alpha)$;*

---

[2] Recall that a set of strings Θ is called a prefix set if no word of Θ is a prefix of another word of Θ [CR94].

− for a non-empty set-instance node $\{T_1; \ldots; T_n\}$ of label α, $enc(\{T_1; \ldots; T_n\})$ = $start(\alpha) \cdot enc(T_{i_1}) \cdot \ldots \cdot enc(T_{i_n}) \cdot end(\alpha)$, where set elements have been recursively ordered according to $<_\Delta$; empty set-instances are encoded by $start(\alpha) \cdot end(\alpha)$.

We distinguish between *loose* and *strict* mark-up encodings, based on the encoding of empty sets. Suppose U contains a null value *null*. Given a set type σ, we define its *null instance*, $null(\sigma)$ as an instance whose tree is obtained from σ by replacing each leaf node U with a leaf node *null*. A *strict mark-up encoding* is defined as a loose mark-up encoding with the following difference: the encoding of an instance I is the encoding of instance I' obtained by replacing in I each empty set-instance of a type σ by $null(\sigma)$.

The definition of loose (strict) mark-up encoding can be extended also to types. In this case, function *enc* associates a *regular expression* $enc(\sigma)$ over $(\Sigma \cup \Delta)^*$ with each type σ as follows:

− for a leaf node U labeled α, $enc(U) = start(\alpha) \cdot (\Delta)^+ \cdot end(\alpha)$;
− a tuple node is encoded as above;
− for a set node $\{T\}$ with label α, $enc(\{T\}) = start(\alpha) \cdot (enc(T))^* \cdot end(\alpha)$; $(enc(\{T\}) = start(\alpha) \cdot (enc(T))^+ \cdot end(\alpha)$ for strict encoding);

Since the mark-up encoding of an instance is a string in $(\Sigma \cup \Delta)^*$, and the mark-up encoding of a type is a regular expression over $(\Sigma \cup \Delta)^*$, we can establish a close correspondence with the theory of regular languages; in fact, the class of mark-up encodings has the following property. As usual, we note $L(exp)$, the language defined by a regular expression exp.

Proposition 1. *Given a (strict/loose) mark-up encoding enc based on a structure $(\Sigma, \Delta, <_\Delta, \delta, tag)$, then, for each instance I of type σ, $enc(I) \in L(enc(\sigma))$.*

Figure 2 shows several types and instances with their corresponding encodings with $\Delta = \{1, 2, 3, \textbf{NULL}\}$, and Σ containing any character not in Δ. Note that empty sets are encoded with null values in the strict mark-up encoding, while they are simply omitted in the loose mark-up encoding.

For a collection of instances $\mathcal{J}$, we denote by $enc(\mathcal{J})$, the collection of encoded instances of $\mathcal{J}$. The class of mark-up encodings verify the following fundamental property, which states that the choice of a specific encoding is irrelevant.

Theorem 2. *For all mark-up encodings enc, enc′ over the same Σ, Δ, δ, and all set-rich collections of instances $\mathcal{J}, \mathcal{J}'$ of type σ, if $enc(\mathcal{J}) = enc'(\mathcal{J}')$, then $\mathcal{J} = \mathcal{J}'$.*

The proof is made by induction on the nesting of the instances. Theorem 2 has the fundamental consequence, that the decoding can be done without knowledge of the encoding function. In the next section, we investigate the SFP in this context.

$\sigma_1 = [\text{U}, \{[\text{U}, \text{U}]\}]$
strict mark-up encoding
`<t>e`Δ^+`/e<s>(<t>e`Δ^+`/ee`Δ^+`/e</t>)`$^+$`</s></t>`
loose mark-up encoding
`<t>e`Δ^+`/e<s>(<t>e`Δ^+`/ee`Δ^+`/e</t>)`*`</s></t>`
$\sigma_2 = [\text{U}, \{[\text{U}]\}]$
strict mark-up encoding
`romareges`Δ^+`unl(ae`Δ^+`iacta)`$^+$`tpqr`
loose mark-up encoding
`romareges`Δ^+`unl(ae`Δ^+`iacta)`*`tpqr`
$I_1 = [1, \{\}]$ *of type* σ_1
strict mark-up encoding
`<t>e1/e<s><t>eNULL/eeNULL/e</t></s></t>`
loose mark-up encoding
`<t>e1/e<s></s></t>`
$I_2 = [1, \{[2]; [3]\}]$ *of type* σ_2
strict mark-up encoding
`romareges11unlae22iactaae33iactatpqr`
loose mark-up encoding
same as strict

Fig. 2. Examples of encodings

3 Schema Finding for Mark-Up Encodings

In this section, we introduce several algorithms to solve the SFP problem assuming mark-up encodings. We first restate the problem in this special framework:

Definition 4. *Schema Finding Problem for Mark-up Encodings*
Input: Σ, Δ, δ *as defined above, and a finite collection* W *of strings of* $(\Sigma \cup \Delta)^*$.
Output: *A type* σ, *and a collection* C *of instances of type* σ, *such that there is a mark-up encoding enc such that* $enc : C \to W$ *is a bijection*.

For simplicity, we focus in the sequel on inputs consisting of a finite collection of encodings $enc(I_1), enc(I_2), \ldots, enc(I_n)$ of instances $I_1, I_2, \ldots, I_n$ of a nested tuple type σ, according to some mark-up encoding function enc. Our algorithms work on encoded instances, and progressively construct the type by generating *templates*. Templates generalize both types and instances, and represent partially specified types. Together with templates, we introduce a reflexive *subsumption* relation between templates, denoted by $\preceq$, which extends the relationship between a type and its instances. $T = [\text{c}, \{[\text{U}]\}]$ and $T' = [\text{U}, \{[\text{a}, \text{U}]; [\text{a}, \text{U}]; [\text{a}, \text{U}]\}]$ are examples of templates. It is easy to see that they correspond to partially specified types. More specifically, T subsumes any tuple of two attributes, the first one being a c, and the second one any set of monadic tuples. T' subsumes any tuple of two attributes, the second one being a set of exactly three binary tuples, having a as first attribute. Types and instances of Figure 2 provide more examples of templates, satisfying the relation: type σ_1 subsumes T', and σ_2 subsumes T. Templates and the subsumption relation can be formally defined as follows:

- Every element $u \in U$ is a *constant* template; a constant template subsumes itself.
- U, the basic type, is a *basic* template; the basic template, U, subsumes every template in $dom(U)$.
- If $T_1, \ldots, T_n$ are templates, then $[T_1, \ldots, T_n]$ is a *tuple* template; a tuple template, $[T_1, \ldots, T_n]$ subsumes any template in $\{[t_1, \ldots, t_n] \mid t_i \preceq T_i)\}$.
- If T is a template, then $\{T\}$ is a *set* template; a set template, $\{T\}$, subsumes any template in $\mathcal{P}_f(\{t \mid t \preceq T\})$.
- If $T_1, \ldots, T_k$ are templates, then $T = \{T_1; \ldots; T_k\}$ is a *set instance* template; $k \geq 0$ is called the *cardinality* of T; a set instance template subsumes any template in $\{\{a_1; \ldots; a_k\} \mid a_i \preceq T_i\}$.

It is easy to see that: (*i*) every type is a template, constructed using only tuple, set and basic sub-templates; (*ii*) every instance of a type is itself a template, made of tuple, set-instance and constant sub-templates. In the following, we blur the distinction between a types or an instance and the corresponding template. Note also that each template corresponding to a type subsumes all of its instances.

We denote by $\mathcal{T}$ the universe of all templates. The relation $\preceq$ defines a partial order on the set $\mathcal{T}$.[3] We say that two templates T_1, T_2 are *homogeneous* if they admit a common ancestor, that is, there exists a template $T \in \mathcal{T}$ such that $T_1 \preceq T$ and $T_2 \preceq T$. Intuitively, two templates are homogeneous if they represent objects that are subsumed by the same type. It is now easy to see that, for each maximal set of homogeneous templates, $\mathcal{T}_H$, $(\mathcal{T}_H, \preceq)$ is a join-semilattice. Given a template T, we denote by $\mathcal{H}(T)$ the class of all templates homogenous to T. In the following, unless explicitly specified, we will always refer to join-semilattices of homogeneous templates. Given a finite collection S of homogeneous templates, LUB(S) will denote the least upper bound of elements in S in the corresponding join-semilattice.

Consider the relationship between a type and its instances. Since a type subsumes all of its instances, given a set of instances $\mathcal{I} = \{I_1, \ldots, I_n\}$ of some type σ, σ is a common upper bound of $\mathcal{I}$ in the join-semilattice of templates homogeneous to σ, $\mathcal{H}(\sigma)$. The following proposition shows that, if $\mathcal{I}$ makes full use of its type according to the definition given in Section 2, then this upper bound is the least one.

Theorem 3. *Given a set of instances* $\mathcal{I} = \{I_1, \ldots, I_n\}$ *of type* σ, $\mathcal{I}$ *is rich for* σ *iff* $\sigma = $ LUB($\mathcal{I}$).

---

[3] Similar orderings for database types have been used also in other frameworks; see, for example, [Oho90].

This result shows that solving the schema finding problem amounts to computing the least upper bound of a set of instances according to the template subsumption relation. However, we are not dealing with abstract objects, but with strings that encode them. We next show how to solve the problem using regular expressions.

First, note that the tree representation of types and instances, the tree labeling function and the notion of mark-up encoding introduced in Section 2 extend immediately to templates. There is a close relationship between template subsumption, $\preceq$, and the familiar concept of containment, $\subseteq$, between regular expressions, as stated by the following theorem.

Theorem 4. *Given a set-rich collection* $\mathcal{I} = \{I_1, \ldots I_n\}$ *of instances of a type* σ, *and a mark-up encoding enc, let us call* $enc(\mathcal{H}(\sigma))$ *the image of* $\mathcal{H}(\sigma)$ *according to enc. Then,* $(enc(\mathcal{H}(\sigma)), \subseteq)$ *is a join-semilattice, and:* $\mathrm{LUB}_\subseteq(enc(I_1), \ldots, enc(I_n))$ $= enc(\mathrm{LUB}_\preceq(I_1, \ldots, I_n))$

Another important fact is the following:

Proposition 2. *Given an encoding* $enc(T)$ *of a set-instance free template* T, *it is possible to derive* T *from* $enc(T)$ *in linear time.*

Theorem 4 and Proposition 2 suggest that we can solve the schema finding problem working on strings and join-semilattices of regular expressions.[4] Given a set of encoded instances of a nested tuple type σ, $\mathcal{E} = \{e_1, \ldots, c_n\}$ according to some mark-up encoding, the strategy to solve the schema finding problem is: (i) to find the regular expression encoding σ as the least upper bound $e_\sigma = \mathrm{LUB}_\subseteq(\mathcal{E})$; (ii) from the regular expression, to construct σ; (iii) based on the grammar defined by e_σ, from each e_j to derive a representation of an instance I_j of σ.

3.1   Schema Finding with Strict Mark-Up

Let us first consider the case in which inputs are encoded using a *strict* mark-up encoding function. Recall that, for every join-semilattice, the least upper bound operator is associative, and therefore, given a set of elements, $\mathcal{E}$, we can progressively compute the least upper bound of the set, independently of the order $e_1, \ldots e_k$ for elements in $\mathcal{E}$, based on the following iterative algorithm.

$$\begin{cases} lub_1 & = e_1 \\ lub_{i+1} = \mathrm{LUB}(lub_i, e_{i+1}), & \text{for } i = 2, \ldots, k \end{cases}$$

Equations above suggest an efficient on-line strategy to solve the schema finding problem with mark-up encoding, assuming we know how to compute least upper bounds of regular expressions. Note that computing upper bounds of regular

---

[4] With respect to Theorem 4, note that the two join-semilattices, $(\mathcal{H}(\sigma), \preceq)$ and $(enc(\mathcal{H}(\sigma)), \subseteq)$, are not in general isomorphic. This is due to the fact that the notion of subsumption between set and set-instance templates is essentially order-independent, whereas containment between regular expressions depends on the actual order according to which elements in set instances are listed.

expression implies testing containment. The containment problem for regular expression is complete for PSPACE [Pap94]. However, in this context, we deal with rather simplified regular expressions, for which we prove that the containment problem is in PTIME. This is due to the very limited use of union – essentially only as a part of Δ^+ – and to the fact that subexpressions are clearly marked using tags.

We have developed an algorithm, called matchSchema, that computes the least upper bound of two expressions of this sort in polynomial time, as follows:

Theorem 5. *Given two regular expressions e_1, e_2 corresponding to encodings of homogeneous templates $T_1, T_2 \in \mathcal{T}_H$, according to encoding enc, let $n = max(|e_1|, |e_2|)$. Algorithm matchSchema computes $\text{LUB}(e_1, e_2) \in enc(\mathcal{T}_H)$ in time $\mathcal{O}(n^2 log(n))$.*

Algorithm matchSchema tries to align the two input expressions. In presence of mismatches, it attempts to dynamically change the inputs, and then recursively align again. Every time an input is changed, it is transformed into a new regular expression, corresponding to a template that subsumes the previous one. The algorithm terminates when, by successive changes, the two input have been transformed into a common regular expression, which is the least upper bound.

The procedure findSets is the core of the algorithm. It tries to find repeated contiguous patterns of the form w^n corresponding to elements of set instances inside a regular expression, and replace them by $(w)^+$. This process is far from being a trivial task, and implies a number of subtleties. First, the procedure is recursive, since sets may contain nested sets. Second, not all contiguous squares actually correspond to sets of homogeneous elements. To see this, consider the following tuple: [a{[b{[b...]; here, square {[b is due to a repetition of structure at different levels, and not to instances of a set.

Note that, in the case the input collection of encoded instances is not rich for its type, the on-line algorithm computes a regular expression e which corresponds to a template subsumed by σ, that is, to a partially specified type. However, if the input is set-rich, we can recover the schema.

Proposition 3. *Given a set of regular expressions $\mathcal{E} = \{e_1, \ldots, e_n\}$ corresponding to instances of some type σ according to mark-up encoding enc. If $\mathcal{E}$ is set-rich with respect to σ, then: $e = \text{LUB}(e_1, \ldots, e_n) \preceq enc(\sigma)$ and σ can be built from e in linear time wrt the size of e.*

The proof follows from the fact that, since $\mathcal{E}$ is set-rich, e is set-instance free, and therefore, by Proposition 2, σ is uniquely identified. Proposition 3 is very useful in a number of practical cases, as discussed in Section 4. Based on matchSchema, we can define algorithm schemaFinding1 to solve the SFP for strict mark-up encodings as follows: the algorithm progressively loads the encoded tuples and compares them; it first applies matchSchema on the first two tuples and then iteratively applies matchSchema on the previously obtained regular expression and each new tuple. Algorithm schemaFinding1 works on-line, using a buffer of size bounded by the size of the longest encoded tuple. Since matchSchema runs in polynomial time, the overall computation is polynomial.

3.2   Schema Finding with Loose Mark-Up

Consider now the schema finding problem in the case of loose mark-up encodings. In this case, empty sets are encoded simply by the start and end tags, so that their inner structure is not visible. Algorithm matchSchema fails on instances containing empty sets under loose encoding.

We define the notion of *empty-set free template* as a template T such that all subtrees of T corresponding to set-instance templates have cardinality greater than 0. A template is said to have *empty sets* otherwise. The following proposition justifies the use of Algorithm matchSchema on loose mark-up encodings.

Proposition 4. *Given a loose mark-up encoding function, enc, and two regular expressions, e_1, e_2 corresponding to encodings of homogeneous templates T_1, T_2, call e' the output of* matchSchema *on e_1, e_2; then: (i) if both T_1, T_2 are empty-set free templates, then $e' = \text{LUB}(T_1, T_2)$; (ii) if only one of T_1, T_2 is empty-set free, then $e' = null$.*

Based on Proposition 4, we can develop a polynomial on-line strategy for solving the schema-finding problem with loose mark-up encoding, with a slightly more demanding notion of richness, and a larger buffer. We say that a set of instances $\mathcal{I}$ of a type σ is *strongly rich* for σ if the subset of $\mathcal{I}$ of empty-set free instances is rich for σ. Intuitively, as far as sets are concerned, this corresponds to requiring that, for each set subtree of σ, there are at least two different non-empty cardinalities.

In this case, an on-line algorithm – let us call it schemaFinding2 – for solving the schema-finding problem in case of loose mark-up encoding can be informally described as follows; suppose $e_1, \ldots, e_n$ denote the input:

1. schemaFinding2 works on a data structure which is an array of templates, Templ, which initially contains e_1;
2. each e_i, $i = 2, \ldots, n$ is sequentially compared with templates in Templ using Algorithm matchSchema; we say that an e_i matches a template T if matchSchema(T, e_i) is not null; if a matching template is found, the match is recorded and the next instance is examined; if no matching template is found in Templ, e_i is added to Templ as a new template;
3. at the end, several regular expressions will be generated in Templ; if the input was strongly rich, there is at least one expression e_σ in which all sets have been marked; a simple scan of Templ allows to identify e_σ, since it is the expression with the maximum number of marked sets (corresponding to +-subexpressions); by replacing each + with * in e_σ, we have a grammar for parsing encoded instances and build representatives.

The difference between algorithms schemaFinding1 and schemaFinding2 is that the latter has a buffer-size bounded by the size of the loaded tuples (versus the size of a single tuple) and its running time is bounded by a polynomial in the size of the loaded tuples.

4   Schema Finding on the Web

Frequently, Web sites have a rather tight structure; for example, a large number of organizations are now providing a Web access to their information systems and databases. Pages are generated on-the-fly by executing queries on the database and returning results in HTML format, which clearly reflect the regularities in the initial database. However, schema finding techniques are needed to re-discover such regularities in files.

We claim that the techniques presented in this paper, enriched by simple heuristics, can effectively support schema finding on the Web. The notion of mark-up encoding is in fact inspired by SGML-like mark-up languages, of which HTML is an example. In these languages, *tags* – i.e., clearly identifiable pieces of code – are used to mark data inside the document, with two main goals: defining the logical role of a piece of information (like titles, paragraphs, lists etc.) and contribute to the layout on the browser. Consider for example a university department Web site which has been generated automatically starting from a database, a case that is becoming rather frequent. Suppose, for example, the database contains a nested relation *Professor* $\{[Name, email, ResearchGroup, Courses: \{[Code, Title]\}]\}$, and that for each professor, i.e., for each tuple in the relation, an HTML page like the following has been generated:

```
<HTML><BODY BGCOLOR="FFFFFF">
<H1><IMG SRC="deptsymbol.gif">
        John Doe </H1>
<TT> doe@inf.uniroma3.it </TT>
<HR><A HREF="db.html">
        Database Group </A>
<HR><UL>
  <LI><B> OS134 </B>
        <I> Operating Systems </I>
  <LI><B> DB201 </B>
        <I> Databases </I>
  <LI>...
</UL></BODY> </HTML>
```

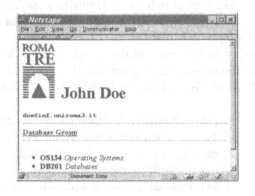

These HTML pages can be easily turned into mark-up encodings of the orig-inal tuples. In fact, roughly speaking, tags are used in the page to encode the original database structure, and strings to encode data. First, constants in the database are strings, i.e, words in the latin alphabet (let us denote it Σ_{latin}) and are therefore encoded by themselves, that is, function δ is the identity function. Second, we may use a simple pre-processing of HTML code to distinguish tags from other strings and replace the former with special tokens from an alphabet Σ_{tag}. Note that this has to be done with special care, since URLs, i.e., refer-ences to other pages, are embedded inside tags <A> and </A>; since URLs are to be considered as meaningful attributes of a page, the tokenization process should extract URLs from <A> tags and treat them as strings in the data alpha-bet, Σ_{latin}. A similar treatment is needed for images. In this way, pages in our departmental site are transformed into strings over $(\Sigma_{latin} \cup \Sigma_{tag})^*$ which are actually mark-up encodings, according to the definition given in Section 2.

Now, simple heuristics can be used to identify collections of pages with homogeneous structure inside the site; we will get to this later on in this section; for now, suppose that in the department site there is a page containing the list of all professors, with links to their respective pages, which can thus be easily identified. We can run our algorithms on such collection of pre-processed pages, and derive the following grammar, from which the nested schema is easily found:

```
<HTML> <BODY BGCOLOR="FFFFFF">
<H1><IMG SRC="deptsymbol.gif"> Σ*latin </H1><HR>
<TT> Σ*latin </TT> <A HREF=" Σ*latin "> Σ*latin </A>
<HR><UL> (<LI><B> Σ*latin </B> <I> Σ*latin </I>)* </UL>
</BODY> </HTML>
```

After this schema has been derived, a human operator can examine the schema and – by looking at actual pages on the site – associate a semantics to each attribute, allowing in this way to tell names from e-mails. Note also that a parser for the grammar is a natural wrapper for the pages.

It might be argued that the example above has a rather strong separation between data and structure in the page. Indeed, in many cases, this separation will be less strict. In fact, to improve readability, often the *role* of data inside a page is marked not only using tags, but also by means of attribute names, comments, remarks. With respect to the HTML page above, beside tags, also constant strings – like "e-mail", "Research Group", "List of courses" – could be used in the encoding. The presence of these "metadata" can somehow complicate the schema finding process, since pages will contain pieces of information that are not in the original database. Interestingly, the techniques developed in Section 3 allow to deal correctly with these situations. In fact, our algorithms will detect that all pages of professors contain the same constant strings, which therefore represent metadata and can be excluded from the schema. (These strings common to all pages can be nicely used instead to automatically suggest a semantics for attributes.)

As mentioned above, another important issue in this context consists in finding groups of homogeneous pages in a site, which can then be processed by the algorithms. There are several empirical ways to do this: for example, by taking collections of pages inside the same physical directory, or all pages linked to the same list. Also, several tools exist that navigate a site and produce a map of the site content, thus giving a graphical representation of the site topology, which may help in identifying homogeneous groups of pages. Let us briefly mention that, under the reasonable assumption that pages containing different information do have different features, our algorithms can be easily extended in such a way as to load the whole site, compare pages and cluster them in different types. In fact, it is easy to see that, whenever two pages of different types, containing perhaps different tags are compared, the algorithms returns a null common schema, thus identifying the mismatch.

5 Conclusion

The algorithms have only been tested on a few samples yet. Nevertheless, we are rather optimistic. Indeed, the number of tuples that are necessary to recover the schema of a nested relation seems very low. Consider random instances with a probability p that, for a given label α, two instances have all sets with label α of equal cardinality. Then, the probability that a collection of n instances has all sets with label α of the same cardinality is $(1 - p^{n-1})$. Assuming that the probabilities are independent for different labels, then, the probability, that a collection of n instances with k set labels is set-rich, is $(1 - p^{n-1})^k$. So, for example if $p = \frac{1}{2}$, the probability that the schema of a relation with 5 sets in its type is found after looking at 10 tuples is 99%! The previous observation leads to a linear time algorithm for extracting the schema and loading the tuples in the right format. Indeed, once the schema is obtained (in an amount of time which in average depends only upon the schema size), checking that a tuple is of the right form, and loading it can be done in linear time.

In the present paper, we have concentrated on abstract data consisting of nested relations. A natural and useful extension would be to allow union types and therefore heterogeneous sets to model semi-structured data [Abi97] which, in this context, seems fundamental. The algorithms developed here can be adapted to nested heterogeneous sets with the following outcome. We were able to extract a type which is subsumed by the original nested type with union, but we have no formal results yet in this case.

We are now implementing our algorithms as part of a system for schema-finding on the Web. The system downloads HTML pages from a target Web site and tries to infer their common structure. Although the techniques we propose are far from being a final solution to this problem, our experiences tell us that they represent a promising starting point. In fact, in all cases in which pages do comply with a tight structure, our algorithms have been able to correctly recover the type. Also, we show that in average only a small number of tuples is needed to identify the schema, thus providing a linear behavior of the method. We are now working to extend the framework in order to handle pages with "exceptions" [CM98], i.e., pages containing features that slightly depart from the common type.

Acknowledgments The authors would like to thank Pino Di Battista for helpful comments on on-line algorithms and Valter Crescenzi, who helped in the implementation of the algorithms.

References

[AB95]   S. Abiteboul and C. Beeri. On the power of languages for the manipulation of complex objects. *The VLDB Journal*, 4(4):117–138, 1995.

[Abi97]   S. Abiteboul. Querying semi-structured data. In *ICDT'97*.

[ACC+97]   S. Abiteboul, S. Cluet, V. Christophides, T. Milo, G. Moerkotte, and J. Siméon. Querying documents in object databases. *Journal of Digital Libraries*, 1(1):5–19, April 1997.

[Ade98]   B. Adelberg. NoDoSE – a tool for semi-automatically extracting structured and semistructured data from text documents. In *SIGMOD'98*.

[AHV94]   S. Abiteboul, R. Hull, and V. Vianu. *Foundations of Databases*. Addison-Wesley, 1994.

[AK97]   N. Ashish and C. Knoblock. Wrapper generation for semistructured Internet sources. In *Proceedings of the Workshop on the Management of Semistructured Data (in conjunction with SIGMOD'97)*.

[AM97]   P. Atzeni and G. Mecca. Cut and Paste. In *PODS'97*.

[AMM97]   P. Atzeni, G. Mecca, and P. Merialdo. To Weave the Web. In *VLDB'97*.

[Bri98]   D. Brin. Extracting patterns and relations from the World Wide Web. In *Proceedings of the Workshop on the Web and Databases (WebDB'98) (in conjunction with EDBT'98)*.

[CM98]   V. Crescenzi and G. Mecca. Grammars have exceptions. *Information Systems*, 1998. Special Issue on Semistructured Data, to appear.

[CR94]   M. Crochemore and W. Rytter. *Text Algorithms*. Oxford University Press, 1994.

[GV95]   S. Grumbach and V. Vianu. Tractable query languages for complex object databases. *Journal of Computer and System Sciences*, 51(2):149–167, 1995.

[HGMC+97] J. Hammer, H. Garcia-Molina, J. Cho, R. Aranha, and A. Crespo. Extracting semistructured information from the Web. In *Proceedings of the Workshop on the Management of Semistructured Data (in conjunction with ACM SIGMOD, 1997)*.

[HK93]   K. Han and H. J. Kim. Prediction of common folding structures of homologous RNAs. *Nucleic Acids Research*, 21(5):1251–1257, 1993.

[Hul88]   R. Hull. A survey of theoretical research on typed complex database objects. In J. Paredaens, editor, *Databases*, pages 193–256. Academic Press, 1988.

[ISO86]   ISO. International Organization for Standardization. ISO-8879: Information Processing – Text and Office Systems - Standard Generalized Markup Language (SGML), October 1986.

[KWD97]   N. Kushmerick, D. S. Weld, and R. Doorenbos. Wrapper induction for information extraction. In *International Joint Conference on Artificial Intelligence (IJCAI'97)*, 1997.

[Las98]   E. R. Lassettre. Olympic records for data at the 1998 Nagano Games. In *SIGMOD'98*. Industrial Session.

[MMM98]   G. Mecca, A. Mendelzon, and P. Merialdo. Efficient queries over Web views. In *EDBT'98*.

[Nag]   Nagano 1998 Winter Olympics Web site. http://www.nagano.olympic.-org.

[NAM98]   S. Nestorov, S. Abiteboul, and R. Motwani. Extracting schema from semistructured data. In *SIGMOD*, 1998.

[Oho90]   A. Ohori. Semantics of types for database objects. *Theoretical Computer Science*, 76(1):53–91, 1990.

[Pap94]   C. H. Papadimitriou. *Computational Complexity*. Addison-Wesley, 1994.

[Wat89]   M.S. Waterman. *Mathematical Methods for DNA Sequences*. CRC Press, 1989.

Tableau Techniques for Querying Information Sources through Global Schemas

Gösta Grahne[1] and Alberto O. Mendelzon[2]

[1] Department of Computer Science, Concordia University
Montreal, Quebec, Canada H3G 1M8
grahne@cs.concordia.ca
[2] Department of Computer Science, University of Toronto
Toronto, Ontario, Canada M5S 3H5
mendel@cs.toronto.edu

Abstract. The foundational homomorphism techniques introduced by Chandra and Merlin for testing containment of conjunctive queries have recently attracted renewed interest due to their central role in information integration applications. We show that generalizations of the classical *tableau* representation of conjunctive queries are useful for computing query answers in information integration systems where information sources are modeled as views defined on a virtual global schema. We consider a general situation where sources may or may not be known to be correct and complete. We characterize the set of answers to a global query and give algorithms to compute a finite representation of this possibly infinite set, as well as its *certain* and *possible* approximations. We show how to rewrite a global query in terms of the sources in two special cases, and show that one of these is equivalent to the Information Manifold rewriting of Levy *et al.*

1 Introduction

Information Integration systems [Ull97] aim to provide a uniform query interface to multiple heterogeneous sources. One particular and useful way of viewing these systems, first proposed within the Information Manifold project [LRO96], is to postulate a *global schema* (called a world view) that provides a unifying data model for all the information sources. A query processor is in charge of accepting queries written in terms of this global schema, translating them to queries on the appropriate sources, and assembling the answers into a global answer. Each source is modeled as a *materialized view* defined in terms of the global relations, which are virtual. Note the reversal of the classical model: instead of thinking of views as virtual artifacts defined on stored relations, we think of the views as stored, and the relations that the views are defined on as virtual. [1]

---

[1] Whether the views are actually stored at each source or materialized by other means, and whether they consist of relations or semi-structured objects or files are issues irrelevant to our discussion and hidden from the query processor by appropriate wrappers.

Catriel Beeri, Peter Buneman (Eds.): ICDT'99, LNCS 1540, pp. 332–347, 1998.

A question of semantics now arises: what is the meaning of a query? Since a query is expressed in terms of the global schema, and the sources implicitly represent an instance of this global schema, it would be natural –at least conceptually– to reconstruct the global database represented by the views and apply the query to this global database. There are at least two issues that must be resolved for this to work.

First, the database represented by a set of sources may not be unique; in fact, it may not even exist. For two trivial examples: first, suppose we have a single information source, which is defined as the projection on attribute A of the global binary relation $R(A, B)$. For any given set of tuples stored at the source, there are many (perhaps an infinite number) of possible global databases. Second, suppose we have not one, but two sources, both storing the projection on A as before; one contains the single tuple $\langle a_1 \rangle$, and the other one the single tuple $\langle a_2 \rangle$; then there is *no* global database whose projections equal these two sources. In sum, the first issue is: what database or databases are represented by a given set of sources?

Second, suppose we have identified the set of databases that are represented by a given set of sources. Applying the query to each database and producing all possible answers may be impossible (e.g. if there is an infinite number of such answers) or undesirable. The second issue is: how do we produce a single compact representation of these multiple answers, or an approximation to them if we so desire?

In this paper, we explore answers to both questions. Before overviewing the results, let us make the example above more concrete. Consider a schema for storing information about the first round of the World Cup Soccer Tournament. Suppose global relation *Team(Country,Group)* represents a list of all teams giving the name of the country and the group to which the country has been assigned for first round play.

Suppose first that the only source, S_{Team}, stores a unary relation listing all the countries that are participating in the first round. The corresponding view mapping is given by the conjunctive query:

$$S_{Team}(x) \leftarrow Team(x, y).$$

What global databases are represented by S_{Team}? They are all the relations *Team* such that the view mapping applied to *Team* produces exactly the given instance of S_{Team}, that is:

$$S_{Team} = \pi_{Country}(Team).$$

In this case, we say the view is both *sound* and *complete*.

On the other hand, suppose the only source is S_{Qual}, which contains the list of all teams that participated in the qualifying round. This is a strict superset of the teams that will actually be playing in the tournament. Since the global schema says nothing about the qualifying round, the only reasonable view mapping is still

$$S_{Qual}(x) \leftarrow Team(x, y).$$

However, now we understand that this is just an approximation, and that the actual database could be any relation whose projection on *Country* produces a *subset* of the source S_{Qual},[2] that is:

$$S_{Qual} \supseteq \pi_{Country}(Team).$$

In this case, we say the view is *complete* (since it lists every possible team) but not sound (since it lists teams that are not in the first round.)

Finally, suppose the only source is S_{Tube}, listing those teams whose games will be televised. Again, the best way to represent the view mapping (since there is no information about television in the global schema) is by

$$S_{Tube}(x) \leftarrow Team(x, y).$$

In this case, every team listed in S_{Tube} corresponds to some tuple in the ideal *Team* relation, but there are tuples in this ideal relation not represented in S_{Tube}. Thus, we take as the set of represented databases all the relations *Team* that satisfy

$$S_{Tube} \subseteq \pi_{Country}(Team).$$

In this case, we say the view is sound, but not complete.

In sum, we will annotate each source, not only with the view mapping that is associated with it, but also with the knowledge of whether this view is guaranteed to be sound, or complete, or both. We will say a global database is *represented* by a given set of (annotated) sources when applying the view mappings to this database produces a subset of every complete source and a superset of every sound source.

In the example, if we had *both* the complete source S_{Qual} and the sound source S_{Tube}, the databases represented by them would be all those that contained *at least* all the countries in S_{Tube} and *at most* those in S_{Qual}. If we had the sound and complete source S_{Team} (with or without the other two), then databases would be constrained to contain exactly the teams listed in this source. Note that it is possible for a given set of source instances to be inconsistent with the source annotations; for example, if S_{Team} mentions a team not listed in S_{Qual}, or omits one mentioned in S_{Tube}. In such a case, the set of represented databases is empty.

The outline of the paper is as follows. In Section 2 we formalize the model above. In order to finitely represent infinite sets of databases, we introduce *templates*, and show how to associate with each set of source instances a template that characterizes all databases represented by the sources. A template is a vector of consisting of tableaux [ASU79] and a set of constraints. Our constraints are related to the egd's of Beeri and Vardi [BV81]. In Section 3 we present our results. First we give a syntactic characterization of consistent sets of sources in terms of their templates. Then, we give an algorithm for evaluating a conjunctive

---

[2] Actually, only relations with 32 tuples in them qualify, since there are 32 teams in the first round, but we ignore this level of detail in our model.

query, expressed on the global schema, using only the given source instances. The algorithm uses the template generated from the source instances and produces as output another template that describes all the answers, one for each represented database. We also show how to compute two natural approximations to this set: the union (the approximation by *possibility*) and the intersection (the approximation by *certainty*) of all the answers.

Next, we study the complexity of conjunctive query evaluation. We show that consistency is coNP-complete in general, but consistency and query evaluation become polynomial when we have only sound or only complete sources. These results extend and generalize earlier ones of Abiteboul and Duschka [AD98].

Finally, in Section 4 we show how to rewrite a query on the global schema in terms of the sources, in two cases: when all sources are sound and the certain semantics is of interest, and when all sources are complete and the possible semantics is sought. This is an optimization over building the template and applying the generic method, since the cost of building the template is linear in the size of all the source instances but there may be only a few out of many sources that are relevant to the query; the rewritings will only use the relevant sources. We show that the all-sound, certain-answer rewriting is equivalent to (although different from) the Information Manifold rewriting described by Levy *et al.* in [LM*95] without any formal justification. In fact, this was the original motivation for our work: providing semantics for the mysterious Information Manifold algorithm.

2   The Model

In this section we first introduce global databases. A global database is a standard multirelational database. We then introduce database templates, a tool for representing sets of global databases. Finally, we define the concept of source collections, modeling a set of sources that we want to amalgamate.

For basic terminology and concepts regarding databases we refer to [AHV95].

Global Databases

Let **rel** be a countably infinite set $\{R, S, \ldots, R_1, R_2, \ldots, S_1, S_2 \ldots\}$ of *global relation names*, Let **dom** be a countably infinite set $\{a, b, \ldots, a_1, a_2, \ldots, b_1, b_2, \ldots\}$ of *constants*, and let **var** be a countably infinite set $\{x, y, \ldots, x_1, x_2, \ldots, y_1, y_2, \ldots\}$ of *variables*.

Associated with each relation name R is a positive integer $arity(R)$, which is the arity of R. A *fact* over R is an expression of the form $R(a_1, \ldots, a_k)$, where $k = arity(R)$.

Let $\mathbf{R} = \{R_1, R_2, \ldots, R_n\}$ be a set of *global relation names*. A set of global relation names will sometimes also be called a *global schema*. A *global database* D over $\mathbf{R}$ is a is a finite set of facts, each fact being over some $R_i \in \mathbf{R}$.

Template Databases

We now introduce templates, which are a generalization of tableaux intended to represent concisely a large or infinite number of possible database instances.

Let R be a global relation name. An *atom* over R is an expression of the form $R(e_1, \ldots, e_k)$, where $k = arity(R)$ and e_i is in **dom** $\cup$ **var**. Note that an atom containing only constants is the same as a fact.

Let **R** $= \{R_1, R_2, \ldots, R_n\}$ be a set of global relation names. A *tableau* T over **R** is a finite set of atoms over the R_i:s. Note that the same variable might appear in several atoms in T.

A *constraint* over **R** is a pair (U, Θ), where U is a tableau over **R** and Θ is a finite set of substitutions of the form $\{x_1/a_1, x_2/a_2, \ldots, x_p/a_p\}$, where all the x_i:s are distinct variables appearing in U.

Finally, a *database template* T over **R** is a tuple $\langle T_1, T_2, \ldots, T_m, C \rangle$, where each T_i is a tableau over **R** and C is a finite set of constraints over **R**.

Example 1. Let $T = \langle T_1, T_2, C \rangle$, where $T_1 = \{R(a, x), S(b, c), S(b', c)\}$, $T_2 = \{R(a', b'), S(b', c)\}$, and $C = \{(R(a, z), \{\{z/b\}, \{z/b'\}\})\}$. This template contains two tableaux, and one constraint with two substitutions.

A *valuation*, is a finite partial mapping from **var** $\cup$ **dom** to **dom** that is the identity on **dom**. Valuations, like $x_i \mapsto a_i$, for $i \in [1, p]$, will usually be given in the form of substitutions $\{x_1/a_1, \ldots, x_p/a_p\}$. The identity on constants is omitted in this notation. Two valuations are *compatible* if they agree on the variables on which both are defined.

A database template T on schema **R** $= \{R_1, R_2, \ldots, R_n\}$ represents a set of global databases on **R**. This set is denoted $rep(T)$, and it is defined by

$$rep(T) = \{D \; : \; \text{there is a valuation } \vartheta \text{ and a tableau } T_i \text{ in } T,$$
$$\text{such that } \vartheta(T_i) \subseteq D,$$
$$\text{and for all } (U, \Theta) \in C \text{ in } T, \text{ and valuations } \sigma,$$
$$\text{if } \sigma(U) \subseteq D \text{ then there is a } \theta \in \Theta \text{ such that } \sigma \text{ and } \theta \text{ are compatible}\}.$$

The definition says that a database D is represented by template T if there is a tableau T_i in T, such that when all variables in T_i are replaced by some constants, the set of facts thus obtained is a subset of D. This is the "sound" part of T. Furthermore, the database D has to satisfy the "completeness" restrictions encoded in the constraints (U, Θ) in C: Whenever it is possible to embed the tableau U in D, the mapping used for the embedding must be extendible to one of the substitutions in Θ.

Example 2. Consider the template $T = \langle T_1, T_2, C \rangle$ from Example 1. The template T represents the three databases $\{R(a, b), S(b, c), S(b', c)\}$, $\{R(a, b'), S(b, c), S(b', c)\}$, $\{R(a', b'), S(b', c)\}$, and any of their supersets satisfying the constraint saying that whenever a occurs in the first component of R, then the second component has to be b or b'. For instance, $\{R(a, b), R(a, b'), S(b, c), S(b', c)\}$ is a database in $rep(T)$, while $\{R(a, c), R(a, b'), S(b, c), S(b', c)\}$ is not in $rep(T)$.

Note the disjunctive role of the several tableaux in a template, similar to the *flocks* of [FKUV86]. Note also that the constraints can encode the pure closed world assumption. For instance, the closed world interpretation of a relation with the two facts $R(a, b)$ and $R(c, d)$, can be expressed as the template $\langle T, C \rangle$, with $T = \{R(a, b), R(c, d)\}$, and $C = \{(\{R(x, y), \{\{x/a, y/b\}, \{x/c, y/d\}\})\}$.

Chasing a Tableau

We now introduce a binary relation $\mathcal{R}_{(U, \{\theta\})}$ between tableaux, where the relation is parameterized by a constraint with a singleton binding set. The idea is that T and T' are related by $\mathcal{R}_{(U, \{\theta\})}$ when U can be embedded into T by a valuation and then this valuation and θ are applied to T to obtain T'. More formally, we say that U *applies* to T through σ when there is a valuation σ such that $\sigma(U) \subseteq T$. Then T *satisfies* $(U, \{\theta\})$ wrt σ if U applies to T and $\theta(U)$ and $\sigma(U)$ can be unified. Let T and T' be tableaux. Then T $\mathcal{R}_{(U, \{\theta\})}$ T', if and only if U applies to T through σ and, either T satisfies $(U, \{\theta\})$ wrt σ, in which case $T' = mgu(\theta(U), \sigma(U))(T)$, or T does not satisfy $(U, \{\theta\})$ wrt σ, in which case $T' = \bot$. [3]

Then let (U, Θ) be a general constraint. We define $\mathcal{R}_{(U, \Theta)} = \bigcup_{\theta \in \Theta} \mathcal{R}_{(U, \{\theta\})}$. If C is a set of constraints we set $\mathcal{R}_C = \bigcup_{(U, \Theta) \in C} \mathcal{R}_{(U, \Theta)}$. Finally, let $\mathcal{R}_C^*$ be the transitive closure of $\mathcal{R}_C$.

It is straightforward to show that $\mathcal{R}_C$ is well-founded, i. e. for any tableau T, the set $\{T' : T \mathcal{R}_C^* T'\}$ is finite. This set therefore contains some maximal elements, i. e. tableaux T', such that for no tableau T'' does $T' \mathcal{R}_C T''$ hold. We can now define the *chase* of a tableau T with a set of constraints C, denoted $C(T)$, to be the set of maximal elements in $\{T' : T \mathcal{R}_C^* T'\}$, provided the last set is nonempty. Otherwise $C(T) = \{T\}$. In the template $\langle T_1, T_2, C \rangle$ from Example 1 we have $C(T_1) = \{\{R(a, b), S(b, c), S(b'c)\}, \{R(a, b'), S(b, c), S(b'c)\}\}$, and $C(T_2) = T_2$. For another example, let $T = \{R(a, x), R(y, d)\}$, and let $C = (\{R(a, u)\}, \{u/b\}, \{u/b'\}) \cup (\{R(w, d)\}, \{w/c\}, \{w/c'\})$, Then one maximal chain in the "chasing sequence" is

$$\{R(a, x), R(y, d)\} \mathcal{R}_C \{R(a, b), R(y, d)\} \mathcal{R}_C \{R(a, b), R(c, d)\}.$$

Another maximal chain is

$$\{R(a, x), R(y, d)\} \mathcal{R}_C \{R(x, b), R(c', d)\} \mathcal{R}_C \{R(a, b), R(c', d)\}.$$

It is easy to verify that

$$C(T) = \{\{R(a, b), R(c, d)\},$$
$$\{R(a, b), R(c', d)\},$$
$$\{R(a, b'), R(c, d)\},$$
$$\{R(a, b'), R(c', d)\}\}.$$

In general, the chase has the following property.

---

[3] *mgu* means *most general unifier*, see e. g. [AHV95], and $\bot$ represents the inconsistent tableau; no U can be applied to $\bot$, and no valuation can be applied to $\bot$.

Theorem 1. *Let* $T = \langle T_1, \ldots, T_n, C \rangle$ *be a database template, and let* $\{T'_1, \ldots, T'_s\}$ $= \bigcup_{i \in [1,n]} C(T_i)$. *Then* $rep(T) = rep(\langle T'_1, \ldots, T'_s, C \rangle)$.

A fundamental question for a template database T is whether $rep(T)$ is non-empty, that is, whether T is consistent. The next theorem gives a syntactic condition.

Theorem 2. *Let* $T = \langle T_1, \ldots, T_n, C \rangle$ *be a database template. Then* $rep(T) \neq \emptyset$ *if and only if there is a tableau* T_i *in* T, *such that* $\perp \notin C(T_i)$.

Source Collections

Let **loc** be a countably infinite set $\{V, U, \ldots V_1, V_2, \ldots, U_1, U_2, \ldots\}$ of *local relation names*. The local relation names have arities, and atoms over local relation names are defined in the same way as atoms over global relation names.

A *view definition* φ is a conjunctive query

$$head(\varphi) \leftarrow body(\varphi),$$

where $body(\varphi)$ is a sequence $b_1, b_2, \ldots, b_n$, where each b_i is an atom over a global relation name, and $head(\varphi)$ is an atom over a local relation name V. We also assume that all variables occurring in $head(\varphi)$ also occur in $body(\varphi)$, i. e. that the query φ is *safe*. The conjunctive query φ can be applied to a database D in the usual way, resulting in a set of facts $\varphi(D)$ over V.

A *view extension* for a view φ is a finite set of facts over the relation name V in the head of the view definition φ. Such an extension will be denoted v.

A *source* S is triple consisting of a view definition φ, a set containing one or both of the labels *open* and *closed*, and a view extension v for φ. Sources are called open, closed, or clopen (closed and open) according to their labels. Sometimes open sources will be called *sound*, and closed sources called *complete*. Clopen sources will be called sound and complete.

A *source collection* S is a finite set of sources. The *(global) schema* of S, denoted $sch(S)$ is the set consisting of all the global relation names occurring in the bodies of the defining views of the sources in S. The *description* of S, denoted $desc(S)$ is obtained from S by dropping the extension from every triple in S. The *extension* of a source collection S, denoted $ext(S)$, is the union of all view extensions in it. In other words, a source collection S has *two* "schemas," $sch(S)$ which is the "global world view," and $desc(S)$, which describes the sources' soundness/completeness and defining views. Source collections S have *one* extension, $ext(S)$, which for each source S_i is a set of facts over the defining view-head relation name.

A source collection S defines a set of possible databases, denoted $poss(S)$, as follows:

$$poss(S) = \{D \text{ over } sch(S) :$$
$$v_i \subseteq \varphi_i(D) \text{ for all open sources } S_i \in S$$
$$v_j \supseteq \varphi_j(D) \text{ for all closed sources } S_j \in S\}$$
$$v_k = \varphi_k(D) \text{ for all clopen sources } S_k \in S\}$$

Note that there are source collections, such as S containing the two sources $\langle\{V_1(x) \leftarrow R(x,y), \{open\}, \{V_1(a)\}\rangle$, and $\langle V_2(u) \leftarrow R(u,w), \{closed\}, \{V_2(b)\}\rangle$, for which $poss(S)$ is empty. This is because the extension of V_1 requires that there be a tuple in every possible database with an a in its first column, while the extension of V_2 requires that every possible database must have only b's in its first column. Such source collections are called *inconsistent*. If $poss(S)$ is nonempty the source collection is said to be *consistent*. We will see in Theorem 4 below that consistency of source collections can be characterized syntactically through database templates and the chase.

3   Querying Source Collections

In this section we first show how templates can be used to query source collections, by extending conjunctive queries to operate over templates. We then analyze the computational complexity of querying source collections. The complexity turns out to be coNP-complete.

Query Evaluation

Let S be source collection, and Q a conjunctive query, such that the atoms in the body of Q are atoms over relation names in $sch(S)$, and the head of Q is an atom over an relation name in the set $\{ans, ans_1, ans_2, \ldots\}$. Now Q applied to S defines the following set of possible answers:

$$Q(S) = \{Q(D) \; : \; D \in poss(S)\}.$$

This (exact) answer can be approximated from below as

$$Q_*(S) = \bigcap_{D \in poss(S)} Q(D),$$

and from above as

$$Q^*(S) = \bigcup_{D \in poss(S)} Q(D).$$

The problem begging for a solution is how to compute the answers to queries on source collections. Towards this end we shall first construct a database template over the global relation names. This database template will represent the set of possible databases for S. Let $\mathbf{R}$ be a global schema. We define a function (T, C) from sources with defining view φ, where the body of φ consists of atoms over relation names in $\mathbf{R}$, to template databases over $\mathbf{R}$. Given a source $S_i = \langle \varphi_i, labels, v_i \rangle$, we set $T(S_i) = \{t \; : \; t \text{ in } body(\varphi_i)\theta \text{ and } head(\varphi_i)\theta = u$, for some $u \in v_i$ and assignment $\theta\}$, provided $open \in labels$. Otherwise $T(S_i) = \emptyset$. If $closed \in labels$ we set $C(S_i) = (U, \Theta)$, where U consists of all atoms in the body of φ_i, and $\Theta = \{\theta \; : \; head(\varphi_i)\theta = u$, for some $u \in v_i\}$. Otherwise $C(S_i) = \emptyset$. Finally, we set

$$T(S) = \left\langle \bigcup_{S_i \in S} T(S_i), \bigcup_{S_i \in S} C(S_i) \right\rangle.$$

Example 3. Consider $S = \{S_1, S_2, S_3\}$, where $S_1 = \langle V_1(u, w) \leftarrow S(u, w), \{open\},$
$\{V_1(b, c), V_1(b', c)\}\rangle$, $S_2 = \langle V_2(v) \leftarrow R(v, x), \{open\}, \{V_2(a)\}\rangle$, and $S_3 = \langle V_3(z)$
$\leftarrow R(a, z), \{closed\}, \{V_3(b), V_3(b')\}\rangle$. Then $\mathcal{T}(S) = \langle T_1, C \rangle$, where $T_1 = \{R(a, x),$
$S(b, c), S(b', c)\}$, and $C = \{(R(a, z), \{\{z/b\}, \{z/b'\}\})\}$.

Note that T_1 and C above are from Example 1. The $\mathcal{T}$-function will always
construct templates with a single tableau. Templates with multiple tableaux
are produced by the chase process or by query evaluation. Query evaluation is
explained below.

The database templates constructed by the function $\mathcal{T}$ have the following
desirable property.

Theorem 3. $rep(\mathcal{T}(S)) = poss(S)$.

We will now return to the issue of consistency of a source collection. Using
the characterization in Theorem 2 together with Theorem 3 we can prove the
following.

Theorem 4. *Let S be a source collection and $\mathcal{T}(S) = \langle T, C \rangle$. Then S is consistent if and only if $\perp \notin C(T)$.*

Corollary 1. *If no source in a collection S is closed, then S is consistent. Likewise, if no source in a collection S is open, then S is consistent.*

For an example of an inconsistent source collection, consider the collection
S from Section 2, where S contains the two sources $\langle \{V_1(x) \leftarrow R(x, y), \{open\},$
$\{V_1(a)\}\rangle$, and $\langle V_2(u) \leftarrow R(u, w), \{closed\}, \{V_2(b)\}\rangle$. We will now have $\mathcal{T}(S) =$
$\langle T, C \rangle$, where $T = \{R(a, y)\}$, and $C = \langle \{R(u, w)\}, \{\{u/b\}\}\rangle$. It is easy to see
that $C(T) = \perp$, and that $poss(S)$ is empty.

We then return to the issue of evaluating queries over global relations given
only the local relations in a source collection S. Since we are able to construct
a database template $\mathcal{T}$ representing all databases in $poss(S)$ it is is natural
to extend the standard query evaluation mechanism to operate on database
templates.

Let $\mathcal{T} = \langle T_1, \ldots, T_n, C \rangle$ be a database template over **R**. Given a conjunctive
query $Q = ans(x) \leftarrow R_1(x_1), \ldots, R_n(x_m)$ where each R_i is a relation name in
R, our evaluation proceeds as follows. Let $\{T_1', \ldots, T_s'\} = \bigcup_{i \in [1, n]} C(T_i)$. Then
define $\widehat{Q}(\mathcal{T}) = \langle T_1'', \ldots, T_q'', \emptyset \rangle$, where each T_j'', $j \in [1, q]$ is equal to a $\widehat{Q}_\kappa(T_i')$,
for some $i \in [1, s]$ and substitution κ. Here

$$\widehat{Q}_\kappa(T_i') = \{ans(x)\sigma : \sigma \text{ is an } mgu \text{ for } \{R_i(x_i)\}_{i=1}^m \text{ and subset of } T_i',$$
$$\text{and } \sigma \text{ is compatible with } \kappa\},$$

Note that there can be only finitely many distinct T_j'':s (modulo renaming). In
computing the unifiers used in $\widehat{Q}_\kappa(T_i')$ we always try to substitute variables or
constants from T_i' for variables in the query. For the inconsistent tableau $\perp$, we
set $\widehat{Q}_\kappa(\perp) = \perp$.

As an illustration, suppose our query Q is $ans(z, u, w) \leftarrow R(z, u), S(u, w)$. If our database template T is $\langle T_1, T_2, C \rangle$ from Example 1, then the query evaluation proceeds as follows: First we chase the tableaux in T with C obtaining the three tableaux $\{R(a, b), S(b, c), S(b', c)\}$, $\{R(a, b'), S(b, c), S(b'c)\}$, and $\{R(a', b'), S(b', c)\}$. Then we apply $\widehat{Q}_\kappa$ to each of these tableaux, getting the results $\{ans(a, b, c)\}$, $\{ans(a, b', c)\}$, and $\{ans(a', b', c)\}$. In this example we only need to use one substitution κ, namely the identity substitution $\{\}$. For another example, let $T = \langle T, C \rangle$, where $T = \{R(a, x), R(a', x), S(b, c), S(y, c')\}$, and $C = \emptyset$. For our example query Q, we get $\widehat{Q}_{\{x/b\}}(T) = \{ans(a, b, c), ans(a', b, c)\}$, $\widehat{Q}_{\{x/y\}}(T) = \{ans(a, y, c'), ans(a', y, c')\}$, and $\widehat{Q}_{\{\}}(T) = \emptyset$. These are all the answer tableaux; no other substitutions κ will yield more.

The query evaluation uses the constraints in that the constraints are chased into the tableaux before querying. The template resulting from the query evaluation will have the empty constraint. It is clear that we thus loose some information. However, the query result will be *coinitially* equivalent to the desired one. Two sets of databases are coinitial if the have the same set of $\subseteq$ minimal elements (see [IL84]). The coinitiality relation will be denoted $\approx$. Our extended semantics now has the following correctness property:

Theorem 5. $rep(\widehat{Q}(T)) \approx Q(rep(T))$,

where the query on the right-hand side is evaluated pointwise.

Let S be a source collection and Q be a query on $sch(S)$. Together Theorems 3 and 5 give the following method for evaluating Q on S.

Theorem 6.   *1.* $Q(S) \approx \widehat{Q}(T(S))$.
2. $Q_*(S) = \cap\, rep(\widehat{Q}(T(S)))$.
3. $Q^*(S) \approx \cup\, rep(\widehat{Q}(T(S)))$.

The Computational Complexity of Querying Sources

In general, template databases have the following complexity.

Theorem 7. *Given a database template T, testing whether $rep(T) \neq \emptyset$ is coNP-complete.*

For the lower bound we use a reduction from the non-containment of tableau queries, which is known to be a coNP-complete problem [CM77,ASU79]. Let U_1 and U_2 be tableau queries. Without loss of generality we can assume that the summary rows of U_1 and U_2 are the same, say $\langle x_1, \ldots, x_p \rangle$. Our task is to construct a template T, such that $rep(T) \neq \emptyset$ if and only if U_1 is not contained in U_2. Let therefore $T = \langle T, (U, \{\theta\}) \rangle$, where T equals the rows of U_1, except that each summary variable x_i has been substituted with a distinct constant a_i. Let U be the rows of U_2, and $\theta = \{x_1/b_1, \ldots, x_p/b_p\}$, where $a_i \neq b_i$. Now it is easy to see that T is inconsistent if and only if there is a containment mapping from U_2 to U_1.

As outlined in Theorem 6 we have a general method that given a source collection S evaluates the answer (or the exact or possible answer) on the template $\mathcal{T}(S)$. On the other hand, Theorem 7 says that a template database might have an intricate combinatorial structure. In the template resulting from query evaluation we have chased out this combinatorial structure. It is clear the the resulting template can be intractably large. The following theorem says that there probably is no way to overcome this intractability.

Theorem 8. *1. If S contains both sound and complete sources the problem of testing whether $poss(S)$ is nonempty is coNP-complete.*

2. *If S contains both sound and complete sources the problem of testing whether a given tuple t is in $Q_*(S)$ is coNP-complete.*

3. *If S contains both sound and complete sources the problem of testing whether a given tuple t is in $Q^*(S)$ is coNP-complete.*

As an aside we note that Theorem 5.1 in [AD98] falls out as a special case of Theorem 8.

If S contains only sound or only complete sources query evaluation becomes tractable.

Theorem 9. *If S contains only sound or only complete sources the consistency of $poss(S)$ as well as $Q_*(S)$ and $Q^*(S)$ can be tested/computed in time polynomial in the number of tuples in the extension of S. (In the case where $Q^*(S)$ is infinite we only report this fact, we don't output all tuples.)*

4   Query Optimization through Rewriting

In practice one would be most interested in computing $Q_*(S)$ or $Q^*(S)$. It is clear that computing $Q_*(S)$ or $Q^*(S)$ from $\widehat{Q}(\mathcal{T}(S))$ might involve a lot of redundant work, since computing $\mathcal{T}(S)$ amounts to constructing the tableaux and constraints corresponding to *all* view-extensions, whereas the global relations mentioned in the body of Q might occur in only a few view definitions. Furthermore, the query might have selections and joins that could be computed directly at the sources. Take for example the open view definitions $\varphi_1 =_{df} V_1(x,y) \leftarrow R(x,y)$, $\varphi_2 =_{df} V_2(u,v) \leftarrow S(u,v)$. and the query $Q =_{df} ans(a,z) \leftarrow R(a,w), S(w,z)$. Obviously it is more efficient to "push the selection and join," and evaluate the query $ans(a,z) \leftarrow V_1(a,w), V_2(w,z)$, on the view extensions v_1 and v_2, rather that obtaining $Q_*(S)$ from $\widehat{Q}$ computed on the tableau constructed from v_1 and v_2 and possibly a large number of other sources.

We shall thus consider the following problem:

Let $\Phi = \{\langle \varphi_1, \{.\}\rangle \ldots, \langle \varphi_n, \{.\}\rangle\}$ be a set of source descriptions where the view definitions have heads $V_1, \ldots, V_n$, and let $\{R_1, \ldots, R_m\}$ be the relation names occurring in the bodies of the φ_i:s. Given a conjunctive query Q where $body(Q)$ contains only global relation names in $\{R_1, \ldots, R_m\}$ find a query $rew(Q)$, where the body of $rew(Q)$ only mentions view relation names in $\{V_1, \ldots, V_n\}$, and $head(rew(Q))$ is compatible with $head(Q)$, such that the following condition holds: For all source collections S with $desc(S) = \Phi$ and $ext(S) = v$ it is true that

1. (Certain answer): $rew(Q)(v) = Q_*(S)$, or
2. (Possible answer): $rew(Q)(v) = Q^*(S)$.

The queries $rew(Q)$ above are called *rewritings* of Q with respect to Φ. If the rewriting satisfies condition 1 it is called a *certainty rewriting*, and if it satisfies condition 2 it is called a *possibility rewriting*.

Certainty Rewritings

Given a query Q on $\{R_1, \ldots, R_m\}$ we shall now construct the desired rewriting on $\{V_1, \ldots, V_n\}$ for the certain answer. It is easy to show, that if all views are closed, then the certain answer is always empty. We will consider the case where all views are open.

The rewriting for the certain answer can be obtained according to the following recipe: Let L be a subset of the atoms in the bodies of the view-definitions $\varphi_1, \ldots, \varphi_n$, such that L unifies with the set of atoms in $body(Q)$. Let the *mgu* that achieves this unification be θ. If θ does not equate any view variable x to any other view variable or constant, unless x appears in the head of its view, then do the following. Choose a subset $\{\varphi_{i_1}, \ldots, \varphi_{i_k}\}$ of the view queries such that every atom in L occurs in some $body(\varphi_{i_j})$, every $body(\varphi_{i_j})$ contains at least one atom in L, and such that the query

$$Q' = head(Q)\theta \leftarrow head(\varphi_{i_1})\theta, \ldots, head(\varphi_{i_k})\theta,$$

is safe (i. e. all variables in the head occur in the body). Consider now the queries Q' and

$$Q'' = head(Q)\theta \leftarrow body(\varphi_{i_1})\theta, \ldots, body(\varphi_{i_k})\theta.$$

It is clear that if Q' exists then the query Q'' is the composition of the query Q' with the view-definition $\langle \varphi_{i_1}, \ldots, \varphi_{i_k} \rangle$. Let $rew_1(Q)$ be the union of all all possible Q':s thus constructed.[4]

The query $rew_1(Q)$ is the rewriting of Q achieving the desired result. Formally we have:

Theorem 10. *Let S be a collection of open sources where $ext(S) = v$, and let Q be a query on $sch(S)$. Then*

$$rew_1(Q)(v) = Q_*(S).$$

---

[4] There is a finite number (modulo renaming) of such Q':s since each one is based on a subset L of the atoms in the bodies of the view queries, and there is a unique (up to renaming) *mgu* for each pair of atom sets. Furthermore, there is a finite number of ways of choosing a "covering" subset of the view-queries given L.

For a simple example, suppose the global database schema has one relation *Flights(Source, Destination, Airline)*. We have two open sources: The flights by Air Canada, and the ones by Canadian Airlines. The definitions of these views are $AC(x, y) \leftarrow Flights(x, y, \text{ac})$, and $CP(x', y') \leftarrow Flights(x', y', \text{cp})$. Suppose we would like to find all connections from Toronto to Jerusalem with one change of planes. The query Q is[5]

$$ans(\text{toronto}, u, v, u, \text{jerusalem}, w) \leftarrow$$
$$Flights(\text{toronto}, u, v), Flights(u, \text{jerusalem}, w).$$

Now $rew_1(Q)$ will be the union of four queries, of which for instance

$$ans(\text{toronto}, u, \text{ac}, u, \text{jerusalem}, \text{cp}) \leftarrow AC(\text{toronto}, u), CP(u, \text{jerusalem}),$$

is obtained through the *mgu* $\{x/\text{toronto}, y/u, v/\text{ac}, x'/u, y'/\text{jerusalem}, w/\text{cp}\}$. The union of the four queries gives the certain answer: indeed, the only connections we can for sure assert are those by Air Canada – Air Canada, Air Canada – Canadian Airlines, Canadian Airlines – Air Canada, and Canadian Airlines – Canadian Airlines.

We have seen that $rew_1(Q)$ is a "sound and complete" rewriting of a query Q with respect to the certain answer on a collection of open views. It turns out that $rew_1(Q)$ is equivalent to a rewriting technique used in the Information Manifold project [LM*95]. Formally, let $manifold(Q)$ be the union of all conjunctive queries P with no more atoms in their bodies than Q and no constants other than those appearing in Q or the view definitions, such that the expansion P' of P through the view definitions is contained in Q. Then we have:

Theorem 11. $rew_1(Q) \equiv manifold(Q)$.

For algorithmic purposes note the following: Suppose that there are n sources, and that the size of the body of view-definition φ_i is b_i, with $B = max\{b_i : i \in [1, n]\}$, $b = \Sigma_{i=1}^n b_i$, and the global query has a body consisting of m atoms. A straightforward implementation of the Information Manifold rewriting technique runs in time $\mathcal{O}(n^{n \times B} \times n^m)$, whereas a straightforward implementation of our technique based on unification requires time $\mathcal{O}(b^m)$. We see that our unification-based rewriting technique is polynomial in the source descriptions and the the number of sources and exponential in the size of the global query. The Information Manifold rewriting technique is polynomial in the number of sources and exponential both in the size of the source descriptions and the global query. However, the following result –indicating that there is little chance of getting rid of the global query size in the exponent– follows easily from [LM*95].

Theorem 12. *Let* $\Phi = \{\langle\varphi_1, \{\text{open}\}\rangle, \ldots, \langle\varphi_n, \{\text{open}\}\rangle\}$, *be a set of source descriptions. Given a conjunctive query* Q *using only the relation names in the bodies of the* φ_i:s, *the problem of whether there exists a certainty rewriting of* Q *with respect to* Φ *is NP-complete.*

---

[5] In the example toronto, jerusalem, ac, and cp are constants.

Possibility Rewritings

For the possible answer we note that it is straightforward to show that if all sources in S are open, then $Q^*(S)$ is always infinite. Here we treat the case where all views are closed.

For this consider each $body(\varphi_i)$ of the view definitions φ_i. For each containment mapping h_{i_j} from $body(\varphi_i)$ to $body(Q)$ set Q'_{i_j} to $head(Q) \leftarrow h_{i_j}(head(\varphi_i))$. If there are no containment mappings h_{i_j}, then no Q'_{i_j} exists. Suppose wlog that we found containment mappings for $i \in [1, k], k \leq n$, and for each such i we found m_i different containment mappings. We then set $rew_2(Q) =$

$$head(Q) \leftarrow h_{1_1}(head(\varphi_1)), \ldots, h_{1_{m_1}}(head(\varphi_1)),$$
$$\ldots,$$
$$h_{k_1}(head(\varphi_k)), \ldots, h_{k_{m_k}}(head(\varphi_k))$$

provided this query is safe. If it isn't safe or if there are no Q'_{i_j}:s, then $rew_2(Q)$ is undefined.

We can now show that the rewriting has the desired property.

Theorem 13. *Let S be a collection of closed sources where $ext(S) = v$, and let Q be a query on $sch(S)$. Then*

$$rew_2(Q)(v) = Q^*(S).$$

For an example, let us return to the World Cup Soccer Tournament from the introduction. Suppose we only have the closed source S_{Qual} available. Recall that this source was defined by

$$S_{Qual}(x) \leftarrow Team(x, y).$$

Suppose we would like to have a list of all possible matches in the first round. Our query Q is then

$$ans(u, v) \leftarrow Team(u, w), Team(v, w).$$

We are now able to compute the possible answer Q^* by evaluating $rew_2(Q) =$

$$ans(u, v) \leftarrow S_{Qual}(u), S_{Qual}(v)$$

on the closed source. The rewriting was obtained as $ans(u, v) \leftarrow h_1(S_{Qual}(x))$, $h_2(S_{Qual}(y))$, where $h_1 = \{x/u, y/w\}$ and $h_2 = \{x/v, y/w\}$. Clearly, the pair of teams actually playing against each other in the first round will be found only among the elements of the Cartesian product $S_{Qual} \times S_{Qual}$.

As in Theorem 12 it turns out that the rewriting is intractable in the global query size.

Theorem 14. *Let $\Phi = \{\langle\varphi_1, \{closed\}\rangle, \ldots, \langle\varphi_n, \{closed\}\rangle\}$, be a set of source descriptions. Given a conjunctive query Q using only the relation names in the bodies of the φ_i:s, the problem of whether there exists a possibility rewriting of Q with respect to Φ is NP-complete.*

5 Related Work

Many works deal with finite representations of infinite sets of databases, both in the constraint database literature [KKR90,vdM93] and in the literature on uncertain and indefinite databases [AKG91,Gra91,IL84,Men84]. We will not go into details; for surveys of these fields see [Kan95] and [vdM98].

The work of Motro [Mot97] is close in spirit and motivation to ours; however, Motro assumes the existence of a "real world" global database instead of modeling the uncertainty in the sources by associating a set of databases with them; this makes it difficult to give precise meaning to his ideas.

In a recent paper [AD98], Abiteboul and Duschka study the special case in which all sources are sound, or all sources are sound and complete, but do not formulate the more general problem. On the other hand, they consider more general view definitions and queries than conjunctive ones.

The idea of sources as views on the global schema goes back to the GMAP project [TSI94]. It was subsequently popularized by the Information Manifold project [LRO96,LM*95], which introduced the query algorithm that we characterize in this paper. In a related paper, Levy [Lev96] studies sources that are complete over some subset of their domain and show how to use them to obtain exact answers.

Finally, we mention two special cases: Suppose the global database consists of one relation, and all sources are defined by projections. Then if all sources are open the certain answer corresponds to the *weak instance window function* [MRW86] with no dependencies, and if all sources are clopen, then the only possible global database is the notorious *universal relation* [Ull82].

Acknowledgments

We thank NSERC, IRIS and Concordia FRDP for their support, and Anthony Tomasic for pointing out Motro's work [Mot97].

References

[AD98]   Abiteboul S., O. M. Duschka: Complexity of Answering Queries Using Materialized Views. *Proc. 9th Annual ACM Symp. on the Theory of Computing*, pp. 254–263.

[AHV95]   Abiteboul S., R. Hull, and V. Vianu. *Foundations of Databases*. Addison-Wesley, Reading Ma. 1995.

[AKG91]   Abiteboul S., P. C. Kanellakis, G. Grahne. On the Representation and Querying of Sets of Possible Worlds. *Theoretical Computer Science* 78:1, 1991, pp. 158–187

[ASU79]   Aho A. V., Y. Sagiv, J. D. Ullman. Equivalences Among Relational Expressions. *SIAM J. Comput.* 8:2, 1979, pp. 218–246

[BV81]   Beeri C, M. Y. Vardi. The Implication Problem for Data Dependencies. *Proc. 8th International Colloquium on Automata, Languages and Programming*, pp. 73–85

[CM77]   Chandra A. K. and Merlin P. M. Optimal implementation of conjunctive queries in relational databases. *Conference Record of the 9th Annual ACM Symposium on Theory of Computing*, pp. 77–90.

[FKUV86]   Fagin R., G. M. Kuper, J. D. Ullman, M. Y. Vardi. Updating Logical Databases. In P. C. Kanellakis and F. Preparata (Editors) *Advances in Computing Research, Vol. 3*, pp. 1–18. JAI Press Inc., Greenwich, CT, 1986.

[Gra91]   Grahne G. *The Problem of Incomplete Information in Relational Databases*. Lecture Notes in Computer Science, vol. 554. Springer-Verlag, Berlin 1991.

[IL84]   Imielinski T, W. Lipski Jr. Incomplete Information in Relational Databases. *J. ACM* **31**:4, 1984, pp. 761–791

[Kan95]   Kanellakis P. C. Constraint Programming and Database Languages: A Tutorial. *Proc. 14th ACM Symp. on Principles of Database Systems*, pp. 46–53.

[KKR90]   Kanellakis P. C., G. M. Kuper, P. Z. Revesz. Constraint Query Languages. *Proc. 9th ACM Symp. on Principles of Database Systems*, pp. 299–313.

[Lev96]   Levy A. Y. Obtaining Complete Answers from Incomplete Databases. *Proc. 22nd Int'l. Conf. on Very Large Databases*, pp. 402 412.

[LM*95]   Levy A. Y., A. O. Mendelzon, Y. Sagiv, D. Srivastava: Answering Queries Using Views. *Proc. 14th ACM Symp. on Principles of Database Systems*, pp. 95–104.

[LRO96]   Levy A. Y., A. Rajaraman and J. J. Ordille. Querying Heterogeneous Information Sources Using Source Descriptions. *Proc. 22nd Int'l. Conf. on Very Large Databases*, pp. 251–262.

[MRW86]   Maier D., D. Rozenshtein, D. S. Warren. Window Functions. In P. C. Kanellakis and F. Preparata (Editors) *Advances in Computing Research, Vol. 3*, pp. 213–246, JAI Press Inc., Greenwich, CT, 1986.

[Men84]   Mendelzon A. O. Database States and Their Tableaux. *ACM Trans. on Databases Systems* **9**:2, 1984, pp. 264–282

[Mot97]   Motro A. Multiplex: A Formal Model for Multidatabases and Its Implementation. Technical Report ISSE-TR-95-103.

[vdM93]   van der Meyden R. Recursively Indefinite Databases, *Theoretical Computer Science* 116(1,2), 1993, pp. 151–194

[vdM98]   van der Meyden R. Logical Approaches to Incomplete Information: A Survey. In J. Chomicki and G. Saake (Editors) *Logics for Databases and Information Systems*. Kluwer Academic Publishers, 1998, pp. 307–356

[TSI94]   Tsatalos, O.G, M.H. Solomon, Y.E. Ioannidis. The GMAP: A Versatile Tool for Physical Data Independence. *Proc. 20th Int'l. Conf. on Very Large Databases*, pp. 367–378.

[Ull82]   Ullman J. D. The U. R. Strikes Back. *Proc. 1st ACM Symp. on Principles of Database Systems*, pp. 10–22.

[Ull97]   Ullman J. D. Information Integration Using Logical Views. *Proc. 6th Int'l. Symp. on Database Theory*, pp. 19–40.

Optimizing Large Join Queries in Mediation Systems

Ramana Yerneni, Chen Li, Jeffrey Ullman, and Hector Garcia-Molina

Stanford University, USA
{yerneni, chenli, ullman, hector}@cs.stanford.edu

Abstract. In data integration systems, queries posed to a mediator need to be translated into a sequence of queries to the underlying data sources. In a heterogeneous environment, with sources of diverse and limited query capabilities, not all the translations are feasible. In this paper, we study the problem of finding feasible and efficient query plans for mediator systems. We consider conjunctive queries on mediators and model the source capabilities through attribute-binding adornments. We use a simple cost model that focuses on the major costs in mediation systems, those involved with sending queries to sources and getting answers back. Under this metric, we develop two algorithms for source query sequencing – one based on a simple greedy strategy and another based on a partitioning scheme. The first algorithm produces optimal plans in some scenarios, and we show a linear bound on its worst case performance when it misses optimal plans. The second algorithm generates optimal plans in more scenarios, while having no bound on the margin by which it misses the optimal plans. We also report on the results of the experiments that study the performance of the two algorithms.

1 Introduction

Integration systems based on a *mediation* architecture [31] provide users with seamless access to data from many heterogeneous sources. Examples of such systems are TSIMMIS [3], Garlic [8], Information Manifold [14], and DISCO [26]. In these systems, the sources. They translate user queries on integrated views into source queries and postprocessing operations on the source query results. The translation process can be quite challenging when integrating a large number of heterogeneous sources.

One of the important challenges for integration systems is to deal with the diverse capabilities of sources in answering queries [8,15,19]. This problem arises due to the heterogeneity in sources ranging from simple file systems to full-fledged relational databases. The problem we address in this paper is how to generate efficient mediator query plans that respect the limited and diverse capabilities of data sources. In particular, we focus our attention on the kind of queries that are the most expensive in mediation systems, *large join queries*. We propose efficient algorithms to find good plans for such queries.

Catriel Beeri, Peter Buneman (Eds.): ICDT'99, LNCS 1540, pp. 348–364, 1998.
© Springer-Verlag Berlin Heidelberg 1998

1.1   Cost Model

In many applications, the cost of query processing in mediator systems is dominated by the cost of interacting with the sources. Hence, we focus on the costs associated with sending queries to sources. Our results are first stated using a very simple cost model where we count the total number of source queries in a plan as its cost. In spite of the simplicity of the cost model, the optimization problem we are dealing with remains NP-hard. Later in the paper, we show how to extend our main results to a more complex cost model that charges a fixed cost per query plus a variable cost that is proportional to the amount of data transferred.

1.2   Capabilities-Based Plan Generation

We consider mediator systems, where users pose conjunctive queries over integrated views provided by the mediator. These queries are translated into conjunctive queries over the source views to arrive at *logical query plans*. The logical plans deal only with the content descriptions of the sources. That is, they tell the mediator which sources provide the relevant data and what postprocessing operations need to be performed on this data. The logical plans are later translated into *physical plans* that specify details such as the order in which the sources are contacted and the exact queries to be sent. Our goal in this paper is to develop algorithms that will translate a mediator logical plan into an efficient, *feasible* (does not exceed the source capabilities) physical plan. We illustrate the process of translating a logical plan into a physical plan by an example.

Example 1. Consider three sources that provide information about movies, and a mediator that provides an integrated view:

Source	Contents	Must Bind
S_1	R(studio, title)	either studio or title
S_2	S(title, year)	title
S_3	T(title, stars)	title

Mediator View:
Movie(studio,title,year,stars) :-
R(studio,title), S(title,year), T(title,stars)

The "Must Bind" column indicates what attributes must be specified at a source. For instance, queries sent to S_1 must either provide the title or the studio. Suppose the user asks for the titles of all movies produced by Paramount in 1955 in which Gregory Peck starred. That is,

```
ans(title) :- Movie('Paramount', title, '1955', 'Gregory Peck')
```

The mediator would translate this query to the logical plan:

```
ans(title) :- R('Paramount', title), S(title, '1955'), T(title,
                    'Gregory Peck')
```

The logical plan states the information the mediator needs to obtain from the three sources and how it needs to postprocess this information. In this example, the mediator needs to join the results of the three source queries on the title attribute. There are many physical plans that correspond to this logical plan (based on various join orders and join methods). Some of these plans are feasible while others are not. Here are two physical plans for this logical plan:

- Plan P_1: Send query R('Paramount', title) to S_1; send query S(title, '1955') to S_2; and send query T(title, 'Gregory Peck') to S_3. Join the results of the three source queries on the title attribute and return the title values to the user.
- Plan P_2: Get the titles of movies produced by Paramount from source S_1. For each returned title t, send a query to S_2 to get its year and check if it is '1955.' If so, send a query to S_3 to get the stars of movie t. If the set of stars contains 'Gregory Peck,' return t to the user.

In the above plans, the first one is not feasible because the queries to sources S_2 and S_3 do not provide a binding for title. The second one is feasible. There are actually other feasible plans (for instance, we can reverse the S_2 and S_3 queries of P_2). If P_2 is the cheapest feasible plan, the mediator may execute it.

As illustrated by the example, we need to solve the following problem: Given a logical plan and the description of the source capabilities, find feasible physical plans for the logical plan. The central problem is to determine the evaluation order for logical plan subgoals, so that attributes are appropriately bound. Among all the feasible physical plans, pick the most efficient one.

1.3   Related Work

The problem of ordering subgoals to find the best feasible sequence can be viewed as the well known *join-order* problem. More precisely, we can assign *infinite* cost to infeasible sequences and then find the best join order.

The join-order problem has been extensively studied in the literature, and many solutions have been proposed. Some solutions perform a rather exhaustive enumeration of plans, and hence do not scale well [1,2,4,5,8,15,17,19,20,22,29]. In particular, we are interested in Internet scenarios with many sources and subgoals, so these schemes are too expensive. Some other solutions reduce the search space through techniques like *simulated annealing*, *random probes*, or other heuristics [6,11,12,16,18,23,24,25]. While these approaches may generate efficient plans in some cases, they do not have any performance guarantees in terms of the quality of plans generated (i.e., the plans generated by them can be arbitrarily far from the optimal one). Many of these techniques may even fail to generate a feasible plan, while the user query does have a feasible plan.

The remaining solutions [10,13,21] use specific cost models and clever techniques that exploit them to produce optimal join orders efficiently. While these solutions are very good for the join-order problem where those cost models are appropriate, they are hard to adopt in our context because of two difficulties. The first is that it is not clear how to model the feasibility of mediator query plans in their frameworks. A direct application of their algorithms to the problem we are studying may end up generating infeasible plans, when a feasible plan exists. The second difficulty is that when we use cost models that emphasize the main costs in mediator systems, the optimality guarantees of their algorithms may not hold.

1.4 Our Solution

In this paper, we develop two algorithms that find good feasible plans. The first algorithm runs in $O(n^2)$ time, where n is the number of subgoals in the logical plan. We provide a linear bound on the margin by which this algorithm can miss the optimal plan. Our second algorithm can guarantee optimal plans in more scenarios than the first, although there is no bounded optimality for its plans. Both our algorithms are guaranteed to find a feasible plan, if the user query has a feasible plan. Furthermore, we show through experiments that our algorithms have excellent running time profiles in a variety of scenarios, and very often find optimal or close-to-optimal plans. This combination of efficient, scalable algorithms that generate provably good plans is not achieved by previously known approaches.

2 Preliminaries

In this section, we introduce the notation we use throughout the paper. We also discuss the cost model used in our optimization algorithms.

2.1 Source Relations and Logical Plans

Let $S_1, \ldots, S_m$ be m sources in an integration system. To simplify the presentation, we assume that sources provide their data in the form of relations. If sources have other data models, one could use *wrappers* [9] to create the simple relational view of data. Each source is assumed to provide a single relation. If a source provides multiple relations, we can model it in our framework as a set of logical sources, all having the same physical source. Example 1 showed three sources S_1, S_2 and S_3 providing three relations R, S and T respectively.

A *query* to a source specifies atomic values to a subset of the source relation attributes and obtains the corresponding set of tuples. A source supports a set of access templates on its relation that specify binding adornment requirements for source queries.[1] In Example 1, source S_2 had one access template:

---

[1] We consider source-capabilities described as *bf* adornment patterns that distinguish bound (*b*) and free (*f*) argument positions [27]. The techniques developed in this paper can also be employed to solve the problem of mediator query planning when other source capability description languages are used.

S^{bf}(title, year), while source S_1 had two access templates: R^{bf}(studio, title) and R^{fb}(studio, title).

User queries to the mediator are conjunctive queries on the integrated views provided by the mediator. Each integrated view is defined as a set of conjunctive queries over the source relations. The user query is translated into a logical plan, which is a set of conjunctive queries on the source relations. The answer to the user query is the union of the results of this set of conjunctive queries. Example 1 showed a user query that was a conjunctive query over the *Movie* view, and it was translated into a conjunctive query over the source relations.

In order to find the best feasible plan for a user query, we assume that the mediator processes the logical plan one conjunctive query at a time (as in [3,8,14]). Thus, we reduce the problem of finding the best feasible plan for the user query to the problem of finding the best feasible plan for a conjunctive query in the logical plan. In a way, from now on, we assume without loss of generality that a logical plan has a single conjunctive query over the source relations.

Let the logical plan be $H : - C_1, C_2, \ldots, C_n$. We call each C_i a *subgoal*. Each subgoal specifies a query on one of the source relations by binding a subset of the attributes of the source relation. We refer to the attributes of subgoals in the logical plan as *variables*. In Example 1, the logical plan had three subgoals with four variables, three of which were bound.

2.2   Binding Relations and Source Queries

Given a sequence of n subgoals $C_1, C_2, \ldots, C_n$, we define a corresponding sequence of $n + 1$ *binding relations* $I_0, I_1, \ldots, I_n$. I_0 has as its schema the set of variables bound in the logical plan, and it has a single tuple, denoting the bindings specified in the logical plan. The schema of I_1 is the union of the schema of I_0 and the schema of the source relation of C_1. Its instance is the join of I_0 and the source relation of C_1. Similarly, we define I_2 in terms of I_1 and the source relation of C_2, and so on. The answer to the conjunctive query is defined by a projection operation on I_n.

In order to compute a binding relation I_j, we need to join I_{j-1} with C_j. There are two ways to perform this operation:

1. Use I_0 to send a query to the source of C_j (by binding a subset of its attributes); perform the join of the result of this source query with I_{j-1} at the mediator to obtain I_j.
2. For $j \geq 2$, use I_{j-1} to send a set of queries to the source relation of C_j (by binding a subset of its attributes); union the results of these source queries; perform the join of this union relation with I_{j-1} to obtain I_j.

We call the first kind of source query a *block query* and the second kind a *parameterized query*[2]. Obviously, answering C_j through the first method takes a single source query, while answering it by the second method can take many

---

[2] A parameterized query is different from a *semijoin* where one can send multiple bindings for an attribute in a single query.

source queries. The main reason why we need to consider parameterized queries is that it may not be possible to answer some of the subgoals in the logical plan through block queries. This may be because the access templates for the corresponding source relations require bindings of variables that are not available in the logical plan. In order to answer these subgoals, we must use parameterized queries by executing other subgoals and collecting bindings for the required parameters of C_j.

2.3   The Plan Space

The space of all possible plans for a given user query is defined first by considering all sequences of subgoals in its logical plan. In a sequence, we must then decide on the choice of queries for each subgoal (among the set of block queries and parameterized queries available for the subgoal). We call a plan in this space *feasible* if all the queries in it are answerable by the sources. Note that the number of feasible physical plans, as well as the number of all plans, for a given logical plan can be exponential in the number of subgoals in the logical plan.

Note that the space of plans we consider is similar to the space of left-deep-tree executions of a join query. As stated in the following theorem, we do not miss feasible plans by not considering bushy-tree executions.

Theorem 1. *We do not miss feasible plans because of considering only left-deep-tree executions of the subgoals.*

Proof. For any feasible execution of the logical plan based on a bushy tree of subgoals, we can construct another feasible execution based on a left-deep tree of subgoals (with the same leaf order). This is similar to the *bound-is-easier* assumption of [28]. See the full version of our paper [32] for a detailed proof.

2.4   The Formal Cost Model

Our cost model is defined as follows:

1. The cost of a subgoal in the feasible plan is the number of source queries needed to answer this subgoal.
2. The cost of a feasible plan is the sum of the costs of all the subgoals in the plan.

We develop the main results of the paper in the simple cost model presented above. Later, in Section 5, we will show how to extend these results to more complex cost models. We also consider more practical cost models in Section 6 where we analyze the performance of our algorithms. Here, we note that even in the simple cost model that counts only the number of source queries, the problem of finding the optimal feasible plan is quite hard.

Theorem 2. *The problem of finding the feasible plan with the minimum number of source queries is NP-hard.*

Proof. We reduce the Vertex Cover problem ([7]) to our problem. Since the Vertex Cover problem is NP-complete, our problem is NP-hard.

Given a graph G with n vertices $V_1, \ldots, V_n$, we construct a database and a logical plan as follows. Corresponding to each vertex V_i we define a relation R_i. For all $1 \leq i \leq j \leq n$, if V_i and V_j are connected by an edge in G, R_i and R_j include the attribute A_{ij}. In addition, we define a special attribute X and two special relations R_0 and R_{n+1}. In all, we have a total of $m + 1$ attributes, where m is the number of edges in G. The special attribute X is in the schema of all the relations. The special relation R_{n+1} also has all the attributes A_{ij}. That is, R_0 has only one attribute and R_{n+1} has $m + 1$ attributes. Each relation has a tuple with a value of 1 for each of its attributes. In addition, all relations except R_{n+1} include a second tuple with a value of 2 for all their attributes. Each relation has a single access template: R_0 has no binding requirements, R_1 through R_n require the attribute X to be bound, and R_{n+1} requires all of the attributes to be bound. Finally, the logical plan consists of all the $n + 2$ relations, with no variables bound.

It is obvious that the above construction of the database and the logical plan takes time that is polynomial in the size of G. Now, we show that G has a vertex cover of size k if and only if the logical plan has a feasible physical plan that requires $(n + k + 3)$ source queries.

Suppose G has a vertex cover of size k. Without loss of generality, let it be $V_1, \ldots, V_k$. Consider the physical plan P that first answers the subgoal R_0 with a block query, then answers $R_1, \ldots, R_k, R_{n+1}, R_{k+1}, \ldots, R_n$ using parameterized queries. P is a feasible plan because R_0 has no binding requirements, $R_1, \ldots, R_k$ need X to be bound and X is available from R_0, and $R_1, \ldots, R_k$ will bind all the variables (since $V_1, \ldots, V_k$ is a vertex cover). In P, R_0 is answered by a single source query, $R_1, \ldots, R_k$ and R_{n+1} are answered by two source queries each, and $R_{k+1}, \ldots, R_n$ are answered by one source query each. This gives a total of $(n + k + 3)$ source queries for this plan. Thus, we see that if G has a vertex cover of size k, we have a feasible plan with $(n + k + 3)$ source queries.

Suppose, there is a feasible plan P' with f source queries. In P', the first relation must be R_0, and this subgoal must be answered by a block query (because the logical plan does not bind any variables). All the other subgoals must be answered by parameterized queries. Consider the set of subgoals in P' that are answered before R_{n+1} is answered. Let j be the size of this set of subgoals (excluding R_0). Since R_{n+1} needs all attributes to be bound, the union of the schemas of these j subgoals must be the entire attribute set. That is, the vertices corresponding to these j subgoals form a vertex cover in G. In P', each of these j subgoals takes two source queries, along with R_{n+1}, while the rest of $(n - j)$ subgoals in $R_1, \ldots, R_n$ take one source query each. That is, $f = 1 + 2 * j + 2 + (n - j)$. From this, we see that we can find a vertex cover for G of size $(f - n - 3)$.

Hence, G has a vertex cover of size k if and only if there is a feasible plan with $(n + k + 3)$ source queries. That is, we have reduced the problem of finding the minimum vertex cover in a graph to our problem of finding a feasible plan with minimum source queries.

In our cost model, it turns out that it is safe to restrict the space of plans to those based on left-deep-tree executions of the set of subgoals.

Theorem 3. *We do not miss the optimal plan by not considering the executions of the logical plan based on bushy trees of subgoals.*

Proof. See the full version of our paper [32] for the proof.

3   The CHAIN Algorithm

In this section, we present the CHAIN algorithm for finding the best feasible query plan. This algorithm is based on a greedy strategy of building a single sequence of subgoals that is feasible and efficient.

The CHAIN Algorithm
Input: Logical plan – subgoals and bound variables.
Output: Feasible physical plan.

- Initialize:
  $S \leftarrow \{C_1, C_2, \ldots, C_n\}$ /*set of subgoals in the logical plan*/
  $B \leftarrow$ set of bound variables in the logical plan
  $L \leftarrow \phi$ /* start with an empty sequence */
- Construct the sequence of subgoals:
  while ($S \neq \phi$) do
  $M \leftarrow$ *infinity*;
  $N \leftarrow$ *null*;
  for each subgoal C_i in S do   /* find the cheapest subgoal */
  if (C_i is answerable with B) then
  $c \leftarrow Cost_L(C_i)$;   /* get the cost of this subgoal in sequence L */
  if ($c < M$) then
  $M \leftarrow c$;
  $N \leftarrow C_i$;
  /* If no next answerable subgoal, declare no feasible plan */
  if ($N = null$)
  return(ϕ);
  /* Add next subgoal to plan */
  $L \leftarrow L + N$;
  $S \leftarrow S - \{N\}$;
  $B \leftarrow B \cup \{$variables of $N\}$;
- Return the feasible plan:
  return($Plan(L)$);   /* construct plan from sequence L */

Fig. 1. Algorithm CHAIN

As shown in Figure 1, CHAIN starts by finding all subgoals that are answerable with the initial bindings in the logical plan. It then picks the answerable subgoal with the least cost and computes the additional variables that are now bound due to the chosen subgoal. It repeats the process of finding answerable subgoals, picking the cheapest among them and updating the set of bound variables, until no more subgoals are left or some subgoals are left but none of them is answerable. If there are subgoals left over, CHAIN declares that there is no feasible plan; otherwise it outputs the plan it has constructed.

3.1   Complexity and Optimality of CHAIN

Here we demonstrate: the CHAIN algorithm is very efficient; it is guaranteed to find feasible plans when they exist; and there is a linear bound on the optimality of the plans it generates. Due to space limitations, we have not provided proofs for all the lemmas and theorems. They are available in the full version of the paper [32].

Lemma 1. *CHAIN runs in $O(n^2)$ time, where n is the number of subgoals.* [3]

Lemma 2. *CHAIN will generate a feasible plan, if the logical plan has feasible physical plans.*

Lemma 3. *If the result of the user query is nonempty, and the number of subgoals in the logical plan is less than 3, CHAIN is guaranteed to find the optimal plan.*

Lemma 4. *CHAIN can miss the optimal plan if the logical plan has more than 2 subgoals.*

Proof. We construct a logical plan with 3 subgoals and a database instance that result in CHAIN generating a suboptimal plan.

$R^{bff}(A, B, D)$	$S^{bf}(B, E)$	$T^{bf}(D, F)$
(1, 1, 1)	(1, 1)	(4, 1)
(1, 2, 2)	(2, 1)	(5, 1)
(1, 3, 3)	(3, 1)	(6, 1)
(1, 1, 4)	(4, 1)	(7, 1)

Table 1. Database Instance for Lemma 4

Consider a logical plan $H : -R(1, B, D)$, $S(B, E)$, $T(D, F)$ and the database instance shown in Table 1. For this logical plan and database, CHAIN will generate the plan: $R \to S \to T$, with a total cost of $1 + 3 + 4 = 8$. We observe that a cheaper feasible plan is: $R \to T \to S$, with a total cost of $1 + 4 + 1 = 6$. Thus, CHAIN misses the optimal plan in this case.

---

[3] We are assuming here that finding the cost of a subgoal following a partial sequence takes $O(1)$ time.

It is not difficult to find situations in which the CHAIN algorithm misses the optimal plan. However, surprisingly, there is a linear upper bound on how far its plan can be from the optimal. In fact, we prove a stronger result in Lemma 5.

Lemma 5. *Suppose P^c is the plan generated by CHAIN for a logical plan with n subgoals; P^o is the optimal plan, and E_{max} is the cost of the most expensive subgoal in P^o. Then,*

$$Cost(P^c) \leq n \times E_{max}$$

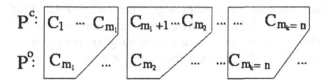

Fig. 2. Proof for Lemma 5

Proof. Without loss of generality, suppose the sequence of subgoals in P^c is $C_1, C_2, \ldots, C_n$. As shown in Figure 2, let the first subgoal in P^o be C_{m_1}. Let G_1 be the prefix of P^c, such that $G_1 = C_1 \ldots C_{m_1}$. When CHAIN chooses C_1, the subgoal C_{m_1} is also answerable. This implies that the cost of C_1 in P^c is less than or equal to the cost of C_{m_1} in P^o. After processing C_1 in P^c, the subgoal C_{m_1} remains answerable and its cost of processing cannot increase. So, if CHAIN has chosen another subgoal C_2 instead of C_{m_1}, once again we can conclude that the cost of C_2 in P^c is not greater than the cost of C_{m_1} in P^o. Finally, at the end of G_1, when C_{m_1} is processed in P^c, we note that the cost of C_{m_1} in P^c is no more than the cost of C_{m_1} in P^o. Thus, the cost of each subgoal of G_1 is less than or equal to the cost of C_{m_1} in P^o.

We call C_{m_1} the first *pivot* in P^o. We define the next pivot C_{m_2} in P^o as follows. C_{m_2} is the first subgoal after C_{m_1} in P^o such that C_{m_2} is not in G_1. Now, we can define the next subsequence G_2 of P^c such that the last subgoal of G_2 is C_{m_2}. The cost of each subgoal in G_2 is less than or equal to the cost of C_{m_2}.

We continue finding the rest of the pivots $C_{m_3}, \ldots, C_{m_k}$ in P^o and the corresponding subsequences $G_3, \ldots, G_k$ in P^c. Based on the above argument, we have

$$\forall C_i \in G_j : (\text{cost of } C_i \text{ in } P^c) \leq (\text{cost of } C_{m_j} \text{ in } P^o)$$

From this, it follows that

$$Cost(P^c) = \sum_{j=1}^{k} \sum_{C_i \in G_j} (\text{cost of } C_i \text{ in } P^c) \leq \sum_{j=1}^{k} |G_j| \times (\text{cost of } C_{m_j} \text{ in } P^o) \leq n \times E_{max}$$

Theorem 4. *CHAIN is n-competitive. That is, the plan generated by CHAIN can be at most n times as expensive as the optimal plan, where n is the number of subgoals.*

Proof. Follows from Lemma 5.

The cost of the plan generated by CHAIN can be arbitrarily close to the cost of the optimal plan multiplied by the number of subgoals; i.e., Theorem 4 cannot be improved. However, in many situations CHAIN yields optimal plans or plans whose cost is very close to that of the optimal plan as demonstrated in Section 6.

4   The PARTITION Algorithm

In this section, we present another algorithm called *PARTITION* for finding efficient feasible plans. PARTITION takes a very different approach to solve the plan generation problem. It is guaranteed to generate optimal plans in more scenarios than CHAIN but has a worse running time.

4.1   PARTITION

The formal description of PARTITION is available in the full version of the paper [32]. Here, we present the essential aspects of the algorithm.

The PARTITION algorithm has two phases. In the first phase, it organizes the subgoals into *clusters* based on the capabilities of the sources. The property satisfied by the clusters generated by the first phase of PARTITION is as follows. All the subgoals in the first cluster are answerable by block queries; all the subgoals in each subsequent cluster are answerable by parameterized queries that use attribute bindings from the subgoals of the earlier clusters. To obtain the clusters, PARTITION keeps track of the set of bound variables V. Initially, V is the set of variables bound in the logical plan. The first phase of PARTITION is divided into many rounds (one per cluster). In each round, the set of answerable subgoals based on the bound variable set V is collected into a new cluster. These subgoals are removed from the set of subgoals that are yet to be picked, and the variables bound by these subgoals are added to V. If in a round of the first phase there are subgoals yet to be picked and none of them is answerable, PARTITION declares that there is no feasible plan for the user query.

In the second phase, PARTITION finds the best subplan for each cluster of subgoals and combines the subplans to arrive at the best overall plan for the user query. The subplan for each cluster is found by enumerating all the sequences of subgoals in the cluster and choosing the one with the least cost.

4.2   Optimality and Complexity of PARTITION

Like the CHAIN algorithm, the PARTITION algorithm always finds feasible plans when they exist. It is guaranteed to find optimal plans in more scenarios than CHAIN. However, when it misses the optimal plans, it can miss them by an unbounded margin. It is also much less efficient than CHAIN, and can take time that is exponential in the number of subgoals of the logical plan. These observations are formally stated by the following lemmas (proofs omitted occasionally due to space limitations).

Lemma 6. *If feasible physical plans exist for a given logical plan, PARTITION is guaranteed to find a feasible plan.*

Lemma 7. *If there are fewer than 3 clusters generated, and the result of the query is nonempty, then PARTITION is guaranteed to find the optimal plan.*

Proof. We proceed by a simple case analysis. There are two cases to consider.

The first case is when there is only one cluster Γ_1. PARTITION finds the best sequence among all the permutations of the subgoals in Γ_1. Since Γ_1 contains all the subgoals of the logical plan, PARTITION will find the best possible sequence.

The second case is when there are two clusters Γ_1 and Γ_2. Let P be the optimal feasible plan. We will show how we can transform P into a plan in the plan space of PARTITION that is at least as good as P.

Let C_i be a subgoal in Γ_1. There are two possibilities: (a) C_i is answered in P by using a block query; (b) C_i is answered in P by using parameterized queries. If C_i is answered by a block query, we make no change to P. Otherwise, we modify P as follows. As the result of the query is not empty, the cost of subgoal C_i (using parameterized queries) in P must be at least 1. Since C_i is in the first cluster, it can be answered by using a block query. So we can modify P by replacing the parameterized queries for C_i with the block query for C_i. Since the cost of a block query can be at most 1, this modification cannot increase the cost of P. For all subgoals in Γ_1, we repeat the above transformation until we get a plan P', in which all the subgoals in Γ_1 are answered by using block queries.

We apply a second transformation to P' with respect to the subgoals in Γ_1. Since all these subgoals are answered by block queries in P', we can move them to the beginning of P' to arrive at a new plan P''. Moving these subgoals ahead of the other subgoals will preserve the feasibility of the plan. It is also true that this transformation cannot increase the cost of the plan. This is because it does not change the cost of these subgoals, and it cannot increase the cost of the other subgoals in the sequence. Hence, P'' cannot be more expensive than P'.

After the two-step transformation, we get a plan P'' that is as good as P. Finally, we note that P'' is in the plan space of PARTITION, and so the plan generated by PARTITION cannot be worse than P''. Thus, the plan found by PARTITION must be as good as the optimal plan.

Lemma 8. *If the number of subgoals in the logical plan does not exceed 3, and the result of the query is not empty, then PARTITION will always find the optimal plan.*

Proof. Follows from Lemma 7.

PARTITION cannot generate the optimal plan in many cases. One can construct logical plans with as few as 4 subgoals that lead the algorithm to generate a sub-optimal plan. Also, PARTITION can miss the optimal plan by a margin that is unbounded by the query parameters.

Lemma 9. *For any integer $m > 0$, there exists a logical plan and a database for which PARTITION generates a plan that is at least m times as expensive as the optimal plan.*

Proof. Refer to [32] for the detailed proof. The essential idea is to construct a logical plan and a database for any given m that will make PARTITION miss the optimal plan by a factor greater than m.

Lemma 10. *The PARTITION algorithm runs in $O(n^2 + (k_1! + k_2! + \ldots + k_p!))$, where n is the number of subgoals in the logical plan, p is the number of clusters found by PARTITION and k_i is the number of subgoals in the ith cluster.* [4]

4.3   Variations of PARTITION

We have seen that the PARTITION algorithm can miss the optimal plan in many scenarios, and in the worst case it has a running time that is exponential in the number of subgoals in the logical plan. In a way, it attempts to strike a balance between running time and the ability to find optimal plans. A naive algorithm that enumerates all sequences of subgoals will always find the optimal plan, but it may take much longer than PARTITION. PARTITION tries to cut down on the running time, and gives up the ability to find optimal plans to a certain extent. Here, we consider two variations of PARTITION that highlight this trade-off.

We call the first variation FILTER. This variation is based on the observation of Lemma 7. FILTER also has two phases like PARTITION. In its first phase, it mimics PARTITION to arrive at the clusters $\Gamma_1, \Gamma_2, \ldots, \Gamma_p$. At the end of the first phase, it keeps the first cluster as is, and collapses all the other clusters into a new second cluster Γ'. That is, it ends up with Γ_1 and Γ'. The second phase of FILTER is identical to that of PARTITION. FILTER is guaranteed to find the optimal plan (as long as the query result is nonempty), but its running time is much worse than PARTITION. Yet, it is more efficient than the naive algorithm that enumerates all plans.

Lemma 11. *If the user query has nonempty result, FILTER will generate the optimal plan.*

Proof. We can prove this lemma in the same way we proved Lemma 7.

Lemma 12. *The running time of FILTER is $O(n^2 + (k_1! + (n - k_1)!)$.* [5]

The second variation of PARTITION is called SCAN. This variation focuses on efficient plan generation. The main idea here is to simplify the second phase

---

[4] If the query result in nonempty, PARTITION can consider just one sequence (instead of $k_1!$) for the first cluster.

[5] If the query result in nonempty, FILTER can consider just one sequence (instead of $k_1!$) for the first cluster.

of PARTITION so that it can run efficiently. The penalty is that SCAN may not generate optimal plans in many cases where PARTITION does.

SCAN also has two phases of processing. The first phase is identical to that of PARTITION. In the second phase, SCAN picks an arbitrary order for each cluster without searching over all the possible orders. This leads to a second phase that runs in $O(n)$ time. Note that since it does not search over the space of subsequences for each cluster, SCAN tends to generate plans that are inferior to those of PARTITION.

Lemma 13. *SCAN runs in $O(n^2)$ time, where n is the number of subgoals in the logical plan.*

5   Other Cost Models

So far, we discussed algorithms that minimize the number of source queries. Now, we consider more complex cost models where different source queries can have different costs.

First, we consider a simple extension (say M_1) where the cost of a query to source S_i is e_i. That is, queries to different sources cost different amounts. Note that in M_1, we still do not charge for the amount of data transferred. Nevertheless, it is strictly more general than the model we discussed in Section 2. All of our results presented so far hold in this new model.

Theorem 5. *In the cost model M_1, Theorem 4 holds. That is, the CHAIN algorithm is n-competitive, where n is the number of subgoals.*

Theorem 6. *In the cost model M_1, Lemma 7 holds. That is, the PARTITION algorithm will find the optimal plan, if there are at most two clusters and the user query has nonempty result.*

Next, we consider a more complex cost model (say M_2) where the data transfer costs are factored in. That is, the cost of a query to source S_i is $e_i + f_i \times$ (size of query result). Note that this cost model is strictly more general than M_1.

Theorem 7. *In the cost model M_2, Theorem 4 holds. That is, the CHAIN algorithm is n-competitive, where n is the number of subgoals.*

Theorem 8. *In the cost model M_2, Lemma 7 does not hold. That is, the PARTITION algorithm cannot guarantee the optimal plan, even when there are at most two clusters.*

We observe that the n-competitiveness of CHAIN holds in any cost model with the following property: the cost of a subgoal in a plan does not increase by postponing its processing to a later time in the plan. We also note that the PARTITION algorithm with two clusters will always find the optimal plan (assuming the query has nonempty result) if block queries cannot cost more than the corresponding parameterized queries. This property holds, for instance, in model M_1 and not in model M_2. When one considers cost models other than those discussed here, these properties may hold in them and consequently CHAIN and PARTITION may yield very good results.

6 Performance Analysis

In this section, we address the questions: How often do PARTITION and CHAIN find the optimal plan? When they miss the optimal plan, what is the expected margin by which they miss? We answer these questions by experiments in a simulated environment. We used both the simple cost model of Section 2.4 as well as the more complex cost model M_2 of Section 5 in our performance analysis. The results did not deviate much from one cost model to the other. The details of the experiments are in [32]. Here, we briefly mention the important results based on the simpler cost model of Section 2.4.

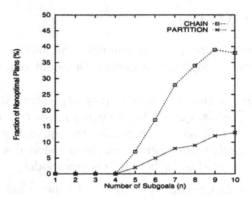

Fig. 3. Rate of Missing Optimal Plans

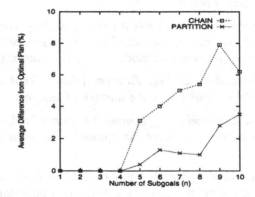

Fig. 4. Margin of Missing Optimal Plans

Figure 3 plots the fraction of the times the algorithms missed the optimal plans vs. number of query subgoals. Over a set of 1000 queries with number of subgoals ranging from 1 to 10, PARTITION generated the optimal plan in more than 95% of the cases, and CHAIN generated the optimal plan more than 75% of the time. This result is surprising because we know that PARTITION can miss optimal plans for queries with as few as 4 subgoals and CHAIN can miss optimal plans for queries with as few as 3 subgoals.

Figure 4 plots the average margin by which generated plans missed the optimal plan vs. the number of query subgoals. Both CHAIN and PARTITION found near-optimal plans over the entire range of queries and, on the average, missed the optimal plan by less than 10%.

In summary, the PARTITION algorithm can have excellent practical performance, even though it gives very few theoretical guarantees. CHAIN also has very good performance, well beyond the theoretical guarantees we proved in Section 3. Finally, comparing the two algorithms, we observe that PARTITION consistently outperforms CHAIN in finding near-optimal plans.

7 Conclusion

In this paper, we considered the problem of query planning in heterogeneous data integration systems based on the mediation approach. We employed a cost model that focuses on the main costs in mediation systems. In this cost model, we developed two algorithms that guarantee the generation of feasible plans (when they exist). We showed that the problem at hand is NP-hard. One of our algorithms runs in polynomial time. It generates optimal plans in many cases and in other cases it has a linear bound on the worst case margin by which it misses the optimal plans. The second algorithm finds optimal plans in more scenarios, but has no bound on the margin of missing the optimal plans in the bad scenarios. We analyzed the performance of our algorithms using simulation experiments and extended our results to more complex cost models.

References

1. P. Apers, A. Hevner, S. Yao. Optimization Algorithms for Distributed Queries. In *IEEE Trans. Software Engineering*, 9(1), 1983.
2. P. Bernstein, N. Goodman, E. Wong, C. Reeve, J. Rothnie. Query Processing in a System for Distributed Databases (SDD-1). In *ACM Trans. Database Systems*, 6(4), 1981.
3. S. Chawathe, H. Garcia-Molina, J. Hammer, K. Ireland, Y. Papakonstantinou, J. Ullman, J. Widom. The TSIMMIS project: Integration of heterogeneous information sources. In *IPSJ*, Japan, 1994.
4. S. Cluet, G. Moerkotte. On the Complexity of Generating Optimal Left-deep Processing Trees with Cross Products. In *ICDT Conference*, 1995.
5. R. Epstein, M. Stonebraker. Analysis of Distributed Database Strategies. In *VLDB Conference*, 1980.
6. C. Galindo-Legaria, A. Pellenkoft, M. Kersten. Fast, Randomized Join Order Selection – Why Use Transformations? In *VLDB Conference*, 1994.
7. M. Garey, D. Johnson. Computers and Intractability: A Guide to the Theory of NP-Completeness. Freeman, San Francisco, 1979.

8. L. Haas, D. Kossman, E.L. Wimmers, J. Yang. Optimizing queries across diverse data sources. In *VLDB Conference*, 1997.
9. J. Hammer, H. Garcia-Molina, S. Nestorov, R. Yerneni, M. Breunig, V. Vassalos. Template-Based Wrappers in the TSIMMIS System. In *SIGMOD Conference*, 1997.
10. T. Ibaraki, T. Kameda. On the Optimal Nesting Order for Computing N-relational Joins. In *ACM Trans. Database Systems*, 9(3), 1984.
11. Y. Ioannidis, Y. Kang. Randomized Algorithms for Optimizing Large Join Queries. In *SIGMOD Conference*, 1990.
12. Y. Ioannidis, E. Wong. Query Optimization by Simulated Annealing. In *SIGMOD Conference*, 1987.
13. R. Krishnamurthy, H. Boral, C. Zaniolo. Optimization of Non-recursive Queries. In *VLDB Conference*, 1986.
14. A. Levy, A. Rajaraman, J. Ordille. Querying Heterogeneous Information Sources Using Source Descriptions. In *VLDB Conference*, 1996.
15. C. Li, R. Yerneni, V. Vassalos, H. Garcia-Molina, Y. Papakonstantinou, J. Ullman, M. Valiveti. Capability Based Mediation in TSIMMIS. In *SIGMOD Conference*, 1998.
16. K. Morris. An algorithm for ordering subgoals in NAIL!. In *ACM PODS*, 1988.
17. K. Ono, G. Lohman. Measuring the Complexity of Join Enumeration in Query Optimization. In *VLDB Conference*, 1990.
18. C. Papadimitriou, K. Steiglitz. Combinatorial Optimization: Algorithms and Complexity. Prentice-Hall, 1982.
19. Y. Papakonstantinou, A. Gupta, L. Haas. Capabilities-based Query Rewriting in Mediator Systems. In *PDIS Conference*, 1996.
20. A. Pellenkoft, C. Galindo-Legaria, M. Kersten. The Complexity of Transformation-Based Join Enumeration. In *VLDB Conference*, 1997.
21. W. Scheufele, G. Moerkotte. On the Comlexity of Generating Optimal Plans with Cartesian Products. In *PODS Conference*, 1997.
22. P. Selinger, M. Adiba. Access Path Selection in Distributed Databases Management Systems. In *Readings in Database Systems*. Edited by M. Stonebraker. Morgan-Kaufman Publishers, 1994.
23. M. Steinbrunn, G. Moerkotte, A. Kemper. Heuristic and Randomized Optimization for the Join Ordering Problem. In *VLDB Journal*, 6(3), 1997.
24. A. Swami. Optimization of Large Join Queries: Combining Heuristic and Combinatorial Techniques. In *SIGMOD Conference*, 1989.
25. A. Swami, A. Gupta. Optimization of Large Join Queries. In *SIGMOD Conference*, 1988.
26. A. Tomasic, L. Raschid, P. Valduriez. Scaling Heterogeneous Databases and the Design of Disco. In *Int. Conf. on Distributed Computing Systems*, 1996.
27. J. Ullman. Principles of Database and Knowledge-base Systems, Volumes I, II. Computer Science Press, Rockville MD.
28. J. Ullman, M. Vardi. The Complexity of Ordering Subgoals. In *ACM PODS*, 1988.
29. B. Vance, D. Maier. Rapid Bushy Join-Order Optimization with Cross Products. In *SIGMOD Conference*, 1996.
30. V. Vassalos, Y. Papakonstantinou. Describing and using query capabilities of heterogeneous sources. In *VLDB Conference*, 1997.
31. G. Wiederhold. Mediators in the Architecture of Future Information Systems. In *IEEE Computer*, 25:38-49, 1992.
32. R. Yerneni, C. Li, J. Ullman, H. Garcia-Molina. Optimizing Large Join Queries in Mediation Systems. http://www-db.stanford.edu/pub/papers/ljq.ps

Incremental $FO(+, <)$ Maintenance of All-Pairs Shortest Paths for Undirected Graphs after Insertions and Deletions

Chaoyi Pang, Ramamohanarao Kotagiri, and Guozhu Dong

Department of Computer Science, The University of Melbourne, Parkville 3052,
Australia, {chaoyi, rao, dong}@cs.mu.oz.au

Abstract. We give incremental algorithms, which support both edge insertions and deletions, for the all-pairs shortest-distance problem (APSD) in weighted undirected graphs. Our algorithms use first-order queries, + (addition) and < (less-than); they store $O(n^2)$ number of tuples, where n is the number of vertices, and have AC^0 data complexity for integer weights. Since $FO(+, <)$ is supported by almost all current database systems, our maintenance algorithms are more appropriate for database applications than non-database query type of maintenance algorithms. Our algorithms can also be extended to duplicate semantics.

1   Introduction

Finding shortest-path information in a graph is one of the most commonly encountered problems in the study of transportation and communication networks and has applications in communication systems, scheduling, computation of network flows, and in the context of document formatting *etc.* Since shortest-path information can be used for routing in a communication network, the possibility of changes to the network, say due to a link failure or a new link being added to the service, makes the incremental shortest-path problem relevant to routing.

Problem statement: We consider the incremental maintenance of the all-pairs shortest distance (which is called the distance problem) in undirected graphs after an edge insertion and an edge deletion. We only consider single edge insertion and single edge deletion operations as the unit changes to the graph. Any distance-modification on an edge could be accomplished through first deleting the edge then followed by adding a new edge with the modified distance between the same vertices.

Contributions: We start from the incremental maintenance algorithm for the all-pairs shortest-distance problem with positive distance on each edge ($APSD > 0$), then extend the maintenance result to the all-pairs shortest-distance problem with non-negative distance on edges ($APSD \geq 0$). A "restricted" reduction result between the $APSD > 0$ case and the $APSD \geq 0$ case is then given. Our maintenance algorithms for the distance problem can be applied to maintain the transitive closure problem in undirected graphs.

Catriel Beeri, Peter Buneman (Eds.): ICDT'99, LNCS 1540, pp. 365–382, 1998.
© Springer-Verlag Berlin Heidelberg 1998

In undirected graphs, the restriction of "non-negative distance" makes each shortest walk between two vertices being a shortest path between the same two vertices. The presence of negative-distance edges implies that shortest walks can be unbounded.

For the distance problem, our algorithms use first-order queries with addition "+" and less-than "<" operations ($FO(+, <)$) to maintain the shortest distance dynamically in undirected graphs after each edge insertion and edge deletion. The time complexity of our algorithms are dominated by "+" and "<" operations (with an upper bound of NC^1). When the distance of each edge in the graph is an integer, our algorithms have AC^0 data complexity [11] (the class of problems that can be solved using polynomially many processors in constant time). To the best of our knowledge, no AC^0 incremental algorithms (even for non-FO algorithms), supporting both edge deletions and edge insertions, for general undirected graphs are previously known. Our algorithms are the first of this kind. Since $FO(+, <)$ is supported by almost all current database system, our incremental maintenance algorithms are more appropriate for database applications than non-FO incremental algorithms. For the maintenance of the transitive closure problem, we keep the "shortest length" (the number of edges on the shortest paths). Our algorithms use simple data structures. The absence of recursion in our algorithms makes additional optimizations possible, as a range of optimization techniques to evaluate relational database queries can be applied to our algorithms. The optimization of recursive queries is significantly harder than that of relational queries.

All our algorithms employ one common technique as the basis for the maintainability results for an edge deletion: They first delete a set of tuples whose existence in the relation depends on the deleted edge; this step may delete more than necessary. Then they correct the wrong deletions by doing the relational natural join of the result of the first step with the modified graph up to two times. This generalises the technique used in [5] for the maintenance of the transitive closure of acyclic digraphs.

Although all the maintenance results in the paper are stated for the *set semantics*, they can be easily extended to the *bag semantics* (multiset).

Related Works: [9] gives a full dynamic algorithm which requires $O(n^2)$ sequential time for an edge insertion and/or an edge cost decrease, and $O(mn + n^2 \log n)$ time for an edge deletion and/or an edge cost increase, where n is the number of vertices and m is the number of edges in the graph. The algorithm in [1] is for graphs with nice topologies such as trees and outerplanar graphs. [4] achieves logarithmic query and update times for planar digraphs through graph decomposition. [10, 12] also consider planar graphs. These previous dynamic algorithms and batch algorithms for the *APSD* problem use elaborate data structures and need a recursive mechanism. Since most commercial database systems are relational database systems, which do not directly support recursion, a more powerful host language is needed for those algorithms to maintain the *APSD* views.

Given a recursive query, the non-recursive incremental evaluation approach uses non-recursive programs to compute the difference of the answers to the query against successive databases between updates. The mechanism used in this approach is called a "First-Order Incremental Evaluation System" in [7] and "Dyn-FO" in [14]. For undirected graphs, reachability, connectivity, bipartiteness and the minimum spanning forests problems have first-order incremental algorithms for edge insertion and edge deletion [6, 14]. [8] considers maintaining views defined by constrained transitive closure queries in directed graph with weights but for insertion only.

Comparing the algorithms of [6, 14] with ours for the transitive closure problem in undirected graphs, their algorithms are based on the maintenance of spanning forests of the given undirected graph while ours are not. Our algorithms are structurally simple and do not need to maintain the order of edges, a successor relation on all vertices. The algorithms based on maintaining spanning forests are hard to convert to solve the $APSD$ problem since the set of all edges on the shortest paths does not necessarily have a "tree-like" structure and, therefore, a single modification to the undirected graph may cause the reconstruction of $O(|V|)$ number of spanning trees (where V is the set of vertices of the graph). Our algorithms also have a unifying scheme of computation, for transitive closure in undirected graphs, in acyclic digraphs [5], and for the $APSD > 0$ (or $APSD \geq 0$) problem in undirected graphs.

Our algorithms are in $FO(+, <)$, using "+" and "<" to add and select the minimum length of paths. The storage demands of our algorithms stay within the same order of magnitude as the algorithm of [6].

As Spira and Pan [17] show, for *directed graphs*, the batch all-pairs shortest-distance problem can, in some sense, be reduced to the problem of updating the solution to the all-pairs shortest-distance problem after an edge deletion. [17] says an incremental algorithm that saves only shortest-distance information cannot, in the worst case, do any better than a batch algorithm. Our results show the statement is not true for the $APSD > 0$ problem in *undirected graphs*.

Organisation: We define some notations in Section 2. In Section 3 we give our incremental algorithm for the distance problem in undirected graphs with each edge having a positive distance. Section 4 extends the maintenance result of Section 3 to the undirected graph with each edge having a non-negative distance. Section 5 shows that the $APSD \geq 0$ problem can be maintained in the same way as that of $APSD > 0$ under certain restrictions and gives a reduction between $APSD > 0$ and $APSD \geq 0$. Section 6 presents some concluding remarks and additional applications of our results.

2 Preliminaries

We assume the reader is familiar with the first-order logic (or the relational calculus). In this section we present some relevant standard terminology of graph theory.

An undirected graph $G = (V, E)$ consists of a finite set of vertices V and a set of edges E such that $E \subseteq \{(u, v) | u, v \in V\}$, where (u, v) is viewed as an unordered pair. Suppose each edge e of G has a distance, which is denoted as $dist(e)$. For example, $dist(e)$ may represent the "weight" of edge e or the time spent to travel between City a and City b where $e = (a, b)$.

In this paper, all graphs mentioned are undirected graphs. We will denote "edge $e = (a, b)$ is in G" simply by $G(a, b)$ (or $G(e)$).

An edge e can be inserted to (or deleted from) a graph G. We use G_{+e} and $G + e$ to denote $G \cup \{e\}$ and use G_{-e} and $G - e$ to denote $G - \{e\}$.

A sequence $u_0 u_1 ... u_n$ $(n > 0)$ of vertices in G is a *walk* (between u_0 and u_n) if (u_{i-1}, u_i) is in G for each $i \in [1..n]$; the sequence is a *path* if it is a walk and $u_i \neq u_j$ for all $0 \leq i < j \leq n$ such that $i \neq 0$ or $j \neq n$. We say $u_i u_{i+1} ... u_{j-1} u_j$ is a subpath of $u_0 u_1 ... u_n$ for all $0 \leq i < j \leq n$; when $i \neq 0$ or $j \neq n$, we call the former path a *real subpath* of the latter path. The *distance* of a path (or a walk) p (denoted as $dist(p)$) is defined as the sum of $dist(e)$ of all edges e on the path (or walk). The *length* of a path (or a walk) p (denoted as $length(p)$) is defined as the number of edges on the path (or walk). Two vertices x and y of G is said to be reachable if there exists a path between x and y in G.

The *shortest-distance (shortest-length*, respectively) path (or walk) between vertex x and vertex y is a *path* (or walk) between x and y with minimum distance (length, respectively). If there is no path between two vertices then the distance (length) is defined to be infinity. A shortest path is a path which has the shortest distance.

We sometimes need to emphasise an ordering of the vertices on a path. We say a path (or walk) p (between vertex u and v) is *from vertex u to vertex v* to imply that p is in the order of $u...v$, and we say a path (or walk) p from u to v *goes through edge $e = (a, b)$ in the order of ab* to imply that p has the form of $p = u...ab...v$.

The all-pairs shortest-distance ($APSD$) problem (the distance problem for short) is to find the shortest distance between every pair of vertices in a graph. A restricted form of the $APSD$ problem is the $APSD > 0$ ($APSD \geq 0$, respectively) problem which restricts each edge in the graph to a positive (non-negative, respectively) distance. We will discuss the $APSD > 0$ ($APSD \geq 0$, respectively) problem when the underlying graph is undirected and, as such, any edge insertion and distance-modification for the undirected graph preserve the property of each edge having a positive (non-negative, respectively) distance.

The all-pairs shortest-path ($APSP$) problem (the path problem for short) is to find the shortest path between every pair of vertices in the graph.

We will usually maintain relations SP_G or SPD_G for each undirected graph G. SP_G is defined as $\{(x, y, d)|$ a shortest path between x and y in G has distance $d\}$. $SP_G(x, y, d)$ is true if and only if the shortest path between x and y in G has distance d. We assume $SP_G(u, u, 0)$ holds for each vertex u of G and $SP_G(x, y, \infty)$ (∞ can expressed by a null value in the database) holds if there is no path between vertex x and vertex y. Similarly to SP_G, we define SPD_G to be $\{(x, y, l, d)|$ the shortest paths between x and y in G have distance d and the least number of edges on all such shortest paths is l}. $SPD_G(x,y,l,d)$ is true if and only if (i) the shortest paths between x and y in G have distance d and (ii) one shortest path between x and y in G passes l number of edges and all other shortest-paths between x and y in G pass no less than l number of edges. When there is no path between vertex x and vertex y in G, we assume $SPD_G(x,y,\infty,\infty)$ holds.

In an undirected graph G with non-negative distance edges, for each vertex u of G, we define $SPD_G(u,u,0,0)$. Clearly, $SPD_G(x,y,0,d)$ implies $(d=0) \wedge (x = y)$. However, $SPD_G(x,y,l,0)$ does not necessarily mean $l = 0$ or $x = y$.

For each binary relation R, we let $\widehat{R} = R \cup \{(u,u)|u$ is a vertex in $R\}$.

Clearly, in an undirected graph G, if $SP_G(u,v,d)$ $(SPD_G(u,v,l,d)$, respectively) holds then $SP_G(v,u,d)$ $(SPD_G(v,u,l,d)$, respectively) holds. The space upper bound needed for storing these relations is $O(|V|^2)$ where V is the set of vertices of G.

Given a set of numbers $\{l_1, l_2, ..., l_k\}$, we use $\min\{l_1, l_2, ..., l_k\}$ to denote the minimum element among the numbers Since the *minimum* operator (min) is applied to a bounded set at a time in our algorithms, it can be replaced by expressions using *less-than* ($<$).

3   Incremental Algorithm for $APSD > 0$

In this section, for an undirected graph G with each edge having a positive distance, we give our incremental maintenance algorithms to find the shortest distance between every pair of vertices after single edge insertion and single edge deletion. The technique for edge insertion is fairly simple and its similar forms have been used previously. The technique for edge deletion is much more involved than that for edge insertion. During the process of edge deletion, we use one property for undirected graphs (Lemma 2): any shortest path of G_{-e} can be regenerated through the join of two shortest paths, which do not pass through edge e, with one edge in G_{-e}. It is because of this property that our algorithms belongs to $FO(+,<)$. The algorithms in this section can be used to incrementally maintain the transitive closure of undirected graphs (by setting SP_G to be $\{(x,y,l)|$ there exists a path between x and y in G and l is the minimum number of edges on such paths $\}$).

The algorithms in this section use the following lemma. Intuitively, it implies that a shortest path can only be built from (other) shortest paths.

Lemma 1. *Given an undirected graph G,*

1. *if path $p = uw_1...w_kv$ $(u = w_0, v = w_{k+1})$ is a shortest path between u and v then any real subpath $q = w_i...w_j$ of p is the shortest path between w_i and w_j, where $0 \leq i < j \leq k+1$.*
2. *if $dist(g) > 0$ for each edge $g \in G$, a walk between two vertices can never be a shortest if it is not a path.*

Proof. 1. Otherwise, suppose subpath $q_1 = w_i...w_j$ is not a shortest path between w_i and w_j. Let a shortest path between w_i and w_j be $q_2 = w_i v_1...v_h w_j$. Then $dist(q_2) < dist(q_1)$ and, for walk $q = uw_1..w_i v_1..v_h, w_j..w_k v$, $dist(q) < dist(p)$. That is contradictory to p being a shortest path, and so the result is proved.

2. Suppose walk $q = u_0 u_1...u_k$ is not a path. Then there exist $0 \le i < j \le k$ such that $u_i = u_j$ and the distance of subwalk $u_i...u_j$ of q is positive. Therefore, $q' = u_0..u_i u_{j+1}..u_k$ must have a shorter distance than q, and q is not a shortest path. $\diamond$

The converse of Lemma 1(1) does not hold. For example, let $G = \{(a, b, 1), (b, c, 1), (a, c, 1)\}$. Then $SP_G(a, b, 1) \wedge SP_G(b, c, 1) \wedge SP_G(a, c, 1)$ holds. The path $a\,b\,c$ is not a shortest path in G, but the subpaths $a\,b$ and $b\,c$ are shortest paths.

3.1   Inserting Edge e to G

The technique for edge insertion is simple. Similar techniques have been used in many recursive algorithms of [16, 2, 3, 1, 15] and in the first-order algorithms of [7, 14].

Theorem 1. *Suppose $dist(g) > 0$ for each edge g of G. When adding a new edge $e = (a, b)$ to G where $dist(e) > 0$, we can construct a formula ψ of $FO(+, <)$ from SP_G and e such that $SP_{G_{+e}} \equiv \psi$.*

Proof. Let

$$\psi(x, y, d) \equiv (\exists d_0, d_1, d_2, d_3, d_4)\ SP_G(x, a, d_1) \wedge SP_G(b, y, d_2) \wedge$$
$$SP_G(x, b, d_3) \wedge SP_G(a, y, d_4) \wedge SP_G(x, y, d_0) \wedge$$
$$(d = min\{dist(e) + d_1 + d_2, dist(e) + d_3 + d_4, d_0\}).$$

Observe that the use of min is applied to a set of three numbers. So it can be replaced by formulas with $<$ operators. Therefore, $\psi \in FO(+, <)$.

We need to show $SP_{G_{+e}} \equiv \psi$. To show that $SP_{G_{+e}} \Rightarrow \psi$, let (x, y, d) be any given tuple of $SP_{G_{+e}}$, Two cases arise:

1. Edge e is not on the shortest paths between x and y. Then $SP_G(x, y, d)$ holds and so $\psi(x, y, d)$ is true.

2. Edge e is on a shortest path between x and y. Let us assume, without loss of generality, the shortest path has the form of $x...w...ab...v...y$. By Lemma 1, since path $x...w...ab...v...y$ is the shortest path in $G + e$, paths $q_1 = x...w...a$ and $q_2 = b...v...y$ are shortest paths and they clearly do not pass through edge e. Therefore, $d = dist(q_1) + dist(q_2) + dist(e)$ and $\psi(x, y, d)$ is true.

To show that $\psi \Rightarrow SP_{G_{+e}}$, let (x, y, d) be a tuple such that $\psi(x, y, d)$ is true. Observe that ψ is selecting the smallest distance d of the shortest paths from x to y that passes through e and the shortest paths from x to y that do not pass through e. This d is clearly the shortest distance from x to y. Hence $SP_{G_{+e}}(x, y, d)$ holds. $\diamond$

Example 1. Let

$$G = \{(a, j, 1), (a, e, 52), (b, c, 7), (b, k, 7), (c, d, 2), (d, e, 2), (e, f, 4),$$
$$(f, g, 6), (g, h, 3), (g, l, 2), (h, i, 8), (h, l, 2), (i, j, 19), (k, l, 6)\}$$

as shown in Figure 3.1(1). The shortest paths between vertices are given in Figure 3.1(2). Consider inserting the edge $\varepsilon = (a, b, 2)$ $(dist(\varepsilon) = 2)$. The shortest paths of $G + \varepsilon$ computed by the algorithm are shown in Figure 3.1(3). For instance, $SP_{G+\varepsilon}(a, c, 9)$ holds since $9 = min\{2 + 7, 45\}$, $G(a, b, 2)$, $SP_G(b, c, 7)$ and $SP_G(a, c, 45)$.

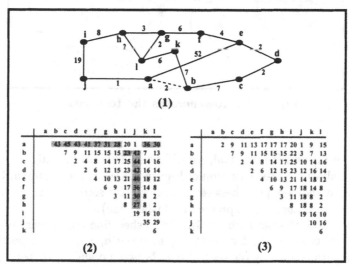

	a	b	c	d	e	f	g	h	i	j	k	l
a		43	45	43	41	37	31	28	20	1	36	30
b			7	9	11	15	15	15	23	42	7	13
c				2	4	8	14	17	25	44	14	16
d					2	6	12	15	23	42	16	14
e						4	10	13	21	40	18	12
f							6	9	17	36	14	8
g								3	11	30	8	2
h									8	27	8	2
i										19	16	10
j											35	29
k												6

(2)

	a	b	c	d	e	f	g	h	i	j	k	l
a		2	9	11	13	17	17	17	20	1	9	15
b			7	9	11	15	15	15	22	3	7	13
c				2	4	8	14	17	25	10	14	16
d					2	6	12	15	23	12	16	14
e						4	10	13	21	14	18	12
f							6	9	17	18	14	8
g								3	11	18	8	2
h									8	18	8	2
i										19	16	10
j											10	16
k												6

(3)

Figure 3.1: Shortest distances

3.2   Deleting Edge e from G

The main result in the section is for edge deletion.

Theorem 2. *For any undirected graph G satisfying $dist(e) > 0$ for each edge e of G, we can construct a formula ψ of $FO(+, <)$ from SP_G and e such that $SP_{G-e} \equiv \psi$.*

To prove Theorem 2 and to construct ψ, we need some lemmas, including the following key lemma.

Lemma 2. *Let $dist(g) > 0$ for each edge g of G. Suppose there exists a shortest path $p_1 = u...ab...v$ from vertex u to vertex v of G which goes through edge $e = (a, b)$ in the order of ab (as shown in Figure 3.2(I)). Let $p_2 = uw_1...w_kv$ $(u = w_0$ and $v = w_{k+1})$ be a shortest path between u and v in $G - e$.*

a. *If a shortest path of G from u to w_i (w_i is on p_2, $1 \leq i \leq k+1$) goes through edge e, then it goes through edge e in the order of ab.*

b. *Similarly, if a shortest path of G from w_i (w_i is on p_2, $0 \leq i \leq k$) to v goes through edge e, then it goes through edge e in the order of ab.*

c. *There exists a vertex w_i ($1 \leq i \leq k+1$) such that for subpaths $p_{21} = uw_1...w_{i-1}$ and $p_{22} = w_i...v$ of p_2, no shortest path of G among vertices $u, w_1, ..., w_{i-1}$ (and $w_i, w_{i+1}, ..., v$) goes through edge e.*

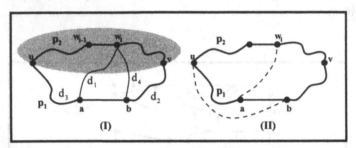

Figure 3.2: Regenerates shortest paths

Proof. Since (a) and (b) are dual, we will prove (a) and (c) only.

For (a), we show that the situation of Figure 3.2(II) cannot happen. Otherwise, there exists a shortest path between u and w_i (for some $0 < i \leq k+1$) which has the form of $u...ba...w_i$ (expressed in dashed line).

Let us denote the path, shown by the dashed line (the lower solid line, respectively), between u and b by $path_{dash}(u, b)$ ($path_{solid}(u, b)$, respectively) and denote the path, shown by the dashed line, between a and w_i by $path_{dash}(a, w_i)$.

By the hypotheses and Lemma 1, the shortest paths between a and b have distance $dist(e)$ and

$$SP_G(a, b, dist(e)) \wedge SP_G(u, a, dist(path_{dash}(u, b)) + dist(e)) \wedge$$
$$SP_G(u, a, dist(path_{solid}(u, b)) - dist(e)) \wedge$$
$$SP_G(u, b, dist(path_{solid}(u, b))) \wedge SP_G(u, b, dist(path_{dash}(u, b))).$$

The formula means that the shortest paths between u and a have a distance of $dist(path_{dash}(u, b)) + dist(e)$ and of $dist(path_{solid}(u, b)) - dist(e)$; the shortest paths between u and b have a distance of $dist(path_{solid}(u, b))$ and of $dist(path_{dash}(u, b))$. Comparing the distance components (the third attribute) of above formula, we have

$$dist(path_{dash}(u, b)) + dist(e) = dist(path_{solid}(u, b)) - dist(e)), \text{ and}$$
$$dist(path_{solid}(u, b)) = dist(path_{dash}(u, b)).$$

Therefore $dist(e) = 0$, contradictory to the hypothesis that $dist(f) > 0$ for each edge f of G.

For (c), we illustrate the situation with Figure 3.2(I). Let i be the smallest integer among $[1...k+1]$ such that a shortest path between u and w_i uses edge e and *every* shortest path between u and w_{i-1} does not use edge e. Since no shortest path from u to u uses e and edge e is on a shortest path between u and v, i exists.

According to the way that vertex w_i is chosen, subpath $p_{21} = u w_1 ... w_{i-1}$ of p_2 is the shortest path between u and w_{i-1} both in G and $G - e$, and there is no shortest path of G among vertices $u, w_1, ..., w_{i-1}$ using edge e. By Lemma 1 and Lemma 2(a),

$$SP_G(u, w_i, d_3 + d_4 + dist(e)) \wedge SP_G(u, a, d_3) \wedge SP_G(b, w_i, d_4) \qquad (1)$$

holds. We now prove that e does not lie on any shortest paths among vertices $w_i, ..., w_k, v$ in G. Otherwise, according to Lemma 1 and Lemma 2(b),

$$SP_G(w_i, v, d_1 + d_2 + dist(e)) \wedge SP_G(w_i, a, d_1) \wedge SP_G(b, v, d_2) \qquad (2)$$

holds. From (1) and (2), since a shortest path between two vertices is not longer than any other paths between the same vertices, we have

$$d_3 + d_4 + dist(e) \le d_3 + d_1, \qquad and \qquad d_1 + d_2 + dist(e) \le d_4 + d_2.$$

It follows that $dist(e) \le 0$, which is contradictory to our positive-distance edge assumption. This implies that edge e does not lie on any shortest path among $w_i, ..., w_k, v$ and therefore, no shortest path among $w_i, ..., w_k, v$ goes through edge e. $\diamond$

Example 2. We now illustrate the above lemma by considering undirected graph $G + \varepsilon$ in Example 1. The shortest path between vertex j ($u = j$ in the Lemma) and vertex d ($v = d$ in the Lemma) is $p_1 = j\,a\,b\,c\,d$. Path $p_2 = j\,i\,h\,g\,f\,e\,d$ is the shortest path between j and d not going through edge ε. In Lemma 2(c), we can let the chosen vertex be h ($w_i = h$ in the Lemma). Therefore, $path(j, i) = j\,i$ is the shortest path between j and i and $path(h, d) = h\,g\,f\,e\,d$ is the shortest path between h and d (no shortest paths among i and j and among h, g, f, e, d go through edge (a, b)) according to Lemma 2(c).

Lemma 2(a) and Lemma 2(b) imply an "ordering" on the vertices of G. They suggest that if one shortest path from an earlier vertex to a later vertex on path p_2 goes through edge e in one "direction" then every shortest path from any earlier vertex to any later vertex on p_2 goes through edge e in the same "direction", so long as the shortest path passes through edge e.

Given an undirected graph G satisfying $dist(g) > 0$ for each edge g of G and an edge $e = (a, b) \in G$, the tuples of SP_G can be classified into two kinds: S_1, the set of tuples (x, y, d) such that no shortest path between x and y in G goes through edge e, and $S_2 = SP_G - S_1$. Lemma 2 implies that each shortest path of $G - e$ which is not in S_1 can be regenerated, through at most two join operations, by those shortest paths which do not go through edge e in G (i.e., in S_1). In order to give a full description, we introduce some formulas.

For edge $e \in G$, let $\Gamma_e^G(x, y, d)$ be a formula stating the fact that there is a shortest path between x and y in G using edge $e = (a, b)$, that is,

$$\Gamma_e^G(x, y, d) \equiv (\exists d_0, d_1, d_2, d_3, d_4) \, SP_G(x, y, d) \wedge [SP_G(x, a, d_1) \wedge$$
$$SP_G(b, y, d_2) \wedge (d = d_1 + d_2 + dist(e)) \vee SP_G(x, b, d_3) \wedge$$
$$SP_G(a, y, d_4) \wedge (d = d_3 + d_4 + dist(e))].$$
$$\Omega_e^G(x, y, d) \equiv SP_G(x, y, d) \wedge \neg\Gamma_e^G(x, y, d).$$

Then $\Omega_e^G(x, y, d)$ states that the shortest paths between x and y in G have distance of d but no such a shortest path uses edge e. With the newly defined formulas, Lemma 2(c) can be rewritten into the following form:

Lemma 2(d): Let $dist(g) > 0$ for each edge g of G. Suppose there exists a shortest path $p_1 = u...ab...v$ from vertex u to vertex v of G which goes through edge $e = (a, b)$ in the order of ab (as shown in Figure 3.2(I)). Let $p_2 = uw_1...w_k v$ ($u = w_0$ and $v = w_{k+1}$) be a shortest path in $G - e$. Then there exists a vertex w_i ($1 \leq i \leq k + 1$) such that for subpaths $p_{21} = uw_1...w_{i-1}$ and $p_{22} = w_i...v$ of p_2, $\Omega_e^G(u, w_{i-1}, dist(p_{21})) \wedge G_{-e}(w_{i-1}, w_i) \wedge \Omega_e^G(w_i, v, dist(p_{22}))$ holds. $\Diamond$

Let

$$\Phi_e^G(x, y, d) \equiv (\exists d_1, d_2)(\exists w_1, w_2) \, \Omega_e^G(x, w_1, d_1) \wedge \widehat{G_{-e}}(w_1, w_2) \wedge$$
$$\Omega_e^G(w_2, y, d_2) \wedge (d = d_1 + dist(w_1, w_2) + d_2).$$

Lemma 3. *Given an undirected graph G satisfying $dist(e) > 0$ for each edge $e \in G$, $SP_{G_{-e}}$ is a subset of Φ_e^G.*

Proof. Suppose $SP_{G_{-e}}(x, y, d)$ holds and we prove $\Phi_e^G(x, y, d)$ is true.

Since $SP_{G_{-e}}(x, y, d)$ holds, there exists a shortest path $p = xw_1...w_k y$ (let $x = w_0$ and $y = w_{k+1}$) in $G - e$ such that $SP_{G_{-e}}(x, y, dist(p))$. Two cases arise: (a) In G, none of the shortest paths between x and y uses edge e. Then $\Omega_e^G(x, y, d)$ is true. Since $\widehat{G_{-e}}(y, y) \wedge \Omega_e^G(y, y, 0)$ is true, $\Omega_e^G(x, y, d)$, $\widehat{G_{-e}}(y, y)$ and $\Omega_e^G(y, y, 0)$ are all true. Therefore, $\Phi_e^G(x, y, d)$ holds. (b) Otherwise. There is a shortest path between x and y in G using edge e. From Lemma 2(d), there exists w_i such that

$$\Omega_e^G(x, w_{i-1}, d_1) \wedge G_{-e}(w_{i-1}, w_i) \wedge \Omega_e^G(w_i, y, d_2) \wedge (d = d_1 + dist(w_{i-1}, w_i) + d_2)$$

is true. Therefore, $\Phi_e^G(x, y, d)$ holds. $\Diamond$

Now, Theorem 2 can be easily proved from Lemma 3.

Proof of Theorem 2 Let $\psi(x, y, d) \equiv \Phi_e^G(x, y, d) \wedge (\forall d') \, [\Phi_e^G(x, y, d') \rightarrow (d \leq d')]$ Clearly, formula ψ is in $FO(+, <)$. From Lemma 3, we know $SP_{G_{-e}} \subseteq \psi$. On the other hand, suppose $\psi(x, y, d)$ holds. By the definition of $SP_{G_{-e}}$, there exists d' such that $SP_{G_{-e}}(x, y, d')$ holds. Since $SP_{G_{-e}} \subseteq \psi$, $\psi(x, y, d')$ holds. By the definition of ψ, there is at most one d'' for tuple (x, y) such that $\psi(x, y, d'')$ holds. So $d = d'$. Thus $\psi \subseteq SP_{G_{-e}}$. $\Diamond$

Example 3. For a simple illustration of the Theorem, let us consider the undirected graph $G_{+\varepsilon}$ of Example 1. Suppose we delete edge $\varepsilon = (a,b)$. $\Gamma_\varepsilon^{G_{+\varepsilon}}(j,d,12)$ is true since the shortest path $j\ a\ b\ c\ d$ $(SP_{G_{+\varepsilon}}(j,d,12)$ holds) between j and d uses edge (a,b). The shortest path between j and d in $G_{+\varepsilon} - (a,b)$ (i.e., G) is path $j\ i\ h\ g\ f\ e\ d$ $(SP_G(j,d,42)$ holds). $\Phi_\varepsilon^{G_{+\varepsilon}}(j,d,42)$ is true since $\Omega_\varepsilon^{G_{+\varepsilon}}(j,i,19)$, $G(i,h)$ and $\Omega_\varepsilon^{G_{+\varepsilon}}(h,d,15)$ all hold and the distance of edge (i,h) is 8.

Lemma 3 reveals why we have such an incremental maintenance result for undirected graphs. It says that the distance of a shortest path in $G-e$ is bounded by the distances of (three) shortest paths in G. A similar result holds for acyclic digraphs, but not for general digraphs.

Without the condition of $dist(g) > 0$ for each edge g of G, the "make-up" steps, in which we regenerate those new shortest paths, may not be completed through a bounded number of join operations.

Example 4. Let G be a connected undirected graph with each edge's distance being 0. Whenever an edge is deleted, each tuple of SP_G will also be deleted by our algorithm, since the shortest path between every two vertices in the graph has the same distance as that of a walk passing the deleted edge.

One interesting implication of above example is that we need to generalise the notion of "the distance of a path" to "the length of derivation", for the incremental maintenance of undirected graphs with non-negative edge distances.

4 Incremental Algorithm for $APSD \geq 0$

At the end of Section 3, we have shown in Example 4 that the general $APSD \geq 0$ problem may not be maintained with only relation SP_G for edge deletion. In this section, we extend the maintenance result of $APSD > 0$ to $APSD \geq 0$ and show such maintenance can be obtained through keeping SPD_G, the extended relation of SP_G by adding one more "attribute" to each tuple. We show that $SPD_{G_{+e}}$ and $SPD_{G_{-e}}$ can be maintained incrementally from G and SPD_G in $FO(+,<)$.

We note that the incremental maintenance algorithm in Section 3 can also be used for the $APSD \geq 0$ problem after non-negative edge insertions and positive edge deletions. This can be proved similarly as those results in Section 3. Our algorithms in this section work for all single edge updates.

The existence of 0-distance edges in an undirected graph G implies that some walks (which are not paths) have the same distance as some paths. When each edge of G has a positive distance, each tuple of SP_G corresponds to paths of G. When G has 0-distance edges, a tuple of SP_G may correspond to walks of G. Thus, after deleting a 0-distance edge, each 0-distance walk which goes through the deleted edge is deleted if we use the algorithm for edge deletion in Section 3. It is this fact that makes the algorithm for edge deletion of Section 3 incorrect for 0-distance-edge deletions. To solve this problem, we will maintain SPD_G instead of SP_G.

The following lemma means that each tuple (x,y,l,d) of SPD_G corresponds to a path and each subpath of the path corresponds to a tuple of SPD_G.

Lemma 4. *Suppose $dist(g) \geq 0$ for each edge g in an undirected graph G and $p = u_0u_1...u_k$ is a walk of G.*

1. *If $SPD_G(u_0, u_k, k, dist(p))$ holds then p is a path.*
2. *If $SPD_G(u_0, u_k, k, dist(p))$ holds then for any subpath $p' = u_iu_{i+1}...u_j$ ($0 \leq i < j \leq k$) of path p, $SPD_G(u_i, u_j, j - i, dist(p'))$ holds.*

Proof. 1. Suppose walk $p = u_0u_1...u_k$ is not a path. Then there exist $0 \leq i < j \leq k$ such that $u_i = u_j$ and the subwalk $u_i...u_j$ of p passes at least one edge. Therefore, $q = u_0..u_iu_{j+1}..u_k$ passes less edges than p does and $dist(q) \leq dist(p)$. It implies that $SPD_G(u_0, u_k, k, dist(p))$ cannot be true.

2. Otherwise, there exists a subpath $q_1 = u_i...u_j$ such that $SPD_G(u_i, u_j, j - i, dist(q_1))$ is not true. Let $q_2 = u_iv_1...v_hu_j$ be a path between u_i and u_j such that $SPD_G(u_i, u_j, h + 1, dist(q_2))$ holds. Since $\neg SPD_G(u_i, u_j, j - i, dist(q_1))$ holds, $(dist(q_2) < dist(q_1)) \vee (h + 1 < j - i)$ holds. Let us consider the walk $q = u_0u_1..u_iv_1..v_hu_j..u_kv$. Clearly, $(dist(q) < dist(p)) \vee (i+h+k-j+1 < k)$ holds. This is contradictory to the fact that $SPD_G(u_0, u_k, k, dist(p))$ holds. Therefore, the result is proved.   ◇

We note that the converse of Lemma 4(1) does not hold. For example, let G be the undirected graph of $\{(a,b,1), (b,c,0), (c,d,0), (b,d,0), (d,e,1)\}$. Then $q = a\ b\ c\ d\ e$ is a path ($dist(p) = 2$). But $\neg SPD_G(a,e,4,2) \wedge SPD_G(a,e,3,2)$ holds.

4.1   Inserting Edge e to G

Theorem 3. *Suppose $dist(g) \geq 0$ for each edge g of G. When adding a new edge $e = (a,b)$ to G where $dist(e) \geq 0$, we can construct a formula φ of $FO(+, <)$ from SPD_G, G and e such that $SPD_{G+e} \equiv \varphi$.*

Proof. Let φ be defined through the following formulas:

$$SP_{G+e}(x,y,d) \equiv (\exists d_0, d_1, d_2, d_3, d_4)(\exists l_0, l_1, l_2, l_3, l_4)\ SPD_G(x, y, l_0, d_0) \wedge$$
$$SPD_G(x, a, l_1, d_1) \wedge SPD_G(b, y, l_2, d_2) \wedge SPD_G(x, b, l_3, d_3) \wedge$$
$$SPD_G(a, y, l_4, d_4) \wedge$$
$$(d = min\{dist(e) + d_1 + d_2, dist(e) + d_3 + d_4, d_0\}).$$

$$\Lambda_e^G(x, y, l, d) \equiv (\exists d_1, d_2, d_3, d_4)(\exists l_1, l_2, l_3, l_4)\ SP_{G+e}(x, y, d) \wedge$$
$$[SPD_G(x, y, l, d) \vee SPD_G(x, a, l_1, d_1) \wedge SPD_G(b, y, l_2, d_2) \wedge$$
$$(d = dist(e) + d_1 + d_2) \wedge (l = l_1 + l_2 + 1) \vee SPD_G(x, b, l_3, d_3) \wedge$$
$$SPD_G(a, y, l_4, d_4) \wedge (d = dist(e) + d_3 + d_4) \wedge (l = l_3 + l_4 + 1)].$$

$$\varphi(x, y, l, d) \equiv \Lambda_e^G(x, y, l, d) \wedge (\forall l')[\Lambda_e^G(x, y, l', d) \to (l \leq l')].$$

Clearly, $\varphi \in FO(+, <)$ since min can be replaced with *less-than* ($<$).

We need to prove $SPD_{G+e} \equiv \varphi$. In $G + e$, let q be a shortest path between x and y passing through l-number of edges such that $SPD_{G+e}(x, y, l, d)$ holds where $d = dist(q)$. Two cases arise:

1. Edge e is not on path q. Then $SP_G(x, y, d) \wedge SPD_G(x, y, l, d)$ holds. From the way that φ is constructed, $SPD_{G_{+e}}(x, y, l, d) \wedge \varphi(x, y, l, d)$ holds.

2. Edge e is on path q. Let us assume, without loss of generality, that path q has the form of $x...w...ab...v...y$. Since $SPD_{G_{+e}}(x, y, l, d)$ holds for path q, by Lemma 4, for subpaths $q_1 = x...w...a$ and $q_2 = b...v...y$, $SPD_G(x, a, l_1, d_1) \wedge SPD_G(b, y, l_2, d_2)$ holds where $d_i = dist(q_i)$ and l_i is the number of edges on path q_i $(i = 1, 2)$. Therefore, $d = d_1 + d_2 + dist(e)$, $l = l_1 + l_2 + 1$ and $SPD_{G_{+e}} \subseteq \Lambda_e^G$ holds. Given a tuple (x, y, l, d) of $SPD_{G_{+e}}$, we claim that for each tuple (x, y, l', d) of Λ_e^G, $l \leq l'$ holds (Otherwise, there is a tuple (x, y, l_w, d) of Λ_e^G such that $l_w < l$. Then there is a walk q_w in G_{+e} such that $dist(q_w) = d$ and $length(q_w) = l_w$. This is contradictory to the definition of $SPD_{G_{+e}}$). Therefore, $SPD_{G_{+e}} \subseteq \varphi$ from the definition of φ.

   On the other hand, suppose $\varphi(x, y, l, d)$ holds. By the definition of $SPD_{G_{+e}}$, there exist d' and l' such that $SPD_{G_{+e}}(x, y, l', d')$ holds. Since $SPD_{G_{+e}} \subseteq \varphi$, $\varphi(x, y, l', d')$ holds. By the definition of φ, there is at most one d'' and one l'' such that $\varphi(x, y, l'', d'')$ holds. So, $d = d'$ and $l - l'$. Thus $\varphi \subseteq SPD_{G_{+e}}$. $\Diamond$

4.2   Deleting Edge e from G

The maintenance result for edge deletion is

Theorem 4. *For any undirected graph G satisfying $dist(e) \geq 0$ for each edge e of G, we can construct a formula φ of $FO(+, <)$ from SPD_G and e such that $SPD_{G_{-e}} \equiv \psi$.*

Similarly to the $APSD > 0$ problem, we need the following lemmas to prove the maintenance result.

Lemma 5. *Suppose $dist(g) \geq 0$ for each edge g of G. In G, let p_1 be a shortest path between vertex u and vertex v which passes through the minimum number of edges of all such shortest paths (i.e., $SPD_G(u, v, l, dist(p_1))$ holds for some l). We assume, without loss of generality, path p_1 goes through edge $e = (a, b)$ in the order of $u...ab...v$ as shown in Figure 3.2(I). Let $p_2 = uw_1...w_k v$ be a shortest path between u and v $(u = w_0, v = w_{k+1})$ in $G - e$ and $SPD_{G_{-e}}(u, v, k + 1, dist(p_2))$ holds.*

a. *If a shortest-path q_1 from u to w_i $(i = 1, ..., k + 1)$ goes through edge e and passes through l_1-number of edges such that $SPD_G(u, w_i, l_1, dist(q_1))$ holds, then path q_1 from u to w_i goes through edge e in the order of ab.*

b. *If a shortest-path q_2 from w_i $(i = 0, ..., k)$ to v goes through edge e and passes through l_2-number of edges such that $SPD_G(w_i, v, l_2, dist(q_2))$ holds, then path q_2 from w_i to v goes through edge e in the order of ab.*

c. *There exists a vertex w_i $(1 \leq i \leq k + 1)$ such that for the subpaths $p_{21} = uw_1...w_{i-1}$ and $p_{22} = w_i...v$ of p_2,*

$$SPD_G(u, w_{i-1}, i - 1, dist(p_{21})) \wedge SPD_G(w_i, v, k + 1 - i, dist(p_{22}))$$

holds and no shortest path among $u, w_1, ..., w_{i-1}$ *($w_i, ..., w_k v$, respectively)
goes through edge e and passes h-number of edges in G satisfying* $h \leq i - 1$
($h \leq k + 1 - i$, respectively).

Proof. Since (a) and (b) are dual, we will prove (a) and (c) only.

For (a), we show that the situation of Figure 3.2(II) cannot happen. Otherwise, there exists a shortest path q' (expressed in dashed line) between u and w_i for some $0 < i \leq k + 1$ such that $SPD_G(u, w_i, k_1 + k_2 + 3, dist(q'))$.

Let us denote the path, shown by the dashed line (solid line, respectively), between vertex u and vertex b by $path_{dash}(u, b)$ ($path_{solid}(u, b)$, respectively) and denote the path, shown by the dashed line, between a and w_i by $path_{dash}(a, w_i)$. By the hypotheses and Lemma 4, the shortest paths from a to b in G have distance $dist(e)$ and

$$SPD_G(a, b, 1, dist(e)) \wedge SPD_G(u, a, k_1 + 2, dist(path_{dash}(u, b)) + dist(e))$$
$$\wedge SPD_G(u, a, h_3, dist(path_{solid}(u, b)) - dist(e))$$
$$\wedge SPD_G(u, b, h_3 + 1, dist(path_{solid}(u, b)))$$
$$\wedge SPD_G(u, b, k_1 + 1, dist(path_{dash}(u, b)))$$

holds. The formula means that the minimum number of edges on shortest paths between u and a is $k_1 + 2$ and h_3; the minimum number of edges on shortest paths between u and b is $k_1 + 1$ and $h_3 + 1$. Comparing the third attribute of each component in the formula, we have an unsatisfiable condition ($h_3 + 1 = k_1 + 1$) $\wedge$ ($k_1 + 2 = h_3$) being true. Therefore, we proved (a).

For (c), we illustrate the situation with Figure 3.2(I). Let i be the smallest integer from $[1...k + 1]$ (i) there is a shortest path p' from u to w_i going through edge e such that $SPD_G(u, w_i, length(p'), dist(p'))$ holds and (ii) any path $p_{uw_{i-1}}$ from u to w_{i-1} satisfying $SPD_G(u, w_{i-1}, length(p_{uw_{i-1}}), dist(p_{uw_{i-1}}))$ does not go through edge e. Since $SPD_G(u, u, 0, 0) \wedge SPD_G(u, v, l, dist(p_1))$ holds, i exists.

Let us consider subpath $p_{21} = u w_1 ... w_{i-1}$ of p_2. Since $SPD_{G_{-e}}(u, v, k + 1, dist(p_2))$ holds, from Lemma 4, $SPD_{G_{-e}}(u, w_{i-1}, i - 1, dist(p_{21}))$ holds. From the way that vertex w_i is chosen and the definition of SPD_G, $SPD_G(u, w_{i-1}, i - 1, dist(p_{21}))$ holds. Therefore, subpath p_{21} satisfies (c).

Let q_3 (q_4, respectively) be the subpath from u to a (from b to w_i, respectively) of p'. Denote $dist(q_h)$ ($length(q_h)$, respectively) by d_h (l_h, respectively) for $h = 3, 4$. According to Lemma 5(a),

$$SPD_G(u, a, l_3, d_3) \wedge SPD_G(b, w_i, l_4, d_4) \wedge \tag{3}$$
$$SPD_G(u, w_i, l_3 + l_4 + 1, d_3 + d_4 + dist(e))$$

holds. We now prove that there is no path p'' of G using edge e among vertices $w_i, ..., w_k, v$ in G such that $SPD_G(w_i, v, length(p''), dist(p''))$ holds. Otherwise, Let q_1 (q_2, respectively) be the subpath from w_i to a (from b to v, respectively) of p''. Denote $dist(q_h)$ ($length(q_h)$, respectively) by d_h (l_h, respectively) for $h = 1, 2$. By Lemma 4 and Lemma 5(b),

$$SPD_G(w_i, v, l_1 + l_2 + 1, d_1 + d_2 + dist(e)) \wedge \tag{4}$$
$$SPD_G(w_i, a, l_1, d_1) \wedge SPD_G(b, v, l_2, d_2)$$

holds. From (4) and (5) and since a shortest path between two vertices is not longer than any path between the same vertices, we have

$$d_3 + d_4 + dist(e) \leq d_3 + d_1, \quad and \quad d_1 + d_2 + dist(e) \leq d_4 + d_2.$$

The formulas imply $dist(e) = 0$ and $d_1 = d_4$. Consequently, from the hypotheses and Lemma 4,

$$SPD_G(a, w_i, l_4 + 1, d_4) \wedge SPD_G(w_i, a, l_1, d_4) \wedge$$
$$SPD_G(b, w_i, l_4, d_4) \wedge SPD_G(w_i, b, l_1 + 1, d_4)$$

holds. Form the above formula and the definition of SPD_G, we have

$$l_4 + 1 = l_1, \quad and \quad l_4 = l_1 + 1.$$

The above formulas imply $1 = 0$. This is contradiction. Thus we proved the result. $\diamond$

For edge $e = (a, b)$ of G, let $\Gamma_e^G(x, y, l, d)$ be a formula expressing those tuples of SPD_G using edge e, that is,

$$\Gamma_e^G(x, y, l, d) \equiv (\exists d_1, d_2, d_3, d_4)(\exists l_1, l_2, l_3, l_4) \; SPD_G(x, y, l, d) \wedge$$
$$[SPD_G(x, a, l_1, d_1) \wedge SPD_G(b, y, l_2, d_2) \wedge (l = l_1 + l_2 + 1) \wedge$$
$$(d = d_1 + d_2 + dist(e)) \vee SPD_G(x, b, l_3, d_3) \wedge SPD_G(a, y, l_4, d_4) \wedge$$
$$(l = l_3 + l_4 + 1) \wedge (d = d_3 + d_4 + dist(e))].$$
$$\Omega_e^G(x, y, l, d) \equiv SPD_G(x, y, l, d) \wedge \neg\Gamma_e^G(x, y, l, d).$$

Thus $\Omega_e^G(x, y, l, d)$ states that the shortest paths between x and y which have distance d and length l do not use edge e. With the newly defined formulas, Lemma 5(c) can be rewritten into the following form:

Lemma 5(d): Suppose $dist(g) \geq 0$ for each edge g of G. In G, let p_1 be a shortest path between vertex u and vertex v which passes through the minimum number of edges of all such shortest paths (i.e., $SPD_G(u, v, l, dist(p_1))$ holds for some l). We assume, without loss of generality, path p_1 goes through edge $e = (a, b)$ in the order of $u...ab...v$ as shown in Figure 3.2(I). Let $p_2 = uw_1...w_kv$ be a shortest path between u and v ($u = w_0$, $v = w_{k+1}$) in $G - e$ and $SPD_{G-e}(u, v, k + 1, dist(p_2))$ holds. Then there exists a vertex w_i ($1 \leq i \leq k + 1$) such that for subpaths $p_{21} = uw_1...w_{i-1}$ and $p_{22} = w_i...v$ of p_2, $\Omega_e^G(u, w_{i-1}, length(p_{21}), dist(p_{21})) \wedge G_{-e}(w_{i-1}, w_i) \wedge \Omega_e^G(w_i, v, length(p_{22}), dist(p_{22}))$ holds. $\diamond$

Let $\Phi_e^G(x, y, l, d)$ be

$$(\exists d_1, d_2)(\exists l_1, l_2)(\exists w_1, w_2) \; \Omega_e^G(x, w_1, l_1, d_1) \wedge \widehat{G_{-e}}(w_1, w_2) \wedge$$
$$\Omega_e^G(w_2, y, l_2, d_2) \wedge [(l = l_1 + l_2 + 1) \wedge (w_1 \neq w_2) \vee (l = l_1 + l_2) \wedge$$
$$(w_1 = w_2)] \wedge (d = d_1 + dist(w_1, w_2) + d_2).$$

The following is the main lemma of the section.

Lemma 6. *Given an undirected graph G satisfying $dist(e) \geq 0$ for each edge $e \in G$, $SPD_{G_{-e}} \subseteq \Phi_e^G$.*

Proof. Suppose $SPD_{G_{-e}}(x, y, l, d)$ holds. We prove $\Phi_e^G(x, y, l, d)$ is true.

Since $SPD_{G_{-e}}(x, y, l, d)$ holds, there exists a shortest path $p = xw_1...w_{l-1}y$ (let $x = w_0$ and $y = w_l$) in $G - e$ such that $SPD_{G_{-e}}(x, y, l, dist(p))$. Two cases arise: (a) None of the shortest paths between x and y use edge e in G. Then $\Omega_e^G(x, y, l, d)$ is true. Since $\widehat{G_{-e}}(y, y) \wedge \Omega_e^G(y, y, 0, 0)$ is true, $\Omega_e^G(x, y, l, d)$, $\widehat{G_{-e}}(y, y)$ and $\Omega_e^G(y, y, 0)$ are all true. Therefore, $\Phi_e^G(x, y, l, d)$ holds. (b) Otherwise. Then there is a shortest path between x and y in G using edge e. From Lemma 2(d), there exists w_i such that

$$(\exists d_1, d_2)(\exists l_1, l_2) \ \Omega_e^G(x, w_{i-1}, l_1, d_1) \wedge \widehat{G_{-e}}(w_{i-1}, w_i) \wedge \Omega_e^G(w_i, y, l_2, d_2)$$
$$\wedge (l = l_1 + l_2 + 1) \wedge (d = d_1 + dist(w_{i-1}, w_i) + d_2).$$

is true. Therefore, $\Phi_e^G(x, y, l, d)$ holds. ◇

Proof of Theorem 2 Let

$$MP_e^G(x, y, l, d) \equiv \Phi_e^G(x, y, l, d) \wedge (\forall d')(\forall l') \ [\Phi_e^G(x, y, l', d') \rightarrow ((d \leq d')], \ and$$
$$\varphi(x, y, l, d) \equiv MP_e^G(x, y, l, d) \wedge (\forall l') \ [MP_e^G(x, y, l', d) \rightarrow (l \leq l')].$$

Clearly, φ is in $FO(+, <)$. We need to prove $SPD_{G_{-e}} \equiv \varphi$.

1. Suppose $SPD_{G_{-e}}(x, y, l, d)$ holds. From Lemma 6, we know $SPD_{G_{-e}} \subseteq \Phi_e^G$. By the definition of $SPD_{G_{-e}}$, $SPD_{G_{-e}} \subseteq MP_e^G$ holds and $SPD_{G_{-e}} \subseteq \varphi$ holds.
2. Suppose $\varphi(x, y, l, d)$ holds. By the definition of $SPD_{G_{-e}}$, there exist d' and l' such that $SPD_{G_{+e}}(x, y, l', d')$ holds. Since $SPD_{G_{-e}} \subseteq \varphi$, $\varphi(x, y, l', d')$ holds. Then there is at most one d'' and one l'' such that $\varphi(x, y, l'', d'')$ holds from the definition of φ. So, $d = d'$ and $l = l'$. Thus $\varphi \subseteq SPD_{G_{-e}}$.

 ◇

5   A Limited Reduction between SP_G and SPD_G

The algorithm for $APSD > 0$ in Section 3 does not need to maintain any auxiliary information during the evaluation while the algorithm for $APSD \geq 0$ in Section 4 does need auxiliary relation. The algorithm for the $APSD \geq 0$ problem can be considered as using the algorithm for $APSD > 0$ twice, once for distance and once for length. in a nested way.

In many practical applications, any modification on the edges of undirected graph G must have some physical limitations, e.g., the amount of information passed through a cable is bounded by the physical property of the cable and the length of cables used is finitely bounded. To model such situations, we assume, for each edge g of $G = (V, E)$, $dist(g)$ is a non-negative integer and n is the upper bound of $|V|$. Under such assumption, the $APSD \geq 0$ problem can be solved by using the method for $APSD > 0$ through redefining the $dist(g)$ with $DIST(g)$ for each edge g of G, where $DIST(g) = dist(g) \times n + 1$. In this way, for a given undirected graph G, we actually construct a new graph G^L, which is the same as G except that distance is defined by "$DIST$" instead of "$dist$". The incremental maintenance of the $APSD \geq 0$ problem for graph G with relation SPD_G is transformed to the maintenance of the $APSD > 0$ problem for graph G^L with relation SP_{G^L}.

The correctness of this transformation is based on the following two facts: (i) For each tuple (x, y, l, d) of SPD_G there is only one tuple (x, y, d_L) of SP_{G^L} where $d_L = d \times n + l$ and, for each tuple (x, y, d_L) of SP_{G^L} there is only one tuple (x, y, d, l) of SPD_G where $d = (d_L \ div \ n)$ and $l = (d_L \ mod \ n)$; (ii) For any two paths p_1 and p_2 between vertex x and vertex y, if $dist(p_1) < dist(p_2)$ then $DIST(p_1) < DIST(p_2)$ holds and if $DIST(p_1) < DIST(p_2)$ then $dist(p_1) \leq dist(p_2)$ holds. Since $DIST(p_1) = dist(p_1) \times n + l_1$ and $DIST(p_2) = dist(p_2) \times n + l_2$, $DIST(p_2) - DIST(p_1) = (dist(p_2) - dist(p_1)) \times n + (l_2 - l_1)$. Therefore, if $dist(p_2) > dist(p_1)$ holds, then $DIST(p_2) - DIST(p_1) \geq n - (n - 1) > 0$ holds. Similarly, we could prove that $dist(p_1) \leq dist(p_2)$ holds if $DIST(p_1) < DIST(p_2)$.

Let $G = (V, E)$ be an undirected graph with restrictions such that $dist(g)$ is an integer for each edge g of G and n is the upper bound of $|V|$. The key point of the algorithm is that $l < n$ holds for each tuple (x, y, l, d) of SPD_G.

6   Concluding Remarks

We have given $FO(+, <)$ algorithms for the incremental maintenance of the $APSD > 0$ problem and the $APSD \geq 0$ problem. Our algorithms have a low parallel complexity and make additional optimizations possible (e.g., the optimization techniques in relational database). These extend earlier results on the maintenance of transitive closure of undirected graphs and the results in [8]. For example, our algorithms for the $APSD \geq 0$ problem can be used to answer queries such as "list the minimum number of cities on a shortest path".

Our results can be applied to the following problems: (i) Although all the maintenance results in the paper are written for *set semantics*, they can be easily extended to *bag semantics* (multiset) by storing the number of alternative shortest paths of a tuple along with the tuple itself. For example, considering the $APSD > 0$ problem, we define SP_G^c to be $\{(x, y, d, c)| \ d$ is the distance of the shortest path between x and y; c is the number of alternative shortest paths between x and $y \ \}$. $SP_G^c(x, y, d, c)$ is true if and only if there exists c alternative shortest paths between x and y in G which have distance of d. The maintenance algorithms are similar to that of SP_G. (ii) Our algorithms can be used to maintain the shortest paths themselves. Refer to [13] for more details.

Acknowledgements: We would like to thank Kevin Glynn for his helpful comments. We are also grateful to the anonymous referees for their very helpful remarks, including spotting an error in an earlier version of the paper. Part of Dong's work was done while visiting Simon Fraser University and George Mason University during his study leave.

References

[1] G. Ausiello, G. F. Italiano, A. M. Spaccamela, and U. Nanni. On-line computation of minimal and maximal length path. *Theor.Comput.Sci., Elsevier Science Publisher*, 95, 2:245–261, 1992.

[2] J. A. Blakeley, P.-A. Larson, and F. W. Tompa. Efficiently updating materialized views. In *Proc. ACM SIGMOD Int. Conf. on Management of Data*, pages 61–71, 1986.

[3] A. L. Buchsbaum, P. C. Kanellakis, and J. S. Vitter. A data structure for arc insertion and regular path finding. In *Proc. ACM-SIAM Symp. on Discrete Algorithms*, 1990.

[4] Hristo N. Djidjev, Grammati E. Pantziou, and Christos D. Zaroliagis. On-line and dynamic algorithms for shortest path problems. In *STACS: Annual Symposium on Theoretical Aspects of Computer Science*, 1995.

[5] G. Dong and C. Pang. Maintaining transitive closure in first-order after node-set and edge-set deletions. *Information Processing Letters*, 62(3):193–199, 1997.

[6] G. Dong and J. Su. Space bounded FOIES. In *Proc. of the ACM Symposium on Principles of Database Systems*, pages 139–150, May 1995.

[7] G. Dong and R. Topor. Incremental evaluation of datalog queries. In *Proc. Int'l Conference on Database Theory*, pages 282–296, Berlin, Germany, October 1992.

[8] Guozhu Dong and Ramamohanarao Kotagiri. Incrementally evaluating constrained transitive closure by conjunctive querie. In *International Conference on Deductive and Object-Oriented Databases*, 1997.

[9] S. Even and H. Gazit. Updating distances in dynamic graphs. *Methods of Operations Research*, 49:371–387, 1985.

[10] E. Feuerstein and A. Marchetti-Spaccamela. Dynamic algorithms for shortest paths in planar graphs. *Theoretical Computer Science*, 116(2):359–371, 1993.

[11] S. Grumbach and J. Su. First-order definability over constraint databases. In *Proceedings of Conference on Constraint Programming*, 1995.

[12] Philip N. Klein, Satish Rao, Monika H. Rauch, and S. Subramanian. Faster shortest-path algorithms for planar graphs. In *Proc. 26th Symp. Theory of Computing*, pages 27–37. Assoc. for Computing Machinery, 1994.

[13] Chaoyi Pang. *Incremental Maintenance Reachability of Graph in First-order and Its extension*. PhD thesis, The University of Melbourne, 1999.

[14] Sushant Patnaik and Neil Immerman. Dyn-FO: A parallel dynamic complexity class. In *Proc. ACM Symp. on Principles of Database Systems*, pages 210–221, 1994.

[15] G. Ramalingam. *Bounded Incremental Computation*. LNCS 1089, 1996.

[16] O. Shmueli and A. Itai. Maintenance of views. In *Sigmod Record*, volume 14(2), pages 240–255, 1984.

[17] P.M.N. Spira and A. Pan. On finding and updating spanning trees and shortest paths. *SIAM Journal on Computing*, 3(4):375–380, September 1975.

A Framework for the Investigation of Aggregate Functions in Database Queries*

Luca Cabibbo and Riccardo Torlone

Dipartimento di Informatica e Automazione, Università di Roma Tre
Via della Vasca Navale, 79 — I-00146 Roma, Italy
{cabibbo,torlone}@dia.uniroma3.it

Abstract. In this paper we present a new approach for studying aggregations in the context of database query languages. Starting from a broad definition of aggregate function, we address our investigation from two different perspectives. We first propose a *declarative* notion of uniform aggregate function that refers to a family of scalar functions uniformly constructed over a vocabulary of basic operators by a bounded Turing Machine. This notion yields an effective tool to study the effect of the embedding of a *class* of built-in aggregate functions in a query language. All the aggregate functions most used in practice are included in this classification. We then present an *operational* notion of aggregate function, by considering a high-order folding constructor, based on structural recursion, devoted to compute numeric aggregations over complex values. We show that numeric folding over a given vocabulary is sometimes not able to compute, by itself, the whole class of uniform aggregate function over the same vocabulary. It turns out however that this limitation can be partially remedied by the restructuring capabilities of a query language.

1 Introduction

Computing aggregations has been always considered an important feature of practical database query languages. This ability is indeed fundamental in specific application domains whose relevance has recently increased; among them, on-line analytical processing (OLAP), decision support, statistical evaluation, and management of geographical data. In spite of this fact, a systematic study of aggregations in the context of query languages has evolved quite slowly. Apart from the work by Klug [13], who formalized extensions of algebra and calculus with aggregates, in the last decade there have been few papers dealing with this subject [7,14,15,16], even if specific aggregate functions of theoretical relevance, like counters, have received special attention [2,8,11].

The general approach to the problem is to study basic properties of formal languages equipped with a specific class of built-in aggregate functions (typically the ones provided by SQL, that is, MIN, MAX, SUM, COUNT and AVG, plus

---

* This work was partially supported by *CNR* and by *MURST*.

Catriel Beeri, Peter Buneman (Eds.): ICDT'99, LNCS 1540, pp. 383–397, 1998.
© Springer-Verlag Berlin Heidelberg 1998

further functions of theoretical interest, like EVEN). Conversely, we would like to attack the problem from a more general perspective, possibly independent of the specific aggregate functions chosen. To do that, we first need to answer a fundamental question: *what is precisely an aggregate function?* It is folk knowledge that a database aggregate function takes a collection of objects (with or without duplicates) as argument, and returns a new value that "summarizes" a numeric property of the collection. This broad definition is clearly too vague to provide clues for answering general questions about query languages with aggregate capabilities.

Our first goal is then trying to refine this definition, in order to provide a solid basis to the whole picture. Borrowing some ideas from the circuit model [12,18], we start by noting that an aggregate function g over a collection s can be effectively described by a family of *scalar* functions (that is, traditional k-ary functions) $G = \{g_0, g_1, g_2, \ldots\}$ such that, for each $k \geq 0$: (i) g_k computes g when s contains exactly k elements; (ii) the result of g_k is invariant under any permutation of its arguments (as g operates on collections rather than sequences); and (iii) g_k is constructed by using a fixed vocabulary of basic operations and constants. To guarantee tractability of this representation in terms of families of scalar functions, we need to set some constraint on the way in which the various g_k are built. We make this constraint precise by introducing a notion of *uniform construction*, stating that a circuit description of each function g_k in G needs to be "easily" generated from k (specifically, from a Turing machine having bounded complexity). In this way, the family G forms a good representative of the aggregate function g, since the computational power is captured by the g_k's themselves rather than by their construction. This approach leads to the definition, in a very natural way, of different and appealing *abstract classes* of aggregate functions: a class is composed of all the aggregate functions that can be represented by a uniform family of functions over a given vocabulary. With the assumption that each scalar function in the vocabulary has constant computational cost, uniform construction indeed guarantees tractability of the aggregate functions so defined.

We are now ready to address the impact of incorporating aggregate functions in a database query language. To this end, we consider a two-sorted algebra for complex values [1], called $\mathcal{CVA}$, over an uninterpreted domain and an interpreted one. In this context, we first study extensions of $\mathcal{CVA}$ with built-in aggregate functions, that is, with operators whose semantics is defined outside the database. We then present a simple constructor, called *folding*, that allows the user to define and apply an aggregation *within* $\mathcal{CVA}$. This operator is based on structural recursion [5] and is defined in terms of a pre function p, an increment function i over the variables acc and $curr$, and a post function q. The application of a folding expression over a collection of complex values s returns a new value by iterating over the elements of s in a natural way: starting from $acc = p(s)$, for each element $curr$ of s (chosen in some arbitrary order) the function i is applied to acc and $curr$; the result is obtained by applying q to the value of acc at the end of the iteration. A constraint on i guarantees that the result of folding over a collection s is indeed independent of the order in which the elements of s are selected during the evaluation. We then restrict our attention to a simplified version of folding devoted to compute *numeric* aggregations: it operates only on multisets of interpreted atomic values and returns a numeric value, without involving complex data types in its evaluation.

We finally relate the abstract notion of uniform aggregate function with this procedural way of computing aggregations. We first show that, even if numeric folding is less expressive than general folding, they have the same expressive power when embedded in $\mathcal{CVA}$; that is, the restructuring capabilities of the algebra overcome the gap in expressiveness. We then show that numeric folding over a given set of scalar functions computes only uniform aggregate functions over the same set of scalar functions, but not all of them. We demonstrate that this limitation can be partially overcome by the restructuring capabilities of a query language. It turns out however that $\mathcal{CVA}$, extended with the folding operator and a vocabulary of scalar functions, is still not able to capture the whole class of uniform aggregate functions over the given vocabulary.

The rest of the paper is devoted to a formalization of the issues discussed in this section and is organized as follows. In Section 2, we introduce the basic notions and present a number of examples of uniform aggregate functions. In Section 3, we introduce the $\mathcal{CVA}$ query language and investigate extensions of $\mathcal{CVA}$ with built-in aggregate functions. The folding operator is introduced in Section 4, where we also characterize an important restriction of it. In Section 5, we relate the expressive power of the various extensions of $\mathcal{CVA}$ with aggregations. Finally, in Section 6, we state a number of interesting open problems.

2   Aggregate Functions

2.1   Basic Definitions

Let us start with a very general definition of aggregate function. Let $\{\!\{\mathcal{N}\}\!\}$ denote the class of *finite multisets* of values from a countably infinite domain $\mathcal{N}$. (Multisets generalize sets, in that they allow an element to occur multiple times.)

Definition 1. *An* aggregate function *over $\mathcal{N}$ is a total function from $\{\!\{\mathcal{N}\}\!\}$ to $\mathcal{N}$, mapping each multiset of values to a value.*

Examples of aggregate functions over numeric domains are sum ($\sum$), product ($\prod$), counting, average, maximum, and minimum. Maximum and minimum are also examples of aggregate functions over collections of non-numeric domains like strings. Note that we require aggregate functions to be *total*; in some cases, this requires some attention. For instance, the sum of a multiset of numbers is always well-defined; conversely, in defining the maximum function MAX, an arbitrary choice for its result over the empty multiset $\{\!\{\}\!\}$ is required.

In the rest of the paper, we will only consider aggregate functions over the domain $\mathbb{Q}$ of the rational numbers.

An important aspect of our approach is that we clearly separate the restructuring capabilities of a query language from its ability to compute aggregations. Specifically, we make a distinction between *aggregate functions* (that is, aggregations over numbers) and *aggregate queries* (that is, queries involving aggregate functions). Under this interpretation, the counting of an arbitrary set (say, of a set of strings) is an aggregate *query*, which can be computed by first mapping each element to some numeric constant (say, 1), and then applying an aggregate *function* that counts the elements of the resulting numeric multiset. Similarly, testing whether two sets are equinumerous can be viewed as an aggregate query accomplished by computing the cardinalities of the sets with an aggregate function, and then checking for their equality. Finally, we note that the maximum function with SQL semantics is an aggregate query that returns a singleton set over non-empty sets and an empty set over empty sets; again, this can be implemented by using a maximum aggregate function together with some restructuring operations.

2.2   Uniform Aggregate Functions

In order to provide a concrete basis for the investigation of aggregations in the context of database queries, we now refine the definition of aggregate function. We first introduce a number of preliminary notions, to develop the following ideas, inspired from the circuit model [12,18]: (i) an aggregate function can be represented by a family of scalar functions; (ii) each scalar function can be described by an arithmetic circuit over a collection of base functions;[1] (iii) uniformity in the construction of a family of circuits guarantees tractability of the represented aggregate function.

A *scalar function* (over $\mathbb{Q}$) is a total function from $\mathbb{Q}^k$ to $\mathbb{Q}$, with $k \geq 0$. (Examples of scalar functions are the nullary functions 0 and 1 and the binary functions $+$, $*$, $-$, and $/$.) An *enumeration* of a multiset $s = \{v_1, \ldots, v_n\}$ is a tuple $\vec{s} = [v_1, \ldots, v_n]$ containing the same elements as s with the same multiplicities, in any of the possible orderings. A *family of functions* is a set G of scalar functions such that, for each $k \geq 0$, there is one function $g_k : \mathbb{Q}^k \to \mathbb{Q}$ in G, called the *k-th component of G*.

We say that a family G of functions *represents* an aggregate function $h : \{\mathbb{Q}\} \to \mathbb{Q}$ if, for each $k \geq 0$, each multiset s of cardinality k, and each enumeration $\vec{s}$ of s, it is the case that $g_k(\vec{s}) = h(s)$, where g_k is the k-th component of G. Note that the above definition implies that only *symmetric* functions can be used in the representation of aggregate functions. We recall that a k-ary function f is symmetric if it remains invariant under any permutation of its arguments, that is, $f(x_1, \ldots, x_k) = f(x_{\sigma(1)}, \ldots, x_{\sigma(k)})$ for every permutation σ on $\{1, \ldots, k\}$.

Let a *vocabulary* be a set of scalar functions over $\mathbb{Q}$. A *circuit* over a vocabulary is a labeled directed acyclic graph whose nodes are either *function nodes* or

---

[1]   Actually, there are other ways to describe scalar functions, such as *straight line programs* and *formulae*, which are essentially equivalent to arithmetic circuits.

are *input nodes*. Each function node is labeled by a function in the vocabulary; a node labeled by a m-ary function has precisely m ingoing arcs (the arcs are ordered). An *input node* is a node with no ingoing arcs labeled by x_i, with $i > 0$. There is one distinguished node with no outgoing arcs, called the *output* of the circuit. A k-*ary circuit* is a circuit with at most k input nodes having different labels from $x_1, \ldots, x_k$. The *semantics* of a k-ary circuit is the k-ary scalar function computed by the circuit in the natural way. A circuit *describes* a scalar function f if its semantics coincides with f. An *encoding* of a circuit is a listing of its nodes, with the respective labels. The *size* of the circuit is the number of its nodes. A *description* of a function f, together with its size, is a circuit that describes f. Examples of circuits are reported in Figure 1.

To guarantee the tractability of a family of functions, we introduce a notion of uniformity. A family G of functions is *uniform* if a description of the n-th component of G can be generated by a deterministic Turing machine using $O(\log n)$ workspace on input 1^n.

Definition 2. *A uniform aggregate function over a vocabulary Ω is an aggregate function that can be represented by a uniform family of functions over Ω.*

As a particular but important case, we call *uniform counting functions* the uniform aggregate functions that can be represented by families of constant functions. We note that, since a constant function does not depend on its arguments, a uniform counting function can be described by a family of circuits without input nodes.

It is worth noting that we use the term "uniform" to mean *logspace uniform*, as it is customary in the context of the circuit model, where several different notions of uniformity are essentially equivalent to *logspace* uniformity. Note also that, as a consequence of the requirement of *logspace* computability in the definition, the size of the description of the n-th component of any uniform family is polynomial in n.

As a first example, Figure 1 shows the first three components of a family describing the average aggregate function AVG over the vocabulary $\Omega_{\mathbb{Q}}$, where $\Omega_{\mathbb{Q}} = \{0, 1, +, -, *, /\}$.

We note that, for each $k > 0$, the left and right subtrees of the output of AVG_k correspond to the k-th component of the aggregate functions SUM and COUNT, respectively. Actually, these three aggregate functions can be defined inductively as follows:

$$
\begin{array}{lll}
\mathrm{SUM}_0 = 0 & \mathrm{SUM}_k = \mathrm{SUM}_{k-1} + x_k & \text{for } k > 0 \\
\mathrm{COUNT}_0 = 0 & \mathrm{COUNT}_k = \mathrm{COUNT}_{k-1} + 1 & \text{for } k > 0 \\
\mathrm{AVG}_0 = 0 & \mathrm{AVG}_k = \mathrm{SUM}_k / \mathrm{COUNT}_k & \text{for } k > 0
\end{array}
$$

Intuitively, the fact that the k-th component of a family can be derived from the previous component in a simple way guarantees uniformity of the family [12].

The vocabulary $\Omega_{\mathbb{Q}}$ can be used to define several other aggregate functions. For example, the function EVEN can be defined as $\mathrm{EVEN}_0 = 1$ and $\mathrm{EVEN}_k = 1 - \mathrm{EVEN}_{k-1}$, for each $k > 0$, in which 0 is interpreted as *false* and 1 as *true*. A

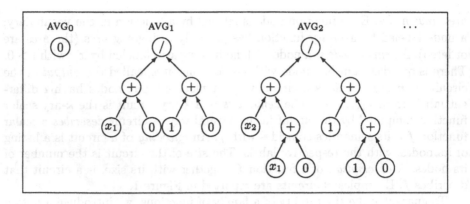

Fig. 1. A circuit representation of the aggregate function AVG

different family for the same function is such that $\text{EVEN}'_{2k} = 1$ and $\text{EVEN}'_{2k+1} = 0$, for each $k \geq 0$. The aggregate function EXP, such that $\text{EXP}_k = 2^k$, can be defined as $\text{EXP}_0 = 1$ and $\text{EXP}_k = double(\text{EXP}_{k-1})$ for $k > 0$, where $double(x) = x + x$. Note that the obvious description $1 + 1 + \ldots + 1$ for EXP_k (with 2^k number of 1's and $2^k - 1$ number of +'s) cannot be generated by a *logspace* computation, since it requires a number of operators which is exponential in k. Further uniform aggregate functions over $\Omega_{\mathbb{Q}}$ are the following: any fixed natural or rational constant c; the function FIB that generates Fibonacci's numbers; the function FATT, such that $\text{FATT}_k = k!$; the function PROD, such that $\text{PROD}_k = x_1 * \ldots * x_k = \prod_{i=1}^{k} x_i$.

Functions like COUNT, EVEN, and EXP do not depend on the actual values of the elements in the argument (multi)set, but rather on the number of elements it contains. According to our definition, these are indeed uniform counting functions.

Although many interesting functions can be defined in terms of $\Omega_{\mathbb{Q}}$, this vocabulary does not allow the definition of the minimum and maximum functions MIN and MAX. To this end, we need to use further scalar functions to take care of order. For instance, using an *ordering* function $\geq: \mathbb{Q} \times \mathbb{Q} \rightarrow \{0,1\}$ and the functions in $\Omega_{\mathbb{Q}}$, it is easy to define also the functions $=$, $\neq$, and $>$. Then, it can be shown that MIN and MAX are uniform aggregate functions over $\Omega_{\mathbb{Q}} \cup \{\geq\}$.

2.3 A Hierarchy of Aggregate Functions

Let $\mathcal{A}(\Omega)$ be the class of uniform aggregate functions over a vocabulary Ω. According to our definition, an element of $\mathcal{A}(\Omega)$ can be represented by a uniform family of functions whose description of the n-th component can be generated by a Turing machine using $O(\log n)$ workspace. Actually, a Turing machine using $O(\log n)$ workspace is essentially equivalent to a program that uses a fixed number of counters, each ranging over $\{1, \ldots, n\}$; it is then apparent that the expressiveness of such a machine increases with the number of available counters. To capture this fact, we now introduce a hierarchy of classes of uniform aggregate functions, as follows.

Definition 3. $\mathcal{A}^k(\Omega)$ *is the class of uniform aggregate functions such that the description of the n-th component has size* $O(n^k)$.

Clearly, $\mathcal{A}(\Omega) = \bigcup_{k \geq 0} \mathcal{A}^k(\Omega)$ and $\mathcal{A}^k(\Omega) \subseteq \mathcal{A}^{k+1}(\Omega)$ for each $k \geq 0$. Actually, it turns out that there are vocabularies for which the above hierarchy is proper.

Lemma 1. *There are a vocabulary* Ω *and a natural* k *such that* $\mathcal{A}^k(\Omega) \subset \mathcal{A}^{k+1}(\Omega)$.

Sketch of proof. Let $\Omega_a = \{0_\oplus, \oplus, \otimes\}$ be an "abstract" vocabulary, where $0_\oplus$ is a constant, $\oplus$ is a commutative binary function, and $\otimes$ is an arbitrary binary function. Consider the uniform aggregate function α over Ω_a such that $\alpha_n = \bigoplus_{i=1,\dots,n}^{j=1,\dots,n} x_i \otimes x_j$, where $\bigoplus$ is defined in terms of $\oplus$ using $0_\oplus$ as "initial value". Since the n-th component α_n contains $O(n^2)$ operators, the function α is in $\mathcal{A}^2(\Omega_a)$ by definition. However, it turns out that α does not belong to $\mathcal{A}^1(\Omega_a)$, since it is not possible to represent its components using a linear number of operators.   □

Remark 1. Let us now briefly discuss the above result. Consider the following "concrete" interpretation $\widetilde{\Omega}_a$ for the abstract vocabulary Ω_a: $0_\oplus$ is 0 (the rational number zero), $\oplus$ is $+$ (addition of rational numbers), and $\otimes$ is $*$ (multiplication of rational numbers); multiplication is distributive over addition. According to this interpretation $\widetilde{\Omega}_a$, the n-th component $\alpha_n = \sum_{i,j} x_i * x_j$ of α can be rewritten as $(\sum_i x_i) * (\sum_j x_j)$, which has $O(n)$ operators, and therefore α belongs to $\mathcal{A}^1(\widetilde{\Omega}_a)$. Conversely, consider the function β such that $\beta_n = \bigoplus_{i,j}^{i \neq j} x_i \otimes x_j$. It is easy to see that β belongs to $\mathcal{A}^2(\Omega_a) - \mathcal{A}^1(\Omega_a)$. Furthermore, even with respect to the interpretation $\widetilde{\Omega}_a$ for the vocabulary Ω_a, the function β belongs to $\mathcal{A}^2(\widetilde{\Omega}_a) - \mathcal{A}^1(\widetilde{\Omega}_a)$. It would belong to $\mathcal{A}^1(\widetilde{\Omega}_a)$ if $\widetilde{\Omega}_a$ contained the difference operator $-$; in this case, β_n can be rewritten as $(\sum_i x_i) * (\sum_j x_j) - (\sum_k x_k * x_k)$. Thus, in general, properties of the aggregate functions in the class $\mathcal{A}(\Omega)$ depend on properties of the scalar functions in the vocabulary Ω.   □

3   A Query Language with Interpreted Functions

In this section we investigate the embedding of a class of aggregate functions within a database query language. We first introduce an algebra for complex values [1], and then extend it with interpreted scalar and aggregate functions.

3.1   The Data Model

We consider a two-sorted data model for complex values, over a countably infinite, uninterpreted domain $\mathcal{D}$ and the interpreted domain $\mathbb{Q}$ of the rational numbers. We fix two further countably infinite disjoint sets: a set $\mathcal{A}$ of *attribute names* and a set $\mathcal{R}$ of *complex-values names*. The *types* of the model are recursively defined as follows: (i) $\mathcal{D}$ and $\mathbb{Q}$ are *atomic* types; (ii) if $\tau_1, \ldots, \tau_k$ are types and $A_1, \ldots, A_k$ are distinct attribute names from $\mathcal{A}$, then $[A_1 : \tau_1, \ldots, A_k : \tau_k]$ is a *tuple* type ($k \geq 0$); and (iii) if τ is a type, then $\{\tau\}$ is a *set* type. The domain of complex values associated with a type is defined in the natural way.

A *database scheme* is a tuple of the form $(s_1 : \tau_1, \ldots, s_n : \tau_n)$, where $s_1, \ldots, s_n$ are distinct complex-values names from $\mathcal{R}$ and each τ_i is a type. A *database instance* is a function mapping each complex-values name s_i to a value of the corresponding type τ_i, for $1 \leq i \leq n$. Note that the s_i's are not required to be *sets* of (complex) values.

3.2   The Complex-Values Algebra

Our reference language, denoted by $\mathcal{CVA}$, is a variant of the complex-values algebra of Abiteboul and Beeri [1] without *powerset*. The language is based on *operators*, similar in spirit to relational algebra operators, and *function constructors*, which are high-order constructors used to apply functions to complex values. We now briefly recall the main features of the language, referring the reader to [1] for further details.

The expressions of the language describe functions[2] from a database scheme to a certain type, which are built by combining operators and function constructors starting from a basic set of functions. More specifically, the *base functions* include constants and complex-values names from $\mathcal{R}$ (viewed as nullary functions), attribute names from $\mathcal{A}$, the identity function *id*, the set constructor $\{\}$, the binary predicates $=$, $\in$, and $\subseteq$, the boolean connectives $\wedge$, $\vee$, and $\neg$. The operators include the set operations $\cup$, $\cap$, and $-$, the cross product (which is a variant of the k-ary Cartesian product), and the set-collapse (which transforms a set of sets into the union of the sets it contains).

The function constructors allow the definition of further functions, as follows:

- the *binary composition* constructor $f \circ g$, where f and g are functions, defines a new function whose meaning is "apply g, then f";
- the *labeled tuple* constructor $[A_1 = f_1, \ldots, A_n = f_n]$, where $f_1, \ldots, f_n$ are unary functions and $A_1, \ldots, A_n$ are distinct attribute names, defines a new function over any type as follows:

$$[A_1 = f_1, \ldots, A_n = f_n](s) = [A_1 : f_1(s), \ldots, A_n : f_n(s)];$$

- the *replace* constructor $replace\langle f \rangle$, where f is a unary function, defines a new function over a set type as: $replace\langle f \rangle(s) = \{f(w) \mid w \in s\}$;
- the *selection* constructor $select\langle c \rangle$, where c is a unary boolean function, defines a new function over a set type as: $select\langle c \rangle(s) = \{w \mid w \in s$ and $c(w)$ is true$\}$.

---

[2] We mainly refer to a general notion of *function* rather than *query* because, in order to include aggregations, it is convenient to relax the assumption that the result of a $\mathcal{CVA}$ expression is a set.

To increase readability, we will often use an intuitive, simplified notation. For example, if A and B are attributes and f is a function, we write $A.B$ instead of $B \circ A$, $A(f)$ instead of $A \circ f$, and $A \in B$ instead of $\in \circ [A, B]$. For the labeled tuple constructor, we write $[A]$ instead of $[A = A]$, and $[A.B]$ instead of $[B = A.B]$ (that is, an attribute takes its name from the name of the last navigated attribute).

As an example, let s_1 and s_2 be complex-values names, having types $\{[A : \mathcal{D}, B : \mathcal{D}]\}$ and $\{[E : \{\mathcal{D}\}, F : \mathcal{D}]\}$, respectively. Then the following expression computes the projection on A and F of the join of s_1 with s_2 based on the condition $B \in E$:

$$replace\langle[X.A, Y.F]\rangle(select\langle X.B \in Y.E\rangle(cross_{[X,Y]}(s_1, s_2))).$$

3.3 Adding Interpreted Functions

Interpreted functions (that is, functions whose semantics is defined outside the database) can be included in CVA in a very natural way [1].

Let us first consider a set Ω of interpreted scalar functions over $\mathbb{Q}$. These functions can be embedded into CVA by simply extending the set of available base functions with those in Ω, and allowing their application through the function constructors. For instance, if $+$ is in Ω, we can extend the tuples of a complex value r of type $\{[A : \mathbb{Q}, B : \mathbb{Q}]\}$ with a further attribute C holding the sum of the values in A and B by means of the expression $replace\langle[A, B, C = A + B]\rangle(r)$.

Let us now consider a set Γ of aggregate functions over $\mathbb{Q}$. In this case we cannot simply extend the base functions with those in Γ, since we could obtain incorrect results. For example, if we need to sum the A components of the tuples in the complex value r above, we cannot use the expression $\text{SUM}(replace\langle A\rangle(r))$, since this would eliminate duplicates before the aggregation. Therefore, we introduce an *aggregate application* constructor $g\{\!\{f\}\!\}$, where g is an aggregate function in Γ and f is any CVA function. For a set s, $g\{\!\{f\}\!\}(s)$ specifies that g has to be applied to the multiset $\{\!\{f(w) \mid w \in s\}\!\}$ rather than to the set $\{f(w) \mid w \in s\}$. Thus, the above function can be computed by means of the expression $\text{SUM}\{\!\{A\}\!\}(r)$.

In the following, we will denote by $CVA + \Omega + \Gamma$ the complex-values algebra extended in this way with the scalar functions in Ω and the aggregate functions in Γ.

3.4 Expressive Power and Complexity

It is well-known that the complex-values algebra CVA is equivalent to a lot of other algebraic or calculus-based languages (without *powerset*) over complex values and nested collections proposed in the literature [5,6,19,20]. It turns out that CVA expresses only functions (over uninterpreted databases) that have PTIME data complexity.

When considering the complexity of functions over numeric interpreted domains, a cost model has to be specified, since it can be defined in several different ways. For instance, it is possible to consider a number as a bit-sequence and define the complexity of a function over a tuple of numbers with respect to the length of the representations of the numbers. However, we prefer to treat numbers as atomic entities, and assume that basic scalar functions are computed in a single step, independently of the magnitude or complexity of the involved numbers [4,10]. Specifically, we assume that the computational cost of any scalar function that we consider is unitary; this is indeed a reasonable choice when arithmetic operations and comparisons over the natural or rational numbers are considered. Under this assumption, the data complexity of $CVA + \Omega$ is in PTIME. Furthermore, if we consider a class Γ of aggregate functions having polynomial time complexity in the size of their input then, by a result in [5], $CVA + \Omega + \Gamma$ remains in PTIME.

By noting that, for a collection Ω of scalar functions, the complexity of evaluating aggregate functions in $A(\Omega)$ is polynomial in the size of their input, the following result easily follows.

Theorem 1. *Let Ω be a collection of scalar functions. Then $CVA + \Omega + A(\Omega)$ has PTIME data complexity.*

4   An Operator for Defining Aggregate Functions

In this section we investigate the introduction, in the query language CVA, of a high-order constructor, called *folding*, that allows us to *define* and *apply* an aggregation. This operator is essentially based on *structural recursion* [5,17].

4.1   Folding Expressions

A *folding signature* is a triple (τ_i, τ_a, τ_o) of types, with the restriction that the type τ_a does not involve the set type constructor. As we will clarify later, this type restriction ensures tractability of folding.

Definition 4. *A folding constructor of signature (τ_i, τ_a, τ_o) is an expression of the form $fold\langle p; i; q\rangle$, where:*

- *p is a CVA function of type $\{\!\{\tau_i\}\!\} \to \tau_a$, called pre-function;*
- *i is a left-commutative[3] CVA function $\tau_i \times \tau_a \to \tau_a$ over the symbols curr and acc, called increment function; and*
- *q is a CVA function of type $\tau_a \to \tau_o$, called post-function.*

A folding $fold\langle p; i; q\rangle$ of signature (τ_i, τ_a, τ_o) defines a function of type $\{\!\{\tau_i\}\!\} \to \tau_o$; the result of applying this function over a collection s is computed iteratively as follows:

> $acc := p(s);$
> **for each** *curr* **in** s **do** $acc := i(curr, acc);$
> **return** $q(acc);$

---

[3] A binary function f is *left-commutative* if it satisfies the condition $f(x_1, f(x_2, y)) = f(x_2, f(x_1, y))$. Commutativity implies left-commutativity, but not vice versa.

Initially, the result of applying the pre-function p to s is assigned to the "accumulator" variable acc. Then, for each element $curr$ of s (chosen in some arbitrary order), the result of applying i to $curr$ and acc is (re)assigned to acc ($curr$ stands for current element). Finally, the result of the whole expression is given by the application of the post-function q to the value of acc at the end of the iteration. It is important to note that, since the function i is left-commutative, the semantics of folding is well-defined, that is, the result is independent of the order in which the elements of s have been selected.

For example, let r be a complex value of type $\{[A : \mathcal{D}, B : \mathbb{Q}]\}$. The count of the tuples in r can be computed by the expression: $fold\langle 0; acc + 1; id\rangle \{\!\!\{id\}\!\!\}(r)$. (Note that we often use the folding constructor together with the aggregate application constructor.) Similarly, the sum of the B components of the tuples in r is given by $fold\langle 0; acc + B(curr); id\rangle \{\!\!\{id\}\!\!\}(r)$ or, equivalently, by $fold\langle 0; acc + curr; id\rangle \{\!\!\{B\}\!\!\}(r)$. The average of the B components can be computed by evaluating the sum and the count in parallel, and then taking their ratio:

$$fold\langle [S = 0, C = 0]; [S = acc.S + curr.B, C = acc.C + 1]; S/C\rangle \{\!\!\{id\}\!\!\}(r).$$

Folding also allows the computation of aggregations over nested sets. For instance, let s be an expression of type $\{[A : \mathcal{D}, B : \{\mathbb{Q}\}]\}$, and assume that we want to extend each tuple by a new component holding the sum of the set of numbers occurring in the B component. This can be obtained by:

$$replace\langle [A, B, C = fold\langle 0; acc + curr; id\rangle \{\!\!\{id\}\!\!\}(B)]\rangle(s).$$

This expression suggests that an SQL query with the *group-by* clause can be specified in this algebra by applying *fold* after a nesting.

The restriction on the type τ_a imposed in the definition of folding signature has been introduced to guarantee tractability of the folding constructor. In fact, the *unrestricted* folding constructor, $fold^{unr}$, in which the accumulator can be of any complex type, can express very complex data manipulations, including *replace*, *set-collapse*, and *powerset*:

$$powerset(s) = fold^{unr}\langle \{\{\}\}; acc \cup replace\langle id \cup \{curr\}\rangle(acc); id\rangle \{\!\!\{id\}\!\!\}(s).$$

4.2   Numeric Folding

We now consider a further constraint on the definition of folding, which essentially allows only the computation of *numeric* aggregations. This is coherent with our approach that tends to make a clear distinction between the restructuring capabilities of a query language and its ability to compute aggregations.

Definition 5. *Let Ω be a vocabulary. A numeric folding over Ω is a folding constructor ϕ that satisfies the following conditions:*

- *the signature of ϕ has the form $(\mathbb{Q}, \tau_a, \mathbb{Q})$, where τ_a is either $\mathbb{Q}$ or $[A_1 : \mathbb{Q}, \ldots, A_k : \mathbb{Q}]$, with $k > 0$;*

– the pre-function, the increment function, and the post-function of ϕ can use only the following functions and constructors: the identity function, binary composition, the labeled tuple constructor, the scalar functions in Ω, the numeric folding constructor, and possibly the attribute names $A_1, \ldots, A_k$.

Definition 6. A counting folding over a vocabulary Ω is a numeric folding over Ω in which the increment function does not use the symbol curr.

Lemma 2. Let Ω be a vocabulary. Then:

– every numeric folding over Ω computes a uniform aggregate function over Ω;
– every counting folding over Ω computes a uniform counting function over Ω.

For instance, $fold\langle 0; acc + curr; id \rangle$ is a numeric folding that computes the aggregate function SUM, whereas $fold\langle 0; acc+1; id \rangle$ is a counting folding that computes the counting function COUNT.

4.3   Expressive Power of Query Languages with Folding

In this section we relate the language $C\mathcal{VA} + \Omega + fold$, in which aggregations are computed using the folding constructor, with $C\mathcal{VA} + \Omega + \overline{fold}$, in which only numeric foldings are allowed. We consider also the weaker languages $C\mathcal{VA} + \Omega + fold^c$ and $C\mathcal{VA} + \Omega + \overline{fold}^c$, in which the former disallows the use of the symbol curr (and thus increment functions cannot refer to the current element while iterating over a collection) and the latter has only the counting folding constructor.

For example, the following is a $C\mathcal{VA} + \Omega + fold$ expression, over the complex value s of type $\{\{\mathcal{D}\}\}$ (a set of sets) that computes the sum of the cardinalities of the sets in s:

$$fold\langle 0; acc + fold\langle 0; acc + 1; id \rangle \{\!\!\{ id \}\!\!\}(curr); id \rangle \{\!\!\{ id \}\!\!\}(s).$$

In the foregoing expression, the outer folding is not numeric (since it applies to a set of sets). There is however an equivalent $C\mathcal{VA} + \Omega + \overline{fold}$ expression:

$$fold\langle 0; acc + curr; id \rangle \{\!\!\{ fold\langle 0; acc + 1; id \rangle \{\!\!\{ 0 \}\!\!\} \}\!\!\}(s).$$

This example suggests that expressions involving generic foldings can be rewritten into expressions involving only numeric foldings, by exploiting the restructuring capabilities of $C\mathcal{VA}$. This is confirmed by the following result.

Theorem 2. Let Ω be a vocabulary. Then:

– $C\mathcal{VA} + \Omega + fold$ and $C\mathcal{VA} + \Omega + \overline{fold}$ have the same expressive power;
– $C\mathcal{VA} + \Omega + fold^c$ and $C\mathcal{VA} + \Omega + \overline{fold}^c$ have the same expressive power.

5 Querying with Aggregate Functions

In this section we study the relationship between the class of aggregate functions that can be expressed by the numeric folding and the class of the uniform aggregate functions, as well as the effect of their inclusion in $CV\!A$.

We first show that numeric folding, considered as a stand-alone operator, is weaker than uniform aggregation. Specifically, the following result states that any aggregate function expressed by a numeric folding can be described by a uniform aggregate function whose description has size linear in the number of its arguments.

Let $\mathcal{F}(\Omega)$ be the class of the aggregate functions computed by numeric foldings over a vocabulary Ω, and $\mathcal{F}^c(\Omega)$ be the class of counting functions defined by counting foldings over Ω. Moreover, let $\mathcal{C}(\Omega)$ be the class of uniform counting functions over Ω.

Theorem 3. *Let Ω be a vocabulary. Then $\mathcal{F}(\Omega) \subseteq \mathcal{A}^1(\Omega)$ and $\mathcal{F}^c(\Omega) \subseteq \mathcal{C}^1(\Omega)$.*

Actually, we conjecture that $\mathcal{F}(\Omega) = \mathcal{A}^1(\Omega)$ and $\mathcal{F}^c(\Omega) = \mathcal{C}^1(\Omega)$, but we do not have a proof at the moment.

Thus, in general, we have that $\mathcal{F}(\Omega) \subseteq \mathcal{A}(\Omega)$ and $\mathcal{F}^c(\Omega) \subseteq \mathcal{C}(\Omega)$ but, according to Lemma 1, there are vocabularies for which the containment is proper, that is, $\mathcal{F}(\Omega) \subset \mathcal{A}(\Omega)$ and $\mathcal{F}^c(\Omega) \subset \mathcal{C}(\Omega)$. These containments suggest that numeric folding presents a limitation in computing aggregate functions, as it is not able to capture an entire class $\mathcal{A}(\Omega)$. On the other hand, it is possible to show that this deficiency can be *partially* remedied by the restructuring capabilities of a query language. For instance, consider again the uniform aggregate function α introduced in the proof of Lemma 1, with $\alpha_n = \bigoplus_{i,j} x_i \otimes x_j$, which belongs to $\mathcal{A}^2(\Omega_a) - \mathcal{A}^1(\Omega_a)$ and, as such, it cannot be expressed as an aggregate *function* by a numeric folding. However, it can be expressed as an aggregate *query* in $CV\!A + \Omega_a + \overline{fold}$, as follows:

$$fold\langle 0_\oplus; acc \oplus curr; id\rangle \{\!\!\{A_1 \otimes A_2\}\!\!\}(cross_{[A_1,A_2]}(id, id)).$$

Lemma 3. *Let Ω be a vocabulary. Then, for each $k > 0$:*

- *there are functions in $\mathcal{A}^k(\Omega) - \mathcal{A}^{k-1}(\Omega)$ that can be expressed in $CV\!A + \Omega + \overline{fold}$;*
- *there are functions in $\mathcal{C}^k(\Omega) - \mathcal{C}^{k-1}(\Omega)$ that can be expressed in $CV\!A + \Omega + \overline{fold}$.*

Actually, there are uniform aggregate functions that cannot be expressed using aggregate queries with folding, showing that, in general, it can be better to have at disposal a language for expressing aggregate functions (such as the uniform ones) outside the database query language.

Theorem 4. *There is a vocabulary Ω such that:*

- $CVA + \Omega + A(\Omega)$ *is more expressive than* $CVA + \Omega + \overline{fold}$;
- $CVA + \Omega + C(\Omega)$ *is more expressive than* $CVA + \Omega + \overline{fold}$.

Sketch of proof. Consider again the abstract vocabulary Ω_a introduced in the proof of Lemma 1, and assume that the binary function $\otimes$ is commutative. Then, the family γ of functions such that $\gamma_n = \bigoplus_{i,j}^{i<j} x_i \otimes x_j$ represents a uniform aggregate function, which belongs to $A^2(\Omega_a) - A^1(\Omega_a)$. It turns out that γ cannot be expressed using $CVA + \Omega_a + \overline{fold}$. $\square$

6   Conclusions and Future Work

We believe that the framework proposed in this paper can be fruitfully used as a formal foundation for further studies on the relationship between aggregate functions and aggregate queries. In particular, the relationship between the classes $CVA + \Omega + \overline{fold}$ and $CVA + \Omega + A(\Omega)$ deserves a deeper investigation.

On one hand, we plan to investigate the implications on considering mutual properties of functions in a vocabulary, such as commutativity, associativity, and distributivity. For instance, the function γ introduced in the proof of Theorem 4 is an aggregate function only if $\otimes$ is commutative. What are the vocabularies for which $CVA + \Omega + \overline{fold}$ and $CVA + \Omega + A(\Omega)$ have the same expressive power?

On the other hand, there are simple *logspace* computations that cannot be easily captured by folding. The definition of the functions β (Remark 1) and γ (proof of Theorem 4) shows that uniform construction can compare indexes of the arguments (as $i < j$ in $\bigoplus_{i,j}^{i<j} x_i \otimes x_j$ and $i \neq j$ in $\bigoplus_{i,j}^{i\neq j} x_i \otimes x_j$). Such a capability can be partially captured by referring to total ordered domains (both $\mathcal{D}$ and $\mathbb{Q}$) and a total order predicate $\geq$ (both as a base function in CVA and in the vocabulary Ω). This extension is another topic that we plan to investigate, first of all by tackling the following claim:

Conjecture 1. Let Ω be a vocabulary. Then $CVA + \Omega + \overline{fold}$ and $CVA + \Omega + A(\Omega)$ have the same expressive power over totally ordered domains.

References

1. S. Abiteboul and C. Beeri. The power of languages for the manipulation of complex values. *The VLDB Journal*, 4(4):727–794, October 1995.
2. M. Benedikt and H. J. Keisler. Expressive power of unary counters. In *International Conference on Data Base Theory*, Springer–Verlag, pages 291–305, 1997.
3. M. Benedikt and L. Libkin. Languages for relational databases over interpreted structures. In *Sixteenth ACM SIGACT SIGMOD SIGART Symp. on Principles of Database Systems*, pages 87–98, 1997.
4. L. Blum, M. Shub, and S. Smale. On a theory of computation and complexity over the real numbers: NP-completeness, recursive functions and universal machines. *Bull. Amer. Math. Soc.*, 21:1–46, 1989.

5. P. Buneman, S. Naqvi, V. Tannen, and L. Wong. Principles of programming with complex objects and collection types. *Theoretical Computer Science*, 149(1):3–48, 1995.
6. L. S. Colby. A recursive algebra for nested relations. *Information Systems*, 15(5):567–582, 1990.
7. M. P. Consens and A. O. Mendelzon. Low complexity aggregation in GraphLog and Datalog. In *International Conference on Data Base Theory*, Springer–Verlag, pages 379–394, 1990.
8. K. Etessami. Counting quantifiers, successor relations, and logarithmic space. *Journal of Computer and Systems Science*, 54(3): 400–411, 1997.
9. E. Grädel and Y. Gurevich. Metafinite model theory. In *Logic and Computational Complexity*, Springer–Verlag, pages 313–366, 1995.
10. E. Grädel and K. Meer. Descriptive complexity theory over the real numbers. In *Twenty-Seventh Annual ACM Symposium on Theory of Computing*, pages 315–324, 1995.
11. S. Grumbach and C. Tollu. On the expressive power of counting. *Theoretical Computer Science*, 149(1):67–99, 1995.
12. R.M. Karp and V. Ramachandran. Parallel algorithms for shared-memory machines. In J. van Leeuwen, editor, *Handbook of Theoretical Computer Science*, volume A, pages 869–941. Elsevier Science Publishers (North-Holland), Amsterdam, 1990.
13. A. Klug. Equivalence of relational algebra and relational calculus query languages having aggregate functions. *Journal of the ACM*, 29(3):699–717, 1982.
14. L. Libkin and L. Wong. New techniques for studying set languages, bag languages and aggregate functions. In *Thirteenth ACM SIGACT SIGMOD SIGART Symp. on Principles of Database Systems*, pages 155–166, 1994.
15. L. Libkin and L. Wong. Query languages for bags and aggregate functions. *Journal of Computer and System Sciences*, 1997. To appear.
16. G. Özsoyoglu, Z. M. Özsoyoglu, V. Matos. Extending relational algebra and relational calculus with set-valued attributes and aggregate functions. *ACM Transactions on Database Systems*, 12(4):566–592, 1987.
17. A. Poulovassilis and C. Small. Algebraic query optimisation for database programming languages. *The VLDB Journal*, 5(2):119–132, April 1996.
18. W. L. Ruzzo. On uniform circuit complexity. *Journal of Computer and Systems Science*, 22: 365–383, 1981.
19. H. Schek and M. H. Scholl. The relational model with relation-valued attributes. *Information Systems*, 11(2):137–147, 1986.
20. S. J. Thomas and P. C. Fisher. Nested relational structures. In *Advances in Computing Research: the theory of database*, JAI Press, 1986.

Discovering Frequent Closed Itemsets for Association Rules

Nicolas Pasquier, Yves Bastide, Rafik Taouil, and Lotfi Lakhal

Laboratoire d'Informatique (LIMOS)
Université Blaise Pascal - Clermont-Ferrand II
Complexe Scientifique des Cézeaux
24, av. des Landais, 63177 Aubière Cedex France
{pasquier,bastide,taouil,lakhal}@libd1.univ-bpclermont.fr

Abstract. In this paper, we address the problem of finding frequent itemsets in a database. Using the closed itemset lattice framework, we show that this problem can be reduced to the problem of finding frequent closed itemsets. Based on this statement, we can construct efficient data mining algorithms by limiting the search space to the closed itemset lattice rather than the subset lattice. Moreover, we show that the set of all frequent closed itemsets suffices to determine a reduced set of association rules, thus addressing another important data mining problem: limiting the number of rules produced without information loss. We propose a new algorithm, called A-Close, using a closure mechanism to find frequent closed itemsets. We realized experiments to compare our approach to the commonly used frequent itemset search approach. Those experiments showed that our approach is very valuable for dense and/or correlated data that represent an important part of existing databases.

1 Introduction

The discovery of association rules was first introduced in [1]. This task consists in determining relationships between sets of items in very large databases. Agrawal's statement of this problem is the following [1, 2]. Let $\mathcal{I} = \{i_1, i_2, \dots, i_m\}$ be a set of m items. Let the database $\mathcal{D} = \{t_1, t_2, \dots, t_n\}$ be a set of n transactions, each one identified by its unique TID. Each transaction t consists of a set of items I from $\mathcal{I}$. If $\|I\| = k$, then I is called a k-itemset. An itemset I is *contained* in a transaction $t \in \mathcal{D}$ if $I \subseteq t$. The support of an itemset I is the percentage of transactions in $\mathcal{D}$ containing I. Association rules are of the form $r : I_1 \xrightarrow{c} I_2$, with $I_1, I_2 \subset \mathcal{I}$ and $I_1 \cap I_2 = \emptyset$. Each association rule r has a support defined as $support(r) = support(I_1 \cup I_2)$ and a confidence c defined as $confidence(r) = support(I_1 \cup I_2) \,/\, support(I_1)$. Given the user defined minimum support *minsup* and minimum confidence *minconf* thresholds, the problem of mining association rules can be divided into two sub-problems [1]:

1. Find all *frequent itemsets* in $\mathcal{D}$, i.e. itemsets with support greater or equal to *minsup*.

Catriel Beeri, Peter Buneman (Eds.): ICDT'99, LNCS 1540, pp. 398–416, 1998.
© Springer-Verlag Berlin Heidelberg 1998

2. For each frequent itemset I_1 found, generate all association rules $I_2 \xrightarrow{c} I_1 - I_2$ where $I_2 \subset I_1$, with confidence c greater or equal to *minconf.*

Once all frequent itemsets and their support are known, the association rule generation is straightforward. Hence, the problem of mining association rules is reduced to the problem of determining frequent itemsets and their support.

Recent works demonstrated that the frequent itemset discovery is also the key stage in the search for episodes from sequences and in finding keys or inclusion as well as functional dependencies from a relation [12]. All existing algorithms use one of the two following approach: a levelwise [12] bottom-up search [2, 5, 13, 16, 17] or a simultaneous bottom-up and top-down search [3, 10, 20]. Although they are dissimilar, all those algorithms explore the *subset lattice* (itemset lattice) for finding frequent itemsets: they all use the basic properties that *all subsets of a frequent itemset are frequent* and that *all supersets of an infrequent itemset are infrequent* in order to prune elements of the itemset lattice.

In this paper, we propose a new efficient algorithm, called A-Close, for finding frequent closed itemsets and their support in a database. Using a closure mechanism based on the *Galois connection*, we define the *closed itemset lattice* which is a sub-order of the itemset lattice, thus often much smaller. This lattice is closely related to the *Galois lattice* [4, 7] also called *concept lattice* [19]. The closed itemset lattice can be used as a formal framework for discovering frequent itemsets given the basic properties that *the support of an itemset I is equal to the support of its closure* and that *the set of maximal frequent itemsets is identical to the set of maximal frequent closed itemsets.* Then, once A-Close has discovered all frequent closed itemsets and their support, we can directly determine the frequent itemsets and their support. Hence, we reduce the problem of mining association rules to the problem of determining frequent closed itemsets and their support.

Using the set of frequent closed itemsets, we can also directly generate a reduced set of association rules without having to determine all frequent itemsets, thus lowering the algorithm computation cost. Moreover, since there can be thousands of association rules holding in a database, reducing the number of rules produced without information loss is an important problem for the understandability of the result [18]. Empirical evaluations comparing A-Close to an optimized version of Apriori showed that they give nearly always equivalent results for weakly correlated data (such as synthetic data) and that A-Close clearly outperforms Apriori for correlated data (such as statistical or text data).

The rest of the paper is organized as follows. In Section 2, we present the closed itemset lattice. In Section 3, we propose a new model for association rules based on the *Galois connection* and we characterize a reduced set of association rules. In Section 4, we describe the A-Close algorithm. Section 5 gives experimental results on synthetic data[1] and census data using the PUMS file for Kansas USA[2] and Section 6 concludes the paper.

---

[1] http://www.almaden.ibm.com/cs/quest/syndata.html

[2] ftp://ftp2.cc.ukans.edu/pub/ippbr/census/pums/pums90ks.zip

2 Closed Itemset Lattices

In this section, we define *data mining context, Galois connection, Galois closure operators, closed itemsets* and *closed itemset lattice*. Interested readers should read [4, 7, 19] for further details on order and lattice theory.

Definition 1 (Data mining context). *A data mining context[3] is a triple $\mathcal{D} = (\mathcal{O}, \mathcal{I}, \mathcal{R})$. $\mathcal{O}$ and $\mathcal{I}$ are finite sets of objects and items respectively. $\mathcal{R} \subseteq \mathcal{O} \times \mathcal{I}$ is a binary relation between objects and items. Each couple $(o, i) \in \mathcal{R}$ denotes the fact that the object $o \in \mathcal{O}$ is related to the item $i \in \mathcal{I}$.*

Definition 2 (Galois connection). *Let $\mathcal{D} = (\mathcal{O}, \mathcal{I}, \mathcal{R})$ be a data mining context. For $O \subseteq \mathcal{O}$ and $I \subseteq \mathcal{I}$, we define:*

$$f(O) \colon 2^{\mathcal{O}} \to 2^{\mathcal{I}} \qquad\qquad g(I) \colon 2^{\mathcal{I}} \to 2^{\mathcal{O}}$$
$$f(O) = \{i \in \mathcal{I} \mid \forall o \in O, (o, i) \in \mathcal{R}\} \qquad g(I) = \{o \in \mathcal{O} \mid \forall i \in I, (o, i) \in \mathcal{R}\}$$

$f(O)$ associates with O the items common to all objects $o \in O$ and $g(I)$ associates with I the objects related to all items $i \in I$. The couple of applications (f, g) is a Galois connection between the power set of $\mathcal{O}$ (i.e. $2^{\mathcal{O}}$) and the power set of $\mathcal{I}$ (i.e. $2^{\mathcal{I}}$). The following properties hold for all $I, I_1, I_2 \subseteq \mathcal{I}$ and $O, O_1, O_2 \subseteq \mathcal{O}$:

(1) $I_1 \subseteq I_2 \Rightarrow g(I_1) \supseteq g(I_2)$ *(1') $O_1 \subseteq O_2 \Rightarrow f(O_1) \supseteq f(O_2)$*
(2) $O \subseteq g(I) \Longleftrightarrow I \subseteq f(O)$

Definition 3 (Galois closure operators). *The operators $h = f \circ g$ in $2^{\mathcal{I}}$ and $h' = g \circ f$ in $2^{\mathcal{O}}$ are Galois closure operators[4]. Given the Galois connection (f, g), the following properties hold for all $I, I_1, I_2 \subseteq \mathcal{I}$ and $O, O_1, O_2 \subseteq \mathcal{O}$ [4, 7, 19]:*

Extension :   *(3) $I \subseteq h(I)$*   *(3') $O \subseteq h'(O)$*
Idempotency :   *(4) $h(h(I)) = h(I)$*   *(4') $h'(h'(O)) = h'(O)$*
Monotonicity : *(5) $I_1 \subseteq I_2 \Rightarrow h(I_1) \subseteq h(I_2)$*   *(5') $O_1 \subseteq O_2 \Rightarrow h'(O_1) \subseteq h'(O_2)$*

Definition 4 (Closed itemsets). *An itemset $C \subseteq \mathcal{I}$ from $\mathcal{D}$ is a closed itemset iff $h(C) = C$. The smallest (minimal) closed itemset containing an itemset I is obtained by applying h to I. We call $h(I)$ the closure of I.*

Definition 5 (Closed itemset lattice). *Let C be the set of closed itemsets derived from $\mathcal{D}$ using the Galois closure operator h. The pair $\mathcal{L}_C = (\mathcal{C}, \leq)$ is a complete lattice called closed itemset lattice. The lattice structure implies two properties:*

i) There exists a partial order on the lattice elements such that, for every elements $C_1, C_2 \in \mathcal{L}_C$, $C_1 \leq C_2$, iff $C_1 \subseteq C_2$[5].

---

[3] By extension, we call database a data mining context afterwards.
[4] Here, we use the following notation: $f \circ g(I) = f(g(I))$ and $g \circ f(O) = g(f(O))$.
[5] C_1 is a sub-closed itemset of C_2 and C_2 is a sup-closed itemset of C_1.

ii) *All subsets of $\mathcal{L}_C$ have one greatest lower bound, the Join element, and one lowest upper bound, the Meet element.*

Below, we give the definitions of the Join and Meet elements extracted from the basic theorem on Galois (concept) lattices [4, 7, 19]. For all $S \subseteq \mathcal{L}_C$:

$$Join\ (S) = h(\bigcup_{C \in S} C), \qquad Meet\ (S) = \bigcap_{C \in S} C$$

OID	Items
1	A C D
2	B C E
3	A B C E
4	B E
5	A B C E

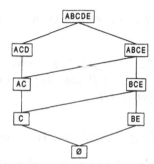

Fig. 1. The data mining context $\mathcal{D}$ and its associated closed itemset lattice.

3   Association Rule Model

In this section, we define *frequent* and *maximal frequent* itemsets and closed itemsets using the Galois connection. We then define *association rules* and *valid association rules*, and we characterise a *reduced set of valid association rules* in a data mining context $\mathcal{D}$.

3.1   Frequent Itemsets

Definition 6 (Itemset support). *Let $I \subseteq \mathcal{I}$ be a set of items from $\mathcal{D}$. The support count of the itemset I in $\mathcal{D}$ is:*

$$support(I) = \frac{\|g(I)\|}{\|\mathcal{O}\|}$$

Definition 7 (Frequent itemsets). *The itemset I is said to be frequent if the support of I in $\mathcal{D}$ is at least minsup. The set L of frequent itemsets in $\mathcal{D}$ is:*

$$L = \{I \subseteq \mathcal{I} \mid support(I) \geq minsup\}$$

Definition 8 (Maximal frequent itemsets). *Let L be the set of frequent itemsets. We define the set M of maximal frequent itemsets in D as:*

$$M = \{I \in L \mid \nexists I' \in L, \ I \subset I'\}$$

Property 1. All subsets of a frequent itemset are frequent (intuitive in [2]).

Proof. Let $I, I' \subseteq \mathcal{I}, I \in L$ and $I' \subseteq I$. According to Property (1) of the Galois connection: $I' \subseteq I \Longrightarrow g(I') \supseteq g(I) \Longrightarrow support(I') \geq support(I) \geq minsup$. So, we get: $I' \in L$.

Property 2. All supersets of an infrequent itemset are infrequent (intuitive in [2]).

Proof. Let $I, I' \subseteq \mathcal{I}, I' \notin L$ and $I' \subseteq I$. According to Property (1) of the Galois connection: $I \supseteq I' \Longrightarrow g(I) \subseteq g(I') \Longrightarrow support(I) \leq support(I') \leq minsup$. So, we get: $I \notin L$.

3.2   Frequent Closed Itemsets

Definition 9 (Frequent closed itemsets). *The closed itemset C is said to be frequent if the support of C in D is at least minsup. We define the set FC of frequent closed itemsets in D as:*

$$FC = \{C \subseteq \mathcal{I} \mid C = h(C) \ \wedge \ support(C) \geq minsup\}$$

Definition 10 (Maximal frequent closed itemsets). *Let FC be the set of frequent closed itemsets. We define the set MC of maximal frequent closed itemsets in D as:*

$$MC = \{C \in FC \mid \nexists C' \in FC, \ C \subset C'\}$$

Property 3. The support of an itemset I is equal to the support of its closure: $support(I) = support(h(I))$.

Proof. Let $I \subseteq \mathcal{I}$ be an itemset. The support of I in $\mathcal{D}$ is: $support(I) = \dfrac{\|g(I)\|}{\|\mathcal{O}\|}$

Now, we consider $h(I)$, the closure of I. Let's show that $h'(g(I)) = g(I)$. We have $g(I) \subseteq h(g(I))$ (extension property of the Galois closure) and $I \subseteq h(I) \Rightarrow g(h(I)) \subseteq g(I)$ (Property (1) of the Galois connection). We deduce that $h'(g(I)) = g(I)$, and therefore we have:

$$support(h(I)) = \frac{\|g(h(I))\|}{\|\mathcal{O}\|} = \frac{\|h'(g(I))\|}{\|\mathcal{O}\|} = \frac{\|g(I)\|}{\|\mathcal{O}\|} = support(I)$$

Property 4. The set of maximal frequent itemsets M is identical to the set of maximal frequent closed itemsets MC.

Proof. It suffices to demonstrate that $\forall I \in M$, I is closed, i.e. $I = h(I)$. Let $I \in M$ be a maximal frequent itemset. According to Property (3) of the Galois connection $I \subseteq h(I)$ and, since I is maximal and $support(h(I)) = support(I) \geq minsup$, we conclude that $I = h(I)$. I is a maximal frequent closed itemset. Since all maximal frequent itemsets are also maximal frequent closed itemsets, we get: $M = MC$.

3.3   Association Rule Semantics

Definition 11 (Association rules). *An association rule is an implication between itemsets of the form $I_1 \xrightarrow{c} I_2$ where $I_1, I_2 \subset \mathcal{I}$ and $I_1 \cap I_2 = \emptyset$. Below, we define the support and confidence (c) of an association rule $r : I_1 \xrightarrow{c} I_2$ using the Galois connection:*

$$support(r) = \frac{\|g(I_1 \cup I_2)\|}{\|\mathcal{O}\|}, \quad confidence(r) = \frac{support(I_1 \cup I_2)}{support(I_1)} = \frac{\|g(I_1 \cup I_2)\|}{\|g(I_1)\|}$$

Definition 12 (Valid association rules). *A valid association rules is an association rules with support and confidence greater or equal to the minsup and minconf thresholds respectively. We define the set $\mathcal{AR}$ of valid association rules in $\mathcal{D}$ using the set MC of maximal frequent closed itemsets as:*

$$\mathcal{AR}(\mathcal{D}, minsup, minconf) = \{r : I_2 \xrightarrow{c} I_1 - I_2,\ I_2 \subset I_1 \mid I_1 \in L = \bigcup_{C \in MC} 2^C\ and$$
$$confidence(r) \geq minconf\}$$

3.4   Reduced Set of Association Rules

Let $I_1, I_2 \subset \mathcal{I}$ and $I_1 \cap I_2 = \emptyset$. An association rule $r : I_1 \xrightarrow{c} I_2$ is an *exact association rule* if $c = 1$. Then, r is noted $r : I_1 \Rightarrow I_2$. An association rule $r : I_1 \xrightarrow{c} I_2$ where $c < 1$ is called an *approximate association rule*. Let $\mathcal{D}$ be a data mining context.

Definition 13 (Pseudo-closed itemsets). *An itemset $I \subseteq \mathcal{I}$ from $\mathcal{D}$ is a pseudo-closed itemset iff $h(I) \neq I$ and $\forall I' \subset I$ such as I' is a pseudo-closed itemset, we have $h(I') \subseteq I$.*

Theorem 1 (Exact association rules basis [8]). *Let P be the set of pseudo-closed itemsets and $\mathcal{R}$ the set of exact association rules in $\mathcal{D}$. The set $\mathcal{E} = \{r : I_1 \Rightarrow h(I_1) - I_1 \mid I_1 \in P\}$ is a basis for all exact association rules. $\forall r' \in \mathcal{R}$ where $confidence(r') = 1 \geq minconf$ we have $\mathcal{E} \models r'$.*

Corollary 1 (Exact valid association rules basis). *Let FP be the set of frequent pseudo-closed itemsets in $\mathcal{D}$. The set $\mathcal{BE} = \{r : I_1 \Rightarrow h(I_1) - I_1 \mid I_1 \in FP\}$ is a basis for all exact valid association rules. $\forall r' \in \mathcal{AR}$ where confidence$(r') = 1$ we have $\mathcal{BE} \models r'$.*

Theorem 2 (Reduced set of approximate association rules [11]). *Let C be the set of closed itemsets and $\mathcal{R}$ the set of approximate association rules in $\mathcal{D}$. The set $\mathcal{A} = \{r : I_1 \xrightarrow{c} I_2 - I_1 \mid I_2 \subset I_1 \wedge I_1, I_2 \in C\}$ is a correct reduced set for all approximate association rules. $\forall r' \in \mathcal{R}$ where minconf $\leq$ confidence$(r') < 1$ we have $\mathcal{A} \models r'$.*

Corollary 2 (Reduced set of approximate valid association rules). *Let FC be the set of frequent closed itemsets in $\mathcal{D}$. The set $\mathcal{BA} = \{r : I_1 \xrightarrow{c} I_2 - I_1 \mid I_2 \subset I_1 \wedge I_1, I_2 \in FC\}$ is a correct reduced set for all approximate valid association rules. $\forall r' \in \mathcal{AR}$ where confidence$(r') \leq 1$ we have $\mathcal{BA} \models r'$.*

4   A-Close Algorithm

In this section, we present our algorithm for finding frequent closed itemsets and their supports in a database. Section 4.1 describes its principle. In Section 4.2 to 4.5, we give the pseudo-close of the algorithm and the sub-functions it uses. Section 4.6 provides an example and the proof of the algorithm correctness.

4.1   A-Close Principle

A closed itemset is a maximal set of items common to a set of objects. For example, in the database $\mathcal{D}$ in Figure 1, the itemset BCE is a closed itemset since it is the maximal set of items common to the objects $\{2, 3, 5\}$. BCE is called a frequent closed itemset for $minsup = 2$ as support$(BCE) = \|\{2, 3, 5\}\| = 3 \geq minsup$. In a basket database, this means that 60% of customers (3 customers on a total of 5) purchase *at most* the items B, C and E. The itemset BC is not a closed itemset since it is not a maximal group of items common to some objects: all customers purchasing the items B and C also purchase the item E. The closed itemset lattice of a finite relation (the database) is dually isomorphic to the Galois lattice [4, 7], also called concept lattice [19].

Based on the closed itemset lattice properties (Section 2 and 3), using the result of A-Close we can generate all frequent itemsets from a database $\mathcal{D}$ through the two following phases:

1. Discover all frequent closed itemsets in $\mathcal{D}$, i.e. itemsets that are closed and have support greater or equal to $minsup$.
2. Derive all frequent itemsets from the frequent closed itemsets found in phase 1. That is generate all subsets of the maximal frequent closed itemsets and derive their support from the frequent closed itemset supports.

A different algorithm for finding frequent closed itemsets and algorithms for deriving frequent itemsets and generating valid association rules are presented in [15].

Using the result of A-Close, we can directly generate the reduced set of valid association rules defined in Section 3.4 instead of determining all frequent itemsets. The procedure is the following:

1. Discover all frequent closed itemsets in $\mathcal{D}$.
2. Determine the exact valid association rule basis: determine the pseudo-closed itemsets in $\mathcal{D}$ and then generate all rules $r : I_1 \xrightarrow{c} I_2 - I_1 \mid I_1 \subset I_2$ where I_2 is a frequent closed itemset and I_1 is a frequent pseudo-closed itemset.
3. Construct the reduced set of approximate valid association rules: generate all rules of the form: $r : I_1 \xrightarrow{c} I_2 - I_1 \mid I_1 \subset I_2$ where I_1 and I_2 are frequent closed itemsets.

In the two cases, the first phase is the most computationally intensive part. After this phase, no more database pass is necessary and the later phases can be solved easily in a straightforward manner. Indeed, the first phase has given us all information needed by the next ones.

A-Close discovers the frequent closed itemsets as follows. Based on the closed itemset properties, it determines a set of *generators* that will give us all frequent closed itemsets by application of the Galois closure operator h. An itemset p is a generator of a closed itemset c if it is one of the smallest itemsets (there can be more than one) that will determine c using the Galois closure operator: $h(p) = c$. For instance, in the database $\mathcal{D}$ (Figure 1), BC and CE are generators of the closed itemset BCE. The itemsets B, C and E are not generators of BCE since $h(C) = C$ and $h(B) = h(E) = BE$. The itemset BCE is not a generator of itself since it includes BC and CE: BCE is not one of the smallest itemsets for which closure is BCE.

The algorithm constructs the set of generators in a levelwise manner: $(i+1)$-generators[6] are created using i-generators in G_i. Then, their support is counted and the useless generators are pruned. According to their supports and the supports of their i-subsets in G_i, infrequent generators and generators that have the same closure as one of their subsets are deleted from G_{i+1}. In the previous example, the support of the generator BCE is the same as the support of generators BC and CE since they have the same closure (Property 3).

Once all frequent useful generators are found, their closures are determined, giving us the set of all frequent closed itemsets. For reducing the cost of the closure computation when possible, we introduce the following optimization. We determine the first iteration of the algorithm for which a $(i+1)$-generator was pruned because it had the same closure as one of its i-subsets. In all iterations preceding the ith one, the generators created are closed and their closure computation is useless. Hence, we can limit the closure computation to generators of size greater or equal to i. For this purpose, the *level* variable indicates the first iteration for which a generator was pruned by this pruning strategy.

---

[6] A generator of size i is called an i-generator.

4.2   Discovering Frequent Closed Itemsets

As in the Apriori algorithm, items are sorted in lexicographic order. The pseudo-code for discovering frequent closed itemsets is given in Algorithm 1. The notation is given in Table 1. In each of the iterations that construct the candidate generators, one pass over the database is necessary in order to count the support of the candidate generators. At the end of the algorithm, one more pass is needed for determining the closures of generators that are not closed. If all generators are closed, this pass is not made.

Set	Field	Contains
G_i	generator	A generator of size i.
	support	Support count of the generator: $support = count(generator)$
G, G'	generator	A generator of size i.
	closure	Closure of the generator: $closure = h(generator)$.
	support	Support count of the generator and its closure: $support = count(closure) = count(generator)$ (Property 3).
FC	closure	Frequent closed itemset (closed itemset with support $\geq$ minsup).
	support	Support count of the frequent closed itemset.

Table 1. Notation

First, the algorithm determines the set G_1 of frequent 1-generators and their support (step 1 to 5). Then, the *level* variable is set to 0 (step 6). In each of the following iterations (step 7 to 9), the AC-Generator function (Section 4.4) is applied to the set of generators G_i, determining the candidate $(i+1)$-generators and their support in G_{i+1} (step 8). This process takes place until G_i is empty. Finally, closures of all generators produced are determined (step 10 to 14). Using the *level* variable, we construct two sets of generators. The set G which contains generators p for which size is less than $level-1$, and so that are closed ($p = h(p)$). The set G' which contains generators for which size is at least $level - 1$, among which some are not closed, and so for which closure computation is necessary. The closures of generators in G' are determined by applying the *AC-Generator* function (Section 4.4) to G' (step 15). Then, all frequent closed itemsets have been produced and their support is known (see Theorem 3).

4.3   Support-Count Function

The function takes the set G_i of frequent i-generators as argument. It returns the set G_i with, for each generator $p \in G_i$, its support count: $support(p) = \|\{o \in \mathcal{O} \mid p \subseteq f(\{o\})\|$. The pseudo-code of the function is given in Algorithm 2.

The Subset function quickly determines which generators are contained in an object[7], i.e. generators that are subsets of f({o}). For this purpose, generators are stored in a *prefix-tree* structure derived from the one proposed in [14].

---

[7] We say that an itemset I is contained in object o if o is related to all items $i \in I$.

Algorithm 1 A-Close algorithm

1) generators in $G_1 \leftarrow$ {1-itemsets};
2) $G_1 \leftarrow$ Support-Count(G_1);
3) **forall** generators $p \in G_1$ **do begin**
4)   **if** (support(p) < minsup) **then delete** p **from** G_1;   // Pruning infrequent
5) **end**
6) *level* $\leftarrow$ 0;
7) **for** ($i \leftarrow$ 1; G_i.generator $\neq \emptyset$; i++) **do begin**
8) $G_{i+1} \leftarrow$ AC-Generator(G_i);   // Creates (i+1)-generators
9) **end**
10) **if** (*level* > 2) **then begin**
11) $G \leftarrow \bigcup\{G_j \mid j < level\text{-}1\}$;   // Those generators are all closed
12)   **forall** generators $p \in G$ **do begin**
13) p.closure $\leftarrow p$.generator;
14)   **end**
15) **end**
16) **if** (*level* $\neq$ 0) **then begin**
17) $G' \leftarrow \bigcup\{G_j \mid j \geq level\text{-}1\}$;   // Some of those generators are not closed
18) $G' \leftarrow$ AC-Closure(G');
19) **end**
20) Answer $FC \leftarrow \{c.closure, c.support | c \in G \cup G'\}$;

Algorithm 2 Support-Count function

1) **forall** objects $o \in O$ **do begin**
2) $G_o \leftarrow$ Subset(G_i.generator,$f(\{o\})$);   // Generators that are subsets of f({o})
3)   **forall** generators $p \in G_o$ **do begin**
4) p.support++;
5)   **end**
6) **end**

4.4   AC-Generator Function

The function takes the set G_i of frequent i-generators as argument. Based on Lemma 1 and 2, it returns the set G_{i+1} of frequent (i+1)-generators. The pseudo-code of the function is given in Algorithm 3.

Lemma 1. *Let I_1, I_2 be two itemsets. We have:*

$$h(I_1 \cup I_2) = h(h(I_1) \cup h(I_2))$$

Proof. Let I_1 and I_2 be two itemsets. According to the extension property of the Galois closure operators:

$$I_1 \subseteq h(I_1) \text{ and } I_2 \subseteq h(I_2) \Longrightarrow I_1 \cup I_2 \subseteq h(I_1) \cup h(I_2)$$
$$\Longrightarrow h(I_1 \cup I_2) \subseteq h(h(I_1) \cup h(I_2)) \tag{1}$$

Obviously, $I_1 \subseteq I_1 \cup I_2$ and $I_2 \subseteq I_1 \cup I_2$. So $h(I_1) \subseteq h(I_1 \cup I_2)$ and $h(I_2) \subseteq h(I_1 \cup I_2)$. According to the idempotency property of the Galois closure operators:

$$h(h(I_1)\cup h(I_2)) \subseteq h(h(I_1\cup I_2)) \implies h(h(I_1)\cup h(I_2)) \subseteq h(I_1\cup I_2) \qquad (2)$$

From (1) and (2), we conclude that $h(I_1 \cup I_2) = h(h(I_1) \cup h(I_2))$.

Lemma 2. *Let I_1 be an itemset and I_2 a subset of I_1 where $support(I_1) = support(I_2)$. Then we have $h(I_1) = h(I_2)$ and $\forall I_3 \subseteq \mathcal{I}$, $h(I_1 \cup I_3) = h(I_2 \cup I_3)$.*

Proof. Let I_1, I_2 be two itemsets where $I_2 \subset I_1$ and $support(I_1) = support(I_2)$. Then, we have that $\|g(I_1)\| = \|g(I_2)\|$ and we deduce that $g(I_1) = g(I_2)$. From this, we conclude $f(g(I_1)) = f(g(I_2)) \implies h(I_1) = h(I_2)$. Let $I_3 \subseteq \mathcal{I}$ be an itemset. Then according to Lemma 1:

$$h(I_1 \cup I_3) = h(h(I_1) \cup h(I_3)) = h(h(I_2) \cup h(I_3)) = h(I_2 \cup I_3)$$

Corollary 3. *Let I be an i-generator and $S = \{s_1, s_2, \dots, s_j\}$ a set of $(i-1)$-subsets of I where $\bigcup_{s \in S} s = I$. If $\exists s \in S$ such as $support(s) = support(I)$, then $h(I) = h(s)$.*

Proof. Derived from Lemma 2.

The AC-Generator function works as follows. We first apply the combinatorial phase of Apriori-Gen [2] to the set of generators G_i in order to obtain a set of candidate $(i+1)$-generators: two generators of size i in G_i with the same first $i-1$ items are joined, producing a new potential generator of size $i+1$ (step 1 to 4). Then, the potential generators produced that will lead to useless computations (infrequent closed itemsets) or redundancies (frequent closed itemsets already produced) are pruned from G_{i+1} as follows.

First, like in Apriori-Gen, G_{i+1} is pruned by removing every candidate $(i+1)$-generator c such that some i-subset of c is not in G_i (step 8 and 9). Using this strategy, we prune two kinds of itemsets: first, all supersets of infrequent generators (that are also infrequent according to Property 2); second, all generators that have the same support as one of their subset and therefore have the same closure (see Theorem 3). Let's take an example. Suppose that the set of frequent closed itemsets G_2 contains the generators AB, AC. The AC-Generator function will create $ABC = AB \cup AC$ as a new potential generator in G_3 and the first pruning will remove ABC since $BC \notin G_2$.

Next, the supports of the remaining candidate generators in G_{i+1} are determined and, based on Property 2, those with support less than *minsup* are deleted from G_{i+1} (step 7).

The third pruning strategy works as follows. For each candidate generator c in G_{i+1}, we test if the support of one of its i-subsets s is equal to the support of c. In that case, the closure of c will be equal to the closure of s (see Corollary 3), so we remove c from G_{i+1} (step 10 to 13). Let's give another example. Suppose that the final set of generators G_2 contains frequent generators AB, AC, BC and their respective supports $3, 2, 3$. The AC-Generator function will create $ABC = AB \cup AC$ as a new potential generator in G_3

Algorithm 3 AC-Generator function

---

1) **insert into** G_{i+1}
2) **select** $p.item_1, p.item_2, \ldots, p.item_i, q.item_i$
3) **from** $G_i \ p, G_i \ q$
4) **where** $p.item_1 = q.item_1, \ldots, p.item_{i-1} = q.item_{i-1}, p.item_i < q.item_i$;

5) **forall** candidate generators $c \in G_{i+1}$ **do begin**
6)   **forall** i-subsets s of c **do begin**
7)   **if** $(s \notin G_i)$ **then delete** c from G_{i+1};
8)   **end**
9) **end**
10) $G_{i+1} \leftarrow$ Support-Count(G_{i+1});
11) **forall** candidate generators $c \in G_{i+1}$ **do begin**
12)   **if** (support$(c) <$ minsup) **then delete** c **from** G_{i+1};   // Pruning infrequent
13)   **else do begin**
14)   **forall** i-subsets s of c **do begin**
15)   **if** (support$(s) =$ support(c)) **then begin**
16)   **delete** c from G_{i+1};
17)   **if** (*level* $= 0$) **then** *level* $\leftarrow i$;   // Iteration number of the first prune
18)   **endif**
29)   **end**
20)   **end**
21) **end**
22) Answer $\leftarrow \bigcup \{c \in G_{i+1}\}$;

---

and suppose it determines its support is 2. The third prune step will remove ABC from G_3 since support$(ABC) =$ support(AC). Indeed, we deduce that closure$(ABC) =$ closure(AC) and the computation of the closure of ABC is useless. For the optimization of the generator closure computation in Algorithm 1, we determine the iteration at which the second prune suppressed a generator (variable *level*).

4.5   AC-Closure Function

The AC-Closure function takes the set of frequent generators G, for which closures must be determined, as argument. It updates G with, for each generator $p \in G$, the closed itemset $p.$closure obtained by applying the closure operator h to p. Algorithm 4 gives the pseudo-code of the function. The method used to compute closures is based on Proposition 1.

Proposition 1. *The closed itemset $h(I)$ corresponding to the closure by h of the itemset I is the intersection of all objects in the database that contain I:*

$$h(I) = \bigcap_{o \in O} \{f(\{o\}) \mid I \subseteq f(\{o\})\}$$

Proof. We define $H = \bigcap_{o \in S} f(\{o\})$ where $S = \{o \in O \mid I \subseteq f(\{o\})\}$. We have $h(I) = f(g(I)) = \bigcap_{o \in g(I)} f(\{o\}) = \bigcap_{o \in S'} f(\{o\})$ where $S' = \{o \in O \mid o \in g(I)\}$.

Let's show that $S' = S$:

$$I \subseteq f(\{o\}) \Longleftrightarrow o \in g(I)$$
$$o \in g(I) \Longleftrightarrow I \subseteq f(g(I)) \subseteq f(\{o\})$$

We conclude that $S = S'$, thus $h(I) = H$.

Algorithm 4 AC-Closure function

---
1) **forall** objects $o \in O$ **do begin**
2) $G_o \leftarrow$ Subset(G.generator,$f(\{o\})$);   // Generators that are subsets of $f(\{o\})$
3)   **forall** generators $p \in G_o$ **do begin**
4)   **if** (p.closure $= \emptyset$) **then** p.closure $\leftarrow f(\{o\})$;
5)   **else** p.closure $\leftarrow p$.closure $\cap f(\{o\})$;
6)   **end**
7) **end**
8) Answer $\leftarrow \bigcup \{p \in G \mid \nexists p' \in G$, closure($p'$)=closure($p$)$\}$;

Using Proposition 1, only one database pass is necessary to compute the closures of the generators. The function works as follows. For each object o in $\mathcal{D}$, the set G_o is created (step 2). G_o contains all generators in G that are subsets of the object itemset $f(\{o\})$. Then, for each generator p in G_o, the associated closed itemset p.closure is updated (step 3 to 6). If the object o is the first one containing the generator, p.closure is empty and the object itemset $f(\{o\})$ is assigned to it (step 4). Otherwise, the intersection between p.closure and the object itemset gives the new p.closure (step 5). At the end, the function returns for each generator p in G, the closed itemset p.closure corresponding to the intersection of all objects containing p.

4.6   Example and Correctness

Figure 2 gives the execution of A-Close for a minimum support of 2 (40%) on the data mining context $\mathcal{D}$ given in Figure 1. First, the algorithm determines the set G_1 of 1-generators and their support (step 1 and 2), and the infrequent generator D is deleted form G_1 (step 3 to 5). Then, generators in G_2 are determined by applying the AC-Generator function to G_1 (step 8): the 2-generators are created by union of generators in G_1, their support is determined and the three pruning strategies are applied. Generators AC and BE are pruned since support(AC) = support(A) and support(BE) = support(B), and the *level* variable is set to 2.

Calling AC-Generator with G_2 produces 3-generators in G_3. The only generator created in G_3 is ABE since only AB and AE have the same first item. The three pruning strategies are applied and the second one removes ABE form G_3 as $BE \notin G_2$. Then, G_3 is empty and the iterative construction of sets G_i terminates (the loop in step 7 to 9 stops).

G_1

Generator	Support
{A}	3
{B}	4
{C}	4
{D}	1
{E}	4

Support-Count $\longrightarrow$

Pruning infrequent generators $\longrightarrow$

G_1

Generator	Support
{A}	3
{B}	4
{C}	4
{E}	4

G_2

Generator	Support
{AB}	2
{AC}	3
{AE}	2
{BC}	3
{BE}	4
{CE}	3

AC-Generator $\longrightarrow$

Pruning $\longrightarrow$

G_2

Generator	Support
{AB}	2
{AE}	2
{BC}	3
{CE}	3

G'

Generator	Closure	Support
{A}	{AC}	3
{B}	{BE}	4
{C}	{C}	4
{E}	{BE}	4
{AB}	{ABCE}	2
{AE}	{ABCE}	2
{BC}	{BCE}	3
{CE}	{BCE}	3

AC-Closure $\longrightarrow$

Pruning $\longrightarrow$

Answer : FC

Closure	Support
{AC}	3
{BE}	4
{C}	4
{ABCE}	2
{BCE}	3

Fig. 2. A-Close frequent closed itemset discovery for $minsup = 2$ (40%)

The sets G and G' are constructed using the *level* variable (step 10 and 11): G is empty and G' contains generators from G_1 and G_2. The closure function AC-Closure is applied to G' and the closures of all generators in G' are determined (step 15). Finally, duplicates closures are removed from G' by AC-Closure and the result is returned to the set FC which therefore contains $AC, BE, C, ABCE$ and BCE, that are all frequent closed itemsets in $\mathcal{D}$.

Lemma 3. *For $p \subseteq \mathcal{I}$ such as $\|p\| > 1$, if $p \notin G_{\|p\|}$ and $support(p) \geq minsup$ then $\exists s_1, s_2 \subseteq \mathcal{I}$, $s_1 \subset s_2 \subseteq p$ and $\|s_1\| = \|s_2\| - 1$ such as $h(s_1) = h(s_2)$ and $s_1 \in G_{\|s_1\|}$.*

Proof. We show this using a recurrence. For $\|p\| = 2$, we have $p = s_2$ and $\exists s_1 \in G_1 \mid s_1 \subset s_2$ and $support(s_1) = support(s_2) \implies h(s_1) = h(s_2)$ (Lemma 3 is obvious). Then, supposing that Lemma 3 is true for $\|p\| = i$, let's show that it is true for $\|p\| = i + 1$. Let $p \subseteq \mathcal{I} \mid \|p\| = i + 1$ and $p \notin G_{\|p\|}$. There are two possible cases:

(1) $\exists p' \subset p \mid \|p'\| = i$ and $p' \notin G_{\|p'\|}$

(2) $\exists p' \subset p \mid \|p'\| = i$ and $p' \in G_{\|p'\|}$ and $\text{support}(p) = \text{support}(p') \Longrightarrow h(p) = h(p')$ (Lemma 2)

If (1) then according to the recurrence hypothesis, $\exists s_1 \subset s_2 \subseteq p' \subset p$ such as $h(s_1) = h(s_2)$ and $s_1 \in G_{\|s_1\|}$. If (2) then we identify s_1 to p' and s_2 to p.

Theorem 3. *The A-Close algorithm generates all frequent closed itemsets.*

Proof. Using a recurrence, we show that $\forall p \subseteq \mathcal{I} \mid \text{support}(p) \geq \text{minsup}$ we have $h(p) \in FC$. We first demonstrate the property for the 1-itemsets: $\forall p \subseteq \mathcal{I}$ where $\|p\| = 1$, if $\text{support}(p) \geq \text{minsup}$ then $p \in G_1 \Rightarrow h(p) \in FC$. Let's suppose that $\forall p \subseteq \mathcal{I}$ such as $\|p\| = i$ we have $h(p) \in FC$. We then demonstrate that $\forall p \subseteq \mathcal{I}$ where $\|p\| = i + 1$ we have $h(p) \in FC$. If $p \in G_{\|p\|}$ then $h(p) \in FC$. Else, if $p \notin G_{\|p\|}$ and according to Lemma 3, we have: $\exists s_1 \subset s_2 \subseteq p \mid s_1 \in G_{\|s_1\|}$ and $h(s_1) = h(s_2)$. Now $h(p) = h(s_2 \cup p - s_2) = h(s_1 \cup p - s_2)$ and $\|s_1 \cup p - s_2\| = i$, therefore in conformity with the recurrence hypothesis we conclude that $h(s_1 \cup p - s_2) \in FC$ and so $h(p) \in FC$.

5   Experimental Results

We implemented the Apriori and A-Close algorithms in C++, both using the same prefix-tree structure that improves Apriori efficiency. Experiments were realized on a 43P240 bi-processor IBM Power-PC running AIX 4.1.5 with a CPU clock rate of 166 MHz, 1GB of main memory and a 9GB disk. Each execution uses only one processor (the application was single-threaded) and was allowed a maximum of 128MB.

Test Data We used two kinds of datasets: synthetic data, that simulate market basket data, and census data, that are typical statistical data. The synthetic datasets were generated using the program described in [2]. The census data were extracted from the Kansas 1990 PUMS file (Public Use Microdata Samples), in the same way as [5] for the PUMS file of Washington (unavailable through Internet at the time of the experiments). Unlike in [5] though, we did not put an upper bound on the support, as this distorts each algorithm results in different ways. We therefore took smaller datasets containing the first 10,000 persons.

Parameter	T10I4D100K	T20I6D100K	C20D10K	C73D10K
Average size of the objects	10	20	20	73
Total number of items	1000	1000	386	2178
Number of objects	100K	100K	10K	10K
Average size of the maximal poten--tially frequent itemsets	4	6	-	-

Table 2. Notation

Results on Synthetic Data Figure 3 shows the execution times of Apriori and A-Close on the datasets T10I4D100K and T20I6D100K. We can observe that both algorithms always give similar results except for executions with *minsup* = 0.5% and 0.33% on T20I6D100. This similitude comes from the fact that data are weakly correlated and sparse in such datasets. Hence, the sets of generators in A-Close and frequent itemsets in Apriori are identical, and the closure mechanism does not help in jumping iterations. In the two cases where Apriori outperforms A-Close, there was in the 4th iteration a generator that has been pruned because it had the same support as one of its subsets. As a consequence, A-Close determined closures of all generators with size greater or equal than 3.

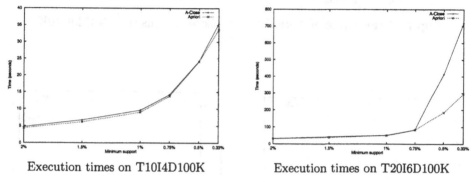

Execution times on T10I4D100K   Execution times on T20I6D100K

Fig. 3. Performance of Apriori and A-Close on synthetic data

Results on Census Data Experiments were conducted on the two census datasets using different *minsup* ranges to get meaningful response times and to accommodate with the memory space limit. Results for the C20D10K and C73D10K datasets are plotted on Figure 4 and 5 respectively. A-Close always significantly outperforms Apriori, for execution times as well as number of database passes. Here, contrarily to the experiments on synthetic data, the differences between execution times can be measured in minutes for C20D10K and in hours for C73D10K. It should furthermore be noted that Apriori could not be run for *minsup* lower than 3% on C20D10K and lower than 70% on C73D10K as it exceeds the memory limit. Census datasets are typical of statistical databases: highly correlated and dense data. Many items being extremely popular, this leads to a huge number of frequent itemsets from which few are closed.

Scale Up Properties on Census Data We finally examined how Apriori and A-Close behave as the object size is increased in census data. The number of objects was fixed to 10,000 and the *minsup* level was set to 10%. The object size varied from 10 (281 total items) up to 24 (408 total items). Apriori could not be run for higher object sizes. Results are shown in Figure 6. We can see here that, the scale up properties of A-Close are far better than those of Apriori.

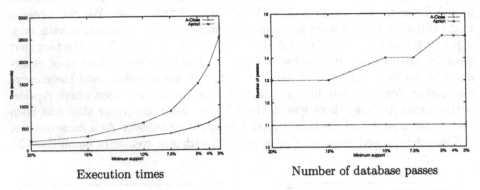

Execution times	Number of database passes

Fig. 4. Performance of Apriori and A-Close on census data C20D10K

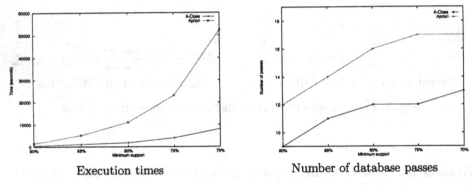

Execution times	Number of database passes

Fig. 5. Performance of Apriori and A-Close on census data C73D10K

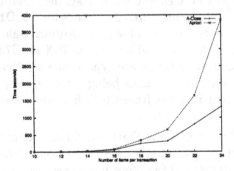

Fig. 6. Scale-up properties of Apriori and A-Close on census data

6   Conclusion

We presented a new algorithm, called A-Close, for discovering frequent closed itemsets in large databases. This algorithm is based on the pruning of the closed itemset lattice instead of the itemset lattice, which is the commonly used approach. This lattice being a sub-order of the itemset lattice, for many datasets, the number of itemsets considered will be significantly reduced. Given the set of frequent closed itemsets and their support, we showed that we can either deduce all frequent itemsets, or construct a reduced set of valid association rules needless the search for frequent itemsets.

We realized experiments in order to compare our approach to the itemset lattice exploration approach. We implemented A-Close and an optimized version of Apriori using prefix-trees. The choice of Apriori leads form the fact that, in practice, it remains one of the most general and powerful algorithms. Those experiments showed that A-Close is very efficient for mining dense and/or correlated data (such as statistical data): on such datasets, the number of itemsets considered and the number of database passes made are significantly reduced compared to those Apriori needs. They also showed that A-Close leads to equivalent performances of the two algorithms for weakly correlated data (such as synthetic data) in which many generators are closed. This leads from the adaptive characteristic of A-Close that consists in determining the first iteration for which it is necessary to compute closures of generators. Such a way, we avoid A-Close many useless closure computations.

We think these results are very interesting since dense and/or correlated data represent an important part of all existing data, and since mining such data is considered as very difficult. Statistical, text, biological and medical data are examples of such correlated data. Supermarket data are weakly correlated and quite sparse, but experimental results showed that mining such data is considerably less difficult than mining correlated data. In the first case, executions take some minutes at most whereas in the second case, executions sometimes take several hours.

Moreover, A-Close gives an efficient unsupervised classification technic: the closed itemset lattice of an order is dually isomorphic to the Dedekind-MacNeille completion of an order [7], which is the smallest lattice associated with an order. The closest work is Ganter's algorithms [9] which work only in main memory. This feature is very interesting since unsupervised classification is another important problem in data mining [6] and in machine learning.

References

[1] R. Agrawal, T. Imielinski, and A. Swami. Mining association rules between sets of items in large databases. *Proceedings of the ACM SIGMOD Int'l Conference on Management of Data*, pages 207–216, May 1993.

[2] R. Agrawal and R. Srikant. Fast algorithms for mining association rules. *Proceedings of the 20th Int'l Conference on Very Large Data Bases*, pages 478–499, June 1994. Expanded version in IBM Research Report RJ9839.

[3] R. J. Bayardo. Efficiently mining long patterns from databases. *Proceedings of the ACM SIGMOD Int'l Conference on Management of Data*, pages 85–93, June 1998.

[4] G. Birkhoff. Lattices theory. In *Coll. Pub. XXV*, volume 25. American Mathematical Society, 1967. Third edition.

[5] S. Brin, R. Motwani, J. D. Ullman, and S. Tsur. Dynamic itemset counting and implication rules for market basket data. *Proceedings of the ACM SIGMOD Int'l Conference on Management of Data*, pages 255–264, May 1997.

[6] M.-S. Chen, J. Han, and P. S. Yu. Data mining: An overview from a database perspective. *IEEE Transactions on Knowledge and Data Engineering*, 8(6):866–883, December 1996.

[7] B. A. Davey and H. A. Priestley. *Introduction to Lattices and Order*. Cambridge University Press, 1994. Fourth edition.

[8] V. Duquenne and L.-L. Guigues. Famille minimale d'implication informatives résultant d'un tableau de données binaires. *Math. Sci. Hum.*, 24(95):5–18, 1986.

[9] B. Ganter and K. Reuter. Finding all closed sets: A general approach. In *Order*, pages 283–290. Kluwer Academic Publishers, 1991.

[10] D. Lin and Z. M. Kedem. Pincer-search: A new algorithm for discovering the maximum frequent set. *Proceedings of the 6th Int'l Conference on Extending Database Technology*, pages 105–119, March 1998.

[11] M. Luxenburger. Implications partielles dans un contexte. *Math. Inf. Sci. Hum.*, 29(113):35–55, 1991.

[12] H. Mannila and H. Toivonen. Levelwise search and borders of theories in knowledge discovery. *Data Mining and Knowledge Discovery*, 1(3):241–258, 1997.

[13] H. Mannila, H. Toivonen, and A. I. Verkamo. Efficient algorithms for discovering association rules. *Proceedings of the AAAI Workshop on Knowledge Discovery in Databases*, pages 181–192, July 1994.

[14] A. M. Mueller. Fast sequential and parallel algorithms for association rules mining: A comparison. Technical report, Faculty of the Graduate School of The University of Maryland, 1995.

[15] N. Pasquier, Y. Bastide, R. Taouil, and L. Lakhal. Pruning closed itemset lattices for association rules. *Proceedings of the BDA French Conference on Advanced Databases*, October 1998. To appear.

[16] A. Savasere, E. Omiecinski, and S. Navathe. An efficient algorithm for mining association rules in larges databases. *Proceedings of the 21th Int'l Conference on Very Large Data Bases*, pages 432–444, September 1995.

[17] H. Toivonen. Sampling large databases for association rules. *Proceedings of the 22nd Int'l Conference on Very Large Data Bases*, pages 134–145, September 1996.

[18] H. Toivonen, M. Klemettinen, P. Ronkainen, K. Hatonen, and H. Mannila. Pruning and grouping discovered association rules. *ECML-95 Workshop on Statistics, Machine Learning, and Knowledge Discovery in Databases*, pages 47–52, April 1995.

[19] R. Wille. Concept lattices and conceptual knowledge systems. *Computers and Mathematics with Applications*, 23:493–515, 1992.

[20] M. J. Zaki, S. Parthasarathy, M. Ogihara, and W. Li. New algorithms for fast discovery of association rules. *Proceedings of the 3rd Int'l Conference on Knowledge Discovery in Databases*, pages 283–286, August 1997.

View Disassembly

Parke Godfrey[1,2] and Jarek Gryz[3]

[1] University of Maryland, College Park MD 20742, U.S.A.,
godfrey@cs.umd.edu,
http://www.cs.umd.edu/~godfrey
[2] U.S. Army Research Laboratory, Adelphi MD 20783, U.S.A.
[3] York University, Toronto ON M3J-1P3, Canada,
jarek@cs.yorku.ca,
http://www.cs.yorku.ca/~jarek

Abstract. We explore a new form of view rewrite called *view disassembly*. The objective is to rewrite views in order to "remove" certain sub-views (or *unfoldings*) of the view. This becomes pertinent for complex views which may defined over other views and which may involve union. Such complex views arise necessarily in environments as data warehousing and mediation over heterogeneous databases. View disassembly can be used for view and query optimization, preserving data security, making use of cached queries and materialized views, and view maintenance.

We provide computational complexity results of view disassembly. We show that the optimal rewrites for disassembled views is at least **NP**-*hard*. However, we provide good news too. We provide an approximation algorithm that has much better run-time behavior. We show a pertinent class of unfoldings for which their removal always results in a simpler disassembled view than the view itself. We also show the complexity to determine when a collection of unfoldings *cover* the view definition.

1 Introduction

Many database applications and environments, such as mediation over heterogeneous database sources and data warehousing for decision support, lead to complex view definitions. Views are often nested, defined over previously defined views, and may involve unions. The union operator is a necessity in mediation, as views in the meta-schema are defined to combine data from disparate sources. In these environments, view definition maintenance is of paramount importance.

There are many reasons why one might want to "remove" components, or *sub-views*, from a given view, or from a query which involves views.[1] Let us call a sub-view an *unfolding* of the view, as the view can be *unfolded* via its definition into more specific sub-views. These reasons include the following.

1. Some unfoldings of the view may be effectively cached from previous queries [2], or may be materialized views [12].

---

[1] In this paper, we use *view* and *query* synonymously.

Catriel Beeri, Peter Buneman (Eds.): ICDT'99, LNCS 1540, pp. 417–434, 1998.
© Springer-Verlag Berlin Heidelberg 1998

2. Some unfoldings may be known to evaluate empty, by reasoning over the integrity constraints [1].
3. Some unfoldings may match protected queries, which, for security, cannot be evaluated for all users [14].
4. Some unfoldings may be subsumed by previously asked queries, so are not of interest to the user.

What does it mean to remove unfolding from a view or query? The modified view or query should not *subsume*—and thus, when evaluated, should never evaluate—the removed unfoldings, but should *subsume* "everything else" of the original view.

In case 1, one might want to separate out certain unfoldings, because they can be evaluated much less expensively (and, in a networked, distributed environment, be evaluated locally). Then, the "remainder query" could be evaluated separately [2]. In case 2, the unfoldings are free to evaluate, since it is known in advance that they must evaluate empty. If the remainder query is less expensive to evaluate than the original, this is an optimization. In case 3, when some unfoldings are protected, this does not mean that the "rest" of the query or view cannot be safely evaluated. In case 4, when a user is asking a series of queries, he or she may just be interested in the stream of answers returning. So any previously seen answers are no longer of interest. In environments in which there are monetary charges for information, there is an additional advantage of not having to pay repeatedly for the same information.

In this paper, we address this problem of how to remove efficiently and correctly sub-views from views. We call this problem *view disassembly*. We present the computational complexities of, and potential algorithmic approaches to, view disassembly tasks. On first consideration, it may seem that the view disassembly problem is trivial, that a view could always be "trimmed" to exclude any given sub-view. On further consideration, however, one quickly sees that this is not true. To remove a sub-view, or especially a collection of sub-views, can be a quite complex task. Certain unfolding removals do, in fact, abide the first intuition: the view's definition can be trimmed to exclude them. We call these unfoldings *simple*, and we characterize these in this paper. In the general case, however, unfoldings require that the view's definition be *rewritten* to effectively remove them. We are interested in *compact* rewrites that accomplish this.

We represent queries and views in Datalog. Thus, we consider databases under the *logic model* [15]. For this paper, we do not consider recursion nor negation. A database **DB** is considered to consist of two parts: the *extensional database* ($\mathbf{E_{DB}}$), a set of atomic facts; and the *intensional database* ($\mathbf{I_{DB}}$), a set of clausal rules. Predicates are designated as either *extensional* or *intensional*. Extensional predicates are defined solely via the facts in the $\mathbf{E_{DB}}$. Intensional predicates are defined solely via the rules in the $\mathbf{I_{DB}}$. Thus, extensional predicates are equivalent to base relations defined by relational *tables* in the relational database realm, and intensional predicates to relational *views*. We shall employ the term *view* to refer to any intensional predicate or any query that uses intensional predicates.

In [7], we called the notion of a view or query with some of its unfoldings (sub-views) "removed" a *discounted query* or *view*, and called the "removed" unfoldings the *unfoldings-to-discount*. A view (or query) can be represented as an AND/OR tree that represents the expansion of its definition via the rules in the I_{DB}. In view disassembly, we consider algebraic rewrites of the view's corresponding AND/OR tree to find AND/OR trees that properly represent the discounted view. Consider the following example.

Example 1. Let there be six relations defined in the database **DB**:

- **Departments** (did, address)
- **Institutes** (did, address)
- **Faculty** (eid, did, rank)
- **Staff** (eid, did, position)
- **Health_Ins** (eid, premium, provider)
- **Life_ins** (eid, premium, provider)

Let there also be three views defined in terms of these relations:

$$academic\_units\,(X,\ Y) \leftarrow departments\,(X,\ Y).$$
$$academic\_units\,(X,\ Y) \leftarrow institutes\,(X,\ Y).$$
$$employees\,(X,\ Y) \leftarrow faculty\,(X,\ Y,\ Z).$$
$$employees\,(X,\ Y) \leftarrow staff\,(X,\ Y,\ Z).$$
$$benefits\,(X,\ Y,\ Z) \leftarrow health\_ins\,(X,\ Y,\ Z).$$
$$benefits\,(X,\ Y,\ Z) \leftarrow life\_ins\,(X,\ Y,\ Z).$$

Define the following query Q that asks for addresses of all academic units with any employees receiving benefits from Ætna:[2]

$$Q: q(Y) \leftarrow a(X,\ Y),\ e(Z,\ X),\ b(Z,\ W,\ ætna).$$

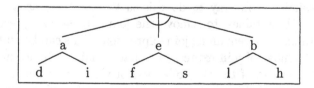

Fig. 1. The AND/OR tree representation of the original query.

Query Q can be represented as parse tree of its relational algebra representation, which is an AND/OR tree, as shown in Figure 1. Evaluating the query—in the order of operations as indicated by its relational algebra representation—is

---

[2] We henceforth abbreviate the predicate names.

equivalent to materializing the nodes of the query's AND/OR tree. We refer to this type of evaluation (and representation) as *bottom-up*. Consider the following three scenarios:

Case 1. Assume that the answers of the following three queries $\mathcal{F}_1$, $\mathcal{F}_2$, and $\mathcal{F}_3$ have been cached. Equivalently, we could assume that these represent materialized views, or that they are known to evaluate empty (by reasoning over integrity constraints). Let f_1, f_2, and f_3 be the corresponding cache predicates.

$$f_1(Y) \leftarrow a(X, Y), f(Z, X, V), b(Z, W, \text{ætna}).$$
$$f_2(Y) \leftarrow d(X, Y), e(Z, X), b(Z, W, \text{ætna}).$$
$$f_3(Y) \leftarrow i(X, Y), s(Z, X, V), b(Z, W, \text{ætna}).$$

Q does not have to be evaluated, since its answer set is equal to the union of answer sets of cached queries.[3] We say that queries $\mathcal{F}_1$, $\mathcal{F}_2$, and $\mathcal{F}_3$ *cover* the query Q.

Case 2. Assume that the following query $\mathcal{F}_4$ has been likewise cached:

$$f_4(Y) \leftarrow d(X, Y), e(Z, X), b(Z, W, \text{ætna}).$$

As $\mathcal{F}_4$ provides a subset of the answer set to Q, we can rewrite Q as Q' to retrieve only the remaining answers:

$$q'(Y) \leftarrow i(X, Y), e(Z, X), b(Z, W, \text{ætna}).$$

Note that unless special tools are available to evaluate efficiently the join of **Academic_Units** $\bowtie$ **Employees**, the rewrite of Q to Q' provides an optimization. In this case, $\mathcal{F}_4$ is a *simple* unfolding of Q (defined in Section 4).

Case 3. Assume that the following query $\mathcal{F}_5$ has been likewise cached.

$$f_5(Y) \leftarrow d(X, Y), f(Z, X, V), l(Z, W, \text{ætna}).$$

Again, we may want to "remove" $\mathcal{F}_5$ from the rest of the query, as its answers are locally available. One way to do this is to rewrite Q as a union of join expressions over base tables, to remove the join expression represented by $\mathcal{F}_5$, and then to evaluate the remaining join expressions. This can be quite inefficient, however. The number of join expressions that remain to be evaluated may be exponential in the size of the the collection of view definitions and the query. Furthermore, we showed in [8] that such an evaluation plan (which we call a *top-down* evaluation plan) may require evaluating the same joins multiple times, and incur the expense that a given answer tuple may be computed many times (whenever base tables overlap). A top-down evaluation of Q from Figure 1 is the union of the eight join expressions from

$$\{d, i\} \times \{f, s\} \times \{h, l\}$$

---

[3] We assume set semantics for answer sets in this paper.

A more efficient evaluation plan, perhaps, for the discounted query can be devised by rewriting the query so that the number of operations (unions plus joins) is minimized. (See Figure 2). As a side effect of this operation, the redundancy in join evaluation, as well as the redundancy in answer tuple computation, is reduced [8].[4]

Clearly, there are many factors that are more important involved in estimating whether one query will evaluate faster than another than merely the size of the query expression. It is quite likely that some well chosen, larger query expression will evaluate faster than the minimum sized expression of the query. However, succinctness of the query expression is an important component which cannot be ignored. Especially when alternative expressions can be exponentially larger than the minimal expression, controlling the succinctness of the query expression is vital. We focus on the succinctness issue in this paper.

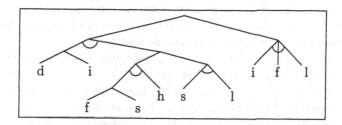

Fig. 2. The AND/OR tree representation of the modified query.

As in *Case 1* above, it may be that the unfoldings-to-discount (removed sub-views) *cover* the view. This means that the discounted view is equivalent to the *null view* (defined to evaluate empty). We present the complexity of deciding coverage in Section 3. In Section 4, we show that there are natural cases when the view can be *always* rewritten into a simpler form. This is true whenever an unfolding-to-discount is *simple*, as in *Case 2* above. In such cases, the rewrite is always an algebraic optimization. In Section 5, we consider the general case of rewriting a view in an algebraically absolute optimal way, as we did in *Case 3* and Figure 2 above. Our goal is to find good view disassemblies; that is, rewrites that result in small AND/OR trees. We aim to optimize over the number of nodes of the resulting AND/OR tree. (An ultimate goal might be to find a rewrite that results in the *smallest* AND/OR tree possible.) We show that the complexity of a sub-case of this task (a sub-class of fairly simple views) is **NP**-*complete* over the size of the view's AND/OR tree. We show the general problem is even harder. In Section 6, we explore approximate optimality. We motivate a rewrite algorithm

---

[4] We have a naïve algorithm that can find the optimal rewrite in the case of a single unfolding-to-discount. Such a result, even for this small example, would be rather difficult to find by hand.

that produces a disassembled view (equivalent semantically to the discounted view expression) for which the complexity is over the number of unfoldings-to-discount, and *not* over the size of the view's AND/OR tree. Hence, this approach is tractable, in general, and can result in rewrites that are reasonably compact.

We do not address in this paper the issue of *determining* when one query semantically *overlaps* with another query; that is, we assume that the unfolding that represents the overlap has already been identified. This, of course, may not be a trivial task. For example, queries $\mathcal{F}_1$, $\mathcal{F}_2$, and $\mathcal{F}_3$ from Example 1 might not have been the original cached queries themselves, but instead could have been constructed from them.

2   Related Work

The work most closely related to view disassembly is [11]. The authors consider queries that involve nested union operations, and propose a technique for rewriting such queries when it is known that some of the joins evaluated as part of the query are empty. The technique in [11] applies, however, only to a class of simple queries, and no complexity issues are addressed.

Another research area related to view disassembly is *multiple query optimization* (MQO) [13]. The goal in multiple query optimization is to optimize batch evaluation of a collection of queries, rather than just a single query. The techniques developed for MQO attempt to find and reuse common sub-expressions from the collection of queries, and are heuristics-based. We do not expect that the MQO techniques could result in the rewrites we propose in this paper. We can exploit the fact that our rewrites involve unfoldings that all come from the same view.

The problem of query tree rewrites for the purpose of optimization has been also considered in the context of deductive databases with recursion. In [9], the problem of detecting and eliminating redundant subgoal occurrences in proof trees generated by programs in the presence of functional dependencies is discussed. In [10], the residue method of [1] is extended to recursive queries.

In [7], we introduced a framework we call *intensional query optimization* which enables rewrites to be applied to non-conjunctive queries and views (that is, ones which involve union). An initial discussion of complexity issues and possible algorithmic solutions appear in [8]. In [7], we present an algorithm which incorporates unfolding removal into the query evaluation procedure. Hence the method in [7] is *not* an explicit query rewrite.

Our work in view disassembly is naturally related with all work on view and query rewrites. However, most all work in view rewrites strives to find views that are semantically *equivalent* with, or *contained* in, the original. View disassembly does not. Rather, we are using rewrites in order to remove *implicitly* components (unfoldings) from the original view. This is a much different goal than that of previous view rewrite work, and so this requires a different treatment. Aside from the work listed above, we are not aware of any work on view rewrites that bears directly on view disassembly.

3   Discounting and Covers

We define a *view* (and, likewise, a *query*) to be a set of atoms. For instance, $\{a, e, b\}$ represents the query/view in Example 1.[5] Some of the atoms may be intensional; that is, they are written with view predicates defined over base table predicates and, perhaps, other views. So since some of atoms may be intensional, the corresponding AND/OR tree (with respect to the $\mathbf{I_{DB}}$'s rules) may involve both joins (ANDs) and unions (ORs).

We provide a formal definition for an *unfolding* of a query.

Definition 1. *Given query sets Q and U, call U a 1-step unfolding of query set Q (denoted by $U \leq^1 Q$) with respect to database $\mathbf{DB}$ iff, given some $q_i \in Q$ and a rule $\langle a \leftarrow b_1, \ldots, b_n. \rangle$ in $\mathbf{I_{DB}}$ such that $q_i\theta \equiv a\theta$ (for most general unifier θ), then*

$$U = (Q - \{q_i\} \cup \{b_1, \ldots, b_n\})\theta$$

Call U_1 simply an unfolding of Q, written as $U_1 \leq Q$, iff there is some finite collection of query sets $U_1, \ldots, U_k$ such that $U_1 \leq^1 \ldots \leq^1 U_k \leq^1 Q$.

An unfolding U is called extensional *iff, for every $q_i \in U$, atom q_i is written with an extensional predicate. Call the unfolding* intensional *otherwise.*

One of the 1-step unfoldings of the query in Example 1 is $\{a, e, l\}$. One of the extensional unfoldings of the query is $\{d, f, h\}$.

An unfolding of a view Q can be *marked* in Q's AND/OR tree. In Example 2 below, the three unfoldings of the view Q considered are shown marked (by labels 1, 2, and 3) in Q's AND/OR tree in Figure 4. In essence, one can think of each unfolding's own AND/OR tree as embedded in the view's AND/OR tree. It is actually these embedded AND/OR trees, rather than the unfoldings themselves, that we seek to remove by rewriting syntactically the view's AND/OR tree.

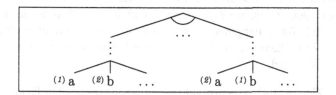

Fig. 3. An AND/OR tree with repeated elements.

---

[5] We ignore the ordering of the atoms in the query, without loss of generality. We also only present "propositional" examples for simplicity's sake. It should to be clear how the examples and techniques apply when the view's variables are explicitly presented.

When the unfoldings-to-discount correspond uniquely to embedded AND/OR trees in the AND/OR tree of the view to be discounted (as they do in Example 2 below), this distinction between *unfoldings*—a semantic notion as are queries—and the (embedded) AND/OR trees that represent them—a syntactic notion—is unimportant. However, the correspondence is not always unique (and, therefore, not always straightforward). This can happen if the same atom appears multiple times in the view's definition (and, hence, AND/OR tree). Consider the AND/OR tree in Figure 3. Does unfolding {a, b, ...} correspond to the embedded AND/OR tree marked by (1) or that marked by (2)? Or does it correspond to both?

To avoid this complication for the sake of this paper, we avoid these ambiguities. We limit ourselves to a sub-class of views for which these ambiguities do not arise: views for which no atom is employed twice in its definition. For this sub-class, the correspondence of unfoldings to embedded AND/OR trees is unique and straigtforward. Since the complexity results we derive in this paper are with respect to this sub-class of views, they provide a legitimate lower bound on the complexity on the view disassembly problems for the class of all views. Certainly, a view query with repetition in its definition presents further opportunities for optimization via rewrites to remove some of the duplication, but we do not consider these rewrite issues here.

Let Q be a view and $\mathcal{U}_1, \ldots, \mathcal{U}_k$ be unfoldings of Q. We define the notation $Q \setminus \{\mathcal{U}_1, \ldots, \mathcal{U}_k\}$ to be a *discounted view* of Q with *unfoldings-to-discount* $\mathcal{U}_1, \ldots, \mathcal{U}_k$. Define **unfolds**$(Q)$ to be the set of all extensional unfoldings of Q. The meaning of $Q \setminus \{\mathcal{U}_1, \ldots, \mathcal{U}_k\}$ is intended to be:

$$\textbf{unfolds}\,(Q) - \left(\bigcup_{i=1}^{k} \textbf{unfolds}\,(\mathcal{U}_i) \right)$$

The first case we ought to consider is when the set of extensional unfoldings of the discounted view is empty. In such a case, we say that the unfoldings-to-discount—that is, the unfoldings that we effectively want to remove—*cover* the view (or query). The degenerate case is $Q \setminus \{Q\}$. At the opposite end of the spectrum is $Q \setminus \textbf{unfolds}\,(Q)$. When a discounted view is covered, the most succinct disassembled view is the *null view*, which we define to evaluate to the empty answer set. Thus, we are interested in how to test when a discounted view is covered. As it happens, there are interesting, and unobvious, cases of discounted views which turn out to be covered. Furthermore, cover detection is computationally hard.

Example 2. $\mathcal{F}_1$, $\mathcal{F}_2$, and $\mathcal{F}_3$ represent three unfoldings of Q in Example 1. Figure 4 shows $\mathcal{F}_1$, $\mathcal{F}_2$, and $\mathcal{F}_3$ marked in the tree from Figure 1 of Example 1. Since $\textbf{unfolds}\,(Q) \subseteq \bigcup_{i=1}^{3} \textbf{unfolds}\,(\mathcal{F}_i)$ the set $\{\mathcal{F}_1, \mathcal{F}_2, \mathcal{F}_3\}$ is a cover of Q.

We establish that determining that a discounted view is covered is *coNP-complete* over the number of unfoldings-to-discount. For a set-theoretic version of this problem that is appropriate to establish computational complexity, the

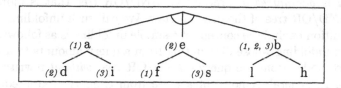

Fig. 4. Cover of the AND/OR tree in Example 2.

input can be considered to be the view's AND/OR tree and the AND/OR trees of the unfoldings-to-discount, and the question is whether the view's AND/OR tree is *covered* by the AND/OR trees of the unfoldings-to-discount.

Definition 2. *A discounted view instance* V *is a pair of an AND/OR tree (which represents the view, and which contains no duplicate atoms) and a list of AND/OR trees (which correspond to the unfoldings-to-discount, and which can be marked uniquely as embedded AND/OR trees in the view's AND/OR tree). Define* **COV** *as the set of all discounted view instances that are covered.*

Theorem 1. COV *is coNP-complete.*

Proof. By reduction from 3-**SAT**.   □

It is perhaps a surprising result that the complexity of deciding the cover question for discounted views is dictated by the number of unfoldings-to-discount, and *not* by the size of the view. This is still bad whenever one has many unfoldings-to-discount to consider. The good news is that the intractability is *independent* of the view definition's complexity. Furthermore, the news for cover detection seems good, in practice. Often, the number of unfoldings being considered is manageably small, so the cover check is tractable. In addition, we have empirically observed [5] that average case for the cover check appears tractable even for significantly more unfoldings-to-discount, even though worst-case is known to be intractable.

Thus, the first step in view disassembly should be to check whether the discounted view is covered. We investigate next what can be done when it is not.

4   Simple Unfoldings

A disassembled view may cost more to evaluate than the original view. A degenerate case is, of course, the case of the disassembled view that is the collection of all the extensional unfoldings. In general, it cannot be guaranteed that the AND/OR tree for a *best* disassembled view would be more compact (hence would require fewer operations to evaluate) than the original view. (Case 3 of Example 1 demonstrated this.) In this section, we define a type of unfolding for which discounting is *guaranteed* to produce an AND/OR tree that is more compact than the AND/OR tree of the original view. We call such unfoldings *simple*.

The intuition behind the concept of a simple unfolding is as follows. We strive to define an unfolding whose discounting from a query amounts to a removal of one or more nodes from the query's AND/OR tree *without* rewriting the rest of the tree. In general, removal of a node from a query tree is equivalent to discounting more than a single unfolding because such a node represents an atom from more than one unfolding. Thus, removal of a node from a query tree amounts to discounting *all* unfoldings that contain the atom represented by the removed node. Hence, if there is a single unfolding U that subsumes all unfoldings affected by a removal of node N but *no other* unfoldings, we are guaranteed that removing N from a query tree of Q results in a query tree for $Q \backslash \{U\}$.

Let us define first the concept of a *choice point atom*. A choice point atom is an atom (in a query or view) that refers to a view defined with a union operator (at the top level).

Definition 3. *Let* $Q = \{q_1, \ldots, q_n\}$ *be a view. Then* q_i *is called a* choice point atom iff *there is more than one rule* $\langle a \leftarrow b_1, \ldots, b_n. \rangle$ *such that* $q_i \theta \equiv a\theta$, *for most general unifier* θ.

All atoms in query Q of Example 1 (that is, a, e, and b) are choice point atoms.

Definition 4. *Let* Q *be a query and* U_0 *be an unfolding of* Q *such that* $U_0 \leq^1 U_1 \leq^1 \ldots \leq^1 U_k = Q$. *Then,* U_0 *is a* simple *unfolding of* Q *iff, for all* $i \leq k$, *the set* $U_i - U_0$ *contains at most one choice point atom.*

Example 3. Let the query Q be as in Example 1, but now assume that **Departments** is also a view defined as follows.

$$d(Y, V) \leftarrow d_1(X, Y, Z), d_2(X, V, W).$$
$$d_1(X, Y, Z) \leftarrow d_{1,1}(X, Y, Z).$$
$$d_1(X, Y, Z) \leftarrow d_{1,2}(X, Y, Z).$$

The query tree for Q in this new database is shown in Figure 5.
Consider the following unfoldings of Q:

$$U_1: \{d, e, b\}$$
$$U_2: \{d_{1,1}, d_2, e, b\}$$
$$U_3: \{d, f, b\}$$

Unfolding U_1 is simple, since $U_1 \leq^1 Q$ and $Q - U_1 = \{a\}$. Removing node d (with the entire subtree rooted at d) produces a tree which contains all unfoldings of the original query Q except for the unfolding U_1 (and all unfoldings subsumed by U_1). In other words, the new tree represents the query $Q \backslash \{U_1\}$. Note that this is clearly a case of optimization. The new tree has fewer operations than the original tree.

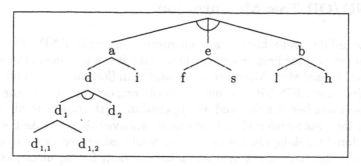

Fig. 5. The AND/OR tree representation of the query of Example 3.

Unfolding $\mathcal{U}_2$ is simple, since $\mathcal{U}_2 \leq^1 \mathcal{U}_4 \leq^1 \mathcal{U}_1 \leq^1 \mathcal{Q}$, for which $\mathcal{U}_4 = \{d_1, d_2, e, b\}$, and we know $\mathcal{U}_4 - \mathcal{U}_2 = \{d_1\}$, $\mathcal{U}_1 - \mathcal{U}_2 = \{d\}$, and $\mathcal{Q} - \mathcal{U}_2 = \{a\}$. Similarly to the case discussed above, it is sufficient to remove node $d_{1,1}$ to produce a tree for $\mathcal{Q}\backslash\{\mathcal{U}_2\}$; no other rewrite is necessary.

Consider unfolding $\mathcal{U}_3$. Now, $\mathcal{Q} - \mathcal{U}_3 = \{e, b\}$. Since both e and b are choice point atoms, the unfolding is not simple. This case illustrates the intuition behind Definition 4. Since $\mathcal{Q} - \mathcal{U}_3 = \{e, b\}$, then there must be at least two atoms in $\mathcal{U}_3$ (they are d and f in this case) that lie under a and e respectively. Since both a and e are choice point atoms, d and f each must have siblings (they are i and s, respectively, in this case). Consider removing d or f (or both) to generate a tree for $\mathcal{Q}\backslash\{\mathcal{U}_3\}$. Removing d from the tree means that an unfolding $\{d, s, b\}$ is also removed; removing f means that $\{i, f, b\}$ is removed as well. Thus, it is not possible to produce a tree for $\mathcal{Q}\backslash\{\mathcal{U}_3\}$ by simple node removal.

It is easy to show that all 1-step unfoldings are simple (Unfolding $\mathcal{U}_1$ in Example 3 is a 1-step unfolding.)

We can now state an optimization theorem.

Theorem 2. *Let $\mathcal{Q}$ be a query and $\mathcal{U}_0$ be a simple unfolding of $\mathcal{Q}$. Then, an AND/OR tree for $\mathcal{Q}\backslash\{\mathcal{U}_0\}$ can be produced by removing one or more nodes from the AND/OR tree for $\mathcal{Q}$.*

Proof. By proof by case.   □

Simple unfoldings are ideal when the goal of disassembly is optimization (that is, the discounted query or view must cost less to evaluate than the original). They are easy to detect (by definition) and remove (as shown for $\mathcal{U}_1$ above). The disassembled view is then *guaranteed* to be smaller than the original view. This means the disassembled view will almost always cost less to evaluate than the original view. It can also be shown that the class of simple unfoldings is the only type of unfolding that guarantees the existence of a disassembled view that has fewer operations than the view.

5   AND/OR Tree Minimization

When the unfoldings-to-discount are not simple, finding an AND/OR tree of the disassembled view requires, in general, more than just a pruning of the AND/OR tree of the original view. Moreover, as we stated in Section 1, one might want to find not just *any* AND/OR tree, but the most *compact* one; that is, the one with the smallest number of union and join operations with respect to all trees that represent the disassembled view. One way to achieve this is to take the union of all extensional unfoldings of the view, remove all that are extensional unfoldings of any unfolding-to-discount, and minimize (by distributing unions over joins) the number of operations in the remaining unfoldings. This procedure is clearly intractable since there can be an exponential number of extensional unfoldings with respect to the size of the view's tree. As it is, we cannot do any better. Finding the most compact tree is intractable, even for very simple views. In this section, we consider a view which is a two-way join over unions of base tables. In a sense, this is the simplest class of views for which the minimization problem is non-trivial (in that this is the least complex view that contains non-simple unfoldings).

Let the view Q be:

$$q \leftarrow a, b.$$

in which a and b are defined as follows:

$$a \leftarrow a_1. \qquad b \leftarrow b_1.$$
$$\vdots \qquad\qquad \vdots$$
$$a \leftarrow a_n. \qquad b \leftarrow b_n.$$

Define the set of unfoldings-to-discount as follows. Let $\mathcal{U}_1 = \{a_{i_1}, b_{j_1}\}, \ldots,$ $\mathcal{U}_l = \{a_{i_l}, b_{j_l}\}$, for $i_k, j_k \in \{1, ..., n\}$, $1 \leq k \leq l$. Assume, without loss of generality, that for every $S \subseteq \{a_1, ..., a_n\}$, there is an atom (with the intensional predicate) A_s defined as: $A_s \leftarrow a_k$ for all $a_k \in S$. We call the collection of all such atoms $\mathcal{A}$; that is,

$$\mathcal{A} = \{A_s \mid S \subseteq \{a_1, ..., a_n\} \text{ and } A_s \leftarrow a_k, \text{ for all } a_k \in S\}$$

Similarly define B_r for all subsets of $\{b_1, ..., b_n\}$. Then, the discounted query can be evaluated as a union of joins over atoms A_s and B_r. We are interested in the maximal pairs of A_s's and B_r's such that none of the unfoldings-to-discount can be found in their cross. (By maximal, it is meant that no super-set of the chosen A_s or no super-set of the B_r chosen would also have this property.) That is, given such a pair A_s and B_r, $a_{i_k} \notin A_s$ or $b_{i_k} \notin B_r$, for $1 \leq k \leq l$. Let C be the collection of all such maximal, consistent pairs of A_s's and B_r's.

$$\mathbf{unfolds}\left(Q \backslash \{\mathcal{U}_1, \ldots \mathcal{U}_l\}\right) = \bigcup_{\langle A_s, B_r \rangle \in C} \mathbf{unfolds}\left(\{A_s, B_r\}\right)$$

Let t be the cardinality of the collection $\mathcal{C}$. This number represents the number of trees that are needed to evaluate the discounted query. Let $\mathcal{W}_i$, $1 \le i \le t$, be a query (unfolding) represented by each such tree and $op(\mathcal{W}_i)$ be the total number (that is, a single join and all unions)[6] of operations required to evaluate $\mathcal{W}_i$. Then, $op(\bigcup_{i=1}^{t} \mathcal{W}_i) = (\bigcup_{i=1}^{t} op(\mathcal{W}_i)) + t - 1$. We also require, without loss of generality, that $\mathcal{W}$'s do not overlap; that is, there does not exist an unfolding U such that $U \le \mathcal{W}_i$, $U \le \mathcal{W}_j$, and $i \ne j$.

We can now state the problem of *Minimization of Discounted Query* as follows.

Definition 5. *Define the class* Minimization of Discounted Query *(MDQ) as follows. An instance is the triplet of a query set $\mathcal{Q}$, a collection of unfoldings-to-discount $\mathcal{U}$, and a positive integer K. An instance belongs to* **MDQ** *iff there is a collection of unfoldings $\mathcal{W}_1, ..., \mathcal{W}_l$ defined as above, such that $op(\bigcup_{i=1}^{t} \mathcal{W}_i) \le K$.*

Theorem 3. *Minimization of Discounted Query* (**MDQ**) *is* **NP***-complete.*

Proof. By reduction from a known **NP**-*hard* problem, minimum order partition into bipartite cliques [3]. □

The **NP**-*completeness* result can be trivially generalized to the case where a and b in the query $\mathcal{Q}$ are defined through different numbers of rules.

The minimization of more complex queries does not remain **NP**-*complete*. Consider a query $\mathcal{Q}=\{p_1, ..., p_n\}$, where each of p_i's is defined through multiple rules as: $\langle p_i \leftarrow p_i^j.\rangle$ for $1 \le j \le k_i$. Since the number of extensional unfoldings for this query is exponential in the size of the original query, verifying the solution cannot be, in general, done in polynomial time. It can be shown, however, that minimization of an arbitrarily complex query—that is, a query for which its AND/OR tree representation is arbitrarily deep (an alternation of ANDs and ORs)—is in the class Π_2^p.

Theorem 4. *Let $\mathcal{Q}$ be an arbitrarily complex query. Then, minimization of $\mathcal{Q}$ is in Π_2^p.*

Proof. It is easy to show that minimization of query's operations is equivalent to minimization of operations in a propositional logic formula, where joins are mapped to conjunctions and unions are mapped to disjunctions. This problem, called *Minimum Equivalent Expression*, is known to be in Π_2^p [4]. □

We conjecture that it may be complete in this class.

---

[6] It is easy to show that the optimal tree for the two-way join view constructed above must be a union of two level trees also. This means that this is a legitimate sub-class of the absolute optimization problem for view trees, thus the general problem is at least **NP**-*hard*.

6   Approximation Solutions

In the previous section, we showed that to find an algebraic rewrite for view disassembly which optimizes absolutely the number of algebraic operations (that is, the size of the AND/OR tree) is intractable. In this section, we investigate an approximation approach. The premise of the approach is to not rewrite the original view's AND/OR tree, but rather to find a collection of unfoldings of the view which "complete" the cover with respect to the unfoldings-to-discount.

This collection, call it C, should have the following properties. Let N be the set of unfoldings-to-discount.

1. $N \cup C$ should be a *cover* of the view; that is, any extensional unfolding of the view is also an unfolding of some unfolding in N or C.
2. No two unfoldings in C should *overlap*; that is, for $U, V \in C$ ($U \neq V$), U and V have no unfolding in common. (Call U and V *pair-wise independent* in this case.)
3. Set C should be *most general*:

   a. no unfolding in C can be refolded at all, and still preserve the above properties; and
   b. for any $U \in C$, $(N \cup C) - \{U\}$ is not a cover of the view.

We present an algorithm to accomplish such a rewrite called the *unfold/refold* algorithm (Algorithm 7). It works as follows. First, find an extensional unfolding which is not subsumed by any of the unfoldings-to-discount or any unfolding in the set C (that is, the unfoldings generated so far). The routine *new_unfolding* performs that step. (This is the co-problem of determining *cover*. Thus, the difficulty depends on the size of the collection of the unfoldings-to-discount.) Second, *refold* the unfolding (that is, find a super-unfolding) such that the super-unfolding does not subsume any of the unfoldings-to-discount. This is performed by the routine *refolding*.[7]

The entire algorithm is then repeated until the unfold step fails; that is, there is no such extensional unfolding, meaning that a cover has been established. On subsequent cycles, during the refold procedure, the unfolding is refolded only insofar as it does not overlap with any unfoldings already in C (condition 2 from above). In the end, *parsimonious* ensures that the unfolding collection C returned is minimal; that is, no member unfolding of C can be removed and leave C still as a cover. The call *parsimonious*(C) can be accomplished in $O(|C|)$, using the results of the last call to *new_unfolding* which had determined that C was, indeed, a cover [5].

At completion, the union of the unfoldings produced is a disassembled view. It is equivalent semantically to the discounted view. The set of the unfoldings unioned with the set of the unfoldings-to-discount is equivalent semantically to the original view.

---

[7] A version of the unfold/refold algorithm is implemented in the Carmin prototype [5]. It efficiently performs the unfold step (hence, the covers test).

```
C := {}
while new_unfolding(Q, N ∪ C, U)
    V := refolding(U, N, C)
    C := C ∪ {V}
return parsimonious(C)
```

Algorithm 1. Unfold/refold algorithm for view disassembly.

Example 4. Consider again Example 1. The algorithm is initialized with $C := \{\}$. Assume that the first extensional unfolding to consider is $V = \{i, f, l\}$. Refolding V, we arrive at an unfolding $\{i, e, b\}$. The next extensional unfolding that does not overlap either with $\{i, e, b\}$ or with the unfolding-to-discount (which is $\{d, f, l\}$ in this case), is $V = \{d, f, h\}$. Refolding it produces an unfolding $\{d, e, h\}$ (which is pair-wise independent with $\{i, e, b\}$ in C from before). The last remaining extensional unfolding to consider is $V = \{d, s, l\}$. This one cannot be refolded any further. The AND/OR query tree representing the most-general unfoldings is shown in Figure 6.

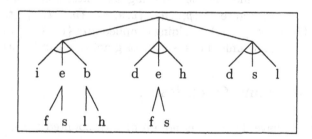

Fig. 6. The result of *unfold/refold* algorithm applied to the query and the unfolding-to-discount of Example 1.

Note that the resulting rewrite in the example has eleven nodes (algebraic operations) compared with nine nodes of the tree in Example 1 which represented the most compact rewrite.

The run-time complexity of the unfold/refold algorithm is dictated by the *new_unfolding* step of each cycle. This depends on the size of the collection of unfoldings generated so far plus the number of unfoldings-to-discount. While this collection remains small, the algorithms is tractable. Only when the collection has grown large does the algorithm tend towards intractable. An advantage of the approach is that a threshold can be set, beyond which the rewrite computation is abandoned. On average, we expect the final cover not to be large.

A variation on the unfold/refold algorithm can be used to find the collection of *most general* unfoldings that are covered by the unfoldings-to-discount. By most general, it is meant that no super-unfolding of those found are covered. This is a generalization of the check for *cover* discussed in Section 3. In the extreme case, if only a single most-general unfolding is found (that is, the view itself), then the discounted view itself is covered.

Ideally, we would always convert the set of unfoldings-to-discount into this *most-general* form. This most-general collection of unfoldings-to-discount is guaranteed always to be smaller (or the same size, at worst) as the initial collection. Thus, it is a better input to the unfold/refold algorithm for view disassembly.

These techniques avail us many tools for rewriting views and queries for a number of purposes. For instance, by finding the most-general unfoldings-to-discount, one also identifies all the most-general simple unfoldings that are entailed by the unfoldings-to-discount. They are just the simple unfoldings that appear in the collection. For view or query optimization, the simple unfoldings can be pruned from the AND/OR tree, resulting in a smaller, simpler tree to evaluate (as shown in Section 4). If we "remove" only the simple unfoldings, but not the others, we are not evaluating the discounted view, but something in-between the view and the discounted view. However, when our goal is optimization, this is acceptable.

Example 5. Consider removing the following six (extensional) unfoldings from the AND/OR tree in Figure 1: $\{p, s, u\}$, $\{p, s, w\}$, $\{p, t, u\}$, $\{p, t, w\}$, $\{r, s, u\}$, and $\{r, s, w\}$. The most-general unfoldings implied are: $\{v_1, s, v_3\}$ and $\{p, v_2, v_3\}$. Both of these are simple unfoldings, so the original tree can be pruned.

7   Conclusions and Open Issues

In this paper, we have defined the notion of a discounted view, which is conceptually the view with some of its sub-views (unfoldings) "removed". We have explored how to rewrite effectively the view into a form equivalent to a discounted view expression, thus "removing" the unfoldings-to-discount. We called such a rewrite a disassembled view. Disassembled views can be used for optimization, data security, and streamlining the query/answer cycle by helping to eliminate answers already seen.

View disassembly, as most forms of view and query rewrites, can be computationally hard. We showed that optimal view disassembly rewrites is at least **NP**-*hard*. However, effective disassembled views can be found which are not necessarily algebraically optimal, but are compact. We explored an approximation approach called the unfold/refold algorithm which can result in compact disassembled views. The complexity of the algorithm is dictated by the number of unfoldings-to-discount, and *not* by the complexity of the view definition to be disassembled. Thus, we have shown there are effective tools for view disassembly.

We also have identified a class of unfoldings we called simple unfoldings which can be easily removed from the view definition to result in a *simpler* view definition. This offers a powerful tool for semantic optimization of views. We also established how we can infer when a collection of unfoldings-to-discount *cover* the original view, meaning that the discounted view is void. This result has general application, and is fundamental to determine when a view is subsumed by a collection of views.

There is much more work to be done on view disassembly. This includes the following.

- If we are to use view disassembly for optimization, we must study how view disassembly can be incorporated with existing query optimization techniques. Clearly cost-based estimates should be used to help determine which view disassemblies appear more promising for the given view, the given database, and the given database system.
- Some applications benefit by view rewrite technology and might further benefit by view disassembly technology. However, rewrites are not always necessary to accomplish the task. In [7] and in recent work, we have been exploring methods to evaluate discounted queries directly, with no need to algebraically rewrite the query. We have seen with initial experimental results that a method we call *tuple tagging* tends to evaluate discounted queries less expensively than the evaluation of the queries themselves. Thus, it is necessary to determine which applications need rewrites, and which can be handled by other means.
- The basic approach of the unfold/refold algorithm needs to be extended for the additional computations discussed in Section 6. It is also possible that a combined approach of the unfold/refold algorithm with other view rewrite procedures might provide generally better performance.
  Sometimes if the original view tree were syntactically rewritten in some given, semantically preserving way, a candidate unfolding could be removed easily, while it cannot be "easily" removed with respect to the original tree as is. We should study how view disassembly could be combined effectively with other semantically preserving view rewrite procedures to enable such rewrites.
- A yet better understanding of the profile of view disassembly complexity, also with respect to other view rewrite techniques, would allow us to build perhaps better view disassembly algorithms. Empirical use of the unfold/refold algorithm, for instance, in data warehousing environments, might also provide more insight.

References

[1] U. Chakravarthy, J. Grant, and J. Minker. Logic-based approach to semantic query optimization. *ACM Transactions on Database Systems*, 15(2):162–207, June 1990.

[2] S. Dar, M. Franklin, B. Jónsson, D. Srivastava, and M. Tan. Semantic data caching and replacement. In *Proceedings of the 22nd International Conference on Very Large Data Bases (VLDB)*, Bombay, India, Sept. 1996.

[3] T. Feder and R. Motwani. Clique partitions, graph compressions and speeding-up algorithms. In *Proceedings of the ACM Sumposium on Theory of Computing*, pages 123–133, 1991.

[4] M. R. Garey and D. S. Johnson. *Computers and Intractability: a Guide to the Theory of NP-Completeness*. A Series of Books in the Mathematical Sciences. W. H. Freeman and Company, New York, 1979.

[5] P. Godfrey. *An Architecture and Implementation for a Cooperative Database System*. PhD thesis, University of Maryland at College Park, College Park, Maryland 20742, 1998.

[6] P. Godfrey and J. Gryz. Intensional query optimization. Technical Report CS-TR-3702, UMIACS-TR-96-72, Dept. of Computer Science, University of Maryland, College Park, MD 20742, Oct. 1996.

[7] P. Godfrey and J. Gryz. Overview of dynamic query evaluation in intensional query optimization. In *Proceedings of Fifth DOOD*, pages 425–426, Montreux, Switzerland, Dec. 1997. Longer version appears as [6].

[8] P. Godfrey, J. Gryz, and J. Minker. Semantic query optimization for bottom-up evaluation. In Z. W. Raś and M. Michalewicz, editors, *Foundations of Intelligent Systems: Proceedings of the 9th International Symposium on Methodologies for Intelligent Systems*, Lecture Notes in Artificial Intelligence 1079, pages 561–571, Berlin, June 1996. Springer.

[9] L. V. S. Lakshmanan and H. Hernandez. Structural query optimization: A uniform framework for semantic query optimization in deductive databases. In *Proceedings of the ACM Symposium on the Principles of Database Systems*, pages 102–114, Denver, Colorado, May 1991.

[10] L. V. S. Lakshmanan and R. Missaoui. Pushing constraints inside recursion: A general framework for semantic optimization of recursive queries. In *Proceedings of the International Conference on Data Engineering*, Taipei, Taiwan, Feb. 1995.

[11] S. Lee, L. J. Henschen, and G. Z. Qadah. Semantic query reformulation in deductive databases. In *Proceedings of the IEEE International Conference on Data Engineering*, pages 232–239. IEEE Computer Society Press, 1991.

[12] A. Y. Levy, A. O. Mendelzon, Y. Sagiv, and D. Srivastava. Answering queries using views. In *Proc. PODS*, pages 95–104, 1995.

[13] T. Sellis and S. Ghosh. On the multiple-query optimization problem. *TKDE*, 2(2):262–266, June 1990.

[14] B. Thuraisingham and W. Ford. Security constraint processing in a multilevel secure distributed database management system. *IEEE Transactions on Knowledge and Data Engineering*, 7(2):274–293, Apr. 1995.

[15] J. D. Ullman. *Principles of Database and Knowledge-Base Systems, Volumes I & II*. Principles of Computer Science Series. Computer Science Press, Incorporated, Rockville, Maryland, 1988/1989.

Answering Queries Using Materialized Views with Disjunctions*

Foto N. Afrati[1], Manolis Gergatsoulis[2], and Theodoros Kavalieros[1]

[1] Dept. of Electrical and Computer Engineering,
National Technical University of Athens,
157 73 Athens, Greece,
{afrati,kavalier}@softlab.ece.ntua.gr
[2] Inst. of Informatics & Telecom.,
N.C.S.R. 'Demokritos',
153 10 A. Paraskevi Attikis, Greece
manolis@iit.demokritos.gr

Abstract. We consider the problem of answering datalog queries using materialized views. More specifically, queries are rewritten to refer to views instead of the base relations over which the queries were originally written. Much work has been done on program rewriting that produces an equivalent query. In the context of information integration, though, the importance of using views to infer as many answers as possible has been pointed out. Formally, the problem is: Given a datalog program $\mathcal{P}$ is there a datalog program $\mathcal{P}_v$ which uses only views as EDB predicates and (i) produces a subset of the answers that $\mathcal{P}$ produces and (ii) any other program $\mathcal{P}'_v$ over the views with property (i) is contained in $\mathcal{P}_v$? In this paper we investigate the problem in the case of disjunctive view definitions.

1 Introduction

A considerable amount of recent work has focused on using materialized views to answer queries [1, 7, 5, 12, 16, 13, 4]. This issue may arise in several situations, e.g., if the relations mentioned in the query are not actually stored or are impossible to consult or are very costly to access. The ability to use views is important in many applications, including information integration, where information sources are considered to store materialized views over a global database schema [2, 19, 14].

Suppose that we want to integrate three databases that provide flight information. These three databases can be seen as views over the EDB predicates $international\_flight(X, Y)$ and $local\_flight(X, Y)$ (which have the meaning that there is a non-stop international flight from a greek city X to city Y and, there is a non-stop local flight from a greek city X to a greek city Y respectively):

---

* This work has been partially supported by the Greek General Secretariat of Research and Technology under the project "Logic Programming Systems and Environments for developing Logic Programs" of $\Pi ENE\Delta'95$, contract no 952.

Catriel Beeri, Peter Buneman (Eds.): ICDT'99, LNCS 1540, pp. 435–452, 1998.

$$v_1(X) : - international\_flight(Athens, X)$$
$$v_1(X) : - international\_flight(Rhodes, X)$$
$$v_2(X, Y) : - local\_flight(X, Athens), local\_flight(Athens, Y)$$
$$v_3(X) : - local\_flight(X, Rhodes)$$

Suppose that the user is interested in whether there is a way to fly from a greek city X to a city Y in another country making at most one intermediate connection in a greek city and then a direct international flight i.e. the following query $\mathcal{P}$, is asked:

$$p(X, Y) : - international\_flight(X, Y)$$
$$p(X, Y) : - local\_flight(X, Z), international\_flight(Z, Y)$$

The user does not have access to the databases that contain the facts in the predicates *international_flight* and *local_flight* but only to the views. Using only the materialized views v_1, v_2 and v_3, it is not possible to find all the answers. The best one can do is to retrieve all the flights that use either the international airport of *Athens* or the international airport of *Rhodes*, i.e. ask the following query $\mathcal{P}_v$, on the available data:

$$p(Athens, Y) : - v_2(W, Rhodes), v_1(Y)$$
$$p(Rhodes, Y) : - v_2(Rhodes, W), v_1(Y)$$
$$p(Athens, Y) : - v_3(Athens), v_1(Y)$$
$$p(X, Y) : - v_3(X), v_2(X, W), v_1(Y)$$

In fact, the program $\mathcal{P}_v$ which is said to be a *retrievable program* (i.e., it contains only the view predicates as EDB predicates), is maximal in the sense that any datalog program which uses only the views v_1, v_2, v_3 as EDB predicates and produces only *correct* answers is contained in $\mathcal{P}$. Such a program is said to be a *retrievable maximally contained program*.

The problem that we consider here is : Given a datalog query and views defined over its EDB predicates, is there a retrievable maximally contained datalog program?

Previous work on this problem is done in [7, 12] where they restricted views to being defined by conjunctive queries, whereas in [8, 6] disjunctive view definitions are considered and is shown how to express a retrievable maximally contained program in disjunctive datalog with inequality. In [1], the problem of computing correct (called *certain*) answers is considered, also, in the general case where views are defined by datalog programs; they investigate the data complexity problem under both the closed world assumption and the open world assumption.

In this paper, we investigate the case where views have disjunctions in their definition. We prove the following results:

a) In the case where both the query and the views are given by non-recursive datalog programs, we identify a non-trivial class of instances of the problem where there exists a retrievable datalog($\neq$) program maximally contained in the query; in this case, we give an algorithm to obtain it; this program computes *all* correct answers. We know, though, that, in general such a program does not exist [1].

b) When the views are defined by recursive datalog programs and the query by non-recursive datalog program, we reduce the problem to that of non-recursive view definitions.

c) In the case the query is given by a recursive datalog program and the views by non-recursive datalog programs, we construct a simple disjunctive logic program, which, applied on a view instance, computes all correct answers whenever it halts. This result is also obtained in [8] under a similar technique. We also show how, in certain cases, this disjunctive program can be transformed into a datalog($\neq$) program thus obtaining the results mentioned in (a) above.

d) Finally, when both the views and the query are given by recursive programs, we prove that it is undecidable whether there exists a non-empty retrievable program $\mathcal{P}_v$. Still, we give a criterion that gives a negative answer, in some special cases. In fact, the undecidability result holds even in the case of simple chain programs [20].

Other related work is done in [5, 16, 13, 4], where the approaches used essentially look for rewritings producing equivalent queries. It is known [13] that the problem of finding a rewriting that produces an equivalent program is NP-complete, in the case, where both the query and the views are defined by disjunctions of conjunctive queries. Other work concern conjunctive queries (the views and the question asked) and include [13, 16] where they give nondeterministic polynomial time algorithms to find either a single retrievable query equivalent to the given query or a set of retrievable queries whose union is contained in the given query Q and that contains any other retrievable datalog query that is contained in Q. Special classes of conjunctive queries are examined in [5].

2 Preliminaries

2.1 Logic Programs and Datalog

A *disjunctive clause* C is a formula of the form [15]

$$A_1 \vee \ldots \vee A_m : - B_1, \ldots, B_n$$

where $m \geq 1$, $n \geq 0$ and $A_1, \ldots, A_m, B_1, \ldots, B_n$ are atoms. If $n = 0$, C is called a *positive disjunctive clause*. If $m = 1$, C is called a *definite clause* or *Horn clause*. A *definite/disjunctive program* is a finite set of definite/disjunctive clauses. A *Datalog program* is a set of function free Horn clauses. A *Datalog($\neq$) program* is a set of function free Horn clauses whose bodies are allowed to contain atoms whose predicate is the built-in inequality predicate ($\neq$). The left hand side of a rule is called the *head* of the rule and the right hand side is the *body* of the rule. A predicate is an *intensional database predicate*, or *IDB predicate*, in a program $\mathcal{P}$ if it appears at the head of a rule in $\mathcal{P}$, otherwise it is an *extensional database (EDB) predicate*. A *conjunctive query* is a single non-recursive function-free Horn rule.

Let D be a finite set. A *database* over domain D is a finite relational structure $\mathcal{D} = (D, r_1, \ldots, r_n)$, where each r_i is a relation over D; a *substructure* of a database is a relational structure $(D', r'_1, \ldots, r'_n)$, where each r'_i contains a subset of the facts contained in r_i.

A *query* is a function from databases (of some fixed type) to relations of fixed arity over the same domain; it has to be *generic*, i.e., invariant under renamings of the domain.

Datalog programs may be viewed as a declarative query language with the following semantics. Let $\mathcal{D}$ be a database, thought of as a collection of facts about the EDB predicates of a program $\mathcal{P}$. Let $Q^k_{\mathcal{P},p}(\mathcal{D})$ be the collection of facts about an IDB predicate p that can be deduced from $\mathcal{D}$ by at most k applications of the rules in $\mathcal{P}$. If we consider p the *goal* predicate (or *output* predicate), then $\mathcal{P}$ expresses a query $Q_{\mathcal{P},p}$, where

$$Q_{\mathcal{P},p}(\mathcal{D}) = \bigcup_{k \geq 0} Q^k_{\mathcal{P},p}(\mathcal{D})$$

We will sometimes write $Q_{\mathcal{P}}$ or $\mathcal{P}_p(\mathcal{D})$ instead of $Q_{\mathcal{P},p}$.

The above definition also gives a particular algorithm to compute $Q_{\mathcal{P},p}$: initialize the IDB predicates to be empty, and repeatedly apply the rules to add tuples to the IDB predicates, until no new tuples can be added. This is known as *bottom-up evaluation*. A *derivation tree* is a tree depicting the bottom up evaluation of a specific derived fact in the IDB. Its nodes are labeled by facts and each node with its children correspond to an instantiation of a rule in $\mathcal{P}$ [18].

Given a datalog program, we can define a *dependency graph*, whose nodes are the predicate names appearing in the rules. There is an edge from the node of predicate p to the node of predicate p' if p' appears in the body of a rule whose head predicate is p. The program is *recursive* if there is a cycle in the dependency graph. We define, also, the *adorned dependency graph* as follows: We assign labels (possible none or more than one) on each edge: Suppose there is a rule with head predicate symbol p and predicate symbol p' appears somewhere in the body; suppose that the i-th argument of p is the same variable as the j-th argument of p'. Then, on edge $e = (p, p')$ we assign a label $l = i \rightarrow j$; we call the pair (e, l) a *p-pair*. We define a *perfect cycle* in the adorned dependency graph to be a sequence of p-pairs $(e_1, l_1), \ldots, (e_k, l_k)$ such that the edges $e_1, \ldots, e_k$ form a cycle and, moreover, the following holds: for all $q = 1, \ldots, k-1$ if $l_q = i \rightarrow j$ then $l_{q+1} = j \rightarrow j'$ for some j' and, if $l_k = i \rightarrow j$ then $l_1 = j \rightarrow j'$ for some j'. We say that a datalog program *has no presistencies* iff there is no perfect cycle in the adorned dependency graph.

Given any datalog program $\mathcal{P}$, we can unwind the rules several times and produce a conjunctive query (over the EDB predicates of $\mathcal{P}$) generated by $\mathcal{P}$. Program $\mathcal{P}$ can, therefore, be viewed as being equivalent to an infinite disjunction of all these conjunctive queries. Considering a conjunctive query, we freeze the body of the query by turning each of the subgoals into facts in a database; we obtain, thus, the *canonical database* of this query. The constants in the canonical database that correspond to variables that also appear in the head of the query are conveniently called *head constants*. If all EDB predicates are binary, we may view a canonical database as a labeled graph. Correspondingly, we can refer to a canonical database *generated* by a datalog program. We say that a datalog program is *connected* iff all head variables of the program rules occur also in the bodies of the corresponding rules and any canonical database (viewed as a hypergraph) is connected.

A *containment mapping* from a conjunctive query Q_1 to a conjunctive query Q_2, is a function, h, that maps all variables of Q_1 on variables of Q_2, so that whenever an atom $p(X_1, X_2, \ldots)$ occurs in Q_1, then an atom $p(h(X_1), h(X_2), \ldots)$ occurs in Q_2.

The following are technical lemmata used in the proof of the main results.

Lemma 1. *Let P be a Datalog program and c a conjunctive query. There exists a positive integer N depending only on the sizes of the program and the query so that the following holds: If there is a conjunctive query c_i generated by P such that there is a containment mapping from c to c_i, then there is a conjunctive query c_j generated by P, of size $< N$, such that there is a containment mapping from c to c_j.*

Proof. First, we note, that, given a sufficiently large conjunctive query generated by a datalog program, we can apply a pumping on it, obtaining a shorter conjunctive query generated by the same program (see [3]).

Suppose c_i is of size $> N$. The containment mapping from c to c_i maps c on at most $|c|$ constants in c_i. Thus, there are $> N - |c|$ constants in c_i that are not involved in this mapping. Consider this "free" part of c_i and do on it a pumping, obtaining, thus a shorter conjunctive query, on which the containment mapping is preserved.   □

Definition 1. *Consider a database. A neighborhood of size k in the database is a connected substructure of size k. If we view the database as the canonical database of a conjunctive query, then, we can refer to neighborhoods in a conjunctive query accordingly.*

Lemma 2. *Suppose two conjunctive queries Q_1, Q_2 such that: each neighborhood of size up to k appears in one query iff it appears in the other. Then, for any conjunctive query Q of size up to k, there is containment mapping from Q to the query Q_1 iff there is containment mapping from Q to Q_2.*

2.2 Retrievable Programs

Let P be any datalog program over EDB predicates $e_1, e_2, \ldots, e_m$ and with output predicate q. Let $v_1, v_2, \ldots, v_n$ be views defined by datalog programs over EDB predicates $e_1, e_2, \ldots, e_m$; call P_V the union of programs that define the views. We want to answer the query Q_P assuming that we do not have access to database relations $e_1, e_2, \ldots, e_m$, but only to views $v_1, \ldots, v_n$; we need a "certain" answer no matter which is the database that yielded the given view instance.

Definition 2. *A* certain *answer to query* Q_P, *given a view instance* $\mathcal{D}_\mathcal{V}$, *is a tuple t such that: for each database $\mathcal{D}$ over $e_1, e_2, \ldots, e_m$ with $\mathcal{D}_\mathcal{V} \subseteq \mathcal{P}_\mathcal{V}(\mathcal{D})$, t belongs to $Q_P(\mathcal{D})$.*

The above definition assumes the open world assumption; under the closed world assumption, the definition requires that $\mathcal{D}_\mathcal{V} = \mathcal{P}_\mathcal{V}(\mathcal{D})$; to compute a certain answer in this case is harder (see [1]).

Let $\mathcal{P}_v$ be a datalog program over EDB predicates $v_1, v_2, \ldots, v_n$. We say that $\mathcal{P}_v$ *is a retrievable program contained* in $\mathcal{P}$ if, for each view instance $\mathcal{D}_\mathcal{V}$, all tuples in $\mathcal{P}_v(\mathcal{D}_\mathcal{V})$ are certain answers.

Example 1. Let views v_1, v_2 be defined over the EDB predicates e_1, e_2, e_3, e_4:

$$v_1(X,Y) : - e_1(X,Y)$$
$$v_1(X,Y) : - e_1(X,Z), e_2(Z,Y)$$
$$v_2(X,Y) : - e_3(X,Y), e_4(Y)$$

and the query $\mathcal{P}$ by:

$$p(X) : - e_3(Y,X), e_1(X,Z)$$

Then a retrievable program maximally contained in $\mathcal{P}_v$, is:

$$p_v(X) : - v_2(Y,X), v_1(X,Z)$$

If $\mathcal{P}_v$ is applied on an instance of v_1, v_2, it will produce a set of answers; this is a subset of the answers which will be produced if query $\mathcal{P}$ is applied on some instance of the relations e_1, e_2, e_3, e_4 which yields the given instance of v_1, v_2. For example, suppose $v_1 = \{(a,b), (b,c), (b,d), (c,f)\}$ and $v_2 = \{(d,a)\}$. Then $\mathcal{P}_v$ will produce the set of answers $\{(a)\}$. A database that yields the above view instance could have been either $\mathcal{D}_1 = \{e_1(a,b), e_1(b,c), e_1(c,f), e_2(c,d), e_3(d,a), e_3(b,c), e_4(a)\}$ or $\mathcal{D}_2 = \{e_1(a,b), e_1(b,d), e_1(c,f), e_2(d,c), e_2(f,g), e_3(d,a), e_3(d,b), e_4(a), e_4(c), e_4(b)\}$ (or infinitely many other alternatives). If we apply $\mathcal{P}$ on $\mathcal{D}_1$, we get the answers $\{(a), (c)\}$, whereas if we apply $\mathcal{P}$ on $\mathcal{D}_2$ we get the answers $\{(a), (b)\}$; tuple (a) is the only answer common to both. It turns out that, for any view instance, program $\mathcal{P}_v$ provably derives exactly those answers that are common to all relational structures over e_1, e_2, e_3, e_4 that yield this view instance. Note, that if the programs that define the views are applied on $\mathcal{D}_2$, then more tuples will be derived than already in the view instance, namely the $v_1(c,g)$ and $v_2(d,b)$. This is called query answering under *the open world assumption* [1], i.e., the available data in the views is assumed to be a subset of the data derived by the view definition programs if they are applied on the non–accessible relations e_1, e_2, e_3, e_4. □

We investigate the following problem: Given a datalog program $\mathcal{P}$ and materialized views $v_1, v_2, \ldots, v_n$, construct a datalog program $\mathcal{P}_v$ with the following properties:

(i) $\mathcal{P}_v$ is a retrievable program contained in $\mathcal{P}$

(ii) Every datalog program that satisfies condition (i) is contained in $\mathcal{P}_v$.

When both conditions (i) and (ii) hold, we say that $\mathcal{P}_v$ is a *retrievable program maximally contained* in $\mathcal{P}$.

A few technical definitions: Given a view instance $\mathcal{D}_\mathcal{V}$, we define an *expansion* of $\mathcal{D}_\mathcal{V}$ to be any database (over $e_1, \ldots, e_m$) that results from $\mathcal{D}_\mathcal{V}$ after replacing the view facts with facts that are implied by one of the conjunctive queries produced from the view definitions (i.e., assuming the rules contain only EDB predicates in their bodies, we unify each tuple from $\mathcal{D}_\mathcal{V}$ with the head of some rule, freeze the rest of the variables in the body of the rule and replace the view fact by the facts in the body). We denote an expansion of $\mathcal{D}_\mathcal{V}$ by $R(\mathcal{D}_\mathcal{V}))$. E.g., in example 1, if $\mathcal{D}_\mathcal{V} = \{v_1(a, b), v_2(b, c)\}$, then an expansion is $R(\mathcal{D}_\mathcal{V}) = \{e_1(a, 1), e_2(1, b), e_3(b, c), e_4(c)\}$.

3   Retrievable Disjunctive Programs

Let $\mathcal{P}$ be any datalog program with output predicate q and $v_1, v_2, \ldots, v_n$ be views given by non–recursive datalog programs over the predicates of $\mathcal{P}$. We will construct in the following a disjunctive logic program $\mathcal{P}_{disj}$ and we will show that it is maximally contained in $\mathcal{P}$.

In fact, we construct a program $\mathcal{P}_{disj}$ which differs from being a datalog program in that it might contain disjunctions and function symbols in the head of some rules (which we call $\mathcal{V}^{-1}$–rules).

The construction is easy: $\mathcal{P}_{disj}$ contains: (i) all the rules of $\mathcal{P}$ except the ones that contain as subgoals EDB predicates which do not appear in any of the programs of the views and ii) For each view v_i, we complete its definition, i.e., we construct a collection of (possibly) disjunctive clauses as follows: We rewrite the definition of the view v_i as a disjunction of conjunctive queries. For this we rewrite each rule by renaming the head variables and possibly by introducing equalities in the bodies of the rules so as all the rules of the view definition have the same atom $v_i(X_1, \ldots, X_m)$ in their heads. Then, we replace all occurrences of each existential variable by a function (Skolem function) of the form $f(X_1, \ldots, X_m)$, where $X_1, \ldots, X_m$ are all variables in the head of the rule and f is a function symbol such that for each existential variable we use a different function symbol. We then take the disjunction of the bodies of the rules and rewrite it as a conjunction of disjuncts. For each disjunct, we create a new rule with this disjunct in the head and the atom $v_i(X_1, \ldots, X_m)$ in the body. Finally, all equalities are moved in the body as inequalities. The clauses obtained by applying this process to all view definitions are called $\mathcal{V}^{-1}$–rules.

Example 2. Assume that there are two materialized views v_1 and v_2 available defined as follows

$$v_1(X, Z) : - \; e(X, Y), r(Y, Z)$$
$$v_2(X, X) : - \; e(X, X)$$
$$v_2(X, Z) : - \; r(X, Y), e(Y, Z)$$

where e and r are EDB predicates.

We construct the $\mathcal{V}^{-1}$-rules as follows: By completing the definition of v_1 we take:

$$v_1(X, Z) \rightarrow \exists Y[e(X, Y) \wedge r(Y, Z)]$$

We introduce a Skolem function in order to eliminate the existential variable Y. We get

$$v_1(X, Z) \rightarrow e(X, f(X, Z)) \wedge r(f(X, Z), Z)$$

¿From this we obtain the following clauses

$$e(X, f(X, Z)) : - v_1(X, Z)$$
$$r(f(X, Z), Z) : - v_1(X, Z)$$

Now we complete the definition of v_2

$$v_2(X, Z) \rightarrow [Z = X \wedge e(X, X)] \vee \exists Y[r(X, Y) \wedge e(Y, Z)]$$

and introduce a Skolem function in order to eliminate the existential variable Y. We get

$$v_2(X, Z) \rightarrow [Z = X \wedge e(X, X)] \vee [r(X, g(X, Z)) \wedge e(g(X, Z), Z)]$$

transforming the right hand side into conjunctive normal form, we finally get

$$Z = X \vee r(X, g(X, Z)) : - v_2(X, Z)$$
$$Z = X \vee e(g(X, Z), Z) : - v_2(X, Z)$$
$$e(X, X) \vee r(X, g(X, Z)) : - v_2(X, Z)$$
$$e(X, X) \vee e(g(X, Z), Z) : - v_2(X, Z)$$

Moving equalities to the right hand side, we finally get the following $\mathcal{V}^{-1}$-rules:

$$r(X, g(X, Z)) : - v_2(X, Z), Z \neq X$$
$$e(g(X, Z), Z) : - v_2(X, Z), Z \neq X$$
$$e(X, X) \vee r(X, g(X, Z)) : - v_2(X, Z)$$
$$e(X, X) \vee e(g(X, Z), Z) : - v_2(X, Z)$$

□

We view $\mathcal{P}_{disj}$ as a program over the EDB predicates $v_1, v_2, \ldots, v_n$. The computation of program $\mathcal{P}_{disj}$ applied on a database $\mathcal{D}$ is considered in the usual bottom up fashion only that now a) it computes disjunctions of facts [15] and b) by firing a datalog rule we mean: either we unify each subgoal with an already derived fact or we unify the subgoal with a disjunct in an already derived disjunction of facts; in the latter case the rest of the disjuncts will appear in the newly derived disjunctive fact together with the head literal and other disjuncts resulting possibly from other subgoals. (Observe that $\mathcal{V}^{-1}$-rules will be used only in the first step of the bottom up evaluation.) Derivation trees for this bottom up evaluation are defined in the usual way only that the labels on the nodes are disjunctions of facts. In the following, we will refer to a derivation tree with nodes labeled by either facts or disjunctions of facts as a *disjunctive derivation tree*.

We will refer to the *output database* of program P_{disj} applied on an input database, meaning the database that contains only the atomic facts without function symbols computed by P_{disj}.

We say that program P_{disj} is *contained* in (*equivalent* to, respectively) a datalog program P iff for any input database, the output database computed by P_{disj} is contained in (is equal to, respectively) the output database computed by P. If every disjunctive datalog program contained in P is also contained in P_{disj}, we say that P_{disj} is a *retrievable* disjunctive datalog program *maximally contained* in P.

Theorem 1. *Let P be any datalog program and $v_1, \ldots, v_n$ be views given by non-recursive datalog programs over the EDB predicates of P; let P_{disj} be the disjunctive program constructed from P and the views. Then, program P_{disj} is a retrievable disjunctive datalog($\neq$) program maximally contained in P.*

Proof. (Sketch) The program P_{disj} contains (i) rules of P without view subgoals and (ii) non-recursive V^{-1}–rules. Therefore, it can be equivalently thought of as program P applied on databases having disjunctions as facts. (i.e., those facts that are derived by V^{-1}–rules).

One direction is easy: P_{disj} uses resolution in the bottom up evaluation we described, therefore it computes all the logical consequences of P applied on a particular disjunctive database, namely the one containing the disjunctive facts over EDB predicates of P implied by the view facts and their definitions in terms of the EDB predicates of P. Hence P_{disj} is contained in any retrievable program maximally contained in P.

For the other direction, we argue as follows: Let P_v be a maximally contained retrievable datalog program. Consider an arbitrary database D over the EDB predicates $v_1, \ldots, v_n$ of P. Let $q(\mathbf{a})$ be a fact computed by P_v. Consider all possible expansions of D derived by replacing a view fact by a collection of facts derived from one of the conjunctions which define this view. Because P_v is contained in P, for any expansion database, fact $q(\mathbf{a})$ is computed by P; therefore, for each expansion database, there is at least one derivation tree which derives $q(\mathbf{a})$. Let T be an arbitrary collection containing at least one such derivation tree for each expansion database. It suffices to prove that there is a finite derivation tree of P_{disj} that computes $q(\mathbf{a})$ in D.

We conveniently define the *merging* of two (disjunctive) derivation trees, T_1 and T_2: We choose a leaf of T_2. We identify this leaf with the root of T_1 and label this node by the disjunction of the two labels. The rest of the nodes are left as are (in fact, we hang tree T_1 from T_2) only that some of the labels are changed: The label in the root of T_1 appears in the disjunction in every node of the path from the particular leaf to the root of T_2. The label of the leaf of T_1 appears in the disjunction in every node on a number of paths (arbitrary chosen) each leading from the root to a leaf of T_1.

The rest of the proof involves a combinatorial argument to show the following lemma:

Lemma 3. *There is a collection T of derivation trees as defined above, such that the following holds: Considering as initialization set the set of derivation trees T, there is a sequence of mergings that produces a disjunctive derivation tree of program P_{disj} which computes $q(\mathbf{a})$ in D.*

□

4   Queries and Views Defined by Non-recursive Programs

In this section we consider the case of non-recursive query datalog programs and views defined by datalog programs without recursion as well.

Theorem 2. *Suppose that the program defining the query is a non-recursive connected datalog program and the programs defining the views are all non-recursive datalog programs. Suppose that there exists a retrievable datalog program maximally contained in the query, which has no persistencies. Then there exists a retrievable datalog program maximally contained in the query which is non-recursive.*

Proof. (Sketch): Let P be the program defining the query and suppose there is a retrievable datalog program maximally contained in the query, call it P_v. Suppose P_v is recursive. Consider any canonical database of P_v and suppose D is an expansion of this canonical database. Consider the conjunctive query generated by P, say Q, such as there is a containment mapping from Q to D (D being viewed as a conjunctive query). Since P_v has no persistencies, any canonical database, and hence D as well, is of low ($<$ a function of the size of the program) degree. Moreover Q is connected; consequently, the image of Q in D may involve only a limited number ($<$ a function of the sizes of the programs) of constants of the domain of D. Therefore P_v is contained in a retrievable program which itself is contained in the query, a contradiction.

□

We, next, present a procedure which produces a retrievable program, whenever the instance of the problem obeys certain conditions. We show that if the procedure reaches a datalog program then this is a retrievable program maximally contained in the query.

Our procedure proceeds in two steps: a) From P_{disj} we try to obtain a Horn program P_{Horn} which might contain function symbols and b) In the case we find a Horn program in the previous step, we eliminate from P_{Horn} the function symbols deriving the final program P_v. The elimination of function symbols is done in a bottom up fashion as in [7, 12]. Note that in step (a) we might not obtain a Horn program.

In the first step, we try to obtain program P_{Horn} by applying program transformation rules to P_{disj}. The basic transformation rule that we use is *unfolding* [10]. Unfolding in disjunctive logic programs is an extension of the unfolding in

Horn clause programs. In general, the application of the unfolding rule consists of a sequence of elementary unfolding steps. Suppose that we have to unfold (elementary unfolding) a clause C at a body atom B using a clause D at a head atom B'. Suppose that θ is the most general unifier of B and B'. Then we get a clause whose body is the body of C after replacing the atom B by the body of D and whose head is the disjunction of the head of C with the head atoms of D except B'. In this clause we apply the unifier θ. Now in order to unfold a clause R at a chosen body atom B, we have to use all program clauses, which have a head atom unifiable with B. If we have more than one such head atoms we use the clause in all possible ways. Moreover, in the later case we have also to unfold the initial clause using the clauses obtained by the previous elementary unfolding steps if they also have head atoms unifiable with B and so on. The set of clauses obtained in this way, denoted by $unfold(C, B)$, may replace clause R in the program. For more details about the unfolding operation, see [10].

Besides unfolding, some clause deletion rules [9] are used, which preserve the semantics of a disjunctive logic program, (thus, we discard useless clauses). More specifically, a) we can delete a clause which is a variant of another program clause, b) we can delete a clause which is a tautology (i.e. there is an atom which appears in both the head and the body of the clause), c) we can delete a failing clause (i.e. a clause which has an atom in its body which does not unify with any head atom of the program clauses), d) we can delete a clauses which is subsumed by another program clause. We say that a clause C subsumes another clause D if there exists a substitution θ such that $head(C\theta) \subseteq head(D)$ and $body(C\theta) \subseteq body(D)$. All these deletion rules preserve the equivalence of the disjunctive programs [9].

In the following, we will also use *factoring* [15]. If two head atoms of a disjunctive clause C have a most general unifier θ then $C\theta$ is a *factor* of C. When we say that we take the *factoring closure* of a program we mean that we add to the program all factors obtained by applying factoring to all program clauses in all possible ways.

All the transformation rules presented so far preserve the equivalence of programs. Now we present, through the following two lemmas, two deletion rules, which although they do not preserve the equivalence of programs, they preserve the set of the atoms of the query predicate which are logical consequences of the programs.

Lemma 4. *Let $\mathcal{P}$ be a disjunctive logic program, p be a predicate in $\mathcal{P}$ and C be a clause in $\mathcal{P}$ of the form*

$$A_1 \vee \ldots \vee A_m : - B_1, \ldots, B_n$$

Suppose that there is an atom A_j in $\{A_1, \ldots, A_m\}$ whose predicate is different from p, such that there is no clause in $\mathcal{P}$ with a body atom which unifies with A_j. Let $\mathcal{P}' = \mathcal{P} - \{C\}$. Then, for any database $\mathcal{D}$, $\mathcal{P}'_p(\mathcal{D}) = \mathcal{P}_p(\mathcal{D})$.

Lemma 5. *Let $\mathcal{P}$ be a disjunctive logic program, p be a predicate in $\mathcal{P}$ and C be a clause in $\mathcal{P}$ of the form*

$$A_1 \vee \ldots \vee A_m : - B_1, \ldots, B_n$$

Suppose that there is no clause in $\mathcal{P}$ with a body atom whose predicate is p. Suppose also that $\mathcal{P}$ is closed under factoring and that there are two or more atoms in the head of C whose predicate is p. Let $\mathcal{P}' = \mathcal{P} - \{C\}$. Then, for any database $\mathcal{D}$, $\mathcal{P}'_p(\mathcal{D}) = \mathcal{P}_p(\mathcal{D})$.

In the following, we present an algorithm which gives a systematic way to apply the above described operations on $\mathcal{V}^{-1} \cup \mathcal{P}$ deriving, in certain cases, a retrievable datalog($\neq$) program maximally contained in $\mathcal{P}$. We suppose, without loss of generality, that all predicates appearing in the body of rules of the query program are EDB predicates (as the program is non-recursive, we can always obtain a program of this form by applying unfolding to all IDB body atoms).

Procedure:
  Input: $\mathcal{V}^{-1}$, $\mathcal{P}$.
  Output: $\mathcal{P}_{der}$.
begin
  - Let $P = \mathcal{P} \cup \mathcal{V}^{-1}$.
  - Let S_p be the set of EDB predicates in $\mathcal{P}$.
  while $S_p \neq \{\ \}$ and *check2* is true **do**
      begin
        - Select a predicate e from S_p.
        while *check1(e)* is true **and** *check2* is true **do**
            begin
              - Select a clause D from P whose body contains an atom B
                whose predicate is e.
              - Unfold D at B by P. Let $P' = (P - \{D\}) \cup unfold(D, B)$.
              - Let P'' be the obtained from P' by getting
                the factoring closure of the clauses in $unfold(D, B)$.
              - Let P''' be the program obtained from P'' by
                applying the deletion rules.
              - Let $P = P'''$.
            end
          Let $S_p = S_p - \{e\}$.
      end
end.

The condition *check1(e)* is *true* if: *There is a clause in P with a body atom whose predicate is 'e'.*

The condition *check2* is *true* if: *There is no clause in P with an EDB atom E_1 in its body which unifies with an EDB atom E_2 in the head of the same clause.*

Example 3. Consider the following datalog program $\mathcal{P}$

$$
\begin{array}{ll}
(1) & p(X) :- e(X,Y), r(Y) \\
(2) & p(X) :- e(Y,X), s(X) \\
(3) & p(X) :- e(X,X)
\end{array}
$$

and assume that there are two materialized views v_1 and v_2 available

$$
\begin{array}{ll}
(4) & v_1(X,Y) :- r(X), s(Y) \\
(5) & v_2(X,Y) :- e(X,Y) \\
(6) & v_2(X,Y) :- e(Y,X)
\end{array}
$$

Applying the procedure described in the previous section, we get $\mathcal{P}_{disj}$ which contains the rules (1)-(3) and the following $\mathcal{V}^{-1}$-rules:

$$
\begin{array}{ll}
(7) & r(X) :- v_1(X,Y) \\
(8) & s(Y) :- v_1(X,Y) \\
(9) & e(X,Y) \vee e(Y,X) :- v_2(X,Y)
\end{array}
$$

Now we apply the procedure described above in order to obtain a datalog program which has the same atomic results as P_{disj}.

We unfold (1) at '$e(X,Y)$' using (9). We get a new equivalent program, which contains the clauses $P_1 = \{2,3,7,8,9,10,11,12\}$, where:

$$
\begin{array}{ll}
(10) & p(X) \vee e(Y,X) :- v_2(X,Y), r(Y) \\
(11) & p(X) \vee e(Y,X) :- v_2(Y,X), r(Y) \\
(12) & p(X) \vee p(Y) :- v_2(Y,X), r(X), r(Y)
\end{array}
$$

Unfolding (2) at '$e(X,Y)$' using (9), (10), (11) we get $P_2 = \{3,7,\ 8,9,10,\ 11,12,13,\ 14,\ 15,16,17\}$, where:

$$
\begin{array}{ll}
(13) & p(X) \vee e(X,Y) :- v_2(Y,X), s(X) \\
(14) & p(X) \vee e(X,Y) :- v_2(X,Y), s(X) \\
(15) & p(X) \vee p(Y) :- v_2(Y,X), s(X), s(X) \\
(16) & p(X) :- v_2(X,Y), r(Y), s(X) \\
(17) & p(X) :- v_2(Y,X), r(Y), s(X)
\end{array}
$$

Finally, unfolding (3) at '$e(X,X)$' using (9), (10), (11), (13), (14) we get $P_3 = \{7,8,9,10,11,12,13,\ 14,\ 15,16,\ 17,18,\ 19,20,21,22,23,24\}$, where:

$$
\begin{array}{ll}
(18) & p(X) \vee e(X,X) :- v_2(X,X) \\
(19) & p(X) \vee e(X,X) :- v_2(X,X) \\
(20) & p(X) :- v_2(X,X) \\
(21) & p(X) :- v_2(X,X), r(X) \\
(22) & p(X) :- v_2(X,X), r(X) \\
(23) & p(X) :- v_2(X,X), s(X) \\
(24) & p(X) :- v_2(X,X), s(X)
\end{array}
$$

Taking the factoring closure of the program, we get from clauses (12) and (15) the clauses:

$$(25) \qquad p(X) :- v_2(X,X), r(X), r(X)$$
$$(26) \qquad p(X) :- v_2(X,X), s(X), s(X)$$

which are also added to the program. Clauses (19), (22), (24), (25) can be deleted since they are variants of other program clauses. Clauses (18), (21), (23) and (26) can be deleted since they are subsumed by clause (20). Clauses (9), (10), (11), (13) and (14) can be deleted because of lemma 4 (i.e. the atom with the predicate 'e' does not occur in any program clause). Finally, clauses (12) and (15) can be deleted from the program because of lemma 5. Therefore, the program obtained so far is $\{7, 8, 16, 17, 20\}$. Now, unfolding the EDB atoms in the bodies of (16) and (17) and deleting the redundant clauses we finally get:

$$p(X) :- v_2(X,X)$$
$$p(Y) :- v_2(X,Y), v_1(Z_1,Y), v_1(X,Z_2)$$
$$p(X) :- v_2(X,Y), v_1(Z_1,X), v_1(Y,Z_2)$$

This program is a retrievable Datalog program maximally contained in $\mathcal{P}$.   □

Concerning the procedure described above we can prove the following theorem.

Theorem 3. *The following hold for the procedure above:*

1. *The procedure always terminates.*
2. *Suppose that by applying the procedure above to a program P_{disj} we get a program P_{der} whose clause bodies do not contain any EDB atom. Then P_{der} is a non-recursive datalog($\neq$) program which is maximally contained in P.*

In the following we give a syntactic sufficient condition for the algorithm to end up with a datalog($\neq$) program.

Sufficient condition: *Consider the $\mathcal{V}^{-1}$-rules and the query program $\mathcal{P}$. For each rule in $\mathcal{P}$ there is at most one atom in its body whose predicate occurs in the head of a (non-trivial) disjunctive $\mathcal{V}^{-1}$-rule.*

Theorem 4. *If the sufficient condition holds for a a set of $\mathcal{V}^{-1}$-rules and a query program $\mathcal{P}$ then by applying the procedure to $\mathcal{V}^{-1} \cup \mathcal{P}$ we get a retrievable maximally contained non-recursive datalog($\neq$) program.*

5   Recursive Views

In the case where the views are given by recursive datalog programs and the query by a non-recursive datalog program $\mathcal{P}$, the problem of computing a retrievable program maximally contained in $\mathcal{P}$ is reduced to that of non-recursive view definitions (following lemma).

Lemma 6. *Let $\mathcal{P}$ be any non-recursive datalog program and $v_1, \ldots, v_n$ be views given by any datalog programs over the EDB predicates of $\mathcal{P}$. Then, there exists a positive integer N depending only on the sizes of the programs so that the following holds:*

Consider a new set of views $v_1', \ldots v_m'$ with view definitions $\mathcal{P}_{v_1'}, \mathcal{P}_{v_2'}, \ldots, \mathcal{P}_{v_m'}$ respectively: where $\mathcal{P}_{v_i'}$ is the disjunction of all conjunctive queries that are produced by $\mathcal{P}_{v_i}$ and have size less that N.

If $\mathcal{P}_v$ is a retrievable program contained in $\mathcal{P}$ under the new view definitions, then $\mathcal{P}_v$ is a retrievable program contained in $\mathcal{P}$ under the original view definitions.

Proof. Let c_v be a conjunctive query generated by $\mathcal{P}_v$. Let c_v^{expi} be all expansions of c_v that result after replacing each occurrence of a view atom by one of their new definitions. Then, for each c_v^{expi}, there is a conjunctive query c_i generated by $\mathcal{P}$ and there exists a containment mapping, h_i, from c_i to c_v^{expi}.

Now, obtain all expansions oc_v^{expi}, $i = 1, 2, \ldots$, of c_v considering the original view definitions. Suppose there exists an i such that there is no conjunctive query in $\mathcal{P}$ with a containment mapping on oc_v^{expi}. Then, a view occurrence in c_v has been replaced by a long ($> N = O(2^{s \log s})$, where s is the maximum size of the programs defining the query and the views) conjunctive query $R(v)$; $R(v)$ appears as a subquery in oc_v^{expi}. ¿From oc_v^{expi}, we construct a shorter expansion oc_v^{expj}: We can pump $R(v)$ to get a shorter view expansion which, though, preserves all the neighborhoods of size $\leq m =$the size of the maximum conjunctive query in $\mathcal{P}$ (see lemmata 1, 2). We apply this pumping on all expansions that are longer than N, getting, in the end, an expansion, c_v^{expi}, of c_v under the new view definitions. There exists, though, a conjunctive query of $\mathcal{P}$ with a containment mapping on c_v^{expi}. Since oc_v^{expi} and c_v^{expi} have the same neighborhoods of size up to m, there is a containment mapping also on oc_v^{expi}; this is a contradiction. □

Theorem 5. *Let $\mathcal{P}$ be any non-recursive connected datalog program and $v_1, \ldots, v_n$ be views given by any datalog programs over the EDB predicates of $\mathcal{P}$. Suppose there exists a retrievable datalog program maximally contained in $\mathcal{P}$ which has no persistencies. Then, there exists a retrievable datalog program maximally contained in $\mathcal{P}$ which is non-recursive.*

Proof. An immediate consequence of the preceding lemma, and theorem 2. □

6   Chain Programs

A *chain rule* is a rule over only binary predicates; moreover the first variable in the head is identical to the first variable of the first predicate in the body, the second variable in the head is identical to the last variable of the last predicate in the body and the second variable of the i-th predicate is identical to the first variable of the $i + 1$-th predicate in the body. A *chain program* contains only chain rules. It is easy to see that any conjunctive query generated by a chain program P corresponds to a canonical database which is a simple path spelling a word over the alphabet of the EDB predicate symbols. Thus, we can view a chain program as generating a language over this alphabet; we call this language L_P. Observe that for chain programs, L_P is a context free language.

In the case, though, where both the query and the views are defined by recursive programs, it becomes undecidable to answer the question whether there is a non-empty datalog program that is contained in P and uses only the given views as EDB predicates; it remains undecidable even in the case where both program P and the views are given by chain programs.

The reduction, in the following theorem is done from the containment problem of context free grammars [17, 11]

Theorem 6. *Given a datalog chain program P and views $v_1, v_2, \ldots, v_m$ which are also given by chain programs over the EDB predicates of P, it is undecidable whether there is a non-empty retrievable datalog program P_v contained in P.*

In some cases, though, we can have a negative answer in the question whether there exists a "simple" non–empty retrievable program, as it is stated in the theorem that follows.

Here on, we consider the following situation: A datalog query given by chain program P and materialized views, $v_1, v_2, \ldots, v_m$, over the EDB predicates of P, which are also given by chain programs. Let P_v be a datalog program (not necessarily chain) contained in P that uses only $v_1, v_2, \ldots, v_m$ as EDB predicates.

Consider a datalog program P where both IDB and EDB predicates are binary. Take any conjunctive query c produced by P and take the canonical database of c. We call P *simple* if, for all c, the canonical database (viewed as a directed graph) contains a number of pairwise node-disjoint simple paths with endpoints on the two head constants, i.e., besides the head constants every constant (viewed as a node) has in–degree one and out–degree one. Chain programs are simple.

We need some technical concepts here on pumping lemmas for formal languages. Let w be a word over the alphabet Σ. For fixed positive integer N, we say that $w_i = ux^i v y^i w, i = 1, 2, \ldots$ is a *pumping sequence* for w if $w = uxvyw$ and $|xy| < N$. For context free languages, there exists a positive integer N, such that, for any word in a language, L, longer than N, there exists a pumping sequence $w_i, i = 1, \ldots$, such that $w_i, i = 1, \ldots$ also belongs in the language. We call such a pumping sequence a *proper* pumping sequence *wrto* language L.

Theorem 7. *Let P be a chain program and $v_1, v_2, \ldots, v_m$ views over the EDB predicates of P, which are also given by chain programs $V_1, V_2, \ldots, V_m$, respectively. Suppose there exists a simple retrievable datalog program contained in P. Then there exists a fixed positive integer N (depending only on the sizes of the programs for the views and P), and there is a view definition V_i such that for any word w in L_{V_i}, with $|w| > N$, the following happens: There is a word w_P in L_P such that $w_P = ww'$ and for any proper pumping sequence, $w_1, w_2, \ldots$, of w wrto L_{V_i}, there exists an infinite subsequence $w_{i_1}, w_{i_1+1}, \ldots$ such that $w_{i_1+j}w'$ also belongs to L_P, for all $j = 1, 2, \ldots$.*

For an application, consider the following program $\mathcal{P}$:

$$p(X, Y) : - a(X, Z_1), p(Z_1, Z_2), p(Z_2, Z_3), a(Z_3, Y)$$
$$p(X, Y) : - b(X, Y)$$

and the views:

$$v_1(X, Y) : - a(X, Z_1), v_1(Z_1, Z_2), a(Z_2, Y)$$
$$v_1(X, Y) : - b(X, Z_1), b(Z_1, Y)$$
$$v_2(X, Y) : - a(X, Z_1), v_2(Z_1, Y)$$
$$v_2(X, Y) : - a(X, Y)$$

Theorem 8. *Given the views v_1, v_2, there is no retrievable simple datalog program contained in $\mathcal{P}$.*

Proof. Consider any word $w = w'w''$ of $L_{\mathcal{P}}$ where w' is a sufficiently large word of L_{v_1} (L_{v_2} respectively). Consider a proper pumping sequence of w' wrto L_{v_1} (L_{v_2} respectively), $w_1, w_2, \ldots$. Suppose there exists a retrievable simple program. Then, for infinitely many i's, $w_i w'$ is also a word in $L_{\mathcal{P}}$, according to the theorem above. Observe, though, that any word in $L_{\mathcal{P}}$ longer than four contains $2k + 2$ as and $k + 2$ bs. $w_i w'$ will not retain this balance, therefore it is not a word of $L_{\mathcal{P}}$. □

7 Conclusion

We investigated the problem of answering queries using materialized views. In particular, we searched for a retrievable program maximally contained in the query. In the case the query is defined by a non-recursive datalog program and the views by recursive datalog programs, we reduced the problem to that of non-recursive definitions for both the query and the views. We showed that, in the case where both the query and the views are defined by recursive datalog programs, then the problem becomes easily undecidable; we showed, though, some methods to produce negative results. It would be interesting to further pursue this latter line of research. In the case both the query and the views are defined by non-recursive datalog programs, we showed how, in certain cases, we can produce a retrievable non-recursive datalog($\neq$) program maximally contained in the query. It seems that, further investigation towards this direction will produce interesting results. We are currently working on this.

Acknowledgment: We thank Vassilis Vassalos for helpful discussions.

References

[1] S. Abiteboul and O. Duschka. Complexity of answering queries using materialized views. In *Proc. ACM Symposium on Principles of Database Systems*, 1998.

[2] Serge Abiteboul. Querying semi-structured data. In *Proceedings of the Sixth International Conference on Database Theory*, pages 1–18. Springer-Verlag, 1997.

[3] F. Afrati, S. Cosmadakis, and M. Yannakakis. On datalog vs. polynomial time. *J. Computer and Systems Sciences*, 51(2):117–196, 1995.

[4] Surajit Chaudhuri, Ravi Krishnamurthy, Spyros Potamianos, and Kyuseak Shim. Optimizing queries with materialized views. In *Proceedings of the 11th International Conference on Data Engineering, Los Alamitos, CA*, pages 190–200. IEEE Comput. Soc. Press, 1995.

[5] Chandra Chekuri and Anand Rajaraman. Conjunctive query containment revisited. In *Proceedings of the Sixth International Conference on Database Theory*, pages 56–70. Springer-Verlag, 1997.

[6] Oliver M. Duschka. *Query Planning and Optimization in Information Integration*. PhD thesis, Stanford University, December 1997.

[7] Oliver M. Duschka and Michael R. Genesereth. Answering recursive queries using views. In *Proc. 16th ACM SIGACT-SIGMOD-GIGART Symposium on Principles of Database Systems*, pages 109–116, 1997.

[8] Oliver M. Duschka and Michael R. Genesereth. Query planning with disjunctive sources. In *Proc. of the AAAI-98 Workshop on AI and Information Integration*, 1998.

[9] M. Gergatsoulis. Correctness-preserving transformations for disjunctive logic programs. Demo 97/2, Institute of Informatics & Telecom. NCSR 'Demokritos', 1997.

[10] Manolis Gergatsoulis. Unfold/fold transformations for disjunctive logic programs. *Information Processing Letters*, 62(1):23–29, April 1997.

[11] M. A. Harrison. *Introduction to formal language theory*. Addison-Wesley, 1978.

[12] Nam Huyn. A more aggressive use of views to extract information. Technical Report STAN-CS-TR-96-1577, Stanford University, Computer Science Department, 1996.

[13] Alon Y. Levy, Alberto O. Mendelzon, Yehoshua Sagiv, and Divesh Srivastava. Answering queries using views. In *Proc. 14th ACM SIGACT-SIGMOD-SIGART Symposium on Principles of Database Systems*, pages 95–104, 1995.

[14] Alon Y. Levy, Divest Srivastava, and Thomas Kirk. Data model and query evaluation in global information systems. *Journal of Intelligent Information Systems*, 1995. Special Issue on Networked Information Discovery and Retrieval.

[15] J. Lobo, J. Minker, and A. Rajasekar. *Foundations of Disjunctive Logic Programming*. MIT Press, 1992.

[16] Anand Rajaraman, Yehoshua Sagiv, and Jeffrey D. Ullman. Answering queries using templates with binding patterns. In *Proc. 14th ACM SIGACT-SIGMOD-GIGART Symposium on Principles of Database Systems, San Jose, CA*, 1995.

[17] Oded Shmueli. Decidability and expressiveness aspects of logic queries. In *Proc. 6th ACM SIGACT-SIGMOD-SIGART Symposium on Principles of Database Systems*, pages 237–249, 1987.

[18] Jeffrey D. Ullman. *Principles of Database and Knowledge-Base Systems*, volume I & II. Computer Science Press, 1989.

[19] Jeffrey D. Ullman. Information integration using logical views. In *Proceedings of the Sixth International Conference on Database Theory*, pages 19–40. Springer-Verlag, 1997.

[20] Jeffrey D. Ullman and Allen Van Gelder. Parallel complexity of logical query programs. In *Proc. 27th IEEE Symp. on Foundations of Comp. Sci.*, pages 438–454, 1986.

Selection of Views to Materialize Under a Maintenance Cost Constraint

Himanshu Gupta[1*] and Inderpal Singh Mumick[2]

[1] Stanford University, Stanford, CA 94305, hgupta@db.stanford.edu
[2] Savera Systems, Summit, NJ 07901, mumick@savera.com

Abstract. A data warehouse stores materialized views derived from one or more sources for the purpose of efficiently implementing decision-support or OLAP queries. One of the most important decisions in designing a data warehouse is the selection of materialized views to be maintained at the warehouse. The goal is to select an appropriate set of views that minimizes total query response time and/or the cost of maintaining the selected views, given a limited amount of resource such as materialization time, storage space, or total view maintenance time. In this article, we develop algorithms to select a set of views to materialize in a data warehouse in order to minimize the total query response time under the constraint of a given total view maintenance time. As the above maintenance-cost view-selection problem is extremely intractable, we tackle some special cases and design approximation algorithms. First, we design an approximation greedy algorithm for the maintenance-cost view-selection problem in OR view graphs, which arise in many practical applications, e.g., data cubes. We prove that the query benefit of the solution delivered by the proposed greedy heuristic is within 63% of that of the optimal solution. Second, we also design an A^* heuristic, that delivers an optimal solution, for the general case of AND-OR view graphs. We implemented our algorithms and a performance study of the algorithms shows that the proposed greedy algorithm for OR view graphs almost always delivers an optimal solution.

1 Introduction

A *data warehouse* is a repository of integrated information available for querying and analysis [IK93,HGMW+95,Wid95]. Figure 1 illustrates the architecture of a typical warehouse [WGL+96]. The bottom of the figure depicts the multiple *information sources* of interest. Data that is of interest to the client(s) is derived or copied and integrated into the data warehouse, depicted near the top of the figure. These views stored at the warehouse are often referred to as *materialized views*. The *integerator*, which lies in between the sources and the warehouse, is responsible for maintaining the materialized views at the warehouse in response to changes at the sources [ZGMHW95,CW91,GM95]. This incremental maintenance of views incurs what is known as *maintenance cost*. We use the term maintenance cost interchangeably with *maintenance time*.

---

* Supported by NSF grant IRI-96-31952.

Catriel Beeri, Peter Buneman (Eds.): ICDT'99, LNCS 1540, pp. 453–470, 1998.
© Springer-Verlag Berlin Heidelberg 1998

One of the advantages of such a system is that user queries can be answered using the information stored at the warehouse and need not be translated and shipped to the original source(s) for execution. Also, warehouse data is available for queries even when the original information source(s) are inaccessible due to real-time operations or other reasons. Widom in [Wid95] gives a nice overview of the technical issues that arise in a data warehouse.

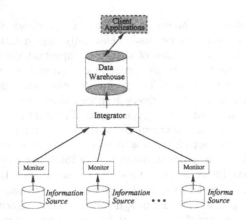

Fig. 1. A typical data warehouse architecture

The selection of which views to materialize is one of the most important decisions in the design of a data warehouse. Earlier work [Gup97] presents a theoretical formulation of the general "view-selection" problem in a data warehouse. Given some resource constraint and a query load to be supported at the warehouse, the *view-selection* problem defined in [Gup97] is to select a set of derived views to materialize, under a given resource constraint, pthat will minimize the sum of total query response time and maintenance time of the selected views. [Gup97] presents near-optimal polynomial-time greedy algorithms for some special cases of the general problem where the resource constraint is disk space.

In this article, we consider the view-selection problem of selecting views to materialize in order to optimize the total query response time, under the constraint that the selected set of views incur less than a given amount of total maintenance time. Hereafter, we will refer to this problem as the *maintenance-cost view-selection* problem. The maintenance-cost view-selection problem is much more difficult than the view-selection problem with a disk-space constraint, because the maintenance cost of a view v depends on the set of other materialized views. For the special case of "OR view graphs," we present a competitive greedy algorithm that provably delivers a near-optimal solution. The OR view graphs, which are view graphs where exactly one view is used to derive another view, arise in many important practical applications. A very important application is that of OLAP warehouses called data cubes, where the candidate views for precomputation (materialization) form an "OR boolean lattice." For the general maintenance-cost view-selection problem that arises in a data warehouse, i.e., for the general case of AND-OR view graphs, we present an A^* heuristic that delivers an optimal solution.

The rest of the paper is organized as follows. The rest of this section gives a brief summary of the related work. In Section 2, we present the motivation for the maintenance-cost view-selection problem and the main contributions of this article. Section 3 presents some preliminary definitions. We define the maintenance-cost view-selection problem formally in Section 4. In Section 5, we present an approximation greedy algorithm for the maintenance-cost view-selection problem in OR view graphs. Section 6 presents an A^* heuristic that delivers an optimal set of views for the maintenance-cost view-selection problem in general AND-OR view graphs. We present our experimental results in Section 7. Finally, we give some concluding remarks in Section 8.

1.1 Related Work

Recently, there has been a lot of interest on the problem of selecting views to materialize in a data warehouse. Harinarayan, Rajaraman and Ullman [HRU96] provide algorithms to select views to materialize in order to minimize the total query response time, for the case of data cubes or other OLAP applications when there are only queries with aggregates over the base relation. The view graphs that arise in OLAP applications are special cases of OR view graphs. The authors in [HRU96] propose a polynomial-time greedy algorithm that delivers a near-optimal solution. Gupta et al. in [GHRU97] extend their results to selection of views *and* indexes in data cubes. Gupta in [Gup97] presents a theoretical formulation of the general view-selection problem in a data warehouse and generalizes the previous results to (i) AND view graphs, where each view has a unique execution plan, (ii) OR view graphs, (iii) OR view graphs with indexes, (iv) AND view graphs with indexes, and some other special cases of AND-OR view graphs. All of the above mentioned works ([HRU96,GHRU97,Gup97]) present approximation algorithms to select a set of structures that minimizes the total query response time under a given *space* constraint; the constraint represents the maximum amount of disk space that can be used to store the materialized views.

Other recent works on the view-selection problem have been as follows. Ross, Srivastava, and Sudarshan in [RSS96], Yang, Karlapalem, and Li in [YKL97], Baralis, Paraboschi, and Teniente in [BPT97], and Theodoratos and Sellis in [TS97] provide various frameworks and heuristics for selection of views in order to optimize the sum of query response time and view maintenance time without any resource constraint. Most of the heuristics presented there are either exhaustive searches or do not have any performance guarantees on the quality of the solution delivered.

Ours is the first article to address the problem of selecting views to materialize in a data warehouse under the constraint of a given amount of total view maintenance time.

2   Motivation and Contributions

Most of the previous work done ([HRU96,GHRU97,Gup97]) on designing poly-nomial-time approximation algorithms that provably deliver a near-optimal so-lution for the view-selection problem suffers from one drawback. The designed algorithms apply only to the case of a disk-space constraint.

Though the previous work has offered significant insight into the nature of the view-selection problem, the constraint considered therein makes the results less applicable in practice because disk-space is very cheap in real life. In practice, the real constraining factor that prevents us from materializing everything at the warehouse is the maintenance time incurred in keeping the materialized views up to date at the warehouse. Usually, changes to the source data are queued and propagated periodically to the warehouse views in a large batch update transaction. The update transaction is usually done overnight, so that the warehouse is available for querying and analysis during the day time. Hence, there is a constraint on the time that can be alloted to the maintenance of materialized views.

In this article, we consider the maintenance-cost view-selection problem which is to select a set of views to materialize in order to minimize the query response time under a constraint of maintenance time. We do not make any assump-tions about the query or the maintenance cost models. It is easy to see that the view-selection problem under a disk-space constraint is only a special case of the maintenance-time view-selection problem, when maintenance cost of each view remains a constant, i.e., the cost of maintaining a view is independent of the set of other materialized views. Thus, the maintenance-cost view-selection problem is trivially NP-hard, since the space-constraint view-selection problem is NP-hard [Gup97].

Now, we explain the main differences between the view-selection problem un-der the space constraint and the maintenance-cost view-selection problem, which makes the maintenance-cost view-selection optimization problem more difficult. In the case of the view-selection problem with space constraint, as the query benefit of a view never increases with materialization of other views, the query-benefit per unit space of a non-selected view always decreases monotonically with the selection of other views. This property is formally defined in [Gup97] as the monotonicity property of the benefit function and is repeated here for convenience.

Definition 1. (Monotonic Property) *A benefit function B, which is used to prioritize views for selection, is said to satisfy the monotonicity property for a set of views M with respect to distinct views V_1 and V_2 if $B(\{V_1, V_2\}, M)$ is less than (or equal to) either $B(\{V_1\}, M)$ or $B(\{V_2\}, M)$.*

In the case of the view-selection problem under space constraint, the query-benefit per unit space function satisfies the above defined monotonicity property for all sets M and views V_1 and V_2. However, for the case of maintenance-cost view-selection problem, the maintenance cost of a view can decrease with selection of other views for materialization and hence, the query-benefit per unit of maintenance-cost of a view can actually increase. Hence, the total maintenance cost of two "dependent" views may be much less than the sum of the maintenance costs of the individual views, causing the query-benefit per unit maintenance-cost of two dependent views to be sometimes much greater than the query-benefit per unit maintenance-cost of either of the individual views. The above described non-monotonic behavior of the query-benefit function makes the maintenance-problem view-selection problem intractable. The non-monotonic behavior of the query-benefit per unit maintenance-cost function is illustrated in Example 2 in Section 5, where it is shown that the simple greedy approaches presented in previous works for the space-constraint view-selection problem could deliver an arbitrarily bad solution when applied to the maintenance-cost view-selection problem.

Contributions In this article, we have identified the maintenance-cost view-selection problem and the difficulty it presents. We develop a couple of algorithms to solve the maintenance-cost view-selection problem within the framework of general query and maintenance cost models. For the maintenance-cost view-selection problem in general OR view graphs, we present a greedy heuristic that selects a _set_ of views at each stage of the algorithm. We prove that the proposed greedy algorithm delivers a near-optimal solution. The OR view graphs, where exactly one view is used to compute another view, arise in many important practical applications. A very important application is that of OLAP warehouses called data cubes, where the candidate views for precomputation (materialization) form an "OR boolean lattice." We also present an A^* heuristic for the general case of AND-OR graphs. Performance studies indicate that the proposed greedy heuristic almost always returns an optimal solution for OR view graphs. The maintenance-cost view-selection was one of the open problems mentioned in [Gup97]. By designing an approximate algorithm for the problem, this article essentially answers one of the open questions raised in [Gup97].

3   Preliminaries

In this section, we present a refinement of a few definitions from [Gup97] used in this article. Throughout this article, we use $V(G)$ and $E(G)$ to denote the _set of vertices_ and _edges_ respectively of a graph G.

Definition 2. (Expression AND-DAG) _An expression AND-DAG for a view, or a query, V is a directed acyclic graph having the base relations (and materialized views) as "sinks" (no outgoing edges) and the node V as a "source" (no incoming edges). If a node/view u has outgoing edges to nodes $v_1, v_2, \ldots, v_k$, then u can be computed from all of the views $v_1, v_2, \ldots, v_k$ and this dependence is indicated by drawing a semicircle, called an AND arc, through the edges $(u, v_1), (u, v_2), \ldots, (u, v_k)$. Such an AND arc has an operator[1] and a query-cost_

---

[1] The operator associated with the AND arc is actually a k-ary function involving operations like join, union, aggregation etc.

associated with it, which is the cost incurred during the computation of u from
$v_1, v_2, \ldots, v_k$.

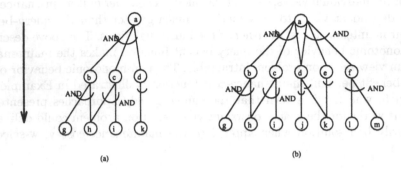

(a)   (b)

Fig. 2. a) An expression AND-DAG b) An expression ANDOR-DAG

Definition 3. (Expression ANDOR-DAG) *An expression ANDOR-DAG for a view or a query V is a directed acyclic graph with V as a source and the base relations as sinks. Each non-sink node v has associated with it one or more AND arcs, where each AND arc binds a subset of the outgoing edges of node v. As in the previous definition, each AND arc has an operator and a cost associated with it. More than one AND arc at a node depicts multiple ways of computing that node.*

Figure 2 shows an example of an expression AND-DAG as well as an expression ANDOR-DAG. In Figure 2 (b), the node a can be computed either from the set of views $\{b, c, d\}$ or $\{d, e, f\}$. The view a can also be computed from the set $\{j, k, f\}$, as d can be computed from j or k and e can be computed from k.

Definition 4. (AND-OR View Graph) *A directed acyclic graph G having the base relations as the sinks is called an AND-OR view graph for the views (or queries) $V_1, V_2, \ldots, V_k$ if for each V_i, there is a subgraph[2] G_i in G that is an expression ANDOR-DAG for V_i. Each node v in an AND-OR view graph has the following parameters associated with it: query-frequency f_v (frequency of the queries on v), update-frequency g_v (frequency of updates on v), and reading-cost R_v (cost incurred in reading the materialized view v). Also, there is a maintenance-cost function UC^3 associated with G, such that for a view v and a*

---

[2] An AND-OR view graph H is called a subgraph of an AND-OR view graph G if $V(H) \subseteq V(G)$, $E(H) \subseteq E(G)$, and each edge e_1 in H is bound with the same set of edges through an AND-arc as it is bound through an AND-arc in G. That is, if $e_1, e_2 \in E(G)$, $e_1 \in E(H)$, and e_1 and e_2 are bound by an AND-arc (which may bind other edges too) in G, then $e_2 \in E(H)$, and e_1 and e_2 are bound with the same AND-arc in H. For example, Figure 2 (a) is a subgraph of Figure 2 (b), but Figure 2 (a) without the edge (c, h) is not.

[3] The function symbol "UC" denotes *update cost*.

set of views M, $UC(v, M)$ gives the cost of maintaining v in presence of the set M of materialized views.

Given a set of queries $Q_1, Q_2, \ldots, Q_k$ to be supported at a warehouse, [Gup97] shows how to construct an AND-OR view graph for the queries.

Definition 5. (Evaluation Cost) *The evaluation cost of an AND-DAG H embedded in an AND-OR view graph G is the sum of the costs associated with the AND arcs in H, plus the sum of the reading costs associated with the sinks/leaves of H.*

Definition 6. (OR View Graphs) *An OR view graph is a special case of an AND-OR view graph, where each AND-arc binds exactly one edge. Hence, in OR view graphs, we omit drawing AND arcs and label the edges, rather than the AND arcs, with query-costs. Also, in OR view graphs, instead of the maintenance cost function UC for the graph, there is a maintenance-cost value associated with each edge (u, v), which is the maintenance cost incurred in maintaining u using the materialized view v. Figure 3 shows an example of an OR view graph $\mathcal{G}$.*

4   The Maintenance-Cost View-Selection Problem

In this section, we present a formal definition of the maintenance-cost view-selection problem which is to select a set of views in order to minimize the total query response time under a given maintenance-cost constraint.

Given an AND-OR view graph G and a quantity S (available maintenance time), the *maintenance-cost view-selection problem* is to select a set of views M, a subset of the nodes in G, that minimizes the total query response time such that the total maintenance time of the set M is less than S.

More formally, let $Q(v, M)$ denote the cost of answering a query v (also a node of G) in the presence of a set M of materialized views. As defined before, $UC(v, M)$ is the cost of maintaining a materialized view v in presence of a set M of materialized views. Given an AND-OR view graph G and a quantity S, the maintenance-cost view-selection problem is to select a set of views/nodes M, that minimizes $\tau(G, M)$, where

$$\tau(G, M) = \sum_{v \in V(G)} f_v Q(v, M),$$

under the constraint that $U(M) \leq S$, where $U(M)$, the *total maintenance time*, is defined as

$$U(M) = \sum_{v \in M} g_v UC(v, M).$$

The view-selection problem under a disk-space constraint can be easily shown to be NP-hard, as there is a straightforward reduction [Gup97] from the **minimum set cover** problem. Thus, the maintenance-cost view-selection problem, which is a more general problem as discussed in Section 2, is trivially NP-hard.

Computing Q(v,M) The cost of answering a query v in presence of M, $Q(v, M)$, in an AND-OR view graph G is actually the evaluation cost of the cheapest AND-DAG H_v for v, such that H_v is a subgraph of G and the sinks of H_v belong to the set $M \cup L$, where L is the set of sinks in G. Here, without loss of generality, we have assumed that the nodes in L, the set of sinks in G, are always available for computation as they represent the base tables at the source(s). Thus, $Q(v, \phi)$ is the cost of answering a query on v directly from the source(s). For the special case of OR view graphs, $Q(v, M)$ is the minimum query-length of a path from v to some $u \in (M \cup L)$, where the *query-length* of a path from v to u is defined as R_u, the reading cost of u, plus the sum of the query-costs associated with the edges on the path.

Computing UC(v,M) in OR view Graphs The quantity $UC(v, M)$, as defined earlier, denotes the maintenance cost of a view v with respect to a selected set of materialized views M, i.e., in presence of the set $M \cup L$. As before, we assume that the set L of base relations in G is always available. In general AND-OR view graphs, the function UC, which depends upon the maintenance cost model being used, is associated with the graph. However, for the special case of OR view graphs, $UC(v, M)$ is computed from the maintenance costs associated with the edges in the graph as follows. The quantity $UC(v, M)$ is defined as the minimum maintenance-length of a path from v to some $u \in (M \cup L) - \{v\}$, where the *maintenance-length* of a path is defined as the sum of the maintenance-costs associated with the edges on the path.[4] The above characterization of $UC(v, M)$ in OR view graphs is without any loss of generality of a maintenance-cost model, because in OR view graphs a view u uses at most one view to help maintain itself.

In the following example, we illustrate the above definitions of Q and UC on OR view graphs.

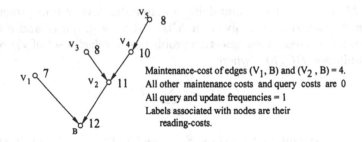

Fig. 3. G: An OR view graph

Example 1. Consider the OR view graph G of Figure 3. In the given OR view graph G, the maintenance-costs and query-costs associated with each edge is

---

[4] Note that the maintenance-length doesn't include the reading cost of the destination as in the query-length of a path.

zero, except for the maintenance-cost of 4 associated with the edges (V_1, B) and (V_2, B). Also, all query and update frequencies are uniformly 1. The label associated with each of the nodes in $\mathcal{G}$ is the reading-cost of the node. Also, the set of sinks $L = \{B\}$.

In the OR view graph $\mathcal{G}$, $Q(V_i, \phi) = 12$ for all $i \leq 5$, because as the query-costs are all zero, the minimum query-length of a path from V_i to B is just the reading-cost of B. Note that $Q(B, \phi) = 12$. Also, as the minimum maintenance-length of a path from a view V_i to B is 4, $UC(V_i, \phi) = 4$ for all $i \leq 5$.

Knapsack Effect We simplify the view-selection problem as in prior discussions ([HRU96,GHRU97,Gup97]) by allowing that a solution may consume "slightly" more than the given amount of constraint. This assumption is made to ignore the **knapsack** component of the view-selection problem. However, when proving performance guarantee of a given algorithm, we compare the solution delivered by the algorithm with an optimal solution that consumes the same amount of resource as that consumed by the delivered solution.

5   Inverted-Tree Greedy Algorithm

In this section, we present a competitive greedy algorithm called the *Inverted-Tree Greedy Algorithm* which delivers a near-optimal solution for the maintenance-cost view-selection problem in OR view graphs.

In the context of view-selection problem, a greedy algorithm was originally proposed in [HRU96] for selection of views in data cubes under a disk-space constraint. Gupta in [Gup97] generalized the results to some special cases of AND-OR view graphs, but still for the constraint of disk space. The greedy algorithms proposed in the context of view-selection work in stages. At each stage, the algorithm picks the "most beneficial" view. The algorithm continues to pick views until the set of selected views take up the given resource constraint. One of the key notions required in designing a greedy algorithm for selection of views is the notion of the "most beneficial" view.

In the greedy heuristics proposed earlier ([HRU96,GHRU97,Gup97]) for selection of views to materialize under a space constraint, views are selected in order of their "query benefits" per unit space consumed. We now define a similar notion of benefit for the maintenance-cost view-selection problem addressed in this article.

Most Beneficial View

Consider an OR view graph G. At a stage, when a set of views M has already been selected for materialization, the *query benefit* $B(C, M)$ associated with a set of views C with respect to M is defined as $\tau(G, M) - \tau(G, M \cup C)$. We define the *effective maintenance-cost* $EU(C, M)$ of C with respect to M as $U(M \cup C) - U(M)$.[5] Based on these two notions, we define the view that has

---

[5] The effective maintenance-cost may be negative. The results in this article hold nevertheless.

the most query-benefit per unit effective maintenance-cost with respect to M as the *most beneficial view* for greedy selection at the stage when the set M has already been selected for materialization.

We illustrate through an example that a *simple greedy* algorithm, that at each stage selects the most beneficial view, as defined above, could deliver an arbitrarily bad solution.

Example 2. Consider the OR view graph $\mathcal{G}$ shown in Figure 3. We assume that the base relation B is materialized and we consider the case when the maintenance-cost constraint is 4 units.

We first compute the query benefit of V_1 at the initial stage when only the base relation B is available (materialized). Recall from Example 1 that $Q(V_i, \phi) = 12$ for all $i \leq 5$ and $Q(B, \phi) = 12$. Thus, $\tau(\mathcal{G}, \phi) = 12 \times 6 = 72$, as all the query frequencies are 1. Also, $Q(V_1, \{V_1\}) = 7$, as the reading-cost of V_1 is 7, $Q(V_i, \{V_1\}) = 12$ for $i = 2, 3, 4, 5$, and $Q(B, \{V_1\}) = 12$. Thus, $\tau(G, \{V_1\}) = 12 \times 5 + 7 = 67$ and thus, the initial query benefit of V_1 is $72 - 67 = 5$. Similarly, the initial query benefits of each of the views V_2, V_3, V_4, and V_5 can be computed to be 4.

Also, $U(\{V_i\}) = UC(V_i, \{V_i\}) = 4$ as the minimum maintenance-length of a path from any V_i to B is 4. Thus, the solution returned by the simple greedy algorithm, that picks the most beneficial view, as defined above, at each stage, is $\{V_1\}$.

It is easy to see that the optimal solution is $\{V_2, V_3, V_4, V_5\}$ with a query benefit of 11 and a total maintenance time of 4. To demonstrate the **non-monotonic** behavior of the benefit function, observe that the query-benefits per unit maintenance-cost of sets $\{V_2\}, \{V_3\}, \{V_2, V_3\}$ are 1, 1, and 7/4 respectively. This non-monotonic behavior is the reason why the simple greedy algorithm that selects views on the basis of their query-benefits per unit maintenance-cost can deliver an arbitrarily bad solution. Figure 4 illustrates through an extended example that the optimal solution can be made to have an arbitrarily high query benefit, while keeping the simple greedy solution unchanged.

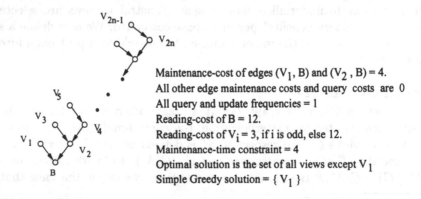

Maintenance-cost of edges (V_1, B) and $(V_2, B) = 4$.
All other edge maintenance costs and query costs are 0
All query and update frequencies = 1
Reading-cost of $B = 12$.
Reading-cost of $V_i = 3$, if i is odd, else 12.
Maintenance-time constraint = 4
Optimal solution is the set of all views except V_1
Simple Greedy solution = $\{ V_1 \}$

Fig. 4. An OR view graph, $\mathcal{H}$, for which simple greedy performs arbitrarily bad

Note that the nodes in the OR view graphs $\mathcal{G}$ and $\mathcal{H}$, presented in Figure 3 and Figure 4 respectively, can be easily mapped into **real queries** involving aggregations over the base data B. The query-costs associated with the edges in $\mathcal{G}$ and $\mathcal{H}$ depict the *linear cost model*, where the cost of answering a query on v using its descendant u is directly proportional to the size of the view u, which in our model of OR view graphs is represented by the reading-cost of u. Notice that the minimum query-length of a path from u to v in $\mathcal{G}$ or $\mathcal{H}$ is R_v, the reading-cost of v. As zero maintenance-costs in the OR view graphs $\mathcal{G}$ and $\mathcal{H}$ can be replaced by extremely small quantities, the OR view graphs $\mathcal{G}$ and $\mathcal{H}$ depict the plausible scenario when the cost of maintaining a view u from a materialized view v be negligible in comparison to the maintenance cost incurred in maintaining a view u directly from the base data B.

Definition 7. (Inverted Tree Set) *A set of nodes R is defined to be an inverted tree set in a directed graph G if there is a subgraph (not necessarily induced) T_R in the transitive closure of G such that the set of vertices of T_R is R, and the inverse graph[6] of T_R is a tree.[7]*
    In the OR view graph $\mathcal{G}$ of Figure 3, any subset of $\{V_2, V_3, V_4, V_5\}$ that includes V_2 forms an inverted tree set. The T_R graph corresponding to the inverted tree set $R = \{V_2, V_3, V_5\}$ has the edges (V_2, V_5) and (V_2, V_3) only.

The motivation for the inverted tree set comes from the following observation, which we prove in Lemma 1. In an OR view graph, an arbitrary set O (in particular an optimal solution O), can be partitioned into inverted tree sets such that the effective maintenance-cost of O with respect to an already materialized set M is greater than the sum of effective-costs of inverted tree sets with respect to M.
    Based on the notion of an inverted tree set, we develop a greedy heuristic called *Inverted-tree Greedy Algorithm* which, at each stage, considers all inverted tree sets in the given view graph and selects the inverted tree set that has the most query-benefit per unit effective maintenance-cost.

Algorithm 1   Inverted-Tree Greedy Algorithm

Given: An OR view graph (G), and a total view maintenance time constraint S
BEGIN
    $M = \phi$; $B_C = 0$;
    repeat
        for each inverted tree set of views T in G such that $T \cap M = \phi$
            if $(EU(T, M) \leq S)$ **and** $(B(T, M)/EU(T, M) > B_C)$
                $B_C = B(T, M)/EU(T, M)$;
                $C = T$;
            endif
        endfor

---

[6] The inverse of a directed graph is the graph with its edges reversed.
[7] A tree is a *connected* graph in which each vertex has exactly one incoming edge.

$M = M \cup C$;
until ($U(M) \geq S$);
return M;
END.   ◇

We prove in Theorem 1 that the Inverted-tree greedy algorithm is guaranteed to deliver a near-optimal solution. In Section 7, we present experimental results that indicate that in practice, the Inverted-tree greedy algorithm almost always returns an optimal solution. We now define a notion of update graphs which is used to prove Lemma 1.

Definition 8. (Update Graph) *Given an OR view graph G and a set of nodes/views O in G. An update graph of O in G is denoted by U_O^G and is a subgraph of G such that $V(U_O^G) = O$, and $E(U_O^G) = \{(v, u) \mid u, v \in O$ and $v(\in O)$ is such that $UC(u, \{v\}) \leq UC(u, \{w\})$ for all $w \in O\}$. We drop the superscript G of U_O^G, whenever evident from context.*

It is easy to see that an update graph is an embedded forest in G. An update graph of O is useful in determining the flow of changes when maintaining the set of views O. An edge (v, u) in an update graph U_O signifies that the view u uses the view v (or its delta tables) to incrementally maintain itself, when the set O is materialized. Figure 5 shows the update graph of $\{V_1, V_2, V_5\}$ in the OR view graph $\mathcal{G}$ of our running example in Figure 3.

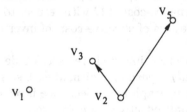

Fig. 5. The update-graph for $\{V_1, V_2, V_3, V_5\}$ in G

Lemma 1 *For a given set of views M, a set of views O in an OR view graph G can be partitioned into inverted tree sets $O_1, O_2, \ldots, O_m$, such that $\sum_{i=1}^{m} EU(O_i, M) \leq EU(O, M)$.*

Proof. Consider the update graph U_O of O in G. By definition, U_O is a forest consisting of m trees, say, $U_1, \ldots, U_m$ for some $m \leq |O|$. Let, $O_i = V(U_i)$, for $i \leq m$.

An edge (y, x) in the update graph U_O implies presence of an edge (x, y) in the transitive closure of G. Thus, an embedded tree U_i in the update graph U_O is an embedded tree in the transitive closure of the inverse graph of G. Hence, the set of vertices O_i is an inverted tree set in G.

For a set of views C, we use $UC(C, M)$ to denote the maintenance cost of the set C w.r.t. M, i.e., $UC(C, M) = \sum_{v \in C} g_v UC(v, M \cup C)$, where $UC(v, M)$ for a view v is as defined in Section 3. Now, the effective maintenance-cost of a set O_i with respect to a set M can be written as $EU(O_i, M) = (UC(O_i, M) + UC(M, O_i)) - U(M) = UC(O_i, M) - (U(M) - UC(M, O_i)) = UC(O_i, M) - Rd(M, O_i)$, where $Rd(M, C)$ is used to denote the reduction in the maintenance time of M due to the set of views C, i.e., $Rd(M, C) = U(M) - UC(M, C)$.

As, no view in a set O_i uses a view in a different set O_j for its maintenance, $UC(O, M) = \sum_{i=1}^{m} UC(O_i, M)$. Also, the reduction in the maintenance cost of M due to the set O is less than the sum of the reductions due to the sets $O_1, \ldots, O_m$, i.e., $Rd(M, O) \leq \sum_{i=1}^{m} Rd(M, O_i)$.

Therefore, as $EU(O, M) = UC(O, M) - Rd(M, O)$, we have $EU(O, M) \geq \sum_{i=1}^{m} EU(O_i, M)$.   □

Theorem 1 *Given an OR view graph G and a total maintenance-time constraint S. The Inverted-tree greedy algorithm (Algorithm 1) returns a solution M such that $U(M) \leq 2S$ and M has a query benefit of at least $(1 - 1/e) = 63\%$ of that of an optimal solution that has a maintenance cost of at most $U(M)$, under the assumption that the optimal solution doesn't have an inverted tree set O_i such that $U(O_i) > S$.*   ∎

The simplifying assumption made in the above algorithm is almost always true, because $U(M)$ is not expected to be much higher than S. The following theorem proves a similar performance guarantee on the solution returned by the Inverted-tree greedy algorithm without the assumption used in Theorem 1.

Theorem 2 *Given an OR view graph G and a total maintenance-time constraint S. The Inverted-tree greedy algorithm (Algorithm 1) returns a solution M such that $U(M) \leq 2S$ and $B(M, \phi)/U(M) \geq 0.5 B(O, \phi)/S$, where O is an optimal solution such that $U(O) <= S$.*   ∎

Dependence of Query and Update Frequencies Note that we have not made any assumptions about the independence of query frequencies and update frequencies of views. In fact, the query frequency of a view may decrease with the materialization of other views. It can be shown that the above performance guarantees hold even when the query frequency of a view decreases with the materialization of other views.

Time Complexity Let G be an OR view graph of size n and A_v be the number of ancestors of a node $v \in V(G)$. The number of inverted tree sets in G that are formed by a node $v \in V(G)$ as its root is 2^{A_v}, because any set of ancestors of v (which become a set of descendants in the inverse graph) form an inverted tree with v and any inverted tree set that has v as its root is formed from v and a subset of its ancestors. Therefore, the total number of inverted tree sets in an OR view graph G and also, the total time complexity of a stage of the Inverted-tree greedy algorithm is $\sum_{v \in V(G)} (2^{A_v})$, which is in the worst case exponential in n.

We note that for the special case of an OR view graph being a *balanced binary tree*, each stage of the Inverted-tree greedy algorithm runs in polynomial time $O(n^2)$, where n is the number of nodes in the graph. The number of inverted tree sets, $T(h)$, in a general balanced tree of height h can also be computed using the following recursion: $T(h) = ((2r)^h - 1)/(r-1) = ((n+1)^2 - 1)/(r-1) = O(n^2/r)$, where $r > 1$ is the branching factor of the tree.

As discussed in Section 7, our experiments show that the Inverted-tree greedy approach takes substantially less time than the A^* algorithm presented in the next section, especially for sparse graphs. Also, the space requirements of the Inverted-tree greedy algorithm is polynomial in the size of graph while that of the A^* heuristic is exponential in the size of the input graph.

6 A^* Heuristic

In this section, we present an A^* heuristic that, given an AND-OR view graph and a quantity S, deliver a set of views M that has an optimal query response time such that the total maintenance cost of M is less than S. Recollect that an A^* algorithm [Nil80] searches for an optimal solution in a search graph where each node represents a candidate solution. Roussopoulos in [Rou82] also demonstrated the use of A^* heuristics for selection of indexes in relational databases.

Let G be an AND-OR view graph instance and S be the total maintenance-time constraint. We first number the set of views (nodes) N of the graph in an inverse topological order $<v_1, v_2, \ldots, v_n>$ so that all the edges (v_i, v_j) in G are such that $i > j$. We use this order of views to define a binary tree T_G of candidate feasible solutions, which is the search tree used by the A^* algorithm to search for an optimal solution. Each node x in T_G has a label $<N_x, M_x>$, where $N_x = \{v_1, v_2, \ldots, v_d\}$ is a set of views that have been considered for possible materialization at x and $M_x (\subset N_x)$, is the set of views chosen for materialization at x. The root of T_G has the label $<\phi, \phi>$, signifying an empty solution. Each node x with a label $<N_x, M_x>$ has two successor nodes $l(x)$ and $r(x)$ with the labels $<N_x \cup \{v_{d+1}\}, M_x>$ and $<N_x \cup \{v_{d+1}\}, M_x \cup \{v_{d+1}\}>$ respectively. The successor $r(x)$ exists only if $M_x \cup \{v_{d+1}\}$ has a total maintenance cost of less than S, the given cost constraint.

We define two functions[8] $g : V(T_G) \mapsto \mathcal{R}$, and $h : V(T_G) \mapsto \mathcal{R}$, where $\mathcal{R}$ is the set of real numbers. For a node $x \in V(T_G)$, with a label $<N_x, M_x>$, the value $g(x)$ is the total query cost of the queries on N_x using the selected views in M_x. That is,

$$g_x = \sum_{v_i \in N_x} f_{v_i} Q(v_i, M_x).$$

The number $h(x)$ is an estimated lower bound on $h^*(x)$ which is defined as the remaining query cost of an optimal solution corresponding to some descendant of x in T_G. In other words, $h(x)$ is a lower bound estimation of $h^*(x) = \tau(G, M_y) -$

---

[8] The function g is not to be confused with the update frequency g_v associated with each view in a view graph.

$g(x)$, where M_y is an optimal solution corresponding to some descendant y of x in T_G.

Algorithm 2   A* Heuristic

Input: G, an AND-OR view graph, and S, the maintenance-cost constraint.
Output: A set of views M selected for materialization.
BEGIN
    Create a tree T_G having just the root A. The label associated with A is
      $<\phi, \phi>$.
    Create a priority queue (heap) $L = <A>$.
    repeat
      Remove x from L, where x has the lowest $g(x) + h(x)$ value in L.
      Let the label of x be $<N_x, M_x>$, where $N_x = \{v_1, v_2, \ldots, v_d\}$ for some
        $d \leq n$.
      if $(d = n)$ **RETURN** M_x.
      Add a successor of x, $l(x)$, with a label $<N_x \cup \{v_{d+1}\}, M_x>$ to the list L.
      if $(U(M_x) < S)$
        Add to L a successor of x, $r(x)$, with a label $<N_x \cup \{v_{d+1}\}$,
          $M_x \cup \{v_{d+1}\}>$.
    until (L is empty);
    RETURN NULL;
END.   ◇

We now show how to compute the value $h(x)$ for a node x in the binary tree T_G. Let $N = V(G)$ be the set of all views/nodes in G. Given a node x, we need to estimate the optimal query cost of the remaining queries in $N - N_x$. Let $s(v) = g_v UC(v, N)$, the minimum maintenance time a view v can have in presence of other materialized views. Also, if a node $v \in V(G)$ is not selected for materialization, queries on v have a minimum query cost of $p(v) = f_v Q(v, N - \{v\})$. Hence, for each view v that is not selected in an optimal solution M_y containing M_x, the remaining query cost accrues by at least $p(v)$. Thus, we fill up the remaining maintenance time available $S - U(M_x)$ with views in $N - N_x$ in the order of their $p(v)/s(v)$ values. The sum of the $f_v Q(v, N - \{v\})$ values for the views left out will give a lower bound on $h^*(x)$, the optimal query cost of the remaining queries. In order to nullify the knapsack effect as mentioned in Section 4, we start with leaving out the view w that has the highest $f_v Q(v, N - \{v\})$ value.

Theorem 3 *The A* algorithm (Algorithm 2) returns an optimal solution.* ∎

The above theorem guarantees the correctness of A^* heuristic. Better lower bounds yield A^* heuristics that will have better performances in terms of the number of nodes explored in T_G. In the worst case, the A^* heuristic can take exponential time in the number of nodes in the view graph. There is no better bounds known for the A^* algorithm in terms of the function $h(x)$ used.

7   Experimental Results

We ran some experiments to determine the quality of the solution delivered and the time taken in practice by the Inverted-tree Greedy algorithm for OR view graphs that arise in practice. We implemented both the algorithms, Inverted-tree Greedy and A^* heuristic, and ran them on random instances of OR view graphs that are balanced trees and directed acyclic OR view graphs with varying edge-densities, and random query and update frequencies. We used a linear cost model [HRU96] for the purposes of our experiments.

We made the following observations. The Inverted-tree Greedy Algorithm (Algorithm 1) returned an optimal solution for almost all (96%) view graph instances. In other cases, the solution returned by the Inverted-tree greedy algorithm had a query benefit of around 95% of the optimal query benefit. For balanced trees and sparse graphs having edge density less than 40%, the Inverted-tree greedy took substantially less time (a factor of 10 to 500) than that taken by the A^* heuristic. With the increase in the edge density, the benefit of Inverted-tree greedy over the A^* heuristic reduces and for very dense graphs, A^* may actually perform marginally better than the Inverted-tree greedy. One should observe that OR view graphs that are expected to arise in practice would be very sparse. For example, the the OR view graph corresponding to a data cube having n dimensions has $\sum_{i=1}^{n}(\binom{n}{i}2^i) = 3^n$ edges and 2^n vertices. Thus, the edge density is approximately $(0.75)^n$, for a given n.

The comparison of the times taken by the Inverted-tree greedy and the A^* heuristic is briefly presented in Figure 6. In all the plots shown in Figures 6, the different view graph instances of the maintenance-cost view-selection problem are plotted on the x-axis. A view graph instance G is represented in terms of N, the number of nodes in G, and S, the maintenance-time constraint. The view graph instances are arranged in the lexicographic order of (N, S), i.e., all the view graphs with smallest N are listed first, in order of their constraint S values. In all the graph plots, the number N varied from 10 to 25, and S varied from the time required to maintain the smallest view to the time required to maintain all views in a given view graph.

8   Conclusions

One of the most important decisions in design of a data warehouse is the selection of views to materialize. The view-selection problem in a data warehouse is to select a set of views to materialize so as to optimize the total query response time, under some resource constraint such as total space and/or the total maintenance time of the materialized views. All the prior work done on the view selection problem considered only a disk-space constraint. In practice, the real constraining factor is the total maintenance time. Hence, in this article, we have considered the maintenance-cost view-selection problem where the constraint is of total maintenance time.

As the maintenance-cost view-selection problem is intractable, we designed an approximation algorithms for the special case of OR view graphs. The OR view graphs arise in many practical applications like data cubes, and other OLAP applications. For the general case of AND-OR view graphs, we designed an A^* heuristic that delivers an optimal solution.

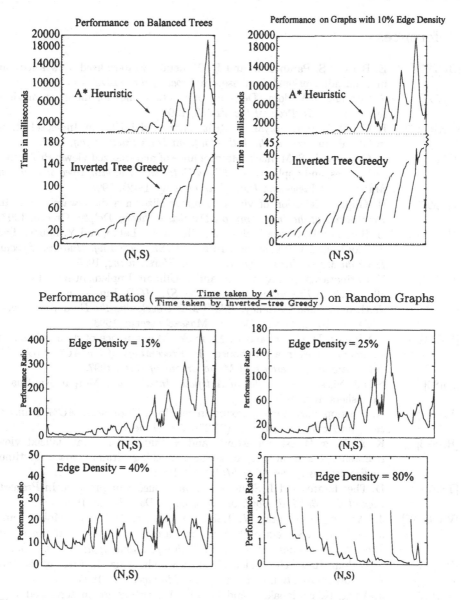

Fig. 6. Experimental Results. The x-axis shows the view graph instances in lexicographic order of their (N, S) values, where N is the number of nodes in the graph and S is the maintenance-time constraint.

Our preliminary experiment results are very encouraging for the Inverted-tree Greedy algorithm. Also, the space requirement of the Inverted-tree greedy heuristic is polynomial in size of the graph, while that of the A^* heuristic grows exponentially in the size of the graph.

References

[BPT97]   E. Baralis, S. Paraboschi, and E. Teniente. Materialized view selection in a multidimensional database. In *Proc. of the VLDB*, 1997.

[CW91]   S. Ceri and J. Widom. Deriving production rules for incremental view maintenance. In *Proc. of the VLDB*, 1991.

[GHRU97]   H. Gupta, V. Harinarayan, A. Rajaraman, and J. Ullman. Index selection in OLAP. In *Proc. of the Intl. Conf. on Data Engineering*, 1997.

[GM95]   A. Gupta and I.S. Mumick. Maintenance of materialized views: Problems, techniques, and applications. *IEEE Data Eng. Bulletin, Special Issue on Materialized Views and Data Warehousing*, 18(2), 1995.

[Gup97]   H. Gupta. Selection of views to materialize in a data warehouse. In *Proceedings of the Intl. Conf. on Database Theory*, Delphi, Greece, 1997.

[HGMW+95]   J. Hammer, H. Garcia-Molina, J. Widom, W. Labio, and Y. Zhuge. The Stanford Data Warehousing Project. *IEEE Data Eng. Bulletin, Special Issue on Materialized Views and Data Warehousing*, 1995.

[HRU96]   V. Harinarayan, A. Rajaraman, and J. Ullman. Implementing data cubes efficiently. In *Proceedings of the ACM SIGMOD*, June 1996.

[IK93]   W.H. Inmon and C. Kelley. *Rdb/VMS: Developing the Data Warehouse*. QED Publishing Group, Boston, Massachussetts, 1993.

[MQM97]   I. Mumick, D. Quass, and B. Mumick. Maintenance of data cubes and summary tables in a warehouse. In *Proceedings of the ACM SIGMOD International Conference of Management of Data*, 1997.

[Nil80]   Nils J. Nilsson. *Principles of Artificial Intelligence*. Morgan Kaufmann Publishers, Inc., 1980.

[Rou82]   N. Roussopoulos. View indexing in relational databases. *ACM Transactions on Database Systems*, 7(2):258–290, June 1982.

[RSS96]   K. A. Ross, Divesh Srivastava, and S. Sudarshan. Materialized view maintenance and integrity constraint checking: Trading space for time. In *Proceedings of the ACM SIGMOD*, 1996.

[TS97]   D. Theodoratos and T. Sellis. Data warehouse configuration. In *Proceedings of the 23rd Intl. Conf. on Very Large Data Bases*, 1997.

[WGL+96]   J. Wiener, H. Gupta, W. Labio, Y. Zhuge, H. Garcia-Molina, and J. Widom. A system prototype for warehouse view maintenance. In *Workshop on Materialized Views: Techniques and Applications*, 1996.

[Wid95]   J. Widom. Research problems in data warehousing. In *Proc. of the Intl. Conf. on Information and Knowledge Management*, 1995.

[YKL97]   J. Yang, K. Karlapalem, and Q. Li. Algorithms for materialized view design in data warehousing environment. In *Proc. of the VLDB*, 1997.

[ZGMHW95]   Y. Zhuge, H. Garcia-Molina, J. Hammer, and J. Widom. View maintenance in a warehousing environment. In *Proc. of the ACM SIGMOD International Conference on Management of Data*, 1995.

The Data Warehouse of Newsgroups

Himanshu Gupta[1]* and Divesh Srivastava[2]

[1] Stanford University, Stanford, CA 94305, USA,
hgupta@db.stanford.edu
[2] AT&T Labs – Research, Florham Park, NJ 07932,
divesh@research.att.com

Abstract. Electronic newsgroups are one of the primary means for the dissemination, exchange and sharing of information. We argue that the current newsgroup model is unsatisfactory, especially when posted articles are relevant to multiple newsgroups. We demonstrate that considerable additional flexibility can be achieved by managing newsgroups in a data warehouse, where each article is a tuple of attribute-value pairs, and each newsgroup is a view on the set of all posted articles. Supporting this paradigm for a large set of newsgroups makes it imperative to efficiently support a very large number of views: this is the key difference between newsgroup data warehouses and conventional data warehouses. We identify two complementary problems concerning the design of such a newsgroup data warehouse. An important design decision that the system needs to make is which newsgroup views to eagerly maintain (i.e., materialize). We demonstrate the intractability of the general newsgroup-selection problem, consider various natural special cases of the problem, and present efficient exact/approximation algorithms and complexity hardness results for them. A second important task concerns the efficient incremental maintenance of the eagerly maintained newsgroups. The newsgroup-maintenance problem for our model of newsgroup definitions is a more general version of the classical point-location problem, and we design an I/O and CPU efficient algorithm for this problem.

1 Introduction

Electronic newsgroups/discussion groups are one of the primary means for the dissemination, exchange and sharing of information on a wide variety of topics. For example, comp.databases and comp.lang.c, typically contain articles relevant to computers and computation, while soc.culture.indian and soc.culture.mexican typically contain articles relevant to some world cultures.

In the current model of posting articles to electronic newsgroups, it is the responsibility of the *author* of an article to determine the newsgroups that are relevant to the article. Placing such a burden on the author of the article has many undesirable consequences, especially since there are thousands of newsgroups currently, and the author of an article may not always know all the relevant newsgroups: (a) articles are often cross-posted to irrelevant newsgroups,

---

* Supported by NSF grant IRI-96-31952.

resulting in flame wars, and (b) articles that are obviously relevant to multiple newsgroups may not be posted to all of them, missing potentially relevant readers. This unsatisfactory situation will only get worse as the number of newsgroups increase.

In this paper, we present a novel model for managing electronic newsgroups that does not suffer from the above mentioned problems; we refer to it as the *Data Warehouse of Newsgroups* (DaWN) model. In the DaWN model, the author of an article "posts" the article to the newsgroup management system, not to any specific newsgroups. Each newsgroup is defined as a view over the set of *all* articles posted to the newsgroup management system, and it is the responsibility of the system to determine all the newsgroups into which a new article must be inserted. Our *newsgroup views* allow the flexible combination of selection conditions on structured attributes of the article, such as its author and posting date, along with selection conditions on unstructured attributes of the article, such as its subject and body. For example, the newsgroup `soc.culture.indian` may be defined to contain all articles posted in the current year, each of whose bodies is similar to at least one of a set of, say, 100 articles that have been manually determined to be representative of this newsgroup. Similarly, the definition of the newsgroup `att.forsale` may require that the organization of the article's author be AT&T. The ability to automatically classify posted articles into newsgroups based on conditions satisfied by multiple structured and unstructured attributes of the article permits very flexible newsgroup definitions. Clearly, the DaWN model has the potential of bringing together the author and targeted readers of an article.

In this paper, we identify and address two complementary problems that arise when newsgroups are defined as views in the DaWN model.

Newsgroup-selection problem: Given a large set of newsgroups, which of these newsgroups should be eagerly maintained (materialized), and which of them should be lazily maintained, in order to conserve system resources while allowing efficient access to the various newsgroups?

We demonstrate that the general *newsgroup-selection problem* is intractable, which motivates a study of special cases that arise in practice. We consider many natural special cases, based on the DaWN model of articles and newsgroups, and present efficient exact/approximation algorithms for them.

Newsgroup-maintenance problem: Given a new article, in which of the possibly large number of materialized newsgroups must the article be inserted?

We expect any article to be contained in very few newsgroups, while the number of newsgroups supported by the data warehouse may be very large. Thus, an algorithm that iteratively checks whether the new article needs to be inserted in each of the newsgroups would be extremely inefficient. We devise an I/O and CPU efficient solution for the *newsgroup-maintenance problem*.

Both the above problems arise in any data warehouse that supports materialized views. What distinguishes DaWN from conventional data warehouses are the following characteristics: (i) the extremely large number of views defined in DaWN, and (ii) the simple form of individual newsgroup views as selections over the set of all posted articles. While we focus on the data warehouse of newsgroups in this paper, our techniques and solutions are more generally applicable to any data warehouse or multi-dimensional database with the above characteristics, such as data warehouses of scientific articles, legal resolutions, and corporate e-mail repositories.

The rest of this paper is organized as follows. In the next section, we briefly describe the DaWN model. In Section 3, we consider the problem of efficiently maintaining materialized newsgroup views, when new articles arrive into the newsgroup system. In Section 4, we discuss the problem of selecting an appropriate set of newsgroup views to eagerly maintain. We present related work for each of the two problems in their respective sections. We end with concluding remarks in Section 5.

2   The DaWN Model

A data warehouse is a large repository of information available for querying and analysis [IK93,HGMW+95,Wid95]. It consists of a set of materialized views over information sources of interest, using which a family of (anticipated) user queries can be answered efficiently. In this paper, we show the advantages of modeling the newsgroup management system as a data warehouse.

2.1   Article Store: The Information Source

A newsgroup article contains information of two types: *header fields*, and a *body*. The header fields of an article are each identified by a keyword and a value. In contrast, the body is viewed as unstructured text. For the purpose of this paper, we model articles as having d attributes, $A_1, A_2, \ldots, A_d$. For header fields of the article, the keyword is the name of the attribute; the body of the article can be treated as the value of an attribute called Body. The various examples in this paper use the commonly specified attributes From, Organization, Date, Subject, and Body of newsgroup articles, with their obvious meanings.

The *article store* is the set of all posted articles. To facilitate answering queries over the article store, various indexes can be built over the article attributes. For example, the article store may maintain an inverted index structure [Fal85] on the Body attribute, and a B-tree on the Date attribute. The article store along with the index structures is the *information source* for the data warehouse of newsgroups.

2.2   Newsgroup Views

An *electronic newsgroup* contains a set of articles. Current day newsgroup management systems support only newsgroups that contain articles that have been explicitly posted to those newsgroups. Here, we focus our attention on news-groups that are defined as *views* over the set of all articles stored in the under-lying article store. The articles in the newsgroups are determined automatically by the newsgroup management system based on the newsgroup definitions, and are *not* explicitly posted to the newsgroups by the authors. Conventional news-groups can also co-exist with such automatically populated newsgroups.

In this paper, we consider newsgroups that are defined as selection views on the article attributes. The *atomic conditions* that are the basis of the newsgroup definitions are of the forms: (a) "attribute *similar-to* typical-article-body *with-threshold* threshold-value", (b) "attribute *contains* value", and (c) "attribute $\{\leq, \geq, =, \neq, <, >\}$ value".

Given an article attribute A_i, an *attribute selection condition* on A_i is an arbitrary boolean expression of atomic conditions on A_i. A *newsgroup-view* defi-nition is a conjunction of attribute selection conditions on the article attributes, i.e., we consider newsgroups V defined using selection conditions of the form

$$\bigwedge_{j \in I} (f_j(A_j))$$

where $I \subseteq \{1, 2, \ldots, d\}$ is known as the *index set* of newsgroup V and $f_j(A_j)$ is an attribute selection condition on attribute A_j. We expect the size of the index set $|I|$ of typical newsgroups, that are defined as views, to be small compared to the total number of article attributes.

For example, the newsgroup att.forsale may be defined as "($\wedge$ (Date ≥ 1 Jan 1998) (Organization = AT&T) (Subject *contains* Sale))". A more inter-esting example defines the newsgroup soc.culture.indian as "($\wedge$ (Date ≥ 1 Jan 1998) ($\vee$ (Body *similar-to* B_1 *with-threshold* T_1) ... (Body *similar-to* B_{100} *with-threshold* T_{100})))", where the various B_i's are the bodies of *typical-articles* that are representative of the newsgroup, and the T_i's are the desired *cosine similarity match* threshold values [SB88]. Both these examples combine the use of conditions on structured and text-valued unstructured attributes.

2.3   The Data Warehouse and Design Decisions

The data warehouse of newsgroups, defined over the article store, allows users to request the set of all articles in any specific newsgroup; this request is referred to as a *newsgroup query* and is the only type of user query supported by the data warehouse. The newsgroup management system may decide to eagerly maintain (materialize) some of the newsgroups; these newsgroups are the materialized views in DaWN, and are kept up to date in response to additions to the article store. Newsgroup queries can be answered using the materialized views stored in the data warehouse and/or the article store. We use the term *newsgroup management system* to refer to the system consisting of the data warehouses and the article store.

Two of the most important decisions in designing DaWN, the data warehouse of newsgroups, are the following: (a) the selection of materialized views to be stored at the warehouse, for a given family of (anticipated) user queries; such a selection is important given limited amount of resources such as storage space and/or total view maintenance time, and (b) the efficient incremental maintenance of the materialized views, for a given family of information source data updates. The warehouse may maintain various indexes for efficient maintenance of the materialized newsgroups. We further discuss the nature and use of these index structures in Section 3.

In the following sections, we address the above two key issues in the design of DaWN, taking into account the special characteristics that distinguish it from conventional data warehouses: (i) the extremely large number of newsgroup views defined in DaWN, and (ii) the simple form of individual newsgroup views as selections over the set of all posted articles.

3   The Newsgroup-Maintenance Problem

In this section, we consider the newsgroup-maintenance problem, i.e., the problem of efficiently updating a large set of materialized newsgroups, in response to new articles being added to the article store. We start with a precise definition of our problem, and present some related work, before describing our I/O and CPU efficient solution for the problem.

3.1   The Problem Definition

We formally define the *newsgroup-maintenance problem* as follows. Let $V_1, \ldots, V_n$ be the large set of materialized newsgroups in the newsgroup system. Given a new article $m = (b_1, b_2, \ldots, b_d)$, we wish to output the subset of newsgroups that are affected by the posting of the article m to the article store, i.e., the set of newsgroups in which m needs to be inserted.

Given the large number of newsgroups in a typical newsgroup data warehouse, the brute force method of sequentially checking each of the newsgroup definitions to determine if the article needs to be inserted into the newsgroup could be very inefficient. The key challenge here is to devise a solution that takes advantage of the specific nature of our problem, wherein the size of the index set of newsgroups is small, compared to the number of attributes of the article.

3.2   Related Work

The work that is most closely related to our problem of newsgroup-maintenance is that on the classical *point-location problem*. The point-location problem is to report all hyper-rectangles from a given set, that contain a given query point. An equivalent problem that has been examined by the database community is that of the predicate matching problem in active databases and forward chaining rule systems [HCKW90]. However, our problem is more general because our problem combines conditions on ordered domains with conditions on unstructured text attributes. Also, each attribute selection condition on an ordered domain may be a general boolean expression of atomic conditions, for example, a *union* of interval ranges.

There has been a considerable amount of work on the point-location problem [EM81,Ede83a,Ede83b,Cha83] on designing optimal *main-memory* algorithms. However, there hasn't been any work reported on designing secondary memory algorithms for the point-location problem, that have optimal worst-case bounds. In contrast, there has been some recent work [KRVV93,RS95,VV96] reported for the dual problem of range-searching. The secondary memory data structures developed for the point-location problem like various R-trees, cell-trees, hB-trees have good average-case behavior for common spatial database problems, but do not have any theoretical worst-case bounds. We refer the reader to [Sam89a,Sam89b] for a survey. We note that *none* of the previously proposed algorithms can take advantage of small index sets of newsgroup views, i.e., all of them treat unspecified selection conditions as intervals covering the entire dimension.

3.3   Independent Search Trees Algorithm

In this subsection, we present our I/O and CPU efficient approach called the *Independent Search Trees Algorithm* for solving the newsgroup-maintenance problem. For ease of understanding, we start with a description of the algorithm for newsgroup definitions where each attribute is an ordered domain, and each selection condition is an atomic condition. Thus, each attribute value is restricted to be in a single interval, i.e., each newsgroup is a hyper-rectangle. Later, we will extend it to handling unstructured text attributes and general boolean expressions in the attribute selection conditions.

Newsgroup-Maintenance of Hyper-Rectangles: Consider n newsgroups $V_1, \ldots, V_n$, where each newsgroup V_i is defined as

$$V_i = \bigwedge_{j \in I_i} (f_{ij})$$

and each f_{ij} is of the form $(A_j \in c_{ij})$ for some interval c_{ij} on the respective ordered domain D_j. The data structure we use consists of d external segment tree structures [RS94] $T_1, T_2, \ldots, T_d$, such that tree T_j stores the intervals $\{c_{ij} \mid j \in I_i, 1 \le i \le n\}$.

We compute the set of affected newsgroups (views) as follows. We keep an array I of size n, where $I[i]$ is initialized to $|I_i|$, the size of the index set of newsgroup V_i. When an article $m = (b_1, b_2, \ldots, b_d)$ arrives, we search for intervals in the external segment trees T_j that contain b_j, for all $1 \le j \le d$. While searching in the segment tree T_j for b_j, when an interval c_{ij} gets hit (which happens when $b_j \in c_{ij}$), the entry $I[i]$ is decremented by 1. If an entry $I[i]$ drops to zero, then the corresponding newsgroup V_i is reported as one of the affected newsgroups. These are precisely the newsgroups in which the article m will have to be inserted.

Handling the "contains" operator: We now extend our Independent Search Trees Algorithm to handle the "contains" operator for unstructured text-valued attributes such as Subject. Thus, the newsgroup definitions may now use the *contains* operator, i.e., f_{ij} can be $(A_j \text{ contains } s_{ij})$ for some string s_{ij} and a text-valued attribute A_j. To incorporate the *contains* operator in our newsgroup definitions, we use *trie* data structures [Fre60] instead of segment trees for text-valued attributes. The question we wish to answer is the following. Given a set of strings $S_j = \{s_{ij} \mid j \in I_i\}$ (from the newsgroup definitions) and a query string b_j (the value of the article attribute A_j), output the set of strings $s_{i_1 j}, s_{i_2 j}, \ldots, s_{i_l j}$ such that b_j *contains* $s_{i_p j}$ for all $p \leq l$. The matching algorithm used in conjunction with the *trie* data structure can be easily modified to answer the above problem. We build a *trie* on the set S_j of data strings. On a query b_j, we search the *trie* data structure for *superstring* matches for each suffix of b_j. The search can be completed in $(|b_j|^2 + l)$ character comparisons, where $|b_j|$ is the size of the query string b_j and l is the number of strings reported. The space requirements of the *trie* data structure is $k|\Sigma|$ characters for storing k strings, where $|\Sigma|$ is the size of the alphabet. Note that the *trie* yields itself to an efficient secondary memory implementation, as it is just a special form of a B-tree.

Handling Selection Conditions on Body *Attribute:* We extend our techniques to general newsgroup definitions that may also use *similar-to with-threshold* predicates on the Body attribute, say A_d. In particular, for a view V_i, we consider

$$f_{id}(A_d) = \bigvee_k (C(A_d, B_{ik}, T_{ik})),$$

where $C(A_d, B_{ik}, T_{ik})$ is used to represent the predicate $(A_d$ *similar-to* B_{ik} *with-threshold* $T_{ik})$. Each B_{ik} here is the body of a typical-article that is representative of the V_i newsgroup.

To handle maintenance of such newsgroup definitions, we build inverted lists $L_1, L_2, \ldots, L_p$, where p is the size of the dictionary (set of *relevant* words). Each typical-article body B_{ik} is represented by a *similarity-vector* $B_{ik} = (w_{ik1}, \ldots, w_{ikp})$, where w_{ikl} is the weight of the lth word in B_{ik}. Let the set of all *distinct* similarity-vectors used in the view definitions be $\mathcal{W}_1, \mathcal{W}_2, \ldots, \mathcal{W}_m$. An inverted list L_l keeps a list of all similarity-vectors $\mathcal{W}_j$'s that have a non-zero weight of the lth word. Also, with each similarity-vector $\mathcal{W}_j$, we keep a list, R_j, of all view definitions that use the similarity-vector $\mathcal{W}_j$ along with the corresponding threshold. In other words, $R_j = \{(i, T_{ik}) | \mathcal{W}_j = B_{ik}\}$, stored as an ordered list in increasing order of the thresholds. We also keep a dot-product integer P_j (initialized to zero).

Let $m = (b_1, b_2, \ldots, b_d)$ be a new article posted to the article store, whose Body attribute value $b_d = (w_{m1}, w_{m2}, \ldots, w_{mp})$ is the word-vector representing the article body. Each b_j for $j < d$ is searched in the external segment tree or trie T_j, as before, with entries in I decremented appropriately. To compute f_{id}, we sequentially scan the inverted list L_l, for each non-zero value w_{ml} in the new article's word-vector b_d. For each $\mathcal{W}_j$ in L_l, we increment the dot-product value P_j associated with $\mathcal{W}_j$ by $(w_{jl} * w_{ml})/|b_d||\mathcal{W}_j|$. After all required inverted lists have been scanned, for each W_j, we scan its list R_j and for each $(i, T_{ik}) \in R_j$, such that $T_{ik} \leq P_j$, we decrement the value of $I[i]$ by 1, making sure that each $I[i]$ is decremented at most once.

Newsgroup-Maintenance of Boolean Expressions: When f_{ij}, the attribute selection condition involving an ordered attribute A_j, is $A_j \notin d_{ij}$ for some interval d_{ij} on domain D_j, we still store d_{ij} in the segment tree T_j. But, whenever d_{ij} is hit (which happens when $b_j \in d_{ij}$), we increase $I[i]$ to d (instead of decrementing by one), guaranteeing that newsgroup V_i is not output. Similarly, we handle f_{ij}'s of the form $\neg(A_j \ contains \ s_{ij})$ or $(\neg(C(A_j, B_{ik}, T_{ik})))$ for an unstructured text-valued attribute A_j. Also, in an entry $I[i]$ of array I, we store the size of *positive index set* of V_i instead of the size of V_i's index set. The positive index set I_i^+ of a view V_i is defined as $\{j \mid (j \in I_i) \wedge (f_{ij} \text{ is either of the form } (A_j \in c_{ij}) \text{ or } (A_j \ contains \ s_{ij}) \text{ or } (C(A_j, B_{ik}, T_{ik})))\}$. Similarly, the *negative index set* I_i^- is defined as $\{j \mid (j \in I_i) \wedge (f_{ij} \text{ is of the form } (A_j \notin d_{ij}) \text{ or } \neg(A_j \ contains \ s_{ij}) \text{ or } \neg(C(A_j, B_{ik}, T_{ik})))\}$.

The generalization to arbitrary boolean expressions for ordered domain attributes is achieved as follows. An arbitrary boolean expression f_{ij} for an arithmetic attribute A_j can be represented as $\bigvee_k (A_j \in c_{ijk})$ or as $\bigwedge_k (A_j \notin d_{ijk})$, for some set of intervals c_{ijk} or d_{ijk} on D_j. A segment tree T_j, corresponding to the attribute A_j, is constructed as including all the intervals c_{ijk} or d_{ijk} and corresponding entries in I are decreased by 1, or increased to d on hits to intervals appropriately. If A_j is an unstructured text-valued attribute, we can easily handle boolean expressions of the type $f_{ij} = (\bigvee_k (A_j \ contains \ s_{ijk}))$ or $f_{ij} = (\bigwedge_k \neg(A_j \ contains \ s_{ijk}))$ for a set of strings s_{ijk}. For the Body attribute A_d, we can handle expressions of the type $f_{id} = \bigvee_k (C(A_d, B_{ik}, T_{ik}))$, or $f_{id} = \bigwedge_k (\neg(C(A_d, B_{ik}, T_{ik})))$. Arbitrary boolean expressions in conjunctive normal form (CNF) for unstructured text attributes using *contains* or *similar-to with-threshold* predicate can also be handled by creating a duplicate attribute for each clause in the CNF boolean expression. We note that $\bigvee_k (C(A_d, B_{ik}, T_{ik}))$ is the only type of boolean expression involving the Body attribute, that we expect in practice.

For general boolean expressions, the definitions of I_i^+ and I_i^- are appropriately extended to $\{j \mid (j \in I_i) \wedge (f_{ij} \text{ is either of the form } \bigvee_k (A_j \in c_{ijk}) \text{ or } \bigvee_k (A_j \ contains \ s_{ijk}) \text{ or } \bigvee_k (C(A_d, B_{ik}, T_{ik})))\}$ and $\{j \mid (j \in I_i) \wedge (f_{ij} \text{ is either of the form } \bigwedge_k (A_j \notin d_{ijk}) \text{ or } \bigwedge_k \neg(A_j \ contains \ s_{ijk}) \text{ or } \bigwedge_k \neg(C(A_d, B_{ik}, T_{ik}))))\}$ respectively.[1]

Handling Unspecified Article Attributes: An article m is inserted into a view V_i based on the values of only those article attributes that belong to V_i's index set I_i. However, an attribute selection condition f_{ij} can be defined to accept or reject an unspecified attribute value. For example, it is reasonable for the selection condition (Organization = "AT&T") to reject articles that have the

---

[1] We assume that $|I_i^+| > 0$ for each i. Else, we will need to keep a list of views with zero $|I_i^+|$ and report them if the entry $I[i] = |I_i^+|$ remains unchanged.

attribute Organization unspecified, while an unspecified attribute value should probably pass the selection condition Organization $\neq$ "AOL".

To handle such cases of unspecified attribute values in articles, we maintain two disjoint integer sets P_j and F_j for each attribute A_j, in addition to its index structure. The *pass* list P_j is defined as $\{i \mid (j \in I_i^+) \land (f_{ij} \text{ accepts unspecified values})\}$. Similarly, *fail* list F_j is defined as $\{i \mid (j \in I_i^-) \land (f_{ij} \text{ rejects unspecified values})\}$. Thus, if an arriving article m has its A_j attribute's value unspecified, we decrement the entry $I[i]$ by one for each $i \in P_j$ and increment $I[i]$ to d for each $i \in F_j$, instead of searching in the index structure of A_j.

CPU Efficient Initialization of Array I: Whenever a new article arrives in the newsgroup management system, we need to initialize *each* entry $I[i]$ of the array I to $|I_i^+|$, the size of the positive index set of V_i. A simple scheme is to explicitly store (in persistent memory) $|I_i^+|$ for each V_i and initialize each of the n entries of I every time a new article arrives. However, since the article is expected to affect only a few newsgroups, initializing all n elements of the array I can be very inefficient. Below, we present an efficient scheme to find the initial values in I, only for potentially relevant newsgroups.

We number the views in such a way that $|I_j^+| \leq |I_k^+|$ for all $1 \leq j < k \leq n$. We define $d - 1$ numbers $t_1, t_2, \ldots, t_{d-1}$, where t_j is such that $|I_{t_j}^+| < |I_{t_j+1}^+|$, i.e., these $d - 1$ numbers define the transition points for the initial values in the array I. If no such t_j exists for some $j < d$, then $t_l = n + 1$ for all $j \leq l < d$. We create a persistent memory array T of size d, where $T[0] = 0$ and $T[i] = t_i$ for $1 \leq i < d$. Since the array T contains only d elements, it is quite small and hence can be maintained in main memory. To find the initial value of $I[i]$, $|I_i^+|$, we find a number x such that $T[x - 1] < i \leq T[x]$ in $O(\log d)$ main-memory time. It is easy to see that $|I_i^+| = x$.

When we have to decrement the value of $I[i]$ for the *first* time, we initialize $I[i]$ to $x - 1$, else we reduce the *current* value of $I[i]$ by 1. How do we find out if $I[i]$ has been decremented before or not? We do this by keeping a bit vector H of size n, where $H[i] = 1$ iff $I[i]$ has been decremented before. Both arrays H and I can reside in main-memory, even when thousands of newsgroups are maintained as materialized views. For each new article that arrives into the newsgroup management system, only the bit vector H needs to be reset to 0, which can be done very efficiently in most systems.

I/O Efficiency: We now analyze the time taken by the above algorithm to output the newsgroups affected, when a new article arrives in the newsgroup management system.

Let B be the I/O block size. We define K_j as the number of intervals in the various newsgroup definitions involving an ordered-domain attribute A_j (equivalently, the number of entries in the segment tree T_j), and m_j as the maximum number of intervals in tree T_j that overlap. Using the optimal external segment tree structure of [RS94], we can perform a search in a segment tree T in $\log_B(p) + 2(t/B)$ number of I/O accesses, where p is the number of entries in

T, and t is the number of intervals output. Let s_j be the number of similarity-vectors that have a non-zero weight in the jth word, where $j \leq p$. Thus, the scan of the jth inverted list L_j takes s_j/B disk accesses. Therefore, the overall query time complexity of the above algorithm is $O(\sum_{j=1}^{d-1} \log_B(K_j) + 2(\sum_{j=1}^{d-1} m_j)/B + (\sum_{j=1}^{p} s_j)/B)$, assuming that there are no conditions involving the *contains* operator. An unspecified value in the attribute A_j of a new article m results in only $(|P_j| + |F_j|)/B$ disk accesses.

Theorem 1. *Consider n newsgroup views whose definitions are conjunctions of arithmetic attribute selection and unstructured attribute selection conditions. Each attribute selection condition on an ordered-domain attribute A_i is a boolean expression of atomic conditions on A_i.*

The Independent Search Trees Algorithm for newsgroup-maintenance is correct and has a maintenance time of $O(\sum_{j=1}^{d-1} \log_B(K_j) + 2(\sum_{j=1}^{d-1} m_j)/B) + (\sum_{j=1}^{p} s_j)/B$ disk accesses, where K_j, m_j, and s_j are defined as above.

If an attribute selection condition for a text attribute A_s uses the contains *operator, the maintenance time required to search the index structure (trie) of A_s is $(|b_j|^2 + m_j)/B$, where $|b_j|$ is the length of b_j, the A_s attribute string value in the arriving article, and m_j is the number of newsgroups that match.*

The update time of the data structure due to an insertion of a new view is $O(\sum_{j=1}^{d} \log_B(K_j)) + s$ disk accesses, where s is the number of non-zero weights in the typical-article bodies of the added view.[2]

One of main features of the above described algorithm is that the time-complexity directly depends upon the total number of *specified* attribute atomic selection conditions, unlike any of the previously proposed algorithms for similar problems.

4   The Newsgroup-Selection Problem

An important decision in the design of the newsgroup system is to select an appropriate set of newsgroups to be eagerly maintained (materialized). The rest of the newsgroups are computed whenever queried, using the other materialized newsgroups and/or the article store. A natural optimization criterion is to minimize the storage space and/or newsgroup maintenance time, while guaranteeing that each newsgroup query can be answered within some threshold.

The query threshold of a newsgroup query is essentially the query-time a user request for the newsgroup can tolerate. Heavily accessed important newsgroups would have low query thresholds, while newsgroups with very low query frequencies could tolerate higher query times. The newsgroup-selection problem is to select the most "beneficial" newsgroups to materialize, so that *all* newsgroup queries can be answered within their respective query-time thresholds. Often, materializing only a small subset of newsgroups will be sufficient to answer each

---

[2] The array T can be maintained periodically.

newsgroup query within its query-time thresholds. This conserves system re-sources and facilitates efficient maintenance of materialized newsgroups.

In this section, we first formulate the general problem of selecting newsgroups to be eagerly maintained (materialized), and show that it is, unfortunately, in-tractable. We then take advantage of our specific model of newsgroup definitions as selection views, and present some efficient exact/approximation algorithms and complexity hardness results for the problems.

As with the previous problem of newsgroup-maintenance, the problems ad-dressed here are more generally applicable to the selection of views to materialize in a data warehouse, when the queries are restricted to selections and unions over the underlying sources of information.

4.1   General Problem of Newsgroup-Selection

Consider a labeled bipartite hypergraph $G = (Q \cup V, E)$, where Q is the set of newsgroup queries and V is a set of candidate newsgroups (views) considered for materialization. The set E is the set of hyperedges, where each hyperedge is of the form $(q, \{v_1, v_2, \ldots, v_l\})$, $q \in Q$, and $v_1, v_2, \ldots, v_l \in V$. Each hyperedge is labeled with a *query-cost* of t, signifying that query q can be answered using the set of views $\{v_1, v_2, \ldots, v_l\}$ incurring a cost of t units. With each query node $q \in Q$, there is a query-cost threshold T_q associated, and with each view node $v \in V$, there is a weight (space cost) $S(v)$ associated. We refer to such a graph as a *query-view* graph. This notion of a query-view graph is similar to that used in [GHRU97], but more general. We now define the *newsgroup-selection* problem.

Newsgroup-Selection Problem: *Given a bipartite query-view hypergraph G defined as above, select a minimum weighted set of views $M \subseteq V$ to materialize such that for each query $q \in Q$ there exists a hyperedge $(q, \{v_1, v_2, \ldots, v_l\})$ in G, where views $v_1, v_2, \ldots, v_l \in M$ and the query-cost associated with the hyperedge is less than T_q.*

The above problem is trivially in NP. As there is a straightforward reduction from minimum set cover to a special case of the newsgroup-selection problem when G has only simple edges, the newsgroup-selection problem is also NP-hard. The newsgroup-selection problem is exactly the problem of minimizing the num-ber of leaves scheduled in a 3-level AND/OR scheduling problem with internal-tree precedence constraints [GM97]. The 2-level version of the AND/OR schedul-ing problem with internal-tree precedence constraints is equivalent to minimum set cover, while the 4-level AND/OR scheduling problem with internal-tree constraints is as hard as the LABEL-COVER [ABSS93,GM97] problem making it quasi-NP-hard[3] to approximate within a factor of $2^{\log^{1-\gamma} n}$ for any $\gamma > 0$. To the best of our knowledge, nothing is known about the 3-level version of the AND/OR scheduling problem with internal tree constraints.

The intractability of the general problem leads us to look at some natural special cases that arise in practice in the context of newsgroup management,

---

[3] That is, this would imply $NP \subseteq DTIME(n^{poly(logn)})$. "A proof of quasi-NP-hardness is good evidence that the problem has no polynomial-time algorithm" [AL95].

and we present efficient algorithms for each of them. Recall that, in Section 2, we allowed newsgroups to be defined only as selection views of a specified form. In such cases, a newsgroup needs only the union ($\cup$) and selection (σ) relational operators to be computed from a set of other newsgroups. However, the above formulation of the newsgroup-selection problem is much more general.

In the next subsection, we restrict the computation of a newsgroup from other newsgroups to just using the selection operator. We handle the case of using both the union and the selection operators in the subsequent subsection.

4.2   Queries as Selections over Views

In this subsection, we focus on the restricted newsgroup-selection problem where newsgroup queries are computed using only selections, either on some material-ized newsgroup in the data warehouse or the article store. For example, if the data warehouse eagerly maintains `comp.databases`, then answering the news-group query `comp.databases.object` requires only a selection over the news-group `comp.databases`. Being a special case of the general newsgroup-selection problem, the above restricted version of the problem helps in better understand-ing of the general problem. Moreover, in some domains, the union operation may be very expensive or not feasible. For example, let the newsgroup V_1 contain all articles whose `Subject` *contains* "computer", and the newsgroup V_2 be the set of all articles whose `Subject` *contains* "compute". Though, V_2 can be computed using V_1 *and* the article store using the selection condition ($\wedge$ (`Subject` *contains* "computer") ($\neg$(`Subject` *contains* "compute"))) on the article store, it may be more efficient to compute V_2 using a simple selection over just the article store.

In the above restricted newsgroup-selection problem where newsgroup queries are computed using only the selection operator, a query uses exactly one view for its computation. Hence, the query-view graph defined earlier will have only simple edges. The restricted newsgroup-problem has a natural reduction from the `minimum set cover` problem and hence is also NP-complete. However, there exists a polynomial-time greedy algorithm that delivers a competitive solution that is within $O(\log n)$ factor of an optimal solution, where n is the number of newsgroup queries. The greedy algorithm used is almost the same as that used to approximate the `weighted set cover` problem [Chv79]. It can be shown that the solution delivered by the greedy algorithm is within $O(\log n)$ of the optimal solution.

So far, we have not taken any advantage of the specific nature of the atomic conditions used in the newsgroup definitions. We now do so, and restrict ourselves to newsgroups defined using arithmetic operators on the article attributes. As the arithmetic operators used in an atomic condition assume an order on the domain, all defined newsgroups form some sort of "orthogonal objects" in the multidimensional space of the article attributes. We take advantage of this fact and formulate a series of problems, presenting exact or approximate algorithms.

Newsgroup-Selection with Ordered Domains Consider an ordered domain D. Consider newsgroups (views or queries) that are ranges over D. In other words, views and queries can be represented as intervals over D. As we restrict our attention to using only the selection operator for computing a query, a query interval q can be computed using a view interval v only if v completely covers q. With each pair (q, v), where v completely covers q, there is a query-cost associated, which is the cost incurred in computing q from v.

We observe here that the techniques used to solve the various problems of one-dimensional queries/views addressed in this section can also be applied to the more general case when the queries involve intervals (ranges) along one dimension and equality selections over other dimensions.

Problem (One-dimensional Selection Queries) *Given interval views V and interval queries Q over an ordered domain D, select a minimum weighted set of interval views M such that each query $q \in Q$ has a view $v \in M$ that completely contains q and answers the query q within its query-cost threshold T_q.*

Let n be the number of query and view intervals. There is an $O(n^2)$ exact dynamic programming algorithm that delivers an optimal solution to the above problem. The algorithm appears in the full version of the paper.

The restricted version of the newsgroup-selection problem considered above is a special case of the view-selection problem in OR view graphs defined in [Gup97] with different optimization criteria and constraints. Gupta [Gup97] presents a simple greedy approach to deliver a solution that is within a constant factor of an optimal solution. In effect, we have taken advantage of the restricted model of the newsgroup definitions and shown that for this special case of the view-selection problem in OR graphs there exists a polynomial-time algorithm that delivers an optimal solution.

Multi-dimension Selection Queries The generalization of the above newsgroup-selection problem to *d-dimensional selection queries*, where each query and view is a d-dimensional hyper-rectangle, doesn't have any better than the $O(\log n)$ approximation algorithm. The newsgroup-selection problem for d-dimensional selection queries can be shown to be NP-complete through a reduction from 3-SAT. In fact, the problem is a more general version of the classical age-old problem of covering points using rectangles in a 2-D plane [FPT81], for which nothing better than an $O(\log n)$ approximation algorithm is known.

Selection over Body Attribute Conditions Consider newsgroups defined by selection conditions of the form $f_{id} = \bigvee_k (C(A_d, B_{ik}, T_{ik}))$ over the Body attribute of the articles. So, an article m belongs to a newsgroup if m is *similar-to* one of the representative typical-article's body B_{ik} with a minimum threshold. A newsgroup query Q can be answered using another materialized newsgroup view V if the set of typical-article bodies of Q is a subset of the set of typical-article bodies of V. The newsgroup-selection problem in this setting can be shown to be exactly the same problem as the NP-complete set cover problem. Thus, allowing selections over the Body attribute makes the newsgroup-selection problem as difficult as the general newsgroup-selection problem with simple edges in the query-view graph.

4.3 Queries as Selections + Unions over Views

In this section, we look at some special cases of the general newsgroup-selection problem, while allowing both selection and union operators for computation of a newsgroup query from other materialized newsgroups. The use of both operators introduces hyperedges in the query-view graph. As mentioned before, the general newsgroup-selection problem involving hyperedges is intractable, hence we take advantage of the restricted model of our newsgroup definitions in designing approximation algorithms.

The newsgroup-selection problem with union and selection operators is a special case of the view-selection problem in AND-OR view graphs considered in [Gup97], with different optimization criteria and constraints. Gupta [Gup97] fails to give any approximation algorithms for the general view-selection problem in AND-OR graphs. We take advantage of the special nature of our problem, and present some polynomial-time approximation algorithms.

One-dimensional Selection/Union Queries Consider an ordered domain D, and let newsgroups be interval ranges over D. In other words, newsgroup views and queries can be represented as intervals over D and a newsgroup query interval can be answered using views $v_1, \ldots, v_l$ if the union of the view intervals covers the query interval completely. There is a query-cost associated with each such pair, which is the cost incurred in computing q from $v_1, v_2, \ldots, v_l$.

Problem (One-dimensional Selection/Union Queries) *Given a set of interval views V and interval queries Q in an ordered domain D, select a minimum weighted set of interval views M such that each query $q \in Q$ has a set of views $v_1, v_2, \ldots, v_l \in M$ that completely cover q and the query-cost associated is less than T_q.*

Consider the following cost model. In addition to a weight associated with each view, let there also be a cost $C(v)$ associated with each view. Let the cost of computing a query q using a set of views $\{v_1, v_2, \ldots, v_l\}$ that cover the query q be defined as $\sum_{i=1}^{l} C(v_i)$, i.e., the sum of the costs of the views used. The above cost model is general enough for all practical purposes.

The problem of one-dimensional selection/union queries with the above cost model can be shown to be NP-complete through a reduction from the NP-complete Partition [GJ79] problem. See the full version of the paper for the reduction. However, if we restrict our attention to the *index cost model* where the cost incurred in computing a query covered by l views is l units (a special case of the general cost model above, where each $C(v) = 1$), we show that there exists an $O(m^{k-1}n^2)$ dynamic programming solution, where m is the maximum overlap between the given queries and k is the maximum individual query-cost threshold (which we expect to be small). The details of the algorithm can be found in the full version of the paper.

The index cost model, where the cost of answering a query q using l views is l units, is based on the following very reasonable implementation. If all the materialized views are indexed along the dimension D, then the cost incurred in computing the query is proportional to l, the total number of index look-ups. Note that the query-costs associated with the edges may not be the actual query costs but could be the normalized query-cost "overheads".

Average Query Cost Constraint A relatively easier problem in the context of the above cost model is when the constraint is on the *total* (or, *average*) query cost instead of having a threshold on each individual query. For such a case, there exists an $O(kn^3)$ time dynamic programming algorithm that delivers a minimum-weighted solution, where $k(\leq n)$ is the average query-cost constraint. The dynamic approach here works by maintaining for each interval $[1, i]$ a list of k solutions, where the jth solution corresponds to the minimum-weighted set of views that covers the queries in $[1, i]$ under the constraint that the total query cost incurred is less than j.

Multi-dimensional Selection/Union Queries Consider next the newsgroup-selection problem where newsgroup queries and views are d-dimensional ranges. In other words, views and queries can be represented as hyper-rectangles in a d-dimensional space and a query hyper-rectangle can be answered using views $v_1, \ldots, v_k$ if the union of the view hyper-rectangles covers the query hyper-rectangle completely. We wish to select a minimum-weighted set of views such that all queries are covered. The simplest version of the problem has no threshold constraints and it is only required to cover all the query rectangles using the materialized views.

The above problem is NP-complete even for the case of two dimensions. We present here a polynomial-time (in n) $O(d \log n)$ approximation algorithm. The space of hyper-rectangular queries can be broken down into $O((2n)^d)$ elementary hyper-rectangles. Thus, the problem of covering the query hyper-rectangles can be reduced to covering the elementary hyper-rectangles with minimum-weighted set of views, which is equivalent to a `weighted set cover` instance having $O((2n)^d)$ elements; this has an $O(d \log n)$ approximation algorithm.

Selection/Union on `Body` Attribute Conditions In this subsection, we consider the case where newsgroup queries, having selection conditions of the form $f_{id} = \bigvee_k (C(A_d, B_{ik}, T_{ik}))$, can be computed using only selection and union over the `Body` attribute predicates of the materialized newsgroup views. Due to the same similarity-vector occurring in the definition of many newsgroups, a newsgroup V can be computed from the materialized newsgroups $V_1, V_2, \ldots, V_k$ if each similarity-vector of V is included in one of the materialized newsgroups.[4] The computation involves computing a selection over each of the relevant newsgroups followed by a union. If some of the similarity-vectors of a non-materialized view V are not covered by the other materialized views, then to answer the newsgroup query V, the article store needs to be accessed to select all articles whose bodies

---

[4] Here, for simplicity, we assume that the threshold corresponding to a particular similarity-vector is the same across different newsgroup views it is used in.

match (using cosine similarity function with the specified threshold) one of the uncovered similarity-vectors.

The cost of accessing a materialized view V, based on a selection over ordered domains, is proportional to the logarithm of the size of V, as it involves searching through efficient data structures like B-trees. In contrast, accessing V based on a selection over an unstructured attribute involves searching through the inverted index data structure. Therefore, when a query is computed as selection and union over the Body attribute using some materialized views and the article store, the cost incurred in accessing the article store is the dominant factor in the total query time. Since each similarity-vector is compared with the inverted index independently, the query cost is proportional to the number of similarity-vectors sent to the article store.

Thus, in the context of newsgroup queries computed as selection/union over the Body attribute, the natural optimization problem is to select a minimum weighted set of newsgroup views to materialize, such that the total number of uncovered similarity-vectors summed over all newsgroup queries is less than a given threshold. From the discussion in the previous paragraph, the threshold on the total number of similarity-vectors summed over all queries translates to a threshold on the average query-cost of a newsgroup query.

The above optimization problem has a greedy $O(\log n)$ approximation algorithm, that at each stage selects the newsgroup that decreases the total number of uncovered body articles (summed over all queries) by most. We omit the details of the proof here.

4.4   Related Work

The newsgroup-selection problem is similar to the view-selection problem defined in [Gup97]. The view-selection problem considered there was to select a set of views for materialization to minimize the query response time under the disk-space constraint. The key differences between the two problems are the different constraint and the minimization goal used.

Previous work on the view selection problem is as follows. Harinarayan et al. [HRU96] provide algorithms to select views to materialize for the case of data cubes, which is a special case of OR-graphs, where a query uses exactly one view to compute itself. The authors in [HRU96] show that the proposed polynomial-time greedy algorithm delivers a solution that is within a constant factor of the optimal solution. Gupta et al. [GHRU97] extend their results to selection of views *and* indexes in data cubes. Gupta [Gup97] presents a theoretical formulation of the general view-selection problem in a data warehouse and generalizes the previous results to general OR view graphs, AND view graphs, OR view graphs with indexes, and AND view graphs with indexes.

The case of one-dimensional selection queries considered here is a special case of the view-selection problem in OR view graphs for which we provided a polynomial time algorithm that delivers an optimal solution. Similarly, the case of one-dimensional selection/union queries is a special case of the view-selection problem in AND-OR view graphs ([Gup97]), which we observe can be solved optimally in polynomial-time for a reasonable cost model. The case of selection/union queries on newsgroups defined using similarity-vectors is also a special case of the general view-selection problem in AND-OR graphs, for which we have designed a provably good approximation algorithm.

In the computational geometry research community, to the best of our knowledge, the specific problems mentioned here haven't been addressed except for the preliminary work done on rectangular covers [FPT81].

5   Conclusions

We have proposed a novel paradigm for newsgroups, the DaWN model, where newsgroups are defined as selection views over the article store. The success of the DaWN model clearly depends on the efficiency with which news readers can continue to access newsgroups. In this paper, we have looked at the two complementary problems that are critical for this efficiency. The first problem is the efficient incremental maintenance of eagerly maintained newsgroups. We have designed an I/O and CPU efficient algorithm for this problem, based on external segment trees, tries, and inverted lists. The second problem is the choice of eagerly maintained (materialized) newsgroups. We have demonstrated the intractability of the general problem, and discussed various special natural cases of the general problem in the context of the DaWN model.

The success of the DaWN model also depends on the precision with which an article can be automatically classified into appropriate newsgroups. This precision will be determined by the newsgroup definitions, in particular by the choice of representative typical-articles. The problem of a good choice of typical-articles for a given newsgroup is orthogonal to the problems/issues addressed in this paper, and is an interesting open problem, where techniques from data mining and data clustering can play a significant role.

We believe that the DaWN model can also serve as the foundation for allowing individual users to enhance the standard newsgroups by defining their personal newsgroups. Such personal newsgroups can be specified using "profiles" of the users that are matched against the article store, and techniques and solutions from dissemination-based systems can be used to advantage here.

References

[ABSS93]   S. Arora, L. Babai, J. Stern, and Z. Sweedyk. The hardness of approximate optima in lattices, codes, and systems of linear equations. In *Proceedings of the Foundations of Computer Science*, 1993.

[AL95]   S. Arora and C. Lund. Hardness of approximations. Technical Report TR-504-95, Princeton University, Computer Science Department, 1995.

[Cha83]   B. Chazelle. Filtering search: A new approach to query-answering. In *Proceeding of the Foundations of Computer Science*, 1983.

[Chv79]   V. Chvatal. A greedy heuristic for the set covering problem. *Mathematics of Operations Research*, 4(3):233–235, 1979.

[Ede83a]   H. Edelsbrunner. A new approach to rectangle intersections, Part I. *International Journal of Computer Mathematics*, 13:209–219, 1983.

[Ede83b]   H. Edelsbrunner. A new approach to rectangle intersections, Part II. *International Journal of Computer Mathematics*, 13:221–229, 1983.

[EM81]   H. Edelsbrunner and H.A. Maurer. On the intersection of orthogonal objects. *Information Processing Letters*, 13(4):177–180, 1981.

[Fal85]   C. Faloutsos. Access methods for text. *ACM Comp. Surveys*, 17(1), 1985.

[FPT81]   R. J. Fowler, M. S. Paterson, and S. L. Tanimoto. Optimal packing and covering in the plane are NP-complete. *Info. Proc. Letters*, 12(3), 1981.

[Fre60]   E. Fredkin. Trie memory. *Communications of the ACM*, 3(9), 1960.

[GJ79]   M. R. Garey, D. J. Johnson. *Computers and Intractability: a Guide to the Theory of NP-Completeness*, Freeman, San Francisco, 1979.

[GHRU97]   H. Gupta, V. Harinarayan, A. Rajaraman, and J. Ullman. Index selection in OLAP. In *Proceedings of the ICDE*, 1997.

[GM97]   M. Goldwasser and R. Motwani. Intractability of assembly sequencing: Unit disks in the plane. In *Proceeding of the Workshop on Algorithms and Data Structures*, August 1997.

[Gup97]   H. Gupta. Selection of views to materialize in a data warehouse. In *Proceedings of the ICDT*, Delphi, Greece., January 1997.

[HCKW90]   E. Hanson, M. Chaabouni, C.-H. Kim, and Y.-W. Wang. A predicate matching algorithm for database rule systems. In *PODS*, 1990.

[HGMW⁺95]   J. Hammer, H. Garcia-Molina, J. Widom, W. Labio, and Y. Zhuge. The Stanford Data Warehousing Project. *IEEE Data Engineering Bulletin, Special Issue on Materialized Views and Data Warehousing*, 18(2), 1995.

[HRU96]   V. Harinarayan, A. Rajaraman, and J. Ullman. Implementing data cubes efficiently. In *SIGMOD*, 1996.

[IK93]   W.H. Inmon and C. Kelley. *Rdb/VMS: Developing the Data Warehouse*. QED Publishing Group, Boston, Massachusetts, 1993.

[KRVV93]   P.C. Kanellakis, S. Ramaswamy, D.E. Vengroff, and J.S. Vitter. Indexing for data models with constraints and classes. In *PODS*, 1993.

[Per94]   M. Persin. Document filtering for fast ranking. *Proc. ACM SIGIR Conf.*, Dublin, Ireland, 1994.

[RS94]   S. Ramaswamy and S. Subramanian. Path caching: A technique in optimal external searching. In *PODS*, 1994.

[RS95]   S. Ramaswamy and S. Subramanian. The p-range tree: A new data structure for range searching in secondary memory. In *SODA*, 1995.

[SB88]   G. Salton and C. Buckley. Term-weighting approaches in automatic text retrieval. *Information Processing & Management*, 24(5), 1988.

[Sam89a]   Hanan Samet. *Applications of Spatial Data Structures: Computer Graphics, Image Processing, and GIS*. Addison-Wesley, 1989.

[Sam89b]   Hanan Samet. *The Design and Analysis of Spatial Data Structures*. Addison-Wesley, 1989.

[VV96]   D.E. Vengroff and J.S. Vitter. Efficient 3-D searching in external memory. In *Proceeding of the STOC*, 1996.

[Wid95]   J. Widom. Research problems in data warehousing. In *Proceedings of the Conference on Info. and Knowledge Management*, 1995.

Author Index

Lecture Notes in Computer Science

For information about Vols. 1–1463
please contact your bookseller or Springer-Verlag